THE TUDOR REGIME

THE TUDOR REGIME

BY

PENRY WILLIAMS

CLARENDON PRESS · OXFORD

1979

Oxford University Press, Walton Street, Oxford OX2 6DP

OXFORD LONDON GLASGOW
NEW YORK TORONTO MELBOURNE WELLINGTON
KUALA LUMPUR SINGAPORE JAKARTA HONG KONG TOKYO
DELHI BOMBAY CALCUTTA MADRAS KARACHI
IBADAN NAIROBI DAR ES SALAAM CAPE TOWN

© *Penry Williams 1979*

Published in the United States by Oxford University Press, New York

British Library Cataloguing in Publication Data

Williams, Penry
   The Tudor regime.
   1. Great Britain—Politics and government—
1485–1603
   I. Title
   354'.41'0009   JN309   79-40424
   ISBN 0-19-822491-5

Printed in Great Britain by
Butler & Tanner Ltd, Frome and London

TO

JUNE

Preface

Most historians of Tudor government have been concerned with institutions. While much work remains to be done in that area, I have adopted a different approach in this book. Without ignoring the institutional framework of the regime, I have concentrated on describing the ways in which government actually worked, the people who ran it, the impact that it made upon society, and the reasons for its survival: in short, I have been more concerned with processes than with structure. After an introductory chapter, in which the regime is set against the social background of the sixteenth century, the first part of the book deals with the apparatus of government: institutions, revenue and expenditure, civil servants, army and navy. The second part examines the impact of the regime upon various aspects of life and the success of different policies. It covers trade, industry, poor-relief, food-supply, law and order, religion, education, and drama. The third part analyses the methods used by the government for maintaining itself and tries to explain its success. It describes the protest movements of the century, the means available to government for securing compliance, the chain of command from the centre to the localities, and the composition of the political élite.

Even a fairly long book, like this one, cannot cover in detail every aspect of so vast a subject, and I have been selective in assessing the impact of government upon different areas of national life. In particular I have not tried to give a complete history of the English Reformation: instead, I have largely limited my discussion of religion to the imposition of Protestantism after 1558, in the belief that until the reign of Elizabeth the changes at the centre had produced only temporary and slender effects upon the religious life of the people. I have discussed foreign policy and war only in the context of their repercussion on domestic government. The complex field of Irish history would have needed a book to itself, so different were Irish society and Irish government from English. Above all, I would stress that this is a book about monarchical rule: the partial self-government of the towns and manors of England—the 'little commonwealths' as John Norden called them—lies outside my brief.

The typescript of this book was substantially completed by the autumn of 1976. Although it was originally accepted by another publisher, it was later withdrawn by mutual consent, and was then offered to the Oxford University Press in the spring of 1978. As a result of this delay, I have been unable to incorporate in it all the most recently published findings of other scholars. As far as possible I have referred in footnotes to relevant works which appeared between September 1976 and April 1978, but I have not always been able to do them full justice in the text itself.

I have become indebted to many people in the course of writing this book. The warden and fellows of New College, Oxford, granted me in all four terms of sabbatical leave, without which it could never have been finished. Successive fellows' secretaries at New College—Miss Pamela Maddox, Miss Stephanie Verhoeven, and Mrs Jane Smedley—patiently and accurately deciphered my handwriting. Dr Roger Schofield most generously allowed me to consult not only his Cambridge Ph.D. thesis, 'Parliamentary Lay Taxation, 1485–1547', but also several unpublished papers on government finance, from all of which I learned a great deal. Dr Joan Thirsk kindly allowed me to read in typescript her Ford Lectures, now published as *Economic Policy and Projects* (Oxford, 1978): this was of great assistance to me in writing chapter V. I have acknowledged several other specific pieces of help in the footnotes. But I wish to say here that colleagues and pupils have aided me more than they can know in discussing, formally and informally, the processes of Tudor government. Above all, I am immensely grateful to the late Mr J. P. Cooper, to Dr Jennifer Loach, to Dr R. A. C. Parker, to Dr P. A. Slack, and to my wife, who all read the book at various stages, in part or in whole, gave me countless stimulating ideas, and saved me from many errors. The book owes much to them: but it owes its defects to myself alone.

LLANIGON
AUGUST, 1978
PENRY WILLIAMS

Contents

Abbreviations

Agrarian History	Joan Thirsk (ed.), *The Agrarian History of England and Wales, 1500–1640*, Vol. IV (Cambridge, 1967).
AmHR	*American Historical Review.*
APC	*Acts of the Privy Council of England*, ed. J. R. Dasent.
BIHR	*Bulletin of the Institute of Historical Research.*
BL	British Library.
CHJ	*Cambridge Historical Journal.*
CPR	*Calendar of Patent Rolls.*
CSPDom	*Calendar of State Papers Domestic.*
DNB	*Dictionary of National Biography.*
EcHR	*Economic History Review.*
EHR	*English Historical Review.*
Ellis	Henry Ellis, *Original Letters, Illustrative of English History* (11 vols., 1824, 1827, 1846).
Elton, *Studies*	G. R. Elton, *Studies in Tudor and Stuart Politics and Government* (2 vols., Cambridge, 1974).
Elton, *TRG*	G. R. Elton, *Tudor Revolution in Government* (Cambridge, 1953).
Hall	E. Hall, *The Union of the two noble and illustre famelies of York and Lancaster* (ed. H. Ellis, 1809).
Hawarde	John Hawarde, *Les reportes del cases in camera stellata, 1593–1609* (ed. W. P. Baildon, 1894).
Haynes	Samuel Haynes, *A Collection of State Papers ... relating to affairs ... from the year 1542 to 1570* (1740).
HJ	*Historical Journal.*
HMC	Historical Manuscripts Commission.
Holdsworth	W. S. Holdsworth, *A History of English Law.*
Hughes & Larkin	P. L. Hughes and J. F. Larkin, *Tudor Royal Proclamations* (3 vols., New Haven & London, 1964–9).
JMH	*Journal of Modern History.*
Journ. Eccl. Hist.	*Journal of Ecclesiastical History.*
Lodge	E. Lodge, *Illustrations of British History* (3 vols., 1791).
LP	*Letters and Papers, Foreign and Domestic, of the Reign of Henry VIII*, ed. J. S. Brewer *et al.* (21 vols., 1862–1932).
LQR	*Law Quarterly Review.*

Murdin	William Murdin, *A collection of state papers relating to affairs ...from 1571 to 1596* (1759).
Nicolas	Sir Harris Nicolas, *Proceedings and Ordinances of the Privy Council of England* (1834–7).
NLW	National Library of Wales.
P&P	*Past and Present.*
PRO	Public Record Office.
TED	R. H. Tawney and Eileen Power, *Tudor Economic Documents* (3 vols., 1924, repr. 1963).
TRHS	*Transactions of the Royal Historical Society.*
VCH	*Victoria County History.*
WHR	*Welsh History Review.*

References to *LP* are to numbers of documents; other references are to pages, unless otherwise stated. The place of publication is London, unless another imprint is given.

INTRODUCTION
The Background to Tudor Politics

All Governments work within an intricate matrix of relationships which form the structure of power within society. In the later middle ages the principal centres of social influence and strength were the castles and households of great noblemen, from which connections and followings spread out in concentric, but often overlapping, circles, forming the lord's 'affinity'. At the centre of each affinity was the noble household, often a peripatetic body moving from one great castle or manorhouse to another. Since the service of a nobleman was an honourable occupation, the household contained men who were well-born and important, as well as humble persons who performed merely menial tasks. The servants of the Duke of Buckingham in 1519 numbered 148 persons, of whom seventeen were gentlemen and nine were gentlewomen. At about the same time Lord Darcy—by no means a great magnate—employed twenty-one gentlemen among his eighty servants. Office in a noble's household or on his estate brought material rewards, prestige, social influence, and the protection of the master. In return, officers owed loyalty and service beyond the conduct of their routine duties. The household was a nucleus whose leading members disseminated the forces of power and influence which they sometimes derived from their lord and sometimes possessed in their own right.[1]

Beyond the immediate horizon of the household servants and the lord's officers stretched the wider, less stable and less easily defined elements of his 'affinity'. Great noblemen increased their followings by retaining men with gifts of fees and annuities, which might often be granted for sinecure offices, or even for the expectation of service. Retaining acquired a bad name at the time and has kept it until recent years. But the existence

---

[1] K. B. McFarlane, *The Nobility of Later Medieval England* (Oxford, 1973), *passim*, esp. 110–11. R. B. Smith, *Land and Politics in the England of Henry VIII* (Oxford, 1970), 137. M. E. James, *Family, Lineage, and Civil Society* (Oxford, 1974), 32–5.

of a body of retainers was essential to the whole mode of noble
life. A lord needed his retainers for display, to exhibit a suitable
degree of grandeur in his own countryside or at court; they were
also important for magnifying his 'worship' or influence, which
enabled him to advance his own cause and with it that of
his dependants. Patronage, good lordship, protection, and
pageantry formed the binding cement of late medieval society.[2]

Retaining became dangerous to society only when the
retinue was very large or when lords recruited men of low rank
for short periods. The assembling of 'mean men' with no specific household function was understandably unpopular and
became the principal target of the legislation against retaining.
Although historians do not find it easy to make the distinction,
there was a line, perceived and accepted by contemporaries,
between the lawful and the unlawful retainer. The problem of
illegal retaining was not easy to solve, but nor was it, for an
able monarch, insoluble. For retinues were not in general very
large. In times of war or rebellion great magnates might
assemble considerable followings: the companies of John of
Gaunt and Lord Hastings have become legendary, and like
many legends have distorted historical understanding. But the
average noble, if such a being existed, seldom spent more than
ten per cent of his income on retainers.[3]

Nor did the leader of an affinity possess unquestioned control
over his followers. Some men might be retained by more than
one lord; allegiances were often fickle and uncertain. The successful deployment of power meant more than the material
ability to hire a private army of retainers. Skill, discretion, and
judgement were essential to the equipment of a political magnate. The straightforward military role of the retinue has probably been exaggerated. For most of the time a retinue was less a
private army than a source of 'worship', influence, and prestige.[4]

[2] McFarlane, op. cit. 104–15. T. B. Pugh, 'The Magnates, Knights, and Gentry',
in *Fifteenth-Century England*, ed. S. B. Chrimes *et al.* (Manchester, 1972), 101–5. Also
N. B. Lewis, 'The Organisation of Indentured Retinues', *TRHS* xxvII (1945); W. H.
Dunham, *Lord Hastings' Indentured Retainers* (Yale, 1955), *passim*.

[3] McFarlane, op. cit. 106–8. A. Cameron, 'The Giving of Livery and Retaining in
Henry VII's Reign', *Renaissance and Modern Studies*, xvIII (1974), esp. 20–2. Pugh, op.
cit. 102–5. M. E. James, *A Tudor Magnate and the Tudor State* (Borthwick Papers, York,
no. 30, 1966), 5–6.

[4] See McFarlane, 'The Wars of the Roses', *Proceedings of the British Academy*, vol. L
(1964), esp. 106 ff.

The old tenurial bonds of landlord and tenant still held firm at the beginning of the sixteenth century. The following of the Cliffords, Earls of Cumberland, was largely, though not very securely, based upon the feudal bond of homage performed by mesne tenants who held their lands by knight-service. The Percies could call up a force of 1,900 tenants from Northumberland, 3,000 from Cumberland, and 6,200 from Yorkshire to fight against the Scots. Such 'feudal' cohorts may have been larger and more impressive in the northern counties, but tenurial service provided lords with a following elsewhere.[5]

The power of a noble following—of household servants, estate officers, tenants, and personal retainers—was never quite enough to secure for its head dominance over a region. Real power came from combining that territorial influence with offices held from the Crown. Even the magnificent Percies needed the Wardenship of the Marches to complete their hegemony on the northern border. Lord Darcy, a substantial but not an outstanding Yorkshire landowner, was steward and constable of the Crown's honours of Knaresborough and Pontefract. Through these offices he controlled a major castle, Pontefract, and led the Crown's own retinue to the wars. The Earl of Cumberland, appointed Warden of the West March, begged Wolsey for the Stewardship of Penrith. Without it he would not have the following to carry out his duties: for 'I have neither land nor men of mine own, of any reputation, near the Borders, than within sixteen mile at the next; so that, without the rule and leading of the King's tenants, it shall be painful and also doubtous to deserve any thanks for me on these Marches.'[6]

This reminds us that the King himself was a great landowner as well as a government. His lands, like those of any other magnate, produced political as well as financial benefits. The royal tenants were his first line of defence and frequent proclamations emphasized that others must not try to add them to their retinues. The King also had a household, whose members owed him their primary duty and allegiance. The Yorkist monarchs were surrounded by two or three hundred men of knightly or

[5] M. E. James, 'The First Earl of Cumberland and the Decline of Northern Feudalism', *Northern History*, I (1966), 48–50. Id., *Tudor Magnate*, 13, 19–20, 27.

[6] R. L. Storey, 'The Wardens of the Marches ... 1377–1489', *EHR* LXXII (1957). Smith, *Land and Politics*, 138–9. *State Papers, Henry VIII*, IV. 420–1: I am grateful to Miss Susan Taylor for this reference.

gentle rank.[7] The number grew under the Tudors. These men formed a reliable corps from which agents could be recruited for missions at home and abroad and from which some could be selected for the higher echelons of state. As late as 1572 Sir Thomas Gargrave told Burghley that the Queen had many seigniories in Yorkshire and that if her officers were resident, well-chosen, and circumspect she could raise from them 2,000 trained men ready for an emergency.[8]

By 1500 the King had absorbed many of the great palatinates which had marked out almost autonomous zones of power in the earlier middle ages. The Duchies of Lancaster and Cornwall and the Earldom of Chester each preserved some independence from the national administrative system, but each was directly controlled by royal officers. Similarly the counties of the Principality of Wales were ruled by their own courts, separate from Westminster; but the courts were royal. A few of the Marcher lordships were still in private hands, but most of the greatest had fallen to the Crown. The only true palatinate to survive intact into the Tudor period was the Bishopric of Durham, from which the King's judicial power was excluded until 1536. Even in Durham however the law administered by the bishop's courts was the common law of the realm, while the bishop himself and his officers were in practice servants of the Crown.[9] In Ireland the royal writ ran hardly at all beyond the boundaries of the Pale and effective power was wielded by such great feudatories as Kildare, Desmond, and Ormonde. But the Marches of Wales, the Bishopric of Durham, and the Anglo-Norman lordships of Ireland were exceptional. By 1500, most of the lordships, honours, and franchises which lay scattered across England preserved only vestiges of their former 'liberties'. Some fifty lordships in the West Riding of Yorkshire survived into the early sixteenth century, but the powers of their lords were confined in the main to financial exactions and relatively minor forms of jurisdiction.[10]

English noblemen had fewer privileges and less regional

---

[7] D. A. L. Morgan, 'The King's Affinity in the Polity of Yorkist England', *TRHS*, 5th ser. xxiii (1973), 1–25.

[8] *CSPDom, Add., 1566–79*, 425.

[9] James, *Family, Lineage, and Civil Society*, ch. ii. W. Rees, *An Historical Atlas of Wales* (Cardiff, 1951), plates 53, 55.

[10] Smith, *Land and Politics*, 43–50.

authority than their contemporaries in mainland Europe. Since England was protected from foreign invasion by the sea the military service of the nobility was less important to the monarchy than it was in France or in the Iberian peninsula. Consequently the nobles had extracted fewer 'liberties'; in particular, they never gained that comfortable exemption from taxation which made the status of the noble in France and Castile so enviable. The great territorial authority of a French magnate put him into a different class from the late fifteenth-century English peer. Military power and judicial independence made the Duc de Berry, for instance, almost a king in his own part of France; of few, if any, English nobles could this be said when the Tudors succeeded.[11] Their strength lay more in influence than in power: it rested upon traditional allegiances, the ties of fee, office, and retainer, the bonds between landlord and tenant, but not—except in Ireland and occasionally in Wales—upon regalian powers of jurisdiction or upon military service. But, while the English magnate lacked the territorial authority of his French counterpart, he made up for this by exercising greater influence at the centre, upon the court. In the relatively small and highly centralized realm of England the magnates were able to press their claims upon the King himself, through household, council, and Parliament.[12]

The magnates of later medieval England were far from all-powerful; and many regions of England were relatively little exposed to their influence. Beneath the uppermost layers of political society knights, esquires, and gentlemen often ran their own localities. Some of them were not much inferior in wealth and status to the lesser barons. Families like the Gascoignes, Tempests, and Saviles in Yorkshire, or the Stradlings and Mansels in Glamorgan, had their traditional followings and their tenants. Although they might attach themselves to a great magnate, they would not be wholly dependent on him and could themselves attract lesser gentlemen and yeomen to their service. Fifteenth-century Cheshire was ruled by an oligarchy of gentry families, about sixty in number, many of them related by marriage; no great lord seems to have interfered in the

[11] P. S. Lewis, *Later Medieval France: the Polity* (1968), 195–9.
[12] R. H. Hilton, *A Medieval Society: the West Midlands at the End of the Thirteenth Century* (1966), ch. ii and pp. 240–1.

conduct of the county community. In a region like the West Midlands, where too there were not many magnates, knights and gentlemen had emerged by the thirteenth century as a 'service' class, supervising county affairs.[13]

Alongside the bastions of aristocratic power stood the secular authority of the Church and its princes. Great bishops and abbots presided over households and estates which rivalled those of all but the most notable magnates. Immediately before the Reformation the monasteries alone drew a net income of £136,000 per annum, the Church as a whole about £270,000 p.a., considerably more than the revenues of the Crown. In the West Riding of Yorkshire the Church's temporal and spiritual income was £11,000 p.a., compared with £15,000 p.a. for the Crown, nobles, and gentry. Great abbeys had lands valued at more than £1,000 per annum. The Archbishop of Canterbury drew over £3,000 p.a. from his demesnes.[14] Ecclesiastical privileges and Church courts protected the clergy from secular interference and gave them at the same time an unwelcome authority over the laity. Although by the fifteenth century the clerical order had lost its monopoly of literacy and learning it still controlled most schools and totally dominated the two universities. Above all, the Church held a commanding surveillance over men's minds. The pulpit was the main vehicle of communication between authority and the masses; and through images, relics, and ceremonies the clergy exercised a powerful hold upon the popular consciousness.

Yet, in spite of its wealth, its estates, its judicial machinery, and its moral influence, the English Church was vulnerable and dependent. Henry VIII might complain that the bishops were 'but half our subjects, yea and scarce our subjects', but no one could have taken him very seriously.[15] Edward IV had achieved effective control over the episcopal bench, and a bishopric had principally become a means of rewarding service to the Crown. The aristocratic prince-bishops of the middle ages—Courtenay,

---

[13] M. J. Bennett, 'A County Community: Social Cohesion among the Cheshire Gentry, 1400–25', *Northern History*, VIII (1973). Hilton, op. cit. 41–61.

[14] Smith, *Land and Politics*, 73. Hilton, op. cit. 26–41. F. R. H. du Boulay, *The Lordship of Canterbury* (1966), ch. v.

[15] G. L. Harriss, 'Medieval Government and Statecraft', *P&P* 25 (1963), 13.

Arundel, Beaufort, Beauchamp—were by the early sixteenth century extinct, their places taken by ecclesiastical lawyers and bureaucrats, whose ties of loyalty bound them to the government rather than to the aristocracy. By contrast with France, where bishoprics were often the preserve of noble families; with the Holy Roman Empire, where commoners were virtually excluded from many of the greater monasteries; and with Castile, where noblemen monopolized the powerful military orders of the Church, the English peerage had little influence or power within the spiritual order. But, at the local level, the Church's officers often lacked the power to maintain ecclesiastical authority, and they had in consequence to turn to nobles and gentlemen for assistance. In general, although the Church pervaded every aspect of national life—economic, legal, intellectual, governmental, and spiritual—it was already, before the Reformation, becoming dangerously dependent upon the secular order.[16]

After the nobles and the clergy, the third great 'estate' of the realm was formed by the lawyers. By 1500 there were 400 lawyers practising at Westminster, with many more working in country towns. Sharing a common education at the Inns of Court and a continuing membership thereafter, they had become a distinct professional group. Legal qualifications gave them not merely custody of the law itself and its profits, but also an entrée into the counsels of great magnates, the administration of boroughs, and the affairs of state. The judges and serjeants at the top of the profession were few in number, but their very rarity and skill conferred upon them a certain immunity and independence.[17]

The law which they practised and upheld was enforced largely—though not exclusively—through royal courts and

[16] R. J. Knecht, 'The Episcopate and the Wars of the Roses', *University of Birmingham Historical Journal*, VI (1957-8). L. B. Smith, *Tudor Prelates and Politics* (1953), *passim*. For a general account of the medieval Church see P. Heath, *The English Parish Clergy on the Eve of the Reformation* (1969) and references given below in ch. VIII.
[17] E. W. Ives, 'Common Lawyers in Pre-Reformation England', *TRHS*, 5th ser. XVIII (1968). Alan Harding, *A Social History of English Law* (1966), 183–90, 206–11. Margaret Hastings, *The Court of Common Pleas in Fifteenth-Century England* (New York, 1947), chs. v, vi.

royal commissions. That did not make it the King's law. In origin it was, or was held to be, the custom of the country. Sir John Davies commented in the early seventeenth century that 'the *Common Law* of England is nothing else but the *Common Custom* of the Realm ... And this *Customary Law* is the most perfect and most excellent, and without comparison the best, to make and preserve a Commonwealth.'[18]

The common law of the late middle ages had developed out of this custom as precedents, proclamations, and statutes were grafted on to it by the actions and interactions of royal judges, feudal lords, Justices of the Peace, and the commons of England. But the appeal of custom, as the fundamental element in law, remained almost as compelling in national affairs as it was in the by-laws of boroughs and manors.

In France, the King was venerated as the sole maker of law, standing above it, while respecting its provisions. In 1527 the Parlement of Paris told Francis I that 'we know well that you are above the laws and that the laws or ordinances cannot constrain you ... But ... you do not wish, nor should you wish, to do all that which you could.'[19] The Kings of England had no independent legislative power and were restrained by something more reliable and less flexible than their consciences. Clause 39 of Magna Carta laid down that no freeman could be imprisoned, dispossessed, outlawed, or exiled, except by a lawful court of his peers and the law of the land. Nearly a century later, Edward II swore at his coronation to 'uphold and protect the laws and rightful customs which the community of the realm will have chosen'.[20] The Statute of Northampton, enacted soon after his death, ordained that the judges should ignore any royal order which disturbed the due course of law. Even in matters of treason the King's power was circumscribed. The great statute of 1352 had been designed as much to curb undue royal encroachments as to protect the person of the monarch. The judges were careful throughout the fourteenth and fifteenth centuries to observe its provisions.[21]

[18] J. G. A. Pocock, *The Ancient Constitution and the Feudal Law* (Cambridge, 1957), 32.

[19] Lewis, *Later Medieval France*, 87.

[20] W. Ullmann, *A History of Political Thought: the Middle Ages* (1965), 153.

[21] Harding, op. cit. 242. J. G. Bellamy, *The Law of Treason in England in the Later Middle Ages* (Cambridge, 1970), ch. iv and p. 202. For other examples see Bellamy,

Respect for the law was maintained not merely by the judges and the professional lawyers but also by the community as a whole. Legal rights and restraints had been defended by the barons in the thirteenth and fourteenth centuries. But they were maintained as well by both Houses of Parliament and by the landowning class. Laws were enforced and moulded by amateur Justices of the Peace in co-operation and in competition with the judges of the Westminster courts.[22] Thus the legal 'estate'—an essential element in the promotion and in the restriction of royal power—contained the professionals in the Inns of Court, the Justices of the Peace, and that resilient compound known as the English common law.

In most European countries the great walled cities ranked beside nobles and bishops as centres of power and influence. The free cities of Germany preserved an independent political life and an autonomous culture. Spanish civilization was based largely upon its towns, exported by the *conquistadores* to the New World. Political and economic life in Italy and in the Low Countries was essentially urban. Not so in England. The second city of the realm, Norwich, had a population of only about 12,000 in 1500. Except for London, no other English town had more than 10,000 inhabitants. Their merchant oligarchs were seldom men of much importance outside the city walls. If they succeeded in life they turned to the country and left the town. Many towns were economically enfeebled in the fifteenth and sixteenth centuries as industry escaped the control of the guilds for the freedom of rural villages. There was one great exception: the City of London. With about 60,000 inhabitants in 1500 and about 200,000 in 1600, it came increasingly to dominate the financial and commercial life of the country. But its political supremacy sprang less from economic power than from the presence of royal residences, the lawcourts, government offices, and the town houses of the great. While its merchant princes were men of consequence and the City was decidedly a force to be

---

Crime and Public Order in England in the Later Middle Ages (1973), 15, and Hastings, op. cit., ch. vi.

[22] B. H. Putnam (ed.), *Proceedings before the Justices of the Peace: Edward III to Richard III* (1938), xlviii–lvi, cxxx, and the remarks by Plucknett, ibid. cxlix.

reckoned with, its interests were too tightly chained to the chariot-wheels of government for it to act as an independent entity during the sixteenth century.[23]

By comparison with the great monarchies of western Europe the kingdom of England was by 1500 relatively compact and united. News could travel rapidly across the country: by means of relays a message could cover 200 miles in two days; and even without them sixty miles a day was possible. Movement for the ordinary traveller was of course much slower: twenty or thirty miles in a day was creditable going.[24] But such progress allowed a reasonable degree of contact between the communities. Monarchs could, without intolerable exertion, display themselves to many of their subjects. Nobles, gentlemen, and their families could visit other counties and the capital. Lords rode from one manor to another, bringing a glimpse of the great world into the villages. Peasants and servants moved over the countryside, driving herds, taking corn to market, and helping their lords to travel.[25]

Landscapes, settlements, and customs varied greatly: no two shires were alike in their economy or in their social structure. The bonds which held together local communities were tough and durable:[26] the consciousness and power of the community is perhaps the most difficult aspect of early modern England for the twentieth-century historian to grasp. But in spite of the variety and cohesion of county and village communities, England was scarcely affected by the regional loyalties which divided contemporary France. The dominance of London— seat of government, finance, and trade—helped to focus national life upon a single centre, which attracted gentlemen and nobles as well as merchants and lawyers, providing a staple for the exchange of ideas and information. The development

[23] J. H. Hexter, 'The Myth of the Middle Class', in *Reappraisals in History* (1961), 93–9. W. G. Hoskins, 'English Provincial Towns in the Early Sixteenth Century', *TRHS*, 5th ser. vi (1956). G. D. Ramsay, *The City of London in International Politics at the Accession of Elizabeth Tudor* (Manchester, 1975), ch. ii. Below, ch. V.

[24] C. A. J. Armstrong, 'Some Examples of the Distribution of News at the Time of the Wars of the Roses', in *Studies Presented to F. M. Powicke* (Oxford, 1948).

[25] Du Boulay, op. cit. 114–16.

[26] M. J. Bennett, *Northern History*, viii (1973).

of the vernacular, in England as in the rest of Europe, was served by the invention of printing: as the sixteenth century drew on, the proportion of books in Latin declined while the demand for texts in English grew. The consequent emergence of a standard language and the growth of London were both by 1500 beginning to produce a greater unity.[27] Only in Ireland and Wales were there strong regional distinctions, loyalties, and antagonisms. In Ireland the barriers and hostilities were complex and durable; but that turbulent island lies outside the scope of this book. In Wales, at the end of the fifteenth century, there were still important differences between Welsh and English: distinctions of legal status, custom, land-tenure, and language were real and sometimes inflammatory; and there was a lively tradition of hostility towards the English in Welsh prophetic poetry. Even so, the Welsh gentry usually co-operated with the English government, entering royal service, fighting the King's wars, holding administrative office, and adopting English ways.[28]

Nor were there many regional institutions interposed between the central government and the shires. Such as did exist—the justices of the Principality of Wales, the wardens of the Scottish border, the Councils in the North and in the Welsh Marches—were essentially agents of the King, used by him to extend the reach of royal power. The realm of England had none of those barriers to national unity erected by provincial estates and *parlements* in France, by the Cortes in the kingdoms of Spain, or by the towns and provinces of the Netherlands.[29]

Unity was fostered by the relatively small size of the population, especially of the political nation. Perhaps 2,000 families really counted in the government of the country and of its shires at the end of the fifteenth century. They were not too many to be known, most of them, by the King and his servants; and they were small enough to form some kind of a community in Parliament. In the Lancastrian period a high proportion of M.P.s sat in more than one Parliament, and there is evidence

[27] Cf. Lewis, op cit. 4–5. L. Febvre and H.-J. Martin, *L'Apparition du livre* (Paris, 1958), 477–8.

[28] Glyn Roberts, 'Wales and England: Antipathy and Sympathy, 1282–1485', *WHR* 1 (1963), repr. in id., *Aspects of Welsh History* (Cardiff, 1969). Rees Davies, 'Race Relations in Post-Conquest Wales', *Trans. Hon. Soc. of Cymmrodorion* (1974/75).

[29] Lewis, op. cit. 1–16, 345–74.

of social contact and cohesion between them. That Parliament could be called 'the body of the whole realm' meant something important: there was no equivalent in the Iberian peninsula; and the Estates-General in France never acquired such authority or significance. Parliament helped to strengthen a national unity of which it was itself a symbol and a product.

The problems confronting government were not easy in 1485, and they grew in complexity and magnitude throughout the sixteenth century. The oldest, and traditionally the most highly regarded, of the monarch's tasks was the preservation of order and the maintenance of law. There are grounds for thinking that during the middle decades of the fifteenth century this task had become more difficult than before. Certainly this was the opinion of the House of Commons in 1450:

> The honour, wealth and prosperity of every prince reigning upon his people standeth most principally upon conservation of his peace, keeping of justice, and due execution of his laws, without which no realm may long endure in quiet nor prosperity: and for lack hereof many murders, manslaughters, rapes, robberies, riots, affrays, and other inconveniences, greater than before, now late have grown within this your realm.[30]

Partisan as this statement was, it indicated what the Commons thought government was about and something of the turmoil into which it had fallen under Henry VI. There is more than one opinion on the disorders of the fifteenth century. Against the run of many earlier historians, the late Bruce McFarlane was inclined to think that, except in the two middle decades, they were no worse than the troubles of the fourteenth. Dr J. G. Bellamy is disposed to reverse this judgement, on account of the especially pernicious organization of crime under the Lancastrians.[31] Perhaps the disagreement does not greatly matter, for it is clear that, throughout both centuries, when the King was abroad or when he was a weakling, order and control deteriorated. The protection given by certain magnates to their criminal dependants, the decrease of the old system of frank-

---

[30] R. L. Storey, *The End of the House of Lancaster* (1966), 59.
[31] McFarlane, *Nobility of Later Medieval England*, 114–21. Bellamy, *Crime and Public Order*, 10, 22.

pledge, and the abandonment after about 1290 of the thoroughly effective general eyres all eroded the system of legal control. Weak government forced men to look to the protection of great magnates. The consequent expansion of baronial retinues weakened government still further; and so the process continued. There is no need to suppose that all, or even many, of the nobility were vicious and brutal. But a few of them certainly were. In October 1455 Nicholas Radford, an elderly and distinguished lawyer, awoke to find one hundred men, led by Sir Thomas Courtenay, son of the Earl of Devon, setting fire to his outhouses. Although Courtenay promised Radford that he would not be harmed, he was in fact stabbed to death. The earl and his son later ordered their men to hold a mock inquest. This brought in a verdict of suicide, after which Radford's servants were forced to give his corpse a heretic's burial. Such brutality was certainly exceptional. But there were brutes around in fifteenth-century England and when they were allowed excessive freedom they could infect society with their habits.[32]

Violence and disorder had of course long been endemic in English society. During the sixteenth century new problems confronted the monarchy and some old ones grew in magnitude and complexity. Although the principal initiative in religious change in England was taken by the Crown, monarchy and nation were soon embroiled in the struggles of contending factions and beliefs. Every sixteenth-century government tried to impose one uniform doctrine and one form of worship within the state; and probably they were right to do so. Religious strife was too bitter and governmental controls were too weak for peaceful coexistence and mutual toleration to be possible. Only a very powerful monarchy, in a country which had been ravaged by a generation of civil strife, could accept and enforce an arrangement like the Edict of Nantes in France. All the Tudor monarchs believed that uniformity of religious practice was essential and that overt deviation from the established Church must be forbidden. Henry VIII, lamenting the difference of opinion among his subjects, by which 'there is begun and sprung among themselves slander and railing each at other', announced his intention 'to reduce his people committed by God to his cure, to unity of opinion, and to increase love

[32] Bellamy, *Crime and Public Order*, 55–7. Storey, op. cit. 167–70.

Introduction

and charity among themselves'.[33] His attitude was typical of the time. It was reinforced by the fear that unorthodox religious opinions might stimulate social unrest; and the agrarian troubles of the 1540s were often attributed to sinister agitation by hedge-priests and Anabaptists.

Religious uniformity and control were made more necessary by international pressures. In the middle of the fifteenth century England had lost all her overseas possessions in France, except Calais. Her kings were therefore no longer obliged to commit their resources to the increasingly difficult and expensive task of defending possessions across the Channel. Edward IV and Henry VII took full advantage of this new situation by husbanding their resources. Henry VIII did attempt to recover territory in northern France for the English Crown, but his success was limited to brief occupations of Tournai, between 1513 and 1519, and of Boulogne from 1544 to 1549.[34] By then England's international position was notably less favourable than it had been in the days of his great predecessor, Henry V, and the demands of warfare were becoming increasingly heavy. Where 30,000 men had once sufficed for a major campaign, the armies that marched and counter-marched through Italy and the Empire rose from 60,000 in the 1530s to more than 100,000 in the 1550s. The techniques of urban fortification had been enormously improved in the fifteenth century by the use of lower and thicker ramparts with projecting bastions from which cross-fire could be deployed. The only English example of this style, known as the *trace italienne*, can still be seen in the walls of Berwick-on-Tweed. More magnificent examples, built by the Venetians against the Turks, survive in Cyprus, at Famagusta and Nicosia, and in Crete, at Iráklion. These defensive walls were almost impregnable to the normal techniques of attack by artillery and mining. Only prolonged siege by a large army could reduce a strongly fortified city; and that was an expensive operation. The Valois and the Habsburgs, ruling large and populous kingdoms, were able to compete in this new world of large-scale, protracted, and costly warfare.[35] But

[33] Hughes & Larkin, i, no. 191: proclamation of April 1539.
[34] R. B. Wernham, *Before the Armada* (1966), chs. i–xii.
[35] For a succinct account of changes in warfare see Geoffrey Parker, *The Army of Flanders and the Spanish Road, 1567–1659* (Cambridge, 1972), 5–21.

English monarchs had neither the resources in manpower nor the apparently bottomless sources of borrowing on which the French and Spanish kings could draw.[36] Except in the years when Henry VIII was trying to outdo Francis I, English statesmen of the Tudor period adjusted sensibly enough to this situation. But permanent isolation from the European conflict was impossible. England lay strategically upon the vital sea-link between Spain and the Netherlands. The Habsburgs and the Valois must attempt to secure either an alliance with England or else some measure of control over her. Hence the interest of Habsburg statesmen in the fate of Mary Tudor; hence the marriage between Mary and Philip of Castile; hence both Philip's long tolerance of Elizabeth I and his eventual support for her rival, Mary Stuart. Hence, too, French support for the Duke of Northumberland and Lady Jane Grey in 1553 and for Wyatt's rebellion in 1554; hence the backing given by France to Mary of Guise and Mary Stuart in Scotland. These dynastic struggles of the two great Catholic powers were heightened and complicated by the religious conflicts of the day. England's enemies tried to exploit religious dissension within the kingdom and to gain support in those neighbouring and disorderly realms, Scotland and Ireland. Even so cautious a statesman as William Cecil, anxious above everything else to avoid the expenses of war, believed England to be menaced by a massive Catholic conspiracy which would eventually unite Spain, France, and the Papacy against her.[37] No doubt he wildly exaggerated the unity of the Catholic powers. But his fears were understandable: the threat, though less than he supposed, was real.

Religious tension and foreign pressure threatened England at a time when economic changes were straining its social fabric. Economic dislocation was nothing new in England. In the fourteenth century bad harvests and plague sharply reduced the population and faced landlords with serious difficulties. The sixteenth century by contrast witnessed a gradual expansion of the population, which probably grew by more than half between 1520 and 1600. Since agricultural production rose more slowly and there was little growth in the

[36] R. B. Outhwaite, 'The Trials of Foreign Borrowing', *EcHR*, 2nd ser. xix (1966).
[37] Haynes, 579 ff.

opportunities for employment, the increase in population brought with it a rise in food-prices of perhaps 300 per cent over the century, an inflation of rents from about 1570, and a serious problem of unemployment. Those who grew surplus food for the market or could raise rents from their tenantry profited accordingly; but those dependent upon fixed incomes and wages suffered a serious reduction in their livelihood.[38]

Periodic slumps in the cloth trade, the existence of a larger class of landless paupers, the high rate of unemployment and underemployment, and the inadequacy of the food-supply seemed to threaten internal security and the safety of property. And if that was not a strong enough incentive to action, the government came under heavy moral pressure from humanist thinkers and religious reformers to better the conditions of life, put an end to social abuses, and relieve misery.[39] Henry Brinkelow, an ex-friar, proposed that a worthy man be appointed to preach four times a week to Parliament, for at least an hour on each occasion, 'and there to tell the lords and burgesses their duties, and to open unto them such matters as are to be reformed in the realm'. Bishop Latimer, preaching before Edward VI, proposed that the clergy play an active role in secular affairs: 'The preacher cannot correct the King, if he be a transgressor of God's word, with the temporal sword; but he must correct and reprove him with the spiritual sword.' Writers, preachers, and administrators were coming to accept—indeed to insist upon—the government's role in social regulation.[40]

Their pleas were directed to an increasingly literate political nation. The demand for reading-matter in the fifteenth century was already encouraging copyists to foreshadow the production of the printing-presses; and in 1478 the Goldsmiths' Company of London forbade anyone to become an apprentice 'without

---

[38] For a more detailed account of economic and social problems, see below, 139-43.

[39] A. B. Ferguson, *The Articulate Citizen and the English Renaissance* (Durham, N.C., 1965). G. R. Elton, *Reform and Renewal* (Cambridge, 1973). W. R. D. Jones, *The Tudor Commonwealth, 1529–1559* (1970). Helen C. White, *Social Criticism in Popular Religious Literature of the Sixteenth Century* (New York, 1944).

[40] H. Brinkelow, *The Complaynt of Roderyck Mors* (Early English Text Soc. xxii, 1874), 7. H. Latimer, *First Sermon before Edward VI*, 8 March 1549. Elton, op. cit., chs. i–iii. See also E. Lamond (ed.), *The Discourse of the Common Weal* (Cambridge, 1893); the author was probably Sir Thomas Smith: see M. Dewar, 'The Authorship of "The Discourse of the Common Weal"', *EcHR* xix (1966).

he can write and read'.[41] The invention of printing both stimulated literacy and was nourished by it, for the presses gave access to far more material than had been available in the past. Such had been the obstacles to knowledge in the middle ages that even scholars had probably been restricted to a few thoroughly known books. In the sixteenth century not only could more people read and write, but they did so with an accustomed fluency that had previously been rare. Reading became for some a normal part of life; and it is striking, though not surprising, to find the third Duke of Norfolk, imprisoned in the Tower in 1547, asking for books so that he might read himself to sleep at night, according to his usual habit.[42] Thus complaints, warnings, exhortations, and proposals for reform were more easily transmitted than they had been in the past and reached an audience increasingly accustomed to absorbing the message of the written word.

None of the problems facing the Tudor monarchy was unprecedented. Disorder had long been endemic; there had been economic crises and peasant revolts before; England had often been threatened by powerful enemies; the Church had sometimes been acutely divided on spiritual issues. But now these difficulties were both more severe and more tightly connected one with another. Spiritual conflict, encouraged by Spain, exposed Britain to military invasion. The ruling classes felt themselves more darkly threatened by social disorders when they saw, or thought they saw, the terrifying spectre of Anabaptism behind peasant protest. An increasingly educated and literate public, stimulated by clerical and lay reformers, expected the government to cure the diseases of the commonwealth. Tudor government needed skills, techniques, and resources beyond those of its predecessors if it was to survive.

[41] Joan Simon, *Education and Society in Tudor England* (Cambridge, 1966), 15.

[42] E. P. Goldschmidt, *Medieval Texts and their First Appearance in Print* (1943), 106–10. H. J. Chaytor, *From Script to Print* (1966), 10. Febvre and Martin, op. cit., chs. iv, vii. Elizabeth L. Eisenstein, 'Some Conjectures about the Impact of Printing on Western Society and Thought', *JMH* XL (1968). T. B. Howell, *A Complete Collection of State Trials* (1816), I. 457.

PART I

The Fabric of Government

I

The Central Machine[1]

Twentieth-century cabinet ministers and their senior officials deal with great issues: they draft legislation, direct foreign policy, shape economic affairs, provide education, and control social services. Governments are expected by the public to have 'policies', based upon general considerations and principles; and they delegate the execution of those policies to their officials. In practice the boundary between the formation of policy and its execution is not always clear, and politicians sometimes complain that officials usurp the higher functions. But it remains true that the cabinet, its members and senior officials concern themselves with broader issues and leave the trivia to underlings.

No such distinction was made in the sixteenth century. The Crown and its officials certainly had to face major issues, but they seldom thought in terms of policy: indeed the word was less often used in the sense of a plan or strategy than to suggest, at its highest, shrewd dealing, and, at its lowest, a disreputable cunning. Business came upon Tudor princes in a continuous stream of the important and the trivial, and they had little in the way of a bureaucratic substructure for deciding matters of executive detail. The character of royal business is apparent in the agenda compiled by leading ministers for the monarch or his Council. A memorandum by Thomas Cromwell in 1533 of matters to be discussed with the King includes things to be said on the departure of the Bavarian ambassador, the interrogation of a friar named Reysbye, the treatment of certain other friars who had been in contact with Rome, the folding of cloth in the north of England, the offer made to the King

---

[1] For an introduction to the institutions of government see A. G. R. Smith, *The Government of Elizabethan England* (1967) and G. R. Elton, *The Tudor Constitution* (Cambridge, 1960). The following general accounts of the Tudor period are recommended: G. R. Elton, *England under the Tudors* (2nd edn., 1974); Conrad Russell, *The Crisis of Parliaments, 1509–1660* (Oxford, 1971); C. S. L. Davies, *Peace, Print and Protestantism* (1976); G. R. Elton, *Reform and Reformation: England, 1509–1558* (1977).

by the executors of Lord Dacre of the South in an important test case, and the affairs of a reputed idiot named Ralph Francis. The note ends with the words 'to remember my Lady Pounder'.[2] At the far end of the century, in June 1596, Lord Burghley drew up a note of matters to be considered by Queen and Council. They included the cost of a pond in St James's Park, the provision of ordnance for St Mawes Castle, the state of fortresses in Kent, the expenses of Sir Francis Drake's recent and final voyage to the Caribbean, the debts of the late Earl of Huntingdon and Sir Thomas Heneage, the answers of the Earl of Pembroke and Sir Richard Bingham to charges made against them, complaints of decays in the Bishopric of Durham, the dispute in the College of Arms between Garter King-at-Arms and Clarencieux, a claim on the barony of Dacre, the voyage of the Earl of Essex and the Lord Admiral to Cadiz, and, rather obscurely, 'order to be taken with Matthew Goodman for the cosener'.[3]

These documents probably represented the more important business of the day—matters which Secretary Cromwell and Lord Treasurer Burghley thought worth a special note. A vast bulk of political time was taken up with the importunacy of subjects: petitions for an office or a wardship or a lease of Crown land; begging letters for pensions; suits for a pardon; requests for the Crown's help in a law-case. Adjudicating such requests was the staple business of the Crown. Perhaps as many as 3,000 had been presented annually to Henry IV.[4] There is no sign that their number had decreased by the sixteenth century. Something of their nature and their variety can be discovered from the signed bills authenticated with the King's stamp at the end of the reign of Henry VIII. A list of such bills for the period 27 April to 31 May 1546 contains 140 separate items. The first twenty-nine involved grants of wardship and the thirtieth the custody of a lunatic. The rest included a grant of the office of yeoman in the Tower, the presentation to the vicarage of Lewisham, and a lease of a royal manor, as well as such significant matters of state as letters to the Regent of Flanders,

[2] *LP* VI. 1370.

[3] PRO, State Papers Domestic, Elizabeth (SP 12), 259/3.

[4] A. L. Brown, 'The Authorization of Letters under the Great Seal', *BIHR* XXXVII (1964), 152–5.

the Earl of Bothwell, the Duke of 'Pomerland', the Duke of Mecklenburg, and the Count de Buren.[5] Requests to Edward VI in June 1552 included relief for the children of the Earl of Surrey, executed in 1547; fee-farms for the King's cofferer, Mr Chitterwood of the Privy Chamber, Dr Leyson, Sir Thomas Dacre, and Sir Ralph Bagenal; £200 for Sir Nicholas le Strange; and a pardon to John Smallwood for inadvertent manslaughter.[6]

Such matters, trivial as they might seem to us, could not be left by even the most negligent monarch wholly to others. Henry VIII's inattention to business was a constant irritation to his servants. In 1536 Sir Ralph Sadler complained: 'I think it will be hard to get any bills signed at this time . . . As ye know, His Grace is always loth to sign.'[7] Some documents could be authenticated with a wooden stamp of the royal signature, perhaps without the King even seeing them. But important matters had to wait on his attention; and, if he chose to withhold it, might wait for some time. In September 1539 Sir Thomas Heneage told Cromwell that he had managed to get three bills signed by Henry, but there were several others for which his successors in office would have to get that difficult authority, the royal signature.[8]

Elizabeth, equally dilatory, would never let such decisions slip out of her control, and she adopted an attitude of determined independence towards her ministers and courtiers. When the voices of Essex and the Cecils combined in unusual harmony to press the claim of Francis Bacon for the office of Solicitor-General, she turned him down. A trivial incident illustrates her close scrutiny of suits for patronage. When John Bull, the great musician, asked for the reversion to the lease of Radnor Forest, the officer in attendance noted that the Queen was disposed to grant it but wanted more information first.[9]

In small matters, as in great, everyday government was the inescapable business of the monarch. But Tudor sovereigns did not take their decisions in isolation from pressure and advice.

[5] PRO, State Papers Domestic, Henry VIII (SP 4), no. 11.
[6] Ibid., Edward VI (SP 10), 14/45. Haynes, 146.
[7] Elton, *TRG* 284, n.4. Cf. ibid. 67–70.
[8] *LP* xiv. ii. 163, 201.
[9] HMC, *Salisbury MSS*, xiii. 422. Cf. E. Hughes, *Studies in Administration and Finance, 1558–1825* (Manchester, 1934), 80–1.

Most of their business was transacted in the royal court, whose
physical setting dictated the rituals of supplication and
patronage. The monarch had a ceremonial life, open to the
whole political nation, and a more secluded—though scarcely
a private—life out of the general view. The boundary between
these two was carefully guarded but was not impassable. The
arrangement of rooms in royal palaces determined where the
boundary lay; and for any understanding of politics some
knowledge of these rooms and their access is essential.

The geography of fifteenth-century palaces had been relatively simple: there was a Great Hall, where ceremonious and
public appearances were made, and the Chamber where the
King withdrew and where only a few could follow him. This
disposition became more complicated in the early sixteenth
century. Some new palaces, like Whitehall and Hampton
Court, had both a Hall and a Great Chamber for grand
occasions. The more restricted arena of the Chamber itself was
divided into the Presence Chamber, where anyone with access
to court might go, and beyond it the Privy Chamber and the
most private apartments, to which entrée was restricted.[10] This
pattern of living was reproduced wherever the peripatetic court
might settle. When Elizabeth visited Burghley's house at Theo-
balds in 1572, he had this courtly pattern superimposed upon
his normal arrangement of rooms: the Hall was converted into
the Great Chamber, the Parlour into the Presence Chamber,
the Dining Chamber into the Privy Chamber, and the Vine
Chamber into the Bedchamber.[11] It was essential that this be
done, since the pattern reflected the realities of political life,
which combined the ceremonious role of the monarch in the
Great Hall, personal contact with the general run of visitors
in the Presence Chamber, and the conduct of confidential business in the Privy Chamber and the Bedchamber. Paul
Hentzner, a German traveller, has described the scene in the
Presence Chamber as the Queen passed through it one Sunday
on her way to chapel. He and his party were admitted by leave
of the Lord Chamberlain and waited with many noblemen,
councillors, and gentlemen for the Queen's appearance. She

---

[10] E. K. Chambers, *The Elizabethan Stage* (Oxford, 1923), I, ch. i. Roy Strong, *Holbein
and Henry VIII* (1967), 29–32.

[11] HMC, *Salisbury MSS*, XIII. 110–11. Cf. also 128, 145, 228.

emerged from her apartment preceded by officers of the household and as she went along 'spoke very graciously, first to one, then to another, whether foreign ministers, or those who attended for different reasons'. In the antechapel petitions were presented to her before she went to her devotions. Ceremony was effectively combined with informal contact.[12]

The people who counted in royal politics were those with access to the restricted areas of the court. Ministers of state, great noblemen, and royal favourites could expect this as a matter of course. But there was another group which is sometimes forgotten: the holders of the most intimate household offices. These men and women were as close to the monarch, and to power, as anyone. The key offices changed between the late fifteenth century and the end of the Tudor period. Under Edward IV, when the palace was still divided between the Great Hall and the Chamber, the knights of the household and the esquires of the body, who slept in the royal bedchamber, were the men to know. Of the latter it was said that 'their business is many secrets'. When John Paston wanted a favour he thought that 'Sir George Brown, Sir James Ratcliff and others of my acquaintance which wait most upon the King and lie nightly in his chamber will put to their good wills'.[13]

As the Privy Chamber developed, the knights of the household and the esquires of the body were converted, around 1518, into a new group, the gentlemen of the Privy Chamber.[14] When Henry VIII dismissed three of these gentlemen and various other household officials in 1519, the Venetian ambassador commented that they had had great authority and had been the 'very soul' of the King. In 1534 William Tyldesley advised Lord Lisle that the best means of getting a favourable answer to his requests would be a letter to some of his friends in the Privy Chamber or to the Lord Chamberlain. The correspondence of John Gates, gentleman of the Chamber in the following decade, shows that many people considered him an effective channel for their suits to the King. Their opinion is confirmed by the authority given to Gates and his colleague, Anthony

[12] P. Hentzner, *Travels in England*, trans. Horace Walpole (1797), 33–7.
[13] A. R. Myers, *The Household of Edward IV* (Manchester, 1959), 111. Lewis, *Later Medieval France*, 123.
[14] Chambers, op. cit. I, ch. ii.

Denny, together with one William Clerk, to sign documents on Henry's behalf with the royal stamp.[15]

Elizabeth, as a queen regnant, had fewer gentlemen of the Privy Chamber, and it may be that their influence was less than in the days of her father. Even so, there was competition for places in it towards the end of her reign, and many of the ageing Chamber officers were trying to bring in their own relatives as their successors. The main point certainly stands: that those in daily contact with the Queen could influence her mind and help their friends. When in 1566 the Queen was hesitating about a grant to the Earl of Leicester, then away from court, John Dudley wrote to the earl suggesting that Mrs Blanche Parry, one of the ladies-in-waiting, be approached. Some men might be able to present their own case: Sir John Harington described how he intended to bring forward a suit of his own by getting into the Privy Chamber before the breakfast covers were placed and waylaying the Queen when she came out of her bedchamber.[16] But such privileged access was for the few: most men had to relay their desires through the élite which manned the doors of power. Some suitors would have friends among this group. Others seem increasingly to have thronged the court hoping to have a chance of pressing their suit upon the Queen or a courtier. Towards the end of Elizabeth's reign arrangements were made to bring more formality into the process. In 1594 the Masters of Requests were allocated a room outside the gates of the court, to which all suitors might be directed. The Masters were to hear the suits and decide which could go forward. It is at present difficult to say how effectively they controlled the flow of petitions. Almost certainly some suitors must have continued to press their claims through courtiers and household servants. But the Masters may have become an important link between monarch and subject.[17]

However, for real power, personal attendance at court was

---

[15] *LP* III. i. 151, 235, 246; VII. 95; Add. I. ii. 1553, 1625; XXI. i. 1537 (nos 31–4). Our knowledge of the Privy Chamber will be greatly increased when Dr D. R. Starkey's thesis, 'The King's Privy Chamber, 1485–1547' (Ph.D., Cambridge, 1974) is published: I learned of it too late to be able to consult it for this book.

[16] *CSPDom, 1601–3*, 115 (282/25). *CSPDom, Add., 1566–79*, 2–4 (13/7). J. Harington, *Nugae Antiquae* (1804), I. 169.

[17] *CPSDom, 1591–4*, 432–3. Attempts to restrict access to the Council were not new. Cf. The Eltham Ordinances, *LP* IV. i. 1939 (p. 863). On the later work of the Masters of Requests see G. E. Aylmer, *The King's Servants* (1961), 13–15.

essential. In 1537 Ralph Sadler complained to Cromwell about the probable consequences of an enforced withdrawal: 'My absence from the court will so much hinder me that I shall never be able to recover.' In 1597 an anonymous friend urged Robert, Earl of Essex: 'Let nothing draw thee from the court; sit in every council . . .' Essex's rash disregard of this advice was ultimately fatal.[18]

A more formal arena of decision-making was the King's, or Queen's, Council, a mutable and complex body, which dealt not only in the making of decisions but also in the dispatch of orders and the adjudication of disputes. This Council had been firmly established as an advisory and executive board by the start of the fifteenth century. A much larger body, the Great Council, still survived at that date, meeting occasionally when the King wanted the views of the notables. It was not to have a long future, although Mary summoned it late in 1553 to announce her proposed marriage to Philip of Castile.[19] The ordinary or continual Council of the fifteenth century was quite small, had a fairly fixed membership, and met two or three times a week, sometimes with the King, sometimes without him. Some of its work was routine, designed to take off the shoulders of the King part of the administrative burden of the realm. Some of it was judicial, when it heard the complaints of private persons. Some of it was concerned with making policy in conjunction with the King, whom it advised on matters of state. Its membership and its political weight varied of course from time to time with the personality of the monarch and with changing circumstances. In the early years of Henry IV's reign it was primarily an official body executing his wishes. After 1406 its advisory role may have become more prominent. During the minority of Henry VI it dominated the government of the country. But, whatever the variations, there existed under the adult Lancastrian Kings a permanent Council whose function was to help the Monarch in governing the country by advising

---

[18] A. J. Slavin, *Politics and Profit* (Cambridge, 1966), 35. *CSPDom, 1595–7*, 532–4 (265/10). On the court in politics, see. J. E. Neale, *The Elizabethan Political Scene* (1948).

[19] *Calendar of State Papers Spanish*, IX. 414. I am grateful to Mrs Loach for this reference.

him on decisions, executing orders, and adjudicating disputes.[20] The Council's role does not seem to have changed drastically under the Yorkists, although its activities are only revealed to us obliquely in the records.[21]

The Council of Henry VII is much better documented, thanks to the survival of various excerpts from its registers. Compared with the Privy Council of Elizabeth's reign it was a large body: 183 councillors attended during the twenty-five years of the reign and sometimes more than forty were present at a single meeting.[22] But this did not prevent it from acting as an effective agency of government. The Council, often in the presence of the King, debated and decided important matters of policy. On 18 June 1486 it agreed on 'a peace to be concluded with the King of Scots ... so that a diet [conference] be taken upon treaty to be made of marriage ...' On 16 November 1504 it discussed the question of peace treaties with the Crowns of Spain and the King of France, referring the matter to the 'good and ripe deliberation' of a small committee. On 12 November 1499, sixty-five councillors, having discussed and rejected the proposal of the Archduke Maximilian to have a resident agent at Calais, received a report from Chief Justice Fyneux on the treasons of Perkin Warbeck and the Earl of Warwick. When the King asked what was to be done, 'all the said councillors and every of them by himself, adviseth, counselleth and prayeth that not only process but execution of justice be also had ...' But these grand issues of policy appear less frequently in the surviving fragments of the register than such routine matters as orders in judicial suits, summonses to men to appear before the Council, inquiries into crimes and misdemeanours, and instructions to local officials.[23]

[20] J. L. Kirby, 'Councils and Councillors of Henry IV', *TRHS*, 5th ser. xiv (1964). A. L. Brown, 'The Commons and the Council in the Reign of Henry IV', *EHR* lxxix (1964). Id., 'The Privy Seal in the Early Fifteenth Century' (D.Phil. thesis, Oxford, 1954). I am much indebted to Dr Brown for allowing me to read and use his valuable thesis. G. L. Harriss, 'Medieval Government and Statecraft', *P&P* 25 (1963), 31–4.

[21] J. R. Lander, 'The Yorkist Council and Administration', *EHR* lxxiii (1958) and 'Council, Administration and Councillors, 1461–1485', *BIHR* xxxii (1959). Professor Lander has effectively rebutted the view that the Council became insignificant under Edward IV.

[22] G. R. Elton, 'Why the History of the Early-Tudor Council Remains Unwritten', *Studies*, i. 308–38. C. G. Bayne and W. H. Dunham, *Select Cases in the Council of Henry VII* (Selden Soc., Vol. 75, 1958), introduction.

[23] Bayne and Dunham, op. cit. 9, 32, 38; see 6–47 *passim*.

While it is not difficult to say in general terms what the Council did under Henry VII, certain problems about its organization are less easily solved. Obviously, some councillors were more trusted than others; equally obviously, when the King was away from Westminster some councillors attended him while others stayed behind. Some historians have concluded from this that the councillors with the King formed an inner ring, which dealt with business of real moment. Such a conclusion is not warranted : there does not appear to have been a clearly distinguished inner group and the more important men were not always those able to leave Westminster to travel with Henry. But since Henry himself regularly attended meetings it is likely that the most significant decisions were taken by the group that was with him, whether it was the larger body sitting at Westminster or a smaller attendant body on progress.[24]

The registers give the impression—in itself plausible—that Henry VII told his Council what he wanted and left it to work out the details. For instance, in December 1506, the Council, meeting for once without the King, was told by the Lord Chancellor that Henry, hearing reports from Kildare of rebellion in Ireland, proposed to lead an expedition 'for the repress of the wild Irish'. He required the Council to 'commune and treat by ripe advisement of convenient provision for the said voyage'. The Council recommended a force of 6,000 men, apart from members of the royal household and men in charge of supplies, backed by 'three great pieces of guns', 400 arquebuses, 60 'falcons' or light cannon, and 500 hand-guns. The general impression of a biddable Council, given by this response, is supported by the comment of a Florentine, Aldo Brandini, that only one man, Sir Reginald Bray, had any influence over the King.[25]

In the early years of the reign of Henry VIII the Council, benefiting from the inexperience of the new King, probably gained weight while pursuing much the same business as before. Its autonomy was, however, short-lived, and although it was probably no less active than it had been under Henry VII, Wolsey's domineering conduct thrust it into subservience.[26] In the

[24] Elton, *Studies*, I. 317–19.
[25] Bayne and Dunham, op. cit. 46. R. Lockyer, *Henry VII* (1968), 130.
[26] W. H. Dunham, 'Wolsey's Rule of the King's Whole Council', *AmHR* XLIX (1944)

first two decades of the reign the Council was very large, containing perhaps as many as seventy members. During the 1530s this number was substantially reduced, and a small, select group was formed, compact enough to act as an advisory and executive board. In 1540 the first volume of the Privy Council's register records only nineteen members. This small Privy Council had its own staff and letter-book; and later, in 1556, it acquired its own seal. The significance of these changes has not yet been agreed by historians. Professor Elton believes that they are part of the revolution in government carried through by Thomas Cromwell, that they produced an entirely new kind of Council—a formal governing board instead of an informal inner ring—and that they achieved a clear demarcation of function between administrative and judicial business, with the Privy Council attending to administration and the Star Chamber—in effect the same people afforced by two judges—carrying out conciliar jurisdiction. Others, myself among them, are not convinced that Cromwell was the sole architect of the Privy Council, which may have been in part the consequence of his fall rather than of his predominance. Although a small Privy Council is different from an informal inner ring, the new body does not seem entirely original, for it had precedents in the fifteenth century and in the early years of Henry VIII. Nor does the demarcation between Privy Council and Star Chamber seem to have been entirely clear, for the Privy Council continued to exercise judicial or quasi-judicial functions.[27]

The 'new' Privy Council which helped Henry VIII to govern between 1540 and 1547 underwent some changes during the reigns of his successors. Protector Somerset held the number of privy councillors around twenty, but under the Duke of Northumberland it rose to more than thirty. The inclusion of half-a-dozen peers who held no significant office suggests that it was

---

and 'Henry VIII's Whole Council and its Parts', *Huntington Library Quarterly*, VII (1943). Elton, *Studies*, I. 312–13. J. A. Guy, *The Cardinal's Court* (1977), ch. ii, gives the most recent account of the Council under Wolsey.

[27] Elton, *TRG* 320–69; *Tudor Constitution*, 87–93, 101–4; *Studies*, I. 308–38; 'Tudor Government: the Points of Contact: ii, The Council', *TRHS*, 5th ser. XXV (1975), 199–203. Penry Williams and G. L. Harriss, 'A Revolution in Tudor History?', *P&P* 25 (1963), 31–4, 48–50. See the reply to this article by G. R. Elton in *P&P* 29 (1964).

beginning to revert to the form of the 1520s, when the Council had included both office-holders and men whose political support was valuable to the Crown. Mary seems at first sight to have carried still further the process of reversion: 'numbers cause great confusion,' remarked Count Feria, Charles V's ambassador. But it is possible that the poor reputation of Mary's Council is based on too credulous a reading of the reports of Imperial envoys. Irked by their failure to secure full English support for Habsburg policies, they may have attributed to factiousness and incompetence what was simply a sensible reluctance to tie England too closely to the Imperial coat-tails. In practice Mary seems to have ruled through a small group of office-holders, using the other councillors for service in the shires and for the provision of general political support. But even if this is so, the Marian Council was distinctly different from the small executive and advisory board of the years 1540–1547.[28]

It was left to Elizabeth to restore this earlier system. Her Privy Council never had more than nineteen members and towards the end of the reign had only eleven. In her early years it met three days a week, but in the final decades was meeting on six or seven. According to John Herbert, who became second Secretary of State in 1600, it had three principal functions: the business of the Queen, in which it 'doth handle principally questions and consultations of state'; disputes between party and party, which might involve either criminal or civil suits or a mixture of the two; and disputes 'wherein the Queen is a party'.[29] Some idea of its business, ranging from the apparently trivial to the significant, can be seen in the contents of its registers for a single day, 21 December 1595. The Privy Council is then found referring to arbitration a dispute between two foreigners, hearing the submission and apology of a merchant for speaking offensively about the Queen, instructing sheriffs to send up a note of the number of prisoners in their gaols, ordering mayors of seaports to prepare private ships to serve in the navy against the expected Spanish invasion, telling its agents

[28] Elton, *Tudor Constitution*, 96, 100. Id., *TRHS* xxv. 203–7. D. E. Hoak, *The King's Council in the Reign of Edward VI* (Cambridge, 1976), esp. ch. ii.
[29] *Tudor Constitution*, 104. *TRHS* xxv. 207–11. For a discussion of the judicial aspects see below, 217, 228.

at the Hague to arrange for the purchase of matches for guns, sending off various warrants, organizing the acquisition of copper for the Queen's service, delegating the decision in a legal action to the J.P.s of Bedfordshire, permitting the taking of a collection on behalf of a Cornish village despoiled by Spaniards, and writing to the Lord Mayor of London about a complaint against his predecessor.[30] Wide as this range of activities would seem to be, the registers omit one vital aspect of the Council's work. They record only action actually taken in the shape of orders and letters sent out; they tell us nothing of discussions about policy, of general decisions taken, of advice tendered to the Queen. Yet such discussions certainly took place, normally without the Queen. On 4 January 1576, for instance, Francis Talbot told his father, the Earl of Shrewsbury, that 'the Council be all at the court; they sit daily and the ambassadors [of France] come to them'. On 4 April 1579, at the height of the debate about the proposed marriage between Elizabeth and the Duke of Anjou, he reported that the Privy Council had met on each of the previous five days from 8.00 a.m. until supper-time.[31]

The effect of such debates upon the making of policy is difficult to assess. Elizabeth certainly had a much tighter control over her Council than her sister had been able to exercise. At the very beginning of the reign William Cecil, by threatening to resign, persuaded her to follow the Council's advice, which was not unanimous, and intervene in Scotland.[32] Later, it became much harder to influence her. In 1562 and again in 1566 the Privy Council urged Elizabeth in vain to marry and secure the succession. In 1578 the Earl of Leicester complained of the Queen's isolation from her councillors: 'Our conference with Her Majesty about affairs is both seldom and slender,' he wrote. Following the death of William the Silent in 1584 a majority of the councillors, with Burghley and Mildmay dissenting, urged direct support for the Dutch rebels. But not until the following May, when the whole Council had united to demand intervention, did she give in. That she did

---

[30] *APC* xxv. 120–30.

[31] Lodge, II. 136, 212.

[32] Conyers Read, *Mr Secretary Cecil and Queen Elizabeth* (1955), 159–61. *Calendar of State Papers, Foreign, 1559–60*, 197, 220.

so then may have been as much the consequence of events as of advice.[33] Elizabeth's Privy Council had a free hand only in executive matters. It could and did reach conclusions upon policy, but the final decision rested with the Queen, who seldom attended meetings and might easily ignore their conclusions.

John Herbert's second and third categories of business were disputes between party and party and disputes 'wherein the Queen is a party'. It is apparent that the Privy Council continued, even after 1540, to be involved in judicial business: but the nature of that involvement can best be studied in the context of the legal system as a whole.[34]

Parliament was the arena in which were made the most formal decisions: laws applicable to the whole realm, superior to any other rules or customs.[35] By the time that Henry VII reached the throne the English Parliament had already become established as a powerful force in government, law, and politics. Its form was settled in the fifteenth century, and well before 1485 there was no longer any doubt that the House of Commons was an integral part of Parliament, as necessary to its existence as the Lords: no statute was valid without its consent. The

[33] R. B. Wernham, *Before the Armada*, 336. Conyers Read, *Mr Secretary Walsingham* (Oxford, 1925), III. 82–3; and *Lord Burghley and Queen Elizabeth* (1960), ch. xvii.
[34] Below, ch. VII.
[35] The following works are important on the medieval background to parliamentary history. S. B. Chrimes, *English Constitutional Ideas in the Fifteenth Century* (Cambridge, 1936). J. S. Roskell, *The Commons in the Parliament of 1422* (Manchester, 1954). E. B. Fryde and E. Miller (eds.), *Historical Studies of the English Parliament* (2 vols., Cambridge, 1970): the introduction and the bibliographical section are a most useful guide to the literature.

The literature on sixteenth-century Parliaments is very large. Especially important are: G. R. Elton, *Studies*, II. 3–61; id., *Reform and Renewal* (Cambridge, 1973); id., 'Tudor Government: the Points of Contact: i, Parliament', *TRHS*, 5th ser. XXIV (1974); S. E. Lehmberg, *The Reformation Parliament, 1529–36* (Cambridge, 1970); id., *The Later Parliaments of Henry VIII, 1536–1547* (Cambridge, 1977); J. E. Neale, *The Elizabethan House of Commons* (1949); id., *Elizabeth I and her Parliaments* (2 vols., 1953, 1957); W. Notestein, *The Winning of the Initiative by the House of Commons* (1924); Fryde and Miller, op. cit. II, especially the article by J. S. Roskell; P. Williams and G. L. Harriss, 'A Revolution in Tudor History?', *P&P* 25 (1963), with comments by J. P. Cooper in ibid., no. 26, and by G. R. Elton in ibid., no. 29. Jennifer Loach, 'Parliamentary Opposition to Mary' (D.Phil. thesis, Oxford, 1974), is an important contribution to which I owe much, and which will, I hope, shortly be published.

composition of both Houses had been defined in broad terms. The nature of the parliamentary peerage had been fixed by 1450; certain peers were by then entitled to a summons.[36] Representation of shires and boroughs had also been determined: the King no longer had discretion to decide which communities might send up M.P.s, although it was of course open to him to make new enfranchisements by royal charter.

Parliament's authority over finance was undisputed. Only parliamentary consent could allow the King to levy the direct taxes known as fifteenths and tenths or the indirect taxes known as tonnage and poundage. He could still ask for benevolences, but the request could have no legal force, however much moral pressure might lie behind it. At certain times Parliament had even exercised the right to appropriate taxes to particular items of expenditure. Between them, Parliament and the King enacted, in the form of statutes, the highest laws of the realm. In theory a statute could do no more than declare existing law; and statutes were cast in a declaratory form. But in practice, not only did the courts accept Parliament's power to make new laws, but a legal distinction was made between statutes which declared old law and those which created new law. In principle statutes might be limited by the natural law; but in effect they were supreme.[37] Towards the end of the fifteenth century the King was beginning to lose his power to amend a statute after it had passed both Houses: the statute as presented to him was coming to be regarded as the final legal form, which he could only reject or accept *in toto*. Both Houses of Parliament had shown independence of the King during the fourteenth and fifteenth centuries. Royal favourites had been impeached; taxation had been refused or stringent conditions attached to its granting. Nor was intransigence simply an expression of magnate power. Members of the House of Commons were often important landowners, with considerable parliamentary experience and the ability to decide things for themselves. But it would be wrong to stress—either in the middle ages or in the sixteenth century—the significance of parliamentary opposition. As Professor Elton has argued, Parliament's importance in England rested on its utility to the monarch, on its readiness to co-operate in the business of ruling.[38]

Under the Tudors, the granting of money continued to be one of the prime parliamentary functions. But it was not the Crown's invariable motive for summoning a Parliament. Several parliamentary sessions under Henry VIII passed without any direct taxes being asked or given;[39] and Mary, at the start of her reign, even remitted the outstanding part of the last subsidy granted under Edward VI, asking nothing from the two parliaments of 1554.[40] Under Elizabeth, however, there was only one parliamentary session in which no subsidy was granted, that of 1572, when the Houses were summoned to deal with 'the great cause' of national security presented by the Ridolfi plot and by Mary, Queen of Scots. Parliament's control over direct taxation thus increased in importance after 1558 as the Crown became more dependent upon that source of revenue. But Tudor Parliaments allowed indirect revenue to slip almost out of their grasp by granting tonnage and poundage, automatically it seems, to each Tudor monarch for life in the first session of each reign.[41]

Legislation by statute greatly increased in importance during the Tudor period. The pretence that statutes merely declared existing law was dropped; they occupied areas of national life which before they had only occasionally entered; they became far more precisely drafted and the judges interpreted them a good deal less freely; they were, by the reign of Elizabeth, the outcome of a definite and recognized procedure. So much is agreed. How far they were supreme in any new and unprecedented sense, whether their advance can be termed revolutionary, how much they owed to the innovatory genius of Thomas Cromwell are questions still open to dispute. But this is not the place to explore further into that particular controversy. It is enough to say that, especially after 1529, Parliament became a more dynamic and a still less dispensable part of English government than it had been before.[42]

[38] Roskell, *Commons in the Parliament of 1422*. Id., in Fryde and Miller, op. cit. II, ch. x. McFarlane, 'Parliament and Bastard Feudalism', *TRHS* XXVI (1944). Elton, *Studies*, II. 51–61.

[39] For instance the sessions of 1529, 1531, 1532, 1533, 1536, 1539.

[40] 1 Mary c. 17.   [41] Roskell, in Fryde and Miller, op. cit. II. 318–19.

[42] Williams and Harriss, *P&P* 25; Elton, ibid., no. 29; id., *Studies*. 51–61.

The effectiveness of statute gained much from the use of the printing-press. In the fourteenth century even judges had been remarkably ignorant of the statutes which they had to enforce; lawcourts sometimes did not even possess copies of particular acts; and the copies which did exist were marred by gross errors. Since the reign of Richard III Acts of Parliament had been regularly printed, and the massive legislation of the 1530s was conveyed by the press to those entrusted with its execution. The commands of statute could now be more complex, elaborate, and precise; texts were uniform; and copies were widely diffused. The strict interpretation of statute, an important feature of the sixteenth century, owed much to the invention of printing.[43]

Discussion of statute raises the important problem of royal proclamations. Some historians have seen signs in the 1530s that the legislative authority of Parliament might have been undermined by the King's power to issue proclamations. Thomas Cromwell expressed pleasure when told by the Lord Chief Justice in 1535 that proclamations were 'of as good effect as any law made by Parliament or otherwise'.[44] Four years later the Crown introduced into the Lords a bill concerning the authority and enforcement of proclamations. This bill was criticized and amended in the Lords; and as the original bill has not survived we cannot know its contents or the government's intentions. The Act of Proclamations, as it was finally passed in 1539, contains in its preamble some resonant phrases about regal power, but added relatively little to the King's authority: proclamations were given a statutory base and a special court was established for their enforcement. The act was repealed in 1547 and its importance was therefore short-lived. Professor Hurstfield has however inferred from the preamble that the government wanted something much more far-reaching than it got: nothing less than unlimited authority to legislate by proclamation. Without the original bill we cannot be certain of the government's objectives; but on balance it seems unlikely that it wished to replace statutory legislation by proclamation.[45]

[43] J. H. Beale, *Bibliography of Early English Law Books* (Cambridge, Mass., 1926). T. F. T. Plucknett, *Statutes and their Interpretation in the First Half of the Fourteenth Century* (Cambridge, 1922), 103–12.

[44] Elton, *Tudor Constitution*, 27.

[45] For the controversy on the Act of Proclamations see Elton, 'Henry VIII's Act of

Even so, proclamations had considerable power, both before and after 1539. Under Henry VIII they were used to suspend, modify, or extend the provisions of statutes: a proclamation of 1540 altered and dispensed with some clauses of a statute on aliens; in 1546 a statute restricting the sale of wool was extended by proclamation to cover counties not mentioned in the original act.[46] Elizabeth and her advisers seem to have been more cavalier. The statute of 1585, making Jesuits, seminarists, and other Catholic priests traitors by virtue of their order was anticipated by a proclamation of 1582.[47] Regulations restricting building in London were first issued by royal proclamation in 1580, many years before the first statutory regulation.[48] By the end of her reign there are signs that some lawyers were concerned at the free use of proclamations. Robert Beale, clerk to the Privy Council, advised councillors and secretaries of state 'to avoid opinion of being new-fangled and a bringer-in of new customs'.[49] However, wide as the law-making powers of proclamations were, it cannot be said that under the Tudors they ever came near to replacing statute. They might occasionally encroach or anticipate, but that was all. The Crown was dependent upon Parliament for its important legislation and for much that was less significant too.[50]

Parliament was not, however, simply an instrument for far-reaching transformations of the law by the Crown. Much of its business was concerned with continuing statutes that would otherwise lapse, repealing some that had become irksome, or modifying others which had revealed weaknesses in operation. Such legislation was essential for the running of government and society. Undramatic in its effect and narrow in its scope, highly forgettable and often forgotten by historians, it

---

Proclamations', *EHR* LXXV (1960), and 'The Rule of Law in Sixteenth-Century England', both reprinted in *Studies*, I. 260–84, 339–54. J. Hurstfield, 'Was there a Tudor Despotism after all?', *TRHS* XVII (1967), repr. in id., *Freedom, Corruption and Government in Elizabethan England* (1973). The most recent and convincing interpretation is in R. W. Heinze, *The Proclamations of the Tudor Kings* (Cambridge, 1976), ch. vi.

[46] Hughes & Larkin, I, nos. 195, 199, 264. Cf. also nos. 198, 202, 207. On the use of proclamations by Protector Somerset see M. L. Bush, *The Government Policy of Protector Somerset* (1975), 131–41, 146–59.

[47] Hughes & Larkin, II, no. 660. 27 Elizabeth c. 2.

[48] Hawarde, 78, 318, 328. Hughes & Larkin, II, no. 649. *CSPDom. 1598–1601*, 115.

[49] Elton, *Tudor Constitution*, 126.

[50] Neale, *Elizabeth I and her Parliaments*, I. 354–5.

made up the bulk of parliamentary business. The session of 1536 is best remembered for the dissolution of the smaller monasteries, the union of England and Wales, the establishment of the Court of Augmentations, and the seizure of franchises by the Crown. Besides these, sixty-three other acts were passed, dealing, *inter alia*, with the preservation of the banks of the Thames, the price of meat, the regulation of the cloth trade, the jointure of Lady Eleanor Clifford, and various exchanges of lands.

Some of these statutes were brought forward, like the better-known acts of state, by the Crown. But others were the work of private groups or individuals, who used Parliament as an arena for advancing their own interests and for settling disputes with their rivals. The politics of the pressure-group were highly developed in Tudor England. Towns like London and York knew how to organize the procedures of Parliament and whom to lobby. Trading guilds and companies manœuvred to have their industry organized to their own advantage or allied with the Crown to do so. To most of the people who used Parliament in this way—and probably to most of its members—it was a complex political organism which, handled carefully, might produce something to their advantage.[51]

As Professor Elton has argued, it was not regarded as a constitutional force which deserved notice only when it was opposing or restricting the Crown. The preoccupation of historians with this constitutional role, with the evolution of privilege and the growth of party, has obscured the essential work of Parliament: discussion and negotiation about the enactment of law. That is not to say that Parliament was subservient. The large question of the limits upon royal power will be discussed in a later chapter, but it can be said now that, although the Crown put pressure upon both Houses, they were capable of obstinacy and independence. Parliament was neither a rubber-stamp nor a makeweight in the constitutional balance. It was an important part of the governmental machine, which helped to pro-

---

[51] Helen Miller, 'London and Parliament in the Reign of Henry VIII', *BIHR* xxxv (1962), repr. in Fryde and Miller, op. cit. II. L. A. Clarkson, 'English Economic Policy in the Sixteenth and Seventeenth Centuries', *BIHR* xxxviii (1965). On the problems of distinguishing between public and private bills see Elton, *Reform and Renewal*, 77–97.

duce—by negotiation, discussion, criticism, and occasional obstruction—a large body of law.[52]

By 1400 a sophisticated machine had been assembled for the transmission, authentication, and execution of the decisions made in the upper echelons of government, and for conducting such recurrent and routine operations as the collection and payment of money. This machine resembled a set of assembly-lines along which orders passed through a series of check-points. The decisions made by King and Council were processed by three institutions—the Signet, the Privy Seal, and the Chancery—though not in every case by all three of them. The King had acquired, in the time of Richard II, an authenticating instrument, the Signet, which was under his own control and was wielded by his personal secretary. Signet and secretary could be used for sending relatively informal letters to the King's subjects or for activating other parts of the executive machine: the Signet Office was the instrument most often used for disseminating the King's personal commands. More formal was the Privy Seal office, where King or Council had their administrative orders drawn up in traditional and, if necessary, legal language, and authenticated by the older and more important Privy Seal. Essentially this was a writing-office, which could send instructions to royal officials or foreign courts and could authorize proceedings in the most formal parts of the machine, Chancery and Exchequer. Chancery was the oldest and most solemn part of the whole apparatus. It alone could authenticate documents with the Great Seal, which was in its custody, and issue orders that required full legal backing, such as grants of land, appointments to offices, and treaties with foreign powers. Although there were some routine matters, such as the issue of legal writs, where it could act on its own initiative, for any matter of permanent importance it needed a warrant for its action from the Privy Seal or the Signet: usually only the former would be sufficient.[53]

[52] Elton, *Reform and Renewal*, ch. vii. Id., *Studies*, II. 3–18, 59–61. Id., *TRHS* XXIV (1974). Below, 399–402.

[53] A. L. Brown, 'The Privy Seal in the Early Fifteenth Century' (D.Phil. thesis, Oxford, 1954). Elton, *TRG* 270 ff. B. P. Wolffe, *The Crown Lands, 1461–1536* (1970), 120–39. S. B. Chrimes, *An Introduction to the Administrative History of Medieval England* (Oxford, 1959), ch. vi.

The whole process can be illustrated by a linear diagram.

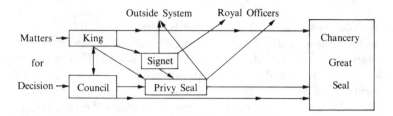

This diagram necessarily oversimplifies a very complicated set of operations. There were two possible starting-points for any decision, the King and the Council, which might of course discuss the matter jointly. From either of these points there were several paths to be taken: a few orders could go directly to the Great Seal, but most had initially to go either to the Signet or to the Privy Seal, sometimes to both. Decisions by the Council usually went to the Privy Seal for transmission; orders from the King might go there or might go first to the Signet. The notion that Signet and Privy Seal were political rivals, the one working for the King, the other for a baronial council, is false. Both were part of the same system. The choice of path to be taken depended upon the degree of formality required, the circumstance of the moment, and pure chance.[54]

Financial operations were mainly handled, until Yorkist times, by the Exchequer, which was responsible for collecting the King's revenue, banking his liquid wealth, if any, arranging for payments to his creditors, and auditing official accounts. The Upper Exchequer conducted the audits in the manner of a lawcourt. Anyone who handled the King's money was 'charged' with the revenues he had received or collected and had to acquit himself before the Barons of the Exchequer by showing what he had done with it. The Lower Exchequer, also called the Exchequer of Receipt—misleadingly so, since it paid money out as well—took in revenue from royal collectors and handed over receipts in the form of tallies, which could then be presented in the Upper Exchequer at the audit.[55]

---

[54] Brown, op. cit. Id., 'Authorization of Letters under the Great Seal', *BIHR* xxxvii (1964).

[55] Chrimes, op. cit. 52–66, 147, 210–13, 264. Elton, *TRG* 20–30.

The receipt of money and the audit of accounts were routine operations which the Exchequer conducted all the time without needing any instruction or authorization for doing so. But before it could pay money out it would require a warrant. Such warrants might authorize single payments or a regular series; and they could come either from Chancery or from the Privy Seal. To complicate matters further, however, the Crown might use one of its local officials for paying creditors: in that case the official would receive a warrant, which he would take, with his receipt, to the Exchequer when presenting his account. The flow of warrants and decisions can again be shown in a diagram.

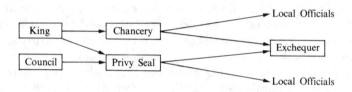

The main purpose of the Exchequer was to prevent the Crown from being defrauded by its own officials. In a cumbersome way it seems to have done this fairly effectively, for it was difficult for an official to embezzle royal money without being exposed in the long run, although the run was often so long that he was dead before it finished. Its accounting system also enabled the Exchequer to provide the King with fairly realistic statements of his revenue, expenditure, and debts.[56] The Exchequer's secondary function was the payment of the King's debts; provided that the King had some money for discharging them, it performed this task efficiently but slowly. The Exchequer was not really designed to provide the King with a store of liquid cash and it was no part of its role to expand existing sources of revenue, invent new ones, or curb royal expenditure. The weakness of the system lay not so much in the Exchequer's faulty handling of the business for which it was intended, as in the absence of any institution responsible for developing or supervising the whole field of royal finance.[57]

[56] Cf. J. L. Kirby, 'The Issues of the Lancastrian Exchequer', *BIHR* xxiv (1951).
[57] G. L. Harriss, 'Medieval Government and Statecraft', *P&P* 25 (1963), 26–7. Kirby, op. cit.

There were two financial institutions which lay outside the Exchequer's control. One was the court of the Duchy of Lancaster, which administered the lands gained by the Crown at the accession of Henry of Lancaster in 1399. These lands were kept separate from the remainder of the Crown estates, and the court of the Duchy kept its own accounts. Much more important than the Duchy was the royal household, whose financial institutions, the Chamber and the Wardrobe, not only consumed a large part of the Crown's income but also assisted, from time to time, in national government.[58]

There were of course other institutions of central government, which cannot be given more than a bare mention here. The College of Arms, founded in 1483, made and authenticated grants of arms, while its heralds were often used by the Crown to treat with foreign powers or with rebels. Both the army and the navy had rudimentary organizations: naval supplies were provided by a clerk acting under the spasmodic supervision of the Lord Admiral while specific operations continued to be mounted by *ad hoc* commissions.

Before we proceed to the changes brought about in this system by the Yorkist and Tudor sovereigns, certain general observations must be made about medieval administration. First, government was obviously very much royal government, although the King was helped in making decisions by the Council. Second, the institutions of government, apart from the Council, did little more than process decisions made elsewhere. Most of the work of the Signet Office, the Privy Seal Office, and Chancery was routine, although the Signet was the vehicle for less formal expressions of the royal will. The heads of these offices might be men of authority and influence, but they owed little of this to the departments over which they presided. They were important because of their social standing or because others listened to them in Council. The Lord Privy Seal, for instance, was usually a man of political consequence, but he stood aloof from the mechanical operations of the office. The one occasional exception was the Lord Treasurer, who sometimes, but certainly not always, gained authority from his access to the royal accounts: Ralph, Lord Cromwell, is a case in point.

[58] R. Somerville, *History of the Duchy of Lancaster*, Vol. I, *1265–1603* (1953), chs. xiii–xvi.

Third, by contrast with a modern bureaucracy, the departments of medieval government were only to a small extent defined by areas in which they worked. Again, the Exchequer is exceptional: finance was kept separate from other functions of government. But the other institutions were distinguished by their position in the 'assembly-line' rather than the kind of business with which they dealt.[59]

From 1471 there were important developments in the executive system. The creation of the Privy Council has already been discussed;[60] and it now remains to consider the changes in the Secretaryship of State, military and naval administration, finance, and the royal household.

Under Edward IV the business of both Secretary and Signet increased, and after his death the office of Secretary was not suspended during the minority of Edward V, as it had been when Henry VI was a child. The Secretary had in fact become a public officer, no longer merely the personal assistant of the monarch. By 1532 his office rivalled that of the Privy Seal, and in that year began the greatest development of the Secretaryship, when Thomas Cromwell was appointed to the post. It is difficult to say how much of Cromwell's considerable power derived from this office and how much of his personal authority rubbed off on to its subsequent holders. Certainly his successors were lesser men than he and wielded less authority; after 1540, until at any rate the reign of Elizabeth, the office was to some extent what its holder made of it. But the Secretary had come to stay as the hub of the administrative process. As the clearing-house for information and orders he and his officers had replaced the Privy Seal. Whether he was more than that, whether he carried weight with the monarch or the Council, was up to him.[61]

His functions ranged from the fixed and formal to the highly uncertain. Robert Cecil, who knew what he was talking about, commented that, while all other officers had a clear and defined

---

[59] Brown, 'The Privy Seal'. Kirby, op. cit.

[60] Above, 27–33.

[61] A. J. Otway-Ruthven, *The King's Secretary and the Signet Office in the Fifteenth Century* (Cambridge, 1939). Elton, *TRG*, ch. iv. F. M. G. Evans, *The Principal Secretary of State* (Manchester, 1923), chs. i–iii.

authority, 'to the Secretary, out of a confidence and singular affection, there is a liberty to negotiate at discretion at home and abroad, with friends and enemies, all matters of speech and intelligence'. By then, at the end of the century, the Secretary's power was his for the taking. Forty years earlier, in the days of Ralph Sadler and Thomas Wriothesley, it had been much more hardly won.[62]

The most formal part of his work lay in his control of the Signet Office, which was mainly concerned with the authentication of documents on their way to the Privy Seal, Chancery, or Exchequer. While most of this was routine, the Secretary was in a position to expedite or delay the royal grants of patronage which had to pass the Signet.[63] More important was his role as a linkman. The Secretary instructed the Crown's officers at home and overseas. In close touch with the monarch, he was the best informed and most constantly attendant councillor. He acted as the principal connection between King, Council, and Parliament; for, until Robert Cecil went to the Lords in 1604, the Secretary was invariably a commoner and was normally the Crown's principal mouthpiece in the Lower House. The Secretary was also responsible for collecting and storing the vast and increasing mass of information required by sixteenth-century governments. To him came the reports about the militia and its armaments, the loyalties and affiliations of the country gentry, the names of recusants, the affairs of Ireland, and the politics of foreign countries.[64]

To help him in his work the Secretary had formal and informal support. The formal support came from the Signet Office, which had been given definite shape in the fifteenth century. For duties of a less routine kind the Secretary had the help of two secretaries for foreign tongues—Latin and French—and of his own personal staff. With the departure of one Secretary and the arrival of another, the office staff—apart of course from the members of the Signet Office—normally changed completely; not until the early seventeenth century did a permanent bureaucratic organization begin to appear beneath the Secretary of State.[65]

---

[62] Quoted in Evans, op. cit. 59. See A. J. Slavin, *Politics and Profit*, 51–60.
[63] Slavin, loc. cit.　　　　　　　[64] Evans, op. cit., chs. ii, iii, xi.
[65] A. G. R. Smith, 'The Secretariat of the Cecils', *EHR* LXXXIII (1968).

In consequence the great stores of information collected by the Secretaries were never fully accessible. Robert Beale, Clerk to the Privy Council, insisting that the Secretary must know almost everything about the affairs of England and her neighbours, recommended that the essential material be stored in ten or twelve great books: one would contain treaties; another would list recusants; a third would deal with the Councils in the Marches and in the North; and so on.[66] But his recommendations were not followed. 'There hath been found of late great confusion in the keeping of loose papers,' wrote Nicholas Faunt, one of Walsingham's assistants. Many state documents were regarded as the officer's private property.[67] A few weeks after Burghley's death one Dr James was paid by the Privy Council to remove the Lord Treasurer's papers from his house: the great collections at Hatfield and in the Lansdowne MSS show how limited was his success; and later efforts by Thomas Wilson to establish a state paper office during the reign of James I seem also to have been largely vain. The failure to set up a working system for filing and recovering information shows how defective the organization of the Secretary's office still was at the end of the Tudor period.[68]

Other executive agents began to appear in the course of the sixteenth century. The navy, greatly expanded under Henry VIII, required something more than the single clerk who had managed its affairs under the distant and often negligible supervision of the Lord Admiral. More officers were created, such as the surveyor and rigger, the vice-admiral, and the master of naval ordnance. By 1546 there was a permanent committee, the Navy Board, for the management of naval administration.[69] With no standing army the Crown did not require any equivalent military body. But it did need permanent supervision of weapons, gunpowder, and equipment; and this was provided by the emergence under Henry VIII of a centralized Ordnance Office. In some ways the most striking development was the

[66] C. Read, *Mr Secretary Walsingham*, i. 423-43.

[67] Faunt's treatise is edited by C. Hughes, *EHR* xx (1903), 499-508.

[68] *APC* xxix. 178. *Thirtieth Report of the Deputy-Keeper of the Public Records* (1869), 212-223.

[69] C. S. L. Davies, 'The Administration of the Royal Navy under Henry VIII and the Origins of the Navy Board', *EHR* lxxx (1965).

growth, during the sixteenth century, of a permanent diplomatic service. In the fifteenth century embassies were usually temporary missions for the fulfilment of particular purposes. By the end of the sixteenth, England had followed the current continental practice of keeping permanent ambassadors or agents in most foreign capitals. Their duties were varied: to send back information to England, to negotiate with the government to which they were accredited, and, occasionally, to stir up trouble abroad. As yet there was no career structure for diplomats and there was no separate foreign office: contact with envoys was one of the main duties of the Secretary of State.[70]

The history of financial institutions under the Yorkists and early Tudors is far from straightforward.[71] From 1471 there was built up an informal 'system' of government finance, which operated alongside, and to some extent in co-operation with, the old Exchequer. In essence this was less a system than the resort by the Crown to whatever means came to hand for raising and controlling money. It is consequently difficult to describe in a brief space, and the following account attempts only to indicate some basic features of government finance between 1471 and about 1534.

To bring the Crown out of the poverty and debt which had marked most of the reign of Henry VI, both Edward IV and Richard III used professional receivers, auditors, and surveyors to increase the revenue from Crown lands; and much of this larger income was paid, neither to the Exchequer nor to the Crown's creditors, but to the Chamber of the royal Household, where it was at the disposal of the King. For a brief period after his accession Henry VII allowed the old Exchequer system to revive; but from about 1493 he reverted to the methods of his immediate predecessors. Revenues from Crown lands went increasingly to the Chamber rather than to the Exchequer and money was stored in the Jewel House of the Household. The operations of the Chamber officials and other financial officers were now supervised by the Office of General Surveyors, a committee of the royal Council acting as a board of audit. Several

---

[70] G. Mattingley, *Renaissance Diplomacy* (1955), chs. xxv, xxvi.
[71] See below, ch. II for an analysis of revenue and expenditure.

commissioners were appointed by Henry VII to exploit new or revived forms of revenue; and some new offices were invented. Of these, one, the Office of Wards, survived into the seventeenth century; another, the powerful Surveyor of the King's Prerogative, lasted only for five years.[72]

On the accession of Henry VIII some attempt was made to give cohesion and formality to these arrangements with the statutory establishment of the Office of General Surveyors. But otherwise the informal processes of the Chamber continued to dominate royal finance until the 1530s. The advantages of the innovations brought about by Edward IV and Henry VII lay in the professional supervision of royal estates, the speedy collection of revenues, the rigorous exploitation of all forms of Crown income, and the availability of liquid cash. Their principal drawback lay in their informality, which demanded the constant supervision of an active King.[73]

The Chamber and its attendant offices were capable of managing the traditional revenues of the Crown. But neither they nor an unreformed Exchequer could handle the large new sources of income brought into being by Henry VIII's breach with Rome: the first fruits of bishoprics, the tenths of all ecclesiastical benefices, the revenue from the renting and sale of monastic lands. To manage these Thomas Cromwell invented two totally new institutions, the Court of First Fruits and the Court of Augmentations. In 1540 he transformed the office of Wards, formed in 1503, into the Court of Wards, to which was joined the office of Liveries in 1542. Of all these, Augmentations was probably the most remarkable, since its accounting processes were modern and it used a more rational system for collecting revenues than did the old Exchequer.[74]

The Cromwellian reforms, inventive and effective as they were, produced an extraordinary diversity of financial departments. Six unco-ordinated offices were used for receiving revenue: the old Exchequer, the King's Chamber—by now

[72] B. P. Wolffe, 'Henry VII's Land Revenues and Chamber Finance', *EHR* LXXIX (1964). Id., *The Crown Lands, 1461–1536* (1970), 45–50, and docts. nos. 16, 17. W. C. Richardson, *Tudor Chamber Administration* (Baton Rouge, 1952), *passim*. Elton, *TRG* 23–30, 160–9. Richardson, 'The Surveyor of the King's Prerogative', *EHR* LVI (1941).

[73] Wolffe, *Crown Lands*, intro. Richardson, *Tudor Chamber Administration*, *passim*.

[74] Elton, *TRG*, ch. iii. Richardson, *Tudor Chamber Administration*, ch. vi. Id., *The History of the Court of Augmentations* (Baton Rouge, 1961), *passim*.

reverting to its old function of a domestic household treasury— the Court of Wards and Liveries, the Duchy of Lancaster, the Court of Augmentations, and the Court of First Fruits. There was also the Office of General Surveyors, converted into a court in 1542, which audited various accounts but received no revenues. Such a system was effectively harnessed by the energy and skill of Thomas Cromwell; but deprived of his control after 1540 it became corrupt, inefficient, and unpopular. Some changes came about on the death of Henry VIII, when the General Surveyors were absorbed into Augmentations, but it was apparent that more drastic reforms were needed. Of the various solutions proposed in 1552 by a commission of investigation, a rather curious and irrational compromise was adopted two years later. First Fruits and Augmentations, together with General Surveyors, were absorbed into a reformed Exchequer. The Chamber became solely a domestic household institution, but Wards and the Duchy of Lancaster maintained an independent existence. While there was therefore a move towards a single national agency of finance, this was not fully achieved and the divisions which remained had no obvious rationale. Nevertheless, the Exchequer was, from 1554 onwards, the central and predominant financial institution, the national treasury.[75]

Many of the experiments and creations of the Yorkists and the first two Tudors had been pushed aside, leaving the old system of Exchequer finance in command. But this system had undergone some important changes. The Lord Treasurer, long a figurehead, was once again the Crown's financial manager: the careers of Paulet, Burghley, and Salisbury testify to his power. Beneath the Treasurer, the Chancellor of the Exchequer came to exercise an effective supervision both of receipt and of audit. The Augmentations structure of local receivers and auditors was preserved for certain branches of the revenue; and very much more modern and efficient methods of accountancy were applied to most operations. The system was therefore very different from that of the Lancastrians. But it still suffered from several of the defects of the medieval Exchequer: it was very

---

[75] Elton, loc. cit. Richardson, *Tudor Chamber Administration*, 305–442. Id., *Augmentations, passim*, esp. ch. xiii. Id., *The Report of the Royal Commission of 1552* (Morgantown, W. Virginia, 1974).

slow; it had not the machinery to expand the available sources of revenue; and it had no effective control over expenditure.[76]

Although it is difficult, in reading the Black Book of Edward IV and the Household Ordinances of his reign, always to distinguish what reformers wanted from what they actually achieved, the main lines of the Yorkist Household can be distinguished; and those lines remained pretty much the same until the eighteenth century. By the end of the fifteenth century the royal Household was divided into two principal sections, *Domus Regiae Magnificenciae* and *Domus Providenciae*, the world of display and the world of provisioning: or, as they were later called, the Chamber and the Household-below-Stairs.[77]

The Chamber, which I have already mentioned in connection with the political life of the court, was the area in which the monarch lived and moved. Under the Yorkists it seems to have consisted of the Great Chamber or Hall, for public entertainments, the Chamber itself, and the Bedchamber, consisting of the private apartments. It was supervised by the Chamberlain, who was generally a nobleman close to the King: Lord Hastings under Edward IV, Lord Lovel under Richard III. Beneath his control were two other officers significant in royal government, the Treasurer of the Chamber and the King's Secretary. Both these men, under the Yorkists, were more concerned with national administration than with the domestic affairs of the household. The more strictly domestic staff of the Chamber ranged from the four esquires of the body through the fairly honorific bannerets, knights of the household, and chaplains to a range of lesser men: grooms, pages, yeomen, doctors, surgeons, barbers, minstrels, masters of grammar, messengers; and so on.

The other part of this diarchy, the Household-below-Stairs, sometimes confusingly called merely the Household, was run by the Lord Steward and was concerned with the material

[76] Elton, *TRG* 223–58. Id., 'War in the Exchequer', in *Elizabethan Government and Society*, ed. S. T. Bindoff *et al.* (1961). S. E. Lehmberg, *Sir Walter Mildmay and Tudor Government* (Austin, Texas, 1964). The researches of Mr C. H. D. Coleman of Cambridge will, when complete, add greatly to our knowledge of Elizabethan finance.

[77] The first four paragraphs of this section are mainly drawn from A. R. Myers, *The Household of Edward IV* (Manchester, 1959).

provisioning of the court and with auditing its accounts. The role of the Lord Steward was to provide the utmost royal magnificence at the lowest possible cost. He was assisted in this formidable task by the Treasurer and the Controller of the Household, the cofferer, two clerks, and the chief clerk of controlment. Together they made up the Board of the Greencloth, named, like the Exchequer, from the cloth which covered their working table. The Steward was generally a nobleman of the highest rank: the Earls of Kent, Worcester, Essex, and Surrey held the office under the Yorkist Kings. The Treasurer and Controller were usually knights, men of substance and promise: Sir John Howard, later Duke of Norfolk, was Treasurer from *c.* 1467 to 1474; Sir William Parr was Controller from *c.* 1471 to 1475. Since these three principal officers were likely to be often absent from court on royal business, much of the daily supervision of the Household economy fell on the cofferer, the two clerks of the Greencloth, and the clerk of controlment. They kept in the counting-house a book recording the attendances of all officers of the court and supervised payments, provisioning, and accounting. Beneath them were the usual departments associated with a great medieval household: bakehouse, pantry, spicery, laundry.[78]

Apart from these two central institutions of the court, the Chamber and the Household-below-Stairs, there were several offices, known later as 'the standing offices', which had once been a part of the royal Household and had now moved to its fringes. Of these the most important were the Great Wardrobe, which supplied furnishings and clothing, the office of Works, which was responsible for buildings, the Ordnance, and the Mint.

Under Edward IV and Henry VII there were, as we have seen, developments in national administration which brought the Treasurer of the Chamber and the Keeper of the Jewel House into great prominence, and it may well be that their importance overshadowed the officers of the Lord Steward's department.[79] In consequence, for much of the Yorkist and early Tudor periods, the control of the Greencloth over the Household's economy may have been less strict than was originally

[78] A. R. Myers, *The Household of Edward IV*, 160.
[79] Above, 46–7. Myers, op. cit. 49, n.2.

intended. Probably by 1519 and certainly by 1526 the management of the Household needed reform, for, as Wolsey's Eltham Ordinances pointed out, 'officers and ministers of his Household being employed to the making of provisions and other things concerning the wars, the accustomed good order of his said Household hath been greatly hindered'. Those ordinances and Cromwell's later reforms of 1539–40 attempted to remedy the defects. Between them they reduced the number of officers and assigned specific duties to those that remained. Cromwell's ordinances reorganized the Board of Greencloth, giving practical responsibility for day-to-day management to the cofferer and adding to the board four new officers, the Masters of the Household. Cromwell and Henry VIII also promoted the Lord Steward to the grander title of Lord Great Master of the Household, perhaps intending that this officer should exercise a unified control over both Chamber and Household-below-Stairs. If this was the intention it came to nothing, for the title was abolished in 1554. Thereafter, the personal control of the Lord Steward over the running of the household was probably slender, since the post was often left unfilled.[80]

Three other Tudor changes in the Household are worth mentioning. First, and most important, was the division of the Chamber into the Presence Chamber and the Privy Chamber. The change, which cannot be dated with any certainty, had been achieved by about 1513, and its significance has already been discussed.[81] Second, the King was provided with various forms of bodyguard: the Yeomen of the Guard, created in 1485, and the gentlemen-pensioners or 'spears' created in 1509.[82] Third, a Revels officer was created; there were various temporary appointments from 1494 and a permanent establishment from 1545. He was in charge of costumes and scenery for plays and masques, and was responsible also for 'perusing and reforming of plays' when necessary.[83]

---

[80] Elton, *TRG* 375–6, 395, and ch. vi, *passim*. A. P. Newton, 'Tudor Reforms in the Royal Household', in *Tudor Studies*, ed. R. W. Seton-Watson (1924). E. K. Chambers, *The Elizabethan Stage*, I. 35 and n.2.

[81] Chambers, op. cit. 42–8. Above, 24–5.

[82] Chambers, op. cit. 47. Elton, *TRG* 382, dates the origins of the King's spears in Cromwell's regime. But the evidence for this is not wholly clear. See *LP* I. i. 244, 511; I. ii, 1843; XIII. ii. 1111; XIV. ii. 783.

[83] Chambers, op. cit., ch. iii, esp. 86–7.

The significance of the Tudor reforms in the royal Household is not very easily assessed. It is clear that after the prolonged and intensive use by Edward IV, Henry VII, and Henry VIII of such officers as the Treasurer of the Chamber and the Keeper of the Jewel House, the Chamber offices ceased from about 1540 to play a major part in national administration, although the *holders* of the major offices—the Chamberlain, the Treasurer of the Household, the Controller, and the Vice-Chamberlain—were usually influential political figures. National government and household administration were from the middle of the sixteenth century separate entities. It is less clear how far the Household itself differed after 1540 from the Household of the Yorkists. The basic organization of the later Tudor Household is clearly foreshadowed in the Black Book and Ordinances of Edward IV; and the controlling system devised by Cromwell in 1539–40 is not in essentials different from that expounded in the Black Book. On one view, Professor Elton's, the organization described in the Edwardian ordinances 'bore little relation to reality'; it was Cromwell who gave concrete and lasting form to otherwise pious aspirations. On another, Cromwell simply revived and improved an older structure. While it is clear enough that by 1519 the Household system badly needed reform, it is less clear that the Edwardian system existed only on paper. As a blueprint Cromwell's reforms were not entirely original. They may however have achieved a realization of theoretical proposals: but we cannot be certain about that until further research has been undertaken into the workings of the Household.[84]

Did executive and financial government undergo a substantial transformation during the Tudor period? Was it better fitted than before to handle the increasingly complex business of the sixteenth-century state? Certainly, important changes were made. Some of these, like the reforms in the royal Household, were largely a matter of tidying up existing arrangements. Some, like the creation of the Surveyor of the King's Prerogative and the Court of Augmentations, were innovatory but temporary. Others, like the establishment of the Court of Wards,

[84] Elton, *TRG* 40–3. Newton, op. cit. Myers, op. cit. 48–9.

were permanent. The reforms at the Exchequer, which re-emerged in 1554 as the central office of royal finance, were significant in altering its detailed procedure but left unchanged its fundamental nature and purpose: it was still designed to receive cash, pay the royal debts, and audit accounts, not to exercise full control over national finances by drawing up budgets, monitoring expenditure, and increasing revenues.

On the executive side, the Navy Board and the Ordnance Office supervised military and naval supplies. The establishment of permanent ambassadors marked the beginnings of a diplomatic service. The small, defined, Privy Council and the Secretaries of State provided continuous direction and co-ordination in the affairs of state. Above all, the style of government was changing during the sixteenth century, a change that is reflected in the records of state. During the middle ages the most important records were at least in some degree legal instruments: whether they transferred land, appointed men to office, warranted expenditure, acquitted revenue officers of their charge, or summoned litigants to court, they conveyed some kind of legally valid authority. Proper authorization was essential and was provided by the seals which played so large a role in medieval government. These great series of legal documents survived into and beyond the sixteenth century: letters patent, letters close, privy seal warrants, signet warrants, legal writs. But their importance was overlaid by the less formal and increasingly numerous letters of the type found in the state papers, the Privy Council's register, and private collections: letters that conveyed information, advice, admonition, and informal orders; documents that were not bound by the rigid formularies of legal requirement.[85]

This transformation resulted in part from the growing threats to political, religious, and social security, which necessitated good intelligence-work and a flexible system of command. It was made possible by more widespread literacy, which increased the flow of information. The supreme importance of communications, in every sense, put a premium upon the man who was prepared to handle great sheaves of paper, the man at the desk, the bureaucrat. Yet government was not in any strict sense bureaucratic. Decisions were made at the top, by

[85] Elton, *The Sources of History: England, 1200–1640* (1969), 66–75.

monarch, Council, or minister, not, as in a modern bureaucracy, by officials in the lower and middle echelons, who then mostly carried out routine tasks.[86] Nor was the Secretary of State, the hub of the whole system, able to rely upon an effective permanent staff: apart from the clerks in the Signet Office, his assistants were his personal servants, who left office with him.[87] Thanks in part to the inventive energy of Thomas Cromwell and the long, tireless service of the Cecils, there developed some sort of working tradition; but there was little of the bureaucratic foundation which alone could provide continuity and organization. Men like Thomas Cromwell, William Paget, William Cecil, Francis Walsingham, and Robert Cecil gained an unrivalled knowledge of affairs and could effectively operate the machine. But its smooth running depended very much upon their personal skill and devotion.

This chapter has been concerned with the central machinery for making and executing the decisions of the Crown. However, the structure of government also contained an elaborate system of courts for enforcing commands, punishing criminals, and adjudicating disputes between the subjects of the realm. This judicial system will be briefly analysed below—as a prelude to the discussion of crime, law, and disorder in chapter VII. In the localities the Crown worked through a multitude of officials, agencies, commissions, and private persons. These links between the central government and the regions will be related in succeeding chapters to the functions and policies of government, before the chains of command between the centre and the shires are reviewed as a whole in chapter XII.

[86] M. Albrow, *Bureaucracy* (1970), for a discussion of the term. Williams and Harriss, *P&P* 25. Elton, ibid., no. 29.

[87] A. G. R. Smith, 'The Secretariat of the Cecils', *EHR* LXXXIII (1968).

II

The Financial Resources of Government

Estimating the revenue and expenditure of late medieval and early modern governments is a hazardous business. Rulers seldom had any exact notion of their financial situation and the historian cannot be confident of establishing one. Many records have disappeared, and those which survive are difficult to interpret. They were not usually intended to produce a modern type of financial statement and only very rough approximations can be wrung out of them. But as long as we bear these limitations in mind we can, to some extent, assess the muscle of the political machine. An estimate of royal revenue indicates not only the ability of the government to meet its commitments, but also its capacity to extract money from its subjects.[1]

It is customary for historians to distinguish between the ordinary and the extraordinary revenues of the Crown, between, that is to say, its recurrent, peacetime income and those occasional sums derived during wars or other emergencies from parliamentary grants or benevolences. No such distinction was known in the middle ages and it is essentially the creation of later administrators and writers. Nevertheless, provided that its artificiality is kept in mind, it has its uses, since it enables us to treat separately the revenues over which the monarch had more or less independent control and those which depended to a great extent upon the consent of others.[2]

Of the ordinary revenues, money from Crown lands had come, by 1485, to provide the King with a major part of his income. But it was almost equalled by the customs duties, which, although not strictly speaking part of the Crown's inheritance, were granted by Parliament throughout the Tudor

---

[1] The only general published account of Tudor finance is F. C. Dietz, *English Public Finance, 1485–1641* (2 vols., 2nd edn., 1964). Many of its figures have been corrected by recent research and others probably still require correction.

[2] B. P. Wolffe, *The Crown Lands, 1461–1536* (1970), 15–28.

period for the life of each monarch, to be used as he wished. Indisputably part of the Crown's personal income were the various feudal dues, paid by those who held land by military tenures. These included the King's wardship of heirs succeeding to their lands as minors, the obligation of heirs to pay for 'livery', or possession, of their properties on entering their inheritance, and the royal right to profit from giving unmarried heirs and heiresses in marriage. The monarch was also entitled, as the fount of justice, to the profits of his lawcourts. Chartered towns paid him annual rents, known as fee-farms, in return for their privileges. He received the profits of the Mint, which were, in the middle of the sixteenth century, very large. Finally, there was purveyance. In origin a feudal revenue, this was the right of the King to buy household supplies at less than their market price. By the end of the sixteenth century it had been compounded for a cash payment from the counties and had thus become a straightforward tax.

Extraordinary revenues derived from the general obligation of the King's subjects to aid him in times of emergency. The aid might take the form of personal service or of cash. By the fourteenth century the principal form of financial assistance was the direct tax known as a fifteenth and tenth. Requiring parliamentary consent, it involved a levy of one-tenth on property in the royal demesne, towns, and cities, and one-fifteenth elsewhere. However, in 1334 Edward III had agreed that this tax should become a stereotyped levy based upon fixed quotas for each locality. Although the Lancastrian and Yorkist monarchs occasionally tried to replace it with taxes assessed directly on individual incomes, resistance proved too strong, and the fifteenth and tenth still held its own in 1485 as the established form of parliamentary taxation.[3]

Other extraordinary revenues were more closely linked with feudal obligations. As feudal overlord the King could demand an aid for certain specific purposes: the ransom of his own body if he were captured in war, the knighting of his eldest son, and the marriage of his eldest daughter. Connected with these

[3] R. S. Schofield, 'Parliamentary Lay Taxation, 1485–1547' (unpublished Ph.D. thesis, Cambridge, 1963), ch. iii. Dr Schofield's invaluable thesis is the most important authority on direct taxation in the early Tudor period. I am most grateful to him for lending me his copy and for allowing me to draw upon it freely. See also Dietz, op. cit. 1. 13–18.

feudal aids was the levy known as distraint of knighthood. Henry III originated the practice of forcing landowners to take up knighthood, in order apparently to recruit cavalrymen for an overseas campaign. Under his successors, it was also exploited as a source of revenue by allowing men to pay a fine for exemption.[4]

Finally, the King could resort to borrowing. One way of raising loans was to go to the market, paying interest at the high rates then demanded. In spite of ecclesiastical prohibitions on usury, the Lancastrians and their predecessors had certainly borrowed at interest, often surreptitiously. Alternatively, the King could demand an interest-free loan from his subjects. Henry VII, asking for such a loan in 1496, told his people that 'this is a thing of so great weight and importance as may not be failed, and therefore fail ye not thereof for your said part ... as ye intend the good and honour of us and of this our realm; and as ye tender also the weal and surety of yourself'. Although there was no legal compulsion, the moral obligation to pay was strong.[5]

The Lancastrian monarchy had depended heavily upon the customs duties for its normal revenue. In 1433 indirect taxes contributed about £27,000 per annum to a net revenue of £36,000. The net yield from the Crown lands is difficult to estimate but probably came to about £6,750, with the Duchy of Lancaster contributing another £2,500. The Crown relied very much upon borrowing and was already sliding deep into debt. This situation began to change under the Yorkists as Edward IV built up the royal estates and improved their management. He brought to the Crown the lands of his own family and added the estates of some of his defeated enemies. By the reign of Richard III lands were probably providing the Crown with between £20,000 and £25,000 per annum, a significant improvement on 1433.[6]

Henry VII continued this exploitation of the Crown estates,

---

[4] M. Powicke, *Military Obligations in Medieval England* (Oxford, 1962), ch. iv and 103–10, 170–81. J. Hurstfield, *The Queen's Wards* (1958), 176.

[5] A. Steel, *The Receipt of the Exchequer* (Cambridge, 1954). K. B. McFarlane, 'Loans to the Lancastrian Kings', *CHJ* ix (1947). G. L. Harriss, 'Aids, Loans and Benevolences', *HJ* vi (1963).

[6] J. L. Kirby, 'The Issues of the Lancastrian Exchequer', *BIHR* xxiv (1951). Wolffe, op. cit. 37–8 and sect. iii.

which were far more extensive than they had been in 1433. The lands of York, Warwick, Spencer, and Salisbury were part of the royal inheritance, to which Henry added his own patrimony and the property of several landowners attainted in the course of his reign. He was fortunate in having few relatives who could make any serious encroachment on his endowments: he had no brothers; his uncle Jasper died in 1495; and his elder son Arthur died in 1502, leaving him with only one surviving son for whom provision had to be made. Although his servants were adequately rewarded, Henry resisted the temptation to lavish massive grants upon his supporters and he had no favourites. In consequence the Crown estates were by the time of his death probably larger than they had ever been before. They were also effectively administered, since Henry continued to exert the tight control established by his Yorkist predecessors. Good luck, a close fist, and administrative skills pushed the land revenues up to £42,000 per annum by 1509, about four times their level in 1433.[7]

Henry's total ordinary income at the close of his reign was probably about £113,000 to which the customs contributed £40,000. His extraordinary revenue came, in the nature of things, in irregular bursts, mostly concentrated in his first ten years. From 1487 to 1496, he raised about £250,000 in parliamentary taxes, to which the benevolence of 1491 added some £60,000. After 1496 Henry resorted to Parliament only once, in 1504, when he was granted £30,000 as an aid for the knighting of his eldest son—by then dead—and the marriage of his elder daughter. Thus in the first twelve years of his reign he received an average of about £26,000 per annum from extraordinary revenue and over the reign as a whole about £13,500 per annum.[8] Given the growth in his ordinary income and the difficulty of estimating its size in the early years of his reign, it would not be very useful to work out an average of the total revenue over the whole reign. But it is unlikely that over any five-year period it exceeded the £120,000 per annum enjoyed by Richard II. The income of Henry Tudor was perhaps three times that of Henry VI in 1433, but it was not of an order of magnitude greatly different from that of the richer medieval

[7] Wolffe, op. cit., sect. ii.

[8] Figures derived from Schofield, thesis, Table 40 (opp. p. 416).

kings. The achievement of Edward IV and Henry VII lay less in the size of their income than in their creation of a landed estate which gave them a substantial revenue over which they had complete control.

Henry was not the miser which later historians have labelled him. He understood that monarchs must make a show and his court life was suitably magnificent. His household accounts reveal an attachment to robust and expensive pleasures: £5 went to pay his card debts; £2. 13s. 4d. to a man who brought him a lion; £30 to a young damsel who danced. He rewarded good service generously but not extravagantly. For purposes of this kind his revenue, though comparatively small by continental standards, was adequate. The legend that he amassed a large fortune in gold and jewels is certainly false. But he was able to lend some £300,000 to the Habsburgs in return for political support against pretenders; and he probably left his son a credit balance of about one year's ordinary income. Although this is less dramatic than the traditional stories of his riches, it represents a solid achievement.[9]

The financial history of the reign of Henry VIII falls conveniently into two phases: the years before and those after the breach with Rome. For most of the period before 1533 the domestic side of the royal account was fairly satisfactory. Household expenditure rose gradually from about £13,000 per annum in 1509 to some £25,000 per annum in the late 1530s. At the same time, until the dissolution of the monasteries, the yield from Crown lands was declining slowly; and the return from customs duties was diminishing as well. But until about 1530 these developments do not seem to have caused any serious anxiety.[10]

The major strain on revenue was imposed by the demands of war. In this early part of the reign there were two periods of fighting. During the first, which lasted from 1511 to 1514, there were two small expeditions and three major ones.

[9] A. F. Pollard, *The Reign of Henry VII from Contemporary Sources* (1913–14), I, 263; II, 229. B. P. Wolffe, 'Henry VII's Landed Revenues', *EHR* LXXIX (1964), esp. 253, n.2 and 254, n.1.

[10] Dietz, op. cit. I. 88–90.

Professor Dietz estimates the total cost of the wages and equipment of these armies at £892,000, to which should be added about £20,000, lent to the Emperor Maximilian.[11]

Between 1513 and 1516 Parliament consented to four grants of revenue which effectively revolutionized the system of direct taxation in England. The traditional, fixed-yield tax of fifteenths and tenths was preserved, but a new tax, the subsidy, was developed alongside it, based upon direct assessments of individual wealth, by contrast with the stereotyped geograpical quotas of the older tax. Attempts had of course been made before 1513 to link taxation more directly to personal riches, but they had been unpopular and, in general, ineffective. The subsidy of 1513 was assessed partly on status and partly on income: peers paid according to their rank, commoners according to property or revenue. The subsidies of 1514, 1515, and 1516 abandoned the separate assessment of the peerage by rank and levied taxation entirely according to income. The new directly assessed tax had come to stay as the main supplement to the King's ordinary revenue; although fifteenths and tenths were generally granted in conjunction with subsidies for the rest of the century, the latter were much more productive.[12] Dramatic as the change in the system was, its actual contribution to the royal war-effort in these years was less impressive. Parliamentary revenues brought in about £300,000 between 1512 and 1517, only one-third of military expenditure. The remaining costs of war had to be met from the surplus on the ordinary account and the balance left by Henry VII. It is significant that a popular monarch, making war at the very start of his reign, after a long period of peace, could only raise such inadequate sums.[13]

The next phase of heavy expenditure began in 1522 and lasted until 1525. It included a large expedition to France in 1522, an attack on the Scots and a major invasion of France in 1523, and an abortive plan for a third French campaign after the capture of Francis I at Pavia in 1525. Wolsey met the first crisis by ordering the levy of a forced loan. Commissioners were

[11] Dietz, op. cit. I. 90–1.
[12] 3 Henry VIII c. 22; 4 Henry VIII c. 19; 5 Henry VIII c. 18; 6 Henry VIII c. 26. For the significance of these taxes see Schofield, thesis, ch. iv.
[13] Dietz, op. cit. I. 93. Schofield, thesis, Table 40.

appointed in every shire to assess men for the loan under pretence of discovering what arms they should bear under the Statute of Winchester. They were told to enter in a book the goods and income of all men. When that was done, the true purpose of the operation would be revealed and commissioners would demand the loan from each subject according to his wealth. The Crown just about reached its target of £260,000 from this device. Initially, it promised repayment out of a future parliamentary grant, but most lenders, possibly all, were still waiting to be repaid in 1529, when Parliament absolved the King from all obligation to redeem this debt.[14]

In the following year, 1523, Wolsey demanded a parliamentary subsidy of 4*s.* in the pound, which was intended to raise £800,000. After angry remonstrances in the Commons a much lighter graded tax was eventually granted to run over four years. This ought in theory to have raised the amount demanded by Wolsey, but would have taken much longer to collect. In practice there was resistance to the levying of the first instalment and collection proved increasingly difficult. The first year's yield produced £72,000, the second £66,000, the third £5,800, and the fourth £9,400. The total reached only a little over £150,000, less than 20 per cent of Wolsey's original demand.[15]

The next levy proposed by Wolsey met with an even more humiliating defeat. With the capture of Francis I at Pavia in 1525, Henry saw—or claimed to see—an opportunity of seizing the French throne. To support his claim the Council asked for an 'amicable grant'—an unparliamentary levy—of one-sixth on the income of the laity and one-third on the income of the clergy. I shall describe later the hostile response to this demand, putting it into the context of sixteenth-century protest and rebellion. It is enough to say here that the opposition was successful and that Henry had to withdraw the levy, blaming Wolsey for its inception.[16]

The years from 1522 to 1525 revealed the dangerous frailty

---

[14] *LP* III. ii. 2483 (3), 2484; IV. iii, app. 37; Add. I. i. 455. Also IV i. 214, 417. Dietz, op. cit. I. 94 gives £350,000 as the total raised, but this seems rather high. 21 Henry VIII c. 24.

[15] Dietz, op. cit. I. 94. *LP* IV. iii, app. 6; IV. i. 377–8, 969. Cf. III. ii. 2483 (3), 3082. 14 & 15 Henry VIII c. 16. Schofield, thesis, Table 40.

[16] Below, ch. X.

of the Crown's financial base. In four years Henry may, at best, have added about £100,000 per annum to his ordinary revenue, and fairly soon the taxpayers had called a halt to further intervention abroad. Like Charles II in the following century, Henry tried to secure a pension from France. Since the reign of Henry VII, the French King had paid a substantial sum to England, which was increased to 150,000 francs per annum when Tournai was returned to France in 1519. In 1525 Francis I agreed to pay 100,000 crowns (about £25,000) annually for the rest of Henry's life, and in 1527 he promised 60,000 crowns per annum after Henry's death.[17] But these were hardly large enough to alleviate the serious financial strains engendered by war, and payment was suspended when the divorce crisis made Henry diplomatically dependent on French support. By 1534 the financial situation of the English Crown was decidedly precarious. Household expenses were rising; Henry had grandiose schemes for new royal palaces; revolt threatened in Ireland; and the foreign consequences of his first divorce seemed likely to prove expensive. His revenue was slowly sinking and his subjects had shown themselves resistant to demands for aid.

In 1534 Thomas Cromwell opened his campaign for restoring the Crown's finances. He began by securing from Parliament a fifteenth and tenth, combined with a subsidy, the first to be levied in time of peace.[18] Since it involved a fresh assessment of wealth it encountered some hostility. At Norwich, where the local authorities had assessed no one at more than £100, the Duke of Norfolk asked the King for a letter, 'commanding me ... to speak roundly to all such as do not honestly ... make their said certificates'. Later, the tax was one of the principal grievances of the Pilgrimage of Grace. But levied over a period of three years it brought in about £80,000 and became the prototype for later subsidies.[19]

[17] Dietz, op. cit. I. 99–102.
[18] G. R. Elton, 'Taxation for War and Peace in Early Tudor England', in J. M. Winton (ed.), *War and Economic Development* (Cambridge, 1975), 35–6. 26 Henry VIII c. 19.
[19] Schofield, thesis, Table 40. *State Papers, Henry VIII*, II. 276–7. Cf. *LP* xi. 470. 32 Henry VIII c. 50.

More of Cromwell's attention was, however, given to increasing the landed revenues of the Crown, a matter wholly neglected by Wolsey. Fresh forms of income were uncovered; old sources were improved; and a new administrative machine was created to deal with the influx of wealth. Best known of the new sources were the revenues of the Church. First fruits and tenths, which had previously gone to Rome, came after 1534 to the King: he received a tenth of the annual revenue of every clerical benefice and a sum equivalent to the whole of the first year's income of every newly appointed bishop. The income from this source came to £40,000 per annum up to 1540, but, following the dissolution of the monasteries, fell to about £20,000.[20] Much more substantial were the resources derived from the dissolution, by which the Crown acquired, between 1536 and 1539, land worth £135,000–140,000 per annum. A good deal of this was sold off early on to provide the Crown with an immediate supply of cash. Between 1536 and 1544 the Court of Augmentations, set up to deal with monastic lands, took in almost £900,000, an annual average of £112,390, roughly equal to the whole of Henry VII's ordinary income at his death.[21]

The Crown also acted to stop the evasion of feudal dues by means of the 'use'. The danger that a landowner's heir would have to pay livery on succeeding to his estate, and, if a minor, would have to become a ward of the Crown, could be avoided if the landowner himself, during his lifetime, enfeoffed trustees with the lands, reserving to the 'use' of himself and his heirs the annual income. On his death there were then no freehold estates to pass and therefore no liability to feudal dues. Henry VII had attempted, with some success, to limit the consequences of this evasion, and after 1529 Henry VIII went further still. Beginning with a bargain struck between the Crown and the nobles, and then moving into a skilful attack in the lawcourts, the government managed to persuade Parliament into passing in 1536 the great Statute of Uses which turned the 'use' into a legal estate and abolished completely this method of evasion. Resentment and resistance followed, notably in the Pilgrimage of Grace; and although the Crown

---

[20] 26 Henry VIII c. 3. Elton, *TRG* 190, 198.
[21] W. C. Richardson, *Tudor Chamber Administration* (Baton Rouge, 1952), 322–6.

was able to ride that storm, it agreed in 1540 to replace the
Statute of Uses with a much milder enactment, the Statute of
Wills, which in effect allowed landowners to avoid feudal incidents on two-thirds of their lands. It was a remarkable defeat.[22]
But, even so, thanks in part to the new legislation, in part to
the administrative machinery of the Court of Wards, and in
part to the provision that monastic lands be sold as tenancies-
in-chief, the income from feudal dues rose from £4,434 in 1542
to an average of £7,700 per annum in the first three years of
Edward VI. In general it may be said that 'Cromwell's decade'
saw a doubling of the ordinary revenue of the Crown—though
it also saw an increased expenditure, especially on the household, administration, defence, and Ireland.[23]

Had the government been able to avoid foreign war its situation would have been highly satisfactory. But rumours of war
were being sounded by 1539 and in 1542 there began almost
a decade of fighting. Open war was declared against Scotland
in 1542 and against France in 1543; campaigns were mounted
against the Scots in 1542, 1544, and 1545; a small expedition
was sent to Flanders in 1543 and a large one to France in 1544.
In 1545 and again in 1546 England had to be defended from
invasion and Boulogne from siege. The death of Henry VIII
brought no immediate relief. Somerset invaded Scotland in
1547 and saddled his government with the cost of maintaining
garrisons there. In 1549 the French King, by now allied to Scotland, besieged Boulogne. Not until March 1550 was Somerset's
successor, Northumberland, able to bring the war to an end.
There were other expensive emergencies during this decade.
The imposition of royal control and of Protestant doctrines in
Ireland began a prolonged and heavy drain upon the royal
purse, while in 1549 troops had to be found and paid for putting
down risings in East Anglia, the South-West, the Midlands, and
the South.

In 1540, the Crown extracted from Parliament four fifteenths
and tenths, together with a subsidy payable over two years. This
raised about £77,000. But much more was needed, and in 1542

[22] J. M. W. Bean, *The Decline of English Feudalism* (Manchester, 1968), esp. ch. vi.
E. W. Ives, 'The Genesis of the Statute of Uses', *EHR* LXXXII (1967). 27 Henry
VIII c. 10.
[23] H. E. Bell, *Introduction to the Court of Wards* (Cambridge, 1953), 47–8.

the government resorted, as it had done in 1522, to a forced loan. Letters under the privy seal were prepared by the thousand, and instructions were sent to the chief commissioners in each shire. Those of the royal subjects who 'may and will gladly strain themselves' were asked to contribute to a loan, which would be repaid within two years. In spite of some grumbling in London, the loan was a triumphant success, bringing in £112,000. The Imperial ambassador reported that the willing lenders never expected to see their money again: their pessimism was justified, since Parliament remitted all obligation on the King to repay, just as it had done in 1529.[24]

A further subsidy was granted in 1543. Spread over three years it brought in £187,000.[25] But the massive invasion of France in 1544 proved to be more than twice as expensive as the government had estimated: it cost nearly £650,000 instead of the predicted £250,000. In December Secretary Paget set out the position with gloomy—and inaccurate—figures. The tenor of his argument was that the Parliament due to meet in February 1545 could not provide enough money in time. It would be less burdensome to the poor and more profitable to the King if Parliament were prorogued and a benevolence demanded.[26] This frank proposal for unparliamentary taxation was accepted by the King, and orders were sent out to the appointed commissioners in January. The tax was not to fall upon the very poor: only those with incomes of £2 per annum or goods of £3. 6s. 8d. were to be approached. The rate suggested was 8d. per pound for incomes and possessions worth less than £20, 1s. per pound over that figure. The commissioners were given detailed orders on the best way to proceed: they were not to summon more than twelve men at once and were to speak to each man alone, reminding him of the King's work on his behalf. Anyone alleging poverty was to be charged with ingratitude, but if he persisted in his refusal he was to have his name taken and be told to keep the matter secret.[27] The fate laid up for such a man is revealed by the story of Alderman

[24] 32 Henry VIII c. 20. *LP* XVII. 188, 190, 194, 280. Dietz, op. cit. I. 164–5. 35 Henry VIII c. 12. Schofield, thesis, Table 40. I am grateful to Dr Schofield for allowing me to quote from an unpublished paper his figures for the yield of this loan and of other loans and benevolences.

[25] 34 & 35 Henry VIII c. 27. Schofield, thesis, Table 40.   [26] Haynes, 54–6.

[27] C. Wriothesley, *A Chronicle of England* (Camden Soc., n.s. XL, 1875) I. 151, gives

Reed of London, who, 'upon a disobedient stomach', refused to pay and gave a bad example to his fellow citizens. He was pressed into the ranks of the northern army, 'whereby he might somewhat be instructed of the difference between the sitting quietly in his house, and the travail and danger which others daily do sustain'.[28]

Whether the tactics of individual approach divided possible dissidents, or Alderman Reed's fate terrified them, there was none of the anger or recalcitrance that had greeted the 'amicable grant' twenty years before. There were a few complaints of poverty and the money was slow to come in from Norfolk and Yorkshire. But elsewhere people seemed positively anxious to supply the King with treasure. Sir Anthony Browne reported from Surrey that he would have thought it hard to get the money in so quickly had he not experienced the goodwill of the people; and Sir Thomas Darcy claimed that men were actually saying, 'if this be too little his Grace shall have more'. Dr Schofield estimates that the benevolence brought £125,000 to the King. Considering that the last instalment of the 1543 subsidy was still being paid the achievement is remarkable.[29]

Even so the necessities of war continued to strain the King's resources, and the Parliament that met in November 1545 was persuaded to vote yet another subsidy, together with two fifteenths and tenths.[30] This time the subsidy was in the form of an annual tax payable for two years, with the rates on a sliding scale as before. Moveables were taxed relatively more lightly than before, land more heavily. But the general impact of this tax was heavier than its predecessor. The subsidy yielded £196,000 and the fifteenths and tenths joined to it another £29,000.[31] Yet even this was insufficient for the needs of a King who was indebted to the sum of £270,000. The only solution was another benevolence. The arguments about just quarrels with our ancient enemy, the French, were given yet another outing; commissioners were appointed in May 1546 and armed

---

a different figure of 2*s*. in the pound. *LP* xx. i. 85 gives yet another rate. See also *LP* xx. ii, app. 4; xx. i. 17–18, 52.

[28] Lodge, I. 71–7, 81–3. Wriothesley, *Chronicle*, loc. cit. *APC* I. 284. Reed is said to have been taken prisoner and later ransomed.

[29] *LP* xx. i. 85, 101, 604, 999. Dietz, op. cit. I. 166. Ex inf. R. S. Schofield.

[30] *LP* xx. ii. 211–13, 324, 366, 453, 729, 738.

[31] 37 Henry VIII c. 25. Dietz, op. cit. I. 162. Schofield, thesis, Table 40.

with instructions similar to the previous set. There were a few complaints of poverty, but no signs of serious opposition; and the revenue began to flow in, reaching about £60,000.[32]

In all, the forced loan of 1542, the benevolences of 1544 and 1545, the parliamentary taxes of 1540, 1543, and 1545, together with clerical subsidies and lesser taxes, brought in about £1 m. in just over seven years.[33] Comparison of this figure with the Crown's revenue from these sources earlier in the reign shows that Henry had achieved a powerful grip upon the nation. The taxes of 1512–15 mostly went off at half-cock, each successive subsidy being voted to remedy the deficiencies of the last: they added only about £75,000 per annum to the Crown's revenues. In the four years 1522–5 the King may have got as much as £100,000 per annum from forced loans and subsidies, but his foreign adventures were brought to a sudden and ignominious halt by the refusal to pay the 'amicable grant'. In the seven years from 1540 to 1547 these sources brought in about £140,000 per annum and the King was able to pile one impost on another without the taxpayers showing any sign of wilting. Perhaps his tactics were more skilful; perhaps the gentry were reconciled to paying taxes by the prospect of gain from monastic lands; perhaps the King was wise in these last years to avoid taxing the poor, from whom overt resistance had come in the past; perhaps there was a genuine fear of invasion from France.

But successful as the Crown was in extracting money from its subjects, it was nowhere near successful enough. The total cost of war and defence between 1539 and 1547 was over two million pounds, about twice the yield of forced loans, benevolences, and subsidies. Henry was forced to use the surplus on his ordinary revenue, to sell monastic lands, debase the coinage, and borrow on the Antwerp exchange. Sales of monastic lands brought in perhaps £800,000 between 1539 and 1547; by then two-thirds of these lands had been sold and given away. Debasement of the coinage led Wriothesley to call the Mint 'our holy anchor'; its profits were such that he told Paget to keep its operations secret, 'for if it should come out that men's things coming thither be thus employed, it would make them with-

---

[32] Ex inf. R. S. Schofield. *LP* xx. ii. 738, 769; xxi. i. 844, 970 (30, 31), 1041; xxi. ii. 135, 366, 454. *State Papers, Henry VIII*, I. 842, 847, 879. Lodge, I. 85.

[33] Dietz, op. cit. I. 166–7. Schofield, thesis, Table 40 and private information.

draw and so bring a lack'.[34] Stephen Vaughan began to fish
for loans on the Antwerp market in 1544 and negotiated some
large borrowings. In all, between 1544 and 1546 Vaughan borrowed £272,000 in Antwerp, of which £100,000 was still outstanding when Henry died. These loans, at rates varying
between 10 per cent and 18 per cent, were useful for helping
the Crown over its successive liquidity crises, but, since none
was for more than twelve months and some were for less, they
failed to lighten the Crown's burden in the long run.[35]

Under Edward VI the war cost a further £1,387,000, to
which parliamentary taxes contributed only a small fraction.
Protector Somerset's government was lucky to receive
£112,000, the second instalment of the subsidy voted in 1545.
It then launched, in 1548, an experimental tax of 1s. in the
pound on moveables, together with a poll-tax on sheep of 3d.
per ewe and 2d. per wether, and a form of excise on woollen
cloth. These taxes, to be imposed annually for three years, were
intended both to raise revenue and to prevent the conversion
of arable land to pasture. Before any cash was received from
the sheep tax it was repealed and a fourth year of the property
tax substituted in its place. This produced an average of £46,000
per annum for four years. Thus the total revenue from direct
taxes in Edward's reign, up to 1551, was only about £300,000,
less than a quarter of the cost of the war.[36] Some of this deficit
was made up by a further encroachment upon the lands of the
Church; the chantries were dissolved in 1548 and episcopal
property came under pressure towards the end of the reign.
Sales of lands from these and other sources produced about
£428,000. The debasement of the coinage, begun by Henry
VIII, continued until 1551, by which time the Crown had
reaped from it a profit of £1,200,000.[37]

A document drawn up in 1552 summarized the unhappy

[34] Dietz, op. cit. 1. 147–9. *LP* xx. ii. 457. C. E. Challis, 'The Debasement of the
Coinage, 1542–51', *EcHR* xx (1967).

[35] W. C. Richardson, *Stephen Vaughan: Financial Agent of Henry VIII* (Baton Rouge,
1953), chs. v–vii. See also id., 'Some Financial Expedients of Henry VII', *EcHR* vii
(1954/55). Dietz, op. cit. 1. 167–74.

[36] Dietz, *Finances of Edward VI and Mary* (Smith College Studies in History, III, 1918),
135. 2 & 3 Edward VI c. 36; 3 & 4 Edward VI c. 23. M. W. Beresford, 'The Poll
Tax and Census of Sheep, 1549', *Agricultural History Review*, I & II (1953–4).

[37] Dietz, *English Public Finance*, I. 183 and n., 198. Challis, op. cit.

story of the previous ten years. In all, nearly $3\frac{1}{2}$ million pounds had been spent on war and defence from 1540 until 1552. Boulogne had cost £1,342,000, Calais and Guisnes £371,000, the wars against Scotland £954,000, naval warfare £479,000, the expedition of 1544 £26,500 (which is surely too low), the upkeep of forts in England £291,000, the suppression of rebellions £27,000. The royal debts stood at £235,000 in October 1552, of which £110,700 was owed abroad and £125,000 in England. This was evidently regarded as a heavy burden by the English government, although it was the merest tumulus compared with the great Everest of debts owed by the Emperor Charles V. The English Crown had escaped large-scale indebtedness by selling Crown lands, which produced 32 per cent of the total revenue raised for war, and by debasing the coinage, which produced just about as much. Direct taxation—including forced loans and benevolences—produced only about 35 per cent. Although the Crown avoided a large debt it did so only by reducing its own revenue and patronage and by imposing the serious social burdens of debasement.[38]

The domestic account was also in poor shape. By 1547 customs revenue had declined to about £20,000 per annum.[39] Land revenues, although boosted by the dissolution, had already been eroded by massive sales. By 1551 the ordinary revenue was estimated at only £170,000. Inflation, the extravagance of Henry VIII, and the greed of his son's councillors combined to push up expenditure. The royal household cost £56,000 in 1550/51, compared with only £25,000 in 1538/39; pensions and annuities ate up £20,000; and permanent garrisons, the navy, and the ordnance absorbed £80,000.[40]

In 1553 Northumberland appealed to Parliament for a peacetime grant of two fifteenths and tenths and a subsidy of 2s. in the pound on landed incomes, 1s. 4d. in the pound on personal property over £20.[41] Before any of this reached the Exchequer Edward was dead and his sister Mary had waived her right to all but the two fifteenths and tenths. In spite of this generous beginning the financial management of Mary's

---

[38] PRO, State Papers Domestic, Edward VI (SP 10), 15/11, 13, 42, 73.
[39] Ibid. 2/13.
[40] Dietz, *English Public Finance*, I. 140–1, 190–1.
[41] Ibid. 200–1. 7 Edward VI c. 12.

reign was highly successful. She inherited from her brother a methodical and intelligent Treasurer, the Marquis of Winchester; and she also took over the conclusions of committees which had been investigating the Crown's finances under Edward VI. The expenses of government were reduced and even household costs were kept in hand. It is true that Mary's return of first fruits and tenths to the Church robbed the Crown of some revenue; but as this gesture also charged the Church with the duty of paying clerical and monastic pensions, the actual loss to the Crown was slight. In other respects careful management and a firm hand pushed up the royal income. Revenue from monastic lands rose from £27,000 in 1552/53, to £48,000 in 1556–7. More dramatic still was the rise in customs duties. For years the yield from customs had been declining, in part because the rates were allowed to lag well behind the rise in prices, in part because of bad management. Customs revenue stood at *c.* £40,000 per annum in 1509; in the last years of Henry VIII's reign it was still at that figure; by 1550/51 it had fallen to £26,000. By raising the rates and the valuations of goods on which customs were charged in May 1558, Mary was able to boost the yield from £29,000 in 1556/57 to £83,000 in 1558/59, a startling increase, from which her successor benefited, not she herself. Finally, she raised a forced loan, never repaid, of £109,000.[42]

Elizabeth's financial inheritance was not entirely unfavourable. It is true that Mary left debts of something between £150,000 and £200,000. But she had also, by a fortunate piece of incompetence on the part of her soldiers, lost Calais, which cost about £25,000 per annum, and, by a remarkably firm piece of action, had dramatically increased the revenue from tonnage and poundage.[43] In the early years of her reign Elizabeth was faced with an urgent crisis on her northern border, and in 1562–4 she pursued an expensive adventure into France. But from 1564 until 1585 England was mostly at peace with her neighbours, even if that peace was sometimes fragile.

[42] Dietz, *English Public Finance*, I. 203–5, 206n., 208, 212–13. G. D. Ramsay, *The City of London in International Politics*, 150–3. I owe information on the loan to Dr Schofield.
[43] Dietz, *English Public Finance*, II. 7 and n. PRO, State Papers Domestic, Edward VI 5/25; Mary (SP 11), 13/28.

The ordinary revenue of the Crown fluctuated throughout Elizabeth's reign: it is impossible to make anything better than highly approximate estimates. During the first decade it seems, on average, to have run below £200,000, although it sometimes exceeded that figure. By the end of the century it had risen to more than £300,000 per annum.[44] Set against the background of inflation this rise is less impressive than it looks at first sight. Grain prices in the last five years of Elizabeth's reign were 75 per cent higher than in the first five years; but wages and industrial prices had risen much less steeply. It is extremely difficult to construct a cost-of-living index for governmental expenditure and the most one can say is that, very roughly, the ordinary revenue of the Crown probably kept pace with inflation, but did not increase in real terms to meet the larger calls being made upon government.[45]

The staple elements in the ordinary revenue revealed some major points of weakness. Income from Crown lands stood in 1559 at about £66,000 per annum, to which should be added about £12,000 from the lands of the Duchy of Lancaster. By the end of the reign total land revenue came to about £100,000, a rise of nearly 25 per cent, compared with a price rise of about 75 per cent. In part of course this poor showing was the result of massive land sales at the beginning and at the end of Elizabeth's reign: in all, lands to the annual value of £25,000 were sold. But the Crown's management of its property was too indulgent. Rents on new takings rose hardly at all on Crown lands between the 1550s and the 1590s, whereas on the Seymour estates they increased fivefold and on the Herbert lands by 80 per cent. It is not surprising, in view of these figures, that surveys made in 1608 suggest that Crown rents were often 60 per cent below an economic rental.[46]

---

[44] Dietz, *The Exchequer in Elizabeth's Reign* (Smith College Studies, VIII. ii, 1923), 80–90. W. R. Scott, *The Constitution and Finance of . . . Joint-Stock Companies* (Cambridge, 1910–12) III, div. xv.

[45] For the price-rise see *Agrarian History*, Table VI, 846–50 and E. H. Phelps Brown and Sheila Hopkins, 'Seven Centuries of the Prices of Consumables', *Economica*, n.s. XXIII (1956), repr. in P. Ramsey (ed.), *The Price Revolution in Sixteenth-Century England* (1971).

[46] Dietz, *English Public Finance*, II. 296, 302. R. B. Outhwaite, 'The Price of Crown Land', *EcHR* XX (1967), 231, 240. G. R. Batho, 'Landlords in England', in *Agrarian History*, 272–3. E. Kerridge, 'The Movement of Rent, 1540–1640', *EcHR* VI (1953/54). *CSPDom, 1601–3*, 176–8.

The income from customs dues, which had risen sharply in the first year of the reign, thanks to Mary's reforms, was remarkably sluggish thereafter. It fell from £89,000 in 1558/59 to about £60,000 per annum in the mid-1570s. Thereafter it rose again to about £91,000 per annum in the last five years of the reign, little more than it had been at the start.[47] At a time of rising prices this is a feeble performance; but the reason for it is not difficult to find. Customs duties were of two kinds, specific and *ad valorem*. The specific duties, imposed on imported wines and on exported wool and cloth, were rated upon the quantity of the goods traded: the duties on wine and wool were certainly high, perhaps as much as 80 per cent on French wine and 37 per cent on wool; that on cloth was 5–6 per cent. But whether high or low they did not change throughout the reign. Thus, as prices rose, the effective rate of duty fell: the amount yielded was the same, but it represented a smaller proportion of the value of the goods. One might expect the *ad valorem* duties to have risen with increasing prices. But these duties were levied, not upon the actual value of the goods, but upon the official value given in the Books of Rates. These listed virtually every possible object that might be traded, from ABCs or spelling-books to yarn, including harp-strings by the gross, opium by the pound, and weasel-skins by the dozen, attaching to each a value from which duty would be calculated. The Book issued in 1558 had given fairly realistic values and had thus helped to increase the revenue; thenceforward the values remained almost unchanged until the reign of James I. Nominal duties of 5 per cent had gradually been eroded to something less than 3 per cent.[48]

Similar conservatism is reflected in the treatment of revenue from feudal dues. In the reign of Edward VI the income of the Court of Wards had averaged £11,000 per annum, rising to more than £15,000 per annum under Mary. A higher income still was achieved in the first four years of Elizabeth, but the feudal revenue then fell back to between £12,000 and £14,000 per annum until 1598, when an upward movement began once more. Adjusting this income to allow for the rise in prices, it seems that the real income fell by more than one-third. This

[47] Dietz, *Exchequer in Elizabeth's Reign*, 80–90.
[48] T. S. Willan, *A Tudor Book of Rates* (Manchester, 1962), *passim*, esp. intro.

was a revenue capable of startling, if unpopular, growth: in its peak year, 1638/39, it reached £83,000, six times the average for the reign of Elizabeth. Yet Lord Burghley, Master of the Wards from 1561 to 1598, made no attempt to exploit this revenue to the full: his period of control witnessed an immediate fall in the court's income, which remained at a low level until his son took over. Robert Cecil then showed what could be done by raising the profits of wardship from £14,700 in 1597/98 to £22,300 in 1601/02.[49]

Given the conservative treatment of revenues from lands, customs, and feudal dues it is remarkable that the peacetime account of the Crown should have remained so healthy. There was an accumulated credit balance of £300,000 by 1584; and even at the end of the reign the Crown had an annual surplus on the ordinary account. How was this managed? In part it was done by exploiting as fully as possible many small miscellaneous sources of income, such as fines on recusants and the revenues of vacant episcopal sees; in part by careful and economic management—the household expenses were kept rigidly down in an age of inflation and the building of royal palaces was brought to an end; in part by rewarding courtiers and officials from wardships and monopolies. The surplus was also the product of parliamentary taxation in time of peace.[50]

Elizabeth was remarkable among Tudor monarchs for her consistent use of subsidies during peacetime. Cromwell had secured a peacetime subsidy in 1534 and Northumberland got another in 1553, but most of the latter was remitted by Mary. She herself however called for a subsidy in 1555. Elizabeth's subsidy of 1559 could be justified by the expense of the war with France that was just ending, that of 1563 by the expedition to France. But the seven fifteenths and tenths and the three and two-thirds subsidies granted from 1566 to 1581 could only be justified by the threat rather than the reality of war. From 1559 until 1584, years of almost unbroken peace, direct taxation from laity and clergy rose above £20,000 in sixteen out of the twenty-three years for which figures are available.[51]

[49] J. Hurstfield, 'The Profits of Fiscal Feudalism', *EcHR* VIII (1955/56). Bell, *Court of Wards*, Table A.

[50] Scott, *Joint-Stock Companies*, III. 485–527.

[51] The figures for direct taxation are taken from *Statutes of the Realm*; Dietz, *Public Finance*, II. 392n.; id., *Exchequer in Elizabeth's Reign*, 80–9.

This increasing reliance upon parliamentary taxation was probably a necessary consequence of the cautious attitude adopted towards the ordinary revenues of the Crown. Yet if Elizabeth relied more heavily than her predecessors on direct taxation to carry her through the years of peace, she showed a greater reluctance than her father to squeeze the country heavily in times of war. In the last decade of her reign the yield of direct taxes, clerical subsidies, and forced loans averaged about £144,000 per annum, much the same in cash terms as Henry got in the last seven years of his reign. But it was, in real terms, very much less if one allows for rising prices. In part this was probably due to a steady relaxation in the rigour of tax assessments. This lenience is most dramatically revealed in the tax assessments of the peerage. For the subsidy of 1534, thirty-nine noble families were assessed: their average income was said to be £921, fifteen of them were assessed at over £1,000, and the highest income noted was £2,266. In 1571 the average had fallen to £487, only nine out of fifty-eight were rated above £1,000, and the highest was £2,133. In 1601 the average had fallen still further, to £311, while only one family was rated above £1,000 and the highest income was £1,400. This general trend can be seen in microcosm in the career of Lord Burghley: at his death he was still assessed at £133. 6s. 8d., the figure that he had returned before he became a peer. It contrasts markedly with the £4,000 per annum at which one of his biographers rated his income.[52] There is no reason to suppose that the rest of the propertied classes were any more heavily burdened than the peerage. Sir Walter Raleigh said that the incomes entered in the subsidy books represented 'not the hundredth part of our wealth'.[53] Sir Horatio Palavicino, an exceptionally wealthy man, complained when his income was assessed at £80. Roger, Lord North, admitted that as a subsidy commissioner he had let men off lightly in Cambridgeshire: everyone was known to be worth ten times his assessment in goods and six times in land; some were worth twenty or thirty times their assessments. In 1598 the Privy Council had to instruct commissioners to produce more realistic returns and to

[52] Helen Miller, 'Subsidy Assessments of the Peerage', *BIHR* xxviii (1955).
[53] Ibid. 23.

assess J.P.s at a minimum of £20.[54] The effect of this lenience was that the yield of 4s. in the pound on landed incomes and 2s. 8d. on goods actually fell during Elizabeth's reign—a period of rising prices and of growing prosperity for the propertied classes—from about £140,000 at the beginning of the reign to about £85,000 at the end. To a large extent of course the Queen was able to make up for the loss by grants of double, triple, and even quadruple subsidies, but in doing so she may have encouraged resistance. An effectively assessed tax on incomes rises automatically with prices and incomes: the Elizabethan subsidy could only rise by being multiplied or imposed more frequently.[55]

Like her father Elizabeth could only pay for war by resorting to forced loans, benevolences, and various other devices that proved unpopular in the long run, although, to her credit, she never debased the coinage. In 1600, a benevolence was asked, to which the lawyers seem to have responded favourably but the gentry with some reluctance. Privy seals were sent out for forced loans from about 1590.[56] But these were far from sufficient. In the last twelve years of her reign the war cost £3½m., to which parliamentary grants, benevolences, and forced loans contributed about £1,800,000. The balance was paid by dissipating the surplus built up earlier, selling Crown lands to the capital value of £520,000, securing prize-money of £200,000 from privateering, transferring sums from domestic revenue, and by various expedients of a politically unhealthy kind.[57]

For instance, the use of purveyance began to attract criticism in the last fifteen years of the reign. It had never been popular and complaints about it had been voiced in the fifteenth century. The main, and probably well-founded, objection concerned the corruption of the purveyors. In the latter part of Elizabeth's reign Burghley began a reform of the system of purveyance, partly perhaps as a response to criticism, partly in an effort to direct the profits of purveyance away from the officials and towards the Crown. Originally, purveyors bought supplies

---

[54] HMC, *Salisbury Papers*, III, 428; VIII. 274, 547. F. Peck, *Desiderata Curiosa* (1779) I. 123.

[55] Dietz, *Public Finance*, II. 392–3.

[56] HMC, *Salisbury Papers*, IX. 58; XI, 355; XII, 197; XIII, 391–2. *CSPDom, 1598–1601*, 163, 515. *APC* XXX. 27–31. *Bacon Papers* (Camden Soc., 1915), 95 ff.

[57] Scott, op. cit. III, div. XV, esp. 526–7.

or requisitioned transport at fixed rates below the market price. They were reimbursed by purchasing-officers in the household and took a percentage commission on what they bought. From about 1570, and more intensively from about 1590, a system of compounding was brought in, under which each county made an agreement with the Crown to levy a tax or composition to cover the difference between the royal price and the market price for the amount that the shire was required to supply. The local officers, usually J.P.s, and known as undertakers, then bought goods at market prices and sold them to the household at royal prices. This system would seem on the face of it to have freed the counties from the corrupt and intrusive purveyors while guaranteeing the Crown's interests. In practice this did not happen. Purveyors seem still to have operated even in counties which had compounded. More serious, the business of assessing a county rate met with strong resistance and directed criticism against the Crown itself rather than its purveyors. But however bitter the resentment against purveyance, it was too valuable for the Crown to surrender. By the beginning of James's reign it was probably worth about £35,000 per annum.[58]

In the last fifteen years of her reign Elizabeth also made increasing demands on her subjects for ships or for money in lieu of ships. The Crown had long had an unquestioned right to commandeer ships from coastal towns. In 1588 the Queen levied about eighty, of which thirty came from London. Further levies of ships were made in 1591, 1594, 1595, 1596, 1599, and 1603. Gradually the burden was extended from the ports to the whole of the coastal shires, and then to inland towns and counties. Whereas the original demand had been for actual ships, the Crown began in the 1590s to ask for money instead. Finally, in 1603 a plan was devised, though never executed, for every county, inland and coastal, to contribute money to standing fleets for the protection of merchant shipping. The original requisition of ships was uncontested, although many towns protested that they were too poor to provide what was asked. But the extension of the tax—for that is what it had

---

[58] A. Woodworth, 'Purveyance for the Royal Household in the Reign of Queen Elizabeth', *Trans. American Philosophical Soc.*, n.s. xxxv (1945). G. E. Aylmer, 'The Last Years of Purveyance, 1610–1660', *EcHR* x (1957). Alan Everitt, in *Agrarian History*, 516–19.

become—to inland areas aroused resentment and opposition.[59]

The land forces also burdened the localities with new taxes. The training of the militia was costly, for men were paid a wage of 8*d*. a day during training, usually for ten days in the year, and the purchase of equipment and ammunition had to be added to this. Training programmes might cost a county as much as £400 per annum in the 1580s and considerably more later. Forces levied for service overseas had to be fitted out with uniforms and conveyed to ports of embarkation. The expenses of this were known as coat-and-conduct money, part of which was reimbursed by the Crown but most of which was borne by the counties. Large sums might also be required for fortifications, especially from 1588 onwards. The total expenditure varied very much from shire to shire and from year to year. Norfolk paid £4,000 in 1588 on fortifications, coat-and-conduct money, ammunition, and other military objectives. Northamptonshire paid £1,000 in coat-and-conduct money alone, though as an inland shire its expenses on fortification would have been much less than Norfolk's. However, even the inland counties might find themselves paying as much in local military taxes as they did for the subsidy; and coastal shires might well pay more.[60]

Finally, there is the matter of Crown borrowing. Compared with her predecessors Elizabeth was poorly placed to raise loans, especially during her later years. In the first part of her reign she relied mainly upon the Antwerp money-market, where her debts in 1560 exceeded £272,000. But there were real disadvantages attached to foreign borrowing: exchange-rates were often unfavourable, interest-rates were high, and the Queen had no political control over her creditors. Even before the Antwerp market collapsed in the 1570s, the government was trying to make itself independent. After 1574 there was little money to be had from Antwerp in any case, and Elizabeth had to rely upon domestic resources, which were adequate only for private borrowing. The Crown needed larger sums for

<hr>

[59] Ada H. Lewis, *A Study of Elizabethan Ship-Money* (Philadelphia, 1958), *passim*.

[60] Lindsay Boynton, *The Elizabethan Militia, 1558–1638* (1967), 27, 93, 106, 116, 132–3, 157–8, 166, 170, 177–80. Below, ch. iv, for the military background to these taxes. I am grateful to Mr J. P. Cooper for emphasizing to me the importance of local taxation.

longer periods than London financiers could provide. In consequence, royal borrowing after 1574 largely took the form of interest-free 'forced loans'. This had obvious advantages for the government, but set political limits to the sums that might be raised.[61]

To sum up, Henry VII had restored royal revenues to a thoroughly adequate level by exploiting traditional sources and by building up the Crown estates. His son's attack upon the Church gave him a massive influx of land revenues, while the potential yield of feudal sources was increased by the stricter definition of the law of uses. Yet the massive land-sales of the 1540s and later decades effectively ended the promise of an independent income: Elizabeth's revenue from Crown estates in 1603 was only about double that of Henry VII in a time of much higher prices. Mary's authoritarian treatment of customs duties might have compensated for that decline, had not Elizabeth and Burghley allowed inflation to erode their true value.

The composition of the Crown's ordinary revenue changed several times in the late fifteenth and sixteenth centuries. Edward IV and Henry VII made land revenue far more important than it had been in the past, until by 1509 it slightly exceeded the yield from customs. Under Henry VIII the landed income rose while customs revenue fell, so that by the 1540s the Crown estates were easily the most important part of the ordinary revenue. In the second half of the century this trend was reversed. Customs duties rose under Mary and landed income fell in real terms: by 1603 the two were nearly level, as they had been in 1509. But the potential growth of the two sources was vastly different. Crown lands had been so much reduced in size that the most efficient management could not have increased their yield to the point at which they might have made any significant impact on royal finances. But customs duties—and to a lesser extent feudal dues—were a growth stock. The real rate of duty was very low in 1603 and there was a massive commercial wealth to be exploited. Unfortunately,

    [61] R. B. Outhwaite, 'The Trials of Foreign Borrowing', *EcHR*, 2nd ser. XIX (1966). R. Ashton, *The Crown and the Money-Market* (Oxford, 1960), ch. i. G. D. Ramsay, *The City of London in International Politics*, 50–2.

although Parliament had done little to exercise its authority over them during the Tudor period, customs duties were not fully under the Crown's control. Once the government began to exploit their possibilities by raising the true rate of duty and levying special impositions, Parliament remembered its powers and sought to recapture the commanding heights which it had surrendered. The revenue with the greatest financial potential became politically vulnerable when the Crown tried to make the potential actual. Nor was this all. Elizabeth, throughout her reign, relied for peacetime revenue upon parliamentary grants. She had gone a long way towards admitting that the King could not live of his own.

The history of parliamentary taxation in the Tudor period shows a greater degree of innovation. Although the Lancastrians had relied principally upon the archaic fifteenths and tenths they had occasionally tried some experiments. Henry VII attempted one with little success. But the demands of war under his son made imperative some addition to fifteenths and tenths. From 1513 they were invariably granted in conjunction with some form of subsidy designed to tax property and incomes more effectively by means of direct assessments of individual wealth. What had been occasional in the fifteenth century now became a general rule.[62] For fifty years the precise form of the subsidies varied: that of 1513 combined a tax on rank for the nobles with an income or property tax for commoners; that of 1514 taxed wages as well as landed incomes and property; in 1540 only those with landed incomes or property above £20 had to pay. However, in Mary's reign the rate was fixed at 4s. in the pound for landed incomes, and 2s. 8d. in the pound for other property; and the subsidy remained fixed at that level for the rest of the century. It is worth noticing that while the subsidy was levied on the *income* from land, it fell on the *capital* value of other forms of property and was therefore heavier for merchants and townsmen. As the form of the subsidy became fixed, tax-assessments became stereotyped; by 1603 their relation to actual wealth was remote.

All in all the Tudor monarchs made no permanent addition to the financial resources of the Crown. Henry VII extended the Crown estates; Henry VIII added to them monastic lands

[62] Schofield, thesis, ch. iv.

and developed the subsidy; Mary restored the value of the customs duties. But these gains were ultimately lost, especially in the second half of the century. Sales of land began about 1540 and continued until Stuart times. Inflation eroded the revenue from land and commerce. The tax-base of the subsidy steadily narrowed. Domestic sources of credit were never adequate. The solid financial foundations required by a modern state had not been laid by 1603. With careful management and unadventurous policies the Crown could, however, keep afloat.

III

The Servants of the Crown

In 1641 an attorney of the Council in the Marches, Richard Lloyd, defending that court against its enemies, claimed that 'it is as necessary for princes to have places of preferment to prefer servants of merit as money in their Exchequer'. Neither Elizabeth nor James, he said, had allowed the Duchy of Lancaster to be absorbed into the Exchequer, because the abolition of its offices would have deprived them of valuable rewards for their servants. No more should Charles I tolerate the destruction of the Marcher Council. In making this claim Lloyd described very well one of the two important functions of early modern bureaucracy. Not only did it administer, but it was also a source of political rewards, through which the monarch could foster loyalty to his regime.[1]

For this reason the range of offices was in some ways wider than we would think normal in a modern bureaucracy; and, since the winning of support was quite as important as the conduct of business, influential men were able to accumulate posts. Sir Edward Belknap, Surveyor of the King's Prerogative under Henry VII, later became Surveyor of the King's Wards, Surveyor of the royal mines in Devonshire, and Auditor of the Exchequer. He was also constable of Warwick Castle, steward of Warwick, steward of six Crown lordships in the same county, and chief butler of the realm.[2] At the end of the sixteenth century William Cecil, Lord Burghley, was Lord Treasurer, Master of the Court of Wards, master of the game in Husburne, Hampshire, steward of Bristol, steward of Westminster, steward of the Bishopric of Coventry and Lichfield, steward of the lands of the Bishop of Winchester in Hampshire and Wiltshire,

---

[1] Huntington Lib., California, MS EL 7466. Cf. J. Fortescue, *Governance of England*, ed. Plummer (Oxford, 1885), ch. xvii. See R. Mousnier, *La Vénalité des offices sous Henri IV et Louis XIII* (Rouen, 1945). W. T. MacCaffrey, 'Place and Patronage', in *Elizabethan Government and Society*, ed. S. T. Bindoff *et al.* (1961).

[2] *LP* II. 617, 618, 1127. W. C. Richardson, 'The Surveyor of the King's Prerogative', *EcHR* LVI (1941).

steward of the possessions of Trinity College, Cambridge, master of the game to the Bishop of Chichester, and steward of the lands of the Bishop of St David's. Office involved not merely the central posts of government but stewardships on the estates of the Crown and other appointments.[3]

Governmental pluralism was not of course peculiar to the early modern period. Today the skilled administrator and the ambitious politician collect the chairmanships of those entwined committees which control affairs at local and national level. In the sixteenth century they sought posts in estate administration, which brought a small fee to their holders but were probably more important as signs of royal favour and sources of patronage.

Although the offices in the royal administration ranged into fields that today seem inappropriate for the bureaucrat, they were in other ways much more constricted. Offices that occupy millions of cubic feet in our contemporary administrative buildings did not then exist, and the government had virtually no paid agents in the localities. The steward of a lordship or the master of the royal game might guard the Crown's interests as a landlord—or put in a deputy to do so—but he was not concerned with the collection of taxes, the maintenance of order, and the execution of justice. Those tasks were mostly left to the Justices of the Peace and other commissioners, or to such lesser men as constables and overseers of the poor. While J.P.s received a small allowance for attending sessions, they were, like other local commissioners, largely unpaid—though not necessarily unrewarded—for their services. For that reason I have excluded them from this chapter, which is concerned with men holding offices of profit under the Crown.[4]

By the close of the fourteenth century English Kings had at their disposal a small but effective group of civil servants, most of whom were in clerical orders. In the middle ranks of the service, Chancery was staffed entirely with clerics; the clerks of the Privy Seal and of the Signet were in minor orders; offices in

[3] HMC, *Salisbury MSS*, VIII. 552. B. P. Wolffe, *The Crown Lands*, 39–40.

[4] J. H. Gleason, *The Justices of the Peace in England* (Oxford, 1969), *passim*. Below, ch. XII.

the Exchequer were shared between laymen and clerics. Of the higher officers of state in the fourteenth century most were in holy orders and many could reasonably expect a bishopric as the reward of their secular labours. But their clerical vestments weighed lightly upon them: faced with conflicting claims on their time and loyalty from Church and Crown, they almost invariably obeyed the secular authority. Paid in part by the Crown and in part by ecclesiastical benefices, they were Crown servants first and ministers of God only in a fairly casual sense. Normally they held their offices during the King's pleasure and could therefore be replaced when they were no longer fit for duty. This was a tolerably painless process since they could generally be provided to a clerical living in their retirement.[5]

In the thirteenth and fourteenth centuries the laity began to enter the lawcourts.[6] Elsewhere, the major infiltration seems to have occurred in the course of the fifteenth century: the Signet Office had a predominantly lay staff from 1437, the Exchequer from 1500, if not before.[7] By the end of the fifteenth century fewer Chancery officials were clerics than in mid-century, and more of them had had a legal education. The new courts and departments established under the Tudors were from the beginning staffed by laymen: there was no question of clerical officials being appointed to the Courts of Wards or Augmentations. In regional courts like the Councils in the North and the Marches of Wales, bishops might be appointed to the presidency and other clerics could sit upon the bench, but the offices of profit went to laymen. By the reign of Elizabeth, if not before, the laity had prised away the clerical grip upon the governmental machine: it was to be disastrously, but only briefly, restored in part during the reign of Charles I.[8]

Since clerics had been essentially servants of the Crown rather than of the Church, the change may not be thought to have made much difference. But in practice the intrusion of

[5] T. F. Tout, 'The English Civil Service in the Fourteenth Century', in *Collected Papers*, III (Manchester, 1934), 191–222. J. C. Sainty, 'The Tenure of Offices in the Exchequer', *EHR* LXXX (1965). A. L. Brown, 'The Privy Seal' (D. Phil. thesis, Oxford, 1954), ch. vii. J. Otway-Ruthven, *The King's Secretary*, ch. viii.

[6] A. Harding, *A Social History of English Law*, 167–9.

[7] Otway-Ruthven, op. cit., ch. viii. Sainty, op. cit. 451–4.

[8] G. E. Aylmer, *The King's Servants*, 429–31. N. Pronay, 'Chancellor, Chancery, and Council', in *British Government and Administration*, ed. H. Hearder and H. R. Loyn (Cardiff, 1974).

the laity into government service made it rather less like a twentieth-century bureaucracy than it had been in the later middle ages. The clergy had a financial independence which the laity lacked. Substantially rewarded as they often were from ecclesiastical revenues they constituted only a minor burden on the Crown. They could retire from their bureaucratic labours to clerical benefices, and they had—at any rate officially—no children to provide for. Lay officers were more dependent on the rewards of their secular offices to provide for themselves and for their families. The point was neatly put by that modest and spiritual man, Sir Thomas More, in a letter to Erasmus in 1516. Clerical ambassadors, said More, were much more comfortably off than laymen who were sent on embassies, since they had no families to support and could always be rewarded with clerical livings. Erasmus was certainly a man to appreciate that sort of point.[9]

Considerations of this kind probably help to account for some interesting changes in the tenure of offices during the fifteenth and sixteenth centuries. Official posts could be held by four principal types of tenure: *durante bene placito*, or during the King's pleasure, which was the least secure; *quam diu se bene gesserit*, or during good behaviour, which placed the holder a little more firmly in the saddle; for life, which made him virtually irremovable from his office, although he could, for flagrant misdemeanours, be suspended from its functions; and hereditary tenure, which converted the post to a transmissible freehold property.[10] Mr J. C. Sainty's analysis of posts in the Exchequer shows that in the fourteenth century the important offices of Chancellor, King's Chamberlain, and King's Remembrancer were all held by their clerical occupants during the King's pleasure or during good behaviour. In the course of the fifteenth century all three offices came into lay hands, which held them, from mid-century, for life. The correlation between lay takeover of offices and their conversion to life tenure is high in the Exchequer.[11] Although supporting evidence from other departments is so far lacking, there is at least *prima facie* ground for saying that the intrusion of laymen into the bureaucracy

[9] *LP* ii. i. 1552.
[10] For some less common types of tenure see Aylmer, op. cit. 122–3.
[11] Sainty, op. cit. 451–4.

brought about the conversion of offices into a form of life property. If this did in fact happen, it can be plausibly explained by the anxiety of lay landowners to provide for their families and by their inability to browse on retirement in clerical pastures.

It does not follow from this that all offices were held by life tenures in the sixteenth century. Senior Household officials like the Treasurer of the Chamber, the Chamberlain, the Vice-Chamberlain, the Captain of the Guard, the Controller of the Household, and the Treasurer of the Household evidently held their posts under the Tudors without a patent and at the pleasure of the monarch, although by the reign of Charles I many of them had acquired a life interest.[12] The judges of the royal courts and such major officers of state as the Lord Treasurer, the Lord Chancellor, the Lord Keeper, the Lord Admiral, and the Secretaries of State held by royal pleasure or during good behaviour throughout the sixteenth and the seventeenth centuries.[13] While dependence on the King's pleasure may have been nominally less secure than the other forms of tenure, in practice there was probably not much difference between them. Lord Buckhurst even tried to argue, rather implausibly, that a patent of office *quam diu se bene gesserit* automatically became void on the misbehaviour of the holder, and that therefore this type of tenure was less secure than *durante bene placito*.[14]

At the other end of the scale there were a few offices which were formally and legally hereditary. The Earls of Oxford claimed a hereditary right in the posts of Lord Great Chamberlain, keeper of Waltham Forest, and constable of Colchester Castle.[15] The office of Earl Marshal was to all intents and purposes the heritable property of the Howard family, although it was lost to them for several decades after the attainder of the fourth Duke of Norfolk in 1572. Some quite humble posts, like that of the usher of the Exchequer, were also hereditary.[16]

In the middle range of officialdom life tenures were much

[12] Aylmer, op. cit. 106.

[13] Ibid. 106–13. A. J. Slavin, *Politics and Profit*, 161.

[14] HMC, *Salisbury MSS*, IX. 346, 348. Contrast the view given by Aylmer, op. cit. 108.

[15] *LP*, VII. 594.

[16] Aylmer, op. cit. 107–8.

more common, though certainly not invariable. In the Exchequer, as we have seen, they had come by the sixteenth century to be usual even for so important an officer as the Chancellor. At the Council in the Marches of Wales the Queen's Attorney, the Queen's Solicitor, the Clerk of the Council, and the Clerk of the Signet all held by life patents. A proposal by the Lord President in 1591 to convert the tenure of the Attorney and the Solicitor to 'good behaviour' came to nothing. The same tenure seems to have been usual for officials in most lawcourts— except for the judges—and in such administrative departments as the Signet Office and the Privy Seal Office.[17]

Life tenure did not however give complete and uniform security. Men involved in the upper reaches of political life might not necessarily find in it an adequate protection. At the beginning of Mary's reign Sir Ralph Sadler was not saved from ejection from the office of Master of the Great Wardrobe; yet his life tenure did preserve him as Keeper of the Hanaper in Chancery from 1535 until 1587.[18] Much later, in the reign of Charles I, another officer of the Hanaper, George Mynne, was found guilty in Star Chamber of exacting excessive fees. In spite of his being convicted and fined, he could not be removed from office, although he was forbidden to execute its functions. Yet even when he was sequestered and suspended he still kept his privileges and immunities as an officer of Chancery.[19]

Accompanying the spread of life tenures was the pursuit of reversions. A reversion was the grant of the right of succession to an office, made during the lifetime and tenancy of an existing holder. The earliest reversions to Exchequer offices were granted during the fifteenth century; they became frequent during the sixteenth.[20] In time it became customary to grant more than one reversion to an office, so that a queue of expectant administrators could be seen waiting to step successively into a dead man's shoes. Reversionary grants were not necessarily harmful. They could well be given to an officer's deputy or underling, assuring him of promotion when the time came. But they could also be used to reward courtiers who were wholly

---

[17] P. Williams, *Council in the Marches* (Cardiff, 1958), 151, 156, 159. BL Harleian MS 6995, f. 41.

[18] Slavin, op. cit. 161–2.   [19] Aylmer, op. cit. 117–21.

[20] Ibid. 72, 96–106. Sainty, op. cit. 452–4, 457, 461–6.

inexperienced in the work, or to turn life tenures into hereditary ones. By skilful use of reversions the Osborne family controlled the office of Treasurer's Remembrancer from 1552 to 1674, with only a single complete break, while the Fanshawes established a hereditary regime in the post of King's Remembrancer from 1561 to 1675 with only brief appearances from other families.[21] At the Court of Wards the offices of Auditor and Receiver became virtually hereditary in the families of Tooke and Fleetwood.[22] In 1538 the Earl of Sussex claimed to hold the reversion of the Lord Stewardship. In 1589 Richard Lane asked for the reversion to the post of attorney in the Court of Requests, having acted as deputy in the office for eighteen or nineteen years. In the 1590s it appeared that there were already two reversioners to the post of Clerk to the Privy Seal, when a request came from Edward Reynolds for a third.[23]

Even if they had not acquired reversions, the sons of office-holders did their best to step quickly into the posts of their dead or dying fathers. Lord Strange wrote to Robert Cecil in 1593 that since his father, the Earl of Derby, was unlikely to live long, he wished to be given the earl's office of Chamberlain of Chester. Five days later, after the earl had died, he wrote again asking to succeed his father as Lord-Lieutenant of Cheshire and Lancashire.[24] William, Lord Herbert, showed a similar anxiety during the last days of his father, the second Earl of Pembroke, in 1601. He first requested leave of absence from court to stay with the dying earl at Wilton, in order to prevent him from giving his inheritance elsewhere. A few days later he begged for the offices held by his father and complained that it would be a great disgrace to him if they were granted to anyone else.[25]

The multiplication of life tenures, the scramble for reversions, and the attempt to make posts hereditary are all indications that offices were coming to be regarded as forms of property rather than as jobs to be done. Like other property-owners, officials began to use subordinates in the running of their affairs. Just as a rector would put in a vicar or curate to care for the

---

[21] Sainty, op. cit. 463n.

[22] H. E. Bell, *The Court of Wards and Liveries*, 24–5.

[23] *LP* xiii. ii. 5. *CSPDom, Add., 1580–1625*, 265. HMC, *Salisbury*, vii. 332, 419.

[24] HMC, *Salisbury*, iv. 376, 378, 392, 411, 446, 465. Cf. Lodge, ii. 395, 339–400; iii. 24–7.

[25] HMC, *Salisbury*, xi. 3, 9, 13–14, 91–2, 99.

souls in his parish, or a landlord would employ a bailiff or steward to manage his estates, so an officer would appoint a deputy
to conduct the business of the office, usually for a small pit-
tance, while he himself enjoyed the bulk of the proceeds. The
great officers of state were not allowed to create deputies. Just
occasionally a lesser official might eschew them: Sir Edward
Hoby, for instance, told Robert Cecil in 1599 that he would
like an office in reversion, since this would give him something
to do; he would not exercise the post by deputy.[26] But such
an attitude was unusual. Most men liked, if they could manage
it, to collect as many offices as possible, and, having done so,
they were forced to use deputies for performing the work. This
practice of employing deputies made possible bureaucratic
pluralism. Sir Ralph Sadler, for instance, was not only Secretary of State from 1540 to 1543, he was also Master of the Great
Wardrobe from 1543 to 1553, Keeper of the Hanaper in Chancery from 1535 until his death in 1587, and notary in Chancery
from 1534. The Secretaryship had to be exercised in person,
but the other three involved no more than complex routine
duties and could be delegated. Sadler's activities as a notary
in Chancery remain obscure. At the Wardrobe, he undertook
a good deal of the accounting work himself, but used three of
his own dependants—Hales, Raylton, and Cotton—when he
was too busy. Hales came to be important also at the
Hanaper, where he started by being termed 'clerk' or 'deputy'
and ended by becoming Sadler's co-tenant of the office. Hales
himself was used by Sadler informally on government business
and turned to Sadler's other protégés for securing the office.
Without employing his own servants as agents and deputies
Sadler obviously could not have managed his group of offices;
as it was he complained of seldom going to bed before midnight
and generally waking by 4.00 a.m.[27]

   In some departments an elaborate hierarchy of deputies
enabled pluralism to spread like a weed. At the Council in the
Marches of Wales the offices of Secretary, Clerk to the Council,
and Clerk of the Signet all came to be grouped together in the
same hands. From about 1563 until his death in 1590 they were
held by Charles Fox, although he had to share the Signet with

[26] Aylmer, op. cit. 125–6. HMC, *Salisbury*, ix. 181.
[27] Slavin, op. cit. 161–71.

John Dudley; and in 1590 Fox was succeeded by Fulke Greville, who had already taken over Dudley's share of the Signet and had acquired reversions to the Clerkship of the Council in 1577 and the Secretaryship in 1583. Neither Fox nor Greville could perform all his duties, and after 1598, when he became Treasurer of the Navy, Greville had no intention of performing any of them. Fox executed the office of Secretary himself and made the Council's Examiner, Thomas Sherer, his deputy as Clerk of the Council. Greville continued Sherer as his deputy for the two clerkships until Sherer's death in 1598 and after that he appointed John Powell. Thomas Sherer seems to have worked conscientiously as Fox's deputy, but he could not of course carry out his own functions as Examiner and these had to be performed by deputies, described as 'men of small credit' and 'young men unsworn'. In 1586 the President, the Earl of Pembroke, reported that the Examiner's office was 'furthest out of course of any one thing in that court'.[28] Pluralists were to be found in most courts. For instance, John Williams, Treasurer of Augmentations from 1544 to 1554, was receiver for Buckinghamshire, steward or bailiff in nine manors, joint steward with his son of cathedral lands in Oxfordshire, ranger of Witney Chase, steward and master of the game in the honour of Grafton, warden of the forests of Salcey and Whittlewood.[29]

Men secured their offices in various ways, but never by the modern paths of examination and interview. Some, as we have seen, inherited posts from their fathers. But most had to struggle with their rivals up what Bacon called the 'winding stair' of preferment. The right of appointment to an office was a valuable possession, itself often disputed between great men or between departmental heads and the Crown. At the Council in the Marches of Wales the principal officers were appointed by letters patent from the monarch. Only such lesser functionaries as the pursuivants were appointed by the Lord President.[30] In Chancery the Lord Chancellor appointed the Master in Chancery and the twenty-four cursitors; the Master of the Rolls appointed the Six Clerks, the examiners, the clerks of the

[28] Williams, op. cit. 157–67, 302.
[29] W. C. Richardson, *The Court of Augmentations*, 220–6.
[30] Williams, op. cit., ch. viii.

petty bag, and various minor officials; the monarch was left
with the Registers, whom he 'captured' in 1549, the sealer and
chafe-wax, and various newly established clerkships.[31] In the
Exchequer the Crown secured control over various offices in
the course of the sixteenth century: it gained the Treasurer's
Remembrancer in 1505, the Clerk of the Pipe in 1508, the Tel-
lers of the Receipt in 1528, the Revenue Auditors in 1532, the
Marshal of the Exchequer in 1592. Various offices remained
in the gift of the Lord Treasurer and the Chancellor of the
Exchequer, but they were mostly of a subordinate kind.[32] It
seems clear that the Crown had greater powers of nomination
in the more newly established institutions, that within all departments it was more likely to nominate to the most recently
created offices, and that it was trying, with some measure of
success, to extend its powers.[33]

But this is to talk of the nominal or official method of
appointment. To say that the Crown had the right of
appointment is to say only that it had at least the possibility
of a voice, not that it necessarily exercised any real right of selection. One must look behind the legal forms to see how offices
were filled in practice. Since the monarch obviously could not
be subjected to a direct barrage of demand from all comers,
certain informal roads to royal favour came to be established,
controlled by gate-keepers with access to the sovereign.[34] Thus
the state papers and personal archives of men prominent at
court are filled with requests for office. To take a few examples:
J. Uvedale asked Thomas Cromwell in 1537 to find him a place
with the King or with Prince Edward; Ralph Sadler asked
Cromwell to help him obtain from the Bishop of London the
keepership of a park in Essex; John Varney wanted Cromwell
to get the King's signature approving his petition for a life
patent of his stewardship of Berkhamsted and King's Langley;
Lord Sheffield hinted to Robert Cecil that he would like the
vacant position of Lord Chamberlain; and so on.[35]

[31] W. J. Jones, *The Elizabethan Court of Chancery*, 104, 119, 136, 145, 154, 157–8, 161–4.
Aylmer, op. cit. 71–3.

[32] Sainty, op. cit. 457–61.   [33] Aylmer, op. cit. 69–74.

[34] J. E. Neale, 'The Elizabethan Political Scene', *Proceedings of the British Academy*,
xxxiv (1948). MacCaffrey, op. cit.

[35] *LP* xii. ii. 1192, 1336; xiii. ii. 243, 843. HMC, *Salisbury*, vi. 297, 301, 313–14, 342,
360.

One way of distributing offices was of course by sale, which became extremely common in late medieval and early modern Europe. In France, where the traffic was open and legal, a special department of state, the *Bureau des Parties Casuelles*, was created to administer it.[36] In England the sale of offices was illegal and no such department existed. Yet there is abundant evidence that offices were bought and sold, although the discretion with which this had to be done makes it difficult to measure the flow of business. The phrase 'sale of office' covers several different sorts of transaction. Payment could be made to the monarch himself or it could be made to the current holder of the office.[37] Both systems operated in Valois and Bourbon France: under Louis XIII new offices were generally purchased from the King, old ones from their existing holder. Alternatively payment might be made to the head of the department concerned, or money might be spent not so much in buying the office itself as on the influence necessary for securing it. In 1534, according to a report from John Hussey to Lord Lisle, Henry VIII announced that if offices were being sold, as they daily were, he himself would have the advantage from it. Hussey went on to suggest to Lisle that he might pay the King 1,000 marks to exchange his present post for the captaincy of Guisnes.[38] There is not much sign that the King did in fact profit from the sale of offices; but others certainly could and did. Thomas Cromwell was offered £100 for his help in obtaining the post of justice in North Wales; J. Lucas proposed to give him £10 for wine—literally a *pourboire*—if appointed King's Solicitor.[39]

In the later years of Henry VIII and in the reign of his successor the practice of selling seems to have grown and prices to have risen. In 1551–2 a statute was carried forbidding the sale of offices; sellers were to be deprived of their interest and title in the office, purchasers to be disabled from holding it.[40] It is difficult to find out whether or not the statute had any

[36] Mousnier, *Vénalité des offices, passim*. K. J. Swart, *Sale of Offices in the Seventeenth Century* (Hague, 1949), *passim*.

[37] Aylmer, op. cit. 85–8, 225–39.

[38] *LP* vii. 386.

[39] Ibid., Add. i. i. 798; xii. ii. 1160. See also ibid. viii. 22; xiv. i. 231; Add. i. i. 1070.

[40] Richardson, *Augmentations*, 164. 5 & 6 Edward VI c. 16.

real impact. In 1556 William Cecil rather primly referred to a request from Henry Cobham, 'pretending it an offence to sell an office'. By the last decade of the century there is however abundant evidence of offers being made for posts. In 1592 Sir Thomas Sherley offered £200 for an office, while two years later he was expressing shocked—but rather unconvincing—indignation at the rumour that he was being paid £4,600 for his own position as Treasurer of the Wars. William Hulbert offered Burghley 100 angels if he would get the post of customer at Bristol transferred to J. Dowlie, who had probably bought it from Hulbert; Henry Goldingham promised £100 for the post of controller of the customs at Ipswich; and Herbert Croft wrote that Richard Davis was offering the same amount for a judgeship in Wales.[41] The Earl of Pembroke was accused of displacing all the attorneys at the Council in the Marches and forcing them to buy back their offices from him. This charge may not be true; but there is no doubt that a later President, the Earl of Bridgewater, took an entrance fee of £100 from new attorneys in the reign of Charles I.[42] Two men, Edward More and William Hickman, offered £1,000 for the office of Receiver of the Court of Wards. Most interesting of all is the Queen's order that Mr Dobson, the Clerk of Statutes, should pay £100 per annum to Lady Denny for his office. Dobson also had to pay the Queen £1,100, which was the debt owed her by Sir Edward Denny, the previous holder.[43] After this it is a relief to find a letter from Attorney-General Coke, opposing the appointment of one Wiseman as Clerk of Outlawries and insisting that this was not an office which should be bought or sold.[44]

How much control had the monarch over appointments to offices which legally were in his gift? Naturally enough he was subjected to the influence and sales-talk of courtiers and patrons; but this is a hazard faced by anyone with the power of appointment. Probably the field of his choice was narrowed by the inability of men without friends at court to make an

[41] Haynes, 443. *CSPDom, 1591–4*, 233, 347, 425. HMC, *Salisbury*, IV. 558, 579; X. 31.

[42] PRO, State Papers Domestic, Elizabeth (SP 12), 197/20. Penry Williams, 'The Activity of the Council in the Marches in the Seventeenth Century', *WHR* I. no. 2 (1961).

[43] HMC, *Salisbury*, IV. 497, 501, 529, 531; X, 80, 90, 91, 122.

[44] Ibid. IV. 511.

application. But a monarch with a mind of his, or her, own could certainly exercise choice, at least over the major posts. When, in the 1590s, Essex failed to get the Attorneyship for Francis Bacon, he sought for his protégé the vacant post of Solicitor. Although he was supported in this by his own rivals, Burghley and Robert Cecil, Elizabeth, confronted with this powerful alliance, appointed another man.[45] That Elizabeth needed careful handling is shown in a letter to Burghley from Henry Savile, who wanted Burghley's help in a suit because his commendation, coming in cold blood and sober judgement, would weigh more heavily with the Queen than 'all the affectionate speech' of the Earl of Essex.[46] In the case of minor posts the monarch's influence was likely to be less firmly and more sporadically exercised. Signs that there had been loss of control appear at the very beginning of James's reign when commissioners hearing private suits to the King were ordered not to give reversions to places of consequence.[47]

Two particular features of the system of office-holding may have eroded royal control. The habit of giving reversions had become well established by the sixteenth century. It did not of course necessarily destroy the monarch's power of choice. But, in practice, if allowed to get out of hand, it firmly mortgaged the future. Four, five, even six or seven reversioners might be appointed for a single place; and, while all might have been appointed by the King initially, this queue of hopefuls stretching into the future certainly deprived him of choice when the office became vacant. The system of reversion could also be used, as we have seen, to establish something near to *de facto* hereditary tenure. But toleration of large numbers of reversioners seems to have been a feature of the reign of James I rather than the Tudors.[48]

The other element which affected royal control was the practice of appointing deputies. The monarch might name the officer himself, but if that officer had the power of naming a deputy the Crown had no influence at all in choosing the person who actually did the work. At the Council in the Marches the

[45] W. B. Devereux, *Lives and Letters of the Earls of Essex* (1853), 1. 284–8, 313–14.
[46] HMC, *Salisbury*, v. 188.
[47] *CSPDom, Add., 1580–1625*, 424.
[48] Sainty, op. cit. 461–3.

office of Queen's Attorney was held from 1559 to about 1592 by John Price. But in 1579 Price was suspended from his office by Star Chamber for forgery. Since he held by patent he could not be displaced and the work was executed by his deputy, Thomas Atkins, who turned out to be as dishonest and self-seeking as his principal. Yet, however strong the complaints against him, Atkins could not be removed.[49]

The rewards of office flowed in the sixteenth century down many tributary channels, not, as today, in the single river of salaries. The annual wage formed of course one of these nourishing streams, but it was far from being the largest. The principal Secretary of State had a salary of £100 per annum from the Crown, the Lord Admiral got £200, the Master of the Court of Wards £233. 6s. 8d., the Clerk of Wards £20. The Queen's Attorney at Ludlow got £13. 6s. 8d., her Solicitor £10. Even making the most lavish allowance for the greater purchasing power of money in the sixteenth century, one cannot consider these sums very generous for officials of such standing. Beside the total rewards such men expected and obtained they are minute.[50]

The bulk of an officer's direct revenue came, not from the Crown's salary, but from fees paid by the subjects of the realm for each official act: payment, in other words, was by piece-rate. When John Hawarde, a lawyer, was summoned from his rooms in the Temple to attend the Privy Council at Greenwich he had to pay Mr Ward, the Clerk of the Council, a royal for recording his appearance, 6s. 8d. for his entering into a bond, and 6s. 8d. for the bond itself. The messenger of the Queen's Chamber, who summoned Hawarde, got £1. 6s. 8d. for a very short journey—apparently being paid at 4d. a mile—and a retainer of 6s. 8d. Hawarde thus had to pay out quite largely for a service that he had never requested. At the Court of Wards, the Clerk of the Court received fees for forty-eight separate acts. To sue out the livery of lands worth £22. 7s. 4d. per

---

[49] Williams, *Council in the Marches*, 149–57.

[50] Neale, 'Elizabethan Political Scene'. Bell, *Court of Wards*, 34. Williams, *Council in the Marches*, 150. MacCaffrey, op. cit. 110–22.

annum a man would have to pay in all £45. 6s. 6d. in fees to officers of Wards, Chancery, and Exchequer. By these means all officials, whether they were attached to lawcourts, the Privy Council, the Privy Seal, the Signet, or the Ordnance, accumulated substantial revenues.[51]

But this was not all: officers could expect intermittent, unofficial, and indirect rewards from Crown and people.[52] The Crown, niggardly with salaries, was often generous with occasional *douceurs* and indirect payments. Royal favour took on substantial material form in wardships, pensions, annuities, leases of Crown land, trading licences, and monopolies. Food and lodging at court for an officer and his servants was surprisingly valuable in spite of all attempts at economy in the royal Household. Wardships granted by Burghley between 1594 and 1598 often went to reward such servants of the State as Sir John Wolley, Latin Secretary, Sir John Fortescue, Chancellor of the Exchequer, John Herbert, Master of Requests, and Robert Beale, Clerk of the Privy Council.[53] Henry VII granted annuities ranging from £126. 13s. 4d. to Thomas Lovell as constable of the Tower and of Nottingham Castle, through payments of £33. 6s. 8d. to his squires of the body, to 12d. a day for John Burwell, plumber. Some of them, including those given to squires of the body, were for life, others during the royal pleasure.[54]

Regulations governing trade and industry could be turned to the profit of courtiers and officials. The Earl of Leicester got £750 per annum from the customs. The Earl of Cumberland had a profitable licence to export undressed cloth, which he was able to sell to merchants.[55] In 1576 Simon Bowyer, gentleman usher to Queen Elizabeth, was granted a licence to buy and sell 500 sarplers of wool in the following ten years; and in 1590 he received a commission to act as sole informer against those who infringed certain statutes controlling the wool trade. Sir Walter Raleigh, Captain of the Guard, had a monopoly for playing-cards. In 1598 Lord Buckhurst, the Lord Treasurer,

[51] Hawarde, 112. Bell, op. cit. 193–205. Hurstfield, *Queen's Wards*, 81, 173–5. Evans, *Principal Secretary of State*, ch. ix.
[52] See in general MacCaffrey, op. cit.
[53] Hurstfield, op. cit. 125–7, 347–8.
[54] *LP* II. i. 2736; III. i. 999, 1000.
[55] MacCaffrey, op. cit. 114–15, 120–1. HMC, *Salisbury*, XIII. 67.

and Sir Robert Cecil, Secretary of State, acquired Sir John Packington's starch monopoly.[56]

The indirect rewards from private sources were often discreetly conveyed and cannot therefore be easily measured. Thomas Wriothesley, promoted Secretary of State in 1540, had previously been 'private secretary' to Thomas Cromwell. Among the bribes offered him were 'as good a gelding as you ever rode' and 'an ambling nag'.[57] Michael Hickes, Lord Burghley's personal assistant, had similar offers from men who wanted the path to official favour cleared for them. Men like Hickes and Wriothesley, confidential men of business for the great, relied almost entirely upon such *douceurs*.[58] But the great men themselves also accepted them. Lord Burghley received, over the last two years of his life, £3,103. 6s. 8d. from the purchasers of eleven wardships. These transactions provided the Queen with a mere £906. 13s. 4d. At his death Burghley's silver and gold plate was worth £14,000–£15,000; much of it probably came from gifts made by aspirants for favour.[59] At Christmas 1602 Robert Cecil received presents from nineteen individuals, while the Merchant Adventurers gave him 'one great standing bowl in a case', which he sold, undeterred by sentiment. Several of the gifts were costly, including a cup of gold and a crystal salt-set.[60]

For men at the top the rewards of office and political influence were huge. Professor Slavin estimates that Sir Ralph Sadler was receiving £600 from fees and gratuities in connection with his work in Chancery, £900–£1,000 from the Secretaryship and the Signet.[61] The landed wealth of Lord Burghley, derived ultimately from the profits of office, was estimated at the time of his death at £4,000 per annum, almost certainly too low a figure.[62] Professor Stone has assessed Robert Cecil's income from political offices between 1608 and 1612 at

[56] P. J. Bowden, *The Wool Trade in Tudor and Stuart England* (2nd edn., 1971), 131–3, 146–9. L. Stone, 'The Fruits of Office', in *Essays in the Economic and Social History of Tudor and Stuart England*, ed. F. J. Fisher (Cambridge, 1961). Below, 157–65.

[57] Slavin, *Politics and Profit*, 49–50.

[58] A. G. R. Smith, 'The Secretariat of the Cecils, *c.* 1580–1612', *EHR* LXXXIII (1968), 486–9. Hurstfield, *Queen's Wards*, 264. Neale, 'Elizabethan Political Scene'.

[59] Hurstfield, *Queen's Wards*, 267–8, 276–82. Neale, loc. cit.

[60] HMC, *Salisbury MSS*, XIV. 527.

[61] Slavin, op. cit. 171–87.

[62] F. Peck, *Desiderata Curiosa* (1779), I. 27.

£6,900 per annum, of which £3,000 came from Wards and £2,800 at least from the Treasurership. But there were other, less visible, receipts, such as his pension from Spain, which came to between £1,000 and £1,500 each year. Most lucrative of all, at the end of his life, was his farm of the customs on imported silks, which provided him with £1,333 per annum up to 1610 and £7,000 per annum for the next two years.[63]

The mere computation of Cecil's revenue from the profits of office, while striking enough in itself, is an inadequate reflection of the gains. At his father's death in 1598 he inherited about £1,800 per annum in land. By 1612 he had acquired a territorial estate valued at £6,000 per annum; he had built a sumptuous palace at Hatfield and two town houses in the Strand— Great Salisbury House and Little Salisbury House; he had put up an elaborate commercial structure, the New Exchange; and he had bought potentially valuable building-plots in St Martin's Lane. This great outlay of capital was not of course achieved simply by the diversion of surplus income from office. Much was done by raising huge loans—over £60,000 in his last four years. But none of it would have been possible without Cecil's political influence and contacts, as well as his official revenue. In about fourteen years, a younger son, with the inheritance equivalent to that of a major gentleman, had transformed himself into a grandee.[64]

Office in the higher levels of royal service did, however, involve some element of risk. When Elizabeth offered the post of Lord Chamberlain to her cousin, Lord Hunsdon, Governor of Berwick, he was strongly advised against acceptance by Robert Vernon, the surveyor of victuals at Berwick. Vernon admitted that the post had its attractions: the Lord Chamberlain had the best lodgings at court, could recommend his friends for offices, and was continually in attendance on the Queen 'to take any advantage of time and occasion' for the presentation of suits. But against this Vernon warned Hunsdon that the great elevation of the Lord Chamberlain's position would arouse jealousy, involve heavy expenses, tie him to the court, and expose him to disgrace for any errors that he might commit. Vernon

---

[63] L. Stone, 'The Fruits of Office', in Fisher (ed.), *Essays in the Economic and Social History of Tudor and Stuart England.*

[64] Ibid. Id., *Family and Fortune* (Oxford, 1973), chs. i–iii.

had good reason for wanting to keep Hunsdon at Berwick, since the governor owed him money; and his assessment of the benefits and drawbacks was not unbiased. While he set out very clearly the risks of court office, his letter may have exaggerated them. Hunsdon was able to retain his governorship of Berwick *in absentia* while exercising the post of Lord Chamberlain. In this he was following the ordinary practice of court officials, who were exceptionally well placed to collect offices in plurality: the first Earl of Pembroke held thirty-eight posts in addition to his place in the Privy Chamber. Such posts might not carry a large salary, for although Henry VIII had evidently raised the wages of household officials, Elizabeth held them down in a period of rising prices. But the perquisites and the influence which court office brought with it were probably, for most men, adequate compensation. Hunsdon himself died in debt, but it is impossible to say whether this was the consequence of high expenses at court or whether he was typical: in the upper reaches of royal service, where conspicuous consumption was demanded, much would depend upon luck.[65]

In the middle ranges the risks were less, and although the prospects were obviously more modest, profits were assured. The combined offices of Clerk to the Council and Clerk of the Signet at the Council in the Marches brought in £900 per annum in fees towards the end of the century. Each of the Six Clerks in Chancery was reputedly worth £3,000 annually; while this sum was certainly exaggerated, even half of it would have been a substantial amount.[66] To grasp their real magnitude these figures need to be set against the incomes of other social groups. Professor Stone has estimated that the average landed income of the peerage was £2,140 in 1559 and £3,020 in 1602. For a Yorkshire gentleman in the reign of Henry VIII £400 per annum would be a very substantial income indeed and several of the upper gentry would be content with between £200 and £400. At the end of the century Thomas Wilson estimated that a knight was worth between £1,000 and £2,000 per annum, an ordinary J.P. between £500 and £1,000. Thus official incomes at the top of the ladder exceeded those of the

---

[65] L. Stone, 'Office under Queen Elizabeth', *HJ* x (1967). R. C. Braddock, 'The Rewards of Office-holding in Tudor England', *Journal of British Studies*, XIV (1975).
[66] Williams, *Council in the Marches*, 164. W. J. Jones, *Elizabethan Chancery*, 135.

average peer; and on the middle rungs they equalled those of the upper gentry.[67]

It is difficult to say whether the rewards of office increased in real terms during the Tudor period. The Master of the Rolls got £310 per annum in the 1530s, £1,300 by the end of the century, £1,600 in the 1630s.[68] The Auditor of the Exchequer got £200 in the 1580s, £1,500 in the 1630s. Even allowing for inflation both these posts did well, but the gain in real terms was not enormous. Robert Cecil's total benefits from office in terms of influence and contacts probably brought him more than Sadler's £2,600; but, once again, the increase was not huge when set beside the rise in prices. It is unlikely that there was a smoothly rising escalator of official fortunes, more probable that times of bonanza were separated by periods when rewards rose slowly. Two periods were especially prosperous for courtiers and officials: one was the minority of Edward VI and the other was the reign of James I, when the Scottish monarch bid lavishly for the favour of his new subjects.[69]

Payment by piece-rate had important consequences for relations between officers and for the attitude of the bureaucracy towards reform. The more functions that an official could accumulate the larger his income, both from fees and from gratuities. Royal servants were therefore anxious to extend the boundaries of their bureaucratic empires whenever possible, and to defend them against encroachment at all times. Frontier disputes were common in many departments, but two illustrations will be sufficient. At the Council in the Marches of Wales the line between the duties of the Queen's Attorney and the Queen's Solicitor was only very faintly and uncertainly drawn. While both officers were intended to act on the Crown's behalf at Ludlow, the Attorney seems to have had the task of conducting cases in court, the Solicitor of supervising their preparation.

---

[67] L. Stone, *Crisis of the Aristocracy* (Oxford, 1965), app. ix, xi. R. B. Smith, *Land and Politics in the England of Henry VIII*, 134–5. Dr Smith's figures for Yorkshire are based on subsidy figures, which are not very reliable. T. Wilson, 'The State of England (1600)', ed. F. J. Fisher (Camden Miscellany xvi, 1936), 23–4.

[68] Jones, op. cit. 52–3. C. S. L. Davies, 'The Administration of the Royal Navy under Henry VIII', *EHR* lxxx (1965), 282–8.

[69] Hurstfield, *Queen's Wards*, 279. Braddock, op. cit.

But there were many lucrative functions which occupied a debatable ground between the two officers and which John Price, the Attorney, tried to annex. As a contemporary remarked of one of Price's memoranda, 'Price his notes in substance seek to make his office commodious.'[70] A similar dispute occurred in the Elizabethan Exchequer between the Writer of the Tallies and the Clerk of the Pells. Both had the broadly similar functions of recording, in different ways, payments into and out of the Exchequer of Receipt; but from the middle of the sixteenth century the older office, the Clerkship of the Pells, was being encroached upon by the Writer of the Tallies.[71] There was no real administrative virtue in both officers recording entries, and the Writer of the Tallies seems to have done the work in a more effective manner. But from 1555 to 1602 there was almost continuous dispute. Vincent Skinner, the Writer of the Tallies, complained that 'the distraction I have had about quarrels to my place have hindered me much and now so utterly discouraged me that the service I intended to have done I could not ...'[72] Disrupting such quarrels might be: they were hardly surprising. When there were no ladders of promotion nor any annual increments in a professional salary, office-holders had a strong incentive to extend the boundaries of their posts.[73]

While officers struggled with each other to improve their own positions they often united to block any attempts at reform by the Crown. Alteration of their procedures would disturb their fees and was thus resisted. Since offices were regarded as a form of property, reform could be stigmatized as an encroachment upon freehold. When the Earl of Pembroke, as President of the Council in the Marches, tried to reform that court, its Solicitor, John Amyas, commented: 'I perceive there shall few men's estates here be unsearched.'[74] His use of the word 'estates' is revealing. When reforms were proposed in Star Chamber Francis Bacon said that he considered it to be 'standing with

[70] PRO, State Papers Domestic, Elizabeth (SP 12), 109/12, 37. Williams, *Council in the Marches*, 149–57.

[71] G. R. Elton, 'The Elizabethan Exchequer: War in the Receipt', in *Elizabethan Government and Society*, ed. Bindoff, 213–48.

[72] Ibid. 245.

[73] Jones, *Chancery*, 170–1. Ibid. 70–8, for the dispute between Parker and the Six Clerks.

[74] PRO, State Papers Domestic, Elizabeth (SP 12), 197/20. Williams, *Council in the Marches*, 177.

all equity and reason that new orders or favours should not frustrate ancient fees'.[75] Indignation came to be most heated when a new office was proposed by the Crown. When, in 1594, John Parker obtained a grant of a new office for keeping pleadings in Chancery, two of the Six Clerks, who had done his work previously, wrote that 'the King by his letters patents may not oust the common people of their rights and inheritance which they have in the common law of this land'. Nothing could better illustrate the conservatism of official interests.[76]

What was the quality of the Tudor bureaucracy? Obviously its qualities varied considerably and are in any case difficult to assess. One can begin on fairly firm ground by asking how many officials had the necessary qualifications and experience for their work. Very few wholly unqualified men were to be found at the summit of the administration. The outstanding figures, like Wolsey, Cromwell, Burghley, Robert Cecil, and Walsingham, had high intellectual gifts and underwent a rigorous training. All the Secretaries of State had educational training and experience in government to fit them for their posts. Admittedly the Lord Treasurers were, until the appointment of Paulet in 1552, unqualified noblemen; but they were not usually expected to perform any serious duties. Once the Lord Treasurer became a working officer the post was filled with trained administrators, although their intellectual training had been literary rather than numerate: Lionel Cranfield was probably the first really numerate Lord Treasurer. The Tudor Lord Chancellors and Lord Keepers were all trained in the civil or the common law; and some of them—Wolsey, More, Gardiner, Nicholas Bacon, and Egerton—were outstandingly able.[77] Of Elizabeth's Chancellors and Keepers only Hatton reached the woolsack without having a distinguished legal career behind him; and Hatton was a perfectly competent administrator.

In the middle ranges the quality of officials may have been deteriorating—at any rate in some departments—before 1600.

---

[75] J. Spedding *et al.*, *Works of Francis Bacon* (1862), IX (Vol. II of *Letters and Life*), 57–60.

[76] Jones, *Chancery*, 70–8, esp. 73.

[77] Ibid., chs. i, ii.

A key post at the Council in the Marches of Wales came into the hands of a wholly untrained man, Fulke Greville, through his friendship with Philip Sidney. As Secretary, Clerk of the Council, and Clerk of the Signet at Ludlow, Greville was probably the most important person there next to the President and the Chief Justice. Yet he had no qualifications for the post and showed no sign of wishing to acquire any. But Greville was at least an able man, who in other offices showed some worth. His seventeenth-century successors, Adam Newton and Lord Goring, were absentee courtiers with no interest in the Council beyond the fees which it brought them. It is not yet possible to say how common the practice of appointing absentee courtiers to administrative posts had become by 1603.[78] At the Exchequer the use of reversions was to allow unqualified and inexperienced men into the department under James I; but the deterioration does not seem to have begun before his accession.[79] At the Court of Wards the Tooke family were making the office of auditor hereditary in the last years of Elizabeth, but it was still possible for an active reformer like John Hare to be appointed Clerk; inexperienced men began to be appointed to offices in this court under James.[80]

Were Tudor officials corrupt? This question is much harder to answer. The accepted standards of political morality differed from our own; evidence is hard to come by and difficult to interpret. When gifts and gratuities were a normal part of official incomes the line between the acceptable and the reprehensible was hard to draw.[81] However, charges of corruption were certainly made at the time, and one must try to discover how firmly they were based.

In one area—the handling of government money—the boundary between peculation and honest dealing was clearly marked. It was considered as wrong then as it is now to embezzle the Crown's revenues. But the frailty of the accounting system made such corruption relatively simple. John Beau-

---

[78] Williams, *Council in the Marches*, ch. viii and app. iii; also 160–1. Id., *WHR*, i, no. 2, 150–1.

[79] Sainty, *EHR* LXXX. 461–3, 474.

[80] Bell, *Court of Wards*, ch. ii.

[81] J. Hurstfield, 'Political Corruption in Modern England', *History*, LII (1967), repr. in *Freedom, Corruption and Government in Elizabethan England*, 197. Id., *Queen's Wards*, ch. x.

mont, Receiver-General at the Court of Wards under Edward VI, showed two ways in which it could be done. While receiving money due to the court, Beaumont omitted to enter the receipts in his books and pocketed the proceeds. This was straight-forward theft. His other method was to enter sums received as arrears, while putting the cash to his own uses. In this way he was taking from the Crown a 'forced' and interest-free loan. By these two means Beaumont defrauded Crown and subjects of £20,000. It is no wonder that the judges in Star Chamber condemned 'so foul matters as we think have seldom appeared in any man'. Yet, in spite of the lesson of Beaumont's fraud, a later Receiver, George Goring, was able to repeat his second method and 'borrow' from Queen Elizabeth at least £19,000.[82]

The Court of Wards was not the only department whose officials embezzled money. In 1579 court-messengers were con-demned in Star Chamber to have their ears lopped off for steal-ing £3,000 from the Crown in seven years.[83] During Leicester's expedition to the Netherlands, in 1586-7, rapacious pay-masters and army treasurers raided the military budget.[84] John Williams, Master of the Jewels and Treasurer of Augmentations under Henry VIII, avoided rendering any accounts whatever during his eight years at the Jewel-House, piled up large arrears in Augmentations, and embezzled £31,000 which were not entered in the books. Charged with malfeasance, he pleaded carelessness. The incident did no harm to his career for he went on to become a peer and Lord President of the Council in the Marches.[85]

A second form of corruption was dishonest dealing by the officers of the law. The boundary between probity and fraud was much more difficult to draw in this area. The words used by Lord Bacon when he was arraigned for corruption as Lord Chancellor in 1621 illustrate the problem. Bacon said that there were three kinds of gift that might be offered to a judge: the first were bribes given in advance to pervert the course of jus-tice; the second were presents given when the judge thought the case was over, although in fact it still had some way to run;

[82] Id., *Queen's Wards*, 199-208.
[83] Lodge, ii. 205-6.
[84] J. E. Neale, 'Elizabeth and the Netherlands', *EHR* xlv (1930).
[85] W. C. Richardson, *Augmentations*, 164-5, 205-7, 230-3, 243-5, 266-8, 329-31.

the third were presents given when the case really was over.
While the first were certainly corrupt, Bacon claimed to be as
innocent of these 'as any born upon St Innocent's Day'. He
confessed that he might inadvertently have been guilty of the
second on occasion and freely admitted to taking gifts of the
third kind, which he regarded as entirely permissible. It seems
that he was only proved guilty on one count of perverting the
actual course of justice, but even so, the practice of a judge
receiving presents at all made perversion more likely, and
Bacon's ingenious distinctions may be thought to differentiate
between degrees of corruption rather than between guilt and
innocence. Bacon's case, occurring as it did after eighteen years
of Stuart rule, cannot be taken as evidence for judicial corruption under the Tudors. It does however reveal the problems
of definition and interpretation.[86]

But the accusations against Bacon were often foreshadowed
in Tudor times. John Beaumont, who moved in 1550 from the
Court of Wards to the Mastership of the Rolls, was as corrupt
in his second post as he had been greedy in the first. He was
charged with and was probably guilty of forgery, subornation
of a jury, and concealment of a felony.[87] But there is not much
other evidence of dishonest dealing by judges in Chancery at
this time. At the Council in the Marches of Wales one or two
of the judges were tainted by charges of corruption. Sir John
Throckmorton, Chief Justice of Chester, was accused by the
Privy Council of slackness and greed; and in 1579 he was fined
1,000 marks in Star Chamber for forging a legal document.
Edmund Walter was accused of taking bribes to acquit a murderer at Great Sessions, but his defence leaves some presumption
in his favour. Richard Broughton, legal agent to the Earl of
Essex and second justice in the Anglesey circuit, was fined £200
and removed from the commission of the peace for illegally taking bribes. But Lord Zouch, President of the Council, who was
no friend to the professional judges there, discounted the notion
that they were taking bribes: 'I mean not money to any magistrate,' he remarked. If one turns from the professional judges
to the nobles and gentry who were members of the Council in

---

[86] Hurstfield, *History*, LII, 22–3.
[87] Id., *Queen's Wards*, 199–206. W. K. Jordan (ed.), *The Chronicle and Political Papers of King Edward VI* (1966), 109, 128–9.

the Marches, high-handedness and corruption become more apparent. Sir William Herbert of Swansea was fined 1,000 marks in Star Chamber for disorderly riots in Cardiff; Edward, Lord Stafford, refused to allow the sheriff of Shropshire to execute judgement against him in a dispute over Cawes Castle; Sir Thomas Throckmorton of Tortworth, Gloucestershire, was fined 2,000 marks and removed from his offices for accepting bribes and maintaining quarrels. But these offences largely concerned the local activities and oppressions of the landowners; only Throckmorton's misdeeds involved the Council and that very indirectly.[88]

Much clearer signs of corruption are apparent in the officials of the Council in the Marches. Two of Elizabeth's Attorneys, John Price and Thomas Atkins, were certainly guilty of abusing justice: Price forged those parts of a document that had been eaten by mice and Atkins took bribes from men charged before the Council. There is evidence, admittedly not conclusive, that Charles Fox, the Secretary, was corrupt as well as greedy.[89] The same may well be true of other courts. In Star Chamber it was the clerk of the court, William Mill, not the judges, who was accused of injustice. Lord Keeper Egerton said of Mill that 'the subjects have been abused and "polled" these fourteen years past by Mill'. Later on Mill was reinstated by the Queen, but suspicions against him remained.[90]

The third possibility of corruption lay in the acceptance of gifts by government servants other than judges. Such gratuities were, as I have shown, common form at this time. Were they in themselves corrupt? Professor Hurstfield has argued that they were not, and that, provided no harm was done to the state, it would be anachronistic for the historian to object to them. They were, he says, essential to the working of government when the Crown's revenue was too small to enable it to pay its officials 'salaries appropriate to their rank and responsibilities'.[91] This is certainly true of lesser men at the royal court. Michael Hickes, Burghley's Secretary, was in no way diffident about taking presents, for men in his position could not have lived without them and the practice was part of conventional

[88] Williams, *Council in the Marches*, 266, 273–5, 302, 306–11.
[89] Ibid. 150–2.   [90] Hawarde, 94. *CSPDom, 1598–1601*, 542.
[91] Hurstfield, *History*, LII.

behaviour.[92] But the moral rules applied to men at the top seem
to have been ambiguous. Robert Cecil evidently rebuffed Sir
Arthur Gorges when the latter sent him a present in 1603, for
Gorges wrote in a hurt tone that he had only followed 'the common custom and usual compliment of the time'.[93] Cecil had
expressed his own attitude at great length and less clarity a year
or two before this. The Earl of Northumberland had given him
a coach and four horses, 'a gift greater than I was beholding
for to any subject'. Had he been able to argue with Northumberland before the present arrived he would have refused it,
for four reasons. First, 'gifts of value' should not pass between
'those whose minds condemn all the knots that utility can fasten
...' Second, Cecil had recently helped Northumberland in a
profitable suit and feared that his assistance would now be mis-
interpreted. Third, Cecil's enemies might think that Northumberland found him 'either facile or not clear from servile ends'.
Fourth, the Queen herself might come to suspect Cecil of being
influenced by the gift. These were certainly powerful arguments
for sending the coach back, but they did not prevail. The coach
and horses had, after all, arrived; and they stayed where they
were. As Cecil said, 'But what should I now call back yester-
day?'[94]

Faced with this combination of forced scrupulosity and ingenious casuistry it is hard to believe that gratuities were an
entirely natural and accepted part of the system. Gifts of a
modest size were of course perfectly tolerable. But Cecil's con-
torted prose reveals an uneasy conscience about receiving
objects of great splendour; and, since no one would claim for
Cecil a moral sensitivity above the average, his hesitations probably reflect the conventional morality. Yet he and others certainly accepted large presents. Northumberland's coach-and-
four was a minor matter beside the pension that Cecil took from
Spain: £1,000 per annum from 1603, later increased to £1,500
per annum, crowned by a payment of no less than £12,500 in
1607/08. Whether or not this affected Cecil's handling of
English policy is hard to say: but even if it did not, it was surely
by his own standards, improper. Cecil also used his official position to promote privateering voyages in the Mediterranean,

[92] Smith *EHR* LXXXIII. A. G. R. Smith, *Servant of the Cecils* (1977), ch. iii.
[93] HMC, *Salisbury MSS*, XII. 27.   [94] Ibid. X 347.

from which he drew moderate but dubious profits. Since his privateering interests encouraged him to favour the continuance of war, they may have balanced the pension from Spain in forming his attitude to the peace negotiations.[95] But one cannot really accept the notion that gifts of this kind were necessary to provide officials with incomes 'appropriate to their rank and responsibilities'. Cecil's yearly income from politics at the end of his life was nearly £7,000 without the presents from Spain and other hidden receipts; that might be thought sufficient.

The Crown's servants in the sixteenth century were in many ways less effective as administrative instruments than had been their predecessors in the fourteenth and early fifteenth centuries. Life tenures, pluralism, and the employment of deputies reduced the monarchy's control over its own officers. Payment by fees generated demarcation disputes. The conception of office as a form of property made its holders rigid and conservative. Furthermore, the royal servants of sixteenth-century England were very few in number. Under Elizabeth about 600 officers administered the Crown's lands and a further 600 served the other departments of state.[96] Therefore, in a population of about five millions, there was one royal officer for approximately every 4,000 inhabitants. Most of these officials, apart from the land-officers, operated at the centre and the Crown had virtually no local bureaucracy: to enforce its commands it must rely upon the unpaid assistance of the propertied classes. By contrast the French monarchy of the early seventeenth century employed 40,000 officers, roughly one for every 400 inhabitants, giving a density of bureaucrats ten times that of England; and many of the French officials served in regional or local government. The French monarchy probably benefited little from this horde of officials, who lay, in the words of a contemporary Englishman, 'as thick as the grass-hoppers in Egypt'.

[95] Stone, *Family and Fortune*, 17. For corruption in the Admiralty, H. A. Lloyd, 'Corruption and Sir John Trevor', *Trans. Hon. Soc. of Cymmrodorion* (1975). For Cecil and the privateers, K. R. Andrews, 'Sir Robert Cecil and Mediterranean Plunder', *EHR* LXXXVII (1972), and 'Caribbean Rivalry and the Anglo-Spanish Peace of 1604', *History*, LIX (1974).

[96] MacCaffrey, 'Place and Patronage', in *Elizabethan Government and Society*. Wolffe, *Crown Lands*, 39–40, 63.

But France, perhaps the most heavily governed nation in early modern Europe, serves to show how lightly bureaucracy weighed upon the population of England.[97]

[97] A. L. Moote, *The Revolt of the Judges* (Princeton, 1971), 6–7. Martin Wolfe, *The Fiscal System of Renaissance France* (Yale, 1972), 133n., 136.

IV

Force and Arms

Until the middle of the thirteenth century English kings had
drawn their military strength in part from feudal warriors who
owed services in return for land, in part from the obligation
of every able-bodied man to muster with the national militia
for the defence of the realm, and in part—probably a substantial part—from hired mercenaries.[1] As the feudal levies became
increasingly neglected and enfeebled, Henry III and his son
had come to rely heavily on the men of the national militia.
Each man was obliged by successive assizes of arms, culminating in the Statute of Winchester (1285), to carry arms according
to his station in life. Yet this force could never provide more
than a pool of untrained and amateur fighters, useful for home
defence, but inadequate for offensive warfare. Edward I's campaigns in Wales and Scotland were accordingly fought by
armies which combined archers drawn from the local communities and mounted troops raised by private contracts with
noblemen and war-lords. Both groups were under some legal
obligation to serve the King, but both had to be paid for any
military service performed outside their own shires; and this
necessity to pay wages made warfare expensive. Edward III,
confronted with immense commitments in the French wars,
had resorted to Parliament for help in the form of taxation. But
he also tried—as indeed his father had done with resounding
failure—to extend military obligations by demanding compulsory service abroad, by raising the quota of personal weapons
exacted under the Statute of Winchester, and by insisting that
the counties pay their own levies even when they were fighting
outside their own shires. In all these attempts he too failed. As
his wars continued he had in consequence to rely largely upon
contract armies, recruited through landowners, who drew upon
their tenants, household servants, and personal retainers. This

[1] This paragraph is largely based on Michael Powicke, *Military Obligations in
Medieval England* (Oxford, 1962).

provided an effective nucleus of trained, armed, and largely voluntary soldiers, while incurring some of the risks associated with the name of 'bastard feudalism'. The communal levies, although they remained important in times of civil strife and invasion, were reduced to the role of mere auxiliaries on overseas campaigns.[2]

The Tudor monarchs thus inherited a 'system' of military recruitment based partly upon a contract army used mainly, but not always, for service abroad, and partly upon the national militia, composed in theory of every able-bodied man aged between sixteen and sixty, and responsible largely for home defence. Both forces were under some general obligation to serve the king, although financial inducements reinforced this obligation for the private retinues. But it is hard to believe that the contract armies were wholly composed of real volunteers. Their leaders were doubtless willing enough to fight, but many of the rank-and-file were probably persuaded into service by their lords. At the bottom end of society the peasant may not have found much difference between recruitment into a retinue and compulsory service in the militia.[3] But for the Crown there was a real distinction. With contract armies it had to rely upon the privately recruited and privately led forces of the nobility, whereas the militia was raised by landowners acting as royal agents under the authority of commissions for muster or array.

Until 1453 providing troops for campaigns abroad had been the most pressing need for English monarchs, as the Lancastrian Kings sought first to extend and then to preserve their continental possessions. But from the final defeats of the 1450s until the death of Henry VII continental expeditions were only occasional flurries set in long periods of peace; of all our overseas possessions Calais alone remained. The protection of the dynasty against invading usurpers or internal revolts became a more urgent matter than intervention across the Channel. But with the accession of Henry VIII in 1509 the siren-calls of military glory were once more heeded, and for many of the

---

[2] In addition to Powicke, op. cit., see A. E. Prince, 'The Strength of English Armies in the Reign of Edward III', *EHR* xlvi (1931); N. B. Lewis, 'Recruitment and Organization of a Contract Army', *BIHR* xxxvii (1964); J. W. Sherburne, 'Indentured Retinues and English Expeditions to France, 1369–80', *EHR* lxxix (1964).

[3] For a different view, see H. J. Hewitt, *The Organization of War under Edward III* (Manchester, 1966), ch. ii.

first twenty years of his reign the new King was actively fighting
on the northern border or in France. After a peaceful intermis-
sion in the 1530s, French and Scottish wars again dominated
English politics until the Duke of Northumberland made peace
in 1551; and on Mary's accession relations with France once
more deteriorated until open and disastrous war was joined in
1557. The loss of Calais early in 1558 was significant in more
ways than one: it symbolized both the failure of the Catholic
Queen and the final withdrawal of England from possessions
in Europe. Not that Mary's successor accepted the loss: for
thirty years the sober and cautious Elizabeth hankered for the
return of Calais. Her dream was, fortunately, vain. In practice,
after the failure of her French expedition in 1562, England was
committed only to defensive wars. Intervention on the Continent was merely intended to ward off threats to English
security, and increasingly our strongest defence lay in ships
rather than in soldiers.[4]

At the same time the government had almost constantly to
maintain a vigilant defence against internal rebellion. Except
between 1509 and about 1534 there were few years exempt from
the threat, rumour, or reality of a rising.[5] Many of these turned
out to be mere fantasies; others were minor affrays. But in the
absence of a police force the Crown had to rely upon private
retinues or the national militia for maintaining internal
security.

During the reigns of the first two Tudor monarchs expeditionary forces continued largely to be raised through landowners. In 1492 Henry VII mustered an army of 12,000 men
mostly from the retinues of noblemen and gentlemen. Some of
these retinues were very large: Lord Willoughby de Broke and
Lord Daubeny each provided ten spears and 300 archers, Sir
Robert Curzon 500 men. An agreement between the King and
the Earl of Kent describes the procedure. It bound the earl to
supply six men-at-arms, twenty-one mounted archers, and sixty
archers on foot; rates of pay were fixed; wages were to be paid
through the earl; and detailed regulations were laid down

[4] On Tudor foreign policy, see R. B. Wernham, *Before the Armada* (1966).
[5] Below, ch. X.

concerning the allocation of ransoms won for prisoners. This dependence upon the followings of individuals is further illustrated by a signet letter to Sir Henry Willoughby in 1505. The King reminded Willoughby that although retaining was forbidden by statute he was empowered to license trustworthy men to keep retainers for the good of the realm. Willoughby was to keep men in readiness 'conveniently horsed and harnessed, to do unto us service as well within our realm as elsewhere at our wages'. Possibly Henry VII intended by this proposal to establish a trained reserve of men; if that is so the scheme came to nothing.[6]

Henry VIII was also dependent on the retinues of his subjects. A list of 1512 is headed: 'these persons whose names follow have the King's letters sent to them to make and record the numbers following'. The names include Sir Alexander Baynham, twenty men; Sir Thomas Blount, twelve men; and so on. Broadly speaking, recruitment for the campaign of 1512 was drawn from two categories: those noblemen and gentlemen who served in person with their men, and those who stayed at home and sent a following.[7]

A letter written that year by Lord Darcy, an important northern baron, to the Earl of Surrey, showed how a landowner could raise his following. Darcy will, he says, attend Surrey on the Scottish campaign with eighty gentlemen and 2,000 other able men. In his company would be Sir Thomas Metham with forty men, Sir Ralph Rider with twenty-four, Sir William Skargill with thirty, and others up to a total of 410. A further 500 would come from Darcy's own household and lands; and a large contingent of 1,114 from 'my offices whereof I am steward', which presumably referred to the royal and episcopal lordships in which Darcy held stewardships. Thus he drew upon a following of local gentlemen, his private estates and house-

---

[6] A. Cameron, 'The Giving of Livery and Retaining in Henry VII's Reign', *Renaissance and Modern Studies*, XVIII (1974), 22–4. Dr J. J. Goring's typescript thesis, 'The Military Obligations of the English People, 1511–48' (Ph.D., London, 1955) is the most complete introduction to the subject of Tudor recruitment. See also his 'Social Change and Military Decline in Mid-Tudor England', *History*, LX (1975). T. Rymer, *Foedera*, XII. 477, for indentures with Kent. HMC, *Middleton MSS*, 131–2 and Cameron, op. cit. 25, n.3 for Willoughby's letter. Also, C. G. Cruickshank, *Army Royal* (Oxford, 1969), ch. xiii.

[7] PRO, State Papers Domestic, Henry VIII (SP 1), 1/2 ff. 111–14; 1/229 ff. 48–52 (*LP* I. i. 1176).

hold, and the royal lordships which he controlled. In practice he would be leading the King's own tenants, who would make up more than half his retinue. This should warn us against supposing that the 'retinues' of great men necessarily consisted entirely of their personal retainers.[8] The confused and haphazard nature of military recruitment is illustrated by the force raised for the campaign of 1513. Some men were levied by towns: Boston sent twenty-three. Some were raised by ecclesiastical dignitaries: the Bishop of Carlisle sent fifty-one. The great majority was supplied by private landowners in contingents ranging from the twenty-five men of Sir John Speke to the 420 of Lord Ferrers.[9]

Relatively little attention was paid to the county levies in the early part of the reign of Henry VIII. When invasion threatened in 1512, Sir Edward Poynings, Lord Warden of the Cinque Ports, was issued with a commission of array for mustering forces in the five ports; and similar commissions were sent to the sheriffs and J.P.s of various coastal shires. In the following January Sir John Lisle and Sir William Sandys were appointed chief captains of the 'power' of Wiltshire against any attempted French attack. Borough corporations were ordered to keep lists of able-bodied men, so that they could be recruited for foreign service or mustered for home defence.[10] However, in 1522, when war again seemed imminent, Wolsey initiated a much more ambitious project. The commission issued for general musters in March of that year ordered an inquiry into the able-bodied men in every shire, their arms, their wealth, and the name of the lord 'whom they belong unto'. The purpose was financial as well as military, for the survey was intended as the foundation of a massive forced loan as well as a roll-call of the militia.[11] Few returns have survived and those that have vary greatly in their quality. But they do almost always record the names of able-bodied men and their arms. A contemporary summary of the returns records that in twenty-eight counties 128,250 men were mustered, of whom 43,034 were archers,

---

[8] *LP* I. i. 1363. Cf. II. i. 471. Darcy's arithmetic is often wrong in his totals.

[9] *LP* I. i. 1176 (3). Cf. I. ii. 2051–4.

[10] *LP* I. i. 1360, 1365 (24), 1596. HMC, *Twelfth Report*, App. IX, *Records of the Corporation of Gloucester*, 438.

[11] J. J. Goring, 'The General Proscription of 1522', *EHR* LXXXVI (1971). Above, 60–1.

82,877 were billmen, and 2,338 had no weapons.[12] The government was able to use this information to force men to buy arms and armour according to their wealth; it certainly became better informed; and this may have enabled it to improve the standard of the militia.[13]

The armies for the ensuing campaigns in France were however levied yet again on the old system. Letters had already been sent in January 1522 to all nobles and gentlemen, ordering them to put themselves and their servants in readiness and to inform the King of the numbers that they could raise.[14] The Marquis of Dorset told Sir John Trevelyan that he had been instructed to attend the King with as many men as he could get; accordingly he asked Trevelyan to supply three or four good archers 'to abide with me' at the King's wages. Possibly the information provided by the general muster helped the government to increase the numbers raised. But it is unlikely to have had much effect, since the returns from some counties concealed the essential facts about the 'powers' of individuals. Even when the Crown did increase quotas it met the same reluctance and evasion that frustrated its efforts to raise money in 1523 and 1525.[15]

Troops were raised to suppress rebellion by much the same means as they were levied for campaigns overseas. During the Pilgrimage of Grace, letters missive in standard form were dispatched to nobles and gentlemen ordering them to attend the commander of the royal army with a following of their servants, tenants, and friends.[16] On this basis a substantial force was raised. The Duke of Norfolk provided 600 men, the Marquis of Exeter, soon to be executed for treason, 500, Lord Ferrers 1,000. The gentlemen were mostly arrayed in counties, but each seems to have brought his own contingent to make up the county's levy. The Crown relied not only on the retainers of the great but also upon the resources of scores of lesser men. John Langholme of Conisholme in Lincolnshire is a case in point. Although he belonged only to the middling gentry, the inventory to his will records that he possessed five 'jakes' (pro-

---

[12] *LP* iv. i. 972.   [13] Goring, op. cit. 694–700.
[14] *LP* iii. ii. 2012. Cf. ibid. iv. i. 644.
[15] *Trevelyan Papers* (Camden Soc., 1872), 11. Goring, op. cit. 695–7. Above, 60–1.
[16] *LP* xi. 556–7, 562, 579, 874.

tective coats), one pair of almain rivets (thigh-pieces), eight pairs of splints (for the arms), and two helmets; the value of his armour came to 10 per cent of the total value of the contents of his house. Langholme could have fitted out two men completely and contributed towards the equipment of three or four more. Although he was probably better equipped than many of his contemporaries, his inventory shows that even a small country house contained a miniature armoury. The cumulative total of all these contingents—an army of more than 19,000— was impressive, indeed alarmingly so, since many of the enthusiastic gentry supplied more men than had been required of them and the Duke of Norfolk was embarrassed at having more troops than he could clothe, pay, or feed.[17]

In 1539, with a threatening situation abroad, the King's ministers gave close attention to the needs of home defence. Commissioners were appointed to organize the system of warnings by beacons; local gentlemen were ordered to inspect all possible landing-places in the coastal shires; fortresses were repaired and armed; new blockhouses were built. At Harwich the inhabitants rallied enthusiastically to dig trenches and raise defences. 'You should', reported Lord Audley, 'have seen women and children work with shovels in the trenches and bulwarks there.'[18] The government also tried to put the shire militia on to a more effective basis. A long and careful memorandum appeared in the hand of Ralph Sadler, then one of Cromwell's confidential clerks, for 'ordering of the manrede of this the king's realm'.[19] The word 'manrede' invokes the sense both of homage and of the men upon whom a lord can call in time of war. The memorandum itself bears out this dual meaning. It urges both a better organization of the nation's manpower and the securing of the allegiance of the King's officers. The King was to have a book made of all offices and

---

[17] *LP* xi. 580, 727, 738, 775–6, 803. J. Cornwall, 'The Squire of Conisholme', in *Rural Change and Urban Growth, 1500–1800*, ed. C. W. Chalklin and M. A. Havinden (1974). John Langholme himself had died in 1528, but the military equipment of his heir was probably much the same eight years later.

[18] *LP* xiv. i. 682. Cf. ibid. 398–400, 529, 538, 564, 573, 596, etc.

[19] PRO, State Papers Domestic, Henry VIII (SP 1), vol. 144, ff. 205–15 (*LP* xiv. i. 643).

stewardships in his gift with the names of the officers and the number of able men under their command. Musters of these men were to be taken at once. Commissioners were to be appointed by the King in each shire to muster annually the able-bodied men from the King's lordships; if the numbers were insufficient for defence, noblemen and gentlemen were to muster the men on their own lordships. Officers and landowners were to take an oath always to be ready with their men to assist the King and the shire commissioners, and gentlemen of substance were to be sworn to be servants to the King and no other. The scheme does not seem to have been put into effect. No commissioners were appointed and the oaths do not seem to have been taken. But it shows something of the government's attitude. The King was in the first place calling upon the manpower of his own lordships through the agency of his own land officers; only if that were insufficient would he summon the tenants of nobles and gentry. He still considered himself the greatest lord of the realm and he urgently needed information about his dependants.

The principles behind Sadler's memorandum were however being tacitly abandoned. The threat to national security was too severe to be met by the forces of the royal lordships alone, and shire musters were held to ensure that all able-bodied men, whether or not they were the King's tenants, kept their proper complement of arms.[20] In London, on 8 May 1539, the better armed and armoured of the inhabitants were ordered to parade before the King 'in white hose and cleanly shod'. Men of substance exploited the occasion to display their riches as well as their loyalty, wearing coats of silk, gilding their pikes, covering their breastplates with silver. One is reminded of those Dutch seventeenth-century group portraits in which the burghers are depicted proudly displaying their uniforms. About 20,000 men were reported to have assembled to the east of the City, where all the fields were 'covered in men in bright harness with glistening weapons'. They then marched in three 'battles' through the streets to Westminster, where they paraded before the King.[21] Elsewhere the musters were probably a good deal less glam-

[20] *LP* xiv. i. 398–400, 652–4, 692, 695, 839, 898; xiv. ii, app. 15.

[21] T. Lott, 'Account of the Muster of the Citizens of London', *Archaeologia*, xxxii (1847), 30–7. *LP* xiv. i. 940–1; Add. i. ii. 1412.

orous. But they provided the Crown with detailed information about its resources. In each shire the commissioners noted down, hundred by hundred, parish by parish, the names of able-bodied men and sent these nominal rolls to the central government. Only a few signs of dissent or unease were voiced. The men of Nottinghamshire were reported to be far from courageous at the thought of war. By contrast, Sir Richard Rich, after extolling the virtues of the men of Essex, asked whether it would be thought wise to leave arms in their hands when the emergency was over.[22]

The information collected in 1539 was checked and brought up to date three years later, when musters were held in every parish to determine the number of armed men; and the next year muster-books were again made in every shire south of the River Trent.[23] But the sources of recruitment for the Scottish campaigns of 1542 and 1543 remained unchanged. The King dispatched letters missive in September 1542, telling the recipients that 'we have appointed you to give your personal attendance' on the Duke of Norfolk, the principal commander, and ordering 'you therefore immediately ... to put yourself with all such able men you can make and furnish for the war of your servants, tenants, and others ... in such order and readiness as you may set forth with the same within one hour after you shall be commanded so to do ...'[24]

The army raised for the Flanders campaign in 1543 was based upon the information contained in the muster-books. But the troops were still recruited by individuals, although they were later amalgamated into county bands. The Kentish contingent, for instance, consisted of ten horsemen and 100 foot-soldiers from the Archbishop of Canterbury, 100 foot-soldiers each from Lord Cobham and Mr Wyatt, twenty foot-soldiers from Sir Henry Isley, twelve from George Blage, ten each from four other gentlemen, and five from Antony Thwaites.[25] The move towards county organization was taken a step further in the following year. A muster-book was prepared showing first what troops could be raised by members of the royal council.

[22] *LP* xiv. i. 692, 839.
[23] *LP* xvii. 631, 882; xviii. i. 661; ii. 221, 234. *State Papers, Henry VIII*, i. 744.
[24] J. Bain (ed.), *The Hamilton Papers* (Edinburgh, 1890), i, no. 155. *APC* i. 24, 89. *LP* xvii. 751; app. A, 16.
[25] *LP* xviii. i. 832. Cf. ibid., Add. i. ii. 1589.

The Duke of Suffolk certified that 'with 300 of his tenants in Lincolnshire, able men and meet to serve, and with his household servants he can make 100 horsemen with demilances and javelins, either upon good horses or good geldings, 100 archers and 300 billmen'. Similar promises, though usually for smaller numbers, were made by other councillors, noblemen, and officers of the privy chamber. But having covered the notables of society and the court, the muster-book proceeded county by county, to list the contingents of knights, esquires, and gentlemen. Initially troops were raised by individuals, but were then arranged into shire groups. Reinforcements were apparently levied on a county basis by direct order to the J.P.s.[26]

In 1545 the landowners, pressed for years past to provide troops, began to show signs of resentment and apathy. Sir Edward Acton answered the royal summons by complaining that not only was he sick himself but that many of his servants had died since the previous campaign. Similar protests were made by others.[27] In two counties, Cheshire and Cambridgeshire, the Crown seems to have used muster-commissioners from the first, although it evidently still regarded recruitment through individual landowners as the normal system.[28] But by September of that year and in January 1546 the Privy Council was turning for recruitment to sheriffs and muster-commissioners in the shires. Letters missive were now sent to them, with a quota allocated to each county. A book of levies prepared in 1546 listed the able-bodied men, not against their lords, but against the muster-commissioners or the company-commanders.[29]

By this time the threat of invasion was stimulating a more effective system of county defence. Coastal forts were repaired and commanders appointed; beacons were prepared; and three vast armies each 30,000 strong were assembled under the commands of Norfolk, Suffolk, and Russell. These troops were levied by counties and were mostly held in a state of readiness

[26] PRO, State Papers Domestic, Henry VIII (SP 1), vol. 184 (*LP* xix. i. 273). Also *LP* xix. i. 271–2, 274–6, 361, 440, 632; xix. ii. 253, 292, 397, 452. HMC, *Bath Papers*, iv. 58.

[27] *LP* xx. i. 573; ii. 604, 618, 824.

[28] *LP* xx. i. 538, 574, 903.

[29] *LP* xx. ii. 367, 429. *APC* i. 214–19, 313. PRO, State Papers Domestic, Henry VIII (SP 1), vol. 213 (*LP* xxi. i. 91).

in their own shires, although some were sent to strengthen
the Isles of Wight and Sheppey. By 1546 the county commissioners for musters occupied a more clearly defined and
permanent position in the country's military structure. They
were beginning to be responsible not only for home defence
but also for the recruitment of expeditionary forces; and the
signs are that county organization was adequate for these
purposes.[30]

Apart from native English troops, foreign mercenaries were
from time to time employed by Henry VIII at home and
abroad. Although he hired some 5,000 men for the French campaign of 1513, mercenaries do not seem to have been contemplated again until 1539 when abortive plans were made for
using foreign troops in home defence.[31] After further unsuccessful negotiations in 1542 Henry secured 1,700 horsemen and
4,000 foot-soldiers from the Count of Egmont and Christopher
de Landenberg for the campaign of 1544. Although these men
came from mainland Europe, Henry also hired 1,000 Irish foot-
soldiers that year. The Earl of Hertford complained that these
Irish kern were undisciplined and poorly trained; presumably
they were also cheap.[32] Foreign troops probably reached a
higher military standard, but they too had their drawbacks:
Spanish, Italian, and German mercenaries stationed on the
northern border quarrelled with the householders on whom
they were billeted, refused to eat English food, and would not
pay for their lodgings. They stayed in England for not much
more than a year.[33] In the last two years of the reign Henry
turned increasingly to mercenaries for his overseas campaigns
and in the autumn of 1546 he was dangerously dependent upon
foreign cavalry. As William Paget commented to his colleague,
William Petre, 'You see what case we are in, that we are
enforced for the strength of horsemen to use strangers, the which
at every time leave us in the dirt ...' Trouble, according to
Paget, stemmed from Henry's refusal to pay enough to the
English cavalryman, who got only £1 per month compared

[30] *State Papers, Henry VIII*, I. 785; x. 466–8. *LP* xx. i. 671–3, 717, 958, 1078, 1081
(33), 1329–34; xxi. i. 67, 91, 363.
[31] *LP* I. i. 1412, 1745; I. ii. 1939, 1950, 2050–4, 2062, 2835; xiv. i. 489–90; xiv. ii,
app. 13.
[32] *LP* xix. i. 208, 245–7, 419, 438, 448, 471, 473, 477, 575, etc.
[33] Ibid. xx. i. 535, 555, 596, 630, 787, 901; xx. ii. 457; xxi. i. 274, 289.

with the foreigner's £3, and not surprisingly, to use Paget's phrase, 'his heart is killed'.[34]

The defects of the Henrician system of military defence and recruitment may by now be apparent. Reliance upon the servants, tenants, and followers of the landowning class perpetuated a social danger and seems to have been less than effective militarily. Complaints and excuses from the gentry suggest that their co-operation could not always be assumed. Yet the alternatives were not very hopeful. Paget indicated the weaknesses of a mercenary army; and the national militia, armed with archaic weapons, wholly untrained, and virtually unorganized, was only a potential substitute. A suggestion had been made in the 1530s for a standing army, to be maintained from the revenues of the dissolved monasteries; it had not been adopted. A more realistic plan was put forward to Protector Somerset by Sir Thomas Wyatt of Kent and a group of his friends. They urged that sea defences alone were not adequate against 'an obstinate emperor fierce and proud of his late victorious [*sic*] war with his armed soldiers, or against a French king that feareth no other ill neighbour but us ...' The Privy Council must establish a store of armour, encourage armaments manufacture at home, and raise an army fit to suppress rebellion, repel invasion, aid our allies, and conquer foreign lands.[35]

It is impossible to tell whether Wyatt's advocacy had any direct impact upon the Council's policy. Yet within a generation military organization and recruitment had been substantially, though slowly, altered, to some extent along the lines he had prescribed. Reforms had already been initiated under Henry VIII and further changes were made in the reign of his son; but traditional ways were well entrenched and nothing approaching a new military system—or even a system at all—had emerged by 1558.

In the early years of Edward's reign the Council seems to have contemplated a much greater use of mercenary troops. Italians and Germans were employed to put down Ket's rebel-

[34] *LP* XXI. i. 172, 473–4, 531–5, 581, 687. *State Papers, Henry VIII*, XI. 117–18. W. C. Richardson, *Stephen Vaughan*, ch. v.

[35] L. Stone, 'The Political Programme of Thomas Cromwell', *BIHR* XXIV (1951). Cf. G. R. Elton, 'Parliamentary Drafts, 1529–40', ibid. xxv (1952), 126–30. D. M. Loades, *The Papers of George Wyatt Esquire* (Camden Soc., 4th ser. v, 1968), 55–9, 163–80. See Goring, *History*, LX (1975).

lion in Norfolk and foreign soldiers appeared again on the northern border. But the money for their permanent maintenance was not available and in 1552 the mercenary force had to be sent back to the Continent.[36] In practice Edward VI's government had still to rely upon the services of landowners and their followings. In April 1550 licences were issued for the Council and certain members of the Privy Chamber to keep a total of 2,340 retainers, a substantial force, probably intended for domestic security. Cavalry was raised almost entirely by summonses to individuals. A muster-book of about 1548 provides 'an abstract of all the horses to be found by taxation throughout the kingdom'. It lists the contribution to be made by privy councillors, members of the royal household, peers, and then by the gentlemen of each county. Foot-soldiers too were often levied by requests to landowners to provide a quota from their servants, tenants, and 'favourers'. But increasingly they were drawn from the county contingents, selected and assembled by muster-commissioners.[37] It would be a mistake to suppose that there were two exclusive systems of recruitment: a 'semi-feudal' method operated through landowners and a county system conducted through muster-commissions. The Crown called both on individuals and on county communities to supply its needs.[38]

But although the methods of recruitment and assembling troops remained haphazard during the reigns of Edward VI and Mary, the pressure exerted by rebellion within and war without were forcing their governments to establish new methods of control over the county militia. The appointment of muster-commissioners for assembling and reviewing this force provided neither the necessary continuity of command, nor, more important, the concentration of responsibility essential for political stability in the shires. Partly for that reason and partly because the Duke of Northumberland was determined to establish and perpetuate his own political authority,

[36] *APC* II. 166, 268, 272–6, etc.; III. 43. Dietz, *English Public Finance*, I. 196–7.
[37] W. K. Jordan (ed.), *The Chronicle and Political Papers of King Edward VI* (1966), 24. Cf. ibid. 50, 58, 94, 100, 107, 123–4. PRO, State Papers Domestic, Edward VI (SP 10), 5/17; 2/1; 2/2; 8/1, 2; 8/50; 9/46–50. Ibid., Mary (SP 11), 11/32, 33. *APC* II. 118; IV. 300; VI. 87. *CSPDom, Add., 1547–65*, 353.
[38] HMC, *Buccleuch and Queensberry Papers*, I. 222. Cf. State Papers Domestic, Mary, 11/31; 12/3, 6–11, 22–5, 44.

in 1550–1 the Crown extended to every county an office which had been used only sporadically in the past: the lord-lieutenancy. The commissions of lieutenancy authorized their holders 'to be the king's lieutenant within the said counties for the levying of men, and to fight against the king's enemies'. For many years the office of Lord-Lieutenant was temporary, used in times of emergency and then allowed to lapse. It may be that the advantages of a unified command in each county were thought to be outweighed by the dangers of setting up provincial satraps.[39]

Under Elizabeth commissions of lieutenancy were issued during the dangerous years at the beginning of her reign and once more in 1569. But until the onset of open war with Spain in 1585 Lieutenants were appointed only when they were needed and for a limited period. From that year it became usual, though not absolutely invariable, for every shire to have its Lieutenant, responsible for supervising the musters of the militia, encouraging horse-breeding and archery, maintaining county armouries, and levying men for foreign service. It was however impossible for one man to carry out such tasks unaided, particularly as many of the Lieutenants were, like Burghley, Knollys, Hatton, and Howard of Effingham, preoccupied with the business of the central government, and others, like the President of the Council in the Marches of Wales, had to cover several counties.[40] To assist them the Crown appointed as deputy lieutenants two to six of the most prominent knights and gentlemen of each county. Like their superiors they were at first occasional rather than permanent officers, but from the year of the Armada each county had either deputies or men who were that in all but title. Below the deputy lieutenants most counties appointed other gentlemen as captains to command particular companies of the militia. Especially at the beginning of Elizabeth's reign these captains seem often to have been unsuitable for their commands—too old, too little experienced in war, or too bookish. But some genuine effort was made to improve their quality, with a modest success, in the later years

---

[39] G. Scott Thomson, *Lords Lieutenant in the Sixteenth Century* (1923), 14–39, 149–51. *APC* III. 258–9; IV. 49, 276–8.

[40] Scott Thomson, op. cit. 35–59. J. C. Sainty, *Lieutenants of Counties, 1585–1642* (*BIHR* Supplement, 1970).

of the century.[41] The captains however had necessarily to be local gentry, since the militiamen were thought unlikely to follow anyone else: 'the gentlemen of the counties', wrote John Peyton, 'are the only captains to draw the persons or the purses of the common people into martial actions'; and local gentlemen qualified and willing to train their soldiers might not always be found.[42] The government tried therefore to persuade every county to hire a professional soldier as muster-master to do the real work of training. Paid at first by the Crown, the muster-master was generally accepted by the counties and provided a useful check upon the local officers; but when, after the Armada, the Crown demanded that the counties pay the muster-master's salary, the local gentry protested. The J.P.s of Cornwall, for instance, complained in 1595 against the appointment of Captain Peyton as their muster-master: there was no place in Cornwall for a man who insisted on holding training sessions during the winter and demanded a salary from them for doing so, and they offered him money to go away.[43] However, while all was very far from perfect, the counties had, by the end of the sixteenth century, a command structure which was potentially, and probably in practice, more effective than the temporary *ad hoc* muster commissions of the past.

The second half of the century also saw the beginning of regular training for the militia. Under the Statute of Winchester of 1285 all able-bodied men were required to bear arms according to their station, but there was no provision that they be trained in their use. This was reinforced by two statutes of Mary's reign, which brought the requirement for weapons up to date, by demanding pikes, harquebuses, and other modern equipment in place of the swords, knives, and bows of the thirteenth century, and imposed penalties for absence from the musters. But only at the beginning of Elizabeth's reign did the Crown show an interest in teaching men to handle their weapons. During the first decade some effort was put into training the militia, but more vigorous action was prompted by the rising of 1569.[44] When relations with Spain were frayed and

---

[41] Scott Thomson, op. cit. 60–73. Lindsay Boynton, *The Elizabethan Militia* (1967), 96–107. See Boynton, *passim*, for much of what follows.

[42] Boynton, op. cit. 102.

[43] Ibid. 105–7, 180–1. HMC, *Salisbury MSS*, v. 419.

[44] 4 & 5 Philip and Mary, cc. 2, 3. I have been much helped in this and other militia

the northern earls rebelled in the hope of support from Alba,
England could no longer rely upon an uninstructed rustic mob
to repel invasion and insurrection. Since no government could
hope to find the money for training the entire militia, the
answer was found in a form of selective service. About one-tenth
of the militia would be instructed. The Queen wanted 'perfect
knowledge' of the total number—which came to about
180,000: 'and out of that total ... to have a convenient and
sufficient number of the most able to be chosen and collected
to be by the reasonable charge of the inhabitants in every shire
tried, armed and weaponed, and so consequently taught and
trained for to use, handle and exercise their horses, armour,
shot and other weapons...'[45] The central government cease-
lessly badgered local officials to compile lists of men and arms:
the state papers are filled with the replies to these inquiries.
From about 1580 the Crown exploited modern techniques by
sending out printed questionnaires on which each county's
muster-returns could be entered in a standard form. The
Council ordered that an improved warning-system be provided
by pinnaces at sea and by beacons on land; that county
armouries be set up for storing weapons; and that coastal forts
be repaired. The records of Quarter Sessions show that the
regulations were enforced by the prosecution of men who failed
to meet their obligations. But since the trained bands and the
other sinews of defence were never tested by invasion their
quality cannot be assessed. However, in 1588 England had a
defence-force of 26,000 armed men, organized into companies
and trained up to a point: 'a thing', as Walsingham observed,
'never put into execution in any of Her Majesty's predecessors'
time'.[46]

The organization and operation of national defence had been
wholly recast and largely improved during the second half of
the sixteenth century. The methods of recruiting armies for
overseas campaigns were also changed. Foreign mercenaries

---

matters by the thesis of Mr R. Vella-Bonavita, 'The English Militia, 1558–1580' (M.A.
thesis, Manchester, 1972).

[45] C. G. Cruickshank, *Elizabeth's Army* (2nd edn., Oxford, 1966), 24.

[46] Vella-Bonavita, op. cit. 236. S. A. H. Burne, *Staffordshire Quarter Sessions Records*
(William Salt Soc.), III. 144–5, 156, 157, 206; IV. 107, 294–7, etc. J. Goring and Joan
Wake, *Northamptonshire Lieutenancy Papers, 1580–1614* (Northants. Record Soc. XXVII,
1975). Boynton, 125; and chs. iv and v for a general assessment of the militia.

were never directly employed by Elizabeth, and foot-soldiers were now largely raised from the county musters.[47] The revolt of 1569 was suppressed by shire levies, not, like the Pilgrimage of Grace, by the retainers of noblemen and gentlemen. Almost throughout Elizabeth's reign the government insisted that the trained bands should be exempted from foreign service, for security at home was considered more important than victory overseas.[48] In consequence, since the trained bands were usually chosen from the more respectable classes, there was always a danger that expeditionary forces would be made up of weaklings and rogues. 'In London', said Barnaby Rich, 'when they set forth soldiers, either they scour their prisons of thieves or their streets of rogues and vagabonds ...'[49] Towards the end of the reign, when the Irish rebellion had reached its most critical stage, the Queen did bring herself to order the dispatch to Ireland of members of the trained bands, unless men as good could be found among the untrained; but it was an unusual step. In the 1590s the Privy Council ordered the enlistment of vagabonds and of prisoners awaiting trial. By 1602 it was becoming desperate and Manningham recorded in his diary that there had been 'a strange, confused pressing of soldiers', with men thrust beneath the hatches of ships, 'like calves in a stall'.[50]

But while the bulk of the troops, especially of infantrymen, was raised from the county militia, expeditionary forces often included two other groups. Gentlemen volunteers served in the Netherlands from 1570, and in 1585 more than 2,000 of them were incorporated in the army of the Earl of Leicester. Cavalrymen were still largely recruited by personal summons to individual noblemen and gentlemen; and foot-soldiers were still occasionally raised in this way. In 1585 the Earl of Leicester wrote two hundred letters to his servants and friends, requesting them to prepare themselves for service in the Low Countries. The only one of these letters to survive—that written to Sir John Wynn of Gwydir—asks him to furnish 'your self of

[47] Cruickshank, op. cit., chs. i and ii. On the legality of impressment, below, 398–9.

[48] W. A. Phillips, 'The Trained Soldiers of Salop', *Trans. Salop. Arch. Soc.*, 2nd ser. II, esp. document vi. Lodge, II. 340. HMC, *Salisbury MSS*, XII. 478.

[49] Cruickshank, op. cit. 26. For another view, H.M.C., *Salisbury*, IV. 4–5.

[50] *CSPDom, 1601–3*, 117–18. APC XXIII. 151; XXXII. 27, 36–9. Manningham, *Diary* (Camden Soc., 1868), 42. Cf. *Trevelyan Papers* (Camden Soc., 1872), 40. H. A. Lloyd, *The Rouen Campaign, 1590–92* (Oxford, 1973), ch. v.

a good horse and arms to serve your sovereign under me'.
Leicester hoped that Wynn might be able to raise other men
and horses, since Leicester wished to be accompanied by 'my
good friends and servants'. Wynn did not himself go, but
several of Leicester's other followers, from England and from
Wales, joined this expedition.[51]

The alteration in the composition and recruitment of royal
armies went part of the way towards providing the Crown with
what Professor Stone has called the 'royal monopoly of violence', as trained bands and militia began to make redundant,
for national purposes, the baronial retinues on which the
monarchy had once depended.[52] A nobleman's retinue had
generally been composed of three elements; his household servants; retainers bound by indenture to do him service; and men
recruited for short periods of emergency and tied to their lord
by wearing his livery. A great man's followers might serve him
in various ways—as cooks, chaplains, musicians, lawyers,
estate-managers. But most of the third category—the temporary retainers—served him as warriors, who could be summoned when he was in trouble or when the King demanded
a contingent for war.[53] However much social odium they might
incur, such men were essential to the Crown as the nucleus of
its armed forces.

Royal policy in the fifteenth and sixteenth centuries was
aimed at controlling retinues and at preventing their misbehaviour, not at their abolition. A statute of 1390 forbade anyone
but a peer to retain other men. Edward IV's act of 1468 prohibited the retaining of anyone other than a 'menial servant,
officer or man learned in the... law'; in practice the permission
to retain lawful servants made the act less restrictive than it
might at first have seemed. Henry VII's statute of 1487 forbade
the retaining of the King's own tenants; and this became a constant theme of Tudor legislation.[54] In 1504 Parliament carried
the famous statute *De Retentionibus Illicitis*, for long thought by

---

[51] S. L. Adams, 'The Gentry of North Wales and the Earl of Leicester's Expedition
to the Netherlands', *WHR* VII (1974). For another exception to the normal system,
see J. J. N. McGurk, 'The Clergy and the Militia, 1580–1610', *History*, LX (1975).

[52] Stone, *Crisis of the Aristocracy*, ch. v.   [53] Above, 1–3.

[54] 8 Edward IV c. 2. 3 Henry VII c. 15.

historians to have swept England bare of retainers. It neither did this nor intended it. Reasserting the prohibitions of 1468, this statute, which remained in force only during the lifetime of Henry VII, forbade any man to retain another without the King's licence to do so. The system remained in being, but its control rested more securely in royal hands. With the death of Henry VII this statute lapsed and retaining became subject once again to the act of 1468. Thereafter the Crown used proclamation rather than statute in its legal pronouncements on the matter. But these were designed to advertise the law rather than to change it.[55] In 1511 Henry VIII ordered that 'no manner of man, of what degree or condition he be, make no retainers' other than the law allowed. Similar proclamations were still being issued in the reign of Elizabeth.[56]

Whatever the law might be, the practice of retaining continued well into the sixteenth century and was not, in spite of the statute of 1390, confined to the titled peerage. Impressive bands of men were mustered by noblemen and others under Henry VIII. Although he had been heavily fined for illegal retaining in 1507, Lord Abergavenny mustered 984 men for the King in May 1514. In 1520 the Duke of Buckingham ordered 300 or 400 of his servants to accompany him to Wales. The social status of these retainers was often high: of the 122 servants of the Marquis of Exeter in 1538, nineteen were gentlemen and five were gentlewomen.[57] Retaining continued after the death of Henry VIII. Licences to retain were lavishly handed out under Edward VI. In 1554 a Spanish envoy described the arrival of the Earl of Pembroke at the opening of Parliament, accompanied by 300 retainers, forty-four of whom were gentlemen in black velvet cloaks, with gold tassels and gold chains. Mary issued licences for 2,139 retainers, and Elizabeth permitted 962 in her first thirteen years. Under Mary most of these licences were issued to knights and esquires; but under Elizabeth they were allocated almost exclusively to noblemen.[58]

[55] 19 Henry VII c. 14. Cameron, 'Giving of Livery', *Ren. and Mod. Studies*, XVIII, is the best recent account of the subject. Also, W. H. Dunham, *Lord Hastings' Indentured Retainers*.

[56] Hughes & Larkin, I, nos. 62, 67; II, nos. 582, 664.

[57] *LP* I. ii. 2912; II. 471; III. i. 1070; XIII. ii. 755.

[58] Dunham, op. cit. 109–10. BL Lansdowne MS 14, f. 2. Rymer, *Foedera*, XV. 234, 712. Below, 222–4. *Calendar of State Papers Spanish*, XIII. 82.

Knowing the methods of recruitment used under Elizabeth we might expect to find the practice of retaining in decline as the Crown came to rely increasingly upon the trained bands and the militia. Numbers do indeed seem to have fallen off, but landlords still sought able-bodied and serviceable men for their tenantry. In 1577 Gilbert Talbot wrote to his father, the Earl of Shrewsbury, that after buying the estate of Lord Grey of Wilton he 'might be able to attend on your lordship with a thousand tall fellows to follow your lordship's directions'.[59] Lord St John rejected an Irishman for the tenancy of one of his Glamorgan farms, 'for that he is an alien born, and besides no meet man of personage to go with me if it should please the Queen's Majesty to call me to any service ...'[60] Indeed, many men, as late as 1588, were anxious to enter a noble retinue, since this would exempt them from service with the trained bands or the militia. Early in the reign of James I a summary of the muster-returns reported that there were 140,000 armed men in the militia and 7,500 horse. Besides these, noblemen and prelates could provide 20,000 armed men and 4,000 horse. Thus more than one-third of the horsemen were supplied from private retinues.[61]

At a higher social level, eleven J.P.s in south-west Wales were described as 'serving-men in livery ... belonging to the Earl of Essex'; and as late as 1595 the government issued an order threatening to remove from the commission of the peace any man who belonged to the retinue of another.[62] This produced a tetchy protest from the Earl of Essex, who wrote that 'although I am very loth to leave the name of master to so many honest gentlemen in Wales, as out of their love desire to serve and follow me, and as hold the place of justice', yet he would rather 'free them from retaining unto me than that in this respect they should lose any jot of their former reputations'. He would readily sever the formal ties of retainer, confident that 'I have their love without further ceremonies'. The loyalty of many of his Welsh followers at the

[59] Lodge, ii. 152–3.

[60] J. M. Traherne, *Stradling Correspondence* (1840), 95.

[61] M. Bateson, *Leicester Records* (Cambridge, 1899–1905) iii, no. 247. HMC, *Salisbury MSS*, v. 323. *APC* xvi. 127, 144, 179. *CSPDom, 1581–90*, 507. HMC, *Montagu of Beaulieu MSS*, 80–2: I owe this reference to Mr J. P. Cooper.

[62] BL Lansdowne MS 53, f. 182. Hawarde, 21. *CSPDom, 1595–7*, 47.

time of his harebrained rising in 1601 proves him to have been right.[63]

Not merely did the engagement of retainers survive the development of the trained bands, but at times of crisis the government often preferred to put its trust in noble retinues. When the Armada approached, nobles, courtiers, and prelates provided 16,000 men from their private followings for the Queen's bodyguard; only 5,000 were drawn from the militia for that special purpose. When invasion once more threatened, in 1599, the Privy Council instructed noblemen to come to court with as many horsemen as they could gather for the protection of the Queen.[64] After enclosure riots had broken out in 1607, the Earl of Shrewsbury wrote that the gentlemen of the Midlands, having found 'great backwardness' in the trained bands, had used cavalry as much as possible and 'as many foot of their own servants and followers as they could trust'.[65]

Retaining therefore continued as a political and social force until the end of the sixteenth century. Although the Crown depended upon it far less for military power by 1600 than it had in 1485, baronial retinues still played a part in warfare and in national security. Their impact upon the social order and their changing significance in the whole structure of social power will be discussed in later chapters.[66]

The loss, during the fifteenth century, of all English possessions in France, except Calais, and the failure of Henry VIII to reconquer England's medieval 'empire' turned the Channel into the country's first line of defence. Naval power was now at least as necessary to national security as were land forces. At the same time opportunities opened up across the oceans in Africa, America, and the East Indies. The rich trades in bullion, slaves, sugar, and spices were vital to Spain and Portugal, attractive to Englishmen. Profits were to be made by trade and plunder; and England's principal enemy in the Elizabethan era could be wounded by attacks upon her imperial lifeline across the

[63] BL Harleian MS 6997, f. 74. PRO, State Papers Domestic, Elizabeth (SP 12), 252/42. Williams, *Council in the Marches*, 282–9.

[64] Boynton, op. cit. 161. HMC, *Foljambe MSS (15th Report*, App. V), 57, 84, 97.

[65] Lodge, III. 320–1.

[66] Below, chs. X, XIII.

Atlantic. Thus the benefits of offensive warfare upon the oceans combined with the necessity of defence in home waters to raise the importance of sea warfare. In response, the striking power of English ships became greater than ever before.

Henry VII inherited only about six royal ships, built five more, and captured one. Some of these were lost or decayed, and only five were passed on to his son in 1509. Henry VIII greatly increased the size of the navy, building 46 ships, buying 26, and capturing 13. By the end of his reign there were in all 53 royal ships, of which 28 were above 100 tons. Elizabeth inherited between 20 and 25 ships of this size and left 29 at her death. The Tudors had thus increased the size of their navy from the very low level of 1485; but even so it was not much bigger than the navy of Henry V, who owned 37 ships, at least 17 of them above 100 tons.[67]

This increase in the size of the navy was matched by a permanent improvement in its organization. In 1509 only one official, the clerk of ships, administered naval affairs, under the usually inactive supervision of the Lord Admiral. During the reign of Henry VIII several new offices were created and in 1546 the Navy Board was established, with responsibility for all naval administration. Particularly important was William Gonson, clerk of ships under Henry VIII, his son Benjamin, treasurer from 1549, and Sir John Hawkins, who succeeded Gonson in 1578. Hawkins brought to the Navy Board seafaring experience, which enabled him to improve the design of ships, cutting down high superstructures and making the vessels more seaworthy.[68]

Under Henry VIII the fire-power of English warships was magnified, thanks in part to the great production of ordnance by English ironworks, which led Europe in the manufacture of cannon until about 1620. The improvement of naval armament was assisted by Hawkins, who concentrated upon long-range, medium-weight guns—culverins, demi-culverins, sakers, and minions—by contrast with the short-range, heavy

---

[67] M. Oppenheim, *A History of the Administration of the Royal Navy, 1509–1660* (1896), 12, 35, 48–53, 100, 109, 114–26. J. S. Corbett, *Drake and the Tudor Navy* (1899), i, ch. xii.

[68] C. S. L. Davies, 'The Administration of the Royal Navy under Henry VIII', *EHR* LXXX (1965). J. A. Williamson, *The Age of Drake* (1946), ch. xiv. Oppenheim, op. cit. 145–65.

cannon of the Spaniards. In the fighting conditions of the Armada, when the English ships stood off from their enemies, the longer range was decisive.[69]

In one respect there was no change in the navy during the sixteenth century. The Crown never acquired a permanent corps of naval officers or sailors. The commanders of its ships were drawn either from the nobility or from privateer captains who had been fighting the Spaniards on their own account. Drake was only the most famous of such men. He had had his forerunners under Henry VIII, and many of his contemporaries, like Frobisher and Fenton, had won their battle experience as explorers and privateers. Their crews were drawn from the general body of merchant seamen.[70]

In the sixteenth century English striking power at sea depended only in part upon the official navy. More of it was mobilized from private resources, drawn into service by the hope of profit. From the reign of Henry VIII sea captains penetrated the waters of Africa and the New World, hoping to take a share of the new riches. Since the Spanish and Portuguese governments prohibited any commerce with foreigners in their overseas possessions, totally peaceful trade was never possible, and after the destruction of Hawkins's ships at St Juan de Ulloa in 1567 English merchantmen increasingly turned to forceful exploitation and to plunder. Until 1585 their depredations upon Spanish shipping received no recognition from the Crown; but in that year the Admiralty first issued letters of reprisal, which authorized merchants to seek revenge for any injuries inflicted upon them by the Spaniards. This inaugurated the formal system of privateering, which grew rapidly until the end of the century.[71]

Between 1585 and 1591, 236 privateering vessels were operating, most of them pinnaces, but at least 41 of more than 100 tons. By 1598 the proportion of large ships had increased: out

---

[69] Oppenheim, op. cit. 54–6. H. R. Schubert, *History of the British Iron and Steel Industry* (1957), 246 ff. M. Lewis, *The Spanish Armada* (1966 edn.), 77–87. Id., 'Armada Guns', *Mariner's Mirror*, XXVIII–XXIX (1942–3).

[70] G. Connell-Smith, *Fore-runners of Drake* (1954). Lewis, *Armada*, ch. vi. G. V. Scammell, 'War at Sea under the Early Tudors', *Archaeologia Aeliana*, XXXVIII–XXXIX (1960–1).

[71] K. R. Andrews, *Elizabethan Privateering* (Cambridge, 1964), chs. i. ii. Id., *Drake's Voyages* (1970 edn.), chs. i, ii.

of 86 sailing in that year, 30 were above 100 tons.[72] Their captains included amateur gentlemen and professional seamen, and the most successful of them were backed by London merchants. These ships and their men carried on continuous irregular warfare against the Spaniards, inflicting some damage upon the Iberian economy and providing a reservoir of ships, manpower, skill, and experience upon which the Queen could draw for large-scale operations.

Most of the sea campaigns of Elizabeth's reign were conducted on a 'joint-stock' basis, the Crown co-operating with the privateers. A Venetian agent, Scaramelli, reported that

The Queen's ships do not amount to more than fifteen or sixteen, as her revenue cannot support a greater charge; and so the whole strength of the nation rests on the vast number of small privateers, which are supported and increase to that dangerous extent which everyone recognizes; and to ensure this support, the privateers make the ministers partners in the profits ...[73]

Scaramelli certainly underestimated the number of the Queen's own ships; but he was right to stress, even though he exaggerated it, the role of the privateers. For Drake's West India voyage in 1585 the Queen supplied two ships out of about 22, and £10,000 of the total capital investment of £60,000. She contributed a larger proportion to the Cadiz expedition of 1587: four warships and two pinnaces in a fleet of 17 warships and six pinnaces. In the enormous fleet of 150 ships sent to Portugal in 1589 only seven belonged to the Queen, although she put up nearly half the capital. Thus the royal navy formed only a small part of the attacking forces of England in the war against Spain. The bulk of the ships and the money came from privateers and merchants, who were in the business for profit. In consequence, the objectives of each campaign were divided between the demands of strategy and the hopes of plunder. In some instances, notably the Portugal expedition, this conflict of aims was disastrous. The one exception was the campaign against the Armada. The Queen provided 34 ships, of which 19 were over 200 tons; these were supported by 34 auxiliaries above 200 tons and various smaller vessels. In this defensive

[72] Andrews, *Privateering*, 32–3.
[73] Andrews, 'Sir Robert Cecil and Mediterranean Plunder', *EHR* LXXXVII (1972), 532.

battle there was no question of plunder and the forces were effectively united under one command, with a single aim.[74]

The large role played in sea warfare by the search for profit made naval administration especially vulnerable to the inroads of corruption. The Lord Admiral, responsible to the Crown for the navy, was also responsible, through the Admiralty court, for the regulation of privateering. The court issued letters of reprisal, heard complaints from shipowners, and judged cases of piracy. But the material interests of the Lord Admiral and his subordinates were heavily involved in privateering. The Admiral received 10 per cent of all prizes; and both he and his officials had a stake in many of the ventures. In consequence, neutral merchants whose ships were plundered found redress hard to obtain; letters of reprisal were freely traded; and regulations were easily flouted. Since the Crown itself hoped to profit from plunder it was none too scrupulous about restraining the excesses of the privateers; and the line between privateering and piracy, never easily drawn, became faint. Equally important, the personal interests of men like Robert Cecil and Lord Admiral Nottingham became so heavily engaged in privateering ventures that their attitudes to the conduct of foreign policy were inevitably affected.[75]

The Tudor monarchs substantially transformed the organization and balance of England's armed force. Home defence on land was entrusted to a partially trained militia, placed under a permanent structure of command in each county. Although the Crown still used the retainers of the great, it was less dependent on them by the final quarter of the sixteenth century. It relied instead upon a part-time, unpaid force, largely commanded by inexperienced amateurs. Since they were never tested by invasion or by large-scale rebellion, the strength and effectiveness of these trained bands cannot be assessed: one can only say that

---

[74] Andrews, *Drake's Voyages*, 115–16, 134–7, 159–68, 188. Lewis, *Armada*, ch. v. J. P. Cooper and Joan Thirsk, *Seventeenth-Century Economic Documents* (Oxford, 1972), 434–6.

[75] Andrews, *Privateering*, ch. ii. H. A. Lloyd, 'Corruption and Sir John Trevor', *Trans. Hon. Soc. of Cymmrodorion* (1975). L. M. Hill, 'The Admiralty Circuit of 1591', *HJ* xiv (1971). Andrews, *EHR* lxxxvii. Id., 'Caribbean Rivalry and the Anglo-Spanish Peace of 1604', *History*, lix (1974).

England now possessed a large, armed, partly trained, and organized force for home defence, and that this was in practice, if not in principle, an innovation.

Henry VIII had mounted large and well-armed expeditionary forces by calling upon the followings of noblemen and gentlemen. In 1513, he put into France an army of 35,000 men, which was at least as big as any of the armies then fighting in Italy. Throughout his reign he was well served by able commanders from the nobility, who were fully experienced in warfare: men like the second and third Dukes of Norfolk, the Duke of Suffolk, the Earl of Shrewsbury, Lord Russell, Edward Seymour, and John Dudley. As the sixteenth century wore on, continental armies became larger. Charles V sent 60,000 men into Lombardy in 1536–7; in 1552 he raised 109,000 men in Germany. Philip II's army in Flanders was 86,000 strong, and that was only one of his many commitments. Tudor armies, by contrast, became smaller. Elizabeth sent only 4,000 troops into France under Willoughby in 1589, and rather fewer under Essex two years later. In the second half of the sixteenth century England was fighting on the Continent only as an auxiliary. Two of Elizabeth's commanders were disasters: Lord Grey of Wilton in the Scottish campaign of 1560 and the Earl of Leicester in the Netherlands in 1585–6. Another, Essex, was imaginative and bold, but was finally defeated in Ireland by politics, ill-luck, and his own temperament. Several—Vere, Willoughby, Williams, and the Norris brothers—were highly competent. One, Mountjoy, was outstandingly and ruthlessly successful. But, in general, Elizabethan noblemen lacked the experience of land warfare which their predecessors had enjoyed under her father.[76]

At sea the story was different. Thanks to its encouragement of privateers, the Crown was able to mobilize a striking power which was at least the equal of England's rivals. The Spanish and English fleets in the Armada campaign each numbered between sixty and seventy first-line ships; and while the Spaniards carried heavier guns, the English were stronger in long-range cannon.[77] The 'royal monopoly of violence', in-

---

[76] For the size of armies see G. Parker, *The Army of Flanders and the Spanish Road, 1567–1659* (Cambridge, 1972), 6. For two contrasting Tudor campaigns: Cruickshank, *Army Royal* and Lloyd, *The Rouen Campaign.*   [77] Lewis, *Armada*, ch. v.

complete on land, was non-existent at sea. Just as the attractions of plunder and profit in France had helped to fill the ranks of English armies during the Hundred Years War, so they were the best recruiting agents for service in the Atlantic under Elizabeth. The less the Crown's control over its forces and the greater its reliance upon profit-seeking entrepreneurs, the more weighty its striking power; but a price had to be paid in the frustrations produced by divergent aims and disunited commands. Highly impressive in defence, English sea-power wasted much of its effectiveness in attack.

Conspicuous as were the defects in all branches of the land and sea forces, the Tudor monarchs were nevertheless much more successful at raising armies and navies than they were—at any rate in the second half of the century—at raising money. The conservatism of Elizabethan finance and the erosion of royal revenue form a bleak contrast to the creation of the trained bands and the English successes at sea. While the influential classes were tight with their money, they were willing enough to co-operate in the mustering and levying of their social inferiors in the militia. They were also, some of them, sufficiently attracted by the glamour of war to serve as captains or as gentlemen-volunteers. Above all, noblemen, gentlemen, seamen, and merchants, excited by the prospect of windfalls at sea, swelled the numbers of English privateers. None of these incentives was present when it came to paying taxes.[78]

[78] Restrictions of space have prevented me from exploring problems of military supply. See: C. S. L. Davies, 'Provisions for Armies, 1509–1550', *EcHR* xvii (1964); A. E. Everitt, in *Agrarian History*, iv. 519–23; Cruickshank, *Army Royal*, ch. v.; below, 186.

PART II

The Impact of Government

V

The Regulation of Trade and Industry

Many voices were raised during the sixteenth century in protest at the social dislocation, misery, and disorder of the time. Henry Brinklow, in the *Complaynt of Roderyck Mors*, published in about 1542, lamented the depopulation of villages: 'For by your oppressors and extortioners, how be the towns and villages decayed? Where as were viii, x, xii, yea xvi households and more, is now but a sheep-house and ii or iii shepherds.'[1] The author of the *Discourse of the Common Weal* (probably Sir Thomas Smith) asserted in 1549 that all parts of the country, except London, were impoverished: 'Not only the good towns are decayed sore in their houses, streets and other buildings, but also the country in their highways and bridges; for such poverty reigneth everywhere that few men have so much to spare as they may give anything to the reparation of such ways, bridges and other common easements.'[2] In the same year the anonymous author of *Policies to Reduce this Realm unto a Prosperous Wealth and Estate* complained that 'scantness and dearth of victual' had forced many people to leave their homes and caused 'great discord and tumults to rise between the commonalty and the magistrates'.[3] Lord Burghley, in 1581, maintained that the whole country was being impoverished by an unfavourable balance of trade.[4]

Some people in sixteenth-century England obviously prospered—houses, furniture, clothes, tombs, and wills bear witness to that prosperity—but they did not advertise their

[1] H. Brinklow, *The Complaynt of Roderyck Mors* (ed. J. M. Cowper, Early English Text Soc., 1874), 48–9. For the literature of complaint see Whitney R. D. Jones, *The Tudor Commonwealth 1529–1559* (1970), chs. vi–ix. A good general introduction to the sixteenth-century economy is Peter Ramsey, *Tudor Economic Problems* (1963).

[2] Elizabeth Lamond (ed.), *A Discourse of the Common Weal of this Realm of England*, 16.

[3] *TED* III. 315.

[4] *TED* II. 24.

contentment. Economic comment in the sixteenth century emanated largely from the poor and unfortunate, or from those who spoke on their behalf. Quite naturally it emphasized the darker face of the human condition. That dark face, even if it was not the only one, certainly existed; and there was general agreement that poverty, misfortune, and dislocation could not be ignored by the government.

Two major trends underlay the economic changes of the sixteenth century: the growth of population and the inflation of prices. Even the most general movements of population are difficult to plot, given the available evidence, and no reliable figures can be established. But it seems that following a century of decline and stagnation, the English population began to rise in the second half of the fifteenth century and continued to grow during the sixteenth, in spite of occasional setbacks.[5] By the reign of Elizabeth, Sir Humfrey Gilbert was probably expressing received opinion when he said that 'England is pestered with people'.[6]

One consequence of this growth, unaccompanied as it was by a comparable increase in agrarian production, was a rise in prices, especially in food-prices. Although the inflation was mild by the standards of our own days it seemed shocking and unnatural to the men of the time. The long-term price rise was accelerated by high government expenditure in wartime, by the mid-century debasement of the coinage, and, possibly, in the second half of the century, by an inflow of bullion.[7] In the years 1551–5 grain prices were 180 per cent higher than they had been in the first five years of the century; fifty years later, in 1601–5 they had risen by a further 45 per cent, giving a rise of more than 300 per cent for the century as a whole. Moreover these broad figures conceal massive fluctuations: average grain prices from 1596 to 1600 for instance were more than 50 per cent higher than for 1591–5 and nearly 50 per cent higher than for the following quinquennium. Families on fixed incomes

[5] J. D. Chambers, *Population, Economy and Society in Pre-Industrial England* (Oxford, 1972). J. Cornwall, 'English Population in the Early Sixteenth Century', *EcHR* xxiii (1970). M. Drake, 'An Elementary Exercise in Parish Register Demography', ibid. xiv (1962). T. H. Hollingsworth, *Historical Demography* (1969), appendix 3.

[6] Chambers, op. cit. 27.

[7] For discussion of the causes of inflation see P. Ramsey (ed.), *The Price Revolution in Sixteenth-Century England* (1971).

found their standard of living threatened; and as a growing population entered the labour-market the real wages of urban workers were reduced by almost 50 per cent over the century.[8] With food-prices and population rising, rents also increased; and although substantial farmers producing for the market could sustain the high burden of rent and still profit from rising prices, the subsistence farmer—the cottager or small husbandman—was often forced off the land in the competition for holdings.[9] Growing sheep-flocks, the property of landlords and richer farmers, encroached upon the common pastures, squeezing out the animals of the poorer tenants; and some landowners, especially in the midlands, converted arable land to pasture in order to feed their beasts.[10]

Unfortunately, the expansion of industry was insufficient to provide employment for the surplus population. The market for cloth was subject to volatile movements of demand. When sales went well it was easy for the clothiers, who needed little fixed capital, to expand their operations; when demand slackened the extra labour could easily be laid off. Fluctuations of the market, especially in the 1540s and 1550s, brought hardship and unemployment to spinners and weavers. The size of the unemployed and landless population cannot be estimated, but it was large enough to frighten property-owners and to shock moralists. William Lambarde, speaking in 1594, was conscious of the connection between population and poverty: younger marriages and the absence of plague had, he said, brought more people into the world and created a new class of poor.[11]

While some areas of the country prospered from rising exports, high prices, and expanding industry, others fell into depression. The long-established clothing industries of English towns had in the fifteenth century begun to suffer from competition with domestic manufacture in the large villages of the West Riding, East Anglia, Wiltshire, and the West Country. Some towns—Worcester, for instance—were able to recover from the consequent depression and to emerge in the later sixteenth cen-

[8] Figures for grain-prices are based on *Agrarian History*, vi, Table VI. See also E. H. Phelps Brown and Sheila Hopkins, 'Seven Centuries of the Prices of Consumables', *Economica*, n.s. xxiii (1956), repr. in Ramsey, op. cit.

[9] *Agrarian History*, chs. iv, vii, ix.

[10] *Agrarian History*, ch. iv.

[11] Conyers Read (ed.), *William Lambarde and Local Government* (Cornell, 1962), 181.

tury with a prosperous clothing industry. But others, such as Lincoln, York, and Coventry, were in serious trouble. Furthermore, as foreign trade became increasingly concentrated upon London, the old 'out-ports', such as Southampton, decayed. Many English towns, deprived of their original mercantile and industrial functions, became mere social centres and markets. London, by contrast, grew from about 60,000 inhabitants in 1500 to 200,000 in 1600. Its merchants dominated the country's trade and finance, while its markets drew food from the surrounding counties.[12]

Yet the changing pattern of overseas trade threatened the prosperity of even some London merchants. Expansion of exports in manufactured cloth deprived the Staplers of their principal trading commodity, raw wool. The growth of the textile industry led—or was alleged to lead—to a decline in the quality of cloth. The weakness of the Antwerp market in the 1550s and its ultimate collapse in the 1580s forced English merchants to look elsewhere for outlets.

Throughout the sixteenth century the Crown was subjected to continuous and often conflicting pressures, forcing its intervention. Unemployment and vagrancy threatened—or seemed to threaten—the security of property and person. Rising and fluctuating prices upset normal expectations and caused acute hardship to the poor. Uncertain harvests, rising population, and the growth of metropolitan London necessitated some regulation of the food-supply. Landlords, yeoman farmers, and other employers wanted an assured supply of labour; tenants demanded protection from the racking of rents and the enclosure of the common lands; English merchants sought protection from their foreign rivals; established trading companies insisted upon the exclusion of interlopers; declining towns wanted a defence against the depredations of London; wool merchants complained about competition from cloth merchants; traders urged the Crown to regulate the quality of industrial products; and consumers of all kinds blamed the middleman for their difficulties and urged the Crown into increasingly complex measures for the control of marketing. The Crown itself was involved directly in economic life as landlord, minter of cur-

[12] P. Clark and P. A. Slack, *Crisis and Order in English Towns* (1972), intro. A. D. Dyer, *The City of Worcester in the Sixteenth Century* (Leicester, 1973), chs. viii, ix.

rency, and debtor; indirectly as the recipient of taxes. In its own interests it was concerned to moderate inflation, maintain the value of the pound against foreign currencies, and preserve the quality of industrial products.

Tudor monarchs were not the first to intervene in the economic activities of their subjects; many, perhaps most, of the commercial and industrial regulations of the sixteenth century had precedents in earlier times. Medieval governments had been concerned with the issue of coinage, prohibition of bullion-exports, supervision of the quality of cloth, and the control of foreign trade. But the volume, range, and complexity of Tudor regulation outstripped the ambitions of previous monarchs and their Parliaments.

However, it would be wrong to suppose that the mass of regulations issued in the sixteenth century was inspired solely by the Crown. Often the initiative came from unofficial, not from governmental, quarters. Many measures were proposed by interested trading corporations.[13] Some were the product of local or regional pressure.[14] Others were devised by well-connected individuals.[15] Most powerful and strenuous of all the interest-groups was the Company of Merchant Adventurers, whose main occupation lay in exporting cloth to the Netherlands and northern Germany. Although, for much of the sixteenth century, the company had its headquarters at Antwerp, its leading members lived in London. Their wealth dominated the capital and brought them the preponderant voice in its

[13] On the interplay of forces behind regulation in the next century see J. P. Cooper, 'Economic Regulation and the Cloth Industry in Seventeenth-Century England', *TRHS*, 5th ser. xx (1970). For examples see 5 Elizabeth c. 8; L. A. Clarkson, 'English Economic Policy in the Sixteenth and Seventeenth Centuries: the Case of the Leather Industry', *BIHR* xxxviii (1965); 5 & 6 Edward VI c. 7; P. J. Bowden, *The Wool Trade in Tudor and Stuart England* (1962, repr. 1971), 112–21.

[14] For example, 1 Edward VI c. 6. 2 & 3 Philip & Mary c. 13. Bowden, op. cit. 118–21. T. C. Mendenhall, *The Shrewsbury Drapers and the Welsh Wool Trade* (Oxford, 1953), 14–18, 124–6. A. D. Dyer, *The City of Worcester in the Sixteenth Century*, 113–14. 25 Henry VIII c. 18. 5 & 6 Edward VI c. 6. 4 & 5 Philip and Mary c. 5.

[15] e.g. Menna Prestwich, *Cranfield* (Oxford, 1966), 67–9. Mrs Prestwich's book contains many other examples of such projects. For a comprehensive account, see Joan Thirsk, *Economic Policy and Projects* (Oxford, 1978). I am very grateful to Mrs Thirsk for letting me see her work in typescript. Below, 157–65.

government. The total value of cloth exports at mid-century amounted to nearly £1 million per annum, a large proportion of the country's wealth: the trade was of great importance to landowners, whose pastures produced the raw material, and to the government, which depended heavily upon the levy of customs duties and upon the loans which the City could provide. Close links developed between the government and such leading London financiers as Sir Thomas Gresham.[16]

Historians have for some time been sceptical about the notion of any coherent Tudor economic policy based upon a body of theory. While many regulations were not the work of government at all, those promoted by the Crown were often the response to a specific situation or to particular pressures rather than the elaboration of some conscious and durable strategy. Fear of insurrection, the needs of defence, concern to preserve the value of the pound and a stock of bullion, the importance of maintaining the quality of industrial products and hence of exports, the protection of employment, and, above all perhaps, the Crown's thirst for revenue all prompted interference in economic and social life. The preoccupations of government mingled with the pressures of vested interest and hopeful speculation to produce a lush *bouillabaisse* of regulation that defies any attempt by the historian to subject it to precise and schematic analysis. But it seems that everyone accepted the principle of government intervention in economic affairs, however much they might protest when controls were applied to themselves.[17]

In the Tudor period about 300 parliamentary statutes were passed to regulate economic affairs, the majority of which— perhaps 250—were known as 'penal statutes'. These created a specific offence, laid down financial penalties, and normally offered a proportion of the fine to successful prosecutors. For

[16] G. D. Ramsay, *The City of London in International Politics*, ch. ii.

[17] F. J. Fisher, 'Commercial Trends and Policy in Sixteenth-Century England', *EcHR*, 1st ser. x (1939/40). L. Stone, 'State Control in Sixteenth-Century England', ibid. XVII (1947). J. D. Gould, 'The Crisis in the Export Trade', *EHR* LXXI (1956). For a useful summary of the points at issue, see P. Ramsey, *Tudor Economic Policy*, 163–73. For seventeenth-century policy see B. E. Supple, *Commercial Crisis and Change in England, 1600–1642* (Cambridge, 1964).

example, the 'act touching weavers' of 1555 forbade clothiers living outside corporate towns to possess more than one loom: offenders were to be fined £1. Of 115 penal statutes still in force in the middle of the reign of James I, about twenty-five had been carried under Henry VIII, eleven under Edward VI, thirty under Elizabeth, and nineteen under James himself.[18] Other statutes were positive rather than prohibitive, demanding or permitting specific actions: for instance, the act for 'setting of the poor on work', passed in 1576, instructed local officers to provide stocks of raw material on which the poor could be employed, ordered the appointment of governors of the poor, and authorized the governors to lay down rules of work.[19] Many of the statutes carried in the Tudor century were trivial, local in scope, or temporary in duration. But many were important in themselves and their cumulative bulk is awesome.

Many statutes were emphasized, amplified, modified, or even suspended by royal proclamations. For example, a proclamation of April 1549 ordered each clothier to seal his own cloth—a traditional regulation; limited the amount by which cloths could be stretched; forbade the use of chalk, flock, flour, or starch on cloth; and laid down rules for measurement. Sometimes statutes proved too rigid in framework for the diverse industries of the country and proclamations allowed exemptions. The clothiers of East Anglia protested to the Privy Council that they were unable to comply with the provisions of statute and were consequently granted separate orders of their own.[20]

More specific instructions were issued by the Privy Council and the executive officers of the Crown. The Council Register contains letters ranging from the revocation of Hanse privileges to instructions for relieving a bankrupt clothier in Newbury.[21] An increasingly elaborate system of licences, patents, and monopolies was also employed to control the volume, type, and direction of trade and industry. Licences exempted individuals from the operation of certain statutes: Lord Hunsdon, for instance, was licensed to export 20,000 undressed woollen cloths,

[18] 2 & 3 Philip & Mary c. 11. *TED* I, 185. M. W. Beresford, 'The Common Informer, the Penal Statutes and Economic Regulation', *EcHR*, 2nd ser. x (1957/58).

[19] 18 Elizabeth c. 3. *TED* II. 331.

[20] Hughes & Larkin, I, no. 328; III, no. 720.

[21] e.g. *APC* III. 487; IV. 274, 278; XXVII. 230; XXVIII. 372.

a right which he sold to various merchants.[22] In the second half of the century foreign trade was almost entirely conducted—officially that is—by the great chartered companies: the Staplers exporting raw wool, the Merchant Adventurers trading with the Netherlands and North Germany in everything except raw wool, the Barbary Company dealing with Morocco, the Spanish Company with the Iberian peninsula, the Levant Company with the eastern Mediterranean, the Eastland Company with the Baltic, the Muscovy Company with Russia, and the East India Company with India and south-east Asia. Each of these companies traded under charters which gave them a monopoly in their own areas, although these monopolies were not of course easily enforced against interlopers. Under Elizabeth other forms of monopoly were granted for domestic manufacture and trade. Inventors and industrial entrepreneurs were encouraged by their protection, although monopolies were extended into areas in which such encouragement was neither needed nor deserved.[23]

This complex arrangement of regulatory obstacles and exhortations covered almost every aspect of social welfare, agrarian management, labour relations, industry, commerce, and finance. Statutes and proclamations attempted to control the nature, extent, and direction of foreign trade, the location of industry and the quality of its products, the qualifications of craftsmen, the marketing of food and other commodities, the export of bullion, the rate of exchange, the issue of currency, the problem of usury, the manufacture of armaments, the spread of new building around London, the upkeep of highways, the rate of wages, and the treatment of the poor.[24]

Enforcement of these regulations depended primarily upon the operation of the courts of law. Infringements of penal statutes could be brought before almost the whole range of law-courts from the lowest in the hundreds to the highest at West-

---

[22] *CSPDom, Add., 1580–1625*, 385. See P. J. Bowden, *The Wool Trade*, ch. v for a discussion of licences. G. D. Ramsay, *The City of London*, ch. ii, explains the background to this licence.

[23] For a brief but comprehensive survey, P. Ramsey, *Tudor Economic Problems*, ch. ii. W. R. Scott, *The Constitution and Finance of . . . Joint-Stock Companies* (3 vols., Cambridge, 1910–12), *passim*. Ramsay, *City of London*, *passim*. For monopolies, below, 157–65.

[24] See V. Ponko, *The Privy Council and the Spirit of Elizabethan Economic Management* (Trans. American Philosophical Soc., n.s. 58, 1968). Holdsworth, IV. 314–402.

minster. The 'petty sessions' or hundredal courts held by high constables were charged with the duties of arresting clothiers who failed to pay the correct wages to their employees, enforcing terms of service upon labourers, compelling men to work at harvest-time, prosecuting engrossers of grain, and registering contracts of service; but their main preoccupation lay in the preservation of order.[25] Boroughs had several courts roughly equivalent to these 'petty sessions' and it is likely that they were more energetically concerned than their rural counterparts with the enforcement of economic regulations. At Worcester, for instance, the 'view of frankpledge', similar to a court leet, met three times a year to fix maximum prices, regulate wages, license victuallers and ale-sellers, and punish those who charged excessive prices. Weekly—sometimes daily—inspection of markets was made by the two aldermen of Worcester, who had the power to confiscate over-priced or defective goods, and held in addition a quarterly court in the Guildhall for levying fines.[26]

The local courts most celebrated for the enforcement of economic regulation were of course Quarter Sessions. Lambarde's phrase about the 'stacks of statutes' burdening the shoulders of the justices has burrowed its way into most historical textbooks. The list of penal statutes on economic affairs over which Quarter Sessions had jurisdiction is certainly long. The final Tudor edition of Lambarde's *Eirenarcha* lists more than eighty statutes concerned with economic or social offences. They govern usury, the forestalling and engrossing of grain, the making of malt, the sale of cattle, the prices of food and drink, the manufacture of leather, woollen yarn, arrowheads, tiles, wax, and cloth, the export of victuals, weights and measures, husbandry and tillage, terms of apprenticeship and of other forms of service, and the upkeep of roads.[27] The biennial courts of assize were empowered to hear at least as many offences as Quarter Sessions. At the regional level the Councils in the North and in the Marches of Wales were both authorized to try offenders

---

[25] W. Lambarde, *The Duties of Constables* (1619), 29–34. Margaret G. Davies, *The Enforcement of English Apprenticeship, 1563–1642* (Cambridge, Mass., 1956). Mrs Davies's book provides the best account of enforcement agencies and I have used it extensively in what follows.

[26] A. D. Dyer, *The City of Worcester*, 50–1, 114, 199, 203–5.

[27] Lambarde, *Eirenarcha* (1602), 425–55. See P. Ramsey, *Tudor Economic Problems*, ch. v on the scope of penal statutes.

against penal statutes. At Westminster offences against penal statutes were occasionally brought before King's Bench, Common Pleas, or Star Chamber. But the most important central court for the trial of economic offences was the Exchequer. From the mid-1540s the number of informations brought before this court grew rapidly and remained high until 1617.[28]

Effective economic regulation obviously depends upon the available methods of detecting and prosecuting offenders. Without a police force or a cadre of inspectors, the Tudor regime had to rely in part upon the slender apparatus of local law-enforcement and in part upon common informers, private individuals who stood to gain from a successful prosecution.[29] On the 'public' side of the fence petty and high constables were the soldiers-of-the-line in the battle—not exactly unremitting— against economic offenders. Their role was to discover and report offences to their superiors, the Justices of the Peace. The justices themselves played a relatively small role in detection and prosecution, although they could, acting out of sessions, discipline servants who left their masters before their time was up, prohibit ale-selling, determine weights and measures, and punish clothiers who failed to pay the official wages to their workers. The main role of the justices was to hear, at Quarter Sessions, cases brought to them by the constables, by juries of presentment from each hundred, or by the grand jury of the county. Boroughs generally had their own officers charged with enforcing particular regulations. The city of Worcester appointed official cloth-searchers in 1557, who inspected cloths brought to them by the fullers at the Guildhall and who also had the right of entering the houses of fullers and weavers to check their equipment.[30]

Specialized officers were available for enforcing the law in two fields of economic activity, and not surprisingly these were the areas to which government attached the greatest importance: foreign trade and the cloth industry. A staff of customs officials had been set up in the fourteenth century and the Tudors inherited twenty-seven officers in London and a much

[28] Penry Williams, *The Council in the Marches*, 51. Beresford, 'Common Informer', *EcHR* x (1957/58).

[29] Davies, op. cit. *passim*. G. R. Elton, 'Informing for Profit', *CHJ* xi (1954).

[30] Lambarde, *Eirenarcha* (1619), 330–64. Davies, op. cit. 198–205. Dyer, op. cit. 114.

more slender provision elsewhere. In the reigns of Mary and Elizabeth, Lord Treasurer Winchester tried to bring the system under more effective control, laying down instructions for customs officers, appointing general surveyors, and establishing many more customers in the provincial ports. Under Elizabeth a series of experiments was attempted, oscillating between direct exploitation and farming: the machinery of customs administration became more complex but never particularly effective.[31] Edward I had created the office of aulnager in cloth-manufacturing districts to measure the length of cloth in each roll. Long before the sixteenth century aulnagers had apparently ceased to regulate the quantity or quality of cloth manufactured, and exporters demanded a more effective system of inspection. Overseers of cloth were appointed in the West Country under a statute of 1550, and then two years later, each town was ordered to appoint a cloth-searcher. Local supervision did not however satisfy the merchant lobby and a special London aulnager with five assistants was appointed in 1560; but his powers were eroded by the lawcourts in 1589-91, before being abolished in 1607.[32] One other special official was appointed by the Crown, this time in a new and expanding industry: the growing of woad. In 1587 the Privy Council announced the relaxation of its previous prohibition on the cultivation of woad and appointed a surveyor to ensure that it was sown only in suitable places.[33] But on the whole the great volume of regulation, imposed in the sixteenth century by statute and proclamation, was unaccompanied by the provision of any bureaucratic machinery for its enforcement.

In consequence the main burden of prosecution fell upon the private activities of common informers. Some informers were professionals who made at least a part of their living from the business, others were evidently moved by personal hostility to the accused or by the spirit of business competition. Of

[31] A. P. Newton, 'The Establishment of the Great Farm of the Custom', *TRHS*, 4th ser. 1 (1918). F. C. Dietz, 'Elizabethan Customs Administration', *EHR* xlv (1930). G. D. Ramsay, *English Overseas Trade during the Centuries of Emergence* (1957), 176–91. W. R. B. Robinson, 'The Establishment of Royal Customs in Glamorgan and Monmouthshire', *Bulletin of the Board of Celtic Studies*, xxiii (1970).

[32] 3 & 4 Edward VI c. 2. 5 & 6 Edward VI c. 6. G. D. Ramsay, *The Wiltshire Woollen Industry in the Sixteenth and Seventeenth Centuries* (Oxford, 1943, repr. 1965), ch. iv.

[33] *CSPDom, Add., 1580–1625*, 207.

the prosecutions brought under the statute of apprentices, informers—professional and amateur—were responsible in Elizabeth's reign for more than 90 per cent. By contrast with the presentments made by a public officer or jury, the informer proceeded by what was called a 'qui tam' information: if successful this led to an indictment by the presentment jury. The informer's object was either to secure a conviction, when he would be awarded a proportion of the fine, or a composition with the defendant under licence from the court. Thus private profit was enlisted as a means of law-enforcement.[34]

The exclusive right of prosecution in certain types of case was sometimes granted by the Crown to individuals or to syndicates. By 1575 several licences had been issued which apparently carried such powers of prosecution: to Sir Ralph Bagenal and two others for offences by the clergy; to Oliver Dawbenay for concealments of customs; to Ralph Lane for the import of prohibited goods; to Mr Middleman for failure to import bowstaves and the unlicensed shipping of wine; to Henry Mackwilliams and Robert Colshill for cases of usury, preservation of woods, the assizes of fuel and leather, transporting victuals, and keeping too many sheep. These licences had evidently stirred resentment and were revoked that year.[35] But similar patents were issued in later years. Simon Bowyer was in 1590 commissioned as sole informer under the statute of 1552 governing the marketing of wool. Neither the Crown nor Bowyer intended that other common informers should end their operations; the object was rather that they should pay him a proportion of their profits.[36]

The informer was naturally out for profit, but the revenue derived from successful prosecution or licensed compositions was hardly sufficient, when legal costs had been met, to provide a reasonable living. Informers turned therefore to illegal sources of gain: they made unlicensed compositions with defendants after actions had begun, or they extorted blackmail from offenders by abstaining from prosecutions in return for a bribe.[37] Not surprisingly informers acquired an evil reputation.

[34] M. G. Davies, *Apprenticeship*, 275, Table I, and part i, *passim*. Lambarde, *Eirenarcha* (1619), 485. [35] *APC* VIII. 370.
[36] Bowden, *Wool Trade*, 146–54. Davies, op. cit. 31–9. J. Hurstfield, *Queen's Waras*, 36–45. Beresford, 'Common Informer', *EcHR* x, 232–3, esp. footnotes.
[37] Davies, *Apprenticeship*, 50–62.

In the middle of the sixteenth century Bishop Latimer had called for the appointment of more promoters, or informers, who would prosecute offenders: 'for God's sake make some promoters', he pleaded. His cry would hardly have been echoed fifty years later. Lambarde claimed that 'promoters and informers [are] like flies that feed upon the sores of diseased cattle'. They hunt, he said, 'for private gain and are not led by zeal of justice'. Sir John Stafford was censured in Star Chamber for acting as an informer, since they were mostly 'of the meaner and worst kind of people'.[38]

Various proposals were made to purify the system of informers or to supplant it with something better. A scheme was suggested under Edward VI for the appointment of special commissioners, charged with the execution of penal statutes; but there is no evidence that it was put into effect.[39] In 1565 J.P.s were ordered to deal with extortionate informers; but again there is no sign of any action. Sometimes local justices acted in Quarter Sessions against offenders; and the occasional informer was punished in Star Chamber. But such attempts were sporadic.[40] Three statutes were carried through Parliament under Elizabeth. The first, in 1576, was intended to tighten procedure and to prevent unlicensed compositions with defendants; the second made that act perpetual; the third, passed in 1589, forbade the bringing of informations except in the county where the offence was committed, and transferred certain types of case from Westminster to assizes and Quarter Sessions. It is unlikely that any of them had much effect. The strong financial benefits brought by informers to the Crown made reform unlikely; and it was not until 1624 that the activities of the common informer were effectively curbed.[41]

The impact of the penal statutes upon the lawcourts was probably less than their range and number might lead one to expect. Lambarde's complaint about the burden imposed on

[38] H. Latimer, *Sermons* (Parker Soc., 1844), I, 279. Lambarde, *Eirenarcha* (1619), 401. Hawarde, 331–2. Conyers Read (ed.), *Lambarde and Local Government*, 107.

[39] PRO, State Papers Domestic, Edward VI (SP 10), 14/16, 17.

[40] Hawarde, 63, 300. *Staffordshire Quarter Sessions Rolls*, IV. 338. *West Riding Sessions Rolls*, 101–2.

[41] 18 Elizabeth c. 5. 27 Elizabeth c. 10. 31 Elizabeth c. 5. Davies, *Apprenticeship*, ch. iii.

J.P.s by the 'stacks of statutes' is hardly borne out by the records of Quarter Sessions. The justices there dealt with breaches of the laws of apprenticeship, with engrossing, with stretching of cloth, with various marketing offences, and with a few breaches of the laws about dyeing cloth and making malt. Lambarde's own notebook and his charges to juries show little concern about economic penal statutes, except those governing highways, alehouses, vagabonds, and the corn-supply. Most of the statutes enumerated in the *Eirenarcha* are either unmentioned in the printed Quarter Sessions records or appear very rarely in just one or two shires. On this kind of subject statistics can be misleading, but the figures extracted from the true bills found in the Middlesex Quarter Sessions' records confirm the general impression derived from other counties: only forestalling, engrossing, and infringements of the apprenticeship laws leave any mark on the rolls, and that mark is a small one. Tudor J.P.s were mainly concerned with the traditional offences of assault, forcible entry, disorderly conduct, riot, bastardy, alehouses, petty larceny, and unlawful games.[42]

At assizes, to judge from the evidence of Sussex, economic offences were heard even less frequently than at Quarter Sessions. The assize judges were mainly concerned with murder, homicide, infanticide, rape, grand larceny, burglary, petty larceny, and recusancy. The records of the Council in the Marches for the sixteenth century have largely disappeared; but the few surviving lists of fines suggest that penal statutes figured very little in the Council's business. For the year ending in Michaelmas 1602, sixteen fines were levied for offences against penal statutes, 270 for riots, and 197 for sexual misdemeanours; this seems to have been a fairly typical year.[43]

The court most affected by Tudor legislation was undoubtedly the Exchequer. Relatively few informations were brought before it in the early Tudor period, but its business began to expand rapidly from the mid-1540s. The 1560s saw the end of this rapid growth in business but the number of prose-

[42] *Lambarde and Local Government, passim.* This paragraph is based upon Lambarde and upon the printed Quarter Sessions records of Caernarvonshire, Lancashire, Middlesex, Staffordshire, Wiltshire, and the West Riding. See especially J. C. Jeaffreson, *Middlesex County Records* (1886–7), II. 239–314.

[43] J. S. Cockburn (ed.), *Calendar of Assize Records; Sussex Indictments; Elizabeth I* (1975), *passim.* Williams, *Council in the Marches,* 331.

cutions remained high until a decline began in 1617. During the 1580s an average of 400 prosecutions was brought before Exchequer each Michaelmas term, which suggests that the annual average was probably around 800. Yet even in the Exchequer most penal statutes received little attention. Marketing offences accounted for 43 per cent of prosecutions, infringements of the customs regulations for a further 26 per cent. The remaining 31 per cent of informations were spread fairly evenly between suits involving manufacture, enclosure, labour-regulations, usury, exchange-control, and ecclesiastical offences.[44]

The examination of some sample areas of regulation will test its effectiveness. Much the most intensive study of a Tudor statute is Dr Margaret Davies's book on the enforcement of English apprenticeship laws: indeed this is the only thorough investigation of its kind that has yet appeared. Dr Davies examines the requirement of section 24 of the statute of artificers that a seven-year apprenticeship was necessary for entry into 'every craft, mystery or occupation' then practised in the kingdom.[45]

In the reign of Elizabeth only about 2 per cent of prosecutions for entering a craft without having served an apprenticeship were made by the public agencies of constables or juries: from the fifteen counties analysed by Dr Davies, only fourteen to sixteen prosecutions were brought by officials, about 500 by professional informers, and about 150 by amateur informers.[46] The apathy shown by public prosecutors was shared by the J.P.s and the central government. Although the act of 1563 enjoined J.P.s to hold special sessions of inquiry they very seldom did so, and were usually reluctant to enforce the apprenticeship regulations if there were any danger that this might cause unemployment. The central government did equally little, either in its charges to the judges of assize or in Privy Council letters, to direct the attentions of local rulers to the statute. Nor were

[44] Beresford, 'Common Informer', *EcHR* x (1957/58). Cf. S. B. Chrimes, *Henry VII* (1972), 191–2.

[45] Davies, *Apprenticeship, passim*. 5 Eliz. c. 4.

[46] Davies, *Apprenticeship, passim*.

the few prosecutions brought by public officials at all successful: 80 per cent were inconclusive and only two, in the whole reign of Elizabeth, produced a conviction.[47] This failure is not surprising. Local constables were cautious about incurring the expense of a prosecution and were normally reluctant to incur unpopularity by prosecuting their neighbours; J.P.s, usually landowners, were much more concerned with preventing vagrancy than throwing men out of their occupations; and, if Professor Bindoff is right in suggesting that the apprenticeship clauses of the 1563 act were the work of private interests, the Crown was not interested in the regulations from the start.[48]

It was therefore left to the common informer to bring infringement of the apprenticeship laws before the courts; and of the 650 prosecutions brought by private individuals under Elizabeth, about 500 were the work of professionals. These men were concerned, naturally enough, with making a profit rather than ensuring the health of British industry; and they consequently brought their actions when demand for manufactured goods was high and the call on the labour market was strong. If the professional informers had any effect at all it was probably to hinder the expansion of the cloth industry when times were propitious. But it is unlikely that their work had momentous consequences for the economy. About 80 per cent of their prosecutions were inconclusive and only about 6 per cent resulted in conviction or a licensed composition. Few men are likely to have been driven in consequence from unlawful occupations. At best the common informer kept the existence of the law before the public mind; but he did so at the cost of increasing public resentment.[49]

The enforcement of apprenticeship may well have been typical of those regulations in which local rulers and the central government showed little interest; and these were, to judge from Quarter Sessions records, fairly numerous. But there were regulations with which the Crown had a much more urgent concern. Above all, it was interested in the manufacture of

[47] Davies, *Apprenticeship*, 218–20, 244–56.
[48] Ibid. 218–56. S. T. Bindoff, 'The Making of the Statute of Artificers', in *Elizabethan Government and Society*, ed. Bindoff *et al.*
[49] Davies, *Apprenticeship*, chs. v, vi, and app. ii.

cloth.[50] Considering the prominent place held by textiles in English industry, the great value of cloth exports, and the revenue consequently derived by the Crown, one would expect the regulation of cloth-making to be both extensive and detailed. So indeed it was. Thirty-four acts dealt with traditional woollen manufacture and another ten with worsteds; and these statutes were supplemented by frequent proclamations. The regulations governed the length and breadth of broadcloths, the methods of stretching, techniques of dyeing, and the location of looms.[51]

One part of the legislation attempted to protect urban industries by preventing competition from rural weavers and clothiers. In 1533 the corporation of Worcester complained that the city had been substantially maintained in the past by making woollen cloth, but now suffered because 'divers persons inhabiting and dwelling in the hamlets, thorpes, and villages' near Worcester had taken up the manufacture without being subject to guild regulations. A statute of 1554 lamented in its preamble that the cities and towns of England were 'like to come very shortly to utter destruction, ruin and decay' because of the practices of rural clothiers and retailers. Parliament responded to the appeal from Worcester with a statute restricting cloth-manufacture to that city and the four market-towns of the county. One statute of Mary's reign forbade the retail sale of cloth or other goods in towns by persons living outside them; the other, passed in 1555, limited the number of looms that could be owned by rural clothiers and weavers.[52]

The statute limiting cloth-manufacture to Worcester and the market-towns of the county seems to have had some success. At any rate, there is evidence that the regulations were enforced, that the clothiers of Worcester prospered, and that rural weaving did not increase until late in the sixteenth century. But elsewhere this statute seems to have been very little applied. Rural industry flourished in Wiltshire, Lancashire, and the West Riding. The act of 1555 was little enforced

[50] The wool trade was another area in which the government was closely concerned. See Bowden, *The Wool Trade*, chs. iv–vi, on that topic.

[51] Ramsey, *Tudor Economic Problems*, 147. Cf. Hughes & Larkin, I, nos. 152, 166, 198, 328; III, nos. 720, 744. G. D. Ramsay, *The Wiltshire Woollen Industry*, ch. iv.

[52] 25 Henry VIII c. 18. 1 & 2 Philip & Mary c. 7. 2 & 3 Philip & Mary c. 11. *TED* I, 173, 119, 185.

and old clothing towns like York and Beverley continued to decay.[53]

There was a long series of Tudor statutes attempting to prevent abuses in manufacture and to improve the quality of English cloth. The demand for this legislation came from exporters, major clothiers, who hoped to drive out less skilful competitors, and even from Henry IV of France. The most detailed and massive statute, passed in 1552, laid down specific rules for different types of cloth and different regions, covering methods of manufacture, stretching, and dyeing. It was by no means the last of the series, however, and the final years of Elizabeth's reign saw the passage of two stringent statutes against excessive stretching, or 'tentering', of cloth.[54]

The high tone and impressive bulk of these statutes sadly contrasts with their achievement. John Leake, writing in 1577, complained that no serious attempt was made to enforce the law and that even the J.P.s, fearful that unemployment might result from the dismissal of poor workmen, allowed the statutes to be 'covered as it were under a bushel'.[55] Other evidence suggests that he was right. The local aulnagers were usually more concerned with collecting fees than with examining cloth. For a few years in the middle of the century a more rigorous system of central inspection was achieved by the appointment in 1560 of a London aulnager and five assistants. But their activities soon diminished and by 1570 the rules were once again being laxly observed.[56] Leake commented that the best cloth came from the West Country, Worcester, and Kent. There is some evidence that regulations were enforced by town officials in Worcester; but the Wiltshire industry, although its products may have been better than those of other regions, was not very thoroughly supervised.[57] In Yorkshire, Lancashire, and Wales control was at best sporadic, at worst non-existent. Orders by

[53] A. D. Dyer, *The City of Worcester*, ch. ix. H. Heaton, *The Yorkshire Woollen and Worsted Industries* (Oxford, 1920), ch. ii. Ramsay, *Wiltshire Woollen Industry*, 17–18, 58–9. Norman Lowe, *The Lancashire Textile Industry in the Sixteenth Century* (Chetham Soc., 3rd ser., vol. 20, 1972), 82–4.

[54] 5 & 6 Edward VI c. 6. Cf. 6 Henry VIII c. 9; 27 Henry VIII c. 12; 3 & 4 Edward VI c. 2; 39 Elizabeth c. 20; 43 Elizabeth c. 10.

[55] *TED* III. 220–1.

[56] 3 & 4 Edward VI c. 2. 5 & 6 Edward VI c. 6. Ramsay, *The Wiltshire Woollen Industry*, 53–8.

[57] *TED* III, 217. Dyer, *Worcester*, loc. cit. Ramsay, loc. cit.

the Privy Council in 1600–1 to enforce the rules against stretching met with protest from the local J.P.s and only the most grudging and occasional action.[58]

Although the Crown's intervention in economic affairs was mainly negative and prohibitory—designed to prevent people from committing particular actions—it did, especially in the third quarter of the sixteenth century, take positive steps to encourage certain industries. In 1550 English manufactures were still, except for cloth, relatively primitive, and the country therefore depended upon foreign imports for a large range of goods, including luxury items and armaments. This threatened the balance of payments and the value of the pound, endangered national security, and deprived native Englishmen of employment. To some extent the drain of bullion could be slowed by prohibitions on the import of unnecessary luxuries, and such measures were often advocated. But more positive steps were also needed. In consequence the Crown, especially under the direction and advice of William Cecil, tried to encourage the importation of foreign skills rather than foreign goods, so that native industries might be developed.[59]

For the first half of the century England had depended on France for supplies of salt, a vital commodity. Early in the reign of Elizabeth civil dissensions in France damaged this trade and pushed up the price. William Cecil procured a licence for Jasper Seler, a German financier, to manufacture white salt and invited him to England. Cecil's object was partly fiscal—to make money for the Crown; partly personal—to make money for himself; and partly national—to secure supplies of cheap salt.[60] His active role in the encouragement of industrial enterprise is again evident in a letter fron Daniel Höchstetter, a German, to Alderman Duckett of London. Höchsetter was engaged in searching for sources of copper in the north and wrote

---

[58] *APC* xxx. 481, 602–4, 606; xxxi. 78, 111, 387–9, 445–6, 473. Heaton, op. cit., ch. iv. Lowe, op. cit., ch. vi. T. C. Mendenhall, *The Shrewsbury Drapers and the Welsh Wool Trade* (Oxford, 1953), 20–5. G. D. Ramsay, 'The Distribution of the Cloth Industry, 1561–62', *EHR* LVII (1942).

[59] On government sponsorship of projects see Joan Thirsk, *Economic Policy and Projects*, esp. chs. ii, iii.

[60] E. Hughes, 'The English Monopoly of Salt, 1563–71', *EHR* XL (1925).

enthusiastically about Cecil's help: 'It is joyful news to us to understand that Master Secretary hath shewed himself so friendly and forward in this our work of our mineral and that his money hath been so ready with the first, and also so willing for the next, payment . . .'[61]

The principal means of encouraging the development of new industries or new processes was the grant of patents by the Crown. These licensed the patentees to employ their special techniques, build equipment, and sell their products. They usually gave some degree of protection in the form of a temporary monopoly. An early industrial monopoly was granted in 1552 for making glass. Under Elizabeth such patents became much more frequent, some going to foreigners and some to native entrepreneurs.[62]

In two instances the issue of patents led to the formation of joint-stock companies for exploiting material resources and new processes. Daniel Höchstetter and his partner, Thomas Thurland, were granted the sole right to search for and mine copper in the counties of northern England, the South-West, Wales, Gloucestershire, and Worcestershire; after discovering copper in Cumberland they set up a joint-stock company, the Mines Royal, with twenty-four shareholders. At the same time William Humfrey, a London goldsmith, and a German iron-maker, Christopher Schütz, secured two patents: one for the sole right to mine and work metals in the counties not already included in the grant to Thurland and Höchstetter; the other for a monopoly of mining calamine, making brass, 'battering' metals into plates, and making wire. In 1568 these rights were entrusted to a second joint-stock company, the Mineral and Battery Company. The story of these two companies was as complex as their enterprises were unsuccessful. The operations of the Mineral and Battery Company were divided into three sections. An ironworks, for making wire, was established at Tintern by Humfrey and Schütz, but was leased out to a succes-

[61] W. Cunningham, *The Growth of English Industry and Commerce* (3rd edn., Cambridge, 1903), II. 59.

[62] Harold G. Fox, *Monopolies and Patents* (Toronto, 1947), ch. vi. Fox's book is the most recent general treatment of the subject in print. See also E. W. Hulme, 'The History of the Patent System', *LQR* XII, XVI (1896, 1900), W. H. Price, *The English Patents of Monopoly* (1900), and E. P. Cheyney, *History of England from the Defeat of the Armada to the Death of Elizabeth* (1926), II. 284–310.

sion of farmers from 1570. Humfrey then went to Beauchief Abbey in Derbyshire, where he established the second branch of the company's activities, lead-mining. The third branch, the manufacture of brass, was established by John Brode at Isleworth in 1587 under licence from the Mineral and Battery Company.[63] The wire-works at Tintern took many years to establish on a sound footing; but eventually successive lessees built up the works until they were said to have employed 5,000 people by 1597. This figure probably included men indirectly dependent on the Tintern wire-works for employment as well as the main labour-force; and it may also have included the families of workmen. Even so, it suggests that the enterprise had grown to a considerable size.[64]

The finances of the English copper-mines are better documented and reveal a long story of frustrated endeavour and low profits. Production from the Keswick mines averaged only thirty-four tons per annum between 1567 and 1600, falling to an average of only twenty-one tons for the next four decades. During the first eight years of operation the Company of Mines Royal spent £52,000 to acquire a gross revenue of £30,000. They then, not surprisingly, leased out the mines, principally to Daniel Höchstetter and his sons. English ores, by comparison with those of the Tyrol and Sweden, were of poor quality and contained little silver, an element essential to the success of the Hungarian copper-mines. Demand for copper in England was not high and was often met by imports which were priced below the Cumberland copper. Only the business-like persistence of the Höchstetter family kept English copper-mining in existence until 1640.[65]

These two great joint-stock industrial companies were exceptional in the history of Elizabethan enterprise. Most of the early patents for the development of new or imported processes were given to one or two individuals only. In the early

[63] M. B. Donald, *Elizabethan Copper* (1955), *passim*. Id., *Elizabethan Monopolies* (1961), *passim*. J. W. Gough, *The Rise of the Entrepreneur* (1969), 74–89, 106–15, 115–26, 133–40. *TED* I, 240–62. A. E. Bland, P. A. Brown, R. H. Tawney, *English Economic History: Select Documents* (1914), 427. H. R. Schubert, *History of the British Iron and Steel Industry* (1957), ch. xvii.

[64] Schubert, op. cit. 294–5.

[65] G. Hammersley, 'Technique or Economy?: the Rise and Decline of the Early English Copper Industry', *Business History*, xv (1973).

years of Elizabeth's reign a large number of these patents, which generally included an element of monopoly, went to foreigners. S. Groyett and A. Le Leuryer were given a monopoly for the making of white soap, B. Cranick for draining-engines, Cornelius de Vos for alum and copperas, J. Seler for white salt. Gradually however, the scope, number, and variety of these patents increased.[66] The original patents, granted to protect and encourage new or imported processes, were unobjectionable. But later ones granted a monopoly in a trade or process that was already established, empowered their holders to supervise existing crafts by prosecuting offenders against the penal statutes, or allowed the patentees to infringe existing regulations with impunity. None of these later types of patent could be said to stimulate industry and many of them were regarded as corrupt and oppressive. Moreover, while a large proportion of the earlier patents were awarded to foreigners, who presumably had skills to offer, most of those granted after 1580 went to Englishmen, many of them to favoured courtiers who could contribute little to the economy.[67]

There is at present little evidence available on the working of those patents which were genuinely designed to develop new processes. Since they were generally regarded as legitimate and may have provided both employment and commodities, they were not the target of attack.[68] By contrast, the other types of patent, whose disadvantages were obvious, generated more evidence as a result of the hostility that they aroused. The glass industry provides a useful example both of monopolies and of their reception.

Although a glass industry had existed in England during the middle ages, by 1550 it had virtually disappeared. Consequently there was no opposition to the grant of a monopoly in the manufacture of window-glass to Jean Carré and Anthony Becker in 1567. Carré brought over foreign workmen and set up furnaces for window-glass in the Weald and another for Venetian-style crystal glass in London. After his death in 1572 the monopoly patent for window-glass seems in effect to have

---

[66] Hulme, *LQR* xii. 145–50, gives a list of early patents.

[67] Fox, *Monopolies and Patents*, ch. vi. Hulme, *LQR* xvi. 44–56.

[68] Mr G. D. Duncan's Ph.D thesis (Cambridge) on 'Elizabethan Monopolies, 1558–1585' will, when it is complete, add much to our knowledge of the subject. See also Thirsk, *Economic Policy*, chs. ii–iv.

lapsed. Rival glass-makers established furnaces without any apparent opposition and the industry spread through much of England. Rising demand ensured the growth of window-glass manufacture without the need for any protection by patent. Crystal glass for tableware was however another matter. Jacob Verzelini, who had been brought to England by Carré in 1571, received a monopoly for the making of crystal glass in 1574, having insisted on exclusive rights as a condition of staying in England. By 1590 the manufacture of crystal glass was concentrated in London under Verzelini's patent, while the making of window-glass was scattered and free from monopoly. Both branches of the industry seem to have been flourishing under different types of organization.[69]

In the 1590s there began a struggle for the exclusive control of the industry, which was to end in 1615 with the grant of a monopoly for the making of all forms of glass to Sir Robert Mansel. A reversion to Verzelini's patent, which expired in 1595, was granted to Sir Jerome Bowes, courtier, soldier, and, for a time, English ambassador to Russia. Bowes was of course unable to manage the monopoly himself and entrusted the running to William Turner and William Robson who eliminated competition from Verzelini's sons by getting them imprisoned. They built a furnace at Blackfriars and took over Verzelini's workmen, paying a rent of £500 per annum to Bowes—a rent that he did not always receive. Their control of the industry was far from secure, since they had to face litigation by competitors and imports from abroad. The invention of a process for making glass with coal, perfected in 1611, led to the overthrow of Robson's patent by Sir Edward Larch, and ultimately to a monopoly over the whole industry in the hands of Sir Robert Mansel, treasurer of the navy and vice-admiral of England.

Of all the monopoly industries glass-making was the most successful. It owed its success to high and growing demand, the imported skill of alien craftsmen, and the use of coal instead of timber. The patents of monopoly seem in the early years to have neither helped nor hindered the industry: window-glass manufacturers prospered without one. Between 1595 and about

1614 the patents seem to have hampered growth by encouraging litigation. After 1615 Mansel's patent seems to have had, on the whole, a largely beneficial effect through his efficient organization of the industry.[70]

Major industrial monopolies were also created for paper,[71] saltpetre,[72] starch,[73] salt,[74] and playing-cards. Other forms of patent were issued for the execution of the law. Several allowed their holders to dispense with specific penal statutes or to collect the fines upon them: Sir Edward Dyer dispensed men—for a consideration—from the laws governing tanning; Sir Walter Raleigh issued licences for taverns; William Carr licensed men to brew beer for export; Thomas Cornwallis made grants for the keeping of gaming-houses.[75] The operation of such licences can be understood from the activities of Robert Kirke and William Carter, who obtained a patent allowing them to collect from the inhabitants of East Anglia fines for failing to observe the statute ordering the sowing of one acre of hemp for every sixty acres of arable. In July 1592 within one half-hundred they collected £24. 10s. from twenty-seven men, most of them being mulcted at the rate of 3s. 4d. a year for non-compliance with an almost obsolete law.[76]

It was not surprising that hostility to patents mounted towards the end of the century. Robert Bell had protested against them in the Parliament of 1571; but at that time his seems to have been an isolated voice. In the 1580s and 1590s objections were made by J.P.s, town corporations, the Grocers' Company, and the City of London. Strong protests were lodged in the parliamentary session of 1597. The Crown promised reform and

[70] Godfrey, op. cit., chs. iii–v, xi. D. W. Crossley, 'The Performance of the Glass Industry in Sixteenth-Century England', *EcHR* xxv (1972). *APC* xxix. 101.

[71] D. C. Coleman, *The British Paper Industry, 1495–1860* (Oxford, 1958), 40–54. Gough, op. cit. 233 ff. *TED* ii. 251–4. *APC* xxii. 374; xxix. 106; xxxi. 274. *CSPDom, 1601–3*, 43.

[72] Gough, op. cit. 204–7. Hughes & Larkin, iii, nos. 718, 776. *APC* xx. 21. HMC, *Salisbury*, iv. 263.

[73] HMC, *Salisbury*, iv. 275–6, 499, 556; v. 332, 532; xiii. 559; viii. 172; xiv. 59, 87, 100, 150, 291. *APC* xxiii. 45, 48, 92, 315; xxv. 43, 49, 197, 207, 209, 258, 374; xxvi. 16; xxvii. 118; xxix. 497. Hughes & Larkin, iii, no. 794. Hulme, *LQR* xvi.

[74] Hughes, 'English Monopoly of Salt', *EHR* xl (1925), 334–50. Id., *Studies in Administration and Finance, 1558–1825* (Manchester, 1934), chs. ii, iii. *TED* ii. 254–62.

[75] *TED* ii. 280–6. PRO, State Papers Domestic, Elizabeth (SP 12), 282/28. Cheyney, op. cit. ii. 284–94.

[76] *TED* ii, 267–9.

a few patents were withdrawn. It was not enough. Monopolies became the main issue in the Parliament of 1601, occupying four full sessions and two meetings of committee. One member said that the grievance of monopoly 'bringeth the general profit into a private hand; and the end of all is beggary and bondage to the subject'. Monopolies were thought odious because they raised prices and brought unemployment. No member tried to defend them on principle. The Crown's spokesmen held a modest line, urging the House of Commons to respect the Queen's prerogative by proceeding with a petition rather than a statute. They promised reform and suggested distinctions between those patents which were admittedly odious and those on which judgement might be reserved. The House accepted this line of defence and the debate was followed, within three days, by a royal proclamation. This cancelled the monopolies in salt, vinegar, aqua vitae, salting of fish, train-oil, blubber, poldavies (sailcloth), starch, pots, brushes, and bottles. Other patents were left in being, their lawfulness and convenience to be decided by the common law. Of these the most significant was the monopoly of playing-cards, soon to become the subject of a major test case, *Darcy* v. *Allen*.[77]

The first monopoly of the manufacture and importation of playing-cards had been issued in 1578 to Bowes and Bedingfield. The patentees ran into opposition from the beginning as established card-makers tried to continue their trade. Local authorities, such as the Mayor of Cambridge, were uncooperative. Even the Privy Council was sympathetic to the rivals of the patentees. When Bowes and Bedingfield complained that John Acherley of London had infringed the monopoly, the Council asked the Crown's law-officers to arbitrate, so that Acherley might be allowed to continue in business because he employed many people in card-making. But in 1596 the Council wrote a pained letter to the Lord Mayor of London, 'marvelling' that he should have failed to arrest a carpenter who had infringed this monopoly. They made a number of suggestions about the ways in which the carpenter might be caught: barring his doors and windows; indicting him for absence from

[77] J. E. Neale, *Elizabeth I and her Parliaments, 1584–1601*, 352–6, 376–93. *TED* II. 269–95. Cheyney, op. cit. II. 291–310.

church; disfranchising him from the City.[78] In 1598 the patent passed to Edward Darcy, a groom of the privy chamber, and the Privy Council appointed a small committee to protect his monopoly. The debate of 1601 radically altered the position of patentees. Previously, they had been able to sue offenders in Star Chamber, Chancery, or Exchequer; now cases had to go to Queen's Bench. In 1602 Darcy brought an action against a Londoner named Allen for infringement of his patent. It is evident that Allen had been encouraged by the City authorities to continue making, selling, and importing cards, in order to maintain the privileges of London. Judgement was finally given against the monopolist, first on the ground that the patent restricted employment, second because it raised prices.[79]

The history of monopolies certainly deserves a much fuller examination than it has yet received in print.[80] But even this brief survey shows how a device used originally to encourage new manufactures was soon abused by the patentees and distorted into a means of restriction and price-raising. The earlier monopolies had probably been largely neutral in their economic effect. Much more important than monopoly was the import of alien craftsmen. The manufacture of window-glass prospered after the monopoly had lapsed; the forging of cast-iron cannon succeeded without any monopoly at all. Conversely, the grant of monopoly rights seems to have done little for the makers of salt and paper; or for the miners of copper. Later monopolies—like the grant for starch—hampered existing manufacturers and aroused complaints from consumers. The Crown was faced with opposition, especially from the City of London, before the matter became a major issue in Parliament. The victories won by the Commons in 1601 and by Allen in the lawcourts two years later were however only transient, for James I, after initially expressing sympathy with the opponents of monopoly, soon surrendered to his rapacious

---

[78] HMC, *Salisbury*, II no. 427; VIII, p. 34. *APC* x. 431, 434; XI. 172, 430; XVIII. 186; XXV. 503. *CSPDom, Add., 1580–1625*, 371.

[79] D. Seaborne Davies, 'Further Light on the Case of Monopolies', *LQR* XLVIII (1932). Barbara Malament, 'The "Economic Liberalism" of Sir Edward Coke', *Yale Law Journal*, LXXVI (ii) (1967).

[80] Mr G. D. Duncan's Ph.D thesis (Cambridge) on 'Elizabethan Monopolies, 1558–85', will, when complete, throw light on the whole topic. So does Joan Thirsk, *Economic Policy*, chs. ii–iv.

favourites. By 1621 the abuse was more monstrous than it had ever been.[81]

Probably the Crown's regulation of foreign trade was more effective and therefore more important throughout the sixteenth century than were its attempts—often half-hearted and usually unimpressive—to control the domestic economy. The vitality of the cloth trade was essential to the economic and social health of the nation; the revenue from customs duties formed a large part of the royal income; the government could offer important services to English merchants abroad by extending to them its protection and by negotiating with foreign powers, in return for which merchants were sometimes prepared to comply with its financial demands; and, finally, the concentration of the export trade upon the port of London made control and regulation easier than it ever could be in the scattered English shires. That does not, however, mean that the Crown gave all its favour to the exporters of manufactured cloth. It offered some protection to the Staplers, who depended upon the export of raw wool, although heavy taxation, economic changes, and the loss of Calais combined to extinguish most of their foreign trade. The Navigation Act of 1485—forbidding the import of wine in foreign vessels—was an attempt to encourage English shipping and seamanship, and was succeeded by a more elaborate statute in 1540.[82] The so-called 'political Lent'—ordering the compulsory eating of fish on Wednesdays—had the same purpose. It is hard to say whether or not these measures were in themselves effective, but the volume of English merchant shipping rose in a spectacular fashion: in 1560 there were rather more than 70 ships between 100 and 199 tons, only six above 200; by 1582 these figures had risen to 155 and eighteen respectively. This increase is however as likely to have been the result of developing long-distance trade as of government policy.[83]

[81] Robert Zeller, *The Parliament of 1621* (California, 1971), 21–6. Fox, *Monopolies*, chs. vii–ix.

[82] 1 Henry VII c. 8; cf. 4 Henry VII c. 10. 32 Henry VIII c. 14. 5 & 6 Edward VI c. 18. 1 Elizabeth c. 13.

[83] 5 Elizabeth c. 5. Cf. 13 Eliz. c. 11; 23 Eliz. c. 7; 39 Eliz. c. 10. Ralph Davis, *The Rise of the English Shipping Industry* (1962), ch. i.

More interesting than these measures were the prohibitions laid upon the export of undyed and undressed cloth, measures which vitally affected the nature of the cloth trade. Two acts had been carried before the accession of the Tudors to protect the interests of English fullers. Soon after the accession of Henry VII it was enacted that only cloths valued at less than 40*s.* might be exported in an unfinished state: the finer cloths were to provide employment for English artisans by being dyed, fulled, and shorn before being exported. In the next fifty years, as the price of cloth rose, this threshold was progressively raised until, by 1542, it reached £4 for white cloths and £3 for coloured. The Merchant Adventurers were thus able to export to the Netherlands a large volume of undressed cloth, for which the demand was greater than for cloth finished in England. But the inflation of the next few years was not accompanied by any further adjustment of the threshold. Henceforth the law in effect ordained that all cloth—not merely the best—should be dressed and finished in England. Had the statutes been effectively enforced the Adventurers would have lost a great deal of business. In practice they were evaded by a series of licences, which were profitable to the Crown.[84]

The Merchant Adventurers themselves were granted a licence to export annually 30,000 cloths, perhaps one-third of their total trade. They had to buy licences to export the rest from various individuals, of whom the most important was Robert Dudley, Earl of Leicester, whose licence was bought for £6,666. 13*s.* 4*d.*[85] In the final decade of the century the Merchant Adventurers tried once more to have the threshold raised to £6 for white cloths and £5 for coloureds. They were opposed by the cloth-workers, who evidently derived some benefit from existing legislation in spite of the licences, and also presumably by licensees, actual or aspiring. By this time the major licence was held by Lord Hunsdon, who had transferred it to J. Robinson and other merchants.[86] Other licences were held by Lord Huntingdon for 8,000 cloths, the Earl of Bedford for another 8,000, and Lord Burghley for 12,000. Later a licence was granted to the Earl of Cumberland, in the face of opposition

[84] Ramsay, *City of London*, 44–6. *LP* XVI. 864; XVII. 309.
[85] Ramsay, op. cit. 56.
[86] HMC, *Salisbury*, XIII. 475, 477.

from the Adventurers; he leased it out for a rent of £1,000 per annum. These developments are of interest for two reasons. First, they illustrate the tendency of economic regulation to become either a form of taxation on behalf of the Crown or a source of reward for its favourites and servants. Second, the large sums paid by merchants for the licences and the hostility of the Adventurers to the system suggests that the prohibition on the export of undressed cloth without licence was fairly effectively enforced.[87]

Crown policy also determined the outcome of rivalries between English and foreign merchants trading in London. Since 1474 the German merchants of the Hanseatic League, trading from their headquarters at the Steelyard in Thames Street, had enjoyed preferential treatment over other merchants, both native and foreign. They paid lower rates of duty on both imports and exports and could trade with anyone else in the City; they gave little in return to English merchants in the Hanse towns. When, in the early 1550s, English merchants encountered serious difficulties in their trade, the Hansard position was bound to come under attack. The Crown, in need of credit, was prepared to bargain away these privileges in return for a loan from the Merchant Adventurers. In 1552 the special rights for the Hanse merchants were rescinded. Although Mary restored their privileges to the Germans, this was the beginning of the end for them. Eight years of complicated negotiation, with the Crown constantly swinging the balance, ended with the abrogation of Hansard privileges. After 1560 they continued to trade from England, but in a very limited way; and the role of other foreign merchants diminished with them. Alien traders had won a commanding position by the favour of the Crown in 1474. English merchants captured it in the 1550s and 1560s. The determination of the Crown had been crucial.[88]

The voice of the Crown also helped to decide the direction taken by English exports. From the last decade of the fifteenth century the Company of Merchant Adventurers had established a permanent foothold in Antwerp, which became the

[87] *CSPDom, Add., 1580–1625*, 385, 400–3. HMC, *Salisbury*, viii. 475. *CSPDom, 1601–3*, 80, 164. *Egerton Papers* (Camden Soc. xii), 335.

[88] Ramsay, op. cit. 51, 60–70, 158–73. H. Zins, *England and the Baltic in the Elizabethan Era* (Manchester, 1972), ch. iii.

principal outlet for their monopoly of English trade with the Netherlands in all goods except raw wool. During the first half of the sixteenth century their export of cloth came to be easily the most important component of English commerce, and both the Adventurers and the city of Antwerp benefited accordingly. However economic difficulties began to threaten the Antwerp market in the 1550s, and these were compounded by political disturbances in the first years of the reign of Elizabeth. In 1563 the Spanish rulers of the Netherlands decided, for complex reasons of diplomacy and domestic policy, to prohibit all traffic with England. The English were forced to seek another outlet for their cloth, and ultimately, in 1564, they found one at Emden. Essentially the choice of Emden was a government decision, although it was taken after consultation with the merchants.[89]

The location of the mart for English cloth changed frequently during Elizabeth's reign; and the rapid alterations of policy need not be described in detail here. It is sufficient to say that, although the Adventurers returned to Antwerp in 1565, they were soon forced by turbulent conditions in the Netherlands to look elsewhere. By the end of the century their trade in English cloth had divided into two streams: one flowed to Middelburg, in the United Provinces, the other to various north German ports, principally Emden, Stade, and Hamburg. Although the regulations concerning these foreign marts changed frequently and confusingly, it seems evident that the final decisions rested, as they had done in 1564, with the Privy Council.[90]

The government also played a major role in the establishment of new chartered companies. As trade with the Netherlands became increasingly interrupted from 1550, merchants began to seek other outlets and other sources of supply. A short-lived Company of Merchant Adventurers for Guinea was established in 1553, in the hope of profiting from the African slave-trade, but was killed by Spanish hostility in 1567.[91] A little

---

[89] Ramsay, op. cit. 22–8, 40–4, 189–210, 241–4.

[90] T. S. Willan, *Studies in Elizabethan Foreign Trade*, 49–56. G. D. Ramsay, *English Overseas Trade*, 31–3, 105–6, 215. Cf. J. D. Gould, 'The Crisis in the Export Trade, 1586–1587', *EHR* LXXI (1956).

[91] W. R. Scott, *Joint-Stock Companies*, II. 3–9.

further north, the exchange of cloth and sugar in Morocco seemed an attractive proposition. For most of Elizabeth's reign this commerce was conducted by individual merchants, but for a few years, 1585–97, it came under the control of a monopoly company, the Barbary Co., operating under royal charter. A Spanish Company received a charter in 1577, although it did not trade between 1585 and 1604.[92]

Although the Crown established these three companies by charter it played only a minor part in their trade. Its intervention and backing was far more significant in the trade with Russia. In that despotically ruled country the favour and protection of the Tsar was essential. The Muscovy merchants, founded as a joint-stock company in London by a royal charter in 1555, wanted the Tsar to give them protection, monopoly of trade, and freedom from customs duties. Tsar Ivan was prepared to concede these benefits in return for a political alliance with England, a guarantee of asylum should he be dethroned, and, later, an English bride. The Company got most of their demands, although they lost their monopoly in 1587; the Tsar seems to have achieved only modest diplomatic gains.[93] Similar support from the Crown was given to the Levant Company, which was granted a monopoly of trade with the dominions of the Ottoman Sultan in 1581. In addition to her diplomatic support the Queen reputedly subscribed £40,000 of the company's £80,000 capital. The Eastland Company, trading cloth in return for naval stores and corn from the Baltic, received its charter of monopoly in 1579. Last of the Elizabethan companies—and ultimately the most important of all—was the East India Company, formed in 1600.[94]

At the beginning of the sixteenth century there were only two English chartered trading companies, the Staplers and the Merchant Adventurers. In the second half of that century seven more such companies were founded and trade to most parts

[92] Willan, *Studies*, ch. iv. Pauline Croft, 'Free Trade and the House of Commons, 1605–6' *EcHR* XXVIII (1975), 18.

[93] Willan, *The Early History of the Russia Company, 1553–1603* (Manchester, 1956), *passim*, esp. 7–14, 76–7, 99–100, 107, 110, 161–8, 171, 179.

[94] Ramsay, *Overseas Trade*, 41, 67–8. Scott, op. cit. 83–8. R. W. K. Hinton, *The Eastland Trade and the Common Weal* (Cambridge, 1959), intro. A. C. Wood, *A History of the Levant Company* (1935), chs. i, ii. Zins, op. cit., chs. iii, v.

of Europe was confined—though not in every case permanently—to these monopolistic bodies centred on London.
Officially the greater part of English commerce was corseted
within the tightly drawn garment of government sponsorship.
Reality did not however entirely conform to this model.
Smugglers evaded the customs in England and interlopers
broke into the monopoly trade of the companies abroad. Customs officers were too often dishonest or incompetent, and the
Crown resorted to indirect farming of the duties instead of
building up an effective service. This was hardly a solution to
its problems.[95]

It is impossible to measure the extent of evasion practised
by smugglers and interlopers. Probably it was relatively slight
in the first half of the century when duties were low and the
great bulk of the trade was channelled through London to
Antwerp, and was thus more easily controlled. But the raising
of the duties in 1558, the constant shifting of the Merchant
Adventurers' mart, and the radiation of commerce into new
regions all made control more difficult. The diversion of the
overseas mart from Antwerp to Emden in 1564 seems to have
been accomplished with only a relatively small amount of
evasion.[96] But the frequent shifting of the overseas staple in later
years may well have made policing harder. The chartered
companies did not themselves possess the means to keep out
interlopers and relied upon the coercive mechanism of Privy
Council and royal courts. Although the Council was prepared
to support the monopolies of the chartered companies, it
could not always protect them fully, especially against illicit
trading in other countries. Any conclusions about the extent
of interloping—trading by men who were not members
of companies—must be tentative. But the practice seems to
have been growing in the last two decades of the sixteenth
century: in 1597/98 interlopers shipped to the Netherlands
and Germany a volume of cloth allegedly equivalent to 13 per
cent of the normal cloth exports of the Merchant Adventurers.
Even a joint-stock company, like the Russia Company,
trading in a distant and unwelcoming country, was faced

[95] Ramsay, *Overseas Trade*, 166–206.
[96] Ramsay, *City of London*, 269.

with the threat of private trade by its own servants or by inter-lopers.[97]

The insistence of the companies that their own members trade only at the recognized marts was also difficult to enforce. While Antwerp was the staple for the Merchant Adventurers it seems effectively to have monopolized the export of cloth; but imports came from several other sources. After the mart shifted from Antwerp the monopoly became still less complete, although it is likely that cloth exports continued to go preponderantly to the official ports. In 1598 the Privy Council had to rescind its own orders that all exports by the Adventurers should go to Middelburg in the Netherlands: it allowed export to Emden and, later, to Stade. Despite this regulation many merchants traded illicitly to Hamburg.[98]

However, the growing opposition to the monopolistic power of the chartered companies suggests that their restrictions were at least partially effective. In the middle of Elizabeth's reign the merchants of Hull complained that 'by means of the said companies (the government whereof is ruled only in the City of London) all the whole trade of merchandise is in a manner brought to the City of London'.[99] By 1604 the opposition had grown sufficiently to launch a powerful attack in Parliament. The opponents of the companies, led by Sir Edwin Sandys, claimed that 'the mass of the whole trade of all the realm is in the hands of some two hundred persons at the most ...' The merchants of the outports claimed to be excluded from commerce by the dominance of London; and within London high entry-fees to the companies confined membership to a small handful of rich men. Particularly odious to the critics was the Muscovy Company, 'a strong and shameful monopoly; a monopoly in a monopoly; both abroad and at home ...' The 'free-trade' movement of 1604 was only in part successful, and the complaints of the Hull merchants were probably exaggerated, considering the healthy state of Hull's trade with the Baltic. The doors of the London companies remained closed to outsiders, but the outcry did for a time prevent the creation

[97] Willan, *Studies*, 40–6, 63–4. Id., *Russia Company*, 258, 278–9. On the role of tariffs see id., *A Tudor Book of Rates*, intro. *TED* II. 66.

[98] Willan, *Studies*, 46–64. B. E. Supple, *Commercial Crisis and Change in England, 1600–1642*, 24–5. *TED* II. 66–8.

[99] *TED* II. 49.

of a new French Company and permanently frustrated the revival of the Spanish Company.[100]

Although the earlier part of the sixteenth century was certainly
not free from economic regulation, there does seem to be a contrast between the reigns of the first two Tudors and of their
successors. While medieval and early Tudor governments had
left many activities to the regulation of local authorities and
urban guilds, the Crown tended after 1547 to insist upon certain
general national standards: this is especially noticeable in the
statute of artificers of 1563. The legislation of the latter part of
the century reflected better information and a more flexible
attitude on the part of the government. The cloth act of 1552
embodied a remarkable control of detail in the standards that
it imposed upon different types of cloth and different counties;
the enclosure act of 1597 recognized that uniform regulation
could not be applied to the varied farming regions of England.
Above all, foreign trade had come by the end of the century
to be concentrated in the hands of a few, London-based, monopolistic companies.[101]

But the growing range and detail of statutory prohibition was
not matched by any comparable development of the machinery
of enforcement. More customs officers were appointed; but that
is all. The Justices of the Peace, protesting against the 'stacks
of statutes' laid upon their shoulders, were largely inert. Common informers, who became the Crown's main weapon against
economic offences, did not always find it easy to secure convictions from juries, with whom the ultimate decision lay, and
whose sympathies might be more closely tied to local offenders
than to intrusive informers.[102]

The 'success rate' of enforcement naturally varied. Many
statutes—for instance the apprenticeship regulations—were
seldom invoked. When informations were brought, more often

[100] Joan Thirsk and J. P. Cooper, *Seventeenth-Century Economic Documents* (Oxford,
1972), 436–44; cf. 447–9. *TED* III. 280–304, a defence of the chartered companies.
Robert Ashton, 'The Parliamentary Agitation for Free Trade...', *P&P* 38 (1967).
Cf. ibid., nos. 40, 43. P. Croft, 'Free Trade and the House of Commons, 1605–6', *EcHR*
XXVIII (1975). On Hull's trade to the Baltic see Zins, op. cit. 134–8, 175–6, 180–1.
[101] See references in n.17, above.
[102] G. R. Elton, 'Informing for Profit', *CHJ* XI (1954).

than not they failed to secure a conviction. But it would be a mistake to suppose that such statutes had no effect whatever. Their existence may well have had some deterrent effect even if their breach was seldom the subject of litigation. At the very least such statutes had a fiscal value for the Crown, its agents, and its favourites. But it is less likely that they achieved their stated objectives. The statutes aimed at keeping industry within the towns and out of the countryside were almost entirely ineffective. The laws against abuses in cloth-making may have been an irritant to clothiers; they probably did little to improve the quality of cloth. Early in the reign of Elizabeth the government's policy of attracting alien craftsmen promised well for the development of 'new' industries; but in the end the result was disappointing, except in glass-making. On the other hand the Crown's intervention in foreign trade, even though limited by the inefficiency of the customs service, was probably much more effective in eliminating the Hansard merchants, determining the direction of English exports, and entrusting commerce to the big monopoly companies.

Politically the Crown paid a high price for these limited achievements. The unpopularity of informers undermined respect for the law itself. Patents, licences, and monopolies stirred up the most considerable movement of parliamentary opposition in the reign of Elizabeth—perhaps in the whole Tudor period. The dominance of trade by London was hotly resented by the other ports and by many M.P.s.

VI

Poverty, Labour, and Dearth

The poor of sixteenth-century England were often regarded as a more or less homogeneous, somewhat threatening, and probably shiftless mass.[1] In reality, as the more discerning of sixteenth-century observers and statesmen realized, they were made up of different groups with distinct problems. Those who attracted most attention—at the beginning of the century they were virtually the only ones to attract any attention at all—were the migrant and rootless unemployed who wandered the countryside, notoriously but perhaps mythically in bands of sturdy beggars, more often in ones and twos, seeking relief from their hunger. Some of them were confidence-tricksters and rogues; some were honest men and women deprived of their livelihoods by unrelenting circumstance; others were disbanded soldiers and sailors, the destitute victims of war. Most of them trudged hopefully towards the towns where they expected to find charity or work. Second, there were the old, the sick, the widows, and the orphans. They were of course no new phenomenon; but it is noticeable that widows made up a high proportion of the poor in towns.[2] Third, there were the families which were able to support themselves in good times but were rendered destitute by the sudden calamities of harvest failure, industrial slump, or plague. The problems of this group might be temporary, but they were often desperate and intractable, especially in the towns.[3] Finally, there were the families which were poor but not destitute. The living-standard of wage-earners was declining over the century and they can have had

[1] The standard work on the sixteenth-century poor-law is still E. M. Leonard, *The Early History of English Poor Relief* (1900, repr. 1965). A useful brief introduction, with documents and bibliography, is given by J. F. Pound, *Poverty and Vagrancy in Tudor England* (1971). See also W. K. Jordan, *Philanthropy in England* (1959) and F. Aydelotte, *Elizabethan Rogues and Vagabonds* (Oxford, 1913). A full-scale treatment of the whole subject is badly needed.

[2] K. V. Thomas, *Religion and the Decline of Magic* (1973 edn.), 670–2.

[3] P. A. Slack, 'Poverty and Politics in Salisbury', in Clark and Slack (eds.), *Crisis and Order in English Towns*, 164 ff.

little margin to spare for hard times. Farm-labourers made up 25–30 per cent of the population in the countryside, while in Elizabethan Norwich rather more than 25 per cent of adult males were wage-earners.[4] This however was not a group which society proposed to help. Relief was intended only for the destitute, not for those living, as so many did, on the poverty-line.

Poverty seems to have been most acute in the towns. The size of the problem can be assessed from a remarkable census of the indigent poor carried out in Norwich in 1570; this records about 500 men, over 850 women, and nearly 1,000 children. Together they made up between 20 per cent and 25 per cent of the total English population of the town. Most of them were natives of Norwich but about 300 had arrived in the course of the previous ten years. If one adds to this group about 650 wage-earners and their dependants, admittedly a conjectural figure, it would seem that about half the population of the city was living on or below the poverty-line. These figures were not constant. Epidemics in 1579, 1583–6, and 1590–3 may have reduced the number of poor, at any rate for a time. On the other hand, an influx of aliens in the 1570s probably raised it.[5]

Society was therefore confronted with a set of interlocking tasks. Order and security must be preserved by controlling the migrant poor, inhibiting them from crime, and preventing them from wandering indiscriminately over the countryside. The indigent and the helpless must be relieved. The children of the poor must be fed and trained to support themselves. Rural depopulation must be halted, so that the numbers of the landless be kept within bounds. Grain must be supplied at reasonable prices in times of shortage. Work must be provided for the unemployed. Prices and wages must be controlled during the period of inflation.

Historians of the Tudor poor-law have usually concentrated upon the first three of these tasks: control of vagrants, relief of the 'impotent' poor, and maintenance of orphaned children. But the impact of government upon the problem of poverty can

---

[4] Alan Everitt, in *Agrarian History*, ch. vii. J. F. Pound, 'The Social and Trade Structure of Norwich', *P&P* 34 (1966), 53–5.

[5] J. F. Pound, 'An Elizabethan Census of the Poor', *University of Birmingham Historical Journal*, VIII (1962), 135–62. Id., *The Norwich Census of the Poor, 1570* (Norfolk Record Soc., XL, 1971). John Webb, *Poor Relief in Elizabethan Ipswich* (Suffolk Record Soc. IX, 1966), sect. v. I am grateful for Dr Slack's help with the Norwich figures.

only be fully assessed if they are considered alongside the control of wages, the prevention of enclosure and depopulation, and the supply of food. Moreover, a full understanding of the treatment of the poor is impossible unless one also considers municipal schemes and private charity.

A. *Wages*

The policing of wages, labour-relations, and conditions of employment had long been a responsibility of both national government and town corporations.[6] Boroughs set maximum wages for their inhabitants in the middle ages and in the sixteenth century. The statute of 1389 imposed national maxima for wages, empowering Justices of the Peace to assess actual rates within these limits; and this statute was re-enacted twice in the fifteenth century and again under Henry VIII.[7] The comprehensive Statute of Artificers, carried in 1563, ended the imposition of a uniform, national maximum and instructed J.P.s to assess maxima annually in each shire. It also laid down that the period of hire for a servant or workman should never be less than a year; that masters should not dismiss their servants or servants leave their employment without due cause; that all unmarried persons under thirty trained in a craft should take employment in that craft; that unemployed men should be compulsorily employed in husbandry and unemployed girls in domestic service; and that parish constables could enlist the services of any man to help in reaping the harvest.[8]

The objectives of this statute have been much debated. Its preamble announced, quite correctly, that the wages rated in earlier statutes 'are in divers places too small and not answerable to this time, respecting the advancement of prices of all

---

[6] The main authorities on the regulation of wages are: R. H. Tawney, 'The Assessment of Wages in England by the Justices of the Peace', *Vierteljahrschrift für Social- und Wirtschaftsgeschichte*, XI (1913), and R. K. Kelsall, *Wage Regulation under the Statute of Artificers* (1938). Both are reprinted, with a useful introduction, in W. E. Minchinton (ed.), *Wage Regulation in Pre-Industrial England* (1972). My citations from Tawney and Kelsall are taken from this edition. See also D. M. Woodward, 'The Assessment of Wages', *The Local Historian*, VIII (1969).

[7] 13 Richard II c. 8. Tawney, op. cit. 45–6, 51–2.

[8] 5 Elizabeth c. 4, partly printed in *TED* I. 338 ff. See S. T. Bindoff, 'The Making of the Statute of Artificers', in *Elizabethan Government and Society*, ed. S. T. Bindoff *et al.* (1961).

things belonging to the said servants and labourers'. Yet the provisions of the act laid down maximum not minimum wages, made it an offence to give or to receive higher rates, and compelled men to labour at the official wage. Its origins are more probably to be found in the labour-shortage brought about by a severe epidemic than in any altruistic concern by government or M.P.s to raise wages. Nevertheless, while the framers of the act were evidently most concerned with the provision of labour at a reasonable rate, the substitution of local assessments for a uniform national maximum did at least allow a more flexible wage-structure in a time of inflation.[9]

In one field of economic activity a different approach was used. Some town governments had long fixed *minimum* wages for textile workers and had tried to protect them against exploitation. In 1593 provisions of this kind were debated in Parliament, and in 1595 the Privy Council ordered clothiers to raise their wages so that workmen should not think themselves uncharitably handled in a time of high prices. In 1604 a statute was carried penalizing clothiers who paid their men less than the fixed rate. Presumably textile workers were thought to be especially vulnerable to the fluctuations of the market—as they were—and to need special protection against their employers.[10]

Justices of the Peace were certainly active in making wage assessments under the act of 1563, and a large number of their ratings have survived. There are some ninety assessments and reassessments made in shires and boroughs between 1563 and 1603, although some of these are mere reissues of earlier rates.[11] In fixing wage-rates the justices seem sometimes to have taken into account fluctuations in prices. The J.P.s of Rutland, for instance, concluded their assessment with the remark that it had been drawn 'upon consideration of the great prices of linen, woollen, leather, corn and other victuals'.[12] But more often the justices were concerned to fix their maxima at a point which would ensure an adequate supply of labour, although this was perhaps less consistently their practice in the sixteenth century

---

[9] F. J. Fisher, 'Influenza and Inflation in Tudor England', *EcHR* xviii (1965). Tawney, op. cit. 62–4.

[10] *APC* xxv 44. 1 James I c. 6. Tawney, op. cit. 69–73.

[11] Minchinton, op. cit. 206–34 gives a list of assessments. Examples are to be found in Hughes & Larkin, ii & iii, *passim*.

[12] Minchinton, op. cit. 23. Cf. also ibid. 24, and Kelsall, 159–62.

than it was to become in the course of the seventeenth.[13] Yet, while the need to attract labour by offering a reasonable wage was certainly important, it was not the only consideration, for justices were also determined to prevent excessive wage-demands. The grand jury of Worcestershire echoed a common view when it complained that 'we find the unreasonableness of servants' wages a great grievance, so that servants are grown proud and idle'.[14] Thus the price-rise and the need to attract labour pushed the assessments up, while a strong desire to resist excessive wages kept them down. In the second half of the six-teenth century, with a rising population, it is unlikely that very large increases were needed to attract labour and the second consideration probably weighed the more heavily.

Assessments might be made with due care, but that of course does not ensure that they were enforced. Under the statute of 1563 there were three principal offences: giving excessive wages; receiving them; and refusing to work. Unfortunately sixteenth-century Quarter Sessions records are not as plentiful as one would wish, and on the evidence that survives it is im-possible to estimate with certainty the activity of the justices. Except in Middlesex the printed records for the reign of Eliza-beth are barren of these cases; and even Middlesex produced only a handful. More records have survived for the early seven-teenth century and they contain more examples of wage cases, especially in the North Riding of Yorkshire. Even so, the silence of the records, in so far as one can infer from it, suggests that this was not a very crowded part of the agenda of Quarter Ses-sions.[15]

Yet the apparent inactivity of Quarter Sessions in enforcing the wage regulations does not prove that the law was dis-regarded. Justices might act out-of-sessions. More important, the business of hiring servants and registering agreements was supposed to be conducted at the statute sessions of the head constable in each hundred. Private hiring of servants was dis-couraged, and, in theory at least, the statute sessions should have provided an adequate system of control over wages and the

[13] Tawney, op. cit. 81–2. Kelsall, op. cit. 159–62.

[14] Kelsall, op. cit. 178. Ibid., ch. vi, *passim.*

[15] Jeaffreson, *Middlesex County Records*, 43, 56, 63, 80. W. Ogwen Williams (ed.), *Calendar of the Caernarvonshire Quarter Sessions Records*, I, *1541–1558* (Caernarvonshire His-torical Soc., 1956), 94–5. Kelsall, op. cit., chs. ii, iii. *TED* I. 376–8.

relations between master and servant. Unfortunately the proceedings at these sessions have left few traces and one can say only that they *may* have exercised that control in practice.[16]

In the end however one wants to know whether actual wages coincided with the assessments or diverged from them, whether, that is, government regulation had any real effect. Technically the problem is difficult: we seldom find assessments which coincide in both time and place with information on wages actually paid. It is useless to compare urban wages with rural assessments; or southern wage-rates with northern assessments; or rates from one date and assessments from another. There seems to be agreement that from the middle of the seventeenth century wages exceeded the legal maxima. But the situation in the reign of Elizabeth is rather less clear. At present the balance of evidence seems to lie with the view that wages tended, in some areas at least, to surmount the legal rates. But even so, they were low enough in comparison with the cost of living. Between 1570 and 1600 prices in Chester rose by more than 100 per cent, assessed wages by only 40 per cent; in Rutland prices doubled between 1563 and 1610, whereas assessed wages hardly rose at all. Even if actual wages exceeded the assessments they failed to keep pace with prices.[17]

B. *Enclosure and Depopulation*

From the time of Henry VII the government tried to reduce poverty and to ensure the supply of food by limiting and controlling changes in the agrarian system. Enclosure and depopulation became the scapegoats for peasants, pamphleteers, and sermonizers, who considered them responsible for the uprooting of husbandmen, the destruction of farmhouses, and the shortage of grain.[18] 'Enclosure' was a protean term which included the hedging and cultivation of waste ground, the fencing of a man's own land, the creation of deer-parks, the consolidation of arable

---

[16] Kelsall, op. cit., ch. iv.

[17] Minchinton, op. cit. 26. Tawney, op. cit. 81–5. Kelsall, op. cit. 115–19. D. M. Woodward, in *The Local Historian*, VIII (1969). A. D. Dyer, *City of Worcester*, 51.

[18] The best short account is by Joan Thirsk, *Agrarian History*, ch. iv. R. H. Tawney's classic *The Agrarian Problem in the Sixteenth Century* needs to be read alongside E. Kerridge, *Agrarian Problems in the Sixteenth Century and after* (1969). See also M. W. Beresford, *The Lost Villages of England* (1954).

strips, and the division of common pasture. In its pejorative sense it meant the extinction of common rights over a piece of land, an action which obviously necessitated hedging or fencing. John Hale distinguished clearly between tolerable and prejudicial enclosure in his charge to jurors empanelled in 1548 to investigate the decay of towns:

> But, first, to declare unto you what is meant by this word, *inclosures*. It is not taken where a man doth enclose and hedge in his own proper ground, where no man hath commons. For such inclosure is very beneficial to the commonwealth ... but it is meant thereby, when any man hath taken away and enclosed any other mens commons, or hath pulled down houses of husbandry, and converted the lands from tillage to pasture.[19]

The dissolution of common rights, the 'engrossing' of farms—that is, the amalgamation of two or more farms into one—and the conversion of arable to pasture: these were the sins against the commonwealth, which depopulated the land, created unemployment, and reduced the supply of corn.

The government opened its attack in 1488 with a statute against enclosures in the Isle of Wight and followed it with a general act the next year 'against pulling down of towns'.[20] From that date on, it assaulted the decay of farms and the conversion of arable to pasture in a series of statutes and proclamations which lasted until 1593. Although the legislation became more complicated over the century its chief provisions remained much the same. Land which had been converted to pasture was to be restored to arable; houses which had decayed as the result of engrossing were to be rebuilt. The differences between the statutes lay rather in the means of enforcement than in their content. The act of 1489 allowed only lords of manors to take action against engrossing, a method which proved wholly ineffective since they usually stood to gain from it. In 1536 prosecution by the Crown was made possible. The other difference between the statutes lay in a growing recognition that the farming regions of England varied and could not be covered by a single principle: exceptions were therefore allowed for predominantly pastoral areas. Some other statutory inroads on the problem were attempted from time to time. An

---

[19] *TED* I. 41. [20] Ibid. 4.

act of 1533 limited the number of sheep to be kept by any one man and forbade the engrossing of farms. In March 1549 a tax was imposed on sheep and cloth in the hope of turning land back to the plough; the act was repealed in the following November. Finally, in 1555 it was ordered that men owning more than 120 sheep should keep one cow for every sixty sheep; this act was repealed in 1563.[21]

The other prong of the government's assault was the commission of inquiry. Five such commissions were issued in the sixteenth and early seventeenth centuries: the first, by Wolsey, in 1517; the second and third, by Protector Somerset, in 1548 and 1549; the fourth, by Elizabeth, in 1565/66; and the last, by James I, in 1607. Their intention was to bring to light cases of illegal enclosure and to stimulate prosecution. In addition, offences against the act of 1533 were prosecuted by informers, who took a share of the fine as an inducement.[22]

The major enactments were repealed in 1593 'because of the great plenty and cheapness of grain'. But this was tempting providence too severely. Four disastrous harvests followed in the years 1594–7 and the Parliament which assembled in 1597 passed two statutes, one for the rebuilding of decayed houses of husbandry and the other for restoring to tillage lands that had been converted to pasture since 1588. The debates on this issue in 1597 and again in 1601 show a considerable advance in economic understanding; and this is reflected in the sophistication of the acts themselves. But the control of enclosure through statute was by this time under attack. The tillage act of 1563 was finally repealed in 1624, and after that year the statutes of 1597 were seldom enforced.[23]

How important and effective was the government's onslaught upon engrossing and conversion between 1489 and the end of the sixteenth century? I am not concerned here with

[21] Thirsk, *Agrarian History*, ch. iv gives a summary of the statutes. Beresford, op. cit., ch. iv.

[22] E. F. Gay, 'Inclosures in England', *Quarterly Journ. of Economics*, XVIII (1903); 'Inquisitions of Depopulation in 1517', *TRHS*, n.s. XIV (1900); 'The Midlands Revolt of 1607', ibid. XVIII (1904). J. D. Gould, 'The Inquisitions for Depopulation of 1607', *EHR* LXVII (1952). E. Kerridge, 'The Returns of Inquisitions of Depopulation', *EHR* LXX (1955). On Somerset's agrarian policy, see M. L. Bush, *The Government Policy of Protector Somerset* (1975), ch. iii.

[23] Thirsk, *Agrarian History*, 228–32, 236–7. 39 Elizabeth cc. 1, 2. J. E. Neale, *Elizabeth I and her Parliaments, 1584–1601*, 337–45.

the wider aspects of the enclosure problem, with the question of its effects upon society and the economy, but simply with the impact of government policy upon agrarian change. However, we need first to recall three general points about enclosure and depopulation. First, enclosure had been practised for centuries before the Tudor period. It was neither a new activity nor a new problem. Second, many farmhouses had decayed in the fiteenth century, when the country's population was low, tenants were difficult to find, and landlords had put down land to grass as the most effective economic solution to that problem. The hardship came fifty or more years later when the population had increased once again and ancient common land was no longer available. By then it was too late for the Crown to put matters right. Third, much enclosure in the widest sense of the word was done by consent and agreement between lord and tenant. This was true in the middle ages, in the Tudor period, and in subsequent centuries.[24]

Although enclosure might often be brought about by agreement, landlords sometimes tried to encroach upon the common pastures or to remove tenants in order to engross farms. How successfully did government then protect the peasantry through its statutes, proclamations, courts, and commissions? Customary tenants, legally secured in their estates, could use the lawcourts to establish that security. Manorial custom and the courts probably helped a larger proportion of tenants than was once thought likely by Professor R. H. Tawney; and their existence may often have induced improving landlords to proceed by agreement if they could get it from their tenants.[25] But if a landlord decided to proceed without agreement, the law's defences could prove frail: legal action was expensive and might be prolonged; the orders of a court were not always properly enforced. Legal title and custom did not give complete protection to tenants against an unscrupulous and determined landlord; just how inadequate they may have been in practice we cannot say until more research has been completed.

[24] Reginald Lennard, 'Agrarian History: Some Vistas and Pitfalls', *Agricultural History Review*, xii (1964). I. Blanchard, 'Population-Change, Enclosure, and the Early Tudor Economy', *EcHR* xxiii (1970). M. W. Beresford, *Lost Villages*, chs. v–vi.
[25] Kerridge, op. cit. 32–133, 137–64. Contrast Tawney, *Agrarian Problem, passim.*

Tenants-at-will and leaseholders derived much less protection from their legal status and were consequently more vulnerable to the attacks of their landlords.[26] They had to rely upon the statutes, proclamations, and commissions issued against enclosure, engrossing, and depopulation. Government action brought to light many alleged offences against the statutes: 583 cases were brought in the Court of Exchequer between 1518 and 1568, most of them in the years 1518–30 and 1539–56. This is in its way an impressive achievement. But the positive effect of the litigation was probably less remarkable. To begin with, the great majority of charges, 70 per cent, concerned minor offences where only one house had been destroyed. More disquieting than that, the charges seldom led to any remedy. Penalties could be avoided by requesting pardon, by promising to rebuild decayed houses, and, most frequently, by pleading that the original depopulation had occurred before 1485, the limiting date of the statute. This last plea revealed a significant weakness in the legislation, for, as John Hales observed, 'the chief destruction of towns and decay of houses was before the beginning of King Henry the seventh'. In other words Tudor government was trying to reverse changes which had been made a generation before the first enclosure commissions were issued by Wolsey. This was hardly practicable.[27]

However, it is possible that the existence of the statutes and the threat of prosecution deterred landlords who had not yet enclosed from doing so. The repeal of enclosure legislation in 1593 seems to have been followed by a rapid conversion of arable land to pasture, especially in Leicestershire.[28] Complaints were made about enclosures in Oxfordshire at the end of 1596; and ten years later the 'Midlands Revolt' of 1607 and the subsequent inquiry revealed much enclosing activity in the last decade of the sixteenth century and the first of the seventeenth. This suggests that government action and attitudes may have acted as some restraint upon landlords before 1593. But the statutes of 1597, enacted in the panic of near-famine, evidently had less effect. By then a large body of opinion was

[26] e.g. Kerridge, op. cit. 97, 98, 128. *TED* I. 19, 29. A. Everitt, in *Agrarian History*, 406.

[27] Beresford, op. cit., ch. iv and appendix, Tables 13, 14. Thirsk, *Agrarian History*, ch. iv.

[28] Thirsk, *Agrarian History*, 227–36.

opposed to enclosure legislation in normal times. The acts narrowly survived in 1601 and by 1608 a statute actually allowed enclosure by agreement in six Herefordshire parishes.[29] Statutes were ineffective if a large section of the political nation regarded them as prejudicial. But as long as they were generally accepted they may have had some force. Difficult as it is to measure that force, it may well be that the combination of statute and moral opinion persuaded some landlords into acting in agreement with their tenants, if possible, rather than by compulsion. The cost in material terms of litigation and in social terms of moral disapproval may sometimes have been high enough to dissuade landlords from an arbitrary course: but in the nature of things those landlords have left no records of their decisions.[30]

Obviously, however, some men would not be so dissuaded and their fate might then have to be left to a higher authority. John Norden, the surveyor, who approved of enclosure by agreement, spoke harshly of landlords who depopulated their manors. Their offences were, in his opinion, 'grievously punishable': 'Although the sword of the magistrate pass by such offenders, because they are commonly great, yet doth the hand of God find them out, and suffereth seldom the issue of depopulators to enjoy such extorted revenues many generations.'[31] That takes us rather far beyond the limits of verifiable historical evidence. But it is unlikely that the knowledge of punishment falling from on high would have restrained greedy landlords, any more than the possibility of divine retribution deterred men from buying monastic lands.

C. *Food-supply and Dearth*

Easily the most important concern of the poor was the price and availability of food, especially of corn and bread; and of all the economic questions of the time this caused most anxiety to the government. But the Crown's interest in the supply of food involved not only the relief of the poor, but also provision

---

[29] M. W. Beresford, 'Habitation versus Improvement', in *Essays in the Economic and Social History of Tudor and Stuart England*, ed. F. J. Fisher (1961). 4 James I c. 11.

[30] Thirsk, *Agrarian History*, 254. Kerridge, op. cit. 112 ff., for enclosures by agreement. J. D. Gould, *The Great Debasement* (1970), 149–50.

[31] Kerridge, op. cit. 120–1.

for towns, especially London, for garrisons, for overseas possessions, and for military and naval expeditions.[32]

Supplying food to the population had always of course been
a precarious business. Since transport was slow and information
unreliable, dearth in one area could not always be cured by
moving grain from regions where there was a surplus. Methods
of storing corn were inadequate and often the grain or flour
went musty; therefore it was rare for the surplus of seven good
years to be saved against the needs of the lean years to come.
Although England seems in good harvest years to have produced a sufficiency of corn, poor harvests left a big deficit to
be filled. Those had been the hard facts of survival throughout
the middle ages. In the sixteenth century, a growing population, the expansion of London, and the attractions of pasture
farming—whether for wool or for meat—all sharpened the
hunger of the poor and intensified the worries of the government.

Throughout the sixteenth century the Crown had to find
some point of equilibrium between competing claims. The
demands of London for special treatment were loud and compelling, since the large, hungry population of the City and its
suburbs was uncomfortably near to the seat of government. But
although London might be the most insistent claimant in times
of shortage, the Privy Council could not ignore other towns or
regions whose supplies were low.[33] Until 1558 Calais and its
environs often had to be provided with corn from England, and
for much of the century there were English garrisons in Berwick
and in various Irish towns to be supplied. In wartime the problem became exceptionally acute since large quantities of victuals had to be bought and assembled for the royal armies,
whether they were standing defensively against invasion or setting out for campaigns in Ireland, France, or the Netherlands.
The interests of the consumers—whether private persons, the
royal household, or military forces—were high in the Crown's

---

[32] N. S. B. Gras, *The Evolution of the English Corn Market* (Cambridge, Mass., 1926)
is still the standard work on its subject. It badly needs replacing. For criticisms of Gras,
see V. R. Ponko, 'N. S. B. Gras and Elizabethan Corn Policy', *EcHR* xvii (1964/65).
The most perceptive account of the food market is by Alan Everitt, 'The Marketing
of Agricultural Produce', in *Agrarian History*, ch. viii.

[33] Gras's claim that the interests of London dominated the corn policy of the Tudors
(op. cit., ch. viii) has been effectively refuted by Ponko, op. cit.

priorities. But the growers of corn could not be entirely ignored. If markets and prices were always manipulated in the interests of the buyer, food-supplies would in the long run be diminished: farmers would either be ruined or would turn to other crops. Remarkably, however, in a political society that was dominated by landlords dependent in part upon rents from corn-growing tenants, the government persistently put the interests of consumers before those of producers in framing its policy. Yet to talk of 'policy' is slightly misleading. In a situation that was constantly changing with the weather, the diplomatic position, or military needs, the Crown had to attempt to satisfy all comers as best it could: its measures were short-term and *ad hoc*, but were usually weighted more heavily towards consumers.[34]

Essentially the Crown tried throughout the sixteenth century to control the supply of food in five different ways. First, it sought to prevent the export of grain overseas in time of shortage. This was difficult not only because smuggling was common and customs officials corrupt, but also because much legal trade went by sea, either along the coast from the corn-growing shires to London, or overseas to Ireland, Calais, Boulogne, or the Netherlands. It was not hard for a merchant to load his ship for some legitimate destination and then sail it somewhere else in the expectation of a higher price. Second, the Crown encouraged the import of grain in times of dearth. Sometimes this might be done through the normal commercial channels; occasionally there might be an element of *force majeure*, when the Privy Council ordered that all foreign grain ships driven into English ports should be forced to sell their cargoes on the English market.[35] Third, the Crown tried to ensure that all home-grown corn should be brought to the markets and sold at a fair price. Again, this was difficult, especially in times of scarcity, since farmers naturally preferred, if they could manage it, to hold back their grain in the expectation of higher prices as the year went on. Fourth, it attempted to ensure that corn was moved from well-supplied regions of the realm to those in need. Finally, when corn was abundant, the Crown allowed

[34] Ponko, op. cit. Lack of space prevents me from dealing with the matter of military supply. On this see: B. Pearce, 'Elizabethan Food Policy and the Armed Forces', *EcHR*, 1st ser. XII (1942); C. S. L. Davies, 'Provisions for Armies, *EcHR*, 2nd ser. XVII (1964); A. Everitt in *Agrarian History*, 519–23; C. G. Cruickshank, *Elizabeth's Army*, ch. v.
[35] e.g. *TED* I. 165.

export overseas but tried to keep this within reasonable bounds, so that abundance should not rapidly be converted into scarcity. In brief, one might say that the problem revealed itself on three levels: national—keeping enough corn in the country; regional—providing as equitably as possible for all areas; and local—ensuring that corn got to the ordinary markets.

The Crown put its controls into operation through various instruments. The export of corn was limited by a series of statutes; and statutes also sought to limit the numbers and the activities of corn-merchants, known usually as badgers, who conducted internal trade. The Privy Council issued a series of proclamations, which regulated the corn trade in more detail than statutes could do; and those proclamations were supplemented by frequent letters of instruction—some general, some very specific—to local officials. From time to time county commissioners were appointed with the task of preventing the export of grain and ensuring that supplies came to market. Rigidities in the system were softened by the use of licences, issued by the Council or by local commissioners, to allow named merchants to ship specific quantities of grain. Lastly, the Crown worked with town authorities who had long enforced a system of regulations to control the price of bread and to prevent the most common offences against the marketing of food: 'engrossing', the cornering of excessive quantities of grain; 'forestalling', buying up grain while it was still in the fields or before it came to market; 'regrating', the purchase of corn, not for one's own consumption, but for resale at a profit in the same market or a neighbouring one. Borough corporations could regulate weights and measures, prices, and behaviour at market; and if they were rich enough, they could build up stocks of corn against periods of dearth.[36] But their power was limited to the town itself and they lacked the necessary authority over areas where the corn was grown. Only the central government could extend its control over producers, traders, and consumers; and in a period of rising population and expanding towns such control was essential.

Statutes, although the best known, were probably the least important form of regulation in the sixteenth century. They did however provide the basis on which exports were controlled.

[36] *TED* I. 156–61.

Up to 1534 the export of grain was governed by a fifteenth-century statute which forbade the shipping of corn overseas unless the price fell below a certain threshold; for example a price of 6s. 8d. per quarter for wheat, and lesser sums for other grains. From 1534, all export was forbidden except with a royal licence; then, in 1555, the threshold arrangement returned, with the same price-limits, which had by then become wholly unrealistic. The limiting price was raised to 10s. per quarter for wheat in 1563, and the threshold arrangement continued until 1571, when a new statute allowed export in English ships after proclamation had been issued by the Council acting in consultation with the local officials. Under this arrangement much of the responsibility was placed upon local men, who were expected to inform the Council whether or not sufficient corn was available for export. Finally, this statute was repealed in 1593 and the threshold system restored with higher price-limits to allow for inflation: wheat could be exported when its price fell below 20s. per quarter, and so on down the scale of crops.[37] In practice the statutes were often ignored: when they forbade export it was sometimes permitted by proclamation or licence; when they permitted it, prohibitions were often imposed by the Council. The regulation of corn exports cannot therefore be understood by confining one's view to the statute-book.

Parliamentary enactments also regulated the traffic in grain within the country. Much of the blame for scarcity and high prices was placed, quite unfairly, upon the badgers, who traded in grain and acted as links between growers and consumers. By a statute of 1552 each badger had to be licensed by three J.P.s and was bound to sell his grain either in open market or to another victualler or to private persons for their own use or for the provision of cities, ships, armies, or garrisons. In 1563 these rules were drawn more tightly to ensure that badgers were licensed only in open sessions and that their licences should run only for one year.[38]

In practice surveillance by the Privy Council and by local commissioners was more important than statutory control. From 1491 onwards proclamations were constantly issued to forbid any export of grain: sometimes those with licences were

---

[37] Gras, op. cit., ch. v, sect. iii, for details of this legislation.
[38] Ibid., ch. v, sect. iv. 5 & 6 Edward VI c. 14. 5 Elizabeth c. 12.

forbidden to export; at other times the Council forbade the shipping of corn even when its price fell below the statutory threshold. Less often it relaxed prohibitions in favour of individuals or of specific towns. Reading the registers of the Privy Council one can only be struck by the very detailed supervision which it exercised over the grain trade. The ultimate effectiveness of this supervision is of course open to question, but there can be no doubt that the Council was ready to devote to it a great deal of time and energy.[39]

Up to 1565 the Council relied for the execution of its orders upon the normal officers of local government: sheriffs, J.P.s, town corporations, and customs officers. But in that year, almost accidentally, it brought on to the scene a new body of agents, the commissioners for the restraint of the grain trade. They were initially empowered, as part of the government's campaign for suppressing piracy, to prevent the loading of grain on to any ship without prior notice being given. The intention was to cut off food-supplies from pirate ships. But within a month they were being used to enforce prohibitions on the export of corn from coastal shires. After the original commissions had expired they were renewed in 1576 during a period of dearth and again in the following year. After that they seem to have become more or less a regular part of the machinery of local government, authorized to stop shipments of corn and to license exports.[40]

As well as preventing the loss of corn overseas the Privy Council made some attempt, but on a much less intensive scale, to encourage the import of corn from abroad. In 1546 Stephen Vaughan, acting as the agent of Henry VIII, made various agreements with Antwerp merchants for shipping corn to England. But this direct intervention seems to have been unusual. More often the Crown tried to persuade other men to lay out the necessary capital. Twice at least the Council exhorted the well-to-do in the counties to buy up stocks of corn which could be sold to the poor; but neither effort seems to have met with any success whatsoever. The principal initiatives in importing

[39] Hughes & Larkin, I, no. 26 is the first in a long series. See, for instance, ibid., no. 225 and III, no. 803. *APC* VII. 359. Saunders, *Papers of Nathaniel Bacon* (Camden Soc., 1915), 138.

[40] *APC* VII. 278–80, 309–10; IX. 210; X. 61, 220, 268–9.

corn came from the merchants of London, who had strong reasons for maintaining the City's supplies and a profitable and populous market for their wares. But other towns played a part: the common council of Shrewsbury imported 3,200 bushels of corn from the Baltic in 1596 to supply the poor with bread below the market price.[41]

Quite as intensive as the Council's restriction of exports, and much more vigorous than its promotion of imports, was its determination that home-grown corn should reach the ordinary markets at a reasonable price for the consumer. Throughout the sixteenth century, during times of dearth, the Crown ordered local officials to see the markets supplied. Commissioners were appointed in the autumn of 1527 to search all barns and other storage-places, compile a survey of the available grain, and compel its owners to take it to market for sale.[42] Anyone refusing to sell his corn was to be reported to the Council and ordered to appear before it. Some of the returns made by the commissioners have survived to testify to the remarkable thoroughness with which they carried out their surveys. For instance, William Clopton, searching the hundred of Hynkford in Essex, reported the number of inhabitants in each village, the amount of grain over and above what was required for sowing, and the number of weeks that it would last the inhabitants; and similar returns came in from several other counties.[43] Such searches were made by local commissioners or by J.P.s in several succeeding years of bad harvest: in 1544 and 1545, 1550, 1556, and 1562.[44] During the hard winter years, 1586–7, the Privy Council introduced standing orders to the J.P.s for supplying the markets in time of need. Justices were to discover what corn was available for sale, to bind the owners by recognizance to take it to market, to attend at markets to see that the rules were observed, and to punish forestallers, engrossers, and regraters. Essentially the Privy Council aimed at a controlled distribution, where the price-mechanism would

[41] *LP* xxi. i. 251, 339, etc.; iv. ii. 3625. *APC* xxv. 25. 'Shrewsbury Chronicle', in *Shropshire Arch. Soc. Trans.*, 1st. ser. iii. 335–6.

[42] Hughes & Larkin, i, nos. 118, 121, 125, 127; iii, no. 118.5.

[43] *LP* iv. ii. 3665. Cf. nos. 3712, 3819, 3822. Leonard, *Poor Relief*, 49–52.

[44] Hughes & Larkin, i, nos. 242, 365–6; ii, nos. 430, 490. *APC* i. 258, 261, 284, 300; v. 84, 242, 247. W. J. Ashley, *The Bread of our Forefathers* (Oxford, 1928), 37–43, 179–88. I owe this reference to Dr P. A. Slack.

be held in check by government regulation and the local officers would ensure that corn was sold openly in the public market each week at a fair price. This Book of Orders did not make any dramatic change in the traditional system, or at any rate in the way in which the system was supposed to work. But it provided a firm code of conduct for local officers, which, with frequent renewals and adjustments, became the model for the working of the internal market in grain for the next two centuries.[45]

Under Henry VIII the Crown tried to regulate the price of meat, beer, wine, and sugar by statute and proclamation; and under Edward VI this was extended to cover butter, cheese, and, on one occasion only, grain.[46] But after 1558 the central government seems to have abandoned any attempt at fixing over-all national prices for victuals: wine alone was thereafter subject to maximum prices.[47] Reluctance to fix national prices for grain does not of course mean that the government was unconcerned about the cost of food. Indeed its whole system of control was designed to ensure a supply at reasonable prices. In 1552 the Lord Mayor of London was reprimanded for allowing victuallers to charge so much when prices outside London had fallen; and four years later the commissioners in Bedfordshire were told to moderate the cost of grain.[48] But the Council preferred to act by exhortation and by preserving the traditional patterns of marketing, rather than by imposing a national maximum, which, given wide local variations in the economic price, could not have been enforced.

In general Tudor government tried to make the customary system of trade work in the interest of the consumer. The re-

[45] B. L. Lansdowne MS 48, nos. 50–8 (ff. 116–39), partly printed in Leonard, op. cit. 318–26. Hughes & Larkin, II, no. 686. Bodleian Library, Rawlinson MS B. 285 ff. 66–7. Cf. E. P. Thompson, 'The Moral Economy of the Crowd', *P&P* 50. See also B. Pearce, 'Elizabethan Food Policy and the Armed Forces', *EcHR*, 1st ser. XII (1942). Gras, op. cit. 448–9.

[46] 23 Henry VIII c. 4; 24 Henry VIII cc. 3, 6; 25 Henry VIII cc. 1, 2; 27 Henry VIII c. 9; 33 Henry VIII c. 11. Hughes & Larkin, I, nos. 139, 142, 144, 148–9, 154, 159, 162, 164, 170, 187, 193, 196, 206, 218, 230–1, 336. R. W. Heinze, 'The Pricing of Meat', *HJ* XII (1969). M. L. Bush, *The Government Policy of Protector Somerset* (1975), points out that price-fixing was abandoned by Somerset but restored by Northumberland.

[47] e. g. Hughes & Larkin, II, nos. 529, 539, etc. One exception was the fixing of prices within twenty miles of the royal court in August 1588 (ibid. III, no. 701).

[48] *APC* IV. 51; V. 242.

straints upon exports had been inherited from its predecessors. The detailed supervision of local markets by J.P.s was an attempt to conserve the traditional practice of open sale when economic developments threatened it. The Privy Council also tried to maintain the normal lines of trade between regions in times of dearth, in order to prevent hunger, or even starvation, in the cities and towns. The passage of corn from areas of surplus to areas of shortage had to be smoothed. For instance, in 1586, when J.P.s were understandably trying to prevent grain from leaving their own counties, the Council ordered the Wiltshire justices to allow corn to be sent to Bristol from those parts of their shire which normally supplied that city, the Huntingdon justices to allow the men of Wisbech to buy corn in their county as they generally did, and the justices of Hampshire and Sussex not to hinder the passage of corn to London.[49] The City of London was of course a special case. It bought its corn over a wide area in southern and eastern England, and in times of scarcity some persuasion was needed to ensure that local resentment did not prevent supplies from being moved. In 1576 the Privy Council authorized the City's agents to buy corn in the Rape of Chichester, but suggested that this be done 'in such secret manner as it causeth it not a further dearth in the said county'.[50]

The surveillance of the Privy Council did not stop at controlling the movement of corn. In times of shortage it forbade the use of grain for making starch and it strongly attacked the 'evil custom' of feeding sheep on peas, which were the best stand-by of the poor when corn was scarce. The justices of Hereford-shire were authorized to spend money collected for a house of correction on buying corn for the poor. The clergy were told to encourage abstinence in the well-to-do and patience in the hungry. If attention to detail and constant exhortation could have filled men's stomachs the Privy Council would surely have been successful.[51]

There was however another side to the problem. A run of good harvests might change its terms without solving it. In the

[49] *APC* xiv. 69, 249, 319–20, 338–9, 369. See J. Walter and K. Wrightson, 'Dearth and the Social Order', *P&P* 71 (1976).

[50] *APC* ix. 206. Cf. ibid. xiv. 342, 359; xxv. 55–7.

[51] *APC* xiv. 248, 263–4; xxv. 7. Cf. also ibid. xiv. 236; xxvi. 383–6. The best way of appreciating the Privy Council's activity in times of dearth is to look through *APC*, vols. viii, ix, xiv, xv, xxv, xxvi.

corn-growing districts of East Anglia an abundant harvest threatened farmers with unsold produce unless they were allowed to export. The Privy Council recognized this, but was usually reluctant to abandon all forms of restraint lest the price of grain shoot up. It therefore resorted, most often, to the system of export licences by which limited and restricted amounts could be exported. This system of licences encouraged favouritism or corruption among the officials who issued them and, by creating a near-monopoly, allowed the licensees to profit at the expense of grower and consumer.[52]

How effective in general was the government's policy for food-supply? Certainly the Privy Council pursued its objectives energetically. This was not one of those areas of policy where regulation lay rusting on the junk-heap of governmental intentions. The reports of local commissioners and the Council's own, very detailed, instructions show that the Crown was, by the standards of the time, well informed about supplies of corn in time of dearth. Prosecution of offenders was not uncommon. Merchants trying to export grain illegally were sometimes arrested and punished. Local courts condemned badgers who operated without licences. In the Exchequer marketing offences were easily the most common breaches of penal statutes, although dependence on informers for prosecuting inevitably weakened the impact.[53] On the whole local officials co-operated with the Crown, especially in times of dearth. Town authorities had every reason to do so, and even rural landlords, who might have resented a policy so heavily weighted in favour of the consumer, accepted the need to avoid civil disturbance. Only in times of good harvest did the rural authorities object to the imposition of continued restriction. That the Crown's policy had its effect is shown in those very objections. Norfolk corn-growers complained in 1599 that merchants were so frightened of severe punishment that they were reluctant to buy corn for export.[54]

---

[52] HMC, *Salisbury Papers*, ii, nos. 843, 1140–2, 1148–9, etc. Saunders, *Papers of Nathaniel Bacon*, 136, 142, 143, 147.

[53] e.g. *LP* iv. ii. 4016. Johnson, *Minutes of Proceedings* (Wiltshire), 2–13, 21–3, 27. Jeaffreson, *Middlesex County Records*, 24, 84, 165. Tait, *Lancashire Records*, 60, 72–3. Read, *Lambarde and Local Government*, 161–8. Hawarde, 71, 75, 91, 104. See also M. W. Beresford, 'The Common Informer', *EcHR* x (1957/58).

[54] Gras, op. cit. 234 exaggerates the tension between the Crown and local officers, because he views the government's policy almost entirely in terms of supplying London. Saunders, *Papers of Nathaniel Bacon*, 136.

Obviously there was evasion. The most zealous officials could not watch every creek in which ships might be loaded with grain; and not all officials were zealous. There is positive evidence that shipments of English corn were illegally exported overseas, especially from the 'outports', where supervision of the customs officers was lax.[55] Corn was probably hoarded by rich corn-growers so that they could obtain the highest possible price. Nor are producing areas always likely to have allowed free passage of corn to consuming regions in time of dearth. Large variations in price between town and country, and between the different seasons reveal the weakness of the regulated system of marketing. Such a system could not possibly have worked exactly as intended, for the state simply had not got the resources to force farmers into selling corn if they did not wish to do so. Even the much more formidable and ruthless apparatus of the Terror during the French Revolution could not do that.[56] At a guess it seems likely that the restrictions on export were more effective—because more easily enforced— than regulations demanding the sale of all available corn in the open market.

Whether or not a totally different system—such as the free market advocated by the physiocrats and by English *laissez-faire* economists in the eighteenth century—would have fed the nation better one cannot say.[57] In the circumstances it would have been too drastic a change to be practicable. Given that the traditional pattern was maintained, the Crown's restrictions on exports probably did something to deter the flow of grain out of the country and its regulation of internal trade is likely to have discouraged hoarding and engrossing to some extent. Government intervention perhaps worked as well as political limitations allowed. More intensive controls would have deprived the Crown of the support of its own local agents. In any case it is difficult to assess the precise impact of government policy, partly because there was no single policy, partly because the evidence is defective, and partly because more research needs to be done on the local and regional aspects of food-supply.

[55] *LP* IX. 353; XIV. i. 319, 426; XIX. ii. 803; XX. i. 95. N. J. Williams, 'Francis Shaxton and the Elizabethan Port Books', *EHR* LXVI (1951). P. Croft, 'Free Trade and the House of Commons', *EcHR* XXVIII (1975), 20.

[56] Cf. R. C. Cobb, *The Police and the People* (Oxford, 1970), sect. III, bk iii.

[57] Cobb, loc. cit. E. P. Thompson, *P&P* 50.

D. *The Poor-Laws*

In all the statutes, proclamations, and regulations of the late middle ages and the sixteenth century it was assumed that the poor could be herded into simple and convenient moral categories. The deserving poor could be distinguished from the mischievous, the aged and 'impotent' from the idle and vicious. Until 1576 only those physically unable to work were accounted deserving; but a statute of that year recognized that persons fit and willing to work might be unable to find employment and therefore be worthy of help. Thereafter three categories were established: sturdy beggars or vagabonds, the 'impotent', and the deserving unemployed.[58]

The laws inherited by the Tudors were based upon three statutes of Richard II. The first of these instructed local officers to take sureties of all vagabonds, imprisoning them, if they could not find sureties, until they were dealt with by the Justices of Gaol Delivery. The other two ordered that sturdy vagabonds and servants who had left their masters without licence were to be put in the stocks. Impotent beggars should stay in the towns where they then were, unless they could not be maintained there, in which case they should go elsewhere or return to their birthplaces: they were forbidden to wander at will through the countryside.[59] The early statutes of the Tudor period held to the general lines of this legislation, keeping the poor as far as possible immobile and deterring the able-bodied from idleness by punishment. The first Tudor statute, carried in 1495, slightly reduced the severity of the law, announcing in its preamble that the King wished to secure obedience by 'softer means than by such extreme rigour therefore provided in a statute made in the time of King Richard the Second'. Accordingly vagabonds were not to be imprisoned but to remain in the stocks for three days before being sent home. An impotent beggar should be allowed to beg only in the hundred 'where he last dwelled, or there where he is best known or born'. Self-help was the only relief available; the state permitted men to beg at home and applied a modified severity to those who

[58] 18 Elizabeth c. 3, printed in *TED* II. 331.
[59] 7 Richard II c. 5. 12 Richard II cc. 3, 7.

attempted it elsewhere.[60] Signs of a harsher attitude appeared in 1530 with a proclamation condemning idleness—the idleness of the poor, that is—as the 'mother and root of all vices', and ordering that vagabonds be whipped instead of being merely put in the stocks.[61] This provision was soon put into statutory form in the act of 1531, which gave more detailed force to the repressive measures and instructed J.P.s to give licences to the impotent poor. Although this statute is sometimes described as first making the important distinction between the impotent and able-bodied poor it does not seem to have done more than give greater precision to the existing law. The indigent still had to help themselves, but under licence now from the authorities. That was the limit of government assistance.[62]

It was soon apparent that these limits were too tightly drawn and some important attempts were made to extend the role of the state, influenced perhaps by the remarkable schemes of poor-relief at Ypres. An official bill was drafted, probably by William Marshal, one of Thomas Cromwell's assistants, for the relief of both the able-bodied poor and the impotent. Under the direction of a 'council to avoid vagabonds', those who could work were to be assembled together and employed on 'certain common works', such as the 'making of the haven of Dover', the repair of other harbours, the building of roads and fortresses, and the scouring of watercourses. All this was to be financed by a special tax on income and capital. The impotent poor were to be relieved in their parishes by voluntary alms collected by 'censors or overseers of poverty', responsible to the J.P.s. The casual distribution of alms was forbidden.[63]

In spite of a personal appearance by Henry VIII in Parliament this proposal failed to win support. The statute finally enacted fell a long way short of the ambitious proposals of the draft. There was no 'council to avoid vagabonds', no censors or overseers, no scheme of public works, no compulsory tax. The impotent poor were to be succoured by voluntary alms,

---

[60] 11 Henry VII c. 2, modifying 7 Richard II c. 5. *TED* ii. 298. Cf. 19 Henry VII c. 12.

[61] Hughes & Larkin, i, no. 128. Cf. nos. 118, 131, 132.

[62] 22 Henry VIII c. 12. Pound, *Poverty and Vagrancy*, 39. Jordan, *Philanthropy*, 84.

[63] G. R. Elton, 'An Early Tudor Poor Law', *Studies*, ii. 137–54. Id., *Reform and Renewal*, 73–4, 123–6. Cf. N. Z. Davis, *Society and Culture in Early Modern France* (1975), for schemes of poor-relief in Lyons.

but no special machinery was established for collection or distribution. The able-bodied poor were to be found work, but no
means for doing so was mentioned. Even so, the statute was
a landmark of sorts, since in principle it committed the Crown
for the first time to intervention. But it is unlikely that actual
intervention was in the event forthcoming. The statute was to
remain in force only until the end of the next Parliament—a
common enough proviso. When that Parliament sat, in the very
same year, the act of 1536 was not continued and the act legally
on the statute-book became once more that of 1531. It is possible
that the 1536 act was still thought, wrongly, to be in force, but
it is doubtful whether much was done to execute it.[64]

But, abortive as they were, William Marshal's draft and the
act of 1536 are significant in the development of policy. The
leading role in framing machinery for poor-relief has usually
been assigned by historians to the town corporations, especially
to London, Ipswich, York, Norwich, and Bristol. The implication is that Crown and Parliament trod in the footsteps of the
city fathers.[65] This may well be true of Parliament but it does
not seem always to have been true of the Crown. At times the
Crown was certainly capable of initiative and imagination. The
difficulty lay in persuading Parliament to follow it. That could
apparently be done only after some of the proposals put forward
in Marshal's draft had been tried out in the cities. Even then
the most dramatic of his suggestions—the scheme of compulsory public works—was never taken up. It would evidently be
a mistake to see the history of the poor-law in terms either of
a paternal central government imposing its will or of en-
lightened city fathers showing the way to Parliament. What
actually occurred was a slow but ultimately fruitful interchange
of ideas and experiments.

The harvest of this interchange was slow to ripen. From 1536
until 1563 the state's actions were guided by the principles of

[64] Elton, *Reform and Renewal*, 123–5. 27 Henry VIII c. 25. *LP* x. 494. T. Wright,
Letters Relating to the Suppression of the Monasteries (Camden Soc. xxvi. 1843), 38–9. In
the following Parliament of 1536, the act of 1531 (22 Henry VIII c. 12) was continued
until the end of the next Parliament. The enactment of the 1539 Parliament is somewhat
ambiguous, but almost certainly intended to continue the act of 1531 again. The act
of 1536 had an uncertain, but probably very brief, life.

[65] e.g. Jordan, *Philanthropy*, 86–7; Pound, *Poverty and Vagrancy*, 45, 48; Leonard, *Poor
Relief*, 22, 61–2.

1531. Severe repressive measures were taken against the able-bodied beggars; the others were left to fend for themselves under licence. In 1545 a royal proclamation announced that the King proposed to use 'all such ruffians, vagabonds, master-less men, common players, and evil-disposed persons to serve ... in these his wars, in certain galleys, and other like vessels'.[66] In 1547 all previous laws concerning beggars were repealed and the notorious statute enacted by which vagrants could be branded and enslaved. This act seems to have been too severe for effective enforcement and was repealed two years later.[67] The law then reverted once more to that established by the statute of 1531. Only one further statute was in-troduced before the reign of Elizabeth to alleviate the situation of the impotent poor. In 1552 Parliament ordered that collectors be appointed in town and country parishes, who would 'gently ask' parishioners for alms and distribute them among the poor. Those who refused to contribute were to be admonished first by the parson and then, if necessary, by the bishop: it is significant that the ecclesiastical arm of the state was given this active role. More important perhaps, the statute forbade free-lance begging, which had until then been the normal means of relief. This statute deserves more credit than it has been given, for it resurrected some of the principles of the short-lived act of 1536, which also had discouraged casual alms-giving and arranged for collections to be taken. Perhaps it has been neglected because the dominance of the Duke of Northumber-land has generally been considered a time of harsh repression of the poor, so that the positive achievements of the period have been overlooked.[68]

The reign of Mary saw an interesting, but probably short-term, effort by the Crown to regulate local employment and to prevent vagabondage. Instructions were sent in April 1557 to J.P.s in Yorkshire, ordering them to appoint overseers in each parish. These overseers were to examine the means of support available to every householder: if they found any man without work he should be persuaded to get employment, and hemp,

[66] Hughes & Larkin, I, no. 250.

[67] 1 Edward VI c. 3. 3 & 4 Edward VI c. 16. C. S. L. Davies, 'Slavery and Protector Somerset', *EcHR* XIX (1966).

[68] 5 & 6 Edward VI c. 2. Cf. 2 & 3 Philip & Mary c. 5.

flax, wool, or some other raw material should be provided on which his family could labour. Should this not avail, the man concerned was to be whipped. The remainder of the instructions deal in some detail with the need to discover and arrest any suspicious or seditious persons and to report religious offenders to the heresy commissioners. The document probably resulted as much from fear of dissidence and heresy as from concern for the livelihood of the poor. Even so, it anticipated the statutes of 1572 and 1576, which appointed overseers and ordered the provision of raw materials.[69]

The first twenty years of Elizabeth's reign saw a methodical extension of the role of the state. In 1563 contribution to the poor-box was made compulsory: refusal could ultimately lead to imprisonment. But the contribution was still regarded as a gift—albeit compulsory—of whatever size the donor thought fit.[70] Only in 1572 was the major step taken of instituting a national scheme of taxation. J.P.s were to list the poor in each parish, assess the money needed to maintain them, and appoint overseers for taxing the parishioners. This has been generally and rightly recognized as the major advance in Tudor legislation for the poor. It was followed in 1576 by an act ordering the provision of raw materials—wool, flax, hemp, or iron—on which the able-bodied poor could be set to work. The admission that some men were unemployed as a result of misfortune rather than idleness was grudgingly made: the preamble declared that the object of the act was to ensure that rogues 'may not have any just excuse in saying that they cannot get any service or work'.[71]

The main foundations of the Tudor system of poor relief were established by 1576: a compulsory parish rate levied by overseers and the provision of work for the able-bodied. The two major statutes of 1597 and 1601 did not add any new general principles. But, combined with two other statutes on hospitals and on charities, and with a proclamation of 1598, they drew together the body of previous legislation, greatly clarified the law, and made its implementation a more practical proposition: in particular they entrusted responsibility for relief to

[69] HMC, *Various Collections*, ii: *Wombwell MSS*, 89–92.
[70] 5 Elizabeth c. 3. Pound, *Poverty and Vagrancy*, 45.
[71] 14 Elizabeth c. 5. 18 Elizabeth c. 3. *TED* ii. 328, 331.

parochial overseers, who were subject to the supervision of the J.P.s. The statutes and the proclamation suggest that serious attempts were being made after 1576 to provide for the poor and that the framers of the later legislation had learned from the experience of these attempts. Their attention to detail—particularly in the proclamation of 1598 and the statute of 1601—suggests that they provided something more than a mere set of reserve powers, to be used occasionally as a supplement to private charity. But obviously the extent to which they actually worked must have varied a great deal from one area to another.[72]

In addition to this statutory programme, occasional attempts were made by the Privy Council to urge local employers or officials to prevent unemployment among industrial workers. A sharp fall in cloth exports in 1528 at a time of food shortage alarmed the government, which instructed clothiers to keep their men in work and ordered London merchants to buy up the cloth.[73] In 1564, when the Antwerp market was closed, the Privy Council commanded J.P.s to 'deal soundly' with any clothiers who dismissed workers: they were to be reminded that they had in past years 'had great profit by clothing'.[74] During the crisis of 1586/87 the Council informed the J.P.s of Somerset that the poor spinners and carders of Bath were out of work and short of food, a matter 'of dangerous consequence to the state'. The clothiers were to see them employed once again.[75]

During the second half of the century the repression of rogues who refused to work was not neglected. But, by contrast with the innovations in the system of poor-relief, the measures were relatively conservative—repetitions of or variations upon traditional themes. The 1572 act was certainly the most harsh of Elizabeth's reign. Vagabonds—a term widely defined to include unlicensed and wandering players, fortune-tellers, fencers, bearwards, jugglers, and university scholars—were to be whipped and bored through the ear at their first offence,

[72] 39 Elizabeth cc. 3, 4. Cf. cc. 5, 6. 43 Elizabeth cc. 2, 4, 9. Hughes & Larkin, III, no. 800. *TED* II. 346. Rosalind Mitchison, 'The Making of the Old Scottish Poor Law', *P&P* 63 (1974). For a contrary view to mine see Jordan, *Philanthropy*, ch. v.
[73] *LP* IV. ii. 4012, 4043–4, 4058, 4085, 4129, 4144–5, 4191, 4239, 4276. Hall, 745–6. Leonard, op. cit. 47–9.
[74] Ramsay, *City of London*, 272.
[75] *APC* XIV. 93, 272. Cf. ibid. X. 434; XIV. 7–8; XXVIII. 592–5, 611, 637.

and judged felons at their second, unless they could find someone to stand surety for them, which involved that person taking
them into service. At their third offence they would be treated
as felons without benefit of clergy. The penalties of ear-boring
and death were lifted in 1593, and a statute of 1597 ordered
that dangerous rogues were to be banished overseas or sent permanently to the galleys, while other vagabonds were to be
whipped and sent to houses of correction.[76] These houses of correction were—in a literal sense—the most constructive innovation of Elizabeth's reign for dealing with vagabonds. The act
of 1576 compelled each county to build at least one such house;
in 1597 it was made permissive, but no longer compulsory, for
J.P.s to erect them, but in 1610 they became once again mandatory in each shire. It is not clear whether the relaxation of 1597
was deliberate, nor, if it were so, what may have been the
reason.[77]

In the second half of the century provost-marshals were occasionally appointed for keeping order and punishing vagrants.[78]
Originally their office had been a military post for maintaining
discipline within the army. But in April 1558 the Marquis of
Winchester, as Lord-Lieutenant of various counties, was authorized to suppress rebels by martial law and to appoint a provost-marshal in each county to execute it. He seems to have
appointed at least one provost, Sir Giles Pool in London, and
in August that year a man was killed by one of Sir Giles's
troopers at St James's fair. Another such appointment is
recorded in 1570 for dealing with rogues, but only in 1588 does
the provost-marshal become a familiar figure. One was
appointed in each county to deal with disturbances at the
approach of the Armada.[79] Provosts were mainly used to control the serious disturbances created by disbanded sailors and
soldiers during the last fifteen years of Elizabeth's reign. They
were mostly appointed in London, the Home Counties, and the
shires of the south coast, all of them areas sensitive to the arrival,
passage, or congregation of unpaid and disbanded soldiery.
They were supported by bands of horsemen, paid out of county

[76] 14 Elizabeth c. 5. 35 Elizabeth c. 7. 39 Elizabeth c. 4. *TED* II. 328–9, 354–62.
[77] 18 Elizabeth c. 3. 39 Elizabeth c. 4. 7 James I c. 4.
[78] L. O. J. Boynton, 'The Tudor Provost-Marshal', *EHR* LXXVII (1962).
[79] Hughes & Larkin, II, no. 441. Boynton, op. cit. *APC* VI. 370; XVI. 126.

funds, and were authorized to execute offending vagrants by martial law. By the late 1590s London and the roads leading out of it were becoming alarmingly unsafe and provosts were again appointed in the City and in adjoining counties.[80] In the aftermath of the Essex revolt the Privy Council once more became alarmed at the number of masterless men around London and appointed provosts to ride the highways and drive all 'base persons' from the City and its confines. The Council however instructed them to some moderation, saying that it did not intend that 'the severity and rigours of the proclamation shall be executed against the multitude of such loose people'. They should merely be sent home. Only the seditious and dangerous should be punished.[81]

Over the sixteenth century as a whole, the political nation had markedly changed its attitude towards the impotent, the aged, and the deserving unemployed. Until 1552 the aged, sick, and impotent were expected to help themselves, under licence from the state after 1531; the only positive assistance provided by the government in the first half of the century was its attempt to prevent clothiers from dismissing their workmen in 1528 and the short-lived provisions of 1536. The move towards organized support by the community started, at a national level, with the statute of 1552; it culminated, in the 1570s, with the system of general taxation and the grudging provision of work for the able-bodied. There is thus a change from non-intervention to the licensing of begging, and then, through the provision of compulsory alms-giving, to an organized form of taxation and the creation of work.

No such progression is apparent in the treatment of those considered incorrigibly idle. They were to be repressed severely: that was common ground. But the form of repression swung back and forth from savagery to mere severity. Henry VII's statutes moderated the harshness of earlier laws. The act of 1531 introduced whipping. Following the wars of the 1540s vagabonds could be sent to the galleys, or even, as in 1547, enslaved.

---

[80] Hughes & Larkin, III, nos. 708, 715, 716, 796. *APC* XVIII. 222, 236, 266–7, 420; XIX. 34; XXVI. 118, 352; XXIX. 128, 132, 140. HMC, *Finch Papers*, I. 29. HMC, *Salisbury Papers*, XIII. 417. BL Landsowne MS 60, no. 86 (f. 207). Boynton, op. cit.

[81] *APC* XXXI. 164, 188. Hughes & Larkin, III, no. 809. For references to provosts in the seventeenth century see Hardy, *Hertford Records*, I. 58; *Worcester County Records*, II. lii, 485.

Two years later these draconian measures were repealed and whipping was reinstated. In 1572 extreme severity returned with the boring of ears and the threat of hanging. This was followed in 1576 by the establishment of houses of correction. Although the penalties of ear-boring and hanging were repealed in 1593, martial law, enforced by the provost-marshals, was from time to time imposed, with the added threat of banishment or galley-service. It is possible to see some connection between these changes and social conditions. The severities of 1531 followed serious economic distress in the late 1520s; the punishments of 1545 and 1547 were imposed in a time of war when disbanded soldiery were likely to cause trouble.[82] The imposition of martial law by provost-marshals was again a response to war, combined with the bad harvests of the mid-1590s and the Essex revolt of 1601.

It remains for the moment mysterious why 1572 and 1576 should have seen both harsher measures towards vagabonds and the introduction of compulsory levies for the impotent. Why should M.P.s, who evidently rejected a levy in 1536, have accepted one now? Economic conditions do not explain this, for prices were fairly stable in the 1560s and 1570s. Fears engendered by the rising of 1569 would probably have subsided by 1572. One possible explanation lies in the results of the widespread searches for vagabonds instituted by the Privy Council in 1570–1, perhaps in the aftermath of the rising of the northern earls.[83] The returns of J.P.s may have alarmed the central government and prepared the ground for legislation.[84] It is also possible that certain English towns, like Norwich, under serious pressure from the migrant poor, may have urged new national measures to lift the burden from their own burgesses. They had themselves, for two or three decades, been evolving new forms of policy on which the legislators could draw.

In the first half of the sixteenth century some urban schemes of poor-relief went far beyond anything enacted in Parliament. Since I am in this book mainly concerned with the operations and effectiveness of central government I shall treat these schemes briefly; but this should not obscure their importance.

---

[82] But see C. S. L. Davies, *EcHR* xix. 538, who doubts that conditions of war prompted the act of 1547.

[83] This was suggested to me by Dr Paul Slack.   [84] Below, 211, and n.107.

The City of London started voluntary collections of alms in 1533, and a compulsory local poor-rate was instituted fourteen years later, when the common council ordered that for one year a tax at the rate of half of one-fifteenth on moveables should be paid for the relief of the poor and should replace the earlier voluntary collection. After a year this was replaced by contributions from the City companies. Under Edward VI the two medieval hospitals—St Thomas's and St Bartholomew's—were put on a sounder footing, and a third—Christ's Hospital—was founded for the education of orphans. The old palace of Bridewell was given to the City by the Crown as a house of correction for employing the able-bodied poor.[85]

In the second city of the realm, York, schemes for the control and relief of the poor were started equally early. In 1515 the corporation ordered the wardens of the four wards to distinguish the sturdy beggars from the deserving and to give the latter a badge of recognition. Lists of beggars were kept in 1528, and two years later master-beggars were appointed to remove intruders. In 1550 a weekly poor-rate was imposed; and defaulters were threatened with imprisonment in 1561. In 1574 the poor were settled in the three York hospitals.[86] Norwich started later with poor-relief schemes, but was encouraged to take action by the alarming situation in 1570 when 'the citizens felt themselves aggrieved that the city was so replenished with great numbers, poor people, both men, women and children, to the number of 2,000 and 300 persons'. Indiscriminate alms-giving was forbidden and a compulsory tax levied for the relief of the poor. Vagabonds were placed in a Norwich version of Bridewell, women and children in St Giles's Hospital.[87]

Elsewhere the urban poor were relieved as much by private charity as by municipal regulation. Professor Jordan has calculated that in ten English counties £11,600 was given on average per decade for the relief of the poor in the period 1480–1540, and £39,000 per decade in the following sixty years. The impact of these benefactions can best be illustrated from Ipswich, where Henry Tooley's trust provided a poor-house, known as

[85] Leonard, *Poor Relief*, 25–40. *TED* II. 305–12.
[86] A. G. Dickens, 'Tudor York', in *VCH, Yorkshire: City of York*, 132–5.
[87] Pound, *Univ. of Birmingham Hist. Journ.* VIII. 135–62. *TED* II. 316–26. Leonard, 40–6.

Christ's Hospital, and two sets of almshouses. The Foundation received £161 in rents in 1577/78 and paid out £110 to the poor; in 1597/98 its rents had risen to £398 and its payments to £334. Outdoor relief was mainly provided by a weekly poor-rate, bringing in about £162 per annum in 1574. In Ipswich private benefaction and compulsory subscription seem effectively to have complemented one another.[88]

But there were towns which had neither an effective municipal scheme nor large charitable foundations. Worcester was one of them. Although £20 per annum was devoted to the poor of Worcester in the mid-sixteenth and early seventeenth centuries, the amount given in the last three decades of the sixteenth century was meagre. Municipal levies were ordered in the exceptionally severe times of 1553 and 1556–7; but otherwise this large town of 4,000 inhabitants seems to have relied mainly upon casual alms-giving.[89] The uneven spread of municipal relief and charitable giving produced a dangerous situation. The landless, unemployed, and vagrant poor tended to drift towards the towns hoping for work and food. If some towns were known to be generous or efficient in their schemes of relief they could expect to be flooded with the migrant bands of the destitute.[90] It may be that the voices of their representatives urged a more widespread national scheme in the Parliaments of 1571 and 1572. That must remain at present mere speculation. But it is certain that some such scheme was needed if the efforts of London, York, Norwich, Ipswich, and other towns were not to be frustrated.

How successful were the national schemes begun tentatively in 1563, continued more firmly in 1572 and 1576, completed in 1597 and 1601? Did they replace private charity and municipal initiative as the principal agencies for the relief and control of the poor? Were they operated at all except in years of crisis? How effectively were they supervised? Were the destitute succoured and the bands of migrants kept in their place? Which

---

[88] Jordan, *Philanthropy*, 369. J. Webb, *Poor Relief in Elizabethan Ipswich.*

[89] A. D. Dyer, *The City of Worcester in the Sixteenth Century*, 165–72, 240–3.

[90] P. Clark, 'The Migrant in Kentish Towns', in Clark and Slack (eds.), *Crisis and Order.* P. Styles, 'The Evolution of the Law of Settlement', *Univ. of Birmingham Hist. Journ.* IX (1963), 34–45.

aspects of the law received most attention from the authorities? To these questions only rather tentative answers can be given. Until more studies of poor-relief have been made in both rural and urban communities our knowledge must be incomplete. The preservation of local, and especially parochial, records has been uneven and their investigation has so far been limited.

In rural parishes, where little study has so far been done, it seems that, except in years of acute crisis, the poor were maintained at a very low level of subsistence. In at least four Essex parishes records have survived to show that collections were being made before 1597 and that receipts usually exceeded payments to the poor. There is nothing to suggest that these parochial collections were insufficient in normal times. In Kent there are signs of collections being made before 1597, although these are mostly sporadic. After the 1597 act was passed, parochial regulation seems to have been, in several parts of the county, methodical and adequate. At Shorne, for instance, there were eleven poor people, including William Fox, a lame boy who went about on stilts. The total collected in 1598 came to £9. 14s. 1d. and £7. 0s. 8d. was disbursed. This treatment was not generous, and the poor had to resort to door-to-door begging and casual loans as a supplement to the official benefits. But probably the combination of the poor-rate, charitable bequests, and indiscriminate alms-giving was just sufficient to keep them alive in normal times.[91]

In Norwich the poor-rate, begun before 1572, provided £530 for 237 persons in the early 1570s, rising to 390 persons in 1575. After this decade the Norwich scheme declined, perhaps because of a large influx of aliens. In Ipswich the poor-rate, begun in 1573, was the main source of outdoor relief. In Swansea regular collections, amounting to about £8 per annum, had begun after the act of 1563. At Worcester, on the other hand, parochial collections were meagre, and the corporation depended on a number of expedients, supplemented by a small

[91] F. G. Emmison, 'The Care of the Poor in Elizabethan Essex', *Essex Review* (Sept. 1953). Elizabeth Melling, *Kentish Sources*, IV: *The Poor* (Maidstone, 1964), part i. 12 ff. Cf. also the Bedfordshire evidence in Emmison, 'Poor Relief Accounts of Two Rural Parishes in Bedfordshire, 1563–98', *EcHR*, 1st ser. III (1931/32), and the Norfolk evidence in Pound, *Poverty and Vagrancy*, 80–1. K. V. Thomas, *Religion and the Decline of Magic* (1971), 673.

volume of private charity, which averaged only £5 per annum in the period 1570–1600.[92]

In country districts the main responsibility for the poor lay with the parish; in the towns with the municipality acting through its parishes. The Justice of the Peace had a supervisory role, being given somewhat more direct responsibility by the act of 1572 than he was to have after 1597, when the overseers were firmly allocated the principal responsibility for working the poor-laws. It is difficult to say how much interest was taken by J.P.s before 1570, since Quarter Sessions records are sparse for that period; indeed they are not at all numerous until the last decade of the century. The Wiltshire Quarter Sessions ordered in 1588 that anyone refusing to contribute to poor-relief should be imprisoned, and two persons were fined for that offence at subsequent meetings.[93] But most of the evidence for active intervention by J.P.s comes after the act of 1597. In April 1598 the Essex justices ordered that overseers were to be appointed in all parishes which had none at that time. A general house of correction was to be established at Coxall and twenty-two subsidiary houses in the various hundreds of the shire. A county rate of 1½d. was to be levied weekly from each parish, in addition to the ordinary parochial collection.[94] The West Riding justices ordered the statute to be proclaimed and publicly read. They laid down specific regulations for parishes in time of famine: rather than raise the poor-rate overseers might allow the poor to beg within their own parishes, but not outside; no one resident in a parish for three years could be removed to the place of his birth. A contribution of £33. 6s. 8d. was made for the poor of Richmond and Guisborough, both badly hit by the plague.[95] In Kent and Lancashire county rates were raised from which maimed soldiers could be assisted; and in Kent at least the J.P.s tried to persuade the better-off parishes to help the poorer.[96]

[92] Pound, *Univ. of Birmingham Hist. Journ.* VIII. Webb, op. cit. Dyer, *Worcester,* 165–72. Swansea Corporation Records; Benevolences or Poor Man's Tax, 1563–9.
[93] H. C. Johnson, *Minutes of Proceedings in Sessions, 1563 and 1574–92* (Wiltshire Arch. and Natural Hist. Soc. Records Branch, IV. 1949), 121–2, 123, 135.
[94] *TED* II. 362–4.
[95] J. Lister, *West Riding Sessions Rolls* (Yorks. Arch. Assoc., Record Series, III, 1888), 72–3, 84. *TED* II. 365–8.
[96] Melling, op. cit. 36 ff. J. Tait (ed.), *Lancashire Quarter Sessions Records* (Chetham Soc., n.s. LXXVII, 1917), 141.

The formal proceedings of Quarter Sessions were most important when the responsibility for maintaining a pauper or a child was disputed between two parishes or between the parish and the alleged father. The Privy Council laid down general rules for guidance in such cases and the Justices of Assize could be called upon to interpret the law; but most of the decisions in such cases had to be made by the J.P.s.[97] The West Riding Quarter Sessions heard a case in which a woman and child came begging into the township of 'Northowrom'; they stayed four or five days, and then the woman fell sick. The constable of the village, not wanting to be saddled with the child, carried her, on the point of death, to a poor man's house in the neighbouring village of Shelf, where she died. The inhabitants of Shelf protested that they were unable to support the child, which had only been in their village about three hours before it was orphaned. The justices ordered Northowram to pay one shilling and Shelf 4*d.* weekly for the upbringing of the child, which was to live in Shelf. It is not a pretty story, but it does show the rulers of the county trying to provide some kind of justice in the face of callous neglect by the local constable.[98]

Justices of the Peace were however anything but sentimental about children; and they were especially anxious to prevent the birth of illegitimate babies and to assign, if possible, paternity, so that the father could pay for the maintenance of the child. By a statute of 1576 two justices, acting out of sessions, could punish the parents and arrange for the child's upkeep.[99] Practice varied from one county to another: in some these cases were heard by the whole bench, in others by a pair of justices out of sessions. Most justices, like those in Gloucestershire, were concerned exclusively with the financial aspects of the case: if the child died the parents went unpunished. But in Hertfordshire and Middlesex the parents were usually flogged whatever happened, although the father might escape punishment if the baby died. If possible, both parents were whipped and put in the stocks with a notice proclaiming their crime. But often, in the absence of a proven father, the mother suffered alone. The

[97] Hughes & Larkin, III, no. 800. Cockburn, *History of English Assizes*, 168–70, 173–7.

[98] *TED* II. 365. *West Riding Sessions Rolls*, 39, 42–3, 91 ff.

[99] 18 Elizabeth c. 3. Also 7 James I c. 4.

punishment of the parents of bastards is one of the commoner
entries in Elizabethan Quarter Sessions records, but whipping,
or the threat of it, was probably not a very effective form of
contraception, and it did nothing to solve the primary problem
of maintenance.[100] If possible, a father must be found, but this
could prove difficult if, as in the case of Abigail Sherwood, who
came before William Lambarde, the mother was 'carnally
known' of many men.[101] Elaborate detective-work was then
needed to uncover the true father. Usually the word of the
mother given during childbirth was considered sufficient. But
the well-to-do and the respectable went to some lengths and
expense to avoid the stigma. William Woodward of Staffordshire tried to persuade his servant, John Hall, to confess to being
the father of Joan Wolley's bastard and promised to pay all
the expenses; when Hall refused to co-operate he was dismissed.
Mr Poynter, minister of Wiveton and Blakeney in Norfolk, having got Elizabeth Reve with child, advised her to lie with Sander
Dove and accuse him of being the father. When that scheme
failed William Sayers, known as William the Cripple, was
offered two cows, some money, and a house if he would marry
her. That device also was frustrated and Poynter's misdeeds
were reported to the archbishop.[102]

Justices of the Peace were also very active in the licensing
and suppressing of alehouses. Inns, tippling-houses, alehouses—the variety of names, gradations, and types seems to
be endless—were a constant source of suspicion and alarm to
the authorities. The unlicensed tippling-house was an important
staging-post in the movements of the migrant poor. It was also
the resort of criminals, the source of drunkenness, gambling,
and vice, and a stimulus to the unnecessary consumption of barley.[103] There was every reason, in the eyes of authority, for suppressing unlicensed houses and for being as niggardly as possible
in issuing licences. A good deal of the time of justices was taken

[100] W. B. Willcox, *Gloucestershire, a Study in Local Government, 1590–1640* (New Haven
1940), 67–9. Tait, *Lancashire Records*, 73–4, 83, 98, 102–3, 105. *Minutes of Proceeding
in Sessions* (Wiltshire), *passim*, and Melling, op. cit., *passim* for other instances.

[101] Conyers Read, *Lambarde and Local Government*, 30.

[102] S. A. H. Burne (ed.), *Staffordshire Quarter Sessions Rolls* (William Salt Soc., 1932),
III. 10, 203, 356. H. W. Saunders (ed.), *Official Papers of Sir Nathaniel Bacon* (Camden
Soc., 1915), 18–23.

[103] Clark, 'The Migrant in Kentish Towns', 117 ff. *TED* I. 330–1.

up in this sort of business. Edward Hext, a Somerset J.P., in a famous letter written to Burghley in 1596, complained that alehouses were too easily licensed: he estimated that in Wells alone the alehouses consumed 12,000 bushels of barley malt and acted as disorderly meeting-places for idle rogues. But Hext's letter is too alarmist to be taken as it stands. Tudor J.P.s may not have been as assiduous as their Victorian successors in suppressing rural taverns, but they were certainly alive to the problem.[104]

It is not easy to say how effectively the laws against vagrants were enforced. Under the 1572 act all vagrants not taken into service had to be tried at Quarter Sessions and therefore to be imprisoned before their appearance. The machinery of gaols and legal procedure could hardly have dealt with the numbers involved, and the 1597 act allowed constables and other parish officials to whip vagrants summarily; and in consequence punishment went unrecorded.[105] Such evidence as exists suggests that the laws were enforced in bursts of activity rather than by a constant application. Searches were conducted for vagrants in London during 1519, 1528, and 1546.[106] In 1570–1 the Privy Council evidently demanded widespread searches for vagrants and reports from J.P.s on the results. The certificates sent in suggest a great variation in the numbers of vagrants or in the thoroughness with which local officers conducted their searches, probably in both. In some places all was said to be quiet, in others several beggars were whipped and sent home. For instance, at Southeley, Nottinghamshire, twenty-three beggars were brought before Nicholas Powtrell, J.P., who found that two couples were licensed tinkers, punished the rest and sent them on their way.[107] The Middlesex Quarter Sessions records show no action against vagrants until 1573, when fifteen were punished. In 1575 three vagrants who had been once whipped were hanged for their second offence, according to the harsh statute then in force. This punishment of vagrants seems

[104] Johnson (ed.), *Minutes of Proceedings in Sessions* (Wiltshire), *passim*. *TED* ii. 344–5. Saunders, *Papers of Sir Nathaniel Bacon*, 58–64.

[105] I am grateful to Dr P. A. Slack for information on these points. Lambarde, *Eirenarcha* (1619), 189 ff. gives a full account of the powers of justices out-of-sessions.

[106] *LP* iii. i. 365; Add. i. 609; xxi. i. 147.

[107] *TED* ii. 326–7. Leonard, 80–3. *CSP Dom, 1547–80,* 51/11, 59/1, 60/27 and *passim* for 1570 and 1571.

to follow closely on the statute of 1572 and may well have been a consequence of it. Punishment was regularly imposed until about 1583 when the number of cases began to decline, almost to nothing. The next burst of activity by the Middlesex justices came, perhaps as the consequence of successive bad harvests, in 1590, when seventy-one persons were sentenced to be whipped and branded between October and December.[108] In the City, William Fleetwood, the Recorder, reacted sharply to the news that the Queen had been surrounded by rogues in her coach near Islington in January 1582. Searches were made and eighty-four vagrants brought in for punishment, most of whom came from far afield and few of whom had been in London for more than three or four months.[109] William Lambarde's charges to the special sessions of the Kent Grand Jury suggest that the years 1582 and 1583 may have seen campaigning against vagrants in that county as well.[110]

The Privy Council's greatest fit of concern about vagrants began in 1588 and lasted until the end of the reign. Probably the council became alarmed first at the threat to internal security posed by vagrants at a time of foreign war, and later by the addition of disbanded soldiers and sailors to the gangs of beggars. In June 1588, as the Armada approached, the Lord Mayor of London was ordered to co-operate with the J.P.s of Middlesex and Surrey in a general and secret search to end the nuisance of masterless men roaming the streets; in the following May he was told to press forty to fifty vagrants into service for Flushing. This was the beginning of a series of operations for search and arrest, which continued throughout the 1590s and was associated with the appointment of provost-marshals, discussed above.[111]

Returned soldiers seem to have posed the really acute problem for the government, especially in London, the Home Counties, and the southern shires. Habituated to fighting, understandably disgruntled at their callous treatment, capable of organizing themselves into bands, they alarmed councillors and city fathers by demonstrating for their arrears of pay and

---

[108] J. C. Jeaffreson, *Middlesex County Records* (1886–7), I. 81, 94–6, 101–3, 109, 190–1; and cf. tables on pp. 257–87.

[109] *TED* II. 335–6.

[110] Read, *Lambarde and Local Government*, 168, 173. Cf. also 25, 28–9.

[111] *APC* XVI. 136, 336, 416; XVII. 161. Above, 202.

robbing travellers on the highways out of London. When, in the mid-1590s, successive harvest failures sent the price of corn to unprecedented heights, the disintegration of order seemed near. War and bad harvests in combination were terrifying.[112] But the periodic sweeps and searches could and did produce order. Sir Henry Cocks reported to Burghley in 1589 that the provost and his men had cleaned Hertfordshire of 'bad persons'. The trouble was that such efforts were not kept up; and once the provost and his men retired from the scene the vagrants entered again from the wings.[113]

At most times the menace of the sturdy beggar was probably much less great than those in authority feared. William Lambarde's charges to the Grand Jury mention that many people thought the penalties on vagrants too harsh, and he went to some pains to argue that this was not so and that they must indeed be rigorously executed. That he was right in suspecting a certain lenience or tolerance is suggested by the charges often brought at Quarter Sessions against constables who had failed to prosecute vagabonds.[114] If the respectable freeholders of a Kentish Grand Jury thought the penalties too severe, and if constables were lax in bringing masterless men to justice, it may well be that the menace was not, at least in the 1580s, too alarming. Stories that there were 30,000 masterless men in London were certainly a wild canard, even if they were repeated by a Lord Chief Justice. The accounts by Dekker and Harman of confidence men, tricksters, cutpurses, and so on were perhaps based on a modest reality. They were also brilliant pieces of romantic journalism, which should not mislead us into thinking that every honest citizen went in constant fear of being set upon or bamboozled by rogues.[115] London in the reign of Elizabeth I was probably a safer place than mid-twentieth-century New York, except in those occasional harsh times when

[112] *APC* XVII. 416, 453; XVIII. 47–54; XX. 227; XXII. 129, 150–1; XXIII. 99, 157, 342; XXIV. 193–6; XXIX. 128. *TED* II. 339–46. Hughes & Larkin, III, nos. 736, 762, 777, 796, 809. BL Lansdowne MS 66, nos. 92–5 (ff. 241–7).

[113] Boynton, *EHR* LXXVII. *APC* XVIII. 420.

[114] Read, *Lambarde and Local Government*, 168, 172, 181. Johnson, *Minutes of Proceedings*, 71–3, 83. Tait, *Lancashire Records*, 106. Lister, *West Riding Sessions Rolls*, 118. Cf. S. D'Ewes, *Journals of All the Parliaments of Elizabeth*, 165, where an M.P. in 1571 described the laws against vagrants as 'over-sharp and bloody'. I owe this reference to Dr Slack.

[115] *Manningham's Diary* (Camden Soc., 1868), 73. P. A. Slack, 'Vagrants and Vagrancy in England, 1598–1664', *EcHR* XXVII (1974).

near-famine and the disruptions of war stretched the bonds of government to the uttermost. There were, no doubt, many miserable, rootless, destitute vagrants in Tudor England, but it is unlikely that many of them had the strength to threaten the social order.

Some broad conclusions may now be suggested about the poor of Tudor England and the impact of government regulation upon their condition. First, there can be no reasonable doubt that the real incomes of artisans and farm-labourers fell during the inflation of the sixteenth century. The glamour and brilliance of the Tudor court and the Elizabethan theatre shine against a backdrop of dark suffering for the majority of the population. Except spasmodically in the case of cloth-workers the government did nothing to help the wage-earner; indeed its actions were directed to keeping down his standard of living. Probably however economic forces were doing that effectively enough without assistance from the Crown, and the government's action had little effect in the field of wage-fixing. Second, there was a larger number of landless and dependent wage-earners than in the past. The government did try to limit this number by its agrarian legislation, and may have had some success in persuading landlords to act by agreement with their tenants rather than by arbitrary eviction. But since the real begetter of the landless worker was the rising population there was not much that the Crown could do to halt the trend. By the last quarter of the century the government accepted an obligation to provide work for the willing unemployed by setting up parish stocks and this may have been of some assistance.

Third, the measures of parish relief adopted in the reign of Elizabeth were probably sufficient, with the assistance of charitable bequests and indiscriminate alms-giving to keep the aged and 'impotent' poor alive at a very low level of subsistence during times of normal harvests. Over most of the country these measures, combined with the government's corn policy, helped to avoid widespread starvation. But in the north people did die of hunger in bad years: a report from Newcastle in 1597 spoke of 'sundry starving and dying in our streets and in the fields for lack of bread'; and other parts of northern England were probably still worse off. But in the Midlands and the south-east disease seems to have been a more dangerous killer than hunger—though it is hardly possible to make a clear distinction between the two. How far the government's measures were responsible for this happier fate it is impossible to say.[116]

Finally, the government did succeed after 1550 in its main objective: preventing large-scale riots and disturbances among the poor. As I shall show in a later chapter, even the combination of war and harvest failure in the 1590s produced no serious eruption by the dispossessed.[117]

[116] Andrew Appleby, 'Disease or Famine?', *EcHR* XXVI (1973), esp. 419.
[117] Below, ch. x. Also J. Walter and K. Wrightson, 'Dearth and the Social Order', *P&P* 71 (1976).

VII

Crime, Disorder, and the Law

The Tudors inherited an elaborate system of courts for dealing with crime and with private disputes: most institutions of government were indeed to some degree or other courts of justice. By the fifteenth century there were six main national law-courts. Common Pleas had original jurisdiction over real actions—cases involving landed property—and over some other civil litigation, its main business lying in the field of actions for debt. King's Bench had jurisdiction over felonies and over errors in civil cases from Common Pleas: towards the end of the fifteenth century it was steadily encroaching on the profitable ground of civil litigation. The earliest jurisdiction of Chancery was in common-law cases arising out of its own secretarial business, but the authority delegated to it by King and Council for correcting the deficiencies of common law became far more important: in this authority originated the equity jurisdiction wielded by the Lord Chancellor as the keeper of the King's conscience.[1] The fourth central court was the Exchequer, which had the jurisdiction of a court of pleas when the King's financial rights were in question. Connected with it were at least two courts known as the Exchequer Chamber. One of these, a panel of judges which met in the Exchequer and debated difficult points of law, was related to it only by the accidents of name and place. The other, which was beginning its development in the fifteenth century, was a court of equity similar in its procedure to Chancery.[2] Parliament was still considered to be the highest court of the realm, although in practice it had by 1500

[1] For general accounts of the law see: Alan Harding, *A Social History of English Law* (1966); T. F. T. Plucknett, *A Concise History of the Common Law* (5th edn., 1956); W. S. Holdsworth, *A History of English Law* (16 vols., 1903–52); A. W. B. Simpson, *An Introduction to the History of the Land Law* (1961). On Chancery: N. Pronay, 'The Chancellor, the Chancery and the Council at the End of the Fifteenth Century', in *British Government and Administration*, ed. H. Hearder and H. R. Loyn (Cardiff, 1974).

[2] At least two other courts known as Exchequer Chamber existed before the seventeenth century. One, extant in the middle ages, heard appeals from the Exchequer of Pleas; the other, formed in 1585, heard pleas in error from King's Bench.

shed its judicial functions, except for the trial of peers in the Upper House.[3] Finally, since the authority of all courts stemmed originally from the *curia regis*, the King and his Council still heard petitions and decided disputes. In the fifteenth century they remained, in an active sense, the most powerful court in the land.[4]

At the local level there had developed by the middle of the fourteenth century a system of assizes, connecting the central courts with the localities. The six assize circuits were travelled twice a year by two royal judges, who had authority from commissions of gaol delivery and of *oyer et terminer* to hear all criminal charges and from patents of assize to hear civil actions through the writ of *nisi prius*. Under this procedure cases begun in one of the common-law courts at Westminster could be heard by a local jury in the county concerned, sitting under the assize-judges. Thanks to the assizes the central courts were able to control legal decisions, maintain contact with the localities, and save local jurors the long and objectionable journey to Westminster.[5]

Within the counties themselves commissions of the peace had been firmly established by the fourteenth century. By 1485 Justices of the Peace were exercising powers of jurisdiction over murder, felony, and trespass. Since trespass included offences against economic regulations as well as such familiar misdemeanours as assault, forcible entry, riot, rout, and affray, the authority of the J.P.s extended over every sort of criminal offence except treason. By the fifteenth century the centre of their judicial activity lay in the general sessions of the peace, held four times a year, and later known as the Quarter Sessions.[6]

Below the level of Quarter Sessions and borough councils were the courts of manors and lordships—the courts baron and courts leet. Courts baron dealt with small civil disputes, courts leet with minor assaults and affrays. Although these courts 'belonged' to the lord of the manor and were presided over by

[3] Above, 33.   [4] Above, 27–33.

[5] Harding, *Social History of English Law*, ch. iii. J. S. Cockburn, *A History of English Assizes, 1558–1714* (Cambridge, 1972), chs. i–iii, vii.

[6] Harding, op. cit. 68–74. B. H. Putnam, *Proceedings before the Justices of the Peace in the Fourteenth and Fifteenth Centuries* (1938), intro., *passim*. W. Lambarde, *Eirenarcha* (1581) is the standard contemporary source on the jurisdiction of commissions of the peace.

his steward, the judgements in them were normally given by the suitors to the court, that is to say, by the tenants of the manor. For most men in medieval and sixteenth-century England this was the form of government that most continuously affected them; and it was to a large extent self-government. 'Is not every manor a little commonwealth, whereof the tenants are the members, the Lord the body, and the law the head?' asked John Norden.[7]

At the start of the Tudor period there were then several courts empowered to deal with criminal offences, the principal subject of this chapter: King's Bench, the royal Council, assizes, Quarter Sessions, and courts leet. But the government faced many obstacles in its attempts to enforce law and order. Some of these obstacles were embedded in the social structure and the moral attitudes of the time. Others were the result of technical deficiencies in the lawcourts. The general weakness of Tudor government, and of its predecessors, was its need to rely on the people at large, and especially upon men of influence and power, for many of the functions which are nowadays carried out by soldiers and policemen. Without a standing army or a police force the Crown had to rely upon private persons for protecting their own property, pursuing criminals, suppressing rebellion, and defending the country against invaders. Private persons must therefore have weapons and be ready to use them. The Statute of Winchester laid down in 1285 that 'every man have in his house harness for to keep the peace', and it went on to list the weapons suitable to each rank of society. In theory at least the statute was still in force in 1485, and an act of 1512 ordered its strict execution.[8] A society whose members were encouraged, indeed obliged, to go armed was not easily pacified. The instruments of violence were ready to hand.

The problem went well beyond the unruliness of the untamed masses: its importance lay in the predilection for violence displayed by members of the landed class, the very people who

[7] J. P. Dawson, *A History of the Lay Judges* (Cambridge, Mass., 1960), ch. iv. E. Kerridge, *Agrarian Problems in the Sixteenth Century and After* (1969), 31 and pp. 17–31 for a general yet succinct account of manorial courts.

[8] W. Stubbs, *Select Charters* (9th edn., Oxford, 1913), 468. 3 Henry VIII c. 3; 6 Henry VIII c. 2.

were supposed to assist the Crown. They were not necessarily illiterate thugs and robber barons. Many aristocrats in the fifteenth and sixteenth centuries were educated and cultured men.[9] But culture and education do not always make men pacific; and even if the head of a household was himself aloof from violence his servants and retainers were often not. Servants were touchy, proud, concerned about their honour and that of their masters. They were easily drawn into quarrels and their master was then morally obliged to protect them.

The problem of upper-class violence could be illustrated a dozen times over from the records of the fifteenth century, but one example will be enough.[10] Sir John Wynn of Gwydir in Caernarvonshire, writing in the early seventeenth century, tells of a family feud in late fifteenth-century Snowdonia. Two brothers-in-law had long been engaged in a quarrel, and one of them, Howell ap Rees, prepared an ambush for the other, Evan ap Robert, and hired an assassin to murder him. Howell and his followers attacked Evan's men, 'the bickering grew very hot', fighting lasted all day, but in the end the only man to die was the intended murderer, 'God bringing upon his head the destruction that he meant for another'. While the story shows the undisciplined resort to violence of two important landowners and their reliance upon gangs of retainers, it also reveals that the fights could be relatively innocuous. In a closely knit community, where the ties of kinship were many, men drew back from death-blows and the only man to die was the hired outsider. Significantly, the feud ended later with the death of Evan, 'for his three eldest sons were sister sons to Howell ap Rees ...'[11]

The more technical problems of law-enforcement began, at the very start of the business, with the difficulty of getting prosecutions brought. An offender might be brought for trial at assizes or Quarter Sessions in various different ways, none of which the Crown effectively controlled. Traditionally crimes were brought before the circuit-judges or the J.P.s by presentments made by the grand jury of the county. The grand

[9] K. B. McFarlane, *Nobility of Later Medieval England*, ch. vi.

[10] See above, 12. Also *inter alia*, Stone, *Crisis of the Aristocracy*, ch. v, and Storey, *End of the House of Lancaster*, *passim*.

[11] J. Wynn, *History of the Gwydir Family*, ed. J. Ballinger (Cardiff, 1927), 37–40, 45.

jury might make such presentments out of its own knowledge. More likely it was endorsing, as *billa vera*, accusations which came to it from others: the constables of hundreds had to present miscreants in their own territories; J.P.s brought forward men whom they had bound over or imprisoned out of sessions; private persons, acting as informers, could prefer charges on their own behalf.[12] The technical nomenclature of these proceedings is confusing. Lambarde confidently asserted that presentment was the denunciation by jurors; that information was accusation by private persons; and that indictment was the finding of a true bill by the grand jury on the accusation of another. But the records do not always seem to have followed these neat definitions.[13] However what matters is the evident reluctance of officials to bring forward charges and of grand juries to endorse them.

Even when charges were brought and process issued against the accused, he was not easily brought into court. Unpaid constables were unlikely to exert themselves very hard in the making of arrests. Sheriffs and their officers were too distant to bother and were often content to report simply that a defendant could not be found. Fugitive criminals might escape trial by fleeing into the sanctuary of consecrated ground. Once he was arraigned before the justices and the trial jury, the fate of the accused was uncertain. Trial juries were notoriously unreliable. Supposed to know the facts of a case and therefore to require no evidence from witnesses, they were often ignorant of what had happened. But if they were innocent of first-hand knowledge they might often be primed with loaded and second-hand information by interested parties. They might also be bribed and bullied by the rich and powerful into a partial verdict. Once convicted a man—though not a woman—could claim benefit of clergy and escape hanging for felonies, though not for treason (and not for misdemeanours either). The ability to read became the test, and as literacy spread it became a fairly simple test to pass. Provided that he could read, the convicted

---

[12] J. G. Bellamy, *Crime and Public Order* (1973), ch. v. J. S. Cockburn, *History of Assizes*, 101–18. A. Harding, *Social History of English Law*, 76–8. The best account of prosecution and other aspects of criminal procedure is now J. H. Baker, 'Criminal Courts and Procedure at the Common Law, 1550–1800', in J. S. Cockburn (ed.), *Crime in England*, *1550–1800* (1977), ch. i.

[13] W. Lambarde, *Eirenarcha* (1619), 485–504. Bellamy, op. cit. 122–3.

man would be branded and handed over to the bishop. Unless he was a notorious criminal or unless someone was prepared to object, he was then admitted to compurgation—a process by which twelve or more clerks swore to his innocence, and he was then released. Most such criminous clerks were evidently released, but usually after some years of rigorous imprisonment. They escaped with their lives, but not without punishment.[14]

Throughout the Tudor period Crown and Parliament attempted to remove some of these obstacles to effective execution of the law. Statutes, proclamations, and general exhortations were issued and reissued, sustained and enlivened by the impressive sounds of sixteenth-century rhetoric. Officially the monarchy was supposed to maintain peace and order. 'The King our sovereign lord, having a tender respect to the surety, peace and restfulness of all his true subjects, for the conservation of his peace ...' ran a proclamation of Henry VII.[15] That was received doctrine. In practice the complete suppression of violence, the creation of an effective machinery for prosecution, and the removal of corruption and partiality from trials were impossible. The monarchy had to rely upon landowners for continuous service and could not afford to alienate them by excessive severity or constant nagging. The most it could do was to bring violence within tolerable limits and to make marginal improvements in the execution of the law.

The law relating to retainers was already stringent when Henry VII succeeded to the throne. A statute of 1390 had forbidden commoners to retain men for life, and another of 1468 forbade the giving of liveries to any but household servants and other officers; these were however categories which could be quite widely extended, so that under Edward IV the intentions of the statute were far from being fulfilled. Henry VII's own proclamations and enactments were much more conservative than many historians have thought. They certainly did not intend or demand the destruction of retinues—which would have been well beyond the reach of any monarch. But the statute of 1504 did bring retinues under royal control by insist-

[14] P. Heath, *The English Parish Clergy on the Eve of the Reformation* (1969), 119–34. Bellamy, op. cit., ch. v and 200–1.   [15] Hughes & Larkin, I, no. 16.

ing that no man could keep retainers without licence from the Crown. With Henry's death this statute lapsed and the law rested once again on the act of 1468. Thereafter the Crown relied on proclamations rather than statutes, and the issue of royal licences continued to be the most effective means of controlling retinues.[16]

The Crown also tried to regulate the use of weapons, ensuring that while men possessed the right arms for war, they did not have those which were likely to upset the peace, disturb the social order, or encourage poaching. The growing use of firearms was a particular danger. While a nobleman might be protected from traditional weapons by his skill in swordsmanship or the number of his followers, there was no such guarantee against gunpowder. 'Many a time and oft', wrote a contemporary German, 'it happens that a brave and manly hero is killed by a shot from a craven who would not dare to look him in the face.'[17] The Privy Council expressed a similar fear when ordering the arrest of a murderer in 1612. The murder was particularly heinous since it had been committed in cold blood with a pistol, 'a weapon from which no man can be safe, nor any defence protect'.[18]

In 1514 there appeared the first of a series of statutes against the use of guns.[19] A later act, of 1542, spoke of the 'divers, detestable, and shameful murders, robberies, felonies, riots and routs with crossbows, little short handguns and little hagbuts'. Denouncing in one sentence, the statute nevertheless made concessions in others, by allowing guns that could not be concealed. Men might practise shooting with their guns, provided that these were not less than 36 inches long—or in the case of hagbuts 27 inches—since the defence of the realm required trained marksmen. The act also allowed men living two furlongs outside a town to keep guns for the defence of their houses.[20] Two years later a proclamation allowed still further relaxation: since the defence of the realm necessitated 'subjects skilled and exercised in the feat of shooting in handguns and hagbuts', all

[16] The critical statute is 19 Henry VII c. 14. For other details and references see above, 1–3, and more especially A. Cameron, 'The Giving of Livery ... in Henry VII's Reign', *Renaissance and Modern Studies*, xviii (1974).

[17] J. R. Hale, 'War and Public Opinion in the Fifteenth and Sixteenth Centuries', *P&P* 22 (1962), 29.   [18] T. Rymer, *Foedera*, xvi. 721–2.

[19] 6 Henry VIII c. 13. Cf. Hughes & Larkin, i, no. 121.   [20] 33 Henry VIII c. 6.

penalties on their possession were lifted, provided that they were not used for shooting game near royal palaces or without the permission of the landlord. Such relaxation was dangerous. The 'plague of war' having been removed, the King in 1546 ordered a fresh prohibition; and a statute of 1548 spoke of the damage done to buildings by 'men of light conversation'.[21] These twists and turns neatly illustrate the Crown's dilemma: the demands of war and self-protection pushed it in the direction of permissiveness; the preservation of peace and of game pulled it back to restriction.[22]

While fire-arms were the government's main concern they were not its only worry. Swords were getting longer, rapiers were becoming fashionable. In 1562 the Queen forbade the wearing of 'long swords and rapiers, sharpened in such sort as may appear the usage of them can not tend to defense, which ought to be the very meaning of wearing of weapons in times of peace, but to murder and evident death'. The Council in the Marches of Wales, apprehensive of disturbances at Ludlow fair, told the town bailiffs that 'if they find any ... weapon above six feet long they shall use their discretion to reduce it to a reasonable length'.[23]

Limitations upon retainers and weapons were part of the general attempt to moderate and control social habits. More specific reforms were made in legal procedures. Medieval definitions of crime had developed under the combined and conflicting directions of lawyers in King's Bench, the Commons in Parliament, and the Justices of the Peace in the countryside.[24] The results were often vague and uncertain. Some effort was made under the Tudors to define, and still more effort to extend, the scope of felonies—that is to say, crimes punishable by death. Hunting at night or in disguise, fishing in another's pond at night, taking hawks' eggs from the lands of the King became felonies under Henry VII and Henry VIII.[25] The

---

[21] Hughes & Larkin, I, no. 271; III, no. 225. 5. 2 & 3 Edward VI c. 14.

[22] See also Hughes & Larkin, II, nos. 611, 641; III, no. 766.

[23] Ibid. II, no. 493. Cf. nos. 432, 542. R. Flenley, *A Calendar of the Register of the Council in the Marches of Wales* (1916), 157.

[24] See the section by Plucknett in Putnam (ed.), *Proceedings before the Justices*, cxxxiii–clxi.

[25] 1 Henry VIII c. 7; 31 Henry VIII cc. 2, 12; 32 Henry VIII c. 11. These were repealed by 1 Edward VI c. 12, but were mostly revived by 3 & 4 Edward VI c. 17.

abduction of women was made felony by the second Parliament of Henry VII but reduced under Mary to an offence carrying only the penalty of fine or imprisonment.[26] Servants who stole the goods of their masters were treated as felons from 1529, with a brief interlude under Mary.[27] Buggery with man or beast became a felony under Henry VIII; and although the penalties were reduced under a general act of repeal at the beginning of Mary's reign, the full punishment was restored by the second Parliament of Elizabeth, which uttered the admonition that repeal had led to an increase in the offence.[28] Similarly, witchcraft—the invocation of spirits to gain money, to destroy a person's body, or to provoke the love of another—became felony by a statute of Henry VIII.[29] Although the penalties were reduced by the act of repeal in 1547, the second Parliament of Elizabeth, complaining that offences had subsequently increased, subjected witches to capital punishment at the first offence if the victim died, or otherwise at the second offence.[30] False prophecies, based on the arms of noblemen or gentlemen, became felonies in 1542, but after the repeal of this act with others in 1547 came to be punished by fine and imprisonment.[31] One other 'promotion' of an offence might be mentioned to illustrate the growing severity of the law. Following an attempt by a cook named Richard Roose to poison the Bishop of Rochester, poisoning was made high treason and its perpetrators condemned to death by boiling. This statute also was repealed in 1547.[32]

The general pattern of this legislation shows an extension of capital offences under Henry VII and Henry VIII, a period of respite for criminals in the early part of Edward's reign and again under Mary, with severity reintroduced after 1549 and once more under Elizabeth. This suggests that the Crown was probably at least in part responsible for the extension of felony;

[26] 3 Henry VII c. 3. 4 & 5 Philip & Mary c. 8.
[27] 21 Henry VIII c. 7. 28 Henry VIII c. 2. 1 Mary st. 1, c. 1. 5 Elizabeth c. 10.
[28] 25 Henry VIII c. 6. 28 Henry VIII c. 6. 2 & 3 Edward VI c. 29. 5 Elizabeth c. 17.   [29] 33 Henry VIII c. 8.
[30] 1 Edward VI c. 12. 5 Elizabeth c. 16. K. V. Thomas, *Religion and the Decline of Magic*, ch. xiv, esp. 525–6. See also 1 James I c. 12, and Alan Macfarlane, *Witchcraft in Tudor and Stuart England* (1970), 14–15.
[31] 33 Henry VIII c. 14. 3 & 4 Edward VI c. 15. 5 Elizabeth c. 15 revived the act of Edward VI. See Thomas, op. cit. 471.
[32] 22 Henry VIII c. 9.

but it is likely that the Commons were willing partners in the process. The act against buggery was drafted by the King's judges. The act against poisoning seems to have been the result of Henry VIII's own perturbation at the attempt on the life of Bishop Fisher—ironically enough, since he was a few years later to be himself responsible for Fisher's death. The King himself addressed the House of Lords on the subject and the bill was prepared by his councillors. Reports in 1538 of the use of black magic against the King, Prince Edward, and the Duke of Norfolk *may* have helped forward statutory action against witchcraft: but there is no direct evidence of any connection.[33]

A further extension of capital punishment and some definition of the criminal law was achieved by the sixteenth-century statutes relating to benefit of clergy. These statutes aimed at preventing men from benefiting more than once from their clerical status, at restricting the benefits allowed to men in minor orders, and at removing certain offences from the operation of benefit of clergy. An act of 1489 ordered that all clerks in minor orders convicted of crimes should be branded, 'on the brawn of the left thumb', with M for murder and with T for theft and other felonies. In 1532 benefit of clergy was entirely denied to those in minor orders and in 1540 even those in major orders were to be branded and denied its protection more than once. In practice these statutes probably made little difference; men continued throughout the century to escape hanging merely by being able to read, and there is evidence of branded men successfully escaping death. About 20 per cent of felons obtained their clergy in the late sixteenth and seventeenth centuries.[34]

Perhaps more important was the denial of benefit of clergy for certain crimes. Murder, robbery in church, or on a highway or in the victim's own house ceased to carry it after 1489. Under Henry VIII it was denied to servants stealing from their masters; under Edward VI to men convicted of breaking into a house and putting the owners into dread, of buggery, horse-stealing, robbing houses while the owner was asleep, and of fleeing from one shire into another after stealing; under Mary to

---

[33] Lehmberg, *Reformation Parliament*, 125, 185. *LP* XIII. i. 487; ii. 1200.

[34] 4 Henry VII c. 13. 23 Henry VIII c. 1. 32 Henry VIII c. 3. Heath, *English Parish Clergy*, 119–33. Cockburn, *History of Assizes*, 128–9.

accessories to petty treason and felony; under Elizabeth to men found guilty of 'stealing privily', of rape and burglary, of abducting heiresses, and of breaking into a house and stealing from it in daytime. After 1576 those who successfully claimed their clergy were no longer to be handed over to the Church courts but could be imprisoned in the civil.[35]

There was not a great deal that the Crown or Parliament could do—short of establishing a professional police-force—to ensure that criminals were prosecuted and brought to court. A statute of Henry VII enabled justices of assize and J.P.s to try cases of misdemeanour on information alone, without the grand jury having to find a true bill; but this measure had a short life, and was repealed by the first Parliament of Henry VIII. Two statutes of Mary's reign ordered J.P.s to examine suspects and witnesses in charges of felony, but the acts may well have had only a marginal effect on the actual conduct of prosecutions.[36] Provisions were made to prevent murderers escaping if they struck the fatal wound in one county and the victim died in another, and to punish accessories to robberies living in adjoining counties. Special laws were made to control crime in Wales and to prevent the movement of felons back and forth over the Severn.[37] The main attack on the elusiveness of criminals was made on the privilege of sanctuary. Criminals and debtors could find two sorts of refuge in the later middle ages. A criminal taking refuge in any church had to abjure the realm after forty days or stand trial.[38] But there were certain privileged jurisdictions where the King's writ did not run at all and where wanted men could remain permanently immune from justice. Some were secular lordships, like the lordships of Tyndale in the north or the Marcher lordships of Wales. Others

---

[35] 4 Henry VII c. 2. 27 Henry VIII c. 17. 1 Edward VI c. 12. 2 & 3 Edward VI cc. 29, 33. 5 & 6 Edward VI cc. 9, 10. 4 & 5 Philip & Mary c. 4. 8 Elizabeth c. 4. 18 Elizabeth c. 7. 39 Elizabeth cc. 9, 15. Heath, op. cit. 123–7. See also Plucknett, in Putnam (ed.), *Proceedings before the Justices*, cxl, cxlv, cxlix.

[36] 11 Henry VII c. 3. 1 Henry VIII c. 6. 1 & 2 Philip & Mary c. 13. 2 & 3 Philip & Mary c. 10. J. H. Langbein, *Prosecuting Crime in the Renaissance* (Cambridge, Mass., 1974), part i, attaches great importance to the Marian statutes. But see J. S. Cockburn, 'Early Modern Assize Records as Historical Evidence', *Journ. Soc. Archivists*, v (1975), esp. 226–7.

[37] 2 & 3 Edward VI c. 24. 26 Henry VIII cc. 5, 6, 11, 12.

[38] Isobel D. Thornley, 'The Destruction of Sanctuary', in *Tudor Studies*, ed. R. W. Seton-Watson (1924).

were ecclesiastical franchises, like the notorious sanctuaries of Westminster and St Martin-le-Grand in London. Successive onslaughts were made upon the immunities of secular lordships. Tyndale was brought within royal jurisdication under Henry VII. The jurisdictions of Welsh Marcher lordships were reduced by a series of acts under Henry VIII. Above all, a major statute of 1536 removed the criminal jurisdiction of all liberties into the King's hands. A few years later all the permanent sanctuaries were abolished and only the forty-day refuge in church or churchyard was allowed. This did not completely end the refuges afforded to fugitives; but they were reduced to tolerable proportions, though not so drastically reduced as Thomas Cromwell, who drafted the original but much amended bill, would have liked.[39]

Various statutes were devised to control juries and to prevent them from giving false verdicts. Procedures were introduced to enable parties who thought themselves deprived of justice to bring actions of attaint against the jury. The penalties for suborning witnesses were increased under Elizabeth to £40.[40] The Crown tried to ensure that juries were made up of respectable persons, prosperous enough to resist bribery. Sheriffs were said to omit the better-off from panels and 'return the poorer and simpler sort, least able to discern the causes in question'. But it was difficult here to strike a balance: too high a property-qualification reduced the pool of recruits; too low allowed in the 'poorer sort'.[41]

These were changes made to regulate the procedures of old-established courts. In addition the Tudors developed conciliar jurisdictions intended to fill gaps in the standard common-law procedures. The King's Council had long had power to hear petitions and to regulate the course of the law. Under the Tudors, especially in the reign of Henry VIII, this authority was developed into the more formal jurisdiction of Star Chamber, which had the power to hear misdemeanours, especially riots, perjury, and forgery. The Tudors also put upon a permanent and organized footing two courts tentatively estab-

[39] 11 Henry VII c. 9. 27 Henry VIII c. 24. 1 Edward VI c. 12 somewhat restored sanctuary provisions. They were totally abolished as late as the reign of James I by 21 James I c. 28. Elton, *Reform and Renewal*, 136–8.

[40] 11 Henry VII cc. 24, 25. 23 Henry VIII c. 3. 26 Henry VIII c. 4. 32 Henry VIII c. 9. 5 Elizabeth c. 9. [41] 27 Elizabeth c. 6.

lished under Edward IV, the Councils in the North and the Welsh Marches, with powers very similar to those of Star Chamber. All these had a more rapid and informal procedure than the older courts and were free from the weaknesses of the jury system. It is false to suppose that they administered a new kind of prerogative law. Wolsey's remark about teaching men the 'new law of the Star Chamber' has left a misleading legacy.[42] They administered the normal, established common law of the land, through procedures which were free of some of the restraints and rigidities of other courts; and significantly Star Chamber, under the guise of hearing cases of riot, dealt with a substantial number of civil disputes. During the sixteenth century these courts heard large numbers of cases and occupied a major and envied position in the legal system.[43]

One other change might be mentioned here. Towards the end of the sixteenth century the Crown began to use in peacetime an official who had previously only been seen during war and rebellion. This was the provost-marshal. The first peacetime appointment was apparently made in London in 1570, when a provost was appointed to deal with rogues and vagabonds. In later years they appeared in several shires with a specific warrant to arrest and punish mutinous or disbanded soldiers. But their authority extended only to wandering vagrants, the masterless men so feared by Tudor society. The provost was certainly no lawcourt, but he was very much a legal officer with the power not merely to apprehend, but also summarily to execute miscreants by martial law. Whether that power was exercised at all widely it is difficult to say.[44]

Such were some of the measures by which Crown and Parliament tried to improve—or at any rate to tighten—the execution

---

[42] *LP* II. ii, app. 38 (p. 1539).

[43] T. G. Barnes, 'Star Chamber Mythology', *American Journal of Legal History*, v (1961), 1–11; id., 'Due Process and Slow Process in the Star Chamber', ibid. VI (1962), 221–49. R. R. Reid, *The King's Council in the North* (1921), *passim*. Penry Williams, *The Council in the Marches* (Cardiff, 1958), *passim*. J. A. Guy, 'The Early Tudor Star Chamber', in *Legal History Studies*, ed. Dafydd Jenkins (Cardiff, 1975), 122–8. Id., 'Wolsey, the Council and the Council Courts', *EHR* XCI (1976). J. A. Guy, *The Cardinal's Court*, *passim*. On the civil side Chancery and Requests were developed by the Tudors to remedy defects in that area of jurisdiction.

[44] L. O. J. Boynton, 'The Tudor Provost-Marshal', *EHR* LXXVII (1962). Above, 202.

of the criminal law. How effective were they? It is best to begin with the punishment of the more serious crimes—felonies—and to move on from them to other aspects of the world of violence and disorder.

Although some felonies might be tried in King's Bench and although noble felons were arraigned before their peers, most capital trials were held before assizes and Quarter Sessions. The demarcation between these courts changed during the sixteenth century. At its start Quarter Sessions had the power to try all felonies and almost certainly exercised that power.[45] In the course of the century they tended however to remit grand larcenies—theft of goods over 12*d*., which carried the death penalty—to assizes; and after 1590 the J.P.s were encouraged by their commission to refer there all cases of difficulty. But although Lambarde asserted in 1581 that gaol deliveries were already being held by the assize judges, evidence from his own writings and from other records shows that this was not always so. However, it is likely that in practice capital felonies were usually heard at assizes from the final quarter of the sixteenth century onwards, except in Middlesex, where the Quarter Sessions had an exceptional commission of Gaol Delivery.[46]

But that only compounds our difficulties. While Quarter Sessions records begin to reappear, after a long gap, in the second half of the sixteenth century, the records of assizes are sparse. In effect only those for the Home Circuit have survived for this period. Depositions for the northern circuit begin in 1613 and the western circuit provides an order book from 1629 to 1685. For those cases which mattered most to the accused—cases literally of life and death—our knowledge must remain restricted. Even in Quarter Sessions, where the records of several counties are available, the picture remains incomplete because the survival of records has been uneven: indictments are common enough; the outcome of cases is more difficult to discover.[47]

[45] Under the provisions of 34 Edward III c. 1.

[46] Cockburn, *History of Assizes*, 86–97. Lambarde, *Eirenarcha* (1581), 449. T. G. Barnes, *Somerset, 1625–1640* (Oxford, 1961), 50–3. E. J. Mercer, 'Middlesex County Record Office', *Archives*, v (1963), 30–9.

[47] Cockburn, *History of Assizes*, 333–5. T. G. Barnes, *Somerset Assize Orders, 1629–40* (Somerset Record Soc. LXV, 1959). On the problem of assize records see Cockburn, *Journ. Soc. Archivists*, v (1975). The publication of indictment files for the home circuit has begun in 1975 under the editorship of Dr Cockburn in the PRO series, *Calendar of Assize Records*.

The difficulties of getting criminals prosecuted were certainly not overcome in either assizes or Quarter Sessions. J.P.s were sometimes negligent, and occasionally corrupt, failing to examine miscreants and bring forward indictments. The grand jury, to judge from Lambarde's criticisms, was too often slack in making presentments. In consequence, he said, the Crown had had to fall back upon the unsatisfactory expedient of the common informer. Presentment juries must realize that they were not fixing the fate of the accused but were merely deciding whether or not he should be called to trial. They were far too often content to report *omnia bene* when they ought to proclaim *omnia pessime*.[48]

There is not much sign that Tudor lawcourts were more successful than their predecessors in securing the attendance of the accused. In Staffordshire the returns of writs to Quarter Sessions declare time after time that the party sought is nowhere to be found and has no goods upon which distraint may be made. About 20 per cent of those indicted at Sussex Assizes were not brought before the court.[49]

The effectiveness and justice of the trials themselves are difficult to assess. Criminal cases were dispatched at a gallop in assizes: fifty might be heard in a day. Trial juries were as capricious as presentment juries and the gentlemen on the commission of the peace were not inhibited from partiality.[50] The attitude to evidence was sometimes cavalier. Lord Burghley, generally considered a cautious and judicious man, once remarked in Star Chamber, not, admittedly, in assizes, that although the evidence against a prisoner was slight 'he who is once evil in the highest degree is always presumed to be evil'.[51] Yet the accused was not entirely naked before the caprices of the courtroom. The transfer of serious cases to assizes at least meant that where life and death were in question trained and senior lawyers presided over the proceedings. While judges frequently intervened in trials and made little pretence at impartiality, they sometimes advocated clemency.

---

[48] Cockburn, *History of Assizes*, 103. Conyers Read (ed.), *William Lambarde and Local Government* (Cornell, 1962), 55 ff. Lambarde, *Eirenarcha* (1619), 401.

[49] S. A. H. Burne (ed.), *Staffordshire Quarter Sessions Records* (William Salt Soc., 1931), I. 295 ff. J. S. Cockburn (ed.), *Calendar of Assize Records: Sussex Indictments, Elizabeth I* (1975), *passim*.

[50] Cockburn, *History of Assizes*, 109.   [51] Hawarde, 41–2.

Nicholas Bacon argued that it was 'better for a man to be twice whipped than once hanged' and his attitude may not have been untypical. The evidence suggests that professional judges were by and large more inclined to mercy than the local landowners who sat on the commissions of the peace.[52]

Contemporary opinion seems generally to have held that thieves had much too good a chance of escaping justice. Edward Hext, a Somerset J.P., complained to Burghley in 1596 that most of them were never brought to trial, 'for they are grown so exceeding cunning by their often being in the gaol as the most part are never taken'; his own words contradict his thesis. But he may have been nearer the mark when he claimed that 'the simple countryman and woman ... are of opinion that they would not procure a man's death for all the goods in the world'. The severity of the law may well have hindered its enforcement.[53] The emotional expostulations of men like Hext are not however reliable evidence. Unfortunately statistics drawn from the legal records of the time have also to be approached with great caution.[54] Assize records for Sussex and Essex show clearly that the number of indictments for felony increased during the second half of the sixteenth century, but we cannot say whether this was the result of a rising crime-rate or more vigorous prosecution. Figures for Sussex, Essex, and Middlesex suggest that between 20 per cent and 36 per cent of those brought to trial for felony were acquitted; and that between 20 per cent and 30 per cent were sentenced to hanging. Several of those convicted of felony avoided death: for instance, between 28 per cent and 36 per cent of those found guilty pleaded benefit of clergy. Dr Cockburn has indeed suggested that over the whole period 1558–1714 only 10 per cent of those convicted of capital crimes were actually executed. It is possible that the sixteenth century achieved a higher rate of conviction than the fourteenth, but such comparisons are not very reliable. Given the ease with which an accused man could avoid appearing in court, the evident reluctance of grand juries to return a true bill, the chance of obtaining benefit of clergy, and the possibility of a pardon, criminals had a fair chance of avoiding execution. If Blackstone was right in saying that 'crimes are

---

[52] Cockburn, *History of Assizes*, 125.   [53] *TED* II, 340–1.
[54] Cockburn, *Journ. Soc. Archivists*, V.

more effectually prevented by certainty than by severity of punishment', the deterrent effect of the criminal law was not very great.[55]

One crime—witchcraft—deserves special mention, partly because it has been more carefully studied than others and partly because it illustrates important points about the execution of the law. In late sixteenth-century Essex witchcraft ranked second only to theft in the number of prosecutions at assizes, making up 13 per cent of the total in the 1580s. Between 1560 and 1599, 163 persons, mostly women, were charged with witchcraft at Essex assizes, in 277 separate indictments. However, witchcraft prosecutions were concentrated at assizes and occurred much less often in other courts. If the number of prosecutions in all courts from those Essex villages is counted, witchcraft ranks below sexual offences, absences from church, thefts, and assaults. Even so, the indictment of twenty persons for witchcraft in three villages over forty years shows that it was not an occasional freakish occurrence: it was less common than fornication but more often prosecuted than murder. That was the situation in Essex. In other counties for which we have comparable evidence—those on the Home Circuit—it was much less common and the Essex total exceeded that of the other four counties put together. But, while Essex was clearly exceptional in the south-east, it is possible that some counties in other regions had a large tally of witches.[56]

Evidence of witchcraft, compared with that available for theft, was difficult to get, and a standard manual for J.P.s stated that 'half-proofs are to be allowed and are good causes of suspicion'.[57] These half-proofs secured a large number of convictions. Of the witches indicted at Essex assizes between 1560 and 1680 slightly more than 50 per cent were dismissed or found not guilty, rather fewer than 25 per cent were condemned to death, and about 20 per cent were imprisoned. More than half

---

[55] My figures are drawn from Cockburn, *Sussex Indictments*; J. Samaha, *Law and Order in Historical Perspective: the Case of Elizabethan Essex* (1974); J. C. Jeaffreson, *Middlesex County Records*; and Cockburn, *History of Assizes*, 127–32. They must be treated with caution: until the appearance of Dr Cockburn's introductory volume to the *Calendars of Assize Records* all conclusions on this subject must be regarded as provisional. On trial procedures see Baker in Cockburn (ed.), *Crime in England*, ch. i.

[56] Macfarlane, *Witchcraft in Tudor and Stuart England*, 24–30, 61, 97–8.

[57] Michael Dalton, *Country Justice*, quoted in ibid. 16.

this last group seem to have died in prison. The proportion of acquittals was therefore higher than for other felonies, but the percentage sentenced to hanging was about the same. Since witches were mostly elderly women it is unlikely that they were able to avoid appearance in court by flight, and a higher proportion of accused witches probably stood trial than did accused thieves. The number hanged is high considering that witchcraft only became a capital charge at the second offence.[58]

Almost all prosecutions for witchcraft were begun by private persons who believed themselves to be injured by the witch. The trials were the expression of quarrels and friction between neighbours. There is no evidence of the Crown or its agents trying to suppress witchcraft. The statute against it provided a means by which injured persons could secure a remedy. By prosecuting the witch they might secure revenge, prevent her continuing her practices, and also, so it was thought, lift the curse which she had laid upon them. In this respect the witch-craft trials are typical of much of the apparatus of the criminal law. It was a means for the private redress of injury rather than a machine for imposing some abstract order upon society. The statistics of sixteenth-century crime do not reveal which crimes were most frequently committed but which offences private persons felt sufficiently aggrieved about to prosecute. Hence, in the three sample Essex villages, twenty witches were prosecuted but only five drunkards. It is hard to believe that there were four times as many witches as there were drunkards; but witches were thought to do more harm to others than the inebriated.[59]

Punishment was severe to the point of barbarism. Hanging involved slow strangulation rather than the swift dislocation of the vertebrae; and it usually involved forfeiture of all the felon's goods to the Crown. A felon who wished to preserve his goods for his family might, if he were brave enough, stand mute and refuse to plead guilty or not guilty. He then suffered *peine forte et dure*, being crushed slowly to death by weights placed on top of his body.[60] In the later sixteenth century a penurious govern-

[58] Thomas, *Religion and the Decline of Magic*, 535–57. Macfarlane, op. cit. 57–60.

[59] Thomas, op. cit. 525–7, 546–50, 650–72. There seems to be no evidence that the enacting of statutes against witchcraft was responsible for the apparent rise in the number of prosecutions (Thomas, 549). Macfarlane, op. cit. 98.

[60] HMC, *Buccleuch and Queensberry*, I. 231.

ment decided to use convicted men as oarsmen in the royal galleys. Considering the appalling conditions in which oarsmen
lived and worked such a reprieve may not have been particularly benevolent.[61] Physical mutilation—which had been uncommon in the later middle ages—came back into favour under
the Tudors. A man condemned for forgery and perjury was sentenced to lose both his ears and to be branded on his face with
the letters 'f' and 'p'. Another, who had forged the signature
of councillors, was to lose ears, suffer branding, and serve in
the galleys. No doubt the victims were a continual and peripatetic warning against crime. Imprisonment was considered a
relatively lenient punishment—a reprieve from death. But such
were the conditions in Tudor prisons that the reprieve was often
short.[62]

Women were generally treated more harshly than men. A
woman could not receive benefit of clergy until 1693, although
she might, if pregnant when she stood trial, have for a time
only 'the benefit of her "belly" '. When a man would be hanged
and drawn for treason, high or petty, a woman would be
burned.[63]

The Crown's efforts at reform certainly had no immediate or
magical effect on the nobles and gentry of Tudor England, who
continued to encourage, or at least to tolerate, the use of violence by their followers. In the reign of Henry VIII the Earl
of Derby was charged with commanding his retinue 'in most
riotous manner to keep the king's fair at Whalley', with perverting justice to allow the offenders to escape, with killing the
king's deer, and with sending his servant, Sir Henry Keighley,
and 800 men to turn a chantry priest out of Preston against
the wishes of the townspeople.[64] In 1541 Lord Dacre of the
South was hanged after he and his companions had murdered
a man during a poaching expedition.[65] Hunting, indeed, seems

[61] Hughes & Larkin, I. 329. *Egerton Papers* (Camden Soc. XII, 1840), 116. *APC* XXIV.
486; XXXII. 489. HMC, *Salisbury*, XII. 243. On conditions in galleys see A. Tenenti,
Piracy and the Decline of Venice, 1580–1615 (1967), 112–16.

[62] HMC, *Salisbury*, V. 483. Hawarde, 38. Bellamy, *Crime and Public Order*, 181–5.

[63] Lambarde, *Eirenarcha* (1619), 563, 571.

[64] *LP* III. ii. 1923. Cf. ibid. x. 806.

[65] *LP* XVI. 931, 932, 941, 954, 978, 1019.

often to have given rise to violence—in spite of the statute of 1485 which had drawn attention to the 'great and heinous rebellions, insurrections, riots, robberies, murders and other inconveniences' resulting from hunting in disguise.[66]

This kind of endemic violence continued through the reign of Elizabeth. In Herefordshire the last two decades of the sixteenth century were dominated by the feud between the Crofts and the Coningsbys. In 1584 an ambush was sprung on Thomas Coningsby when he was up in London; and four years later there was another attempt in Hereford. In 1590 the Crofts rode to Quarter Sessions in Hereford with fifty to eighty armed men. On none of these occasions was any serious harm done.[67] A similar feud in Wiltshire had more alarming consequences. After continual bickering between the families of Danvers and Long in Wiltshire, the son of the Danvers family shot dead the heir of the Longs.[68] In 1599 a Londoner named George Fenner wrote that there had lately been many quarrels between persons of quality. The most dramatic of them was the attack by John Stanhope of Rampton, Nottinghamshire, upon Sir Charles Cavendish. Although the attackers were armed with pistols and outnumbered Cavendish by twenty to three, they were beaten off with three or four of their men killed, inflicting only minor wounds on their victims.[69] The point about all these incidents lies in the responsibility of the landowners. As the Council in the Marches wrote about a brawl in Glamorgan, the gentry were most to blame since they were 'of such countenance as ought rather to be conservators of the peace than otherwise'.[70]

Weapons were probably even more difficult to control than gentlemen. A proclamation of 1579 rebuked local officials for

[66] I Henry VII c. 7.
[67] PRO, Star Chamber Proceedings, Elizabeth (St Ch. 5), C 7/27; C 9/32; C 17/6; C 18/6; C 67/3, 6, 28; C 69/31.
[68] Hawarde, 391–3.
[69] *CSPDom, 1598–1601*, 222–3, 226, 238. W. T. MacCaffrey, 'Talbot and Stanhope', *BIHR* xxxiii (1960), 84. C. Holles, *Memorials of the Holles Family* (Camden Soc., 3rd ser. LV, 1937), 90–2.
[70] NLW, Penrice and Margam MS no. L.16. The catalogue of sixteenth-century violence could be almost indefinitely prolonged. For further instances see: Stone, *Crisis of the Aristocracy*, ch. v; James, *Change and Continuity in the Tudor North* and *A Tudor Magnate and the Tudor State* (Borthwick Papers, nos. 27, 30); Williams, 'The Welsh Borderland under Queen Elizabeth', *WHR* I. i (1960).

their failure to enforce the laws against carrying fire-arms. In 1600 the situation seems to have been little better:

Licentiousness hath grown so far as it is usual not only with common and ordinary persons travelling by the highways to carry pistols and other kinds of pieces, but that ruffians and other lewd and dissolute men ... wheresoever they go or ride in the highways and streets, even of London itself ... do in secret manner go provided of such means to do mischief.[71]

While one should not always believe everything that is stated in royal proclamations—their language was always admonitory rather than accurate—the technical development of fire-arms and the growing popularity of rapiers cannot have simplified the task of enforcing order.

Yet this gloomy and violent picture may be distorted. There is no doubt that scenes of violence continued throughout the sixteenth century, but the evidence—especially the evidence of the lawcourts—tends to record the more dramatic episodes rather than uneventful peace. The problem is to discover how far such scenes continued to be common form; and this problem is not simple, for the historian has no thermometer with which to measure the heat of the social body. But there are some pointers which suggest that society was moving towards a more peaceful condition.

Legal evidence shows that Henry VII's government was quick to prosecute for unlawful retaining when it seemed likely to produce disorder. Many cases were brought before King's Bench and the Council; and it seems probable that the violence of retainers and their leaders was to a real extent inhibited. Admittedly this success was not permanent, for noble retinues were again giving trouble in the early years of Henry VIII. Success still depended upon the vigilance of the monarch and his ministers.[72] Yet signs of more permanent change are apparent by the reign of Edward VI. At first sight the struggles of Somerset and Northumberland may seem a mere repetition of the contest, a century before, between an earlier Somerset and the House of York. But there is, I think, a difference. The

[71] Hughes & Larkin, III, no. 804. Cf. ibid. II, no. 641; III, no. 766.
[72] A. Cameron, 'The Giving of Livery', *Renaissance and Modern Studies*, XVIII. 25–35. For examples of prosecution see *Records of the Borough of Nottingham*, III. 36–7, 344; Lodge, I. 26.

events of the late 1540s show restiveness among the peasantry, feuding among the gentry, and a power-struggle in the Council. But the cruel vendettas between magnates which disrupted so many localities in the mid-fifteenth century were not repeated. There was nothing in Edward VI's reign to match in scale the minor private war in the south-west between Courtenays and Bonvilles, the oppressions of the Duke of Suffolk in East Anglia, the Percy–Neville feud in the north, or the murder of Somerset, Northumberland, and Clifford at St Albans. It is also significant that the petitions of the House of Commons in the fourteenth century against noble retainers and their disorders were not repeated in the sixteenth: what had once been a serious grievance to middling landowners seems to have been so no longer.[73] It is possible that the great landowners were restrained from making private war by their fears of peasant unrest, which had been a disturbing feature of the 1540s; but that remains a speculation.

Yet this is only to say that the forceful and violent domination of whole regions by great magnates had come to an end. Are there any signs that the landowning class as a whole was acquiring more peaceful habits in the course of the sixteenth century? One such sign is the repeal in 1628 of many of the fifteenth-century statutes against livery, including the most ambitious of them all, Edward IV's act of 1468. This suggests that the consequences of livery and retaining were no longer thought to be serious.[74]

Another sign is the marked increase in litigation during the second half of the sixteenth century. In the first year of Elizabeth's reign there were brought to the Star Chamber sixty-seven cases, in the last year 732.[75] While there is no record of the number of cases brought to the Council in Wales during the sixteenth century, it was certainly being kept extremely busy: by 1594 it was said to be 2,000 cases behind, while in

[73] B. McFarlane, 'Bastard Feudalism', *BIHR* xx (1943/45). R. L. Storey, *The End of the House of Lancaster, passim.* Above, 12. Storey, 'Liveries and Commissions of the Peace, 1388–90', in *The Reign of Richard II: Essays in Honour of May McKisack*, ed. F. R. H. du Boulay and Caroline Barron (1971), 131–52.

[74] 3 Charles I c. 5. This statute repeals, *inter alia*, 8 Edward IV c. 2. The celebrated statute of Henry VII (19 Henry VII c. 14) only lasted during that king's lifetime.

[75] Elfreda Skelton, 'The Court of Star Chamber in the Reign of Elizabeth' (M.A. thesis, London, 1930), sect. v. I am grateful to Miss Skelton, later Lady Neale, for allowing me to use her material.

1609/10 3,376 cases were brought before it.[76] Equally significant is the type of case being heard. By the early seventeenth
century the Council in Wales was dealing predominantly with
civil cases rather than the misdemeanours and criminal offences
for which it had originally been established. Taken as a whole
the evidence of the lawcourts suggests that men were turning
increasingly to litigation for settling their disputes.[77]

Study of particular groups and regions confirms this suggestion. Professor Stone has demonstrated that 'recorded acts of
violence by the nobility declined sharply after 1600'. In the last
twenty years of the sixteenth century the odds against a peer's
being involved in physical violence were about one to two; by
the reign of Charles I they had lengthened to four to one.[78]
What was true of the peerage seems also to have been true of
the gentry. Some areas remained lawless and disturbed well
into the seventeenth century: only with the union of the crowns
could pacification be begun on the northern border and the
process was slow and arduous. But Wales and its Marches were
generally thought at the time to have been pacified under Elizabeth. When William Gerard, chancellor of Ireland, was advising the Privy Council upon policies for the pacification of that
island, he recommended the scheme of government established
in Wales: 'a better precedent, I told their honours, could not
be found than to imitate the course that reformed Wales'.
Gerard, who had been vice-president of the Council in the
Marches, was in a position to know.[79]

A more detailed study of a single Welsh county, Glamorgan,
reinforces Gerard's view.[80] In the earlier decades of the sixteenth century the lordship of Glamorgan, dominated by the
Earls of Worcester, was ruled with a mixture of laxity and
oppression. The uniting of Wales to England diminished the
influence of the house of Worcester and allowed the intrusion

[76] BL Lansdowne MS 76, ff. 143–4. PRO, State Papers Domestic, James I, 58/61
i. P. Williams, 'Star Chamber and the Council in the Marches', *Bulletin of the Board
of Celtic Studies*, XVI (1956), 287–97.

[77] P. Williams, 'The Activity of the Council in the Marches under the Early Stuarts',
WHR I. ii (1961), 132 ff. Cf. H. E. I. Phillips, 'The Last Years of Star Chamber', *TRHS*,
4th ser. XXI (1939), 117.

[78] Stone, *Crisis of the Aristocracy*, 269 and app. xv.

[79] *Analecta Hibernica*, II. 124. Williams, 'Welsh Borderland', *WHR* I. i (1960), 30–1.

[80] P. Williams, 'Political and Administrative History of Glamorgan', in *Glamorgan
County History*, IV (ed. Glanmor Williams, Cardiff, 1974), ch. iii.

of English methods of administration. But the county continued to be racked with feuds and brawling for most of Elizabeth's reign. George Owen, a Pembrokeshire antiquarian of the day, described the people of Glamorgan as 'very tall and populous, impatient of injuries, and therefore often quarrels with great outrages; thefts in some parts too common; great troops of retainers follow every gentleman'. During the last decade of the century the feuds reached a climax with successive battles in the streets of Cardiff between the Herbert and Matthew families and their retainers. But in the end the Herberts, who seem to have have been the aggressors, were punished by Star Chamber, described by one of their opponents as 'the great blazing star commonly seen at high noon within the meridian of Middlesex'. The head of the family, Sir William, was fined 1,000 marks; two other members of this faction were fined £500 each and removed from the commission of the peace; and so on down the scale.[81] Thereafter the atmosphere of Glamorgan politics changed: only in the more remote areas around Merthyr Tydfil did the gentry continue to fight out their differences; elsewhere they generally resorted to the peaceful arena of the lawcourts.

Although the practice of duelling to some extent replaced the brawls of landlords and their followers, nobles and gentlemen were probably, by the early seventeenth century, becoming more peaceably inclined. The change was not solely the consequence of government action. A shift in power from the peerage to the gentry may, as Professor Stone suggested, have helped to reduce the number of large-scale aristocratic feuds in the middle of the sixteenth century.[82] But, since the gentry's habits changed as markedly as the aristocracy's, it is unlikely that an alteration in the distribution of wealth within the land-owning class can have done much to bring about more peaceable habits.

The withdrawal of England from continental warfare may have been a good deal more important. In the later middle ages the English 'presence' on the mainland of Europe had led to the continuous involvement of the nobles, knights, and gentle-

---

[81] P. Williams, *Glamorgan County History*, IV, 188–91. Similar fines were imposed in the 1590s on the Talbots: see MacCaffrey, *BIHR* XXXIII. 82.

[82] Cf. Stone, *Crisis of the Aristocracy*, ch. v, esp. 263–5.

men in defensive and offensive warfare. The loss in 1453 of the last English possessions in France, except for Calais, diminished both the need for baronial retainers and the commitment to arms of the landowning classes. True, Henry VIII's campaigns in France induced some resurgence of the warlike spirit. But from 1559 until 1585 England was largely at peace, and when expeditionary forces were again sent across the Channel by Elizabeth they seldom contained the wealth of noble names exhibited by the armies of her father.[83]

Most of the landowning class was, during the Tudor epoch, turning away from its traditional training in arms to an education at the universities and the inns of court. It would be naïve to suppose that higher education makes men calmer, more reasonable, or less inclined to violence.[84] But it does provide them with a new set of political skills. However inefficient legal education may have been, something probably rubbed off on to the landed classes during their stay at the inns of court and their apprenticeship on the commissions of the peace. English landowners, assisted by education, their own experience, and the countless law-guides provided for them, became more adroit than before at using the law for themselves and therefore the more ready to resort to it.

Even allowing generously for the social and military changes of the sixteenth century it is likely that the government's measures were in part responsible for diminishing upper-class violence. However cautious and tolerant the Crown may often have been, it was able to show that the men supposed to be 'conservators of peace' could not with impunity terrorize or assault their neighbours. The example of Glamorgan suggests that by 1600 the lesson had been learned.

Although the feuds and affrays of the landed classes and their followers were probably being restrained by the end of the Tudor epoch, town and country were still exposed to the brawls, casual violence, and blood-lettings of peasants, artisans, and labourers. In the final years of Elizabeth's reign these disorders may have grown more intense under the pressures of rising population, poor harvests, and war. Mutinous bands of unpaid soldiers and sailors demonstrated for their rights in the

[83] Ibid. 239, 265.
[84] Ibid., ch. xii. Id., 'The Educational Revolution in England', *P&P* 28 (1964).

capital. Discontented apprentices hatched plots against foreigners. Large bands of vagrant unemployed were reported to be terrifying the inhabitants of London. The hungry poor clamoured for bread and occasionally robbed grain carts.[85]

But these circumstances were unusual. The 'bloods and frays' which made up the business of lesser Elizabethan courts were not. Men were normally armed with dagger or staff; their tempers were quick; and they were not restrained by any 'civilized' notions about violence. There is plenty of evidence about their brawling, but little that allows much comparison with earlier or later periods. However, it seems unlikely that the Tudor period saw much decline in the endemic disorders of the 'ungentle' classes.

There do however seem to be two patches of contrast between the later middle ages and the later sixteenth century. A feature of England in the thirteenth to fifteenth centuries was the criminal or outlaw band. Its archetype in myth was of course Robin Hood, whose heroic reputation in later days reflected popular discontent with the corruption of the law by its officials.[86] But the outlaw band existed in reality as well as in myth. Its leader was usually the son of a gentleman, or even occasionally a nobleman, like Lord John Fitzwalter in fourteenth-century Essex. Its hard core of members may have been quite small in the fourteenth century—about six men, perhaps—but was probably larger—forty to sixty—in the fifteenth. It was ready to be hired out by others—sometimes even by abbeys—who needed to 'persuade' their enemies. Robbery, kidnapping, feuds, and protection-rackets were its usual business.[87]

A few such bands can be found in Tudor England. The moss-troopers of the northern borders, clans of robbers and raiders, were not controlled until the seventeenth century. In the Marches of Wales, before the reign of Elizabeth, many criminal gangs were reported. Illegitimate sons of the Stradling family were said to be terrorizing Glamorgan in the 1530s.[88] By the second half of the century organized criminal bands of outlaws

[85] Conyers Read (ed.), *Lambarde and Local Government*, 83 ff. for a reiterated belief that order was declining in the last years of the century. *APC* XVII. 416, 453; XVIII. 47–9, 54–6; XXIII. 342. See below, 326–7, where these matters are treated more fully.

[86] M. H. Keen, *The Outlaws of Medieval Legend* (1961), *passim*.

[87] Bellamy, *Crime and Public Order*, ch. iii.

[88] Williams, *Glamorgan County History*, IV. 166.

seem, although one cannot be sure, to have become obsolete. The retainers of noblemen and gentry could still be brutal and violent. But they did not live by crime as did the followers of the Folvilles and the Coterels in the fourteenth century. Nor did the outlaw survive as a folk-hero—except, once more, on the northern border where Kinmont Willie and others were still revered in ballads until Stuart times. Robin Hood himself was certainly regarded with suspicion by the Tudor Crown, which tried to suppress the printing of ballads about him. South of the border zone he seems to have had no Tudor counterpart—not at least on land.[89]

There were of course criminal bands in sixteenth-century England, but they were very unlike the violent, hard-riding robbers and kidnappers of the later middle ages; and still more unlike Robin Hood. The criminal bands of Tudor times were the confidence men and tricksters who operated largely in the towns, especially in London. Men or women who pretended to be cripples or fooled the unwary visitor from the country with a promise of riches, these were the criminal elements most celebrated in literature. But they were not much admired.[90]

The world of the trickster was the criminal world of Elizabethan England, as the forest was the criminal world of the middle ages. The conciliar courts of the sixteenth century had originally been intended mainly to suppress riots and crimes of violence: by the early seventeenth century their business seems to have been shifting to conspiracy, fraud, and forgery.[91]

If the organized criminal band had disappeared on land, it was certainly alive and well at sea. Piracy was of course an old problem, and in the fifteenth century the anonymous author of *The Libel of English Policy* had called on the Crown to draw the sword and clear the sea of pirates:

> Then Hankyn Lyons should not be so bold
> To stop us and our ships for to hold
> Unto our shame; he had be beaten thence.[92]

---

[89] *LP* v, p. 551.

[90] F. Aydelotte, *Elizabethan Rogues and Vagabonds* (Oxford, 1913), *passim*.

[91] Williams, *WHR* I. ii (1961).

[92] G. Warner (ed.), *The Lybelle of Englyshe Polycye* (Oxford, 1926), 31. Hankyn Lyons was a notorious pirate of the day.

The growing trade in coastal waters in the late fifteenth and sixteenth centuries provided a still more appetizing prey for pirates operating in the Narrow Seas, St George's Channel, and the Bristol Channel.[93] In 1511 a commission to John Hopton, gentleman usher of the royal bedchamber, asserted, in the exaggerated language of the day, that 'many spoilers, pirates, exiles, and outlaws, arrayed in warlike fashion on the sea, have there assaulted our subjects and faithful lieges, spoiled their ships, goods and merchandise, and are daily busying themselves and intending with all their strength to assault, rob and spoil them'.[94] The task of suppressing the pirates was never easy, for they were skilled sailors, organized in groups, and often protected by such influential landowning families as the Killigrews of Cornwall. Furthermore they were in the game for profit rather than adventure: operating on commercial lines, they were usually careful to avoid the unnecessary cruelty and violence which might have alienated the landsmen on whom they depended to supply them with food and to buy their booty.[95]

At the start of the Tudor period the law for dealing with piracy was defective. From the early fifteenth century jurisdiction over this offence had been taken over by the Admiralty court, which administered the civil, not the common, law. Piracy was therefore no longer treated as a felony and was moreover very difficult to prove, since the civil law demanded either a confession from the criminal or the evidence of impartial witnesses; and in maritime cases such witnesses were not easily found. A statute of 1536, the 'act concerning pirates and robbers of the sea', laid down that trials for piracy could be held in any shire of the realm by royal commission to the Lord Admiral or his deputies and other 'substantial persons', and should be conducted as if they were for felonies committed on land: the case would be heard by a jury, the guilty would be punished by death, and benefit of clergy would not be allowed. This statute produced the anomalous situation that piracy was a felony

---

[93] R. G. Marsden (ed.), *Select Pleas in the Court of Admiralty* (Selden Soc., 1894), Vol. I, intro.

[94] Id., *Documents relating to the Law and Custom of the Sea* (Navy Records Soc., 1915), I, 146–7.

[95] D. Mathew, 'Cornish and Welsh Pirates in the Reign of Elizabeth I', *EHR* xxxix (1924), 337–48. C. L. Ewen, 'Organised Piracy around England in the Sixteenth Century', *Mariner's Mirror*, xxxv (1949), esp. 29–43.

at civil law triable by the common law. But, anomalous or not, the law was now more effectively capable of dealing with the offence, and the revival of the Admiralty court in the 1520s provided a more efficient machinery for executing that law.[96]

The Crown also made sporadic attempts to catch the pirates at sea. John Hopton, the gentleman usher already mentioned, was appointed captain of the ships dispatched to 'seize and subdue all and singular such spoilers, pirates, exiles and outlaws'.[97] In 1572 William Holstock, comptroller of the navy, was given command of the *Swallow* to capture what pirate ships he could; and in 1576 a similar commission was issued to Henry Palmer. These naval sweeps sometimes brought results, as in 1556, when royal ships captured six out of a fleet of ten pirate vessels; but such success was rare.[98]

The only chance of success lay in cutting the pirates off from their land bases. The pirates who preyed on coastal shipping needed ports in which they could refit and friends on shore who would sell them supplies and buy their captured goods. The inhabitants of coastal villages, officers of ports, and even some of the landowners were often ready to co-operate in return for a share of the profits. Under Elizabeth the Crown tried therefore to control piracy from, as it were, the landward side. In 1564 a royal proclamation ordered among other things that no one should supply any pirate with 'victuals, money, apparel for themselves or their vessels', that all pirates coming into port should be instantly arrested, and that no goods taken from pirates should be sold except under the most stringent conditions.[99] Later proclamations ordered that officials who, by 'fraud and greediness', allowed pirated goods to be sold, should be dismissed from their posts, and that any subjects of the realm trafficking with pirates should be punished by martial law. Twice in Elizabeth's reign, in 1563 and in 1577, commissions were issued to the coastal shires for investigating and suppressing piracy.[100]

---

[96] 27 Henry VIII c. 4. E. Coke, *Third Part of the Institutes* (edn. of 1669), ch. xlix. Marsden, *Select Pleas*, Vol. I, *passim*. Cf. *LP* ii. 235; v. 35, for two commissions.

[97] Marsden, *Law and Custom*, i. 147.

[98] Ibid. 191–7, 210, 218. Mathew, op. cit. *Calendar of State Papers Venetian*, vi. i. 536; I am grateful to Dr D. M. Loades for this reference.

[99] Hughes & Larkin, ii, no. 526. Cf. nos. 562, 563.

[100] Ibid. ii, nos. 573, 585, 654; iii, nos. 730, 813. *APC* vii. 278–90; ix. 298. PRO, State Papers Domestic, Elizabeth (SP 12), 110/2, 3; 111/35; 112/5.

The effect of these measures does not seem to have been very impressive. Feuds between local officials often prevented swift action; and sometimes the officers spent more energy and time accusing one another of complicity in piracy than in carrying out the orders of the Crown. In Pembrokeshire, for instance, accusations of piracy came to be more than anything else part of the conflict between Sir John Perrott, the vice-admiral, and Richard Vaughan of Whitland, who had been deputy to his predecessor. If the Crown's agents in West Wales were not themselves helping the pirates—and the evidence is as contradictory as it is colourful—they were certainly not doing much to hinder them.[101] Elsewhere, delicate conflicts of jurisdiction had to be resolved. Lord Huntingdon, president of the Council in the North, reported in 1577 that the Yorkshire commissioners for piracy were very uncertain how to proceed in view of the interests of the Admiralty's deputies, 'whom they are afraid to offend'.[102] In Glamorgan there was a conflict of a more dramatic kind. Two of the commissioners, Sir Edward Stradling and William Matthew, ordered the bailiffs of Cardiff to send them some suspects for questioning. On the refusal of the bailiffs, Stradling and Matthew reported to the Privy Council that they believed the officers of the town to be in league with the pirates. They were met with a furious tirade from the Earl of Pembroke, who felt his honour as Lord of Cardiff and vice-admiral of the region to be impugned. 'Are you alone', he wrote to the commissioners, 'carefully minded to respect the good of your country, or alone authorised to chasten such faults, or continually accustomed to use such integrity in your offices, that neither you may be thought for favour to wink at, or for malice to pry into, offences?'[103]

Stradling and Matthew may however have had good reason for their suspicions. In 1577 the connivance of the men of Cardiff with pirates had become so notorious that the town's merchants, when trading elsewhere, 'dare not well be known or to avow the place of their dwelling at Cardiff'.[104] Two of the county's piracy commissioners reported in the same year

[101] H. A. Lloyd, *The Gentry of South-West Wales* (Cardiff, 1968), 161–7.
[102] *CSPDom, Add., 1566–79,* 521.
[103] *APC* xiv. 143, 168, 203. PRO, State Papers Domestic, Elizabeth (SP 12), 195/ 59. J. M. Traherne, *Stradling Correspondence,* nos. 27, 70, 229.
[104] PRO, State Papers Domestic, Elizabeth, 112/5.

that the townsmen 'have taken a general rule that they will neither accuse one another' nor answer on oath any question that involved themselves. In spite of the difficulties put in the way of their inquiry, the commissioners found reliable evidence that at least four prominent men of the area were in league with the pirates: these were Nicholas Herbert, sheriff of the county and brother of the most important local landowner; William Herbert, an influential burgess; David Roberts, one of the principal customs officers; and Edward Kemeys, a Justice of the Peace.[105]

The government had some successes. In 1577 one of the most famous Elizabethan pirates, John Callice, was captured by the captain of the Isle of Wight. In contrast to the heroic pirates of legend Callice wrote a grovelling confession to Walsingham, in which he bewailed his wicked life, offered his services in cleansing the sea of pirates, whose haunts he reasonably claimed to know, and revealed the names of his colleagues and customers on land and sea. He was not the only one to be caught. But since the risks of piracy were fairly low, the profits large, and the support of officials and landowners often forthcoming, it is doubtful whether the Crown's actions alone would have cleared English waters.[106] Three developments transformed the nature of robbery at sea. One was the war with Spain, which led the Crown to license privateers as part of its naval strategy and so encouraged the growth of oceanic piracy far from English shores. The second was the intrusion of English pirates into the rich sea-pasture of the Mediterranean to loot Venetian merchantmen instead of English traders. The third was the arrival in northern waters of the Barbary pirates. Based on the north African coast they had no need to co-operate with the English. Indeed their cruelty and rapacity soon terrified the inhabitants of the coastal shires, who turned in a few years from protecting pirates against the Crown to imploring the Crown to save them from the pirates.[107]

[105] Ibid. 112/5. Cf. 110/2, 3, 4; 111/1, 35; 112/27; 122/2; 123/39. For Welsh piracy in general see Carys Hughes, 'Wales and Piracy' (M.A. thesis, Swansea, 1937), *passim*; and Glyn Roberts, 'Piracy along the Welsh Coast', *Trans. Neath Antiquarian Soc.*, 2nd ser. II (1931–2), 77–87.
[106] On problems of Admiralty jurisdiction see L. M. Hill, 'The Admiralty Circuit of 1591', *HJ* XIV (1971).
[107] K. R. Andrews, *Elizabethan Privateering* (Cambridge, 1964). A. Tenenti, *Piracy and*

The government's struggle to suppress coastal piracy is an interesting reflection of the difficulties of Tudor administration. The problem differed in many ways from that presented by the feuds and brawls of nobles and gentry on land. Those quarrels sprang less from economic ambition than from a predilection for violence, the unruliness of retainers, too sensitive a regard for honour and face, and the clashes of the hunting-field. Co-operation with pirates was almost entirely prompted by the hope of profit, and was for that reason less easily eliminated. Whether the Crown was faced with active collusion by its own officers with the pirates or by simple inertia, its dependence upon those officers made it almost impossible to suppress coastal piracy until circumstances changed.

Although an enthusiasm on the part of the landed classes for taking their disputes to court instead of relying upon their strong-arm followers was not new in the sixteenth century, it seems to have grown under the Tudors and to have increased the volume of business before the lawcourts. But the settlement of disputes by judge and jury, rather than by force, does not necessarily mean that justice prevailed.

Many of the suits before the courts were undoubtedly brought out of malice or spite rather than any serious desire to settle disputes. According to Justice William Gerard, 'the common sort of the people of Wales for the most part are so malicious, as they force not of their own charge, so they may procure charges to the adversary ...'[108] The Welsh were not alone in this respect. A draft parliamentary bill complained how 'divers troublesome and contentious persons ... intending rather the impoverishment of honest and quiet men by wrongful vexation than looking for any recompense of their pretended damages and feigned complaints ...' had multiplied the cases before Star Chamber. A statute of 1601, 'for the avoiding the infinite number of small and trifling suits', imposed penalties upon sheriffs who issued writs without a warrant.[109]

the Decline of Venice, ch. iv. Lloyd, op. cit. 166–7. Carys Hughes, op. cit., ch. iii. sect. a. On privateering see above, 131–3.

[108] *Y Cymmrodor*, XIII. 153.

[109] BL Harleian MS 6847, f. 133. Cf. Hawarde, 9–10, 52, 81, 93.

Such malicious suits were not only gratifying to the plaintiffs who brought them; they were also lucrative to court officials. Since judges and other officials were allocated the fees paid by litigants in civil cases, their welfare depended upon a satisfactory flow of suits. The attorneys and lesser clerks, in particular, were often not too scrupulous about encouraging litigation. But for the courts themselves and for the workings of justice the situation was serious. A limited number of judges was having to hear an ever increasing flow of suits. By the middle of Elizabeth's reign the Council in the Marches was sitting from six in the morning until six in the evening, so that 'the toil and travail the Council take ... exceedeth the pains taken in any office of justice throughout the realm'.[110] Hearing 1,200 cases each year, the judges must have been so heavily burdened that they could not bring to genuine suits the attention that they needed. Combined with the irritation aroused in defendants and witnesses by the annoyances of malicious litigation, this could and did erode the respect in which the courts were held.[111]

The developing taste for litigation also created conflicts between the courts themselves. When there was no defined structure of appeal-courts and when the limits of jurisdiction were often vaguely drawn, boundary disputes might easily break out. Court officials did their best to attract cases, while litigants found it tactically useful to bring cases before more than one court. A defendant, summoned before one court, would bring a 'cross-action' against the plaintiff in another. For instance, in a dispute over the collegiate church of Holyhead, Hugh Lloyd brought two actions against his opponent, William Maurice, one in Exchequer and one in the Council in the Marches. Maurice retaliated with a counter-suit in Exchequer and another in Star Chamber; and Lloyd replied with a suit in the consistory court at Bangor and yet another in Exchequer.[112] One consequence of such manœuvring was a great increase in litigation and, probably, in the annoyance which it caused. Another was the warfare between courts. This warfare was in no sense a straightforward battle between rival systems—

[110] *Y Cymmrodor*, loc. cit. Cockburn, *History of Assizes*, 135–6.

[111] Williams, *WHR* I. ii; 'The Attack on the Council in the Marches, 1603–1642', *Trans. Hon. Soc. of Cymmrodorion* (1961, part i). See also M. J. Ingram, 'Communities and Courts', in Cockburn (ed.), *Crime in England*, 118 ff.

[112] Williams, *Council in the Marches*, 216–18.

common-law versus prerogative or common-law versus equity: rather was it a complex and multiple series of disputes between courts which operated essentially within a single system.[113] Indeed it was the similarity of the jurisdictions, rather than the difference, which created dissension, for the friction arose more than anything else from competition for cases among men whose livelihood depended upon litigation. But one effect of such competition and conflict was an erosion of judicial authority. The attack upon the Council in the Marches by the Westminster courts produced a massive barrage of propaganda against the Ludlow court. Many of the allegations were probably justified, but the existence of abuses was an argument for reform rather than abolition. As it was, neither the opponents nor the supporters of the court considered the possibility of reform: the opponents demanded total destruction, the defenders were entrenched around the *status quo*. None of this was likely to preserve confidence in the system.[114]

Nor could litigants feel that their disputes would reach an end. One litigant in Chancery was told that success in a suit was only victory for a month.[115] A skilful litigant could keep a case moving from one court to another for years. Even when one party or the other secured a judgement, it was not easily enforced. Defeated litigants sometimes used force and often used delay to hinder the execution of decrees.[116]

More serious was the growing complication of procedure in many of the courts. Institutions like Star Chamber, Chancery, and the regional councils had originally been intended to provide a straightforward and rapid hearing of cases. Gradually the ingenuity of litigants and their lawyers had come to defeat this purpose. In order to prevent malicious litigation or the self-interested manipulation of the judicial machinery, these courts had to elaborate rules and safeguards. In both Chancery and the Council in the Marches a great deal of time was taken up with the hearing of motions in the course of the trial. The duration of suits tended gradually to lengthen, until by the end of the century the average Chancery suit took about three years.

[113] W. J. Jones, *The Elizabethan Chancery*, 18–24, 314–17, and chs. ix–xiii, *passim*.
[114] Williams, *Trans. Hon. Soc. of Cymmrodorion* (1961, part i), and *WHR* I. ii.
[115] Jones, op. cit. 17, 456, 465.
[116] Ibid., 233–5.

A procedure intended to be simple and intelligible was on the way to that complexity and obscurity for which Chancery later became notorious.[117] In spite of its complex and deepening mysteries Chancery still provided a source of remedies for litigants who were hampered in other courts. But its opportunities were much wider for the man who knew how to take them, for the man, that is, with some skill, however amateurish, in the law. For the poor and simple, courts like Chancery and the regional councils presented a maze of narrow, convoluted, and uncharted paths. By the early seventeenth century the lawcourts were beginning to come under heavy attack. The dilatoriness, negligence, and greed of the Chancery officials was condemned with special severity: it was even claimed in 1621 that cases in Chancery lasted twenty or thirty years.[118]

The sixteenth century does seem to have witnessed important changes in the system and in the success of law-enforcement. That is not of course to say that all measures of Crown policy were successful, or even that the Crown expected that they would be. In a society like Tudor England complete conformity and order were impossible. But the predilections of the upper classes for violence seem to have been restrained while their taste for litigation was developed. The control of the central over the local courts was more firmly established, and in some areas a system of jurisdiction was built up where in effect none had been before.[119] Bands of outlaws seem to have disappeared, while criminal gangs concentrated on fraud in London instead of theft in Nottingham Forest. The feelings of protest which had once romanticized men like Robin Hood now attached themselves to new heroes like Francis Drake, whose activities may well have drawn disruptive personalities out of England. In the higher courts fraud and trickery seem to have replaced violence or unlawful assembly as the most popular crimes.

Much of course remained the same. The procedures for catching and punishing ordinary criminals were little

---

[117] Ibid., 82–6, 305–20. Williams, *Council in the Marches*, ch. iii.

[118] Jones, op. cit. 161–2. See D. Veall, *The Popular Movement for Law Reform* (Oxford, 1970) for seventeenth-century material, esp. 32–6.

[119] P. Williams, in *Glamorgan County History*, ed. Glanmor Williams, IV. 197–201.

improved. Punishments became still more brutal and the range of felonies was extended. It became easier to bring prosecutions. But the chances of escaping detection or conviction—though perhaps slightly reduced—were still high; and it is unlikely that Tudor lawcourts had much impact upon the ordinary crime-rate.

One point does however stand out. In the later middle ages the effectiveness of law-enforcement seems to have varied with the personal intervention of the sovereign. The presence of Edward IV in person at trials is said to have been highly effective. In 1482 the council of the Duchy of Lancaster contended that the 'great strifes' of the time could be remedied 'by no person but only by the king himself'.[120] Henry VII and his successors were much less ready than Edward IV to travel the roads of England with their judges, although they frequently interfered, indirectly, in the conduct of cases. Such abstention might have been disastrous in earlier centuries. There is no sign that it was so in the sixteenth.[121]

[120] Bellamy, *Crime and Public Order*, 4–12.

[121] For royal interference in the course of justice, see Jones, *Chancery*, 328–36, and below, 397.

VIII

The Establishment of Protestantism[1]

The roots of English Protestantism can be traced far back into the fourteenth century, when John Wyclif and his Lollard followers began to question some of the fundamental tenets of Roman orthodoxy. Their doctrines persisted throughout the fifteenth century in several places, notably among skilled artisans in London, Bristol, and Coventry, and among weavers, yeomen, and husbandmen in the Thames Valley, the Chilterns, and East Anglia. But well-to-do laymen, who were becoming better educated during the later middle ages, also criticized the Church, demanding both more personal involvement and a more learned clergy. The Church itself was responding to the attractions of education and more of its clergy were graduates by 1500 than before; but in spite of reforms the quality of the priesthood had not improved sufficiently to silence the criticisms of educated and pious laymen. In addition, by the early decades of the sixteenth century, small groups of clerics at both universities, especially at Cambridge, were coming under the influence of Luther.

These pressures for change had however little connection with the dramatic events of the 1530s. Between 1532 and 1536 Henry VIII secured for the Crown legal authority over the Church in England. Convocation surrendered its right to enact new canons without royal assent, papal jurisdiction in ecclesiastical disputes was severed by the Act of Appeals, taxation

[1] I have not tried in this chapter to give a general history of the English Reformation, which obviously needs a book to itself. For that purpose the reader is referred to A. G. Dickens, *The English Reformation* (1964), and Claire Cross, *Church and People, 1450–1660* (1976). I have aimed here at analysing the methods by which the Crown imposed the Reformation upon the nation and the extent to which it was successful. Until 1558 society did no more than acquiesce in the changes and at the accession of Elizabeth England was very far from being Protestant. The country became so largely in the next forty-five years, and for that reason I have concentrated upon that period, giving only a short account of the years 1530–58 to serve as a necessary background to the main part of the chapter.

levied by Rome was transferred to the Crown, the King obtained the right to nominate bishops, and the papal power of dispensing with laws was entrusted to the Archbishop of Canterbury. In 1534 the King was declared Supreme Head of the English Church and, two years later, the power of Rome was finally extinguished in England. Although these acts were revolutionary in their implications, for they transferred control over spiritual affairs to a layman, they met little opposition. The bishops had been cowed by Henry in 1532, when the Upper House of Convocation, thinly attended, agreed to surrender the legislative powers of the Church. The landowning class in general accepted, and in many cases welcomed, the changes. Protests were voiced in the main by men of little significance. Acquiescence was secured largely by the King's pressure on the bishops and by his ability to secure and to preserve the loyalty of the great magnates.[2]

However, the King and his advisers did not stop at the assertion of royal power. They made valuations of all Church revenues to ensure that the Crown secured its full portion of clerical taxes. They dissolved the smaller monasteries in 1536 and the remainder in the course of the next four years. A proclamation of 1536 reduced the number of holy-days, and Royal Injunctions, issued shortly after, demanded adherence to the new laws, forbade the veneration of images, commanded the clergy to instruct their congregations in the Christian faith, and ordered regular preaching in support of the Royal Supremacy. A second set of injunctions, issued in 1538, insisted that an English Bible be placed in every church and again attacked the misuse of images and pilgrimages. These measures touched the priesthood and the laity far more closely than had the Breach with Rome. Opposition was voiced in most parts of England and grew into a major threat in the northern Pilgrimage of Grace. The ultimate defeat of that movement, thanks largely to the refusal of the major court magnates to join the dissidents, ensured that royal control over the Church would not again be seriously challenged.[3]

---

[2] On opposition and enforcement see G. R. Elton, *Policy and Police* (1972), *passim*. My own view differs in some respects from that of Professor Elton: see my review of his book in *EHR* LXXXVIII (1973), 594–7.

[3] Below, ch. X, for the Pilgrimage of Grace.

To enforce these changes the King and his ministers used every available means. They appointed Protestant bishops, like Cranmer, Latimer, Holgate, and Barlow. They employed press and pulpit to justify the Royal Supremacy and they encouraged and rewarded writers of reformist views. In proclamations, injunctions, and circular letters, they commanded conformity to the new laws, securing a statutory extension of the treason laws to include treason by the spoken word alone. They investigated reports and accusations of dissidence with minute care. They ordered the imposition of oaths which tied men to the new policy: all males had to swear to observe the Succession Act of 1534, legitimizing Henry's marriage with Anne Boleyn; bishops, corporate clergy, secular office-holders, and royal tenants were bound to the Supremacy by oath; parish clergy were required to sign a declaration against the Pope.[4] The enforcement of these oaths was at first entrusted to a metropolitan visitation under Cranmer. But the protests of the bishops and the danger that royal control would be shared with the archbishop led to the establishment of the new post of Vicegerent of the Church, under which a layman, Thomas Cromwell, exercised the Royal Supremacy on behalf of his master. The vicegerency itself did not outlast the death of Cromwell in 1540, but its existence, however temporary, demonstrated to the bishops that they were the servants of God *and* of their King, not merely of God alone. The lesson was renewed and emphasized at the beginning of Edward's reign, when statute laid down that bishops would henceforth receive their authority by letters patent from the Crown.[5] Officially the Henrician Reformation established the supremacy of the secular government over the Church and ensured that its principal officers would be royal servants. These changes were received by the clergy with acquiescence rather than conviction. The number of men ordained fell sharply from 1536, suggesting that the uncertainties of the age reduced the attractions of a clerical career. At the same time, paradoxically, the fall in recruitment to the priesthood eased the lot of those already ordained, by diminishing the competition for benefices and promotion: this may well

---

[4] Elton, *Policy and Police*, chs. iv-ix.
[5] S. E. Lehmberg, 'Supremacy and Vicegerency', *EHR* LXXXI (1966). M. Bowker, 'The Supremacy and the Episcopate', *HJ* XVIII (1975).

have led them to accept reforms which would otherwise have been unpalatable.[6]

The achievement of secular control, however, was one thing, the establishment of Protestantism quite another. Some of the government's actions—especially the publication of the Great Bible—assisted the spread of reform. But Protestant doctrines mostly made headway through the endeavours of sympathetic clerics and laymen. Some of these were influential at court, like Cranmer, Cromwell and Queen Katherine Parr, and a much wider circle of reformers expounded the new tenets throughout the country, especially in London.[7] The foundations of the *official* Protestant reformation were laid under Edward VI, when changes in the liturgy introduced an unequivocally Protestant form of worship. These changes were cautiously introduced, beginning with the Order of Communion in 1548 and the First Edwardian Prayer Book of 1549. The former preserved most of the Catholic Mass but prepared the way for more radical changes by providing for the participation of the laity in the ceremony; the latter omitted all reference to the Catholic doctrine of the sacrifice of the Mass, but preserved just enough of the old forms for an orthodox cleric like Stephen Gardiner unwillingly to accept it. However, the Second Prayer Book, issued in 1552, represented a complete break with the old liturgy, abandoning any notion of transubstantiation: the Mass had become the Communion Service, and the new form of worship was statutorily imposed upon the whole nation by an Act of Uniformity. A year later these liturgical changes were complemented by the fully reformed theology of Cranmer's Forty-two Articles. In the course of his reign Edward's government had also destroyed images, confiscated church ornaments, dissolved the chantries, permitted the marriage of priests, imprisoned outspoken opponents of reform, and appointed men like Ridley, Ponet, and Hooper to bishoprics.

Although some radical clerics, like John Knox, were still dis-

---

[6] M. Bowker, 'The Henrician Reformation and the Parish Clergy', *BIHR* L (1977). In some areas however opposition remained: see Christopher Haigh, *Reformation and Resistance in Tudor Lancashire* (Cambridge, 1975), chs. viii, ix.

[7] Cross, *Church and People*, 70–80. It may be that Henry intended to move in a Protestant direction in the last months of his reign. See L. B. Smith, 'Henry VIII and the Protestant Triumph', *AmHR* LXXI (1966) and J. J. Scarisbrick, *Henry VIII* (1968), 470–8, for differing views on this question.

satisfied with the extent of reform, the English Church was officially Protestant by 1553. The same could not be said of the
English nation. The numbers entering the priesthood continued to fall,[8] the parish clergy were mostly unfitted for the
religious instruction of their flocks, and the politicians were
more concerned with the seizure of Church wealth than with
the establishment of spiritual discipline. A few devoted bishops
did what they could to instil the reformed religion into their
sees. Bishop Hooper of Gloucester devoutly preached and cate-
chized, inquired into every parish of his diocese, imposed
penances upon clergy and laity, purged the parish churches
of rood-screens and images. Yet even Hooper, for all his
exceptional energy, was unable to convert his clergy, let alone
the laity, to more than temporary acceptance of the official religion. He and his colleagues needed more time than the brief
reign of Edward VI allowed them.[9]

The loose attachment of the political nation to the Protestant
creed was tested and broken after Edward's death. Although
the landowning classes were adamant in their refusal to restore
ecclesiastical property to the Church and were understandably
frightened that the new government might insist on this being
done, Mary had little difficulty in annulling the doctrinal and
liturgical reforms of her brother and endured only eighteen
months' delay before she was able to return the country to
Roman jurisdiction. The Queen, Bishop Gardiner, and Cardinal Pole have often been criticized for supposedly concentrating
on the destruction of heresy rather than the construction of a
truly Catholic Church. In practice, they were seriously hampered by a shortage of money, information, and time. Even so,
much was done to lay the foundations upon which an orthodox
Church might have been rebuilt had Mary lived longer. Pole's
legatine synod at Westminster provided for the instruction of
the clergy, the government paid close attention to the universities, episcopal visitation of sees was frequent and thorough, and
the Crown restored a considerable amount of revenue to the
Church. These beginnings have naturally been less publicized
than the exile and burning of heretics. Certainly, the experiences

[8] Haigh, *Reformation and Resistance*, ch. x.

[9] F. D. Price, 'Gloucester Diocese under Bishop Hooper, 1551-53', *Trans. Bristol and Gloucester Arch. Soc.* LX (1938). Cross, op. cit. 99-100. Haigh, op. cit., chs. x, xi.

of the exiles had their effect under Elizabeth, in bringing to England advocates of the most radical Swiss doctrines, but there is little sign that their pamphlets had much effect before the death of Mary. Under Elizabeth, John Foxe was able to mobilize the history of the Marian martyrdoms into a superbly effective instrument of propaganda; but they do not seem to have created more than haphazard discontent and opposition at the time. Like her brother, Mary ruled too briefly to accomplish her purpose. She died leaving a country officially reconciled to Roman faith and authority, but in spirit neither fully orthodox nor fully Protestant.[10]

The task of imposing Protestantism in the parishes as well as in the statute-book was left to Elizabeth. The main lines of the Elizabethan Settlement had already been drawn for her by her father and her brother: the Supremacy of the Crown over the Church and its bishops had been fully established by Henry VIII, while a reformed liturgy and a set of doctrinal articles had been promulgated under Edward. The monasteries and the chantries, both representing a Catholic view of religion, had been destroyed, and the brief Marian restoration of monasticism was easily reversed by Elizabeth. It was not difficult for the new Queen to re-establish the Royal Supremacy and to reintroduce a Protestant liturgy. But it was much harder to ensure that her settlement became the religion of her people. In the end that task was successfully accomplished and Elizabethan England became a Protestant nation: the way in which that was done is the main concern of this chapter.

In the early years of Elizabeth's reign the hold of Protestantism upon the country was demonstrably weak. Lay and clerical leaders uttered constant warnings about the strength of Catholic feeling among influential county families; reports from

[10] On religion under Mary see the following works: A. G. Dickens, *The Marian Reaction in the Diocese of York* (St Anthony's Hall pubns., nos. 11 & 12, 1957); D. M. Loades, *The Oxford Martyrs* (1970); id., 'The Enforcement of Reaction, 1553–58', *Journ. Eccl. Hist.* xvi (1965) and 'The Essex Inquisition of 1556', *BIHR* xxxv (1962); Rex H. Pogson, 'Revival and Reform in Mary's Church', *Journ. Eccl. Hist.* xxv (1974) and 'Reginald Pole and the Priorities of Government', *HJ* xviii (1975); A. Meriel Jagger, 'Bonner's Episcopal Visitation of London', *BIHR* xlv (1972); Jennifer Loach, 'Pamphlets and Politics, 1553–58', *BIHR* xlviii (1975); Haigh, *Reformation and Resistance*, ch. xiii. I owe much to discussion of Marian religion by Mrs Loach in seminars.

diocesan bishops were usually pessimistic. In 1562 Bishop Horne of Winchester complained that his own cathedral town would 'continue and be further nursled in superstition and popery' unless its parishes were reorganized.[11] Two years later reports on every diocese were sent to the Privy Council. Instructed to classify the Justices of the Peace as 'favourers of true religion', 'adversaries of true religion', or 'indifferent to religion', the bishops certified 431 as favourable, 157 as adversaries, and 264 as indifferent. Considering that the Crown had by then had five years in which to alter the commissions of the peace these figures were not reassuring, even though some of the 'adversaries' may have been radical Protestants rather than papists. Individual returns were sometimes astonishingly gloomy. The Earl of Bedford was said to have told the Bishop of Durham that on the eastern march of the northern border 'there is never a justice of the peace nor none that he can command as meet for that purpose'. The Bishop of Hereford claimed that in the council of that city 'there is not one that is counted favourable to this religion'.[12] In 1567–8 episcopal visitations of Yorkshire brought to light many survivals of traditional orthodoxy among the parish clergy: almost a decade after the Elizabethan settlement several vicars were still saying communion-services for the dead.[13] A Sussex visitation of 1569 reported that altars still stood in Arundel church, that in Battle the parishioners left the church when the preacher denounced Roman doctrines, and that, except for Lewes and Chichester, 'the whole diocese is very blind and superstitious for want of teaching'.[14]

The established Church had only worn and feeble machinery for imposing control. It was, to begin with, poor. The councillors of Edward VI had taken pickings from the episcopal lands and inflation had eroded rents. The bishopric of Lichfield was said to have been worth £750 per annum in 1537 and only £560 per annum in 1583, when money went less far. Thomas

---

[11] J. E. Paul, 'Hampshire Recusants', *Proceedings of the Hampshire Field Club*, XXI (1958), 63–4.

[12] M. Bateson, *A Collection of Original Letters . . . 1564* (Camden Miscellany, IX, 1893), 15, 65, and *passim*.

[13] A. G. Dickens, 'The First Stages of Romanist Recusancy in Yorkshire', *Yorks. Arch. Journ.* XXXV (1943), 161.

[14] *VCH, Sussex*, II. 25–6. On Lancashire, the most Catholic of all English counties, see Christopher Haigh, *Reformation and Resistance in Tudor Lancashire*, chs. xiii, xiv.

Bentham, appointed to the see at the beginning of Elizabeth's reign, had to spend much of his time and energy in financial management. Tithes had often been impropriated to lay landlords and many parish priests were reduced to the economic level of peasants. The clerical authorities seldom had a voice in the appointment of ministers, for the right to present to livings had in many parishes been taken over by laymen or by urban corporations. Out of 147 presentations made to parochial livings in the see of Lichfield during the 1560s, Bishop Bentham was responsible for only five.[15]

The church had of course an elaborate system for supervising religious life, discovering unorthodox practices, and punishing offenders. From the archbishops' courts of York and Canterbury a complex hierarchy of jurisdictions stretched down through the diocesan courts of the bishops to the courts of the archdeaconries at the bottom of the pyramid. These courts, more than 250 in number, dealt with cases of probate, disputes over payments to the clergy, civil litigation over marriages, and offences against discipline by clergy and laity alike.[16] Beside this edifice of courts stood the equally traditional system of visitations, designed to guide, admonish, and correct the clerical and lay officials in the parishes. Visitations—official tours of inspection—were conducted by archbishops, bishops, bishops' chancellors, and archdeacons at supposedly regular intervals. Usually the visitors issued in advance articles, or questions, to the minister and churchwardens of every parish, concerning the learning and conduct of the priest, the condition of the church fabric, the books and ornaments owned by the parish, and the religious and moral life of the laity. The *acta*,

[15] M. Rosemary O'Day, 'Thomas Bentham, a Case Study', in *Journ. Eccl. Hist.* xxxiii (1972). C. Hill, *Economic Problems of the Church* (Oxford, 1956), *passim*. R. B. Manning, *Religion and Society in Elizabethan Sussex* (Leicester, 1969), chs. ii, iv. Rosemary O'Day and Felicity Heal (eds.), *Change and Continuity* (Leicester, 1976), chs. vi, vii, by Drs Haigh and Shiels.

[16] I have not tried to describe the full panoply of Church courts. For a brief summary see Elton, *Tudor Constitution*, ch. vii. For more extended accounts: W. Holdsworth, *History of English Law*, Vols. i, iv; C. I. A. Ritchie, *The Ecclesiastical Courts of York* (Arbroath, 1956); J. S. Purvis, *Tudor Parish Documents* (Cambridge, 1948); R. Peters, *Oculus Episcopi: Administration in the Archdeaconry of St Albans, 1580–1625* (Manchester, 1963); R. A. Marchant, *The Church under the Law* (Cambridge, 1969); C. Hill, *Society and Puritanism in Pre-Revolutionary England* (1964), ch. viii. Haigh, *Reformation and Resistance*, 227–33. The most recent accounts of the Church courts are given in O'Day and Heal, op. cit., chs. ix and x, by Drs Lander and Houlbrooke.

or records of the visitations, included purely factual statements—inventories of books and ornaments—and the *comperta*,
or charges against clergy and laymen for neglect or misbehaviour. The *comperta* should in principle have been followed by
trials of the offenders in correction courts. The whole process
was, again in principle, rounded off with a set of injunctions
or orders designed to put right the faults discovered in the
course of the visitation.[17]

The bite of the Church courts varied from one diocese, indeed
from one bishop, to another. At Gloucester, under the som-
nolent eye of Bishop Cheyney, the courts were corrupt and inactive. In London, especially in the days of Bancroft, they
operated with effective regularity.[18] So much is not surprising.
But there were certain weaknesses in the system which even the
most strenuous bishop could not wholly overcome and which
rendered the weaker men largely ineffective. Prosecutions
before Church courts and visitations had usually to be brought
by the churchwardens of the parishes, humble men who had
generally been cajoled into their posts, were frightened of offending the village notables, and often resented the very courts
whose agents they were.[19] Even when the churchwardens informed against an offender it was difficult to get him into court.
The ecclesiastical messengers, known as apparitors, were often
open to bribes, and even when they were honest, they could
easily be evaded. More serious still was the declining power of
excommunication, the principal weapon of the Church courts.
In theory excommunication should have held serious spiritual
terrors and also the more immediate threat of imprisonment
by the sheriff for those who failed to seek absolution. After the
Reformation the spiritual terrors were not very vivid and the
ecclesiastical courts seldom called upon the sheriff to act.
Although the Bishop of St Davids complained to the Privy
Council that more than two hundred 'vicious livers' had been

---

[17] W. H. Frere and W. P. M. Kennedy, *Visitation Articles and Injunctions* (Alcuin Club
Collections, vols. 14–16, 1910). Kennedy, *Elizabethan Episcopal Administration* (Alcuin
Club, vols. 25–7, 1924). Marchant, op. cit., ch. iv. Peters, op. cit. Manning, *Religion
and Society*, ch. ii. H. G. Owen, 'The Episcopal Visitation: Its Limits and Limitations
in Elizabethan London', *Journ. Eccl. Hist.* xi (1960).

[18] Owen, op. cit. F. D. Price, 'An Elizabethan Church Official', *Church Quarterly Rev.*
cxxxviii (1939).

[19] Manning, op. cit., ch. ii.

excommunicated in his diocese, the sheriffs could not be persuaded to use coercion. Many excommunicates learned to live under the Church's sentence and those who wanted it lifted could be freed for a small fine.[20] The Church courts were in many ways subject to the same infirmities as the secular. Both were overwhelmed by the press of cases, both lacked an effective machinery of prosecution, both were abused by corrupt officials. But the Church courts seem to have incurred more resentment than the lay and to have had feebler sanctions with which to impose their will. It was not that they were totally powerless or inert: they were indeed busy and interfering, but their power and their activity were enough to irritate, insufficient to compel. It is not surprising that the Bishop of St Davids requested the aid of the Council in the Marches, 'whose authority', he said, 'reacheth to correct where ecclesiastical law is deficient'.[21]

Fortunately for the success of its policies the Crown had stronger weapons to hand than the spiritual courts. Assizes could punish offenders against ecclesiastical discipline and their judges were empowered to exercise a general surveillance over county governments. Until 1587 Quarter Sessions were authorized to impose fines for recusancy, and in many counties were energetic in doing so during the first half of the 1580s. But assize-judges and Justices of the Peace were often too deeply involved in factional politics to bring down the full weight of their authority upon Catholic dissenters.[22]

More effective, particularly in the first half of Elizabeth's reign, were the various ecclesiastical commissions. Once considered to be the product of the royal supremacy, they are now thought to have originated in the various commissions against heresy issued by the Crown in the middle ages. Certainly they had been used by Mary, in spite of her rejection of the royal supremacy, as well as by Elizabeth. The best known of these courts was the High Commission, sitting in London, which had jurisdiction over the whole of England and Wales. But there

---

[20] F. D. Price, 'Elizabethan Apparitors in the Diocese of Gloucester', *Church Quarterly Rev.* CXXXIV (1942). Id., 'The Abuses of Excommunication', *EHR* LVII (1942). C. Hill, *Society and Puritanism*, ch. x. Haigh, op. cit. 235–6. PRO, State Papers Domestic, Elizabeth, 66/26. Cf. O'Day and Heal, op. cit., chs. ix and x, by Lander and Houlbrooke.

[21] PRO, State Papers Domestic, Elizabeth, 131/42.

[22] Cockburn, *History of Assizes*, 189–219.

were several local commissions, of which the most fully documented is the commission for the province of York, which operated as a lawcourt from 1561 to 1641. Technically subordinate to the High Commission in London, this court was in practice an independent body. Other commissions were established at different times for the sees of Canterbury, Durham, Gloucester, Norwich, Chester, Exeter, Salisbury, Winchester, Peterborough, Lincoln, and Carlisle. These courts seem to have been based on individual commissions, separate from the London court, although the High Commission was no doubt able to override them if it wished: they were lesser partners rather than mere offshoots of the superior body. In other sees—and perhaps in these sees for part of the time—panels of the London Commission itself appear to have sat. Although their history is obscure, it seems reasonably certain that special provincial courts existed from early in the reign for the enforcement of the settlement and that as time went on their efforts were supplemented by other courts at diocesan level.[23]

The ecclesiastical commissions, like all other courts, were hindered by the absence of effective prosecutors, by the inadequacies of their officials, and by the constraints imposed by Elizabethan society. But they had advantages over the purely spiritual courts. They combined lay and clerical members, which often enabled them to gain weight and respect in secular society. They could work by a rapid, summary procedure. Above all, they possessed effective sanctions in the power to take bonds, to fine, and to imprison. It is not surprising that bishops and judges thought them essential to the enforcement of religious uniformity: Lord Chief Justice Wray told Burghley in 1576 that only an ecclesiastical commission could put Norfolk in order, since excommunication was of no account; and right at the end of the reign Bishop Cotton of Exeter, after a horrific description of the profanities of his diocese, wrote that 'these

[23] The standard work on ecclesiastical commissions is R. G. Usher, *The Rise and Fall of the High Commission* (1st edn., Oxford, 1913). But the introduction by P. Tyler to the second edition (Oxford, 1968) contains some essential revisions. See also Tyler, 'The Significance of the Ecclesiastical Commission at York', *Northern History*, II (1967); F. D. Price, 'The Commission for Ecclesiastical Clauses for the Diocese of Bristol and Gloucester', *Trans. Bristol and Gloucs. Arch. Soc.* LIX (1937); P. Clark, 'The Ecclesiastical Commission at Canterbury', *Archaeologia Cantiana*, LXXIX (1974); and W. Shiels in ch. vii of O'Day and Heal, op. cit., on Peterborough. On the weaknesses of the York and Chester commissions see Haigh, op. cit. 212–13, 233 ff.

and many such abuses cannot be redressed by a due course of law, and therefore I do most humbly crave the help of an Ecclesiastical Commission, which is afforded to many other bishops, being nearer to London by 120 miles than I am'.[24]

Some of the available evidence—for instance the registers of the Privy Council—gives the impression that for many years the government was indifferent to the dangers of Catholic survival and only began energetic persecution of popish dissenters in about 1575. Perhaps for this reason several historians have depicted the early part of the reign as a time when lack of Catholic leadership rather than vigorous royal action eroded the foundations of the old faith. In his authoritative work on English Catholicism A. O. Meyer attributed its fatal decline to the first decade of the reign and explained its failure, not by the force of state action, but by the 'religious and national sentiments of Englishmen'. In his view Catholic sympathizers slipped into conformity because they were never given a clear warning from Rome of its dangers and because they were naturally loyal to the monarchy.[25] Understandably enough, Catholic historians have preferred to concentrate their attention upon the heroic years of resistance between 1575 and 1603, on which there survives a mass of evidence in manuscript and in print. That the Crown failed in that period to break the Catholic spirit in England has been taken as evidence of the feebleness of government machinery and as confirmation of the view that the establishment of Protestantism occurred by a process of drift or osmosis when Catholics were leaderless and government passive.

I believe that this view is false and that the truth is much more complicated. The Privy Council's unconcern about recusancy in the early years is certainly no proof of government inactivity. Recusancy was seldom prosecuted before 1570 because recusancy then seldom existed: except in one or two counties, such as Lancashire, adherents of the Old Faith were mostly prepared to attend the services of the Anglican Church, while hold-

[24] HMC, *Salisbury*, II, 136–7; X, 450–1; XI, 26, 182. Cf. J. Strype, *Annals of the Reformation* (7 vols., Oxford, 1824), VI. 329.

[25] A. O. Meyer, *England and the Catholic Church under Elizabeth* (1916), 59–73. Cf. J. B. Black, *The England of Elizabeth*, 19, and P. Hughes, *The Reformation in England*, III (1954), 285.

ing their own observances in private. The real task of those early years was the transformation of the established church into a reformed Church. This involved training and beneficing a Protestant clergy, destroying papal trappings in parish churches, teaching the Anglican doctrine, and attracting the political nation to the new order. Once that task was well in hand, by about 1570, the Crown could attack Catholic sympathizers among the gentry. But its campaign was then made immeasurably more difficult by the missionary enterprise of the Counter-Reformation, which reached England during the late 1570s. The government was now confronted not with a large, ill-defined, poorly instructed group of Catholic sympathizers—church-papists as they were called—but with a hard kernel of recusants, sustained by priests who grasped the essentials of their faith and were not prepared to tolerate either compromise or occasional conformity to the Anglican Church.

During the early part of the reign the laws against Catholics were defined in three principal statutes. The Act of Supremacy of 1559 made it obligatory for all priests, temporal officers, and men proceeding to university degrees to take the oath acknowledging the Queen as Supreme Governor of the Church: failure to do so would be penalized by loss of benefice or office. This Act also imposed penalties on anyone who supported the spiritual jurisdiction of the Pope by writing or preaching. The Act of Uniformity imposed a fine of one shilling for every absence from church on a Sunday. A later act of 1563 extended to schoolmasters, lawyers, M.P.s, and other officials the obligation to take the oath, and also made it treason for a man to refuse the oath if it were offered to him a second time.[26]

In this early period the clergy was the main target of the Crown's attack. The Marian bishops, with one exception, refused the oath and were deprived. Commissions were sent to every diocese in the summer of 1559 to secure the submission of the lower clergy. Whether they were asked, as they should have been, to take a formal oath, is improbable. More likely they were merely required to subscribe to a statement of the Queen's supremacy. The evidence of their subscriptions is incomplete, and historians have disagreed about the number that submitted. But there is really no doubt that acceptance was

[26] 1 Elizabeth cc. 1, 2. 5 Elizabeth c. 1.

wide; the only dispute is over the size of the small minority of objectors. In the northern province, out of about 1,000 clergy, 300 were absent and about ninety refused to subscribe. In six sees of the southern province, 1,804 priests subscribed, but we do not know how many were asked.[27]

The upshot of this visitation was apparently satisfactory to the Crown. But submission to the Supremacy was a long step from commitment to the new Protestant liturgy; and the formal submission of the parochial clergy deprived the government of opportunities to replace conservative priests with men more sympathetic to the settlement. There was of course a complete change of personnel at the summit of the hierarchy. The new bishops were all Protestants, though a few, like Cheyney of Gloucester, preferred a less radical brand of reform to the official doctrine of the Thirty-nine Articles. But there were fewer changes in the middle and lower ranks. In Lancashire, a county much attached to the old faith, only ten out of 200 clergy were deprived in the early years of the reign. In the North Riding of Yorkshire only sixteen schoolmasters and priests were dismissed between 1558 and 1582. Perhaps 300 clergy from the whole kingdom were removed from their benefices in the opening stages of the struggle; several more may have fled or resigned. But many who were sympathetic to the old order remained in the parishes.[28]

Even if more clergy had been dismissed for refusing the oath, it is unlikely that they could have been quickly replaced with convinced and trained Protestants. In the see of Chichester, where at least forty-four out of about 290 clergy lost their benefices in the 1560s, Bishop Barlow estimated in 1563 that one-sixth of the parishes had no spiritual care whatever and that almost half the remainder were served only by curates.[29] In the middle

---

[27] For the enforcement of the settlement on the clergy see H. Gee, *The Elizabethan Clergy and the Settlement of Religion* (1898). A different and Catholic view is given by H. N. Birt, *The Elizabethan Religious Settlement* (1907). See also Hughes, *Reformation in England*, III, 38–41. For the northern province, see C. J. Kitching (ed.), *The Royal Visitation of 1559: Act Book for the Northern Province* (Surtees Soc., vol. 187, Gateshead, 1975).

[28] I owe the Lancashire information originally to unpublished lectures by the late Dr G. H. Tupling. See now Haigh, op. cit. 210–16. H. Aveling, *Northern Catholics* (1966), *passim*. See Gee, op. cit., for a general discussion: his estimate of 200 deprived clergy is usually considered to be too low.

[29] Manning, *Religion and Society*, 54–7. J. J. Daeley, 'Pluralism in the Diocese of Canterbury', *Journ. Eccl. Hist.* XVIII (1967), 33–47.

ranges of the clerical command there were probably more deprivations and more vacancies. Of the thirty-five clergy deprived in Chichester diocese up to 1564, thirteen were canons of the cathedral.[30] Inevitably, since the bishops were few and their sees large, they had to rely heavily upon deans, arch-deacons, and cathedral officers to convey sound doctrine and discipline into the parishes. The dependence of Bishop Bentham of Lichfield upon Thomas Lever, archdeacon of Coventry, is a case in point: Lever was allowed, perhaps even encouraged, to hold 'prophesyings'—large religious conferences—to edu-cate the clergy of his archdeaconry.[31] The 'middle-manage-ment' of the sixteenth-century Church was obviously of critical importance for the success of government policy; but its members have not yet had the attention from historians that, as a group, they deserve.

The prime necessity was an educated, Protestant, and preaching clergy, which could mould the religious life of the parishes. Such men could only come from the universities. In spite of the attraction of Oxford and Cambridge for young noblemen and gentlemen, they were still, above all else, nur-series for the upbringing of the clergy; and the government was quietly determined to extend its control over them. Little in the Crown's policy was dramatic or precipitate. Catholic fel-lows of colleges were given plenty of time to conform, and radi-cal Protestants often met tolerance and sometimes sympathy. But the first decade of the reign witnessed the effective trans-formation of most colleges into Protestant institutions, where piety was inculcated more by sermons and informal teaching than by the academic syllabus. By the early seventeenth century the universities had become the most generally accepted route to a clerical living. But this situation was not easily or quickly achieved, and for most of Elizabeth's reign the main role of the universities probably lay more in providing the Church with an active élite of preachers than in creating a fully graduate clergy.[32]

---

[30] Manning, op. cit. 55. Cf. Glanmor Williams, *Welsh Reformation Essays* (Cardiff, 1967), 146–50.

[31] O'Day, *Journ. Eccl. Hist.* XIII. 149.

[32] See below, ch. IX, for further discussion of the impact of government policy on the universities. M. H. Curtis, *Oxford and Cambridge in Transition* (Oxford, 1959), chs. vii, viii. Id., 'The Alienated Intellectuals of Early Stuart England', *P&P* 23 (1962).

Bishops and secular officers lobbied and exhorted patrons in order to insert able men from the universities into influential positions. Bishop Curteys of Chichester got twenty clerics preferred to livings who were 'well able to preach in any learned audience in this realm'; and he trained forty others, 'sufficient enough to preach to any ordinary audience'. Archbishop Grindal brought forty preachers from the universities into the northern province. The Earl of Huntingdon, as Lord President of the North, said of himself: 'I do all that I can to get good preachers planted in the market towns of this country.' His record—in York, Newcastle, Halifax, Leeds, and elsewhere—bears out his claim. Combinations of preachers took it in turns to preach in parish churches or to organize conferences where two or three sermons would be followed by discussion.[33] Puritan propaganda, grinding away at the inadequacies of the clergy and the failure of the bishops to create a preaching ministry, has obscured a real, though obviously incomplete, achievement. In Canterbury diocese the vacant parishes were being filled with incumbents or curates in the early 1570s; the proportion of pluralists among the clergy was declining. The educational standard of parish priests was rising: more of them had degrees. More important, though more difficult to document or to analyse, a higher proportion than before seems to have been concerned with the spiritual mission of the Church. Even in the Welsh sees—obviously poor and supposedly backward—several of the cathedral and parish clergy were men of learning and integrity. It may well be that God's mysterious ways of purifying the Church included inflation: as grain prices rose, the incomes of parochial clergy improved, the number of ordinands increased, and the bishops were able, thanks to the wider choice of men, to raise the standard of incumbents.[34]

H. Kearney, *Scholars and Gentlemen* (1970), ch. i. H. C. Porter, *Reformation and Reaction in Tudor Cambridge* (Cambridge, 1958), part ii.

[33] Manning, op. cit. 64. R. A. Marchant, *The Puritans and the Church Courts in the Diocese of York, 1560–1642* (1960), 16. F. Peck, *Desiderata Curiosa* (1779), 151. Claire Cross, *The Puritan Earl* (1966), 254–69. P. Collinson, 'Lectures by Combination', *BIHR* XLVIII (1975).

[34] Daeley, *Journ. Eccl. Hist.* XVIII (1967). Glanmor Williams, *Welsh Reformation Essays*, 60. P. Tyler, 'The Status of the Elizabethan Parochial Clergy', *Studies in Church History*, IV, ed. G. J. Cuming (Leiden, 1967). R. O'Day, 'The Reformation of the

However, in the early years, the impact of the 'improved' clergy on parish life was slight and sporadic. Many priests remained attached to the old rituals, images, and ornaments of the Roman Church, and the government could not wait for them to die off before purging parochial life of these relics of the past. Persuasion was unlikely to be sufficient, and coercion had to be applied through episcopal visitations, spiritual courts, and the ecclesiastical commissions. Evidence of the early work of the commissions has survived only for the northern province, and such evidence may not be typical. But it seems likely that if the commission at York was actively engaged in extirpating ritualism and superstition, the commission in London was doing the same.[35]

The York commissioners issued sub-commissions to individuals to 'search out certain monuments of superstition' and ordered their destruction. Vestments were torn up, books were burned, statues and images were destroyed. In 1567 the church-wardens of Aysgarth were sentenced to attend the service 'bare-headed, bare-footed and bare-legged', publicly to confess that they had hidden 'certain idols and images undefaced' and also 'certain old papistical books in the Latin tongue', and then, after the communion service, to burn all their images outside the church. The ringing of bells and the burning of candles for the dead were also put down. While the general effect of these suppressive measures cannot be estimated with certainty, it seems probable that from the early 1570s superstitious cere-monies and images in the parish churches were no longer a serious problem. Visitation records of later years are taken up with quite different matters: fornication, working on Sundays, failure to wear the surplice, non-residence, decay of the church fabric, failure to preach or arrange for sermons, but not adherence to the ceremonies of the old faith. The suppression of these visible manifestations was not perhaps unduly difficult, simply because they *were* visible and derived their effect from being seen. Once put down they were not easily restored, since statues and vestments were expensive for a small country parish.

Ministry', in O'Day and Heal, op. cit. As so often, the picture in Lancashire was much less rosy: see Haigh, *Reformation and Resistance*, 236–44.

[35] P. Tyler, *The Ecclesiastical Commission and Catholicism in the North, 1562–77* (1960). J. S. Purvis, *Tudor Parish Documents* (Cambridge, 1948), *passim*.

Their loss was a serious blow to the continued nourishment of the old faith.[36] But there were some areas where local conservatism was sufficiently tough to withstand the pressure of government. In Lancashire especially many symbols of popular Catholicism survived in the parishes beyond the end of the century: as late as 1604 Lancashire people were described as 'signing themselves with the sign of the cross on the forehead at all prayers and blessings'.[37]

In that county a strong body of recusant priests encouraged the laity to abstain from Anglican services and provided the Mass in secret. But elsewhere laymen seem to have been deprived of effective Catholic guidance and most of them apparently attended the services of the established Church, even if they did not always communicate. Except in Lancashire, where the government acted vigorously against recusant gentlemen in 1568, the Privy Council dealt gently with suspect laymen. In most counties there is little sign of that vigorous action from the centre which is apparent after 1575.[38] At York the policy of the commissioners was directed to winning over a few prominent opponents of the settlement by persuasion rather than serious coercion. On the whole they were remarkably lenient. Edward More of Barnborough near Doncaster suffered nothing worse than a public confession and a fine of twenty shillings for continually disturbing church services by brawling and horn-blowing, as well as calling his mother a whore. William Hussey, a highly influential Catholic sympathizer, who possessed Harding's *Epistle to Dr Jewel*, was merely put under comfortable house-arrest. Real severity was shown only towards Sir Thomas Metham and his wife, Lady Edith. The Methams, who refused to conform after all attempts at persuasion had been made, were finally imprisoned.[39]

Provided that Catholic laymen showed a reasonable degree of outward conformity they were seldom molested in the first

[36] Tyler, op. cit., *passim*, esp. 14, 47–50. Purvis, op. cit. 36–59, 144–6. Cf. *APC* viii. 257.   [37] Haigh, op. cit. 216–24.

[38] For Lancashire, Haigh, op. cit. 247–62. More generally, see W. R. Trimble, *The Catholic Laity in England* (Cambridge, Mass., 1964), 45–9. The State Papers and the Acts of the Privy Council both give the impression that, outside Lancashire, the central government was fairly inactive in suppressing the Catholic laity between 1562 and 1569. On Catholic attitudes, see Elliott Rose, *Cases of Conscience* (Cambridge, 1975), ch. vi.

[39] Tyler, *Ecclesiastical Commission*, ch. ii. Cf. Purvis, op. cit. 74–81.

seventeen years of the reign. Up to 1569 and possibly thereafter they did not always have to take the oath of supremacy to remain as Justices of the Peace. The reason is illustrated by Bishop Curteys's career in Sussex. Promoted Bishop of Chichester in 1570, Curteys held off for seven years from confronting the dissident gentry, although he believed, no doubt rightly, that many of them 'pretend well, and yet be not sound in religion'. When he did act against the crypto-catholics he behaved with astonishing lack of tact. Without any warning he summoned thirty-five suspected gentry to a consistory in Chichester Cathedral, where those who turned up were subjected to searching questions about their attendance at church, their relations with exiles, and the conduct of their household. The three most important gentlemen protested to the Privy Council, and Curteys, who was only executing the law, was driven to apologize. The parish clergy and still more the churchwardens, who seldom had any social standing or influence, might be coerced, but the gentry were a different matter. Sudden confrontations had to be avoided. All means short of coercion had to be tried before they were roughly handled.[40]

However the Crown had other resources at its disposal apart from direct coercion. The most important of these was control over appointments to local offices. No wholesale transformation of the ruling establishment was possible, since there were not enough qualified Protestants immediately available and the mesh of local and regional interests could not suddenly be torn apart. But gradually the government could indicate that religious conformity would be rewarded by favour and patronage. In Sussex, an exceptionally conservative shire, the county lieutenancy was held by two Catholic peers, Arundel and Lumley, until 1569. Then, after the northern rising, both were excluded and the lieutenancy entrusted to Buckhurst and de la Warr, both Protestants, and to Montague, a loyal Catholic.[41]

Commissions of the peace were slowly but distinctly remodelled from the very beginning of Elizabeth's reign. Justices appointed by Mary were often removed by her sister: sixteen out of the forty-two Marian J.P.s for Norfolk were excluded from the commission in 1559. In Sussex the changes took place

[40] Manning, *Religion and Society*, ch. iv.
[41] Ibid., ch. xi. Id., 'The Making of a Protestant Aristocracy', *BIHR* XLIX (1976).

later and more slowly: between 1560 and 1565 twenty-five of
the thirty-seven Marian Justices were put out. In neither
county did this produce a uniformly Protestant bench; nor did
it do so elsewhere. The survival of prominent Catholics on the
commissions of the peace in many shires provoked complaints
from bishops, Protestant gentlemen, and reforming clerics. It is
evidence that change was neither as rapid nor as complete as
those men—and perhaps the Privy Council—would have
wished. But historians should not be misled by it into supposing
that there was no change at all.[42]

One powerful set of men was relatively little disturbed by
religious change, since all the Marian assize-judges remained
in office after the Elizabethan settlement. The most drastic step
taken by the government was the demotion of the two Chief
Justices, Browne and Saunders, both strong Catholics, to ordinary judgeships, which each retained until his death. Many of
the judges who rode the assize circuits in the early part of Elizabeth's reign had Catholic sympathies or relatives. Richard Wes-
ton, who rode the Western circuit, was the father-in-law of Sir
Benjamin Tichborne, an obstinate Hampshire papist. John
Walsh and Nicholas Powtrell, on the Northern circuit, were
accused by the Bishop of Carlisle of making 'a good show of
religion in giving their charge', but otherwise showing themselves 'not favourable to any manner or cause of religion, which
the people much mark and talk of'. Only in the 1570s did the
death of existing judges allow the Crown to make new
appointments. The men recruited to the assize circuits in that
decade were not enthusiastically Protestant: they have been described by the most authoritative historian of these courts as
'conservative'. But they were men upon whom the government
could apparently rely for severe action against dissidents, both
Catholic and Puritan.[43]

Until more research has been completed on the officers of
local and central government it will be impossible to give a full
account of the Crown's use of patronage in the establishment
of Protestantism. It is unlikely that the replacement of Catholic

[42] Manning, *Religion and Society*, ch. xii. Cockburn, *History of Assizes*, 189–219. J. H.
Gleason, 'The Personnel of the Commission of the Peace, 1554–64', *Huntington Library
Quarterly*, xviii (1954/55). A. H. Smith, 'The Personnel of the Commission of the Peace,
1554–64: a Reconsideration', ibid. xxii (1958/59).
[43] Cockburn, *History of Assizes*, 192–208.

by Protestant officers proceeded at a uniform rate in each county. Possibly the Privy Council was most concerned to install reliable men in the vulnerable shires of the south and the south-east: this may explain the fairly rapid ejection of Marian J.P.s from the Sussex commission of the peace. The Crown also seems to have been readier to eject J.P.s than professional assize-judges, possibly because the professionals were more difficult to replace, possibly because they held their offices by patent.[44]

From the beginning of the reign Elizabeth's government had exploited the weapons of propaganda from press and pulpit. Preaching was forbidden between December 1558 and April 1559, but when it was once again allowed the Crown methodically encouraged Protestant divines. The preachers at St Paul's Cross, the great centre for sermons in London, were men of strongly Protestant views; and many of them were specifically recommended by William Cecil. In most parishes the congregation had to be content with a reading of the Homilies, for relatively few ministers were licensed to preach. The Queen ordered a new edition of the Homilies, which had been first produced under Edward VI, and commanded that one of them be read every Sunday, except on those days—which should have occurred at least once a quarter—when a sermon was preached by a licensed preacher.[45]

The value of the printing press had been realized since the 1530s, when Thomas Cromwell had been the first of the Crown's servants to exploit it systematically.[46] He had an able successor in William Cecil, who in 1561 prompted Bishop Jewel to write his *Apologia Ecclesiae Anglicanae*. Cecil told Nicholas Throckmorton: 'I have caused an *Apology* to be written but not printed, in the name of the whole clergy, but I stay the publication of it until it may be further pondered.' By January of the following year the pondering was over and the work was published in Latin. It was soon translated into English by Lady

---

[44] Judges rode the assize circuits under the authority of commissions, but they held their posts in the central courts by patent.

[45] Millar Maclure, *The Paul's Cross Sermons, 1534–1642* (Toronto, 1958). Hughes & Larkin, II, nos. 460, 461.

[46] F. le van Baumer, *The Early Tudor Theory of Kingship* (New Haven, 1940), app. A. W. G. Zeeveld, *Foundations of Tudor Policy* (1948), chs. vi, vii. Elton, *Policy and Police*, ch. iv.

Bacon, Cecil's sister-in-law and the wife of Lord Keeper Bacon.[47]

Of still greater significance in the history of propaganda was John Foxe's *Acts and Monuments*, better known as the *Book of Martyrs*. Foxe was fully conscious of the value of the press: 'The Lord', he wrote, 'began to work for His Church not with sword and target to subdue his exalted adversary, but with printing, writing and reading . . .'[48] His massive work had first appeared in Latin in 1559, and the first English edition was published in 1563. Its publisher, John Day, had already received encouragement from the government, for he had been granted patents for printing ABCs as well as books of devotion. Foxe himself was granted a prebend at Salisbury when his *Book of Martyrs* came out. Important as it was in preserving the heroic story of the Protestants under Mary, his work did much more than that. Through rhetoric, history, and pictures it celebrated the triumph of true doctrine in the English nation and their new monarch. The book was powerfully supported by the clerical establishment, and bishops, deans, archdeacons, and canons were ordered to make it readily available in cathedrals and in their homes.[49]

Cecil himself was later to write the *Execution of Justice in England*, a tract expounding and justifying the royal policy towards Catholic missionaries. It was published in English in 1583 and later translated into Latin, French, Dutch, and Italian. It was followed closely in time and importance by *The Copy of a Letter . . . to Don Bernadino Mendoza*, which publicly proclaimed the loyalty of English Catholics to their Queen. Even schoolchildren were subjected to the government's propaganda, for the Privy Council ordered that a grammar-book, *Anglorum Prelia*, with a treatise on the good government of the Queen, should be used in schools instead of such heathen poets as Ovid.[50]

The government did not restrict itself to encouraging the publication of polemic. A statute of 1563 commanded the translation of the Bible and the Book of Common Prayer into Welsh.

[47] Conyers Read, *Mr Secretary Cecil and Queen Elizabeth* (1955), 262.

[48] W. Haller, *Foxe's Book of Martyrs and the Elect Nation* (1963), 110.

[49] Ibid., *passim*, esp. 118–28, 221.

[50] Conyers Read, 'William Cecil and Elizabethan Public Relations', in *Elizabethan Government and Society*, ed. S. T. Bindoff *et al.* 21–55. *APC* XIII. 389.

By 1567 William Salesbury and Richard Davies had completed their translations of the New Testament and the Prayer Book; the Old Testament, translated by William Morgan, appeared in 1588. Thus the scriptures were opened to the Welsh, at least to the literate minority.[51]

By about 1575 the government had probably advanced a long way in the campaign to secure an outward observance of its religious settlement. Although some powerful enclaves of the old faith remained, especially in Lancashire, many had been overrun. But already the balance of forces and the nature of the battle were beginning to change. The rising of the northern earls in 1569 had raised the threat of foreign invasion backed by a subversive Catholic minority. The papal bull of excommunication, the Ridolfi plot, and the Massacre of St Bartholomew's Day had stimulated further *frissons* of alarm. In 1574 the arrival of the first seminarist priests from Douai, expressly destined to overthrow the Protestant settlement, convinced the government that it could no longer accord gentle treatment to a minority which seemed decidedly hostile. The danger was of course nothing like so serious as it appeared. But even so the seminarists did change the nature of English Catholicism. An amorphous group of occasional conformists or 'church-papists' was replaced by a defiant body of recusants under the selfless and co-ordinated leadership of the missionaries.[52]

The Crown's immediate response to the rising of the earls and the bull of excommunication had been the passage of two statutes in 1571, making it treason to bring papal bulls into the country and ordering that anyone leaving the country for more than six months should forfeit his lands: what Mary had unsuccessfully attempted in 1555, Elizabeth now won from Parliament.[53] But executive action was probably more important than the creation of new laws. In the summer of 1575 the Privy

[51] 5 Elizabeth c. 28. G. Williams, *Welsh Reformation Essays*, 60, 185–6, 195–9.

[52] Dickens, *Yorks Arch. Soc, Journ.* xxxv. J. Bossy, 'The Character of Elizabethan Catholicism', in T. Aston (ed.), *Crisis in Europe, 1560–1660* (1965), 229–38. Meyer, *England and the Catholic Church*, ch. ii. Haigh, *Reformation and Resistance*, chs. xvi, xvii. On the subsequent development of English Catholicism see John Bossy's magisterial work, *The English Catholic Community, 1570–1850* (1975).

[53] 13 Elizabeth cc. 2, 3.

Council, which had hitherto left the problem of recusancy to local agencies, opened a campaign against leading Catholic laymen. On 12 August 1575 two J.P.s and six other gentlemen from Staffordshire were called to London and ordered to listen to the persuasions of various bishops. When episcopal arguments failed the gentlemen were called before the Privy Council itself and told that 'considering the little conformity they had as yet shewed, they could not be suffered to return home unless they would more dutifully submit themselves ...'[54] Further conferences with the bishops were arranged and in one or two cases they succeeded. But most of the obstinate gentlemen, including some new arrivals from Devonshire, were for a time imprisoned. Those who failed to conform by the following June were allowed home only on strict conditions: that they would attend on their diocesan bishop for conferences; that they would refrain from any argument against the established religion outside these conferences; that they would not allow 'any unnecessary repair of people to their houses'; and that they would themselves stay in their homes, giving bonds of £400 each to return again to their prisons in the Michaelmas term.[55]

During the next few years the Council turned its weapons of coercion against the recusants of other counties. The gentlemen of Lancashire, Yorkshire, Norfolk, and Suffolk were scrutinized with particular care. A general census of recusants in every diocese, the two universities, and the Inns of Court was ordered. In all this the Council was following on a national scale a policy that had already been adopted for Lancashire. Persuasion and argument were combined with the threat and the reality of prison; a promise of freedom was offered to those who conformed. A remarkably careful, individual attention was given by the Council to each of these important recusants. The attack was aimed at selected and influential targets.[56]

At the same time general orders were issued for removing recusants from the commission of the peace, although those who conformed were assured of restoration. In 1579 the assize-judges were ordered to administer the oath of supremacy to all J.P.s; and in most counties this was evidently done.[57] Gradually the

---

[54] *APC* ix. 17.   [55] Ibid. ix. 13, 17, 40, 46, 75, 105, 110, 145-7.

[56] Ibid. x. 87-8, 94-5 (Nov. 1577).

[57] Ibid. ix. 233, 238, 257. Cockburn, *History of Assizes*, 208.

chief positions of prestige and influence in the counties were being closed to Catholics. By 1587 only one Sussex magistrate was suspected of popery, though others had Catholic relatives. In Glamorgan the members of the prominent family of Turberville were excluded from the commission of the peace after 1564.[58]

In 1581 the Crown turned to legislation. A much heavier fine, of £20 per month, was imposed upon convicted recusants. As an encouragement to prosecution, common informers, as well as churchwardens, were allowed to bring charges of recusancy; and cases might now be heard in the secular courts.[59] Six years later the procedure for convicting recusants was considerably overhauled by a second statute.[60] Conveyances of land made by recusants to avoid payment of fines were rendered void. Once convicted, a recusant had to go on paying the fine until he conformed: no further trials or convictions were needed. If he failed in his payments the Crown might seize his goods and two-thirds of his land, holding them until he died or conformed. The Crown thus acquired the use of the lands and goods, but not a legal title to them. Finally the procedures for indictment and mesne process were drastically simplified in the interests of the Crown. In 1593 further penalties were imposed on recusants: those with lands were to go to their homes and remain within a five-mile limit; those without lands were to abjure the realm. More threatening still, by a neat legal device, the conforming husband of a recusant wife could now be burdened with his wife's fines.[61]

While the legal penalties for recusancy were being stiffened the machinery for imposing them was improved. The 1581 act confined the power of imposing the £20 fine to the J.P.s, the Justices of Assize, and the Court of King's Bench; the 1587 act removed this power from the J.P.s, who presumably could not be trusted to convict. But since this still left the detection and prosecution of offenders very much to chance, from 1583 onwards the Privy Council began to entrust the execution of

---

[58] Manning, *Religion and Society*, ch. xii. Glanmor Williams (ed.), *Glamorgan County History*, IV (1974), 174, 235–9.

[59] 23 Elizabeth c. 1.   [60] 29 Elizabeth c. 6.

[61] 35 Elizabeth c. 2. For the recusancy statutes see H. Bowler, *Recusant Roll No. 2, 1593–94* (Catholic Record Soc. LVII, 1965), ix–xlviii. Cockburn, *History of Assizes*, 209–12.

its policy to specially picked lay recusancy commissioners, who were given fully effective authority to investigate and question suspects in 1591. From the Crown's point of view such commissions had a great advantage: unlike the larger commissions of the peace they could be composed wholly of men known to be actively Protestant. The Crown was using a specially selected group within the county élite: this might not be popular, but it was more likely to be effective.[62]

Alongside its drive against recusants the Crown opened a savage campaign against seminarist priests. The Act of Supremacy of 1559 had laid down penalties for upholding the papal jurisdiction, making a third offence punishable as treason; a further act of 1563 had stiffened the penalty for a first offence; and the statute of 1571 had made it treasonable to bring in papal bulls.[63] In 1581, some years after the entry of seminarists and Jesuits, Parliament authorized the penalties of high treason for anyone claiming the power to absolve subjects from allegiance to the Queen or withdrawing men from obedience to the state.[64] In the following year Queen and Council took the drastic and remarkable step of issuing a proclamation which declared all seminarists and Jesuits to be *ipso facto* traitors. For the first time a conviction for treason could be grounded upon a man's status without his making any overt act or statement. Although this was done in the first place by proclamation only, it was confirmed by statute in 1585. Under the law priests could be executed or banished merely for being priests.[65]

To make the law into reality the Crown needed information about sources of disaffection, actual or potential. Faced with an organized and skilful opposition, William Cecil and Francis Walsingham used secret agents—Robert Bernard, Walter Williams, Thomas Rogers, and Malverney Catlin—to penetrate the English Catholic world. They did not create the sophisticated counter-intelligence system with which legend has credited them; but whereas even the most active of their predecessors,

[62] R. B. Manning, 'Elizabethan Recusancy Commissions', *HJ* xv (1972). Hughes & Larkin, iii, nos. 738–9. T. Rymer, *Foedera*, xvi. 201. Cockburn, *History of Assizes*, 209–12. *APC* xii, 59; xiv, 8; xxii. 203, 211, 213–15, 324, 342.
[63] 1 Elizabeth c. 1. 5 Elizabeth c. 1. 13 Elizabeth c. 2.
[64] 23 Elizabeth c. 1.
[65] Hughes & Larkin, ii, no. 660. Cf. ibid., nos. 650, 655. F. A. Youngs, 'Definitions of Treason in an Elizabethan Proclamation', *HJ* xiv (1971). 27 Elizabeth c. 2.

Thomas Cromwell, had relied only upon casual and unpaid informers, they had to employ professionals. Their efforts were suitably rewarded: between 1570 and 1603, 189 men were martyred and many others imprisoned in Wisbech Castle, Banbury Castle, and other strongholds.[66]

From about 1580 the Crown intensified its campaign to suppress Catholic literature. The censorship of heretical books already had a long history in England. The rudiments of a licensing system had been created in 1530, when approval from the diocesan authorities became necessary before a book could be published.[67] Under Mary, whose government was generally ineffective in executing censorship regulations, a fresh piece of machinery had been introduced when the Stationers' Company received its first charter in 1557. Although this was probably the outcome of commercial lobbying rather than governmental initiative, the Company became an important arm of the law of censorship. At the beginning of Elizabeth's reign the Act of Supremacy had made it a crime to uphold any foreign spiritual jurisdiction by preaching, writing, or publishing; and a committee of privy councillors and clerical dignitaries had been authorized by the injunctions of 1559 to license books for publication. While the power to give or withhold a licence thus lay in theory with a small number of men eminent in Church or State, the execution of the law was in practice entrusted to the Stationers' Company, which acted as the Crown's agent in return for a monopoly of printing and bookselling.[68]

During the first decades of Elizabeth's reign this system had had only a light impact upon writers and publishers. The official committee of censors seems to have been an inactive watchdog and the Wardens of the Stationers' Company had either licensed books themselves or consulted some unofficial

[66] Elton, *Policy and Police*, chs. vii–ix. C. Read, *Mr Secretary Walsingham* (Oxford, 1925), II. 322–36, 415–20. C. F. Nuttall, 'The English Catholic Martyrs, 1535–1680', *Journ. Eccl. Hist.* XXII (1971). Meyer, *England and the Catholic Church*, ch. ii.

[67] Hughes & Larkin, I, nos. 122, 129, etc. E. J. Devereux, 'Elizabeth Barton and Tudor Censorship', *Bulletin of the John Rylands Library*, XLIX (1966). D. M. Loades, 'The Press under the Early Tudors', *Trans. Cambridge Bibliographical Soc.* IV (1964).

[68] G. Pollard, 'The Company of Stationers before 1557', *The Library*, 4th ser. XVIII (1938). W. W. Greg, *Some Aspects and Problems of London Publishing between 1550 and 1650* (Oxford, 1956), ch. i. 1 Elizabeth c. 1. Hughes & Larkin, II, no. 460.

advisers. In 1586 the Crown finally issued more rigorous decrees. The number of presses was restricted, the Wardens of the
Company were given wider powers, and sharper punishments
were devised for a breach of the laws. Two years later a special
panel of twelve preachers was appointed to peruse and authorize books for publication.[69]

Censorship seems to have been fairly successful in restricting
the publication of Catholic works in England. Since there were
few recognized English printers and most of them worked in
London, they could easily be watched, and the lives of clandes-
tine presses were generally short. William Carter, who may
have begun work on his own in about 1575, was imprisoned
in 1579 and hanged in 1583. A rapid flow of subversive works followed the arrival of Campion and Parsons in 1580. But the two
presses established by Parsons were broken up in 1581 after issuing only eight works between them; Richard Rowland, who
published a report on the death of Campion, and Parsons himself soon left the country. A Welsh press was later discovered
in a cave by the sea; but it had produced little. Rather more
Catholic books were printed in England during the last years
of Elizabeth's reign, some of them with official connivance. But
the tolerance of the Crown did not extend far.[70]

A much greater threat came from abroad. John Fowler began printing for the English Catholic market in Louvain in 1565
and later moved to Antwerp. He had many colleagues, rivals,
and successors. In spite of the English government's attempt
to suppress the overseas presses by ambassadorial pressure, they
survived and flourished—not surprisingly. In 1580 William
Fulke listed forty-one Catholic titles printed at home or abroad.
In all, 223 Catholic books were published in the reign of Elizabeth. It is not possible to tell how many of these were printed
at home, how many overseas, since the publishers protected
themselves by omitting or falsifying the imprint. But probably
the great majority were printed in France and Flanders.[71]

From about 1576 the government seems to have become

---

[69] E. Arber, *A Transcript of the Registers of the Company of Stationers of London, 1554–1640* (1875–94), II. 807–12. Greg, op. cit., chs. i, iii.

[70] Youngs, 'Definitions of Treason', *HJ* XIV (1971), 678–85. Leona Rostenberg, *The Minority Press and the English Crown* (Nieuwkoop, 1971), 20–4, 62–3.

[71] Rostenberg, op. cit., chs. ii–iv. A. F. Allison and D. M. Rogers, *A Catalogue of Catholic Books in English … 1558–1640* (Biographical Studies, III, 1956).

acutely aware of this threat. A Privy Council letter of 13 December 1576 to the Lord Warden of the Cinque Ports spoke of 'lewd and evil disposed subjects' who have left their exile in Louvain and Douai and come over with 'divers Popish books and trumperies'.[72] The Lord Warden was to have incoming passengers carefully searched. Later, the importers of forbidden books were more severely dealt with: Gabriel Colford, 'being a most lewd person employed from the fugitives beyond the seas', and his landlord, Thomas Foulkes, were put to the torture of the manacles in Bridewell. A Fleming, Cornelius Waters, was banished after several years' residence for importing seditious books.[73] Orders were sent to the customs officers to search cargoes and seize Catholic literature. Sometimes these orders had their effect. An undated list of books taken from a ship specifies 700 sheets containing *A Miracle Wrought upon an English Woman at Bruxelles*, 367 copies of R. Bristowe's *Motives to the Catholic Faith*, twenty-eight copies of More's *Dialogue of Comfort*, and twenty copies of *A Treatise of Treasons*. But the notoriously corrupt customs officials could often be bribed or evaded. In 1602 Bishop Bancroft asked Robert Cecil to send a 'round and earnest letter' to the surveyor of the London custom-house, ordering a more careful and honest search. Apparently the surveyor's underlings had been confiscating prohibited books and selling them at a profit, thus demonstrating that a market for Catholic literature existed.[74]

England, by contrast with France and the Netherlands, was however relatively well placed to stop the infiltration of subversive propaganda. Her only land frontier—to the north—was not likely to be a serious threat of that kind. But, even so, a good many books got through to private hands. As early as 1565 William Hussey, a Yorkshire gentleman, was charged by the Ecclesiastical Commission with possessing books printed at Louvain, in particular one of William Harding's replies to Bishop Jewel. The frequent searches of recusant houses often uncovered small libraries of prohibited works. In 1585 the Queen was complaining that the anonymous work, *Leicester's*

---

[72] *APC* IX. 248. Cf. ibid. VIII. 331; IX. 35, 37; X. 246.
[73] *APC* XXV. 73, 479; XXVI. 10.
[74] Arber, op. cit. I. 492. HMC, *Salisbury*, XII. 312, 318, 326. Cf. Rostenberg, op. cit., chs. iii, iv.

Commonwealth, 'containing notoriously slanderous and hateful matter' against the Earl had been widely distributed.[75] But the government had some success even if it was only limited. Since Catholic books could only be brought in through secret and trusted channels, they could only support the lives of the devout. They could hardly make much impact on the heretics.

In one respect government censorship was remarkably successful. Before the beginning of Elizabeth's reign, an attack on the traditional drama had opened. A statute of 1543 forbade the playing of interludes contrary to the doctrine of the Church.[76] Edward VI and Mary ordered that all plays must be licensed by privy councillors or the monarch, and Elizabeth, at the start of her reign, delegated this duty to local officials, instructing them to suppress anything that dealt with religion or government. So public an art as the drama was obviously far more exposed to censorship than were books. By 1580 the Corpus Christi plays of York had disappeared and by the end of the century the traditional dramas of the medieval towns were no longer being performed.[77]

By contrast with the execution of the censorship, the operation of the recusancy laws seems to have been half-hearted. Proper enforcement depended upon local co-operation, particularly upon the co-operation of the gentry. Such help might not be given in regions where the local landowners were themselves related to Catholics; and the use of outsiders was often resented, as Bishop Curteys unhappily discovered. Lesser men, such as churchwardens, were inhibited from presenting the offences of the gentry. Even when they were accused, Catholics often failed to answer a summons or moved from one place to another so that it could not be served upon them. Officials could be bribed; and there were in any case too few of them, which forced the Crown to entrust some of its business to private agents, paid by results. Such men were even less likely to enforce the law

[75] Tyler, *Ecclesiastical Commission*, 32–4. Rostenberg, op. cit. 46–7 and chs. iii–iv. Peck, *Desiderata Curiosa*, 158–9.
[76] 34 & 35 Henry VIII c. 1. Hughes & Larkin, i, no. 240.
[77] Hughes & Larkin, i, nos. 344, 371; ii, nos. 390, 458. APC vi. 102, 110, 118, 168–9. A. G. Dickens, 'Tudor York', in *VCH, Yorkshire: City of York* (London, 1961), 152–3. Glynne Wickham, *Early English Stages*, ii (1963), i. chs. iii, iv.

honestly. Catholic estates were often undervalued and their owners were sometimes able to escape the threat of confiscation by the legal devices of trusts and uses. The enormous statutory fines were seldom levied in full. Had they been the Crown would have received £52,000 per annum from the 200 convicted recusants in Worcestershire. In fact only two men paid at the full rate and the Crown received £300 per annum. In Yorkshire only sixteen recusants ever paid the full fine in the reign of Elizabeth; and only one of those paid it over a long period.[78]

But although the recusancy fines were levied inefficiently, recusants were subjected to real economic penalties. Apart from the fines for absence from church they might be punished for harbouring priests or getting their children baptized away from the parish church. Under the acute pressure of war-finance in the 1590s the Crown turned to the recusant gentry for special assistance: the richer among them were made to pay £30, the more modest £15, towards the cost of providing light cavalrymen for the Irish wars. Apart from these penalties, recusants were often deprived of the profits of office in the central and local government.[79] Such losses are of course difficult to assess: the profits of office were not always very real since they could involve heavy outlay; and there is no certainty, or even probability, that a particular family would have sought or obtained office.

Sometimes however the Crown decided to make an example of a prominent Catholic and bring upon him a crushing weight of punishment. Between 1581 and 1605 Sir Thomas Tresham of Rushton paid £8,000 in penalties of various kinds. Out of an income of £3,500 per annum this might not have been ruinous had it been levied at an even rate. But when mortgage facilities were poor, large sums levied at irregular intervals were not easily found, especially by a landowner who was for much of

---

[78] Above, 259–64. Manning, *Religion and Society*, chs. iv–vi. Cockburn, *History of Assizes*, 209–12. Aveling, *Northern Catholics*, 125, 211. Id., 'Catholic Recusants of the W. Riding' (*Proc. Leeds Phil. and Lit. Soc.* x, 1963), 214–5. Peck, *Desiderata Curiosa*, 89. Haigh, *Reformation and Resistance*, 286–90. M. Hodgetts, 'Elizabethan Recusancy in Worcestershire', *Trans. Worcs. Arch. Soc.*, 3rd ser. 1 (1965–7). Cliffe, *Yorkshire Gentry*, 212–8, 221. Rose, *Cases of Conscience*, ch. v.

[79] *APC* xxvii. 588 (although the text here says £3 it must mean £20); xxix. 72, 79, 111, 116, etc.; xxx. 43.

the time in prison; and the heavy payments exacted in the years 1587–95 began the decay of the family fortunes.[80] In all likelihood only a few families suffered treatment of such severity. But in a time of economic change, when a landowner needed to adapt his management to circumstances, the penalties could reduce freedom of manœuvre and erode capital resources. Mr Cliffe has calculated that, among the Yorkshire gentry, about half the recusant families were in financial difficulties, compared with one-third of the Protestants.[81]

Intellectual pressures might seem to have been as important as financial exactions. All schoolmasters had to be licensed by the bishop, and it was forbidden to employ an unlicensed teacher or to send one's children abroad for their education. Under the Act of Supremacy, no one could take a university degree unless he had first subscribed to the oath; and from 1581 Oxford required the oath before a student could matriculate, although Cambridge remained free of this test until the reign of James I.[82] In law Catholics were cut off from an education in their faith. But in practice a large number of families sent children to seminaries and convents abroad, in spite of the risks; and some Catholic families, especially in Lancashire, employed recusant schoolmasters. Since most sons of gentlemen had no desire to proceed to a degree, the tests imposed by the universities were not very burdensome.[83]

At first sight the records and surveys of recusants suggest that monetary and social pressures were utterly ineffective in curbing Catholic numbers. In the West Riding of Yorkshire there were 271 presentments for recusancy in 1575–80, 750 (involving between 1,500 and 2,000 persons) in 1580–2, 1,013 in 1590–5,

---

[80] Mary Finch, *The Wealth of Five Northamptonshire Families* (Northants Record Soc., 1956), 76–8, 179–81. HMC, *Various Collections*, III. 1–154.

[81] Cliffe, op. cit., ch. x. Cf. J. E. Mousley, 'The Fortunes of Some Gentry Families of Elizabethan Sussex', *EcHR*, 2nd ser. XI (1958–59), 478–83. M. E. James, *Family, Lineage, and Civil Society* 137–40.

[82] 1. Elizabeth c. 1. 5 Elizabeth c. 1. 13 Elizabeth c. 3. 23 Elizabeth c. 1. 27 Elizabeth c. 2. Mark H. Curtis, *Oxford and Cambridge in Transition* (Oxford, 1959), 170–2, 194. Below, 304.

[83] Cliffe, op. cit. 184–6, 194–200. Aveling, *Northern Catholics*, 134–5. Haigh, op. cit. 291–2.

and 1,136 in 1603–4. Lancashire recusants rose from 304 in 1578 to 3,516 in 1604. Other counties show a similar increase.[84] These are of course the numbers of persons accused of recusancy; they reflect the energy and determination of local officers as well as the size of the Catholic community. But it seems beyond dispute that the years following the arrival of missionary priests witnessed a rapid increase in the number of recusants, and that the increase continued, rather more slowly, until the beginning of the following century.

Furthermore, the recusant population was surrounded and supported by a less determined group, the 'church-papists', who outwardly conformed to the Anglican settlement but inwardly sympathized with the Catholics. Since they seldom professed their views openly it is hard to discover either their numbers or their attitudes. But they cannot be sharply distinguished from the recusants, and some men seem to have wavered over the years between full-blooded recusancy and occasional conformity. A reliable estimate of Catholic strength must make some allowance for their numbers. One estimate suggests that by the end of the century crypto-Catholics may have been at least as numerous as recusants. In Lancashire a report of 1613 estimates that there were 2,075 recusants and 2,393 non-communicants, making up some 6 per cent or 7 per cent of the county's adult population.[85] Where the Catholic population was so large it was relatively safe to adhere openly to the proscribed religion: a Jesuit reported of Lancashire in 1600 that 'Catholics are so numerous that priests can wander through the villages and countryside with the utmost freedom'.[86] Across the Pennines a Yorkshire census of 1604 records only 1,839 recusants and 622 non-communicants, not more than $1\frac{1}{2}$ per cent of the communicant population. Even this low figure is probably above the average, for Yorkshire was then regarded as 'backward' in religion.[87]

This broadly quantitative approach to the problem, through lists of recusants and non-communicants, has its drawbacks, for

[84] H. Aveling, 'Catholic Recusants of the W. Riding', *Proceedings of Leeds Phil. and Lit. Soc.* x (1963), 205–11, 221. Id., *Northern Catholics*, 99, 169. Dickens, *Yorks. Arch. Soc. Journ.* xxxv. Haigh, op. cit. 276.

[85] Haigh, op. cit. 275–8.   [86] Ibid. 276.

[87] Dickens, 'The Extent and Character of Recusancy in Yorkshire', *Yorks. Arch. Soc. Journ.* xxxvii (1948–51).

much depended upon the efficiency of the government's agents. Dr R. B. Manning, in his study of Sussex, has adopted an alternative approach. Using all available evidence he has investigated the religious complexion of eighty-eight noble and gentry families in that county. At the beginning of Elizabeth's reign there were thirty-three Catholic families and only eighteen Protestant. By the 1580s, fifteen families had emerged as recusant but ten more had Catholic sympathies; and in the following decade sixteen were recusant, three were crypto-Catholic, but twenty-two were Protestant. The number whose attitudes remain unknown is large throughout the reign; but the absence of evidence can probably be taken to indicate conformity.[88]

Inevitably we know most about those areas, Lancashire and Yorkshire in particular, where Catholicism was strongest, for the Crown's attention was constantly directed towards them and Catholic activity was therefore very fully recorded. But elsewhere the evidence suggests a steady erosion of Catholic numbers. One might expect that north-west Wales, cut off by distance, mountains, and language from the seat of authority, would be firmly attached to the old faith. So indeed it was at the beginning of Elizabeth's reign. But in the later decades of the century the region contained few recusants, far fewer than the counties of the Welsh border. An area inaccessible to government was also inaccessible to missionaries, who found few gentry families in North Wales ready to shelter them. Priests could only operate effectively when they were protected within a Catholic circle, and they were in consequence unable, without incurring terrible risks, to move on to the offensive and convert Protestants. Their role had largely to be supportive; they could hardly ever engage in open proselytizing.[89]

The Crown was never able to destroy the convinced recusants; nor was it able to eliminate the missionary priests, for replacements always came for those who were captured. But it did evidently succeed in reducing gradually the size of the Catholic population as a whole and in isolating Catholics in scattered

---

[88] Manning, *Religion and Society*, 238–62.

[89] Glanmor Williams, *Welsh Reformation Essays*, 55–7. E. G. Jones, 'Catholic Recusancy in Denbighshire, Flint and Montgomery', *Trans. Hon. Soc. of Cymmrodorion* (1945). Id., 'The Lleyn Recusancy Case', ibid. (1936). Cf. Cliffe, *Yorkshire Gentry*, 193.

communities or particular regions. The isolation of English Catholics, rather than their number, is in the end of the greatest political consequence. Many of their children had been educated abroad and cut off from their contemporaries. This was admittedly not usually true of the eldest sons, who were generally kept in England, to be educated either by private tutors or with their Protestant contemporaries at the universities.[90] But the dilemma was serious: either Catholics cut themselves off from circles of influence or they risked association with Protestants and the consequent dangers of conformity. By and large they chose isolation. Catholicism was centred in the households of the nobles and gentry, who had to keep themselves isolated simply because the risks of contact with Protestants were too great: priests, vestments, and books might be discovered and prosecution follow. This isolation probably robbed Catholicism of social and political influence. It also lost contact with its popular roots. With the religious drama suppressed and Catholic services held secretly in the houses of recusant nobles and gentry, it became primarily the religion of landed households.[91]

The Catholic community was, with a few exceptions, loyal to the Queen and the political order. At the time of the Armada lay Catholics protested that they would give no support to the invaders. Those nobles and gentlemen who most effectively maintained Catholic households were, like Lord Montague in Sussex, entirely loyal to the Tudor regime.[92] Over this question Catholic laymen and some secular priests came into direct collision with the Jesuit faction, led by Father Parsons, who supported the claims of Philip II and then of the Spanish Infanta to the English succession. The hostility between the Jesuits and the seculars became openly apparent when the Jesuits secured the appointment from Rome of an Archpriest to command all Catholics in England. The secular priests appealed to the Pope against this decision, with the covert support of the English government. In the course of this dispute Robert Cecil opened negotiations with Parsons' opponents. These negotiations did not in the short run produce very much: only thirteen Catholic

---

[90] Cliffe, op. cit. 196–7.

[91] J. Bossy, 'The Character of Elizabethan Catholicism', in T. Aston (ed.), *Crisis in Europe, 1560–1660*. Manning, *Religion and Society*, ch. viii.

[92] Manning, op. cit. 159–65.

priests gave an assurance that they would disobey any command from Rome to subvert the throne. But in doing so they affirmed what was already the position of the Catholic laity and pointed forward to a future in which the Catholic community would accept political allegiance to a Protestant monarch.[93]

The signs are that by the last decade of the century the government—or at least its more influential and perceptive officers—was becoming aware that the Catholic minority was being undermined from within as well as assaulted from without. True, the Crown continued to initiate stiff measures against the Catholics. The act of 1593 restricted recusants to a five-mile radius from their homes; powerful recusancy commissions were issued to execute the law; the more recalcitrant recusants were imprisoned.[94] The Privy Council and its agents remained as concerned as ever to stop the arrival of priests and to destroy those who entered.

But the Privy Council's prime concern in these years was to locate, contain, and oversee the Catholic recusants, its secondary purpose to exploit them as a source of revenue. It achieved the first objective to a great extent by the act of 1593, which kept them firmly in place; the recusancy commissioners showed themselves diligent and efficient in the detective work of discovering recusants; and a large number of priests were kept in Wisbech Castle, where their quarrels were ultimately to tear the Catholic mission apart. It tapped their estates by seizing their horses for the Queen's service and by forcing them to pay a special levy for the provision of light cavalry in Ireland.[95] But a comparison of the state papers and the Privy Council register for the 1590s with the records of the previous decade gives the impression—and this is something that cannot be proved statistically—that the Council was now a good deal less alarmed about the recusants than it had been, rather less concerned to persuade and cajole them into conformity. There were of course parts of the country that still gave grounds for worry. A report on Lancashire and Cheshire bemoaned the emptiness

---

[93] J. Hurstfield, 'The Succession Struggle in Late Elizabethan England', in S. T. Bindoff (ed.), *Elizabethan Government and Society* (1961), 379–89. Hughes, *Reformation in England*, III. 373–96. Bossy, 'Elizabethan Catholicism'.

[94] 35 Elizabeth c. 2.

[95] Manning, *HJ* xv. 32–4. *APC* XXVI. 375; XXVIII. 588; XXIX. 111, 116, etc.

of the churches, the multitude of bastards and drunkards, the immunity of the Catholic priests from punishment, and the power of the recusants.[96] The Council in the North continued to be frightened of Catholic activity in Yorkshire and especially of the use of Groman Abbey near Whitby as a refuge for priests.[97] But these were regions of exceptional concern.

On the whole the Crown was content to contain the threat, which men like Burghley saw mainly in terms of national security. In a memorandum of March 1594 Burghley noted down 'what is fit to be done with the multitude of recusants of the realm'.[98] Lists should be made of certified recusants and the judgements against them; those once imprisoned and released should be incarcerated again if they were unreformed; conforming husbands should be made to pay fines for their recusant wives. All this is severe enough; but Burghley adds that, in order to avoid protest against the imprisonment of recusants, it should be made clear that this is done, not by way of punishment, since many Catholics are known to be loyal, but to convince foreign adversaries that they will get no help from the recusants if they invade. Burghley's attitude was the prelude to the still more flexible policy of his son, Robert Cecil, who remarked in conversation with the Venetian ambassador in James's reign that 'as far as blood goes, rest assured, provided the Catholics keep quiet; but as regards property the laws must be enforced; though even here we shall go dexterously to work and far more gently than in the days of the late Queen'. In spite of the weaknesses of the enforcement machinery and the government's inability to destroy hard-core recusancy, Elizabeth and her officials had so far managed to contain it that it was no longer a political or social force of any magnitude.[99]

This was however achieved at some cost. The Crown could only contain the Catholic threat by calling upon the forces of Protestant conviction; and often enough those forces were a good deal more radical than the Queen would have wished. Many of Elizabeth's bishops, such as Grindal, Hutton, and Curteys, used Puritan preachers to convert their sees to Protestantism.

[96] *CSPDom, 1591–4*, 158–9.
[97] *CSPDom, 1598–1601*, 188, 200, 232–3.
[98] *CSPDom, 1591–4*, 453. Cf. HMC, *Various Collections*, III. 53.
[99] Quotation from J. Hurstfield, 'Church and State, 1558–1612: the Task of the Cecils', in *Studies in Church History*, II (1965), 136.

Conferences and lectures were encouraged by bishops in the sees of Chichester, Peterborough, York, Lincoln, Chester, and possibly elsewhere.[100] In counties where Catholicism was strong Puritan clergy were tolerated and often supported. William Chadderton, Bishop of Chester, was privately reprimanded by Archbishop Sandys for allowing unsupervised conferences of his clergy and for yielding too much to 'general fastings, all the day preaching and praying'. 'The young ministers of these our times grow mad,' commented Sandys; but he did not stop their meeting; indeed he encouraged them as long as the bishop kept them under control. In practice Chadderton seems to have delegated supervision of these exercises to a number of Puritan moderators, who thus acquired a valuable influence.[101] Conferences were not necessarily the agents of Puritan opposition; but they were disliked by the Queen, and from some of them sprang the classical movement of the 1580s.[102]

Catholicism might be contained and a thoroughgoing form of Protestantism established in many parishes. But could one say that the population as a whole was Protestant, or even, in more than a nominal sense, Christian? How many adults understood the basic tenets of their Church? How many attended divine service regularly? Plain ignorance and irreligion were often as shocking to the clergy as Catholic survivals. It is reported that an old man of Cartmel in Lancashire, when told about Jesus Christ, remarked: 'I think I heard of that man you spake of once in a play at Kendal, called Corpus Christi play, where there was a man on a tree and blood ran down.'[103] No doubt the man of Cartmel was exceptional. But there were frequent complaints that parishioners preferred sports to church on Sundays, and were ignorant of the teachings of religion.[104]

While the political nation had largely acquiesced in the rapid alterations of royal policy between 1529 and 1559, the various

---

[100] Strype, *Annals*, III. 133, 325, 472, 477; IV. 544. Manning, *Religion and Society*, ch. x.

[101] Peck, *Desiderata Curiosa*, I. 102. Haigh, *Reformation and Resistance*, ch. xviii.

[102] R. A. Marchant, *The Puritans and the Church Courts*, chs. ii, iii. Manning, op. cit., ch. x. The standard work on Puritanism is P. Collinson, *The Elizabethan Puritan Movement* (1967). See also his important article, 'Lectures by Combination', *BIHR* XLVIII (1975). Haigh, loc. cit.   [103] Haigh, op. cit. 321.

[104] Ibid. 244–6. See also id., 'Puritan Evangelism in the Reign of Elizabeth I', *EHR* XCII (1977).

settlements of Edward VI and Mary had made relatively little impact upon the attitudes and feelings of men and women in the parishes. Elizabeth's task had been the creation of a Protestant nation which could withstand internal dissension and external threat. In this she succeeded. Although an organized recusant community was established in the last thirty years of her reign, it had virtually no chance of restoring Catholicism in England. The reversal of faith that had occurred in 1553 was impossible on the death of Elizabeth, for by then the nation was vociferously Protestant. It was to demonstrate its hatred of popery in the events leading up to the Civil War and in the reign of James II.

The government achieved this transformation without unleashing the furies of dissension and persecution that were visited on less fortunate countries. Religious differences played a part in the faction-fights of certain counties, but they seldom ranged beyond contention for place and preferment.[105] Spontaneous iconoclasm was rare and massacre unknown in Elizabethan England. County societies were generally cohesive and tended to resist attempts by government or fanatics to disrupt them.[106] The Crown itself, however fierce might be its persecution of priests, avoided imposing the oppressive burdens of a Spanish Inquisition. Freedom of press and pulpit was certainly restricted, but it was never wholly stifled by orthodoxy. Although the Crown treated the old Catholic clergy and the new missionary priests severely and sometimes savagely, it handled the recusant gentry with a lighter touch. Occasionally a prominent gentleman like Tresham might be singled out for exemplary punishment, but in general the political nation was pushed towards conformity rather than driven into resistance. Catholicism survived with the protection of local landowners, and became in consequence a religion of noble and gentry households, largely severed from popular roots.

The broad success of Elizabethan Protestantism owed much to its identification with authority. In the first place it was backed by the Crown, and then, as the political nation came into line, by the influence of the regional élites. The machinery

---

[105] e.g. in Norfolk. See A. Hassell Smith, *County and Court* (Oxford, 1974), ch. x.
[106] Manning, *Religion and Society*, 89. Cf. D. M. Loades, 'The Essex Inquisition of 1556', *BIHR* xxxv (1962).

of enforcement, in spite of its obvious and well-publicized weaknesses, applied effective, though spasmodic, coercion. The instruments of patronage, the persuasions of print and pulpit, the support of ardent Puritans, and, in the end, the effluxion of time all played their role. So too did the patriotic appeal against the Catholic threat from abroad. General respect for the policy of the Crown, the formal institutions of Church and State, and the informal pressures of patronage and influence were all necessary ingredients of the Anglican achievement.

IX

Court and Culture

While royal courts and their attendant nobles had long been patrons of European learning, art, architecture, and literature, the religious dissensions and dynastic rivalries of the sixteenth century prompted a more intense glorification of the image of monarchy, a closer shaping of the values extolled in drama, poetry, and painting, and an unprecedented need to develop and control the seats of learning. The consequences can be seen in the portraits, pageants, ceremonies, palaces, prodigy-houses, tombs, and schools of Tudor England. Since shortage of space makes it impossible to examine all of these, this chapter is confined to studying the impact of the state in two fields of learning and culture: the universities and the drama.[1]

Faced with the threat of heresy and dissension Cardinal Wolsey believed that 'it were best to set up learning against learning, and, by introducing able persons to dispute, suspend the laity betwixt fear and controversy'.[2] Universities were places where true doctrine could be kept secure and expounded to the whole nation. They were traditionally the 'nurseries' of the clergy and thus increasingly important as the emphasis upon an educated and preaching ministry gained ground. From the fifteenth century onwards they were also becoming more and more attractive to the laity, who entered them to prepare for the professions, for service to the state, and for polite society. Inhabited mainly by young men—and in the sixteenth century even the dons were mostly under thirty—the universities were both receptive to new ideas and easily disturbed by their intrusion. The Crown had to control them in order to preserve religious uniformity and to prevent internal disagreements from engendering disorder and sedition. It did this by a combination

[1] For some of these other fields see Joan Simon, *Education and Society in Tudor England* (Cambrige, 1966); David Cressy, *Education in Tudor and Stuart England* (1975); Eric Mercer, *English Art, 1555–1625* (Oxford, 1962); Roy Strong, *Tudor and Jacobean Portraits* (2 vols., 1969); id., *Holbein and Henry VIII* (1967); Frances Yates, *Astraea* (1975). Below, 359–71. [2] Simon, op. cit. 145.

of patronage and authority: colleges and chairs were founded, rules and tests imposed.[3]

The government worked through various institutions and officials. The titular head of each university was the Chancellor, originally a resident graduate, but, from the fifteenth century onwards, more often a clerical grandee. Henry VIII began the practice of appointing lay statesmen to the office when Thomas Cromwell became Chancellor of Cambridge University in 1533, but Bishop Longland of Lincoln, a faithful servant of the Crown, remained Chancellor of Oxford. Although the Earl of Hertford, later Duke of Somerset, became Chancellor of Cambridge in 1546 and was succeeded by his great rival, the Duke of Northumberland, in 1550, only one lay Chancellor, Sir John Mason, governed Oxford before 1558. With William Cecil, Chancellor of Cambridge from 1558 until 1598, and Leicester, Chancellor of Oxford from 1564 until 1588, both universities were brought under the rule of men prominent in the central government, who could bring to bear upon them the pressures of patronage and authority. Judicial and executive powers were in practice wielded by the Vice-Chancellors, who presided over the Chancellors' courts, hearing both civil and criminal cases, and fining, imprisoning, or expelling offenders.[4] In the early sixteenth century the influence of the Vice-Chancellors was relatively unimportant beside that of the resident M.A.s assembled in the Senate at Cambridge and in Congregation at Oxford. But gradually, with encouragement from the Crown, the balance of authority was edged away from these large and democratic assemblies of young men into the hands of the Vice-Chancellor and the heads of colleges. Before the Reformation, colleges had played a less important part in the structure of the university than they came to do under Henry VIII and his successors. They were often small and independent bodies, not easily subjected to authority, and by no means every member of the university belonged to one. In the second

[3] The standard histories of the universities are: J. B. Mullinger, *The University of Cambridge* (3 vols., Cambridge, 1873–1911); C. E. Mallet, *A History of the University of Oxford* (3 vols., 1924–7). Cambridge is better served by Mullinger than Oxford is by Mallet, but a new history of Oxford is in active preparation, Vol. iii of which will deal with the period of the Reformation.

[4] H. C. Porter, *Reformation and Reaction in Tudor Cambridge* (Cambridge, 1958), 163–4. W. A. Pantin, *Oxford Life in Oxford Archives* (Oxford, 1972), ch. v.

half of the century it was made impossible to belong to either university without entering a college or one of the few remaining halls. At the same time the government seems to have recognized the heads of houses as the rulers of their fellows and to have supported their authority. External control was provided—sometimes very actively so—by the college visitors, most of whom were bishops and therefore reliable officials of the Crown.

Chancellors, Vice-Chancellors, college visitors, and heads of houses were the permanent university officers through whom the government could work. For executing important changes of policy the Crown instituted occasional visitations of the two universities. Royal visitors were appointed in 1535, 1549, 1556, and 1559. In the reign of Elizabeth the Ecclesiastical Commission was also brought into play, although, as we shall see, its use was rare after about 1573.

Those were the instruments of control. The first major step in the development of royal authority was the issue of injunctions in 1535 under the auspices of Thomas Cromwell, the King's Vicegerent in religious affairs. All officers, doctors, fellows, and scholars of both universities and their colleges were to swear to maintain the King's succession and to obey all statutes for the extirpation of papal authority. Lombard's *Sentences*, the foundation of medieval teaching in theology, were banned, and all divinity lecturers were instructed to base their exposition directly upon the scriptures. Students were to be permitted to read the Bible privately. The 'frivolous' questions and 'obscure' glosses of Duns Scotus were no longer to be taught. The study of canon law was forbidden.[5]

Two sets of visitors, Dr John Price and Dr Thomas Leigh at Cambridge, Dr John London and Dr Richard Layton at Oxford, executed these injunctions. College charters were surrendered to the Crown, valuations of college property commanded. Lectureships were established in Latin, Greek, and Civil Law. At Oxford they set 'Duns in Bocardo' (the town gaol) and triumphantly watched the leaves of old manuscripts blowing round New College quadrangle as a hunting man gathered them up to make 'blawnsheres', a kind of scarecrow for preventing deer from breaking out of a wood. The

[5] C. H. Cooper, *Annals of Cambridge* (5 vols., Cambridge, 1842–1908), I. 374–6.

destruction of traditional learning was, on the surface at least, going forward.[6]

It was continued in the following year by the statute for the dissolution of the monasteries, which removed the monastic colleges from the two universities. In Oxford twelve monastic colleges disappeared, including Gloucester College and Durham College. In many cases their properties passed later to other, secular, colleges, such as St John's. Cambridge, with fewer monastic foundations, was less severely affected. The university viewed the event with suitable deference, expressing the hope that the Crown would convert the monastic houses into new colleges where, instead of 'lazy drones and swarms of impostors', men might be bred up to solid learning and the true gospel.[7]

Two new colleges were in fact founded under Crown auspices towards the end of Henry's reign. At Cambridge, Trinity College, 'of King Henry the Eighth's foundation', was established by letters patent in December 1546. Its revenue of about £1,600 per annum, granted mostly from the property of dissolved colleges in Cambridge, made it the richest in the university.[8] At Oxford the King built, literally, upon foundations laid by Wolsey twenty years before. In place of Cardinal College he established what was first called King's College and later Christ Church, a collegiate foundation attached to the newly established cathedral of Oxford and governed by the dean and chapter. Like Trinity it was well endowed, and with an income of £2,000 per annum became the richest college in either university.[9]

In 1535 the visitors had ordered the establishment of lectureships but had provided no endowment. The colleges were instructed to support them. However, in 1540 the King created and endowed, from the property of Westminster Abbey, five Regius professorships at Cambridge, at annual stipends of £40 each, for the teaching of divinity, civil law, medicine, Hebrew, and Greek. Five similar chairs were founded at Oxford in 1546.[10]

---

[6] Mullinger, op. cit. I. 630; II. 8. Mallet, op. cit. II. 61–3. Simon, op. cit. 198–200.

[7] Mallet, op. cit. II. 71–7. Simon, op. cit. 203.

[8] Cooper, *Annals*, I. 444–52. Mullinger, op cit. II. 81–6.

[9] Mallet, op. cit. II. 39–42.

[10] Cooper, *Annals*, I. 397. Mullinger, op. cit. II. 52. Mallet, op. cit. II. 71. Simon, op. cit. 207.

Under Henry VIII the Crown began a policy of interference in academic appointments which was to continue throughout the sixteenth and seventeenth centuries. When, in 1544, the mastership of Corpus Christi College, Cambridge, fell vacant the King sent a letter to the fellows recommending his own chaplain, Dr Matthew Parker, for the office, trusting that they would 'with one assent condescend to elect him for your Head'. The royal trust was not misplaced: Parker was duly elected and proved to be a diligent and distinguished Master.[11]

By the end of Henry's reign the universities were becoming alarmed at the danger posed to collegiate property by the designs of courtiers and others, for whom the dissolution of the monasteries had supplied a tempting precedent. The threat came closer when plans were made for the destruction of chantries and religious colleges, and for the dispersal of their lands. Queen Katherine Parr, petitioned by the universities, lent them her support; and the King himself expressed surprise that so many fellows of colleges were 'so honestly maintained in living by so little land and rent'.[12] But with the accession of Edward VI the pressure from courtiers was renewed and the chantries were finally dissolved in 1547–8. Fortunately for the universities they found an ally in the Lord Protector, Edward Seymour, Duke of Somerset, who defended them against depredation. 'If learning decay,' he wrote, 'which of wild men maketh civil, of blockish and rash persons wise and godly counsellors, of obstinate rebels obedient subjects, and of evil men good and godly christians, what shall we look for else but barbarism and tumult?'[13]

Somerset was a reformer of the universities as well as their defender, and in 1549 he sent visitors to both Oxford and Cambridge with radical schemes of change. One part of his plan was to promote the teaching of civil law, in order to train men for the practical service of the state. In this he was probably influenced by Thomas Smith, until recently Professor of Civil Law at Cambridge and now a member of the duke's own household.[14] Somerset proposed to merge Clare Hall and Trinity Hall

[11] Cooper, *Annals*, I. 417.

[12] Simon, op. cit. 210–13. *LP* xxi. ii. 296.

[13] M. L. Bush, *The Government Policy of Protector Somerset* (1975), 54.

[14] Margaret Dewar, *Sir Thomas Smith: a Tudor Intellectual in Office* (1964), ch. iv. A similar scheme had been proposed late in the reign of Henry VIII. Cf. *LP* xxi. ii. 321.

at Cambridge into a single institution, King Edward's College, devoted to the study of civil law. The plan met strong opposition from Stephen Gardiner, Master of Trinity Hall, and from the fellows of Clare, who had already sold the hall's plate and books on first hearing rumours of the merger. They were supported by Bishop Ridley, one of the commissioners, who was recalled to London for daring to question the Protector's policy. Although the proposal was never formally and explicitly rescinded, it was silently and gradually abandoned. So too, it seems, was a plan for converting the divinity fellowships at All Souls College, Oxford, into posts for the study of civil law.[15]

The visitors also brought with them proposals for the reform of the university curriculum, which were, for a time, more successful. Latin grammar was excluded from the university syllabus: it was to be taught in schools and no one should be allowed to come up who had not already mastered it. The traditional courses in logic were removed. The course for the B.A. now began with mathematics and proceeded to dialectic, rhetoric, and philosophy.[16] The individual colleges felt the impact of the visitations in severe—and more lasting—ways. Several officers and fellows were expelled or suspended for remaining firm to their Catholic beliefs. In college chapels altars were pulled down, reredoses destroyed, images broken up, and windows smashed. Sheaves of medieval books and manuscripts were burned.[17]

The Edwardian settlement of the universities was however short-lived. At Mary's accession Stephen Gardiner was restored as Chancellor of Cambridge. The Queen instructed the Vice-Chancellors and heads of houses to revoke all statutes, ordinances, and regulations that had been made since the death of her father. In Cambridge the heads of all colleges but three were removed. Vestments and ornaments were

[15] Cooper, *Annals*. II. 26–36. Mullinger, *Cambridge*, II. 133–8. Mallet, *Oxford*, II. 83. J. A. Muller (ed.), *The Letters of Stephen Gardiner* (Cambridge, 1933), 493–5: I owe this reference to Mrs Loach.

[16] Simon, *Education and Society*, 252–4. Mullinger, op. cit. II. 110–13. Mallet, op. cit. II. 84.

[17] Cooper, *Annals*, II. 28–30. Mallet, op. cit. II. 90–1. Anthony à Wood, *History and Antiquities of the University of Oxford*, ed. J. Gutch (Oxford, 1746), 94 ff. John Lamb, *A Collection . . . Illustrative of the History of the University of Cambridge* (1838), 102–54.

resurrected in college chapels. In 1555 Gardiner instructed the Vice-Chancellor of Cambridge that no man should be admitted to office, fellowship, or degree within the university unless he first 'openly in the congregation detested particularly and by articles the heresies lately spread in this realm'.[18]

After Gardiner's death in 1555, Cardinal Pole became Chancellor of Cambridge and in the following year Sir John Mason resigned the chancellorship of Oxford after convocation had agreed to elect Pole in his place.[19] Pole then sent visitors and statutes to both universities. The statutes, which were intended only as an interim measure, laid down procedure for elections and insisted on the observance of the Christian faith.[20] The visitors burned the exhumed bodies of two foreign Protestants, Bucer and Fagius, as well as heretical books and manuscripts; and they restored ecclesiastical ornaments and vestments.[21] But the government was not concerned only with the dangers of heresy and the revival of Catholic ceremony in the colleges. The study of canon law was encouraged; the M.A. course was shortened so that clerics could be produced more rapidly to fill vacant benefices; the Queen granted money for the restoration of the Divinity Schools at Oxford; and three new colleges were founded with royal encouragement—Gonville and Caius at Cambridge, Trinity and St John's at Oxford.[22]

The early Tudor period had witnessed rapid and dramatic changes in both universities. Heads and fellows of colleges were expelled, suspended, and restored. Catholic ceremony and ritual were banned and then revived. Plans for promoting the study of civil law were produced and scotched, while the Edwardian reforms of the curriculum were annulled by Mary. Other changes were more permanent. Books were burned and images destroyed. The monastic colleges disappeared for ever. Scholasticism was rejected in 1535. Regius chairs were founded at both universities. New colleges were established, most of

[18] Mullinger, op. cit. II. 149–55. Cooper, *Annals*, II. 79, 83, 94–6. Mallet, op. cit. II. 94–9.

[19] Andrew Clark, *Register of the University of Oxford* (Oxford, 1887), II. 239.

[20] Cooper, *Annals*, II. 128–9.

[21] Wood, *History*, II. 133–4. Cooper, *Annals*, II. 112–28. Lamb, *Collection*, 181–274.

[22] I am grateful to Mrs Loach for information on the more positive aspects of Marian policy towards the universities.

them by private persons, but two, Trinity, Cambridge, and Christ Church, Oxford, by Henry VIII.

Elizabeth's government was confronted with universities that had been subject for twenty years to conflicting pressures and severe disagreements over religion.[23] It began by issuing commissions for royal visitations of both Oxford and Cambridge. By contrast with the Marian visititation, but following the precedent of 1549, Elizabeth appointed predominantly lay commissions, headed by the two Chancellors, Sir John Mason for Oxford and Sir William Cecil for Cambridge. The visitations were accompanied by the deprivation or resignation of several heads of colleges at both universities. In Cambridge only the Masters of Pembroke and St John's were expelled by the visitors, but four others resigned in the course of 1559. Ten Oxford heads left office for religious reasons between 1559 and 1561. In most colleges some fellows were forced to resign, though the massacre was nowhere so severe as in New College where twenty-one men were removed.[24]

Not until the middle of the 1570s did Elizabeth's government establish Protestantism firmly in all the colleges of Oxford, and even after that date there were popish sympathizers in the university. Once the major visitation was over, pressure seems to have been supplied mainly by the episcopal visitors of colleges. Bishop Horne of Winchester, visitor of Corpus Christi, Magdalen, New College, and Trinity, found all these houses, except Magdalen, disposed to popery. He had to order the removal of popish symbols from New College chapel in 1567, and it was not until 1571 that the rood-loft was taken down.[25] His visitation of Corpus Christi in 1567 was followed by the expulsion of several fellows. In spite of that, the college refused to accept the Queen's nominee, William Cole, as their Warden in 1568 and elected a man suspected of popery. The Queen annulled the election and had Cole installed. In 1570 Horne repri-

[23] I am engaged in research for a fuller account of the relations between the Elizabethan state and Oxford University, which should appear in the forthcoming *History of Oxford University*, Vol. iii; I hope to be able to add substantially to my present remarks on the topic.

[24] Cooper, *Annals*, ii. 154, 158, 172. Porter, *Reformation and Reaction*, 104–7. Mallet, *Oxford*, ii. 105–7. Mark Curtis, *Oxford and Cambridge in Transition*, 286. Wood, *Annals*, ii. 141–7. For this account I have also drawn upon several college histories, too numerous to mention here.

[25] A. H. M. Jones, 'New College', in *VCH, Oxfordshire*, iii. 146.

manded the President and fellows of Trinity for keeping popish monuments and ordered that they be immediately defaced. Six fellows of the college resigned or were deprived in 1571.[26]

The Archbishop of Canterbury, as visitor of Merton, had already encountered serious opposition in 1562. According to the old statutes of the college, on a vacancy in the wardenship, the fellows chose three candidates, from whom the visitor made the final selection. In 1562 the fellows presented five names, all of which were rejected by Archbishop Parker, who nominated John Mann, one of his chaplains. A popish faction, led by the sub-warden, closed the gate against their new Warden. When he finally got in, the sub-warden either boxed his ears or snatched the statute-book from him—the accounts differ. Parker insisted on the admission of Mann and ordered a visitation of the college, at which the sub-warden and various fellows were expelled.[27]

At Cambridge Romanist elements also remained entrenched. Pory, Master of Corpus, and Perne, Master of Peterhouse, both elected under Mary, preserved office and influence for many years. But the most dramatic conflicts between the ecclesiastical authorities and the Cambridge colleges were provoked by Protestant radicals rather than Catholic conservatives. In the early 1560s William Fulke, a young fellow of St John's, preached in the college chapel against the wearing of surplices. Not only did he and other fellows refuse to put on surplices but they audibly hissed at those who did. Supported by the Master, Richard Longworth, this Puritan faction began to dominate the college. Archbishop Parker urged Cecil, in his capacity as Chancellor, to enforce the law: 'execution, execution, execution of laws and orders must be the first and last part of good government,' he wrote. But Cecil drew back from severity, advocating instead gentleness and persuasion. In the end Longworth was expelled by the Bishop of Ely four years after

[26] T. Fowler, *Corpus Christi College* (Oxford, 1893), 124–9. Wood, *Annals*, 164–7. H. E. D. Blakiston, *Trinity College* (1899), 77–80.

[27] G. C. Brodrick, *Memorials of Merton College* (Oxford, 1885), 51–5. J. M. Fletcher, *Registrum Annalium Collegii Mertonensis* (Oxford, 1974), 210–17. Wood, *Annals*, 148–51. *CSPDom, 1547–80*, 17/21; 21/57; 23/31. Romanism remained for some time in the colleges of Balliol, Lincoln, Queen's, and Exeter.

the troubles had begun, and the college moved into a period of relative calm.[28]

Cambridge University was jealous of its independence during the reign of Elizabeth. When the Ecclesiastical Commission interfered in the case of a fellow of Trinity in 1562, the Vice-Chancellor firmly replied that the matter was being heard in the Chancellor's court.[29] In 1568 the Ecclesiastical Commission again interfered, ordering Dr Young of Pembroke, the Vice-Chancellor, to investigate religious disputes in Corpus Christi. Young refused to obey and, when Archbishop Parker summoned the contending parties before him, ordered them not to appear. Not surprisingly this drew a strong protest from the Ecclesiastical Commission that they 'marvelled not a little at what the Vice-Chancellor wrote and did'.[30] At this point the story ends, but the dispute between the University and the Commission was revived five years later, when the new Master of Corpus, Thomas Aldrich, refused to proceed, as he should have done, to the degree of B.D. The Ecclesiastical Commission ordered the Vice-Chancellor to send Aldrich to Lambeth, at which the Vice-Chancellor and heads complained to Burghley that the university's jurisdiction was being encroached. Burghley responded with a characteristic compromise: he suggested that the matter be heard by a mixed body consisting of the archbishop, some of the ecclesiastical commissioners, and two doctors of the university. When the Vice-Chancellor and his deputy refused to accept this proposal, Burghley and Archbishop Parker let the university have its way and referred the matter to the Vice-Chancellor. Having won their point the Vice-Chancellor and heads of houses found the case too difficult for them and handed it back to Parker. But they had secured more than the right to hear a case which they apparently did not want to decide. They had won agreement to their contention that the Ecclesiastical Commission had no *right* of jurisdiction within the university.[31] The commission continued to hear cases involving university men: it summoned John Travers, fellow of Magdalen, Oxford, in 1578,

[28] Porter, *Reformation and Reaction*, ch. vi. See also ch. ix for the dispute over the mastership of St John's, Cambridge, in 1595.

[29] Porter, op. cit. 147.

[30] Ibid. 146–8. Cooper, *Annals*, ii. 235–9. Cf. ibid. 214–15.

[31] Porter, op. cit. 150–63. Curtis, *Oxford and Cambridge in Transition*, 178–82.

and John Rudd, of Christ's, Cambridge, in 1597. But after 1573 it was careful to avoid any challenge to the university authorities.[32]

Although the government was careful to respect the independence of the universities by curbing the activities of the Ecclesiastical Commission, the Queen and her courtiers frequently interfered in the appointment or election of heads of colleges, fellows, professors, and lecturers. In 1579 the Vice-Chancellor and heads at Cambridge protested at the practice whereby courtiers obtained royal mandatory letters for the election of their protégés. Burghley replied on the Queen's behalf that she had intended neither to violate college statutes nor to promote unsuitable persons; those who had procured such letters would be admonished. But he went on to warn the university that there might well be times when the Queen would wish to recommend suitable persons for fellowships and she would then expect compliance.[33] In practice the patronage of Queen and courtiers was continuously exercised throughout the reign. Probably the most persistent promoter of friends and followers was the Earl of Leicester, as Chancellor of Oxford. His most notorious intervention was to insist that the fellows of Lincoln College elect John Underhill as their Rector after they had already chosen another man. But this was only the most dramatic example of his patronage.[34]

Within the two universities control was passing from the democratic assemblies of Senate and Congregation to the Vice-Chancellor and the heads of houses. This was most evident at Cambridge, where the dispute between John Whitgift, Master of Trinity, and Thomas Cartwright, the leading Cambridge Puritan, led to the promulgation of new university statutes in 1570. These greatly increased the power of heads of colleges, who were now authorized to nominate two persons for various university offices, including the Vice-Chancellorship, and for the post of lector; from these two names the Senate chose one. In addition, the heads, together with doctors and senators, chose the *caput senatus*, the steering committee of the Senate,

[32] *APC* x. 250, 354. Curtis, loc. cit.

[33] Cooper, *Annals*, ii. 368–9.

[34] A. Clark, *Lincoln College* (1898), 51–5. For other examples of royal and courtly patronage see *APC* xxiv. 362; xxxii. 229. *CSPDom, 1595–7*, 496; *1598–1601*, 73, 476–7. Anon., *Leycester's Commonwealth* (Antwerp? 1584; repr. London, 1904), 96–100.

which not surprisingly came to consist largely of heads of colleges. The powers of the *caput* itself were increased; and any member was authorized to veto any grace proposed to it. The power of the proctors was reduced and transferred to the Chancellor and his assessors. The Vice-Chancellor was empowered to imprison on his own authority alone. The right to interpret doubtful points was assigned to the Chancellor and the heads of colleges. Within the colleges themselves the heads were given a power of veto over elections.[35]

These statutes were greeted with a petition from 164 members of the university protesting to the Chancellor against the reduction in the power of the Senate. Whitgift and his colleagues replied that the statutes were intended to improve order and to reduce dissension by giving greater authority to the senior and wiser members of the university. Burghley referred the dispute to a committee consisting of the two archbishops and three other bishops, who concluded that there was 'no great cause to make any alteration' in the statutes, which remained in force until 1856.[36]

No new statutes were issued at Oxford until the Laudian reforms of the 1630s, when Hebdomadal Council was created as the executive authority within the university. The power of Congregation was, at the start of Elizabeth's reign, less than that of the Cambridge Senate, since the Vice-Chancellor was chosen by the Chancellor.[37] The dangers of dissension in Oxford were to some extent reduced by the matriculation statute of 1581, which required all students to subscribe to the Thirty-nine Articles and the royal supremacy.[38] In general the powers of the heads of Oxford colleges seem to have grown under Elizabeth, but without the assistance of formal statutory authority.

Some general points emerge from this study of the relations between the Elizabethan state and the universities. First, the Queen herself seldom intervened directly: governmental authority was brought to bear more often by the Chancellors, royal commissioners, and college visitors. Second, the government

[35] Cooper, *Annals*, II. 258–61. Porter, op. cit. 164–6. Lamb, *Collection*, 315–54.
[36] Porter, op. cit. 166–8. Cooper, *Annals*, II. 279–304. Lamb, *Collection*, 355–402.
[37] Clark, *Register*, II. i. 242–3. Curtis, *Oxford and Cambridge in Transition*, 43–4.
[38] Clark, *Register*, II. i. 267–8.

proceeded slowly and tactfully in the imposition of religious uniformity. It worked by persuasion, arbitration, patronage, and advice rather than by diktat. Third, it seems to have encouraged the concentration of power within the hands of oligarchies in each university—as it also did in the towns—since a small group of senior men was more likely to respond favourably to pressure than were assemblies of young dons. But the Crown did not insist upon exact uniformity of government in the two universities. The Cambridge statutes had no counterpart at Oxford until the days of Laud; Oxford imposed a religious test for matriculation in 1581, but Cambridge waited until the reign of James I.

Control of popular drama in the middle ages had rested in the hands of the Church and of those borough corporations where miracle plays and moralities were regularly performed. Tournaments, masques, and interludes at court were organized by the officers of the royal Household. Other entertainments were sponsored by noblemen and gentlemen in the halls of their castles and houses.[39] The pressure, turbulence, and flux of the sixteenth century necessitated stronger direction by the state. Growing fear of vagabonds and masterless men bred hostility to the small companies of wandering players and entertainers, whose freedom from the ordinary restraints of society seemed to endanger the moral and political order. Large gatherings of people at plays stirred up excitement, and at least one, in Norfolk in 1549, triggered revolt.[40] In times of plague close-packed audiences might spread infection. Above all, religious change and conflict brought drama into the forefront of controversy. The traditional miracle plays had grown out of Catholic liturgy and embodied the doctrines of the old faith. They could not be tolerated by a Protestant Church. Dramatic performances could themselves be used on the Protestant side as propaganda against the Pope; and some polemical drama was performed in the middle of the century under the aegis of the Anglican Church. But the more radical reformers under

[39] Glynne Wickham, *Early English Stages, 1300–1660*, 1 (1959), chs. iv, vi, vii.
[40] BL Harleian MS 1576, f. 251.

Elizabeth disapproved of the theatre itself: not only did it encourage immorality, excess, and disorder, but the very notion of acting implied deceit.[41]

The extension of royal control over the theatre was achieved by the twin instruments of regulation and patronage. Players and playhouses were limited in number and subjected to stringent rules, while their plays were licensed by censors. At the same time royal and courtly interest in the drama provided the companies with some part of their income and, more important, with protection against their enemies. But the right to control and to license actors, plays, and playhouses was contested by the Church, the civic authorities, and the servants of the Crown. In the second half of the century the struggle between the actors and their Puritan opponents was reflected in a contrast between the Mayor and aldermen of London on one side and the Privy Council on the other. The issues largely involved public order and morality; but the controversy was given a sharp edge by the considerable financial interests involved in a growing and profitable business.

The government of Henry VIII was aware of the dangers of unregulated drama but did relatively little to control it, beyond the issue of periodic prohibitions. A statute of 1543, which imposed restrictions upon printing and upon the reading of the Bible by the poorer classes, also, as a minor issue, forbade the playing of interludes which contained matter contrary to the teaching of the Church. A proclamation of the following year forbade the performance of any interludes or plays except in the houses of noblemen, gentlemen, and London officials, or in the streets traditionally used for them.[42] Bishop Gardiner, as Chancellor of Cambridge University, objected to the performance there of the Lutheran play, *Pammachius*, on the ground that it was 'so pestiferous as were intolerable'.[43] Thomas Cromwell, by contrast, promoted one of the few full-blooded pieces of Protestant dramatic propaganda in English, John Bale's *King John*, which was probably performed before Henry VIII in 1539. In it John is described as 'a faithful Moses' who had

---

[41] For examples see E. K. Chambers, *The Elizabethan Stage* (Oxford, 1923), IV, app. C, a collection of documents on state control of the theatre.

[42] 34 & 35 Henry VIII c. 1. Hughes & Larkin, I, no. 240.

[43] Wickham, op. cit. II (1963), i. 62.

attempted to bring his people out of the Egyptian captivity of Rome.[44]

The more radical regime of Protector Somerset began by suppressing the Feast of Corpus Christi in 1548. In Norfolk, the disturbances of 1549 led to a prohibition on all plays for two months, and two years later a further proclamation forbade the printing or performance of any plays which had not first been licensed by six members of the Privy Council. Mary maintained a similar system of regulation, although this obviously operated in the reverse direction.[45]

Elizabeth's government was initially content to leave the control of dramatic performances largely in the hands of borough officials and J.P.s. The Privy Council instructed them to prohibit any plays which treated 'either matters of religion or of the governance of the estate of the commonweal ... being no meet matters to be written or treated upon but by men of authority ... nor to be handled before any audience but of grave and discreet persons'. The printing of plays was to be controlled by members of the Ecclesiastical Commission.[46] Before long the traditional miracle plays of provincial towns came under attack. In 1572 Archbishop Grindal and the northern ecclesiastical commission forbade the Yule procession in York; and four years later the Corpus Christi play in Wakefield was suppressed. The last performance of the York miracle plays took place in 1572, and although the populace attempted a revival in 1579 it was frustrated by the authority of Archbishop Grindal and Dean Hutton. These prohibitions were repeated elsewhere and by the end of Elizabeth's reign performances of miracle plays had ceased.[47]

At the same time actors were brought under the control of a system of licences, by which they were authorized to play under the protection of specific noblemen. The earliest such licence was given to the company of the Earl of Leicester in

---

[44] David Bevington, *Tudor Drama and Politics* (Cambridge, Mass., 1968), ch. viii. For the text of *King John* see Edmund Creeth (ed.), *Tudor Plays* (N.Y., 1966) and also intro., p. xxii.

[45] Wickham, op. cit. II. i. 69. Hughes & Larkin, I, nos. 344, 371; II, nos. 390, 407. *APC* VI. 102, 110, 118, 148, 168–9. Lodge, I. 212.

[46] Hughes & Larkin, II, no. 458. Chambers, *Elizabethan Stage*, IV. 264.

[47] P. Tyler, *The Ecclesiastical Commission and Catholicism in the North*, 94–5. *VCH, Yorkshire: City of York*, 152–3. Wickham, op. cit. II. i. 79.

1574. It was followed by the formation of actors' companies under the patronage of Lord Hunsdon, the Lord Chamberlain; the Earl of Nottingham, the Lord Admiral; the Earl of Pembroke; Lord Strange; and the Earl of Worcester. The number of actors was thus limited, their actions controlled, and their existence protected.[48]

Performances at court were presented and regulated by the Master of the Revels, whose office was permanently established in 1545. Edmund Tilney, appointed Master in 1578–79, licensed players in the provinces and censored the text of plays in London and its suburbs, for which he received fees from the acting companies. The City authorities objected to his interference in their traditional preserves but seem in the end to have been overridden.[49] Censorship does not seem to have been extensive. Mary's Council ordered the suppression of *A Sackful of News*; Elizabeth's suppressed Nash's *Isle of Dogs*; Edmund Tilney excised some passages from Antony Munday's *Sir Thomas More*; there was trouble over a performance of *Richard II* at the time of the Essex revolt; and plays attacking the Marprelate tracts were forbidden. Tudor drama was intensely concerned with politics: Skelton's *Magnificence* dealt, by implication, with royal extravagance; *Gorboduc* explicitly posed the question of the succession; and Shakespeare's history plays condemned both tyrants and usurpers. Political and religious comments were certainly not expunged by censorship; but in general the professional playwrights were conformist in doctrine and deferential to established authority.[50]

The most serious conflict about the drama in Tudor times broke out, not over the contents of particular plays, but over the very existence of the theatre. The authorities of the City of London, largely dominated by Puritan sentiment, tried to suppress players and playhouses in the City itself and in its suburbs. As early as 1564 Edmund Grindal, Bishop of London, complained to Cecil about the spread of disease and profanity by players. By the 1580s the City was launching a full-scale

[48] Chambers, op. cit. IV. 268, 272. Wickham, op. cit. II.i. 104–5. Virginia C. Gildersleeve, *Government Regulation of Elizabethan Drama* (N.Y., 1908), 33–4.

[49] Chambers, op. cit. I. 318–22; IV. 271, 279, 285, 306. Gildersleeve, op. cit., ch. ii. *APC* XVIII. 214.

[50] *APC* VI. 168–9; XXVII. 313, 338; XXXI. 346. Chambers, op. cit. I. 318–25. Gildersleeve, op. cit., ch. iii. Bevington, op. cit., *passim*, esp. ch. xviii.

attack upon the drama. The Mayor and his brethren insisted that playhouses encouraged disorder, infection, idleness, immorality, and sedition.[51] The Puritan campaign of the 1580s seems to have had little success and to have died down in the middle of the decade. In about 1592 it was resumed with an eloquent appeal from the Lord Mayor to Archbishop Whitgift. He spoke of the corruption of youth, the withdrawal of apprentices from sermons to theatres, the resort of harlots and cutpurses to the plays, and the slander of true religion: he concluded by asking for the 'banishing of so great an evil out of this City'.[52] The Privy Council, recognizing the dangers of plays in times of plague, and sensitive to the necessity of control, nevertheless opposed abolition. Properly regulated playhouses need not, they argued, be the cause of disorder or immorality; some recreation was desirable for the people; above all, the Queen herself wished to be entertained by professional actors, who must be able to earn a living and to perfect their performances. The Privy Council did not mention, though it can hardly have forgotten, that two of its own members, Hunsdon and Nottingham, patronized companies of actors.[53]

In July 1597, however, the situation seemed to change abruptly. Following a performance at the Swan theatre, by Lord Pembroke's company, of Nash's and Jonson's *Isle of Dogs*, the Privy Council ordered the suspension of all performances during the remaining summer months and the destruction of the three existing playhouses, the Curtain, the Theatre, and the Swan.[54] Events seemed to have played into the hands of the City, and the actors departed for an enforced and uncomfortable provincial tour. But they were back as soon as summer was ended. Nottingham's men were playing at the Rose in October, and the Curtain was reopened in the same month. Legal complexities of ownership frustrated the order for the destruction of playhouses. But the opportunity was taken by London's impresarios for the construction of more modern buildings. Burbage demolished the Theatre in Shoreditch and built instead the Globe in Southwark. Henslowe met this challenge

[51] Chambers, *Elizabethan Stage*, IV. 266–7, 288, 297–302.
[52] Ibid. IV. 307–8. Cf. 316–18, 321. Wickham, op. cit. II. i. 85–90.
[53] Chambers, op. cit. IV. 287, 296.
[54] *APC* XXVII. 313, 338; XXVIII. 33, 327. Chambers, op. cit. IV. 322–5. The fullest account of the sequence of events is in Wickham, op. cit. II. ii. 9–29.

with the construction of the Fortune in Finsbury Fields in 1601.
Early in 1598 the Privy Council reviewed the situation with
a fresh order: two companies only were to be allowed, Hunsdon's and Nottingham's. Then, in 1600, they restricted the
playhouses to two, Burbage's Globe and the Henslowe–Alleyn
Fortune. Such a solution seemed symmetrical and controlled.
But it lasted only for a short time. By the end of 1601 there
were at least five playhouses in operation and about the same
number of companies. Although the Privy Council blamed the
J.P.s of Middlesex and Surrey for their failure to execute orders,
it seems to have connived at an extension of companies patronized by Councillors themselves and their fellow courtiers.[55]

On the accession of James I the theatre was finally and completely subjected to royal control, while the authority of the
City over players and playhouses was brought to an end. The
principal companies of players were taken from their noble
patrons and put under the direct protection of the King, the
Queen, and Prince Henry. There thus began that separation
of the theatre from its popular base which was so marked a
feature of Stuart England.[56]

The impact of the Tudor state upon English drama had been
momentous. Elizabeth and her Ecclesiastical Commissioners,
assisted by Puritan borough officials, had totally suppressed the
traditional amateur drama of the miracle plays, which disappeared from English life for over 300 years. Professional
actors took the place of the amateurs of provincial England;
they were based on London and protected by the court. These
professional companies needed permanent homes, built for
dramatic performances; and they found them in the playhouses
licensed by the Crown and built by impresarios in the London
suburbs. The plays themselves were perused and licensed by
the Master of the Revels. Thus within a year of the Stuart succession royal control and patronage had been effectively established over actors, playhouses, and plays. Drama was no longer
amateur, provincial, and infinitely varied. It had come, under
the pressure of the Reformation and the influence of the state,
to be professional, metropolitan, and courtly.

---

[55] *APC* XXVIII. 327; XXX. 146, 395–8, 411; XXXI. 346; XXXII. 467–8. Chambers, op.
cit. IV. 326–35. Wickham, loc. cit.

[56] Wickham, op. cit. II. ii. 25–9, 159. Chambers, op. cit. IV. 335–6.

PART III

The Maintenance of the Regime

X
Protest and Rebellion

In Tudor England there were two broad types of rebellion and protest.[1] In one the leaders attempted to seize political power for themselves, either by placing their own candidate upon the throne or by putting themselves in places of authority around the monarchy. Some of these manœuvres involved open revolt, such as the campaigns of the pretenders against Henry VII, the overthrow of Somerset in 1549, Wyatt's revolt in 1554, the rebellion of the northern earls in 1569, and Essex's attempted putsch in 1601. Others were planned to begin with the assassination of the monarch and to develop into rebellion from that moment: no conspiracy against the person of an English monarch was successful in the sixteenth century, but these plots were in conception rebellions, even if they miscarried at an early stage. The other type of movement was a protest or demonstration in force rather than a revolt. It was intended to draw the attention of the monarch to grievances and to secure redress. Some of these movements called for positive action by the Crown; others involved passive resistance against the demands of the central government. Such were the Cornish revolt of 1497, the protest against the Amicable Grant of 1525, the Pilgrimage of Grace in 1536-7, Ket's rebellion, and the South-Western rising of 1549. There were many smaller protests, which hardly qualify as rebellions but might easily have exploded into something much larger. Ket's rebellion started with the destruction of enclosures in one Norfolk village. In origin it was not different in kind, though ultimately it was very different in scale, from scores of other enclosure-riots. Thus one needs to look beyond the large set-piece protests at some of the smaller, even more localized, riots if one is to detect all the elements of strain and tension in sixteenth-century England.

[1] I have developed the distinction between different sorts of revolt in 'Rebellion and Revolution in Early Modern England', in *War and Society: Essays in Honour of John Western*, ed. M. R. D. Foot (1973), 223-40.

Obviously it is not possible in one chapter to examine all the riots and protests of the time. My aim here is not to tell the story of these revolts but to exploit their evidence in order to discover the sources of discontent in Tudor Britain, to indicate the styles and modes of 'direct action', and to estimate its effects. I begin with the protest movements and demonstrations, and then turn to the rebellions which aimed at the seizure of power.[2]

In the first fifty years of Tudor rule some of the most serious protests were set off by exorbitant royal demands for revenue. The fourth Earl of Northumberland was killed in 1489 by rioters in Yorkshire while trying to collect taxes on the King's behalf.[3] More straightforward and more dangerous to the Crown was the Cornish revolt of 1497. Led by a lawyer and a blacksmith, the Cornish rebels protested against paying for the King's Scottish war and marched across England to make their case. Many of them were evidently reluctant to fight the royal army and had probably intended no more than a massive demonstration. Their leaders however resolved on something bolder and were destroyed in the battle that followed.[4] In spite of the complaints against Henry VII's methods of raising money and of the very large calls for subsidies in the early years of the reign of his son, there was no other concerted protest until 1525, when Wolsey attempted to levy the Amicable Grant.

After the capture of the French King, Francis I, by imperial troops at the Battle of Pavia, Henry VIII planned to exploit the weakness of his rival by invading France and claiming its throne. Commissioners were appointed in each county to levy a benevolence of one-sixth of the yearly revenue of the laity and one-third that of the clergy. Not only was the tax extremely heavy and imposed without the consent of Parliament, but it followed the large forced loan of 1522 and several weighty subsidies over the previous three years. There was widespread resistance in London, East Anglia, and Kent. Although Wolsey managed to bully the Lord Mayor and aldermen of London

---

[2] Brief accounts of most of the revolts are given in Antony Fletcher, *Tudor Rebellions* (1968), which has a useful bibliography.

[3] See M. E. James, 'The Murder at Cocklodge', *Durham University Journal*, LVII (1965).

[4] A. L. Rowse, *Tudor Cornwall* (1941), ch. vi.

into agreeing to collect the tax, they found the citizens adamant in their refusal to pay. The aldermen were themselves hostile to the tax and were probably glad to blame the general populace for its failure. Summoned again by Wolsey, the Mayor and aldermen claimed that unparliamentary taxes were contrary to a statute of the reign of Richard III and would impoverish the city. To Wolsey's suggestion that statutes made in the time of the usurper, Richard III, were invalid, they replied, rather bravely, that many good acts had been passed in his reign. Asked by Wolsey what they would themselves give, the Mayor replied that his life would be in danger were he to give the King anything, for whatever he and the aldermen might do, the Common Council of the City would grant nothing.[5]

In Kent, Archbishop Warham, the King's chief commissioner for collecting the tax, had to report a general reluctance or inability to pay. 'In good faith,' he wrote, 'I think there is great poverty in Kent and lack of money ...' Remarking that this was the first time in twenty years that he had known men not conformable to reason, Warham told his fellow commissioners to avoid any assemblies 'this holidays and this hot weather'—a strange remark for a letter written on 15 April. He reported to Wolsey that 'the people sore grudgeth and murmureth and speaketh cursedly among themselves'.[6] When Wolsey suggested that he should first persuade some of the better-disposed to agree to a grant, Warham replied that, excellent as this proposal was, fear of the multitude would prevent anyone from paying. The Archbishop of Canterbury found his clergy as hesitant as the laity. They refused to give any money unless it had been properly authorized in Convocation.[7]

The Dukes of Norfolk and Suffolk were principally responsible for assessing and collecting the benevolence in East Anglia. At first they seem to have encountered an unenthusiastic acquiescence, and by the middle of April Norfolk was suggesting to Wolsey that his presence was no longer required. A fortnight later the mood was changing as rumours spread that concessions were being made to the citizens of London. In the middle of May discontented men were assembling at Lavenham and Sudbury. The Dukes treated the offenders sharply,

[5] Hall, 694 ff.　　[6] Ellis, 3rd ser. I, 359–75, *LP* IV. i. 1305, 1306, 1311, 1362.
[7] Ellis, II. 7–12, 29. *LP* IV. i. 1263, 1267; IV. iii, app. 34.

but had nevertheless to report that hostile meetings were being held in Cambridgeshire, Norfolk, Suffolk, and Essex. In the end Henry sensed that resistance was too strong and dropped his demand. Although the ringleaders of resistance were called before Star Chamber they received nothing worse than a reprimand.[8] For the only time in the century a Tudor monarch had been confronted and defeated by his subjects. There were perhaps three reasons for this remarkable outcome. First, London, almost invariably loyal to the Tudors, was adamant and courageous in its resistance. Second, the opposition was spread widely over several counties so that rumours of opposition in one shire encouraged refusal elsewhere. Third, the influential men appointed as collectors—Warham, Norfolk, and Suffolk—while ostensibly performing the Crown's commands, were quick to emphasize the opposition that they encountered. One gets the impression that they were not sorry to tell Henry that all the blame was being laid on Wolsey; and the loss of face suffered by the Cardinal was probably welcome to his enemies.[9]

Never again was resistance to the royal will of a Tudor to be so successful. But there was a similar attempt three years later. In the hard spring and summer of 1528, against a background of dearth and unemployment, the yeomen of Kent petitioned the King for repayment of a forced loan levied some years before. Archbishop Warham, whom they first approached, showed an indiscreet sympathy with their request and was reprimanded for encouraging dissidence. Frustrated by the Crown's refusal, a group of men plotted to capture Wolsey, take him out to sea, and sink his boat. Needless to say their fantasies came to nothing. The Kentish protests of 1528 failed because they had no support from elsewhere or from any notable except Warham.[10] After 1528 there was only one other concerted protest against royal exactions: the Pilgrimage of Grace in 1536. But the Pilgrimage was much else besides. With its failure, the demands for revenue by Tudor monarchs seem to have been accepted without resistance except in Parliament.

The Pilgrimage of Grace was the archetypal protest move-

---

[8] Hall, loc. cit. Ellis, I. 376–81; II. 3–7. *LP* IV. i. 1235, 1241, 1260–1, 1265, 1295, 1318–19, 1321, 1323–5, 1329, 1343, 1345, 1567; IV. iii, app. 36.

[9] *LP* IV. i. 1318.

[10] Ibid. IV. ii. 4173, 4188–91, 4236, 4276, 4296, 4300–1, 4306, 4310, 4351.

ment of the century.[11] Beginning early in October 1536 in Louth, Lincolnshire, it quickly spread north of the Humber, and by the end of the month, after the Lincolnshire rising had collapsed, Yorkshire, Durham, Northumberland, Cumberland, and Westmorland were in revolt. Who were its leaders? Was it a spontaneous uprising of the peasantry? Or were the masses being used by their betters as a shield behind which they could press their opposition to the policies of the Crown? What were the motives of the rebels? Were they seriously concerned with the fate of the monasteries and the spread of heresy, as they themselves claimed, or were they using these events to disguise their real grievances, which were mainly economic? These questions have been much debated and no doubt will continue to arouse disagreement.

The first surge of revolt gives every sign of apparent spontaneity. While a crowd of parishioners was watching the procession at Louth on the Sunday after Michaelmas, Thomas Foster, a yeoman and chorister, said to his neighbour, 'Go we to follow the crosses, for and if they be taken from us we be like to follow them no more.'[12] The rumour that the King intended seizing all church jewels and ornaments had been circulating for some time. It was accompanied by stories that all the remaining abbeys except Westminster would be suppressed, that two or three parish churches would be amalgamated into one, that a special levy would be imposed on sheep, and that men would be taxed for marriages and funerals, and for eating white bread, goose, or capon.[13] Some of these stories were fantastic or improbable; others, as events were to prove, were not far short of the mark. But whatever their credibility these rumours were

---

[11] On other movements of opposition during the 1530s see G. R. Elton, *Policy and Police* (Cambridge, 1972), chs. i–iii. On the Pilgrimage the standard work is still M. H. and Ruth Dodds, *The Pilgrimage of Grace, 1536–37* (2 vols., Cambridge, 1915). See also: A. G. Dickens, 'Secular and Religious Motivation in the Pilgrimage of Grace', *Studies in Church History*, vol. IV, ed. G. J. Cuming (Cambridge, 1967); C. S. L. Davies, 'The Pilgrimage of Grace Reconsidered', *P&P* 41 (1968); Christopher Haigh, *The Last Days of the Lancashire Monasteries and the Pilgrimage of Grace* (Manchester, 1969); M. E. James, 'Obedience and Dissent in Henrician England: the Lincolnshire Rebellion, 1536', *P&P* 48 (1970); R. B. Smith, *Land and Politics in the England of Henry VIII* (Oxford, 1970); Margaret Bowker, 'Lincolnshire, 1536: Heresy, Schism, or Religious Discontent?', *Studies in Church History*, vol. IX, ed. Derek Baker (Cambridge, 1972); M. E. James, *Family, Lineage and Civil Society* (Oxford, 1974), 45–8; id., *Change and Continuity in the Tudor North* (Borthwick Papers, no. 27), 20–31.

[12] *LP* XI. 828 (iii).   [13] Ibid. 768 (ii).

widely believed; for they reflected well-founded anxieties in
provincial society. Three separate commissions were at that
moment touring northern Lincolnshire. One was executing the
statute dissolving the smaller monasteries; a second was assessing the parliamentary subsidy granted in 1534; and a third,
set up by the Bishop of Lincoln, was examining the fitness of
the clergy.[14]

The men most immediately and directly threatened at this
stage were the clergy. Since many of them were in danger of
failing the tests and losing their livelihood it is not surprising
that they should have taken a lead in the revolt. Those humble
men, like William Leech and Nicholas Melton, the cobbler,
who had stirred up the commons in the first twenty-four hours,
fell quickly into the background. Parochial clerics like Thomas
Kendal, vicar of Louth, and William Morland, an ex-monk,
seem then to have taken over the leadership in conjunction with
a group of laymen from the ranks of the yeomanry. It was easy
for the clergy to make common cause with their parishioners,
who genuinely feared for their churches, their religious ornaments, chalices, and images, their saints' days and holidays.[15]

The Lincolnshire gentry began to take over the movement
a few days later. At first men like Thomas Moigne, a middling
landowner, lawyer, and recorder of Lincoln, occupied the
leadership—men, that is, who were not in the front rank of
county society.[16] But they were soon joined by the heads of some
of the foremost Lincolnshire families, like the Dymokes. These
men were later to claim that their participation had been in-
voluntary, that they had been forced by the rebellious commons
to take the lead. This is of course what one would expect them
to say once the movement had been defeated. If true, it would
convict them of pusillanimity. But in some cases at least it was
probably false. Several Lincolnshire gentlemen had reason to
be dissatisfied with the Crown's policy and some of them are
linked with men known to have organized the revolt and to
have paid the rank and file.[17]

North of the Humber one can find similar developments,
although events there are not known in the detail available for
Lincolnshire. Rumours spread throughout the region; the

---

[14] Bowker, op. cit.   [15] Ibid. James, *P&P* 48 (1970), 12–29.
[16] James, *P&P* 48 (1970), 34, 48.   [17] Ibid. 29–68.

peasants seem to have acclaimed the Lincolnshire Pilgrims spontaneously; nobles and gentry later claimed to have been coerced by the rebels into joining them. The complicity of Sir Thomas and Sir Ingram Percy in the revolt and the close connection of many rebel leaders, including Robert Aske himself, with the Earl of Northumberland argues that the Percy connection was more than passively linked with the uprising. Similarly Lord Neville, heir to the Earl of Westmorland, Lord Latimer, and Lord Lumley were involved.[18] Most notorious of all, Thomas, Lord Darcy, constable of Pontefract Castle, surrendered his charge without a fight. His own defence that the castle had run out of supplies and gunpowder after only about one week's siege falls a long way short of credibility. Most of these men had reason for opposition: the Percies were understandably angry at their disinheritance by the King, and Darcy had long been disgruntled at his exclusion from office and at the royal policy of divorce and supremacy.[19] The nobility and gentry as a whole were resentful at the Statute of Uses, which closed some of the routes through which they had been able to avoid the payment of feudal dues to the King. If there may be some remaining doubt over the responsibility of the landowning class for setting the revolt in motion, there is no doubt that they assumed its leadership, and directed its demands towards their own concerns. Even in the north-west, where the economic grievances of the common people played a large role, one can detect the hand of the Percy family and of the gentry, nourishing resentment against the Earl of Cumberland, who had alienated many gentlemen by his harsh policy towards them as a landlord.[20]

Even so, as Dr R. B. Smith has effectively argued, it would be a mistake to write off the Pilgrimage of Grace as a neo-feudal revolt, in which the commons merely followed their traditional lords. The rumours circulating in Lincolnshire and the North may have been inspired by hidden conspirators; but they touched off real fears in the people. Even if the earliest outbreaks were less spontaneous than they appear at first sight,

[18] Smith, *Land and Politics*, 171–3. James, *Change and Continuity*, 21–2. Id., *Family, Lineage and Civil Society*, 46.

[19] Smith, op. cit., ch. v, esp. 205–12.

[20] Ibid. 198–205. M. E. James, 'The First Earl of Cumberland and the Decline of Northern Feudalism', *Northern History*, i (1966).

they came, not because of any appeal to feudal loyalties or tenurial bonds, but because the people were moved by genuine fears and anxieties. These apprehensions seem very much to the fore during the second rising of January 1537, when the gentry, except for Bigod and Roger Lumley, stood aloof and the common people rebelled on their own. The fears were certainly exploited by leaders who stood socially between the peasants and the upper gentry. In Yorkshire Thomas Maunsell, vicar of Brayton, played a leading part in the early stages of the revolt, while William Morland, an ex-monk, and Thomas Kendal, vicar of Louth, played a critical part in Lincolnshire. William Leech, the Lincolnshire leader, and several of his earliest associates came from yeoman stock. Others like Guy Kyme in Lincolnshire had administrative or legal backgrounds. Then there were men of lesser gentry families like Thomas Moigne in Lincolnshire and Robert Aske in Yorkshire; and both of these men had legal experience. Without the leadership and organizing powers of men like this it is hard to believe that the Pilgrimage would have got beyond the stage of isolated and sporadic rioting.[21]

The critical question, which cannot yet be answered with any certainty, is whether these early leaders were themselves being controlled by the upper gentry and the magnates at the very start of the movement. One would not expect to find firm evidence of this and indeed none exists. There are social links between these groups, for instance between Guy Kyme and the Dymokes in Lincolnshire, but it is hard to know how much to make of them.[22]

Any conclusion has to be tentative. But one can probably say, first, that several nobles and upper gentlemen were much more willing than they later admitted to join the movement once it had started. Second, that having joined it they quickly assumed its leadership, by and large controlling its direction. Third, that where great nobles like Derby and Shrewsbury remained loyal to the King their lordships and areas of influence were insulated from revolt: this in itself casts doubt on the claim of others to have been forced into rebellion. Fourth, that in the early stages of the Pilgrimage, both in Lincolnshire

<hr/>

[21] Smith, op. cit. 179–81. James, *P&P* 48 (1970), 16–20, 34 ff. Bowker, op. cit., *passim*.
[22] Cf. James, *P&P* 48 (1970), 25, 30. *LP* xii. i. 70 (xiii), 380.

and Yorkshire, leadership was provided by men of clerical, yeoman, legal, or lesser-gentry backgrounds. Fifth, that there is at present only inferential and uncertain ground for supposing that such men were at the outset inspired, paid, or manipulated by the great landowners, who later took control. Finally, that the mass of Pilgrims were acting from convictions of some kind and from real anxieties, not simply from hierarchical loyalties.

In spite of all the argument about the motives of the Pilgrims—whether they were concerned with the spiritual life of the Church or with economic grievances—the anxieties that lay behind the revolt and that united its followers can, I think, be stated quite simply. Fundamentally the Pilgrims were protesting against an unprecedented intrusion by the Crown into their local communities and traditional ways. The previous years had seen a surge of royal intervention as different sets of commissioners toured the country, investigating the affairs of the monasteries, the possessions of the churches, the taxable wealth of the laity, and the aptitudes of the clergy. Another set of commissioners had in 1534 sworn men throughout the country to an acceptance of the Boleyn marriage; and two years later all office-holders had been made to take a formal oath of supremacy. In August 1536 Cromwell, acting as vicegerent for the king over the Church of England, had issued the first Royal Injunctions for the clergy, demanding from them a higher standard of behaviour.[23] The smaller monasteries had been suppressed by statute in 1536 and many holidays and saints' days had been abolished by the Ten Articles. In 1536 the Statute of Uses had been carried by a reluctant Parliament to prevent landowners from evading feudal dues.[24] Many county families had cause to resent the Crown's landed policy. The Percies had been harried for a decade, with the King and Cromwell exploiting the weakness of the sixth Earl of Northumberland to persuade him into bequeathing his lands to the Crown. In Lincolnshire the gentry resented the intrusions of Charles Brandon, Duke of Suffolk, into the estates of the Willoughby family.[25]

[23] Elton, *Policy and Police*, 222–30, 249.
[24] E. W. Ives, 'The Genesis of the Statute of Uses', *EHR* LXXXII (1967).
[25] J. M. W. Bean, *The Estates of the Percy Family, 1416–1537*, Part iii, ch. iii. James, *P&P* 48 (1970), 39–45.

Saints' days, holidays, monasteries, clerical livings, landed property: all these had been threatened. It is not surprising that men feared worse to come. There is little profit in disputing whether their resentment and opposition was religious, social, or economic. When the Church was a major landowner and when its ceremonies and saints' days marked the passage of the agricultural year these broad distinctions are largely meaningless. There does not seem to have been any lively concern with the doctrines of the Ten Articles.[26] But some men were drawn by their fears for the future into questioning the Royal Supremacy. More were alarmed at the abolition of holidays and the clergy were naturally uneasy at the threat to their livelihood. Perhaps men were more apprehensive for the future than angry about what had happened so far. These apprehensions were focused on a small group of men at court, of whom Thomas Cromwell became the principal scapegoat. Noblemen resented his power in the royal council, and Lord Darcy's outburst against him may well have been typical of their feelings: 'Cromwell, it is thou that art the very original and chief causer of all this rebellion.'[27] The common people were equally hostile. Rumours flew about that the King intended to make Cromwell his heir, and a popular ballad echoed Darcy's sentiments:

> This cursed Cromwell by his great policy,
> In this realm hath caused great exaction.[28]

Ultimately the Pilgrimage was a defence of local communities against the intrusion of Cromwell, his political henchmen, Lord Audley and Sir Richard Rich, and such allegedly heretic bishops as Cranmer and Latimer. But few of the Pilgrims envisaged revolt against the King himself. As Mr Mervyn James has argued, the Pilgrimage followed a well-marked medieval tradition of dissent, in which loyalty to the monarchy and the established order had been combined with protest against tyranny, abuse, low-born favourites, and evil councillors.[29] An anonymous letter of advice to the Pilgrims put the point:

Where it is alleged that we should not take upon us to assign his Grace's Council, it is necessary that virtuous men that loveth the commonwealth

[26] See Bowker, op. cit., on this point.   [27] *LP* XII. i. 976.
[28] F. J. Furnivall and W. R. Morfill, *Ballads from Manuscripts* (1868), I. 301–12.
[29] James, *P&P* 48 (1970), 5–8, 69–78.

should be his council ... Who reads the chronicles of Edward II what jeopardy he was in for Piers de Gavestan, Spencers, and such like councillors ... Richard II was deposed for following the counsel of such like.[30]

Behind this antagonism towards unworthy and wicked councillors, there lay the stark hint of deposition. But it was not a hint that the Pilgrims could take up, as they mostly well knew, for they had no possible candidate for Henry's throne. They had therefore to rely upon the King himself turning against Cromwell, prompted perhaps by the great magnates. But these men—Norfolk, Suffolk, Shrewsbury, and Derby—stayed loyal to the King; Henry kept his nerve; and the possibility of repeating the success over the Amicable Grant was lost. The Pilgrims were faced with the choice between civil war and negotiated peace. Although some of the lesser men may have contemplated open defiance of the monarchy their leaders could not. The people of Uganda used to have a saying that 'without a prince the Baganda do not rebel'.[31] The same might have applied to the Pilgrims: without an alternative monarch they could do little once Henry stood by Cromwell and the 'heretic' bishops.

The Pilgrimage was the last great sixteenth-century movement of this type, in which nobles, gentry, and commons joined, under oath, to see their grievances righted in a context of loyalty to the Crown. Growls of protest were heard in Yorkshire four years later, in 1541, against royal taxation and the shortage of currency. But the major landowners showed no jot of sympathy, and the conspiracy, such as it was, centred on some priests, including Thomas Maunsell, who had escaped unpunished from the Pilgrimage, and various yeomen; only one landowner, Sir John Neville, was involved and he does not seem to have been close to the centre of the plot.[32]

The south-western 'Prayer-Book' rebellion of 1549 caught up many echoes of the Pilgrimage.[33] There had been trouble in

---

[30] *LP* XI. 1244.

[31] M. Gluckman, *Politics, Law and Ritual in Tribal Society* (1965), 149.

[32] A. G. Dickens, 'Sedition and Conspiracy in Yorkshire', *Yorks Arch. Soc. Journ.* XXXIV (1939). See also id., 'Yorkshire Submissions to Henry VIII', *EHR* LIII (1938).

[33] The main work on this revolt is F. Rose-Troup, *The Western Rebellion of 1549* (1913). See also J. Vowell, alias Hooker, *Description of the Citie of Excester* (Devon & Cornwall Record Soc., 1919), Nicholas Pocock, *Troubles Connected with the Prayer-Book of 1549* (Camden Soc. XXXVII, 1884), and Julian Cornwall, *Revolt of the Peasantry, 1549* (1977).

the first two years of Edward's reign when inquiries into church property and jewels, followed by commissions to destroy images, led in 1548 to the murder of William Body, lessee of the archdeaconry of Cornwall and the government's principal agent there. On Whit Sunday 1549 orders for the use of the new Prayer Book led to resistance from parish clergy at Bodmin in Cornwall, and Sampford Courtenay, in Devonshire. By July some 2,000 rebels were advancing on Exeter carrying a banner of the Five Wounds of Christ. Defence of parish churches, religious ornaments, saints' images, and the traditional liturgy seem to have been the principal motive of the protest. But the rebels gathered none of the support from the gentry and nobles which had given strength to the Pilgrimage. Humphrey Arundell of Bodmin and John Winslade of Tregarrick were the only important landowners to support the cause. This certainly antagonized the common people, who began to associate the gentry with the new religion and with the Crown's interference in their parishes. Rumours spread that the gentry intended to destroy them, and some landowners, like Sir Walter Raleigh's father, were lucky to escape with their lives. But there is no satisfactory reason for accepting the view of A. F. Pollard that the religious grievances were merely a cover for social and economic protest.[34] One of the rebel articles demanded a limitation on the number of servants and retainers that might be kept by the gentry. This certainly shows a dislike of the way in which retainers abused the social power of the landowning class. There was a real hostility to the conduct of the gentry during the revolt, but this was probably due to resentment that the gentry were supporting the Crown rather than the local community. Certainly the Crown and its apologists tried to colour the revolt as socially subversive but that is no evidence of its real character. The articles of the rebels are predominantly ecclesiastical in their demands and there is no hint of the agrarian grievances that were agitating the peasantry elsewhere.[35]

But these agitations, which had been mounting in the second

[34] A. F. Pollard, *England under Protector Somerset* (1900), 239. Fletcher, *Tudor Rebellions*, 61–3.

[35] For the rebels' articles and Cranmer's reply see T. Cranmer, *Works*, ed. J. E. Cox (1844–6), 163–87. Also N. Udall in Pocock, op. cit. 145, and Rose-Troup, op. cit., app. K.

half of the decade and reached a climax in 1549, may well explain the refusal of the gentry to repeat that alliance with the common people which had been so marked a feature of the Pilgrimage. Enclosure riots had been sporadic in the Midlands and in East Anglia before the government was confronted with an outburst of protest in the spring and summer of 1549. Somerset, Wiltshire, Oxfordshire, and Norfolk were the most disturbed counties, but there was evidently little contact between them, and the Oxfordshire rebels seem to have been mainly concerned with religion. By contrast with the South-Western rebellion, Ket's revolt was, however, overtly and fundamentally economic.[36] High prices, high rents, enclosures, and the overstocking of commons by the great sheep-flocks of the gentry were the main grievances. But the rebels were also dissatisfied with the poor standard of the clergy and the corrupt self-seeking of local officers. While the men of Devon and Cornwall knew that they were opposing the policies of the royal council, Ket thought with some reason that he had the Protector on his side. But even if Somerset had wished to help the rebels—and neither he nor the so-called 'Commonwealth Party' would countenance rebellion—they could not have resisted the implacable demand of the rest of the Council that the revolt be suppressed. Although Ket himself was a landowner in a small way, somewhere on the borderline between yeoman and minor gentleman, and although the Mayor and aldermen of Norwich initially gave him some support, more from prudence than enthusiasm, he had no backing from the major landowners, except from one J.P. who tried to buy off the 'rebels' with a cartload of provisions. But this was not a movement of the destitute or the dispossessed. Their articles of grievance show them as men concerned with the quality of the priesthood, the standard of government, the conditions and the rents

---

[36] A. Vere Woodman, 'The Buckinghamshire and Oxfordshire Rising of 1549', *Oxoniensa*, XXII (1957). HMC, *Bath Papers*, IV. 109. HMC, *Rutland Papers*, I. 36. PRO, State Papers Domestic, Edward VI (SP 10), 8/32. The standard account of Ket's revolt is F. W. Russell, *Kett's Rebellion in Norfolk* (1859). But see the interpretations by S. T. Bindoff, 'Kett's Rebellion' (Historical Association pamphlet, 1949) and Cornwall, op. cit. The main contemporary accounts are Alexander Neville, trans. R. Wood, *Norfolk Furies* (1623) and Nicholas Sotherton's unpublished narrative in BL Harleian MS 1576, ff. 251–9. On government reaction to the risings of 1549 see M. L. Bush, *The Government Policy of Protector Somerset* (1975), ch. iv.

of tenant farmers. Their aims were conservative and their attitudes those of small landed proprietors or substantial lease-holders.[37]

Like the Pilgrims they acted in a spirit of loyalty to the Crown and the central government. Their movement was a demonstration against local officers and landlords, an appeal to Protector Somerset and the Council. Their articles of grievance show that they hoped for an end to abuses and had no intention of seizing power for themselves. Ket certainly did not think of himself as a rebel. But his protest was the last large-scale demonstration aimed within a context of loyalty at impressing upon the government the need for attending to grievances. The destruction of the 'rebels' by German mercenaries at Dussindale confirmed the futility of such attempts.

The second half of the century had its share of enclosure riots. But there was no longer any expectation that the monarch or the Council would be sympathetic to a major protest. The spokesmen for the oppressed—men like Latimer, Hales, and Crowley—were careful after 1549 to emphasize their abhorrence of revolt.[38] Deprived of any articulate voice to express their grievances or of any hope of sympathy at court the English poor confined themselves to small and localized protests. In the spring of 1586 there was some disturbance in Ipswich, stirred up by a local alderman, against the shipping of bacon to Leicester's troops in the Netherlands; and a Gloucestershire crowd seized some malt, worth £140, that was being shipped down the Severn to Bristol. In 1590 an Essex landowner, Sir John Smythe, warned the government that the war was breeding trouble, since many yeomen and their sons had been killed and rogues had learned the pleasures of idleness and pilfering while on military service abroad. Unless judges abandoned their customary lenience, England might, he said, suffer revolts comparable to the jacqueries in France.[39]

Nothing happened in the next two or three years to bear out Smythe's warnings. But in the middle of the decade appalling harvests pushed food-prices high throughout Europe. Many

[37] For Ket's articles see: BL Harleian MS 304, f. 75, printed in A. E. Bland, P. A. Brown, and R. H. Tawney, *English Economic History: Select Documents* (1914), 247.

[38] e.g. *APC* IV. 371, 377; VII. 137; X. 155; XXVIII. 442; XXIX. 652. R. Crowley, *The Way to Wealth* (Early English Text Soc., 1872).

[39] *APC* XIV. 128, 133; XV. 40, 78. HMC, *Salisbury MSS*, IV. 4–5.

countries were the victims of dearth, famine, and revolt. The rising of the Croquants swept over much of southern France; the great Austrian revolt lasted from 1594 until 1597; Ukrainian peasants rebelled in 1593, Hungarians in 1597. In England average grain prices for the years 1594–8 were 60 per cent above the average for 1589–93; in 1594 the price of grain rose 77 per cent above the level for 1593; and in 1596 it reached its peak, 50 per cent higher than in the previous year and 130 per cent higher than the average for 1589–93. A Somerset J.P., Edward Hext, wrote to Burghley in 1596 in horrified tones of the uncontrolled disorders in his county. He complained that men were saying boldly that 'they must not starve, they will not starve'; and eighty of them had even robbed a cartload of cheese, dividing it up among themselves. In Kent some corn-wagons had been stopped; in Norwich the lower orders had made threatening noises against the Mayor. By 1597 the Privy Council was exhibiting some alarm at disorders in Kent, Sussex, and Norfolk.[40]

Most frightening of all for the Council was the 'revolt' in Oxfordshire in November 1596. Disturbed by the high price of corn after the bad harvest and angry at enclosures carried out by gentlemen in the western part of the county, Bartholomew Steer, a carpenter, and James and Richard Bradshaw, the sons of a miller, tried to stir up the villagers in the region between Oxford and Banbury. Although Steer was probably the originator of the plot, it is interesting to learn that James Bradshaw was expected to raise most supporters, since, as a miller, he was able to travel about freely. Their plan was to raise as many men as possible, throw down enclosures, seize arms from the houses of the gentry, and then, if they were not strong enough to defend themselves at home, march on London to join the discontented apprentices. Steer was reported to have talked in wilder terms of slitting the throats of the gentlemen. A rendezvous was appointed on Enslow Hill, but instead of the two or three hundred men expected, only three arrived to accompany Steer. Inevitably one of the men whom they had approached reported the affair to his master, and the

---

[40] H. Kamen, *The Iron Century* (1971), 335–41. Figures for grain prices are derived from *Agrarian History*, IV. 849. *TED* II. 341. *APC* XXV. 43, 88, 334; XXVII. 55, 88, 92. *CSPDom, 1595–7*, 401, 432–3.

Lord-Lieutenant, Lord Norris, arrested Steer and other ring-leaders. Norris and the county leaders were thoroughly alarmed, and when they were unable to extract confessions suggested that the ringleaders be sent to London for torture and interrogation. To this the Privy Council readily agreed.

The results of the investigation revealed nothing very menacing. Apart from the four men who turned up at the rendezvous, six others were definitely involved, and seven or eight came under some suspicion. Most of the conspirators were single men and artisans in good employment. This made their offence more heinous, for, as Attorney-General Coke commented, they had no good reason for discontent, whereas a man like Symonds, who revealed the plot, had many children and 'therefore should have some colour to rise in respect of hunger'. The tremors of anxiety caused by the conspiracy among the local gentry and at the Council board were wildly disproportionate to the puny force levied by Steer. However, unsuccessful as his rising was, his efforts had some limited result. When he sent up his first report to the Privy Council, Norris asked for instructions about enclosures, 'so that the poor may live'; and in January 1597 the Council sent for some Oxfordshire landowners to question them about their enclosing activities.[41]

Compared with the widespread and prolonged revolts abroad, the outbreaks of discontent in rural England were astonishingly mild and were easily contained by the local powers. Yet the Privy Council had some reason for its seemingly disproportionate fears. London, which had been quiet and orderly since the Evil May Day of 1517, began in the late 1580s to take on a more violent aspect. At first the main threat to the composure of the city fathers and the central government came, as I have described elsewhere, from a combination of disbanded soldiers and sailors with masterless men and vagabonds.[42] But early in the 1590s the serving-men and apprentices of London itself began to add their discontented voices to the protests of unpaid troops. In 1590 some apprentices broke into a lawyer's office in Lincoln's Inn. The following year saw a riot set off by a man called Hackett, which ended in his torture and

[41] *CSPDom, 1595–7*, 316–20, 322–5, 342–5. *APC* xxvi. 364–6, 373–4, 383, 398, 412, 450, 455. HMC, *Salisbury*, vii. 49, 236.
[42] Above, 196–204.

execution.[43] More serious was the 'tumult' which broke out in Southwark during June 1592. According to the Lord Mayor it was caused by the unnecessarily provocative behaviour of the Knight Marshal's men in serving warrants. But discontent seems also to have been stimulated by resentment against foreign artisans. The Privy Council, apprehensive of further outbreaks, ordered that all servants be kept indoors on Midsummer Eve and Midsummer Night, and that no plays or public pastimes be allowed which might 'draw together the baser sort of people'. The Lord Mayor, while promising that he and his colleagues would punish offenders as an example, 'with such caution as is meet to be used in proceeding against multitudes', asked that justice be even-handed and that some disciplinary action be taken also against the men of the Knight Marshal.[44] In the following October there was a riot in Holborn after the execution of a man who had killed an officer. The Privy Council's comments suggest some tension between the central government and the city fathers, whom the Council criticized for giving bail to the offenders.[45]

The most serious troubles occurred in June 1595. When a silk-weaver went to the Lord Mayor's house and criticized his government, the Mayor, evidently astounded at such presumption, decided that he was mad and ordered him to be committed to Bedlam. On the way he was rescued by a crowd of two or three hundred apprentices. In the next week there were riots about butter and fish, followed by another rescue of a prisoner. On this occasion, a serving-man, angered by his brother's ill-treatment by his master, attacked the master and broke open his head. After he had been arrested and sent to the Counter, he was forcibly released by a crowd of apprentices. The man was again arrested together with some of his rescuers and put in irons. After the Mayor had gone to the prison to order their close confinement, he was passed on his return by an apprentice who refused to take off his cap; he too was sent to the Counter for insubordination. Next day a report came in that some apprentices had conspired with disbanded soldiers, who said to them 'you know not your own strength'. Trouble seems to

[43] *APC* xx, 63, 85; xxi. 293, 297, 299–300, 319, 325.
[44] BL Lansdowne MS 71, nos. 15, 17 (ff. 28–32). *APC* xxii. 506, 549; xxiii. 19, 24, 28; xxiv. 187, 200.   [45] *APC* xxiii. 242.

have rumbled on for some years, although in the end no disaster occurred.[46]

The tensions and dissatisfactions underlying these disturbances have yet to be revealed. There was certainly some resentment by the inhabitants against royal officials and against foreign artisans. By 1595 this had been accentuated by hostility among the apprentices towards the city government, especially towards John Spencer, then Lord Mayor. High prices of foodstuffs can hardly have been relevant in the early stages, since the cost of living was relatively low in 1592, but had certainly become a major grievance by 1595.

The rural outbreaks of the following century were in some ways, and surprisingly, more dangerous than the disturbances of the 1590s. Complaints against enclosure in the Midlands set off risings in 1607 in Northamptonshire, Warwickshire, and Leicestershire. They had an effective leader in John Reynolds, nicknamed Captain Pouch, and seem to have achieved some degree of co-ordination. Some called themselves 'levellers' and began to throw down hedges. But they were easily suppressed by the retainers of the local noblemen. Early in the reign of Charles I there were riots in various royal forests, most notably against enclosures in the Forest of Dean; and in 1635 there were serious tumults in Wiltshire against enclosures made by the Crown. But even these occasional outbursts are more remarkable for their mildness and their rarity than for their threat to the government or the social order. Only when the Crown's authority began to crack in 1641 were there more threatening disturbances.[47]

Some common elements in these protest movements can now be discerned. Demonstrations of this sort, which aimed at the redress of grievances rather than the seizure of power, could under the right circumstances achieve some success. But to do so they had to secure the sympathy, if not the open support,

---

[46] HMC, *Salisbury*, v. 248–50. Hughes & Larkin, iii, no. 769. *CSPDom, 1595–7*, 82. BL Lansdowne MS 78, nos. 64–5 (ff. 159–61). *Trevelyan Papers* (Camden Soc., 1863), 101. HMC, *Salisbury*, ix. 191.

[47] E. F. Gay, 'The Midlands Revolt of 1607', *TRHS*, 2nd ser. xviii (1904). Thirsk, *Agrarian History*, 232–6. Lodge, iii. 320–1. HMC, *Hastings Papers*, iv. 192–6. Hawarde, 346. BL Lansdowne MS 90, nos. 23–6. D. G. C. Allen, 'The Rising in the West, 1628–31', *EcHR* v (1952/53). W. B. Willcox, *Gloucestershire*, 192–203. M. Prestwich, *Cranfield* (Oxford, 1966), 569–70.

of some of the great court magnates; and the association of the City of London with any dissidents could give them additional strength. The opponents of the Amicable Grant, themselves strong in the City, were helped by the reluctance of Archbishop Warham and the Dukes of Norfolk and Suffolk resolutely to suppress the protests. Very likely they were none of them sorry to see Cardinal Wolsey, advocate of the Grant, humiliated. In the Pilgrimage of Grace no great magnate, even in the north, gave his support to the protest. The Earl of Cumberland was loyal to the Crown throughout. The Earl of Westmorland detached himself from events. The Earl of Northumberland equivocated. Lord Dacre—surprisingly, in view of his harsh treatment by the Crown—held aloof. The Earl of Shrewsbury, Lord of Hallamshire and the dominant magnate in Derbyshire and Nottinghamshire, gave whole-hearted support to the Crown. The Earl of Derby kept most of Lancashire loyal. The Duke of Norfolk was the King's principal agent in suppressing the revolt. The landowners who gave unequivocal support to the Pilgrims were younger sons or cousins of the great houses, like Lord Neville, younger son of the Earl of Westmorland, Lord Latimer, Sir Thomas and Sir Ingram Percy, Northumberland's brothers; or they were lesser nobles like Lord Darcy, and gentlemen like Sir Robert Constable and Sir Richard Tempest. Many of the Percy clientele were involved, such as Robert Aske, William Stapleton, Sir Stephen Hamerton, and William Babthorpe; but they followed Sir Thomas and Sir Ingram rather than the passive Earl of Northumberland.[48]

After the Pilgrimage landowners gave very little support to this kind of protest.[49] Such dissidence as they showed was expressed in rebellions that were intended to seize power. In the Yorkshire conspiracy of 1541 and the South-Western revolt of 1549 leadership seems to have been assumed by the clergy; very few of the gentry were ready to be involved. The remaining protest movements—the agrarian disturbances of 1549, the Oxfordshire 'revolt' of 1596, the apprentices' riots in London, and the Midlands rising of 1607—could hardly expect support from the landowners, who were the principal targets of attack.

The protest movements of the sixteenth century were largely

---

[48] R. B. Smith, *Land and Politics*, 173–5.
[49] See below, 343–4, for the revolt of 1569.

rural. Although William Cecil thought industrial workers in the clothing districts to be the most dangerous threat to stability—'the people that depend upon making of cloth are of worse condition to be quietly governed than the husband men'—his view was hardly borne out by events.[50] There certainly were disturbances among artisans in times of hardship: there was widespread outcry by weavers against unemployment in 1528; trouble erupted at Taunton in 1536; shoemakers in Wisbech demanded more wages in 1538; Somerset weavers threw down enclosures in 1549; the poor weavers of Norwich supported Ket; and the London apprentices rioted sporadically in the last two decades of the century. But the only serious urban outbreaks were the Evil May Day of 1517 and London's opposition to the Amicable Grant.[51] At other times the urban poor were either strangely quiescent or followed a rural lead. Ket's men got positive support from Norwich, but the South-Western rebels, in spite of some sympathy for their cause among the poor of Exeter, were unable to enter the city. Most strange of all, the painful dislocation of the cloth industry in the fifties and the mid-eighties seems to have provoked no disorder among the weavers. There is a dramatic contrast here with the England of 1381 and with the continental revolts of the sixteenth century. In 1381, although the uprising certainly started in the countryside, it was welcomed into the city by the London poor.[52] In late sixteenth-century France peasant risings seem usually to have enlisted the enthusiastic support of the urban workers.[53] The studies made so far of English towns do not seem to explain this strange passivity. Living conditions were at the best of times harsh; urban oligarchies were excluding all but a few from the benefits of city government; plague and famine often dislocated urban economies and brought with them serious unemployment. There were abundant grounds for protest and riot, yet the city fathers usually maintained an effective control. Peasant revolts by themselves, denied large-scale urban support and leadership, were unlikely to be effective.

[50] *TED* II. 45.

[51] *LP*, Add. I. i. 1058, 1063, 1075; XIII. i. 1454; ii. 57, 84, 91. HMC, *Bath Papers*, IV. 109. Above, 314. Also *LP* II. ii. 3204, 3218, 3230, 3244.

[52] R. B. Dobson, *The Peasants' Revolt of 1381* (1970), 13–15, 155–230. Cf. M. Mollat and P. Wolff, *Popular Revolutions of the Late Middle Ages* (1973) for some continental instances.   [53] Kamen, *Iron Century*, 337.

Connected perhaps with this rural predominance was the failure of these revolts to spread beyond regional boundaries or to achieve any effective co-ordination. Ket's revolt was confined to Norfolk and the fringes of Suffolk. The South-Western rebels stayed in Devon and Cornwall. Both groups might have found support for their religious and agrarian grievances in the southern Midlands; but there is no sign that they sought it. Even the Pilgrimage of Grace, covering five northern counties, never transformed southern sympathy into active support. Only the Cornish peasants in 1497 were prepared to take the initiative and carry the conflict away from their home ground. But they seem to have gained little support on the march to London. Essentially these movements were the protests of local or regional communities against the intrusion of the central government or the exactions of landlords. As such it was difficult for them to evoke a national response; and their peasant supporters were usually reluctant to go far from their fields, especially at harvest-time.

What was the attitude of these rebels towards other social classes? How effectively were they controlled? Does their conduct match the horrifying accounts given by government propaganda? To the apologists of the Crown rebellion was the worst of sins and rebels were a disordered and violent rabble bereft of respect, religion, and sense.[54] Their behaviour, however, flatly contradicts this convenient stereotype. In 1497 the Cornish rebels killed a subsidy commissioner at Taunton, but their march was otherwise peaceful until they encountered the royal troops.[55] The Pilgrimage was almost entirely pacific. The Lincolnshire rebels beat to death Dr Raynes, the bishop's chancellor, and hanged Thomas Wolsey, a servant of the late and unlamented cardinal. But after that the leaders established firm control and very few deaths are reliably recorded. William Body, lessee of the archdeaconry, was murdered in Cornwall in 1548 and a Devonshire J.P. was killed the following year. But the South-Western rebels deliberately sacrificed an advantage when they refrained from bombarding Exeter. A similar pacific discipline was exercised by Ket. Some of the Norfolk gentry were captured, humiliated, and imprisoned. But although the contemporary accounts of the rising are all hostile

[54] Below, 352–4.   [55] Fletcher, *Tudor Rebellions*, 15.

to Ket they produce nothing worse than humiliation to illustrate the brutality of the rebels. Only after York Herald had
proclaimed him a traitor and Norwich had closed its gates to
his men did Ket order an attack upon the city; and even then
there was relatively little bloodshed. Once the Crown had sent
an army against him, under the Marquis of Northampton, the
policy of non-violence was bound to disintegrate. An Italian
mercenary captain was captured and hanged, 'for his apparel
sake', and Lord Sheffield was killed in a skirmish when his horse
got bogged down in a ditch.[56] By then, with the expected sympathy of the Crown denied them, some of the rebels flouted
Ket's discipline; houses in Norwich were burned and looted.
Yet even at this stage there was no jacquerie against the rich.
A similar respect for the persons of their 'betters' was shown
by rioters in Wiltshire in the same year. The peasants were
reported to have pulled down enclosures around the park at
Wilton and elsewhere, 'but harm they do to no person'.[57] They
said that they would obey King, Protector, and Council, but
would not have their common ground taken from them. From
1497 until 1549 the conduct of the 'rebels' supports their claim
that they meant no disobedience to royal authority or to the
laws of the realm. Almost invariably physical violence and
killing was the consequence, not of the original revolts, but of
government suppression.

Nor was there any serious class-conflict, if one limits that term
to an attempt by one class to reduce the wealth and standing
of another. Some of the protests were of course aroused by the
Crown's demands for taxation and involved no hostility
between social groups. When the peasants did attack landowners they did so because they thought that the nobles and
gentry had abused their position, not because they wished to
destroy that position itself. The articles of grievance put forward
by Ket and his followers were highly conservative. Except for
one mysterious and uncharacteristic claim—'that all bond men
may be made free, for God made all free with his precious blood-
shedding'—they asked for rents to be restored to their customary level, as they had been in 1485, and for landlords to be
prevented from overstocking the commons.[58] In almost all these

[56] BL Harleian MS, 1576, f. 256.   [57] HMC, *Rutland Papers*, I. 36.
[58] BL Harleian MS 304, f. 75.

protest movements and riots the peasants acted, not as men determined to overturn the social hierarchy, as the government generally thought, nor as men driven into unreasoning mob-action by hunger and despair, as they were sometimes described at the time and later. They give every sign of acting by what E. P. Thompson has called the 'moral economy' of the crowd.[59] That is to say, they were defending a set of economic relationships which they held to be sanctioned by time, custom, and the traditional order of landed society. The food-riots of the eighteenth century, described by Thompson, were protests against the violation of methods of marketing grain which had been mostly established for the protection of consumers by the Tudor and Stuart regimes. Similarly the enclosure-riots of the sixteenth were not exercises in wanton destruction. The pulling down of enclosures was of course a means of acting positively against abuses, of expressing openly and physically a protest against hardships, just as the destruction of toll-gates by the Rebecca rioters in nineteenth-century Wales was a symbolic protest against grievances and abuses that were less accessible to direct attack. But pulling down hedges and fences was a restoration of the old structure of the landed economy. Deer-parks were made available once more to the beasts of the peasants; common pastures were restored to the community; and rights-of-way, blocked by the encloser's hedges, were opened to the villagers and their flocks.[60] The obstruction of rights-of-way was a severely felt grievance, which could often lead to serious inconvenience, and many enclosure riots seem to have followed from this intrusion. For the right-of-way was then, and is now, a sensitive point in any rural community.

The moral respectability of at least some enclosure riots can be illustrated by some incidents in London in 1592. On 1 August the parishioners of St Martin-in-the-Fields and St Margaret's broke into some closes on the west side of their parishes and opened gaps in the hedges. Next day they went as far as Chelsea and repeated the performance as they moved back eastwards. They also put some beasts into the fields which they had thus opened up. Their claim was that these were common fields which should customarily be thrown open at Lammas-time

---

[59] E. P. Thompson, 'The Moral Economy of the Crowd', *P&P* 51 (1971).
[60] E. Kerridge, *Agrarian Problems of the Sixteenth Century*, 188–9 for examples.

each year. Since much of the land belonged to the Crown, which had sublet it to enclosing farmers, they had already appealed for help to the Lord Treasurer, who had promised an inquiry. Their action was taken in advance of its results but they evidently believed that they had Burghley's support. Even their opponents admitted that they behaved in a peaceful and orderly fashion; and they were led by their constables and other 'men that carried a show of some countenance and government'.[61]

Sometimes the agents of the Crown itself seemed to give moral sanction to the actions of rebels. When Dr Raynes was killed by the Lincolnshire Pilgrims, the sheriff of the county, Edward Dymoke, actually parcelled out the dead man's money and clothes among his murderers.[62] More significant still, the agrarian riots of 1549 followed upon the government commissions of the previous year for the suppression of enclosures. When John Hales accused landowners of taking 'great pains and study' to defeat the laws he was setting up a moral case. He was of course careful to warn his hearers against taking the law into their own hands: he commanded them 'that ye nor none of them [your neighbours] go about to take upon you to be executors of the statutes; to cut up men's hedges and to put down their enclosures'.[63] But such qualifications and injunctions were easily forgotten when, by 1549, the commissions were seen to have had little effect. Rioters at Frome in Somerset claimed that a royal proclamation had authorized them to pull down enclosures. Ket and his men, according to Sotherton, claimed to be enforcing government policy where the commissions had failed.[64]

Although rebels and rioters were conservative in their attitudes, although they could often find some sanction for their actions in government pronouncements, and although true class-conflict was never apparent, the English peasants of the sixteenth century were not as deferential as has sometimes been made out. They might accept the social order but they were often contemptuous of their betters and happy to humiliate

[61] BL Lansdowne MS 71, nos. 18–24 (ff. 34–45).
[62] James, *P&P* 48 (1970), 32.   [63] *TED* I. 39–44.
[64] HMC, *Bath Papers*, IV. 109. BL Harleian MS 1576, f. 251. Cf. Natalie Z. Davies, 'The Rites of Violence', *P&P* 59 (1973), 61–70 for a discussion of the legitimation of 'mob-violence' in sixteenth-century France.

them. Lord Darcy told Somerset Herald that when he and other Pilgrim leaders had been conferring with Norfolk on Doncaster Bridge in December 1536, 'because the lords and we tarried a while about the entreaty our own host would have runned upon us to have killed us, saying that we would betray them'.[65] The rank and file of the Pilgrimage could accept the leadership of their social superiors but they did not have to trust it.

Social hostility is more evident, as one would expect, in 1549. Sotherton's chronicle of Ket's revolt describes the treatment of captured gentry by the rebels: 'indeed they did press their weapons to kill some of those gentlemen brought to them, which they did of such malice, that one Mr Wharton, being herded with a lane of men on both sides ... into the city [of Norwich], they pricked him with their spears and other weapons on purpose to kill, had they [the gentry] not had great help to withstand their malice and cruelty'.[66] I doubt whether Wharton was in much danger. Had anyone seriously wanted to kill a gentleman it could hardly in the circumstances have been difficult; but there is no record of any such killing. Humiliation rather than murder was probably intended.

Social derision was expressed in a stranger way a few days later. After Ket had been proclaimed a traitor and Norwich had closed its gates against him, he and his men attacked the city-walls. One of the rebels, 'putting down his hose, and in derision turning his bare buttocks to our men, with an horrible noise and outcry, filling the air (all men beholding him) did that which a chaste tongue shameth to speak, much more a sober man to write'.[67] Public excretion and, more commonly, public nakedness have been a recurrent form of protest for centuries.[68] By upsetting normal conventions they deride the social order and its morality. In this case the protest lost some of its force when the rebel was shot in the buttocks by a remarkably skilful archer.

Some harsh verbal attacks were made on the propertied classes at the same time. In August 1549 John Chandler, vicar of a village near King's Lynn, said that 'I would the town of

[65] Dodds, *Pilgrimage of Grace*, I. 300–6.
[66] BL Harleian MS 1576, f. 253.
[67] A. Neville, *Norfolk Furies*, E. 3.
[68] Their latest manifestation has been the craze for 'streaking', begun in America about 1972 and carried to Britain in 1974.

Lynn and all the gentlemen there were on fire'. Discontent simmered in Norwich for some years. Robert Burnham, parish clerk of St Gregory's, was reported to have said that 'there are too many gentlemen in England by five hundred'. Margaret Adams remarked in 1550 that 'there are five hundred of Mousehold men [i.e. Ket's followers] that are gone to the Great Turk and to the Dauphin, and will be here again by Midsummer'. Hopes of social justice had not entirely died at Dussindale.[69]

There may be no unbridgeable gulf fixed between the movements which I have been discussing and those rebellions which aimed at the seizure of power by their leaders. Had events moved another way, the Pilgrimage of Grace might perhaps have turned from presenting grievances amid protestations of loyalty to waging war upon the King.[70] On the other side of the divide it may be wrong to place the revolt of the northern earls in 1569 among the assaults upon the seats of power; it is hard to say what the earls intended and doubtful whether they even knew themselves. But even if there were some borderline cases and some movements which could have changed their character, the distinction between the two types of movement seems both real and useful. At one extreme no one could imagine that the opponents of the Amicable Grant or the followers of Ket envisaged themselves or any candidate named by them being promoted to political authority. At the other there can be no flicker of doubt that Lambert Simnel, Perkin Warbeck, and the men behind them did mean to tumble Henry Tudor from the throne; or that the plots against Elizabeth intended her replacement by Mary Stuart.

The plots against Henry VII were, obviously, a continuation of those dynastic struggles which had marked the twenty-five years before he ascended the throne. But as demonstrations of the power of over-mighty subjects they were unimpressive.[71] They relied for their impetus and for their progress upon

---

[69] W. Rye, *Depositions Taken Before the Mayor and Aldermen of Norwich, 1549–67* (Norwich, 1905), 18–66. R. B. Manning, 'Violence and Social Conflict in Mid-Tudor Rebellions', *Journ. Brit. St.* XVI (1977).

[70] C. S. L. Davies, 'Pilgrimage of Grace', *P&P* 41 (1968), 74–6.

[71] See S. B. Chrimes, *Henry VII* (1972), ch. iii for accounts of the various revolts in that reign.

Henry's enemies abroad and upon the fragility of the Tudor hold upon Ireland. The most dangerous threats to the Tudor dynasty all had foreign support and Ireland was continually to weaken the regime by the drain on men and money for suppressing its revolts.

The first of the conspiracies against Henry VII—by Lord Lovel and the Stafford brothers in 1486—showed the weakness of the opposition. Without an alternative candidate for the throne their revolt instantly crumbled. Henry was strongly placed, since there were few male relations of Edward IV: of those who mattered the Earl of Warwick, son of the Duke of Clarence, was in the Tower, and the de la Pole brothers, sons of Edward IV's sister, were for the moment well-disposed. Henry's opponents had therefore to fall back on impostors to provide a figure-head; inevitably these were less effective than a true prince of the blood, and it is noticeable that they had little support in England itself. The first impostor, Lambert Simnel, was well received in Ireland, where Yorkist feeling was strong and the dominant magnate, Kildare, feared that Henry might diminish his independence. Support also came from Henry's most powerful foreign enemy, Margaret of Burgundy, who sent 2,000 German mercenaries. Accompanied by John de la Pole, Earl of Lincoln, Simnel landed in the north with his Irish and German troops, but received little backing in England. The Battle of Stoke in 1487 was hard-fought, but in it Henry Tudor was repelling a German–Irish invasion rather than fighting a civil war.

Perkin Warbeck's career is more sustained and complicated in its detailed chronology. But essentially the same points emerge. His principal support came from Ireland, France, Flanders, and Scotland. His friends in England, notably Sir William Stanley, were eliminated before they had time to act. The one serious rising during Warbeck's period of operations was the Cornish revolt of 1497, which was in no way intended to support him and was a protest against taxation. When he landed in Kent and Cornwall he had no more encouraging a reception than Simnel; and, since he brought with him fewer foreign troops, his defeat was more humiliating.

For about fifty years England was spared violent struggles for power and contests over the throne. Political disputes under

Henry VIII were ruthless, uninhibited, and sometimes bloody, but they took place within the confines of the court. They involved poisoning the King's mind against rival politicians, incumbent ministers, favourites, or queens, and then pressing charges of treason. The manœuvres were squalid and the consequences beastly. But they took place according to the forms of law. The Duke of Buckingham, Anne Boleyn, Thomas Cromwell, and the Earl of Surrey all came to a traitor's death through Henry's gullibility and the manipulation of legal procedures. Cardinal Wolsey only escaped the final stage in the process by dying naturally, as he had himself prophesied, at eight o'clock in the morning. In no instance was it necessary for the conspirators to rally their followers and none of the accused thought of doing so. Everything depended upon the will of the King, and there was, throughout the reign of Henry VIII, no possible alternative monarch who might direct a rebellion against him.[72]

The situation was altered with Henry's death and the succession of Edward VI, as a minor. Until the last year of his life the young Edward was inevitably directed by others: like the king on a chess-board his importance for the game was enormous but his own moves were limited and his dependence upon others was great. The contest for power which developed between Protector Somerset and his enemies therefore followed rules different from those which had governed the play of factions under Henry VIII. In 1549 Somerset had physical possession of the King and, probably, ascendancy over his mind. He also had the support of the 'poor commons', among whom handbills were distributed urging them to support the good duke. But none of this, nor the presence at his side of Archbishop Cranmer and both Secretaries of State, helped him against the opposition of the rest of the Council.[73] He had alienated the politically powerful by trying to reform too many things at once—he issued seventy-five proclamations in thirty-three months of power—by mishandling the wars in Scotland and France, by seeming to be mean in rewarding service, by alleged

[72] Classic instances are recorded in E. W. Ives, 'Faction at the Court of Henry VIII: the Fall of Anne Boleyn', *History*, LVII (1972) and in G. R. Elton, 'Thomas Cromwell's Decline and Fall', *CHJ* x (1951).

[73] W. K. Jordan, *Edward VI: the Young King* (1968), ch. xvi. P. F. Tytler, *England Under the Reigns of Edward VI and Mary* (1839), 205–54.

lenience towards the rebels in Norfolk and the South-West, and by very evident arrogance towards other councillors. As his candid friend, Lord Paget, told him: 'Oh! the commons pray for you, Sir, they say, God save your life.' But for a subject to behave like a King, to use 'great choleric fashions, whensoever you are contraried', that was 'to fall into great danger and peril'.[74] The councillors gathered their powers in London; Russell and Herbert, at the head of the armies which had just defeated the South-Western rebels, refused Somerset the support he asked; the Protector's enemies secured the Tower of London. Retreating from Hampton Court to Windsor, Somerset found that he had not enough food or drink to maintain a defence-force. He had to turn away supporters. His defeat shows that the common people were powerless to save a man whom they thought their friend if the political nation—lords, councillors, and country gentry—were against him.[75]

The failure of Somerset's supplanter, John Dudley, Duke of Northumberland, to place his daughter-in-law, Lady Jane Grey, upon the throne in 1553 again shows the power of the political nation.[76] In spite of the official proclamation of Queen Jane and Northumberland's apparent control over the machinery of government, he could not maintain any hold upon the shires. This was no contest about religion: support for Mary was strongest in East Anglia, where Protestantism was popular; and London, also disposed to the reformed religion, greeted the fall of Queen Jane with bonfires and rejoicing. Without a standing army or the money with which to pay mercenaries, the government machine was little use to Northumberland. The nobles and gentry in the counties seem simply to have refused to countenance the breach with law and custom entailed in the succession of Jane. Once that was clear Northumberland's allies on the Council, who had always been lukewarm at best, began to rat: in the Tower of London,

---

[74] J. Strype, *Ecclesiastical Memorials* (6 vols., Oxford, 1822), II, part ii. 428–9. On Somerset generally, see M. L. Bush, *The Government Policy of Protector Somerset*.

[75] A. J. A. Malkiewicz, 'An Eye-Witness Account of the Coup d'État of October 1549', *EHR* LXX (1955), gives a vivid description of the last days of the Somerset regime.

[76] Jordan, *Edward VI: the Threshold of Power* (1970), ch. xiv. I am not convinced by Professor Jordan's argument that Northumberland was the unwilling pawn of the young King.

where the Council sat, 'each man then began to pluck in his horns'.[77]

In 1549 and 1553 the political nation had twice demonstrated its strength against the most powerful man in the government. But to do so against a reigning monarch was a different matter; and none of the rebellions or plots against a regnant Queen between 1554 and 1603 came near to success. They do however illustrate the very different style in which political struggles were to be played out in the second half of the century. I have argued above that 1549 saw the last, until 1607, of large-scale protest movements, characterized by the presentation of formal sets of grievances and demands.[78] As that type of movement disappeared, real struggles for power began to punctuate later Tudor history. The rebellion of Sir Thomas Wyatt in 1554 was the first attempt since Perkin Warbeck's day to unseat a reigning monarch. Although Wyatt and his friends rejected a proposal to assassinate Mary, they realized that she would never willingly abandon her plan to marry Philip of Castile. Accordingly, although they kept their ultimate plans secret and insisted that they meant no harm to Mary, it is almost certain that they intended to depose her and to put Elizabeth and Edward Courtenay in her place. There may have been some element of Protestant feeling in their motive, but uppermost in their minds and in their appeal for support was alarm at a foreign marriage and at possible Habsburg hegemony. They failed because Mary kept her nerve, London remained loyal, and the great magnates, after some hesitation, supported the Queen.[79]

Wyatt's revolt showed that conventional domestic revolt had little chance of success against a monarch sustained by a sufficient number of magnates. His successor in rebellion, Henry Dudley, planned to overthrow Mary with the support of the French King and mercenary troops, to be paid either by Henry of France or by the theft of £50,000 from Mary's Exchequer.[80] The crucial difference between Wyatt and Dudley was Dudley's realization that it was not enough merely to call upon

[77] J. G. Nichols (ed.), *The Chronicle of Queen Jane and Queen Mary* (Camden Soc., 1850), 9.

[78] Above, 326.

[79] D. M. Loades, *Two Tudor Conspiracies* (Cambridge, 1965), chs. i–iv.

[80] Ibid. 186–98.

the English people to rise: weapons, trained soldiers, money, and foreign backing were essential. Dudley's failure was, as so often, the consequence of bad security among his followers. To get money his plans had to be complicated and many helpers had to be involved: a leak of information was almost inevitable.

Dudley was only the first in a long sequence of conspirators against the Tudor Crown who relied upon foreign helpers. None of his successors seems to have developed such elaborate plans for securing mercenary troops. But from Ridolfi onwards they mostly understood the need for foreign backing; the destruction of the Protestant monarch was to be followed by Spanish intervention on behalf of Mary Stuart or the Infanta. Ridolfi, Throckmorton, Babington, and the others differed in one crucial respect from Wyatt and from Henry Dudley: rebellion was to be set off by the assassination of the monarch, and, in Guy Fawkes's conspiracy, of most of the political nation assembled in Parliament. None of the plots came to anything; but they were conceived as rebellions, even if they miscarried at an early stage. Their failure may invite us to write them off as hare-brained and impractical. But although the participants were mostly incompetent, the invitation should be rejected. Assassination was not, in those times, a difficult matter, as the corpses of Henry III and Henry IV of France, William of Orange, the Regent Moray, Admiral Coligny, and the Duc de Guise bear witness.

The two Elizabethan revolts which got beyond conception to a short-lived birth were rather different. The attitudes and intentions of the Earls of Northumberland and Westmorland in 1569 were not always clear.[81] Northumberland certainly resented the granting of border offices to other men during the first decade of Elizabeth's reign; and in 1567 he had been reconverted to Roman Catholicism. When Mary Stuart fled to England he regarded her as the 'second person' of the realm and determined to protect her position as heir to the throne. This led him into the politics of opposition and into complicity with Norfolk's plan to marry Mary. But it certainly did not commit him to revolt. Indeed, when Norfolk was arrested in the summer

[81] Cuthbert Sharp, *Memorials of the Rebellion of 1569* (1840). R. R. Reid, 'The Rebellion of the Earls, 1569', *TRHS*, 2nd ser. xx (1906). M. E. James, 'The Concept of Order and the Northern Rising of 1569', *P&P* 60 (1973).

of 1569, neither he nor Westmorland wished to rebel. Westmorland, urged by his followers to rise for the sake of religion, rejected the proposal as shameful.[82] His reluctance was overridden by Elizabeth's insistence that the earls should come to court, which not unnaturally frightened them; by the exhortations of their Catholic followers; and by a passionate denunciation of the proposal to surrender by Lady Westmorland, who 'cried out, weeping bitterly, and said: "we and our country were shamed for ever, that now in the end we should seek holes to creep into"'. Having decided to rise, they proclaimed that evil councillors had led the Queen into error, that their own intention was to preserve the true religion, to secure the person of Mary, and to have her declared heir to the throne. They then sought help from the Spanish ambassador.[83]

The earls themselves were fully conscious that rebellion was dishonourable. As M. E. James has demonstrated, theirs was not a feudal revolt in which loyal tenants followed the lead of their overlord. The tenants, especially in Northumberland, were reluctant to enlist, and the earls gave way to pressure from their wives and their officials. They themselves would have regarded protest as honourable only if it kept within the bounds of loyalty. But the world had changed since 1536; by interfering with the succession and by communicating with Spain they had fallen into rebellion proper.[84]

Robert, second Earl of Essex, was not much more convincing as a rebel than the northern earls. He did not intend in 1601 to depose the Queen, nor did he wish to restore the old religion, although there were Catholics among his followers. But he wanted to gain power for himself by ousting from court Robert Cecil and his other enemies; and he was very much concerned to secure the succession of James Stuart, who would, so he thought, restore him to royal favour and its rewards. If the regional and tenurial following of the Percies had been weakened by 1569, that of the Devereux had never been strong and could never have supported a successful revolt. He might have had the backing of some Welsh tenants, had he waited for their arrival. But as it was, his following consisted mainly of younger peers and swordsmen, disgruntled at their exclusion from court

[82] Reid, loc. cit.   [83] Sharp, op. cit. 199.
[84] James, *P&P* 60 (1973), 68–83.

favour. By contrast with all the other protests, revolts, and rebellions of the sixteenth century, which had been launched in the provinces, this was an abortive palace revolution, begun in the Strand and intended to finish in Whitehall. Under Henry VIII a similar take-over bid for court power would have operated through the mind of the King, twisting him into hostility towards the rival faction. But Elizabeth was far too loyal to her principal advisers for such a tactic to succeed; and by 1601 Essex had in any case put himself well beyond the range of such an approach.

Before we turn to consider the consequences of these protest movements and revolts it would be as well to notice a few general features. First, at the beginning and the end of the Tudor period, Ireland played an important role in English rebellion. It acted as a base for opposition to Henry VII, and his attempts to control it through an English deputy ended in failure. At the very end of the sixteenth century it was the undoing of Robert, Earl of Essex—as it has continued to be the ruin of so many English politicians ever since. His unsuccessful campaign and his talk with the rebel Tyrone disgraced him with Elizabeth and led in the end to his last despairing outbreak of 1601. Ireland had of course its own rebellions throughout the century. But Ireland was so little a part of England, was so totally different in its society and in its politics that I have omitted it from this book. It is enough to say that in rebellion as in most other things Ireland preserved its separate identity. By comparison with the pacific revolts of the English, Irish rebellions were brutal and violent. Their savagery was however exceeded by the uncompromisingly cruel response of the English generals. Unable to crush his opponents by his victories in the field, Mountjoy starved out their women and children.[85]

Second, the quality of harvests had, apparently, little to do with the incidence of revolt. The harvest of 1535 was bad, but grain was abundantly reaped in 1536, just before the Pilgrimage of Grace. The harvests of 1546, 1547, and 1548 were all excellent. The three harvests which preceded the rising of the northern earls in 1569 were good; so were the three before the

[85] C. Falls, *Elizabeth's Irish Wars* (1950).

Midlands riots in the summer of 1607. The atrocious harvests of the mid-1580s and mid-1590s caused some outbreaks of disorder, but on no very large scale.[86] The potential leaders of revolt, whether they were nobles, gentlemen, or substantial farmers, were unlikely to be prompted into rebellion by a bad harvest, when they would benefit from high prices. Dearth threatened only the really poor, who had no surplus to sell in the markets; and without leaders from above their protests were likely to be sporadic, disorganized, and ineffective.

Third, the role of religion in the revolts varied. In 1536 the clergy opposed an examination of their pastoral aptitudes, while the laity resented the threat posed by the central government to parish churches and their ornaments. The same hostility to the disturbance of traditional worship appeared in the south-west in 1547–9; and attachment to the old faith was certainly one ingredient in the revolt of 1569. Yet there is no evidence that religion played any part at all in 1553, and not much that it was significant in 1554. In other words, Catholics were prepared to defend their faith—or at any rate its trappings—by force, while Protestants before 1558 were not; and after 1558 they had no need to do so. English Puritans stopped well short of rebellion under Elizabeth.[87] By comparison with Germany, England was little disturbed by the more radical sects. True, the risings of 1549 in the Midlands and East Anglia were sometimes attributed to Anabaptist hedge-priests. But these were a common and convenient scapegoat, and there is not much evidence that they played any part in arousing revolt. By contrast with France and other European countries there were few violent quarrels between different religious factions. Religious protests were generally made by Catholics against the central government, not against their Protestant neighbours; and the Protestants were usually restrained, except perhaps under Edward VI, in their treatment of ecclesiastical images and ornaments.[88]

Fourth, the rebellions show how dangerously exposed government was to the insidious effects of rumour. The Pilgri-

[86] W. G. Hoskins, 'Harvest Fluctuations and English Economic History', *Agric. Hist. Rev.* xii (1964). P. J. Bowden, in *Agrarian History*, ch. ix. C. S. L. Davies, 'Révoltes populaires en Angleterre', *Annales* (1969).

[87] Below, 356–7.

[88] Contrast the situation described by N. Z. Davies, *P&P* 59.

mage of Grace was sparked off by stories that the King would seize church ornaments, pull down churches, and levy new taxes. In 1549 the first protests of Ket and his followers were stimulated by rumours that men elsewhere had risen to destroy enclosures.[89] When reliable news was scarce and times uncertain, men had a lively appetite for information and easily accepted the wildest of stories. These did not always lead to events as dramatic as the risings of 1536 and 1549 but they could make the government wary. In 1509 the story had gone round that the Duke of Buckingham would be protector of England and the Earl of Northumberland would rule north of the Trent. Twenty years later men were saying that the King had died in Wales, and in 1538 there was an unlikely canard that an angel had appeared to Henry VIII and instructed him to go on pilgrimage. In 1545 the French were reported to have landed in the Isle of Wight.[90] Rumours continued to spread unchecked in the second half of the sixteenth century and throughout the seventeenth. In the years 1640–2 the emotional temperature of politics was raised by tales of Catholic plotting; and in 1688 rioting was triggered off in several towns by false reports that Irish troops had landed in England. The great danger of rumour was that, unlike the printed books and pamphlets of Catholic exiles, which could circulate only in the network of recusant country houses, it could infect that 'many-headed monster', the common people.

Did Tudor rebellions achieve any of their aims or fulfil any of the more general functions of revolt in restraining the actions of the monarch or the ruling class? The triumph of Northumberland over Somerset, following the revolts of 1549, united the ruling class and ensured a firmer control by government. Northumberland's social legislation was not markedly harsher than Somerset's, and by making peace with France and thus ultimately reducing government expenditure he may have done more for the poor than the 'good Duke' ever managed. Mary's triumph over Jane Grey can hardly be called a

[89] BL Harleian MS 1576, f. 251. Above, 325.
[90] *LP* I. 157; IV. iii, p. 2281; XIII. ii, no. 62; xx. ii. 159, 186, 190. Elton, *Policy and Police*, ch. ii.

rebellion; but its consequences were momentous and hardly need reiteration. The one general movement which secured its ends was the protest against the Amicable Grant in 1525. That was totally successful in the short run, but seems not to have had any permanent effect in restraining Henry's demands for revenue. Threats of riot in 1528 failed to persuade him to repay the forced loan which had been levied some years earlier; and the taxation levied by him in his last seven years was heavy and continuous.[91] Elizabeth was certainly much more cautious in demanding money from her subjects and she repaid her forced loans. By comparison with France and Castile, England was, especially in the second half of the sixteenth century, a lightly taxed country. It may be that Elizabeth's restraint was fortified by a fear of revolt; if this was so, and it is only a hypothesis, she was moved by the possibility rather than the reality of rebellion.

Fear of revolt and disorder was probably more important in two other fields of government policy. Legislation against depopulation and the steps taken to control the marketing of grain both sprang, in part, from a fear of disorder. It would be difficult to prove any direct connection between a particular revolt and specific statutes or proclamations.[92] Ket's revolt probably discredited the so-called 'Commonwealth party' and some of the social measures enacted under Somerset were repealed. On the other hand an act for the maintenance of tillage was passed in 1552. The Oxfordshire riots of 1596 led to torture and possibly to death for its ringleaders, but it also produced an inquiry into unlawful enclosures in that county. Fear of food-riots probably had a more compelling effect upon government policy, both in the encouragement of tillage and in the control of marketing to ensure that grain was distributed at a reasonable price. E. P. Thompson has argued that in the eighteenth century, while the short-term effects of food-riots may have been counter-productive, the threat of disorder probably stimulated the authorities into enforcing the laws—laws, which had, as he says, been made in the sixteenth and early seventeenth centuries.[93] This may also have been so in the six-

[91] Above, 64–8.   [92] 5 & 6 Edward VI c. 5. *Agrarian History*, 225.
[93] In 'The Moral Economy of the Crowd', *P&P* 50 (1971), 120–6; also ibid. 108–10.

teenth century: it is suggested by a letter from the Privy Council to the Mayor of Norwich in 1595, following reports that the lower orders had been threatening him. He was told to imprison the ringleaders but to take better steps for the relief of the poor.[94] More significantly, the acts for promotion of tillage and against the decay of cottages in 1597 followed the disastrous harvests of that decade.[95]

Some of the aims of the Pilgrimage of Grace were in the long run secured. Although the monasteries were not restored nor the heretic bishops dismissed, the Statute of Uses was repealed in 1540 and replaced by the less demanding Statute of Wills. Northern opposition may possibly have had something to do with this, although the lapse in time is considerable. Thomas Cromwell was removed from power in the same year, and Mary was restored to the succession, as the Pilgrims had demanded, in 1543. But it seems far-fetched to credit the northern rebellion with these achievements.[96]

Rather more noticeable were those consequences of revolt which were not intended by the rebels. Reprisals after the Pilgrimage of Grace were not particularly severe among the gentry and nobility. In Lincolnshire only Lord Hussey's disappearance made any great difference to the social scene. In Yorkshire more noblemen and gentlemen were executed: Lord Darcy, Sir Thomas Percy, Sir Robert Constable, Sir Francis Bigod, Sir Stephen Hamerton, Robert Aske, and a few others.[97] The impact of these executions upon land-ownership was great; but it is important to remember that the major change of these years, the Crown's take-over of the Percy inheritance, had been virtually accomplished before the Pilgrimage and was very probably one of its causes. The rebellion in all likelihood simply accentuated developments in the north that had already begun.[98]

The effects of Norfolk's conspiracy in 1569, the rising of the northern earls in the same year, the Dacre revolt of 1570, and the Ridolfi plot were much more dramatic. Admittedly Dacre power was on the wane in any case and Leonard Dacre's

[94] *APC* xxv. 88.   [95] 39 Elizabeth cc. 1, 2.
[96] But see James, 'Obedience and Dissent', *P&P* 48 (1970), 76–7.
[97] Ibid. 77. R. B. Smith, *Land and Politics*, 207.
[98] Cf. M. E. James, *Change and Continuity in the Tudor North, passim*.

abortive rebellion was its death-blow. But the effects on the other noble houses were destructive. The Neville inheritance was totally lost; the power of the Dukes of Norfolk in East Anglia was ruined; and Percy influence was confined to southern England. Alarmed at the dangers it had encountered, the Crown developed over the next few years the system of trained bands for defence against invasion and revolt.

On the whole it would probably be fair to say that sixteenth-century rebellions did as much to strengthen as to restrain the Crown. They gave it an excuse for eliminating its enemies and they encouraged it to improve its military defences. The plots against Elizabeth's life certainly led to more stringent treason laws and a more brutal suppression of any dissident opinion.[99] Threat of civil disorder, masterless men, and unruly vagabonds helped to make the landed classes loyal to the established order. The Crown's success in riding political storms was remarkable. The combined assaults upon society in the 1590s of war, inflation, and dearth left it unshaken. The Essex rebellion brought only a few hours of disquiet. Above all, the succession of James I passed off smoothly and peacefully, leaving the Cecilian ruling clique as firmly in control as before.

[99] Below, 375–8.

XI

Securing Compliance

No government can rely upon a single method of securing compliance to its orders. Most employ a combination of moral authority, personal appeal, patronage, and physical coercion, while recognizing the need for an identification of interests between the rulers and some at least of the ruled. The Tudor regime was no exception to this, although individual sovereigns naturally differed in the use they made of the various means.

A. *The Doctrines of Authority*

Medieval monarchy had been buttressed by grand conceptions of right and power. In 1455 the House of Lords had declared that the 'high prerogative, pre-eminence, and authority of His Majesty royal, and also the sovereignty of them and all the land was resting and always must rest in his most excellent person'. Secular power was enhanced by spiritual gifts: the King, anointed by the holy oil, had miraculous powers of healing.[1] Yet, whether acting alone or in Parliament, he was subject to natural law. Medieval theorists, such as Aquinas, had taught that resistance to a tyrant was lawful; and the Parliament Rolls had laid down that the deposition of Richard II was justified. These limitations upon the Crown were not very emphatically asserted during the fifteenth century. But nor was the notion of non-resistance, although some men, like Fortescue, were beginning to urge an extension of royal power. It was only under the Tudors that an uncompromising doctrine of total obedience and absolute authority began to be formulated. It was spread the more effectively through an intelligent use of the printing-

[1] S. B. Chrimes, *English Constitutional Ideas in the Fifteenth Century* (Cambridge, 1936), 6. Cf. ibid., ch. i for an account of royal authority in the fifteenth century. Also E. H. Kantorowicz, *The King's Two Bodies* (Princeton, 1957), *passim*, esp. ch. iii and pp. 317–36.

press by Thomas Cromwell, William Cecil, and other ministers of the Crown.[2]

Fundamental to all the arguments for non-resistance were the teachings of religion. The Crown's interpretations of those teachings were set forth with clarity and eloquence in the printed homilies, which were prepared for reading from the pulpit in those churches where the incumbent had no licence to preach. The earliest of the homilies on obedience, published in 1547, proclaimed that on earth God 'hath assigned kings, princes, with other governors under them, all in good and necessary order'.[3] Subjects must remember that in obeying earthly rulers they are obeying God: 'the high power and authority of kings, with their making of laws, judgments, and officers, are the ordinances, not of man, but of God'. The testimony of the scriptures proved that treason was an offence against God: 'let us all therefore fear the most detestable vice of rebellion ever knowing and remembering that he that resisteth common authority, resisteth God and his ordinance'.[4]

Following the disturbances and alarums of the middle of the century, the tone of the Crown's exhortations became more insistent and shrill. In 1549, after the rebellions in Norfolk and the south-west, the Bishop of London was ordered to preach on the doctrine 'that all such as rebel against their prince get unto them damnation'.[5] *The Homily against Disobedience and Wilful Rebellion*, first published after the rising of the northern earls and reprinted many times thereafter, pronounced revolt to be the origin of all other sins. For the blessed state of paradise had been fractured by rebellion:

The first author of ... rebellion, (the root of all vices and mother of all mischiefs), was Lucifer.... Thus became rebellion, as you see, both the first and greatest and the very root of all other sins, and the first and principal cause both of all wordly and bodily miseries ... and, which is infinitely worse than all these ... the very cause of death and damnation eternal also.[6]

[2] F. le van Baumer, *Early Tudor Theory of Kingship*, ch. i. See also ch. iv for theories of obedience and non-resistance. For the press, above, 273. See D. S. Loades, *The Oxford Martyrs* (1970), chs. i–iii for the religious implications of theories of obedience.

[3] *Certain Sermons or Homilies* (printed by Grafton, 1547), sign. N.i.

[4] Ibid., N.ii, O.iii.

[5] PRO, State Papers Domestic, Edward VI (SP 10), 8/37.

[6] *The Two Books of Homilies*, ed. J. Griffiths (London, 1859), 551.

The consequences of rebellion were thought to be heavy, not merely for the rebels themselves, but also for the commonwealth. Sir John Cheke, a justly celebrated humanist scholar, castigated the Norfolk rebels in his *Hurt of Sedition*.[7] Rebellion had left the hay rotting in the fields and allowed the corn to stand unharvested; victuals were 'wastefully and unthriftily spent' in maintaining the rebels; the consequent rise in prices caused the poor to want and the rich to be less able to relieve them. 'After a great dearth cometh a great death; for that when men in great want of meat eat much ill meat, they fill their bodies with ill humours. . . . And so grow great and deadly plagues.' 'Can ye therefore think . . .', he demands rhetorically of the rebels, 'when ye see decay of victuals, the rich pinch, the poor famish, the following of diseases, the greatness of death, the mourning of widows, the pitifulness of the fatherless, and all this misery to come through your unnatural misbehaviour, that ye have not dangerously hurt the commons of your country with a doleful and uncurable wound?' That so intelligent and scholarly a man should have resorted to charges so wild and language so hysterical reveals the fear of social upheaval among the governing classes.

There were, of course, other writers and preachers of the age who showed greater sympathy towards the Norfolk rebels than did Cheke. Bishop Latimer was one; another was Robert Crowley, a London printer who was ordained deacon. Crowley was fully aware of the hardships of the peasants, oppressed as they were by greedy and irresponsible landlords. But however much they were ground down, the peasants should never have taken it into their heads to rebel. 'The devil should never have persuaded thee', he told them, 'that thou mightest revenge thine own wrong.' The false prophets should never have 'caused thee to believe that thou shouldest prevail against them with the sword, under whose government God hath appointed thee to be'. If they had only been patient, God would have delivered them from their troubles.[8]

The doctrine of obedience did not exempt rulers from admonition. *The Mirror for Magistrates*, a popular work

---

[7] Printed in Ralph Holinshed, *Chronicles* (edn. of 1587), III. 1042–55.

[8] Robert Crowley, *The Way to Wealth* (1st edn., 1550; repr. Early English Text Soc. xv), 134.

published early in the reign of Elizabeth, was mainly concerned to show the terrible consequences of rebellion; but it also warned bad princes and governors that they might suffer destruction at the hands of rebellious subjects. The ghost of Richard II was made to say:

> Happy is the prince that hath in wealth the grace
> To follow virtue, keeping vices under,
> But woe to him whose will hath wisdom's place;
> For who so renteth right and law asunder
> On him at length, lo, all the world shall wonder,
> High birth, choice fortune, force, nor Princely mace
> Can warrant King or Kaiser from the case,
> Shame sueth [i.e. follows] sin, as rain drops do the thunder.
> Let Princes therefore virtuous life embrace,
> That wilful pleasures cause them not to blunder.[9]

Although wicked rulers might justly deserve their fate, their destroyers were not to be commended. These men, by rebelling, were agents of the devil; yet they were, however wickedly, carrying out God's will. Rebellion was certainly evil; but wise rulers should remember that men distracted by oppression were easily led into its snares.

In a period of religious turmoil men were bound to ask how they should act under an ungodly or heretical ruler. Was it not legitimate at such a time to rebel? The answer usually given in the first half of the century, by religious radicals and conformists alike, was that such resistance would be sinful. Ungodly and tyrannical princes were sent by God as a punishment for the sins of the community, and consequently any protest against them would amount to a denial of God's will.

But the Christian was not expected to obey unjust commands. Latimer laid down the accepted principles:

When laws are made against God and his word, then I ought more to obey God than man. Then I may refuse to obey with a good conscience: yet for all that, I may not rise up against the magistrates, nor make any uproar; for if I do so, I sin damnably. I must be content to suffer whatsoever God shall lay upon me, yet I may not obey their wicked laws to do them. Only in such a case men may refuse to obey; else in all the other matters we ought to obey.[10]

---

[9] *The Mirror for Magistrates*, ed. Lily B. Campbell (Cambridge, 1938), 111–12.
[10] H. Latimer, *Sermons* (Parker Soc., 1844), I. 371.

Disobedience was legitimate only when the command given was contrary to God's word; and violent resistance was, even then, totally forbidden. The Christian must suffer passively whatever consequences his disobedience might bring; and Latimer did just that.

So austere a doctrine was not likely to survive unchallenged for long. Few men, apart from Cranmer, Latimer, and Ridley, had the astounding courage necessary to realize it in practice; and the restoration of popery under Mary soon convinced the Protestants that the policy of waiting for God to replace her—of 'tarrying for the Godly magistrate'—was likely to postpone for ever the establishment of the true religion. Among the men exiled to the Continent under Mary, two or three began to elaborate theories of resistance. Intellectually the most remarkable of these theories was devised by Bishop Ponet, who envisaged government as a form of trust, undertaken by monarchs for the good of the people. If the rulers failed to respect the natural rights of their subjects or set up as tyrants, the people had a right to resist.[11] This striking anticipation of the doctrines of the French Huguenots and of John Locke seems however to have made little impact at the time. Much less subtle were the writings of Christopher Goodman and John Knox. Goodman's treatise on government, *How Superior Powers Ought to be Obeyed*, was mainly concerned with the conditions necessary for disobedience. He agreed with Latimer that God should always be obeyed before man, but considered non-resistance to be inadequate. Against an ungodly or heretical ruler rebellion was not merely permitted but positively enjoined. The task of deposing a wicked prince belonged in the first place to the lesser magistrates—nobles, judges, Justices of the Peace, and mayors—but if they failed to act, then it was the task of the whole people to restore the rule of God's laws. But they must be certain that they really were rebelling for spiritual and not for personal ends: Wyatt's claim to be acting against the Spanish marriage and not against Mary's religious policy was usually censured by Protestant writers.[12]

The proponents of rebellion were however few in number.

[11] J. Ponet, *A Short Treatise of Politicke Power* (1556).
[12] Christopher Goodman, *How Superior Powers Oght to be Obeyd* (Geneva, 1558). Cf. John Knox, *The Appellation of John Knoxe* (Geneva, 1558).

Ponet, Goodman, and Knox have been studied by historians because they foreshadow later theories of resistance. But their writings were received at the time, even by Protestants, with alarm and antipathy. Some of the exiles themselves regarded Knox's arguments as 'atrocious and horrible calumnies against the queen of England'. Early in the next reign Matthew Parker deplored the consequences of the doctrines of rebellion. If it were agreed that subjects could decide whether or not a monarch was a tyrant, then, he asked, 'What master shall be sure in his bed chamber?'[13]

The arguments in favour of resistance were naturally abhorrent to the government of Elizabeth. But they were taken up after 1558 by some of her Catholic opponents. Cardinal Pole had already challenged the doctrine of obedience in his *De Unitate Ecclesiastica*, and Cardinal Allen's *Defence of Catholics* upheld the subject's power to depose a monarch. Later Catholics went a good deal further than Allen. William Reynolds, echoing some of the ideas of the Protestant Ponet, envisaged government as dependent on the choice of the people, and justified—rather tentatively—the assassination of tyrants. Most Catholic writers, while more cautious than Reynolds about tyrannicide, believed that Elizabeth's government might legitimately be overthrown. Yet, by the end of the century, these doctrines had become unpalatable to the majority of English Catholics. Alarmed by the realities of civil war in France and discouraged by the stability of the Elizabethan Church, they came in practice to embrace obedience to political authority.[14]

One might perhaps expect that the doctrines of resistance propounded by Goodman and Knox would have been used by the Elizabethan Puritans in their attacks upon the Church. One or two separatists, like Barrow, may have denied the fundamental principles of English monarchy. Thomas Cartwright, arguing in favour of a presbyterian system of Church government, may have hinted at a more limited type of monarchy; but he was never very explicit about it. Most of the men who have been labelled Puritan accepted, indeed warmly

[13] Jennifer Loach, 'Pamphlets and Politics, 1553–58', *BIHR* XLVIII (1975).

[14] T. H. Clancy, *Papist Pamphleteers* (Chicago, 1964), esp. 87–106. R. Mousnier, *L'Assassinat d'Henri IV* (Paris, 1964), Bk ii, ch. i. J. Bossy, 'The Character of Elizabethan Catholicism', *P&P* 21 (1962). Above, 280–2.

embraced, the monarchical conceptions of the time. William Perkins, a notable preacher and writer, used words that might almost have issued from the pen of James I : 'God therefore hath given to Kings and to their lawful deputies, power and authority, not only to command and execute his own laws, commanded in his Word; but also to ordain and enact other good and profitable laws of their own.... And further, God hath given these gods upon earth, a power as to make these laws and annex these punishments ...'[15] Since men like Perkins and his Puritan colleagues were courageous and uninhibited about criticizing the Anglican Church, their praise of royal authority cannot be written off as mere sycophancy. To Perkins disobedience was associated with the 'manifold complots and treasons ... that have been conspired and attempted against our Prince and State, by profane men stirred up by the Devil ...'[16]

Behind these monarchical sentiments stood the figure of John Foxe, author of the *Book of Martyrs*, historian and prophet of the English Church, whose writings were, next to the Bible, the most widely read works of sixteenth-century England. Foxe described English history as a prolonged struggle between God's Word and the papal Antichrist, ending with the accession of Elizabeth, the final saviour of true religion. Under Mary she had herself only narrowly escaped martyrdom: such, says Foxe, 'was then the wickedness and rage of that time, wherein what dangers and troubles were among the inferior subjects of this realm of England, may be easily gathered when such a princess ... could not escape without her cross'.[17] Elizabeth's accession allowed the return of the exiles and the restoration of religion; her survival was essential to the rule of Christ. By welding together patriotism and Protestantism Foxe established the monarch as the leader of the nation against the forces of Anti-Christ. Resistance or disobedience to such a leader were out of the question.

By the end of the century the lay opponents of the monarchy were no nearer than the clerical critics of the Church to devising

[15] C. H. and K. George, *The Protestant Mind of the English Reformation, 1570–1640* (Princeton, 1961), 216. See ibid., chs. v, vi for further illustrations.
[16] Ibid. 251.
[17] W. Haller, *Foxe's Book of Martyrs and the Elect Nation* (1963), 127.

an alternative view of government. In 1593 even Peter Went-worth, most passionate of parliamentary critics, in urging the Queen to name a successor, asserted that the Holy Ghost called princes 'Gods and nursing fathers and nursing mothers unto His Church'.[18] Early in the next reign Sir Edward Coke, later to become an outspoken, but not always consistent, antagonist of James I, told the Norwich assizes that the King 'is over us the Lord's anointed, and in these his realms and dominions, in all causes, and over all persons, as well ecclesiastical as civil, next under Jesus Christ, our supreme governor'.[19]

It does not of course follow that clergy and laity accepted the extreme claims for royal authority put forward by James I or believed that the King should be above the law. Latimer admonished his hearers to be 'subjected to all the common laws made by men of authority; by the King's Majesty and his most honourable council, or by a common Parliament'.[20] The most distinguished philosophical defence of obedience, presented by Bishop Hooker in his *Laws of Ecclesiastical Polity*, rested solidly upon the foundation of natural law. Governments, according to Hooker, were established by the consent of men to avoid 'strifes and troubles' that would otherwise be endless. The corruption in human nature is such that 'the Law of Nature doth now require of necessity some kind of regiment'.[21] That rule or 'regiment' was delegated by God in the first place to whole societies, whose approbation gave force to human laws. Those laws, binding because they had the consent of us all, cannot be disobeyed without threatening the 'possibility of sociable life in this world'. 'Of Law', wrote Hooker, 'there can be no less acknowledged, than that her seat is the bosom of God, her voice the harmony of the world.'[22]

This elevated view of the law, principally set out in Book I of the *Ecclesiastical Polity*, was perfectly consonant with a defence of monarchical authority. In Book VIII, which was not published until 1648 and may not be entirely by Hooker, the royal supremacy over the Church was specifically defended.

[18] Neale, *Elizabeth I and her Parliaments, 1584-1601*, 252.

[19] M. Judson, *The Crisis of the Constitution* (New York, 1964), 17.

[20] Latimer, *Sermons*, I, 371. Cf. Baumer, *Early Tudor Theory of Kingship*, 92.

[21] R. Hooker, *Of the Laws of Ecclesiastical Polity*, in *Works*, ed. J. Keble (Oxford, 1888), I, ch. x, esp. 243.

[22] Ibid. I, ch. xvi, esp. 282, 285.

Kings might derive their authority in many ways, by conquest, by direct nomination from God, or by 'agreement and composition' with their subjects. In England 'our laws made concerning religion, do take originally their essence from the power of the whole realm and Church of England ...' But this in no way diminished the obligation to obey the monarch as supreme governor of the Church. Obedience was due to the King, the law, and Parliament, in spiritual affairs as in secular; and no man might claim exemption on the grounds of conscience.[23]

B. *Symbol, Ritual, and Persona*

By and large the arguments for obedience put forward in sixteenth-century England are not very impressive. Endless repetition of scriptural texts, metaphors about the head ruling the feet, stories depicting the sad fates befalling rebels carry little conviction compared with the powerful concepts forged by Bodin across the Channel or by Hobbes and Bossuet in the following century. Intellectually the most compelling political works by sixteenth-century Englishmen were Ponet's *Shorte Treatise of Politike Power* and Hooker's *Laws of Ecclesiastical Polity*. But Ponet advocated resistance to tyranny, and Hooker, although a firm believer in obedience, based political authority upon consent and elevated the law above human agencies. To understand the ready and whole-hearted obedience of sixteenth-century Englishmen one needs to look beyond the intellectual persuasions of the printing-press to the imaginative and emotional environment.

Tudor rule was imposed upon a society that had long been responsive to symbols and ritual. Advocating the use of plays against the Pope in the 1530s, Richard Morison remarked that 'into the common people things sooner enter by the eyes than by the ears; remembering more better that they see than that they hear'. Probably this still held good until the end of the century and beyond. Medieval religion was largely communicated by visual images and liturgical ceremony. Ritual was carried outside the churches into the mystery plays of the streets and into popular festivals. Action and thought were stimulated

[23] Ibid. VIII, ch. ii. 350; ch. vi. 412.

more readily by symbolism than they are today. Although images might be regarded by theologians as bridges by which human understanding could apprehend spiritual matters, they were often thought by laymen to have an inherent power of their own. The emotional power exercised by the rituals and symbols of religion could be exploited too by the secular power. Monarchs and civil government had long ago acquired some attributes of the divine; and in the sixteenth century lawyers borrowed theological concepts to clothe the majesty of the Crown.[24]

During the sixteenth century the notion of the world as a stage and men as actors performing their roles upon it gained a strong hold upon the imagination. Monarchs had a special part to play. They were the principal actors in the ceremony of coronation and from that moment played out their lives both as human and as semi-divine beings. Elizabeth herself commented: 'We princes ... are set on stages, in the sight and view of all the world duly observed.'[25] Thomas More, in his *Richard III*, observed of that King's politics: 'These matters be King's games, as it were stage plays, and for the most part played upon scaffolds.'[26] But monarchs were not the only persons to play upon the stage. Subjects, especially courtiers, had their allotted roles. Castiglione urged the courtier to fashion for himself a contrived identity. The complex ceremony of a royal court was more easily performed by men and women who saw themselves playing and developing particular roles. Political life acquired definition and boundaries when the concept of the world as a stage was accepted.[27]

The mental and emotional world of the Tudor polity is not easily grasped today, when the power of religious images is seldom felt. Ritual is suspect. Political symbols, where they survive, are usually ignored. Monarchs have long tried to pretend that they are—except on special occasions—much like the rest of us. Politicians have usually followed suit, claiming ordinari-

---

[24] See, *inter alia*, Frances Yates, *Astraea* (1975); E. H. Kantorowicz, *The King's Two Bodies*; John Phillips, *The Reformation of Images* (California, 1973); David Bergeron, *English Civic Pageantry* (1971).

[25] Neale, *Elizabeth I and her Parliaments, 1584–1601*, 119.

[26] M. E. James, *P&P* 48 (1970), 71.

[27] Anne Righter, *Shakespeare and the Idea of the Play* (1964), esp. chs. i, iii, v. Stephen Greenblatt, *Sir Walter Raleigh* (New Haven, 1973), 31–52.

ness even when they do not possess it. The dignified part of the constitution has long been separated from the effective; it has also been reduced almost to insignificance. But if we are to comprehend the power of Tudor monarchy, we must recognize the support that it derived from portraiture, ceremonial, pageantry, and panegyric.

From about 1530 subjects were beginning to acquire portraits of the monarch in order to prove their loyalty, and the Tudors responded by presenting an image of kingship grander than anything seen before in England. Up to 1509 royal portraits had generally underplayed the element of majesty. Some Kings, like Richard II, were shown wearing the crown or other symbols of authority, but mostly they appeared much as other men. Apart from the inscription—*Ricardus III Ang. Rex*—there is nothing in the National Portrait Gallery picture of Richard III to tell us that its subject was a King. Michael Sittow's portrait of Henry VII shows a shrewd, rather sad, middle-aged man, holding a red rose. While the sitter is obviously a person of force and intelligence, the picture conveys no charisma or magnificence.[28]

From the time of the breach with Rome the style began to change, perhaps under the promptings of Thomas Cromwell, certainly under the artistic execution of Hans Holbein. Holbein's title-page for the English Bible of 1536 shows Henry VIII with crown and a sword handing down the Word of God to his bishops and to the laity: it was the prototype for many pictures of the monarch as the mouthpiece of the Almighty. In the Holbein cartoon of Henry presenting a charter to the Barbers and Surgeons, the company appears kneeling before a King that is more than human, as if they were venerating a saint. The climax of this glorification of King Henry came with Holbein's painting of the royal portrait group for the privy chamber at Whitehall, which survives now only in copies and in part of the original cartoon. Henry VIII, accompanied by Jane Seymour, Henry VII, and Elizabeth of York, dominates the scene; legs astride, one hand on hip, bulky and resolute, the King outstares the spectator. A foreign observer reported that he felt 'abashed, annihilated', in the

[28] Roy Strong, *Tudor and Jacobean Portraits* (2 vols., 1969), II, plates 290, 508–12, 515–17.

presence of the portrait: it is not difficult to understand his emotions.[29]

Edward VI was too young for such treatment to be convincing, although the Scrots portrait at Hampton Court shows him in a pose that is obviously derived from his father's stance in the Whitehall group. Portraits of Mary Tudor convey very little of the majesty of Kingship: in spite of her fine costumes and splendid jewellery she appears in the paintings by Antonio Mor and Hans Eworth as sour, inhibited, and drab: there is no reflection here of God's image on earth. It was left to Elizabeth to restore and to develop the high conceptions of the royal person created by Henry VIII. She and her advisers set about this task as a matter of deliberate policy. In 1563 a proclamation was drafted, laying down general principles. It began by remarking that 'through the natural desires that all sorts of subjects and people, both noble and mean, hope to procure the portrait and picture of the Queen's majesty's ... person', many painters had tried to reproduce her features but none had 'sufficiently expressed the natural representation of her majesty's person, favour, or grace'. Therefore the Queen, at the request of her councillors, had agreed to sit for her portrait by 'some cunning person', carefully chosen. Until he had finished his work no one else might make any portrait of the Queen; after that, qualified painters, 'that shall be known men of understanding and so thereto hired by the head officers of the places where they shall dwell', could 'follow the said patron or first portrayer'.[30]

While this proclamation may never have been formally executed, it shows what was in the minds of the government. The first positive step towards an official portrait was taken in 1572, when the Queen sat for Nicholas Hilliard. Thereafter various patterns were produced from which copies were made and distributed to hang in the country houses of the day. By contrast with the intensely, almost painfully, human pictures of Mary, the portraits of Elizabeth present a mask—the mask of regality—in grandiose and royal settings. Elaborate symbolism conjures

---

[29] Roy Strong, *Holbein and Henry VIII* (1967), *passim*. Id., 'Holbein's Cartoon for the Barber-Surgeons Group', *Burlington Magazine*, Jan. 1963.

[30] Hughes & Larkin, ii, no. 516. The major authority on the subject is Roy Strong, *Portraits of Queen Elizabeth I* (Oxford, 1963).

up the appropriate political concepts. In Hilliard's portrait she is wearing a Phoenix pendant, symbolizing presumably the rebirth of true religion at the accession; elsewhere she is portrayed against the background of the Armada and, in the 'Ditchley' portrait, standing on the map of England. Looking at these pictures nobody could doubt that she was something more than a woman and nearer to a goddess.

A proper attitude towards government and its policies was also encouraged by the manipulation of images and emblems in public places. When the conduit in Gracechurch Street, London, was restored and redecorated for the entry of Philip into London in 1554, the painter represented Henry VIII holding a sceptre in one hand and a book, entitled *Verbum Dei*, in the other. Bishop Gardiner, noticing this as the royal procession passed by, summoned the painter and accused him of treachery. Presumably a bible in the King's hand was too obvious a reminder of the frontispiece to the English Great Bible and of the whole Henrician Reformation. The offending book was painted out and an innocuous pair of gloves substituted for it. By contrast, under Elizabeth, when the holy rood and the images of saints were removed from the chancel arch in parish churches, the royal arms often replaced them. At Tivetshall in Norfolk a medieval doom-painting on the tympanum was covered over by Elizabeth's own coat of arms. Elevation of Kingship could hardly be carried higher.[31]

Powerful and resplendent images of monarchy were presented in the court life and the public displays of the Tudor period. Court spectacles and entertainments were intended, from long before the Tudor epoch, to promote a proper respect for monarchy. Under Edward IV and to a higher degree under Henry VII the English court was modelled upon the sophisticated and glittering life of the court of Burgundy.[32] Its splendour was already apparent at the tournament arranged in 1501 to celebrate the marriage of Prince Arthur to Katherine of Aragon. The tilting lasted for a week, and each day's proceedings started with a procession of nobles and knights in

[31] J. G. Nichols (ed.), *Chronicle of Queen Jane and Queen Mary* (Camden Soc. XLVIII, 1850), 78. Phillips, *Reformation of Images*, 119–21; plates 28–31.
[32] Most of what follows is based on Sydney Anglo, *Spectacle, Pageantry, and Early Tudor Policy* (Oxford, 1969).

various disguises: the Duke of Buckingham arrived in a pavilion arranged with 'turrets and pinnacles of curious work', William Courtenay as a dragon led by a giant, the Earl of Essex in a green mountain 'with many crags [?], trees, herbs, stones and marvellous beasts', surmounted by a maiden clad 'in her hair'. In the evenings there were banquets and pageants at the court, with indoor spectacles, disguises, and dances. Henry VII used the ceremonial of his court to impress foreign ambassadors with the wealth of his monarchy and to provide a brilliant focus for the social life of the English nobility.[33] Under Henry VIII the King himself stepped into the centre of the spectacle. Energetic, muscular, athletic, and vain, Henry VIII was just the man to excel at the mixture of competitive sport and exhibitionist display which in effect made up the life of a court: for eighteen years from his accession he was a regular and highly successful contestant in the tournaments. The rich and lavish displays at court tournaments were paralleled in the great conferences between Henry and his fellow monarchs, culminating in the meetings with Francis I at the Field of the Cloth of Gold and with Charles V at Gravelines and Calais. The sumptuous extravagance of such occasions certainly impressed foreign observers, one of whom wrote from London: 'The wealth and civilization of the world are here. ... I here perceive very elegant manners, extreme decorum, and very great politeness; and amongst other things there is this most invincible King. ... I consider him to excel all who ever wore a crown.' If Henry made such an impression upon the Apostolic Nuncio, he probably cut an equally magnificent figure among his own courtiers.[34]

While the impact of portrait-painting, tournaments, and court ceremonial was necessarily limited to a small but powerful section of Tudor society, the Crown reached out to a wider public by exploiting progresses, entries, and pageants. Soon after his accession Henry VII went on progress to York, Worcester, Hereford, Gloucester, and Bristol: in each city the municipal authorities received him with displays which emphasized some of the central themes of Tudor propaganda: the union of the Roses; the King's relationship with the martyred Henry

[33] Ibid., ch. iii, esp. 100. Also John Stevens, *Music and Poetry in the Early Tudor Court* (London, 1961), ch. xi.
[34] Anglo, op. cit. 123.

VI; the royal descent from the British prince Cadwallader.[35] The most sophisticated of these displays was the ceremonial entry of Katherine of Aragon into London: an elaborate combination of visual spectacle and verse pointed the moral that Prince Arthur and his bride would achieve honour through virtue.[36] Later pageants lacked both the intellectual subtlety and the mastery of visual effect, but they probably made their point. For instance, in 1539 a water-pageant was held on the Thames off Westminster, with a fight between two barges, one representing the Pope, the other Henry VIII; the Pope and his cardinals were finally defeated, 'and all his men cast over the board into the Thames'.[37]

Elizabeth, obviously enough, could not frame either court life or public displays upon her father's model of muscular and masculine bellicosity. A different style of imagery, quickly devised, was first displayed at her royal entry into London on 14 January 1559, the day before her coronation. The official account of the pageantry describes the City of London as 'a stage wherein was shewed the wonderful spectacle of a noble-hearted princess towards her most loving people; and the people's exceeding comfort in beholding so worthy a sovereign and hearing so prince-like a voice'. Along the route 'scaffolds' had been erected with symbolic scenes, from which children, 'in costly apparel', spoke appropriate verses. At Gracechurch Street, for instance, was an Ark in which sat persons representing the Queen's ancestors, with the roses of York and Lancaster united into a single branch. By the Conduit was a pageant entitled 'the Seat of Worthy Governance', with a royal throne resting upon four virtues each of which was treading down its complementary vice. In the final pageant, in Fleet Street, Elizabeth herself was represented as Deborah, consulting with her Estates for the restoration of good government in Israel: the Protestant message was here made very clear.[38]

This was the first of many public celebrations of Elizabeth's royalty. She used her progresses to display the symbols of monarchy at her subjects' expense. Her ceremonious entry into Bristol in 1574 was followed by allegorical mock battles

[35] Ibid., ch. i.
[36] Ibid., ch. ii. C. L. Kingsford, *Chronicles of London* (Oxford, 1905), 234–52.
[37] Anglo, op. cit. 269–70.   [38] A. F. Pollard (ed.), *Tudor Tracts*, 365–95.

between War and Peace, at a cost to the corporation of £1,000. At Norwich in 1578 the Queen's arrival was marked by a pageant on the appropriate theme of chastity. After 1570 the anniversary of Elizabeth's accession, 17 November, became a public holiday, on which bells were rung, bonfires lit, wine drunk, and ballads sung.[39]

Elizabeth had the sense of drama and the radiant presence to make her appearances enthralling and memorable. Bishop Goodman of Gloucester described, years after the event, how, as a boy of five in 1588, he had run from his house in the Strand one dark evening to see the Queen at Whitehall. As she came out by torchlight the crowd shouted, 'God save your Majesty!' and she replied, 'God bless you all my good people!' Goodman recalls that so vivid an impression was made by the scene,[40] 'for shows and pageants are ever best seen by torchlight, that all the way long we did nothing but talk what an admirable Queen she was, and how we would adventure our lives to do her service'. The significance attached to pageants and royal processions throughout the sixteenth century can be gauged by the attention given to them in contemporary chronicles. The Chronicle of London, generally terse in its entries, gives a highly detailed description of the entry of Prince Arthur and Princess Katherine in 1501, recording all the orations verbatim; Edward Hall gives a large proportion of his space to public and courtly ceremonies; and Henry Machyn's diary, while much preoccupied with funerals, is also highly informative about other processions and shows.[41]

The symbolism and allegory of courtly celebration became bewilderingly complex during Elizabeth's reign. She was, as Dekker put it, known by several names in the literary panegyrics:

> ...Some call her
> Pandora: some Gloriana: some Cynthia: some Belphoebe:
> Some Astraea: all by several names to express several loves...[42]

---

[39] John Nichols, *The Progresses and Public Processions of Queen Elizabeth* (4 vols., 1788–1821), *passim*. Bergeron, *English Civic Pageantry*, ch. i. R. Strong, 'Popular Celebration of Accession Day', *Journ. Warburg and Courtauld Institutes*, xxi (1958). J. E. Neale, 'November 17th', *Essays in Elizabethan History* (1958).

[40] Paul Johnson, *Elizabeth I* (1974), 324.

[41] Kingsford, *Chronicles of London*, *passim*. J. G. Nichols, *Diary of Henry Machyn* (Camden Soc., vol. 42, 1848), *passim*. Hall, *passim*.

[42] Yates, *Astraea*, 29. The research of Mr David Norbrook of Magdalen College,

The wide frame of reference thus provided was fully exploited in the ceremonial and pageantry of the court. At the Accession-Day Tilts, initially organized by Sir Henry Lee of Ditchley, leading courtiers took part, playing symbolic roles in elaborate costume. Other courtly entertainments were presented on private estates when the Queen was on progress. Lee himself organized a reception for her at Woodstock in 1575, where mock combats, mingled with dramatic orations, music, and banquetings, created a golden world of chivalry and romance for the glorification of Elizabeth.[43]

The pinnacle of this courtly celebration was of course attained in Spenser's *Faerie Queene*. As Spenser himself wrote in his 'Letter to Raleigh', the general intention of the poem was 'to fashion a gentleman or noble person in vertuous and gentle discipline'. To this end he adopted a form of historical allegory based upon the life of King Arthur, who, in Spenser's version, went from his own land to seek the Faerie Queene.

'In that Faerie Queene I mean glory in my general intention, but in my particular I conceive the most excellent and glorious person of our sovereign the Queen and her Kingdom in Faery land. And yet in some places else I do otherwise shadow her.' Elizabeth is both a royal Queen and a virtuous and beautiful lady: in the first capacity Spenser calls her Gloriana, in the second Belphoebe.[44]

Central to the poem are the affirmation of monarchical rule, the insistence upon an ordered society, the celebration of justice, praise for Elizabeth's person, and symbolic description of her struggle against the Catholic Church. In Book II the chronicle of Kings of Britain and Faery land is used to glorify Elizabeth's lineage in allegory:

> Ne under Sunne that shines so wide and faire,
> Whence all that lives, does borrow life and light,
> Lives ought, that to her lineage may compaire,

Oxford, on panegyrics to the monarchy will, when it is completed, greatly extend our understanding of this subject and I have very much benefited from reading parts of it in draft.

[43] Yates, op. cit., 'Elizabethan Chivalry'. Bergeron, op. cit., ch. i.

[44] E. Spenser, *The Faerie Queene*, ed. J. C. Smith (Oxford, 1909), II. 485–7. Cf. Kantorowicz, *King's Two Bodies*, chs. i, ii.

Which though from earth it be derived right,
Yet doth it selfe stretch forth to heavens hight...[45]

Spenser did not of course stand alone. Many of his symbols
and images had been foreshadowed in courtly ceremonials and
used by other poets, like Sidney and Peele.[46] For the historian
his work is significant because a great poem, rich in language,
drama, and allusion, celebrates monarchy in general and the
Elizabethan regime in particular. Twentieth-century political
literature of any quality has usually expressed protest and dissent; most of the works written in support of government have
been shallow pieces of flattery or propaganda. But Spenser and
his contemporaries, by making great poetry from the celebration of monarchy, witness more effectively than anything else
to the emotional power of the symbols and the allegories upon
which they were drawing and to the firm foundations laid for
monarchy in the public imagination of the time.

Symbols and pageantry also supported other parts of the
fabric of government. Sir Henry Sidney, as Lord President of
the Council in the Marches, kept St George's Feast in Shrewsbury in 1581 in his knightly robes. He entered the town in a
grand procession, 700 yards long, accompanied by the knights
and gentlemen of his own company, the bailiffs and aldermen
of the town, and the wardens and livery of every craft and
occupation. At his departure the boys of Shrewsbury School
put on an entertainment in which they were dressed as water-
nymphs. Sidney's successor, the Earl of Pembroke, held a lavish
Christmas feast at Ludlow Castle in 1596, at which the guests
played the roles of King Arthur's knights.[47]

Sidney and Pembroke, as Lord Presidents, were representatives of the monarch. But images and ritual were important to
the nobility as a whole. The funerals of nobles, gentlemen, and
urban worthies displayed the greatness of the dead man and
his place in society. The arrangements for a noble funeral were

[45] *Faerie Queene*, II, canto x. 2. For a useful guide to the poem see Rosemary Freeman,
The Faerie Queene (1970). Other crucial passages are v i. 5; ii. 30–54; ix. 40–50; x–
xi.

[46] Cf. Yates, op. cit., part ii.

[47] W. A. Leighton, 'Early Chronicles of Shrewsbury', *Shropshire Arch. Soc. Trans.*, 1st
ser. III (1880), 285–6, 307. H. J. Randall and W. Rees (eds.), 'The Storie of the Lower
Borowes', *South Wales and Monmouthshire Record Soc.* I (n.d.), 74.

made, not by the clergy, but by the heralds, professional custodians of the social hierarchy. The funeral procession of Lord Dacre in 1563 included the Dacre battle-standard, a banner with the family escutcheons, and the lord's coat of arms carried by the heralds themselves. Inside the cathedral his helm, sword, and target were 'offered' at the altar. The corpse of the Duke of Norfolk was attended in 1524 by 900 mourners, and 1,900 guests were present at his funeral-feast. Within the churches, tombs of noblemen and gentlemen provided a permanent, and increasingly expensive, reminder of the family's prestige.[48] The importance of these monuments was recognized by Bishop Stephen Gardiner, who protested that the destruction of church images 'containeth an enterprise to subvert religion and the state of the world with it, and especially the nobility . . .' Elizabeth herself, at the beginning of her reign, condemned the haphazard defacing of ancient monuments. Their destruction was, she said, 'to the offense of all noble and gentle hearts and the extinguishing of the honourable and good memory of sundry virtuous and noble persons deceased . . .'[49] Funerals and tombs, although nominally part of the ecclesiastical world, in practice testified—like the royal coat of arms on chancel arches—to the secular hierarchy of power.

Pageants and processions were also powerful cohesive forces in the life of English towns. Up to the middle of the sixteenth century religious processions and mystery plays were perhaps the most important public acts. But the ceremonies of initiation and oath-taking in the gilds were lively expressions of communal life and valued advertisements of each man's social status. In Coventry—and perhaps elsewhere—the social structure of the town was preserved and enhanced by carefully controlled periods of licence: the Hock Tuesday battles in which women scored a ritual victory over men and the installation of a lord of misrule. In the second half of the century, urban ceremony seems to have become less religious and less communal, more secular and more official. Certainly, in London, the Lord Mayor's Show became increasingly elaborate during

[48] M. E. James, 'Two Tudor Funerals', *Trans. Cumberland and Westmorland Arch. Soc.* LXVI (1966). Stone, *Crisis of the Aristocracy*, 572 ff. E. Mercer, *English Art, 1553–1625* (Oxford, 1962), 218–23. Nichols, *Diary of Henry Machyn* (Camden Soc., 1848), *passim*.
[49] Phillips, *Reformation of Images*, 90. Hughes & Larkin, II, no. 469.

the reign of Elizabeth. Beginning simply as a grand procession it was gradually transformed into a dramatic performance.[50]

By the end of Elizabeth's reign the tone of public acclamation was pitched high and shrill. Elizabeth the Virgin Queen seems almost to have been apotheosized as Mary the Mother of God. A sermon preached at Whitehall three days after her death made the comparison seriously and explicitly. John Dowland recommended his public to sing[51]

Vivat Eliza for an Ave Mari!

Robert Wright, the puritanical chaplain to Lord Rich, complained that the popular ceremonials and religious celebrations for Accession Day were making Elizabeth a God; but he seems to have been alone among the Protestant clergy in his criticism.[52] There was perhaps a danger in all this for the monarchy. Public emotions and loyalties had been for decades linked to the person of Elizabeth; men responded to the symbolism of Elizabeth as Astraea the just Virgin, as the Protestant phoenix, as Gloriana. When James I succeeded to the throne, he took over a monarchy which was regarded as semi-divine but which had come to be personally associated with his predecessor. The loud, perhaps hysterical, praise of Elizabeth pitched expectations high as well; and when those expectations were disappointed, disillusionment was the greater. So it was with James. A few years after his accession men were nostalgically recalling the reign of Elizabeth. Bishop Goodman wrote that after a few years' experience of Scottish government 'the Queen [Elizabeth] did seem to revive. Thus was her memory much magnified—such ringing of bells, such public joy and sermons in commemoration of her ... and in effect, more solemnity and joy in memory of her coronation than was for the coming in of King James.'[53] Within a few years the memory of Elizabeth

---

[50] C. Pythian-Adams, 'Ceremony and the Citizen', in *Crisis and Order in English Towns*, ed. P. A. Slack and P. Clark, 57–85. Righter, *Shakespeare and the Idea of the Play*, ch. i. Bergeron, op. cit., ch. iv. Nichols, *Diary of Henry Machyn*, *passim*.

[51] Strong, *Portraits of Queen Elizabeth*, ch. vii. Yates, op. cit. 78.

[52] Strong, *Journ. Warburg and Courtauld Inst.* XXI.

[53] Neale, 'November 17th', *Essays in Elizabethan History*.

the Protestant heroine was serving as a principal inspiration for the opponents of her successors.

C. *Patronage*

Moral obligation, personal devotion, the symbols of authority, and the rituals of monarchy went far towards securing the co-operation of those who controlled the shires and the lines of communication between court and county: but not, by themselves, far enough. They had to be supplemented by the titles and emoluments which royal patronage could bestow and which were eagerly sought by members of the political nation. The disposition of patronage involved a subtle mixture of providing rewards, placing reliable men in key positions, and educating persons of influence in their duty to the Crown.[54] Comparing James I—unfavourably—with his predecessor, the Earl of Clare described the way in which Elizabeth called out of the counties the men of most ambition, breeding, ability, and fortune, 'to fill the most honourable rooms [offices] of her household servants; by which she honoured them, obliged their kindred and allegiance, and fortified herself'.[55] These men got material rewards as well as honour; and by attendance at court they were exposed to the ceremonials which elevated the monarchy. In securing their loyalty Elizabeth forged useful chains of obedience with their families and followers in the regions.

In an earlier chapter I have described the value of the offices at the disposal of the Crown. The gross revenues of officials far exceeded their nominal salaries and their posts were used as much for rewarding service and loyalty as for performing the tasks of administration. I do not propose to repeat now what has already been said.[56] But offices were not the only sources of wealth available. Pensions and annuities were commonly

[54] The uses of patronage have been well explored by Tudor historians. See especially, J. E. Neale, 'The Elizabethan Political Scene', British Academy Raleigh Lecture, 1948, repr. *Essays in Elizabethan History*; W. MacCaffrey, 'Place and Patronage in Elizabethan Politics', in S. T. Bindoff (ed.), *Elizabethan Government and Society*; J. Hurstfield, *Queen's Wards*, ch. xvi; id., *Freedom, Corruption and Government*, part iii; A. J. Slavin, *Politics and Profit*, 49–58 and chs. viii, ix.

[55] G. Holles, *Memorials of the Holles Family* (Camden Soc., 1937), 94–5.

[56] Above, 94–9.

granted to courtiers. Crown lands might be sold below their economic value or leased at a favourable rent. Episcopal lands were leased for long terms at low rents. Licences to trade and grants of monopoly became common towards the end of the century.[57] Commissions were issued for the discovery of concealed lands—that is to say, lands properly belonging to the Crown, from which it received no rents—and part of the profits of the operation went to the commissioner. Wardships were sold on such favourable terms that the Queen probably received only about £650,000 from the source, while private individuals accumulated some £2 million.[58]

Grants of honour were also important. Men on the make competed as fiercely for the blazons of prestige as for material reward. Promotion to the peerage, to the Order of the Garter, or to knighthood was greedily coveted. Such local officers as Lord-Lieutenant, deputy lieutenant, and Justice of the Peace carried honour as well as influence. Rank and precedence were matters of fierce dispute.[59]

The favour of the Queen and her highest officers was valuable in local disputes and litigation. During the long quarrel in Nottinghamshire between the Talbots and the Stanhopes, involving both lawsuits and strong-arm tactics, Lord Buckhurst warned the Earl of Shrewsbury of the serious disadvantage he lay under by neglecting the court when two of his opponents, John and Michael Stanhope, were strongly entrenched there: 'The continual presence of these two brethren in court, with the near place they hold to Her Majesty, and that which is above all the rest, the especial favour which Her Majesty doth bear unto them, will always prevail with so great advantage against you ...' Sir Robert Sidney made a similar point in advising Sir John Harrington about the conduct of a lawsuit over the title to some land: 'Visit your friends often and please the Queen by all you can, for all the great lawyers do much fear her displeasure.'[60]

[57] Above, 157–65.
[58] Hurstfield, *Queen's Wards*, 345.
[59] e.g. *LP* III, ii, 2103.
[60] W. MacCaffrey, 'Talbot and Stanhope' *BIHR* XXXIII (1960), 78–9. Above, 236. J. Harington, *Nugae Antiquae*, I. 313. For similar examples: E. W. Ives, 'Patronage at the Court of Henry VIII', *Bull. John Rylands Library*, LII (1969/70); A. Cameron, 'A Nottinghamshire Quarrel in the Reign of Henry VII', *BIHR* XLV (1972).

The national cake of patronage was large, but only part of its circumference can be measured: marks of prestige and the exercise of royal influence obviously cannot be estimated in money terms. Desirable as it might be to assess the total volume of royal bounty available and to compare the generosity of different monarchs, it cannot be done with any precision. However, one can say for certain that all the Tudor monarchs recognized the need to be generous in rewarding service; and even the least open-handed of them, Henry VII and Elizabeth, made some of their supporters into rich men. Men like Reginald Bray, Edward Belknap, John Hussey, Thomas Lovell, and Robert Southwell built up substantial fortunes under Henry VII; so did William Cecil, Robert Dudley, the Stanhopes, and others under Elizabeth.[61] But there can be little doubt that the time to be on top, if one were greedy and ambitious, was the reign of Edward VI. Grants of titles abounded from the first few weeks of the reign and the rewards of chantry and episcopal lands were lavishly apportioned. Looking back on his career in 1584 Lord Burghley remarked: 'In my whole time I have not for these twenty-six years been beneficed from Her Majesty so much as I was within four years of King Edward.' He probably undervalued what he had received from Elizabeth, but all the evidence confirms his comment on the reign of her brother.[62]

How valuable was patronage in winning support? Direct evidence of men being persuaded to serve or defend the monarchy by the promise or receipt of patronage is naturally difficult to find. The expectation of giving and receiving was present on both sides; but the links between performance and reward were seldom specific. However, there were occasions when royal bounty won the Crown adherents. In the reign of Mary, her husband Philip gave generous annuities to nobles and courtiers: the Earls of Derby, Shrewsbury, Pembroke, and Arundel got £500 per annum each; others got smaller, but still substantial, sums. The Venetian envoy commented: 'It is true that all members of the Council are devoted to His Majesty [Philip], owing to the great rewards they have had from him.... He found by experience that what my father used to say of this

[61] W. C. Richardson, *Tudor Chamber Administration*, 112, 170, 201, 451–62.
[62] Quotation from Hurstfield, *Queen's Wards*, 279.

Kingdom was perfectly true, that all, from first to last, are venal and do anything for money.'[63] Thomas Wyatt's advice to Henry VIII in 1536 that, in order to quell discontent, he should 'butter the rook's nest' bears this out. And it seems likely that patronage, or fear of its loss, persuaded many men to accept the Protestant regime of Elizabeth.[64]

Patronage was an essential tool for regulating the size of local retinues. Many nobles secured or increased their followings by holding Crown offices. Sir Thomas Lovell's retinue was swollen in the reign of Henry VII by his appointment as keeper of Sherwood Forest and constable of Nottingham Castle. Lord Darcy drew more than 1,000 men for the Scottish campaign of 1512 from royal lordships in which he was steward. Furthermore the appointment of landowners to Crown offices bound them to serve the monarch and prohibited them from serving anyone else.[65]

But like many agreeable dishes, patronage could easily set up unhealthy reactions. While its use was indispensable, its misuse could be extremely damaging. Somerset's refusal to give the reversion of an office to Ambrose Dudley may have helped to harden the enmity of the Earl of Warwick; and the abundant booty available under Edward VI may have raised the temperature of competition.[66] The exclusion of Northumberland from border offices in the early years of Elizabeth almost certainly angered him against the government; and the Essex rising of 1601 was at least in part the jealous reaction of young men to exclusion from court favour. But the most dangerous consequences of the abuse of patronage were to be revealed under James I. The Earl of Clare, so appreciative of Elizabeth's favour to noble and gentle families, was angrily critical of the 'blue-cap Scots' and 'trotting-companions' who filled the Stuart court. Worse was to come when James's handsome favourite, the Duke of Buckingham, became the sole channel through which patronage was dispensed.[67]

[63] *Calendar of State Papers Spanish*, XIII. 454–6. *Calendar of Venetian Papers*, VI. ii, no. 852. Cf. ibid., no. 884.   [64] Quotation from Slavin, op. cit. 158. Above, ch. VIII.

[65] A. Cameron, 'The Giving of Livery', *Renaissance and Modern Studies*, XVIII (1974). *LP* I. i. 1363; II. i. 471. For the use of patronage in the controlling of regions by appointment to office see below, ch. XIII.

[66] A. Malkiewicz, 'The Coup d'État of 1549', *EHR* LXX (1955), 602–4.

[67] R. R. Reid, 'The Rebellion of the Earls, 1569', *TRHS*, 2nd ser. XX (1906). Holles,

D. *Coercion*

Propaganda, symbols, and ritual persuaded men that it was proper to obey, patronage suggested that it might be profitable to do so. Those who ignored or defied these messages could be coerced into obedience by a frightening set of weapons. The most dreadful of these was the law of treason, which condemned its victims to a hideous death and the confiscation of property. Treason had received its earlier statutory definition in 1352, when Parliament pronounced five offences to be treasonous: compassing or imagining the death of the King, his Queen, or his heir; violating the Queen, the King's eldest daughter, or the wife of his heir; levying war against the King within his realm or adhering to his enemies; forging his seal or his coins; and killing certain royal officials and judges. Of these the most important were compassing the King's death and levying war against him. Treason was principally an offence against the persons of the King, his family, and his offices rather than a crime against any such abstraction as the state. But it could sometimes be extended to cover the rather nebulous crime of causing a division between the monarch and his people.[68]

The dissensions and pressures of the sixteenth century made necessary large additions to the scope of treason. Henry VIII had to secure the rights of those whom he named as his heirs— a task rendered more difficult by the inconstancy of his own ideas on this question. In 1534 the Act of Succession, which recognized Elizabeth as Henry's heir, extended the penalties of treason to derogation of the King's marriage with Anne Boleyn and to interference with the lawful succession. The second Act of Succession, in 1536, made it treason to attack the King's third marriage or to refuse the oath of succession. Later additions to the law were made necessary by the King's subsequent matrimonial adventures.[69]

---

loc. cit. MacCaffrey, 'Place and Patronage'. See also Peter Clark, *English Provincial Society from the Reformation to the Revolution; Religion, Politics and Society in Kent, 1500–1640* (1977), 132–8, 257.

[68] 25 Edward III, st. 5, c. 2. J. G. Bellamy, *The Law of Treason in the Later Middle Ages* (Cambridge, 1970), ch. iv and p. 122, n.4. Conrad Russell, 'The Theory of Treason in the Trial of Strafford', *EHR* LXXX (1965), 30–48.

[69] 25 Henry VIII c. 22. G. R. Elton, *Policy and Police*, 275–9. Also 28 Henry VIII c. 7. M. Levine, *Tudor Dynastic Problems, 1460–1571* (1973), intro., sect. iii. One earlier

Under Henry VIII and his successors the penalties of treason were attached to specific offences against the various ecclesiastical settlements. In 1536 refusal to take the oath of supremacy became treason.[70] In the reign of Elizabeth it was made treason to affirm that the Queen was a heretic, to bring in papal bulls, or to claim the authority to absolve subjects from their allegiance. A proclamation of 1582, confirmed by statute in 1585, laid down that all Jesuits and seminary priests were to be 'holden, esteemed, and taken for traitors'. For the first time no overt action or speech was required to incur condemnation for treason: merely *being* a Jesuit or seminarist was enough.[71]

The celebrated treason act of 1534 had a more general application. Although it was born in the turmoil of the breach with Rome, its definition of treason stretched beyond ecclesiastical offences. After prolonged drafting sessions, in which the hand of Thomas Cromwell is apparent, and after serious debate in Parliament, it now became treason maliciously to desire any harm to the King, his Queen, or his heir, even if the desire was expressed only in words. This was not an abrupt departure from the previous practice of the law. For, although the act of 1352 had spoken only of compassing or imagining the King's death, the judges had subsequently interpreted this to include treason by words alone. Thus in 1534 the Crown made plain and explicit what had only been available before by construction. But in doing so it spread much more widely the net in which loose-tongued opponents of royal policy might be caught.[72]

The subsequent history of treason legislation made the law once again less clear. A statute of 1547, at the start of the protectorship of the Duke of Somerset, repealed many of the punitive measures of Henry VIII, including the treason act of 1534. Its preamble announced, with wild optimism, that in calm

---

act deserves mention: the so-called *de facto* act of 1495 (11 Henry VII c. 1). But although this act is still (1978) on the statute-book, it arose out of the special circumstances of the reign of Henry VII and does not seem to have had much practical effect upon the operation of the law of treason in the sixteenth century. See A. M. Honoré, 'Allegiance and the Usurper', *Cambridge Law Journal*, 1967, for a persuasive interpretation.

[70] 28 Henry VIII c. 10. Cf. 35 Henry VIII c. 3.

[71] 13 Elizabeth cc. 1, 2. 23 Elizabeth c. 1. Cf. 5 & 6 Edward VI c. 11. Hughes & Larkin, II, no. 660; also nos. 650, 655. F. A. Youngs, 'Definitions of Treason in an Elizabethan Proclamation', *HJ* XIV (1971). 27 Elizabeth c. 2. Above, 278.

[72] 26 Henry VIII c. 13. Elton, *Policy and Police*, ch. vi. Lehmberg, *Reformation Parliament*, 194–206. Bellamy, *Law of Treason*, 116–23.

weather a lighter form of government could be employed than during times of storm. The repeal was confirmed by the first Parliament of Mary and the uncertainty of the law became apparent in the trial of Sir Nicholas Throckmorton.[73] Two subsequent statutes of Mary partly remedied the obscurity. One held it treason to pray for the Queen's death, but then blunted its own edge by conceding that repentance might be rewarded by a reduction of the penalty. The other enacted that anyone preaching against the title of Philip or of Mary should be imprisoned for life on the first offence and judged a traitor on the second. Not until 1571 was the clarity of the 1534 statute restored. Parliament then enacted that compassing the death or deprivation of the Queen, whether by the spoken or the written word, or by any other action, should be treason.[74] Even this did not satisfy Sir Thomas Gargrave, an influential Yorkshire lawyer, who urged on Burghley the enactment of still sharper laws. The laws of Henry VIII, he wrote, had been called bloody, but those of his daughter were still too gentle. The more savage laws were to come, with the acts against Jesuits, in the following decade.[75]

In the course of the sixteenth century a great many offences were at one time or another held to be treasonous, one or two of which are worth mentioning to indicate how broad the concept of treason was becoming. By the statute of 1352 it had been made treason to counterfeit the great or the privy seal or the King's coins. In 1535-6 this was extended to cover the King's sign manual or signet.[76] More important, the judges resolved in the reign of Henry VIII that an insurrection against the Statute of Labourers, in order to increase wages, should be regarded as levying war against the King and therefore as treason. Following the riots of 1549 Parliament enacted that if twelve or more persons assembled with the purpose of killing a royal councillor or changing the laws, they would be judged guilty of treason unless they dispersed. If forty or more assembled for over two hours, with the object of destroying enclosures or reducing rents, they too would be regarded as

---

[73] 1 Edward VI c. 12. 1 Mary st. 1, c. 1. For Throckmorton's trial, below, 384-6.
[74] 1 & 2 Philip & Mary cc. 9, 10. Cf. 1 Elizabeth c. 5.
[75] 13 Elizabeth c. 1. *CSPDom, Add., 1566-79*, 425.
[76] 27 Henry VIII c. 2.

traitors. This offence was reduced to felony by the second Parliament of Mary, but in practice general protests against enclosure continued to be regarded as treasonous. In 1597 a majority of the judges, consulted about the Oxfordshire rising of the previous year, resolved that, in spite of the Marian statute, where the rioters had 'a general dislike to all manner of enclosures' any assembly to destroy them was a rebellion against the monarch and therefore a form of treason. On the basis of this construction many offences not specifically directed against the monarch could be called treasonous.[77]

Before 1485 a wide range of methods was available to the Crown for trying men accused of treason. Trial by battle—usually the consequence of an 'appeal' or accusation of treason by a private person—was common in the early fifteenth century, although it was slipping into disuse under the Yorkists. Summary trial under the law of arms before the Constable of England in the Court of Chivalry could be employed when the accused had taken up arms openly against the monarch with banners displayed. In such cases the King's own 'record'—or evidence—was taken as sufficient proof. A similar method of trial was favoured by Edward IV and used to great effect by John Tiptoft, Earl of Worcester, as Constable during the disturbed years of the Wars of the Roses. Summary conviction was also possible by martial law, although its early history is obscure. Certain special courts were used from time to time, such as the court of the Steward and Marshal of the Royal Household, and, more important for the future, the court of the Lord High Steward and the peers. Parliament became in the fifteenth century an increasingly useful arena for the trial of treason and the confirmation of penalties imposed by other courts. Up to 1399 Parliament heard 'appeals' of treason by private individuals, but this mode of trial did not survive long into the fifteenth century. Impeachment was used in the first half of the fifteenth century, but not after 1450 until its revival in the seventeenth. More significant than either of these was the Act of Attainder, which was developed during the fifteenth century into an effective method of punishing defendants who were absent—either because they were dead or because they refused to attend for trial. In 1459, for instance, the Yorkist rebels who stayed away from Parliament were condemned on the King's own 'record' of appearing against him with banners unfurled. However, the most common form of trial, in spite of this wide variety of choice, was the ordinary process of the common law before judges of *oyer et terminer* and a jury.[78]

Four of these methods persisted into the sixteenth century. Trial before the Lord High Steward was used against the Earl of Warwick in 1499, the Duke of Buckingham in 1521, and the fourth Duke of Norfolk in 1572, among others. Many of the rebels of 1536–7 and 1569 were condemned by martial law. Acts of Attainder were common between 1533 and 1547: in all, 130 persons were condemned by attainder under Henry VIII, ninety-six for treason and three for heresy. After the middle of the sixteenth century attainder was often employed to confirm penalties imposed after conviction at the common law and to specify the forfeitures of land, but it was not used as a method of trial—if it could be called that—until it was revived to crush Strafford in the Long Parliament.[79] In the sixteenth century, as in the later middle ages, trial of treason was usually held by common-law procedures. King's Bench might hear treasons committed in Middlesex, or men found guilty elsewhere could sometimes have their cases called there for review. Treason cases were quite commonly heard at assizes, but the most important trials were held before specially appointed commissioners of *oyer et terminer*. Empson and Dudley, Thomas More, Anne Boleyn, Nicholas Throckmorton, and most of the Elizabethan Catholic missionaries were tried before such commissioners and a jury. It is worth noting here that neither Quarter Sessions nor Star Chamber nor the Council in the North could try cases of treason, although the Council in the Marches of Wales could do so by its commission of *oyer et terminer*.

Professor Elton has argued that the act of 1534 was an important landmark, not only in its definition of the scope of treason,

[78] G. D. Squibb, *The High Court of Chivalry* (Oxford, 1959), 22–9. Bellamy, op. cit., chs. vi, vii; p. 212. M. H. Keen, 'Treason Trials under the Law of Arms', *TRHS*, 5th ser. XII (1962).

[79] S. E. Lehmberg, 'Parliamentary Attainder in the Reign of Henry VIII', *HJ* XVIII (1975).

but also in its insistence that offenders must be 'lawfully convicted according to the laws and customs of this realm'. 'Here', he writes, 'was an end to all trials of treasons in such courts as that of the constable, by any law of arms, upon notoriety or the King's information, expedients which all had been freely used in previous centuries. The common law had triumphed.'[80] Yet the contrast does not seem quite so plain between the dark days before the reforms of Thomas Cromwell and the triumphant legalism of the years after 1534. Many of the older methods were already obsolete by the reign of Henry VIII. Impeachment had been last used in 1450; trial by battle had become very rare by the time of the Yorkists; trial by the law of arms reached its height under Edward IV and was last used in 1497. Trial by the Lord High Steward continued throughout the sixteenth century and has been regarded by some historians as an instrument of Tudor despotism;[81] but the Crown's selection of peers to constitute this court probably gave it no more leverage than it might get from the sheriff's power to empanel a favourable jury. More important, the use of martial law continued and condemnation of traitors by Acts of Attainder was still being secured in 1547. The triumph of the common law was not complete in 1534. It is true that common-law processes came to be predominant in the sixteenth century. But the change was less dramatic than supposed by Professor Elton and less closely linked to the act of 1534. It had begun earlier and was completed later.

What in practice did common-law trials involve in the sixteenth century? And how important were the other methods of trial still open to the Crown? There is still a great deal of scope for investigating the treason trials of the century. Although the dramatic set-piece occasions of the major state trials are reasonably well known, only Professor Elton, in his research on the 1530s, has made a detailed study of the mass of lesser trials, without which any conclusions are likely to be unbalanced.[82] However, merely by examining the best-known and best-recorded trials we can learn something of the ways

---

[80] Elton, *Policy and Police*, 292.
[81] Vernon Harcourt, *The Lord High Steward and Trial by Peers* (1907), ch. xii. Cf. Elton, *Policy and Police*, 264.
[82] Elton, *Policy and Police*, chs. vii–ix.

in which the law was applied; and that knowledge can then be set against what we know of less famous cases.

Trials before the Lord High Steward show that it was not difficult for the Crown to use the millstones of the law in crushing its enemies. The evidence of treason brought against the Duke of Buckingham in 1521 was slight and implausible. It rested only on conversations reported by three of Buckingham's servants, who had reason to be resentful of their master. The most damaging evidence, by Knyvet, whom the Duke had dismissed from his service, was obviously suspect. Nor was it clear that the Duke had committed treason even if the evidence was to be believed. Buckingham urged that no overt action was alleged against him and therefore he could not be brought within the scope of the act of 1352. To this Chief Justice Fineux replied that 'to intend the death of the King was high treason, and such intention was sufficiently proved by words alone'. In effect this doctrine anticipated the statute of 1534.[83]

The trial in 1572 of the fourth Duke of Norfolk is better documented. There can be little doubt that Norfolk was guilty of conspiring against the Queen and no serious objection can be made against the final judgement. But the proceedings show how heavily the play was loaded in favour of the Crown. Norfolk was allowed no access to a lawyer while he was awaiting trial, and when he asked to be represented by counsel the request was refused by the court. Of all the witnesses who testified against him, only one was actually present in court to have his evidence publicly weighed; the other testimony was simply read out by prosecuting counsel.[84]

But even with such ground rules operating against him a man might secure acquittal. In 1534 William, Lord Dacre, was tried on a charge of collusion with the Scots. The accusation originated in local hatreds and rivalries on the northern border rather than in court politics. But Dacre's enemies had Thomas Cromwell on their side and included the Earls of Northumberland and Cumberland. Although a true bill was found against him in Cumberland, the peers, presided over by Norfolk as

[83] M. Levine, 'The Fall of Edward, Duke of Buckingham', in A. J. Slavin (ed.), *Tudor Men and Institutions* (Baton Rouge, 1972).
[84] T. B. Howell, *A Complete Collection of State Trials* (1816), I. 957–1042. Neville Williams, *Thomas Howard, fourth Duke of Norfolk* (1964), ch. xii.

Lord High Steward, found him not guilty, to most people's astonishment.[85]

If the accused had an outside chance of avoiding conviction in a trial before the Lord High Steward, the course of a bill of Attainder presented him with no opportunity for defence whatever. Thomas Cromwell, for instance, was charged with offences that either fell far short of treason or were wholly fantastic. It is simply not possible to give a moment's credence to the story that Cromwell promised, should the King turn from the path of religious reform, that 'I would fight in the field in mine own person, with my sword in my hand, against him and all other'. The witnesses against him were Sir George Throckmorton, an old enemy, and Sir Richard Rich, whose testimony had already secured the condemnation of Sir Thomas More. They are not the men to convince an impartial observer that Cromwell had uttered the words of a lunatic; but then they had only to convince Henry VIII. Once that was done the passage of the bill through Parliament was assured and seems to have proceeded without any hindrance. Cromwell's only chance of defending himself lay in appeals for mercy to the King. Whatever else it was, the procedure by bill of Attainder was not a trial at common law, or indeed a trial at all.[86]

But of course only a small minority of those condemned for treason suffered before the Lord High Steward or through Act of Attainder. The principal test of the justice of treason trials must rest upon the cases heard by common-law procedures. The major set-piece trials reveal the situation of a man or woman whom the monarch had determined to destroy. In most cases the Crown was careful to ensure that the charges fell within the scope of the treason laws, even if evidence had to be fabricated in order to make the accusations hold. Lord Chancellor Audley gave firm rulings on the question: for example, he wrote of one case that 'the words spoken in March last ... touching appeals will hardly bear treason, but misprision; for there is no express mention made of the King or the Queen'.[87] Obviously there was an area of doubt before the

---

[85] M. E. James, *Change and Continuity in the Tudor North*, 16–19.

[86] Elton, 'Thomas Cromwell's Decline and Fall', in *Studies*, I. 220–30. Lehmberg, 'Parliamentary Attainder', HJ XVIII (1975).

[87] Elton, *Policy and Police*, 302. Cf. ibid. 301–8.

1534 treason act and after its repeal in 1547 over treason by words. Sometimes the judges seem to have accepted, as they did in Buckingham's case, that words alone could constitute treason; in other cases, such as the prophecies of the Nun of Kent, they were much more hesitant.[88] During the period covered by the 1534 statute some men were convicted of treason for words which do not seem to come clearly within the scope of that act. For instance, R. Yule, rector of Sotby, Lincolnshire, was executed for saying that the King's Councillors were 'false harlots'. However, while the Crown was probably anxious to stretch the limits of the law as widely as possible, 'it would', as Professor Elton says, 'be quite wrong to suppose that anything would do'.[89] The one case under Henry VIII in which men were executed for treason when their offences could not conceivably be counted as such was the trial of Empson and Dudley. That their fate was part of a young King's bid for popularity may explain what happened then, but cannot, in the strict sense, justify it.[90]

While the Crown's lawyers were usually scrupulous about the boundaries of treason, they were much less cautious about the evidence required to establish a man's guilt. Three *causes célèbres* will show the hazards run by those accused of treason in major state trials. In 1536 Anne Boleyn, her brother, Lord Rochford, and four other men were tried for treason: Anne was accused of adultery and incest, the men of being her *adulteros et concubinos*, and all of plotting the King's death. If the offences could be proved they could reasonably be held as treason, although the statute under which the Queen was condemned—26 Henry VIII c. 13—had been made to safeguard Anne herself against the adherents of the Pope: it had therefore to be stretched to include Anne herself among its victims. The evidence against the accused rested on vague gossip, one confession extracted by torture, and the obscure death-bed ramblings of a woman, Lady Wingfield, who had died three years before. Although Lord Rochford made a powerful defence at the trial, he and the others were found guilty and executed. Here is a case where a court faction, playing upon a gullible and jealous

[88] *LP* VI. 1445. Elton, *Policy and Police*, 274–5.
[89] M. Bowker, 'Lincolnshire, 1536', in *Studies in Church History*, IX, ed. D. Baker (1972), 199. Elton, *Policy and Police*, 301.   [90] S. B. Chrimes, *Henry VII*, 316–17.

King, was able to manipulate legal process for its own ends. The forms of the law were observed, but Anne herself surely had the right of it when she asked the Constable of the Tower, 'Master Kingston, shall I die without justice?'[91]

Sir Thomas More was the victim of Henry's own anger at the refusal of a trusted servant and friend to follow his will. Imprisoned in the Tower and attainted for refusing to take the oath of supremacy, More avoided for months being drawn into any overt act of treason. He would not acknowledge the King as Supreme Head but he was careful to make no open denial. In the end he was brought to trial on the word of Sir Richard Rich, the Solicitor-General. According to Rich, during a conversation in which the Solicitor was obviously trying to trap him, More had openly denied Parliament's authority to declare the King Head of the Church. The evidence about the trial is confusing. More denied that he had spoken the words alleged against him, argued that it was improbable that having kept silence for so long he should endanger himself by talking to Rich in that way, and asserted that since this was a private conversation about hypothetical cases the words, even if they had been spoken, could not be described as 'malicious', which they necessarily had to be if they were to count as treason under the 1534 act. The evidence against him rested solely on the testimony of Rich and was not supported by two other men who happened to be present at the time. As Professor Elton has suggested, it seems improbable that the Crown totally fabricated the remarks attributed to More; had it wished to do that it could have produced something much more damaging. Very possibly More let himself be led a little further into this swapping of hypothetical cases than was wise. But that cannot be called treason, even under the harsh terms of the 1534 act.[92]

The third case is that of Sir Nicholas Throckmorton, tried in 1554 for complicity in Wyatt's rebellion. The charge was that he conspired with Wyatt and others, encouraging them to rise, but not himself becoming actively involved in the revolt. Throckmorton's defence was severely hampered by a series of

[91] E. W. Ives, 'Faction at the Court of Henry VIII: the Fall of Anne Boleyn', *History*, LVII (1972).

[92] J. D. M. Derrett, 'The Trial of Sir Thomas More', *EHR* LXXIX (1964), has entirely changed the traditional picture of More's trial. See also Elton, *Policy and Police*, 400–20.

rulings from the bench. In common with other men accused of treason he was allowed neither defence counsel nor law-books to assist him. When he wished to call a defence witness his request was overruled. Only one prosecution witness was brought into court; the testimony of the others was merely recorded and Throckmorton had no opportunity to cross-examine them. Chief Justice Bromley refused to read out the act of 1352 when asked by Throckmorton to do so; and the bench showed itself throughout the trial as hostile to the defendant as was prosecuting counsel. In spite of his situation Throckmorton handled his case so skilfully that prosecuting counsel remarked petulantly: 'If I had thought you had been so well furnished with book cases I would have been better provided for you.' Evidently prosecutors in treason trials did not expect to be tested very hard by the defence.

The case turned in effect upon two legal points. First, Throckmorton argued, with great force, that the case against him rested effectively upon only one witness, Cuthbert Vaughan, whereas two were required to condemn a man for treason. The acts of Edward VI which made two witnesses mandatory— they had often been thought desirable before that—had both been repealed by Mary's first Parliament. But it seems to have been far from clear whether the act of repeal abolished the need for two witnesses. Second, and much more important, Throckmorton's defence turned on the repeal in 1547 of the treason act of 1534. This reinstated the statute of 1352 as the basis of the treason laws and, according to Throckmorton, necessitated an overt act, rather than mere words, before treason could be proved. Against this Chief Justice Bromley and prosecuting counsel argued that the 1352 act was not definitive; there were other, 'common-law' treasons not mentioned in it. At this Throckmorton asked, very reasonably, what had been the point of repealing the Henrician act, if the law were simply constructed against him. At least a defendant had known where he stood under the provisions of 1534. He got no answer to his questions.

To the evident surprise and undoubted annoyance of the bench the jury returned a verdict of Not Guilty. On the orders of the judges Throckmorton was kept in prison to face lesser charges and the jurymen accompanied him there. Eight of them were later brought before Star Chamber and fined for bringing in a false verdict: the fines initially imposed were very high—up to £2,000 in three cases—but were reduced later to £220 in five cases and £60 in three.[93]

Throckmorton's trial suggests a number of points about the treason laws of the mid-sixteenth century. First, the state of the law itself was obscure in many ways and the judges were still prepared to interpret statute in a fairly arbitrary manner. Second, the processes of a treason trial were heavily weighted against the accused, but not so heavily as to guarantee absolutely a victory for the prosecution. Trial by jury was still some safeguard, even in a major state trial, if the policies of the Crown were unpopular. Third, the judges were not prepared to overturn the verdict of a jury by ordering a fresh trial, even though the jurymen were harshly treated.

However, it is not enough to examine the major political trials. In that setting Throckmorton's acquittal seems a remarkable, almost miraculous, event. But, as Professor Elton has shown, acquittal is seen to be much more common if the mass of trials is examined. Influence and friendship might encourage a jury to bring in a verdict of Not Guilty. Working in the localities the agents of the Crown were less favourably placed than they were in London to control the legal proceedings. Not, of course, that they did not try. Norfolk's experiences in the north after the Pilgrimage of Grace illustrate both the difficulties of the Crown and its methods of overcoming them. In March 1537 William Levenyng, accused of complicity with Francis Bigod, was acquitted by the majority of the jury. Two months later, Norfolk told Cromwell that he was now better acquainted with the Yorkshire gentlemen and could name a compliant jury for future treason trials. But in spite of such practices some men still got acquitted.[94]

Professor Elton's figures show that, of 883 people involved in charges of treason between 1532 and 1540, about 38 per cent were executed. But as he argues, fairly enough, a large number of the victims were involved in open rebellion or were caught

[93] L. M. Hill, 'The Two-Witness Rule in English Treason Trials', *American Journal of Legal History*, XII (1968). Howell, *State Trials*, I. 869 ff. I am indebted to Mrs Loach for the analysis of this trial in her thesis, 'Opposition to the Crown in Parliament, 1553–58' (1974, Oxford, D.Phil. thesis), 324–34.

[94] Elton, *Policy and Police*, 314–16. Cf. *LP* XIII. i. 519.

up in those court intrigues which brought down Anne Boleyn, the Countess of Salisbury, and Cromwell himself. If we discount open rebels and the victims of major political trials we are left with 562 cases, producing 127 probable executions. The proportion of convictions does not seem unduly high. However, we have to remember that many of these cases involved delations which never resulted in trial. The Crown, as Professor Elton shows, examined reports of treason with reasonable care and rejected a large number of charges. Of the original 562, somewhat over 200 persons are known to have been brought to trial, and of these 127 were probably executed, twenty-two probably acquitted, forty-one pardoned, and thirteen had their convictions quashed. Only just over 10 per cent of those brought to trial were actually acquitted. By the standards of the day, compared with trials for felony, this is a very low figure, just as the 55 per cent executed is a high one. These figures may indicate that the Crown was exceptionally scrupulous in bringing to trial only those men and women of whose guilt it could be sure; or they may suggest that, although it was possible to secure an acquittal, once brought to trial the accused had only an even chance of avoiding death.[95]

Professor Elton is undoubtedly right in denying the existence of a reign of terror in Cromwellian England. Men did not suffer death as the automatic consequence of delation by their neighbours or government agents. The Crown was careful to examine the evidence contained in reports and did not proceed where the offence fell short of treason or the evidence was weak. Nevertheless, we need to bear in mind that, even in these lesser trials, the procedures of the common law were weighted against the accused.

The Crown had the power to secure the summary conviction by martial law of offenders caught in open rebellion. From time to time the Council threatened the use of martial law and summary execution against those who disturbed the peace and order of the realm. A proclamation of 1549 authorized the penalties of martial law upon enclosure rioters; in April 1558 the Marquis of Winchester was empowered, as Lieutenant of twenty-eight shires, to deal with rebels by martial law; and two

[95] Elton, *Policy and Police*, 383–400, esp. the table on p. 387. Although my conclusions are different from those of Professor Elton, I am deeply indebted to his researches.

months later Mary's government promised that it would be applied to anyone found in possession of seditious or heretical books. Under Elizabeth martial law was authorized in 1572 against anyone who assisted pirates, and in 1589 against vagrants, in particular against the disbanded soldiers and sailors who were then molesting the capital. The strains of war, dearth, and inflation led in the last decade of the century to more stringent 'law-and-order' measures, especially in London. The use of provost-marshals to curb and punish masterless men was often associated with proclamations empowering them and other officials to use martial law. Sometimes these seem to have been issued at the request of local officials, such as the Lord Mayor of London, who insisted in 1595 that the disorders of the apprentices could only be curbed by martial law.[96]

But although it was prepared to authorize the use of martial law from time to time the Privy Council would not automatically do so when requested. In 1556 the Earl of Sussex was politely refused authority to exercise it in dealing with seditious persons in Norfolk.[97] Nor does the authority to use martial law seem necessarily to have been employed when it was available. Since the jurisdiction was summary it has left few traces; but one gets the impression that it was often held *in terrorem*, while offenders were in practice dealt with by the ordinary courts. In July 1588 the Council ordered the Lord Steward to proceed by martial law against one Ross for 'lewd speeches'; but a month later it was giving instructions for his indictment at Quarter Sessions. Similarly the provost-marshals appointed in 1589 seem to have preferred sending offenders before the J.P.s to using their own summary powers.[98]

But martial law was used twice in the sixteenth century to savage effect. In 1537 Norfolk, exercising his commission to punish the rebels of the Pilgrimage of Grace and Bigod's revolt, used martial law against a minor rising at Carlisle, which he put down with the King's banners displayed. He executed seventy-four men by this means and remarked that, had he been compelled to use trial by jury, four-fifths of them would have

---

[96] Hughes & Larkin, I, no. 341; II, nos. 441, 443, 585; III, nos. 715–16, 735, 740, 769, 796, 809. BL Lansdowne MS 78, no. 64 (f. 159).

[97] *APC* v. 349. But cf. ibid. VI, 336.

[98] Ibid. XVI. 193, 246. L. O. J. Boynton, 'The Tudor Provost-Marshal', *EHR* LXXVII (1962).

escaped.[99] In 1569 martial law was used more extensively against the adherents of the northern earls. But the Crown was careful to warn its agents against condemning men of any worth except by the common law, since only thus would they forfeit their property: this legal weakness in the martial law may incidentally explain why the Tudor monarchs were usually reluctant to employ it more widely.[100] Its agents acted accordingly. Sir George Bowes 'appointed' seven hundred men to suffer execution and assured the government that those 'executed by the martial law ... was [*sic*] wholly of the meanest of the people, except the alderman of Durham, Plumtree, their preacher, the constables, and a fifty serving men that were executed at Durham'. Probably he was speaking the truth about their condition, but there is reason to believe that he deceived his masters about the number who suffered: although 700 were 'appointed' to die, it seems that many fewer were actually executed.[101]

The law of treason was only the most terrible of the weapons available to the Crown for deterring, frightening, or crushing its opponents. If its enemies were wise or lucky enough to avoid the snares of the treason acts, they might still be trapped by charges of felony and sedition, or subjected to arbitrary imprisonment, torture, and heavy bonds and recognizances. Abbot Whiting of Glastonbury was apparently reluctant to surrender his splendid monastery to the King. In 1539 he was sent to the Tower, the abbey was searched, and his monks interrogated. The investigation produced some evidence of treasonable activity on Whiting's part but the government did not in the end use it; probably it was considered too insubstantial to convince a local jury. Instead, Whiting was charged with 'robbing Glastonbury church', convicted of felony, found guilty by the jury, and hanged. The evidence against him is fragile; and his offence, if he did offend, was trivial in comparison with the legalized robberies committed by Henry VIII.[102]

[99] *LP* xii. i. 468, 479, 498.   [100] *CSPDom, Add., 1566–79*, 169–75.
[101] Cuthbert Sharp, *Memorials of the Rebellion of 1569* (1840), 183–8. H. B. McCall, 'The Rising in the North', *Yorks. Arch. Journ.* xviii (1904–5).
[102] D. Knowles, *The Religious Orders in England*, iii (1959), 379–82, 488 ff.

The laws against sedition and seditious libel were far from clear throughout the sixteenth century. A statute of 1275 had enacted that anyone publishing false news or scandal likely to create discord between the King and his magnates should be imprisoned until he revealed the inventor of the story. This statute, of *scandalum magnatum*, had been re-enacted in the fourteenth century and others had made it a crime to spread scandal against the nobles. But there was still no clearly established statutory offence of publishing scandal against the monarch. Obviously the government could not use the massive deterrent of the treason laws against every minor offender. It needed other laws which could be brought to bear in such cases and the Tudors began to create them by statute, proclamation, and judicial decision.[103] Henry VII ordered by proclamation that men spreading false rumours should be pilloried. In 1538 another proclamation made assault on royal officials punishable by the loss of lands; and a statute of 1543 made it a felony to issue false prophecies based upon the heraldic devices of noblemen.[104] But it was largely left to the children of Henry VIII—or their advisers—to define more closely these 'lesser' political crimes and to attach to them deterrent penalties.

The penalties for spreading false rumours became savage. In 1549 rumour-mongers were to be 'committed into the galley, there to row in chains ... to the example and terror of all other'. That was Protector Somerset's reaction to rumours of defeat in war. Two years later, Northumberland's administration, engaged in complicated manipulation of the currency, ordered six months' imprisonment for spreading false information about the coinage; anyone unable to pay the fine should lose one or both his ears.[105] Under a statute of Edward VI slanders spoken against the King were to be punished by imprisonment and became treason at the third offence. Under Mary specific penalties were prescribed for the uttering of seditious words; and writings against King or Queen, if they fell short of treason, could be punished by the loss of the author's right hand. In 1581 capital punishment was statutorily decreed for

[103] Statute of Westminster, I, c. 34. 2 Richard II st. 1, c. 5. 12 Richard II c.11. A. Harding, *Social History of English Law*, 79–81. The history of the law of sedition is in many respects obscure and needs detailed investigation.

[104] Hughes & Larkin, I, nos. 11, 179. 33 Henry VIII c. 14.

[105] Hughes & Larkin, I, nos. 329, 337, 353, 378.

anyone writing seditious books, while the spreading of seditious rumours could be punished either by the pillory and the loss of ears or by a fine of £200 and six months' imprisonment. A second offence was to be treated as treason.[106] The law relating to spoken, as opposed to written, slander of the monarch was partly clarified by Oldnoll's case in 1558, when the judges laid down that horrible and slanderous words against the Queen could be punished under the statute of 1275 by fine and imprisonment.[107] In the celebrated case, *De Libellis Famosis*, heard in Star Chamber in 1605, the court laid down that libel and calumny were offences against the Law of God, that they were especially repellent if they were committed against magistrates or other public persons, and that it constituted no defence to say that the libel was true. Although these laws and judgements provided adequate legal weapons for the Crown, they never satisfactorily distinguished between treason and sedition. The decision to charge a man with one offence rather than the other seems often to have lain in the political circumstances of the time rather than in any exact legal definition.[108]

But the absence of definition did not much inhibit the government. The Privy Council actively pursued its loose-mouthed subjects, and its register from 1540 to about 1570 is filled with reports about sedition, seditious libel, and rumour-mongering. If the laws were uncertain, the Crown was able to rely upon the summary jurisdiction of the Council. That is not to say that the Council automatically punished anyone against whom charges were laid. It examined the accusations and quite often decided that they were unfounded. But it also handed down whipping, pillorying, and mutilation. In 1546 it ordered John Wyot, a carpenter who had spoken 'lewd words' against the King, to be set on a pillory with his ear nailed to it, 'the same to remain till he should himself either cut it off or pull it off'. For spreading false rumours about Queen Mary, Thomas Sandesborough, a labourer from Stepney, was condemned to

---

[106] 5 & 6 Edward VI c. 11. 1 & 2 Philip & Mary c. 3, renewed by 1 Elizabeth c. 6. 23 Elizabeth c. 2. This brief list of statutes on sedition and slander is far from exhaustive. See Howell, *State Trials*, I. 1271 ff. for Udall's case, in which the prosecution based its charges on 23 Elizabeth c. 2.

[107] James Dyer, *Reports of Cases*, trans. J. Vaillant (Dublin, 1794), II. 155 a.

[108] E. Coke, *Reports*, v. 125 a. Holdsworth, VIII. 339–40, 409–10. Russell, *EHR* LXXX. 32–3. F. Siebert, *Freedom of the Press in England* (Urbana, 1952), 116 ff.

a similar punishment 'to the terror and example of others that would attempt the like'. These punishments were not imposed arbitrarily, but they were imposed summarily.[109]

After about 1570 the registers contain many fewer such entries and it seems likely that the Privy Council then began to refer charges of sedition to Star Chamber, Assizes, and Quarter Sessions: assize records begin to contain such charges from the early 1570s. One can only speculate on the reasons for this. The Council's agenda was certainly becoming uncomfortably full during Elizabeth's reign and it may well have wanted to delegate as much business as possible. Perhaps, too, the legislation on sedition enabled the common-law courts to act, whereas earlier offences had to be left to the Council.[110]

However, the Council preserved its authority to imprison men and women whom it considered dangerous to the state. Recusants were imprisoned in the Fleet at the mere will of the Council, without any form of trial.[111] Members of Parliament were imprisoned for infringing the rule against discussing parliamentary business outside the House. Although Peter Wentworth had been sentenced by the Commons in 1576, he and four others were put in the Tower by the Privy Council in 1587 for conferring about Puritan measures. A few weeks later Job Throckmorton was imprisoned for insulting the King of Scots. Wentworth was in the Tower for four months in 1591 for a book about the succession question; and was back there in 1593 for a stay which lasted until his death in 1597. Four of his colleagues were sent to the Fleet and the lawyer James Morice was confined to the house of a councillor.[112]

By about 1590 arbitrary imprisonment by individual councillors and other royal officials was causing discontent and complaint. The Lord Mayor of London complained that the Knight Marshal's men were making arrests in a peremptory manner. James Morice objected in Parliament about unjust imprisonment. In 1591 the judges asked Hatton and Burghley that

---

[109] For instances see Nicolas, VII. 148–9, 158–9, 179–80, 215–16, 258, 273, 312; *APC* I. 390; V. 27. This is a small sample from a long series.

[110] See, e. g., F. G. Emmison, *Elizabethan Life: Disorder*, ch. iii. J. S. Cockburn (ed.), *Calendar of Assize Records: Sussex Indictments, Elizabeth I* (1975), 71, 88, 105, etc.

[111] *APC* IX, 13–18, 46, 57, 80, 145; X. 310–13; 372.

[112] Neale, *Elizabeth I and her Parliaments*, I. 325–31, 353; II. 157–8, 162–5, 174, 255, 260–6, 267–9.

a curb be put on the committal of men to prison by noblemen and councillors and on the denial of habeas corpus. But the judges admitted that the imprisonment of men for matters of state by Queen or Council was acceptable.[113]

The Tudor Council resorted extensively—and with doubtful legality—to the use of torture. It seems that torture was seldom, if ever, used in England between 1310 and the reign of Edward IV.[114] In this, as in so many other things, what the Yorkists revived the Tudors continued. In 1527 the Duke of Norfolk, a harsh and authoritarian man, suggested to Wolsey that two thieves arrested in Norfolk should be put to the torture to make them give information about their accomplices. In a case at Sussex Assizes there was put in evidence a confession that had been extracted by torture; very creditably the jury refused to accept it. Mark Smeaton's confession at Anne Boleyn's trial in 1536 seems to have been obtained by torture.[115] From then until 1640 orders to put men to the torture were regularly given, usually to get information, sometimes, as in the case of some hawk-stealers, 'to the example of others'. Until 1570 few, if any, tortures were inflicted in the cause of religion; mostly the victims were murderers, thieves, and rioters. But in that year John Felton, who displayed the Bull of Excommunication against Elizabeth, became the first of a long procession of Catholics tortured for reasons of state. Authority to inflict torture was wielded by the Privy Council and by the Council in the Marches of Wales; but there is some evidence that the official torturers, especially the infamous Topcliffe, sometimes acted without proper warrant. Twentieth-century experience of that breed suggests that they would be unlikely to respect legal forms. On one occasion Topcliffe treated a Scotsman suspected of theft with such savagery that his master told the Lord Mayor 'that cannibals would not use any as his servant was used', at which the Lord Mayor was 'somewhat offended'.[116]

Finally, mention should be made of a form of coercion used extensively by Henry VII. He regularly put men under bonds

---

[113] Above, 329. Neale, op. cit. II. 267–79. *APC* XXII. 151, 170, 240, 264, 372. G. W. Prothero, *Select Statutes* (Oxford, 1954 edn.), 446–8.

[114] Bellamy, *Crime and Public Order*, 139–40.

[115] *LP* IV. ii. 3702–3. Elton, *Policy and Police*, 313. Ives, *History*, LVII. 171.

[116] *APC* IV. 284; VII. 273. David Jardine, *A Reading in the Use of Torture* (1837), *passim.* P. Williams, *Council in the Marches*, 56, 94–6. BL Lansdowne MS 71, no. 21 (f. 40).

and recognizances for very large sums of money in order to ensure their obedience. Four-fifths of the nobility were under bond to him at some time or other during his reign. Some of the most powerful nobles were fined huge sums for relatively trivial offences. Most notoriously, Lord Abergavenny was fined £70,000 in King's Bench for unlawful retaining. No one expected that he could or would pay such a fine, but it was used to make him enter a recognizance of £13,000 that he would pay the King £500 per annum for ten years. Another nobleman forced to live under the threat of a bond was the Earl of Kent. He was heavily in debt to the King when he succeeded to his earldom and agreed to a bond by which he undertook to sell no land and grant no office without royal consent; should he break this condition he stood to forfeit £10,000. Henry Tudor successfully harnessed his nobility by these means, but they were understandably unpopular. His son cancelled many of these bonds, but both he and Mary seem to have resorted to this method of securing obedience in future years.[117]

E. *Law, Justice, and Consent*

This lengthy and perhaps repellent description of coercive methods raises fundamental questions about the nature of the regime. Does the use of such methods suggest that Tudor government was arbitrary? Did the dynasty rule through a prerogative power that stood above the law? Did the Crown step beyond the limits, if any, of its legal authority? How far did the Tudors rely upon forcible coercion and how far upon willing and voluntary acquiescence? These questions have recently become the subject of historical controversy; and I want now to take up some of the points in that debate and to relate them to the evidence that has emerged in earlier parts of this chapter.[118]

[117] J. R. Lander, 'Bonds, Coercion and Fear', in *Florilegium Historiale: Essays Presented to W. K. Ferguson*, ed. J. G. Rowe and W. H. Stockdale (Toronto, 1971). Professor J. J. Scarisbrick tells me that he has found instances of such bonds being exacted under Henry VIII, and Mrs Loach has pointed out to me that Mary also used them.

[118] J. Hurstfield, 'Was There a Tudor Despotism after all?', *TRHS*, 5th ser. XVII (1967), repr. *Freedom, Corruption and Government*. G. R. Elton, 'The Rule of Law in Sixteenth-Century England', *Studies*, I, ch. xiv. Also, Elton, *Studies*, I, chs. iii, iv. xvii; II, chs. xxi, xxii. J. P. Cooper, 'Henry VII's Last Years Reconsidered', *HJ* II (1959). C. Russell, 'Theory of Treason', *EHR* LXXX (1965), 35–48.

Securing Compliance

395

First, it seems clear that legal opinion under the Tudors regarded the prerogative as part of the law and as subject to law. Professor Elton has referred to the widely esteemed views of William Staunford, who wrote that prerogative 'had his being by th'order of the common law', and of Justice Brown, who said that 'the King cannot do any wrong, nor will his prerogative be any warrant to him to do any injury to another'.[119] The Commons in 1576 objected to a bill which would have empowered the monarch to regulate apparel by proclamation, on the ground that if such an act were passed 'a proclamation from the prince should take the force of law, which might prove a dangerous precedent in time to come'.[120]

The prerogative was considered, by lawyers at any rate, to be a part of the law. But is there any evidence that the Tudors tried to release it from these established limitations or to use it in a way that was not properly warranted? On two or three occasions they did indeed try to extend their powers of taxation in a way which might conceivably have made them independent of Parliament. Wolsey's proposal for the Amicable Grant is an obvious case in point: it was not merely unpopular but also contrary to a statute of Richard III. But the manœuvre failed. Later in Henry's reign Paget advocated the levy of a benevolence on the ground that it would save the time and trouble of calling Parliament; this time the proposal was acceptable and the tax was collected. Henry twice converted forced loans into benevolences by securing statutes which freed him from the obligation to repay them; and his successors continued to levy both loans and benevolences. This practice might have become a threat to Parliament's control of revenue had it been used regularly and extensively. But benevolences were what their name implied: acts of good will. Milked too often they would dry up. They could never be a threat to parliamentary independence because their use was restricted by political realities.[121]

More dangerous in practice was the Crown's exploitation of customs duties. After 1485 Parliament allowed its control over

---

[119] Elton, 'Rule of Law', 264–5, and *passim* for further evidence on this point.

[120] Neale, *Elizabeth I and her Parliaments*, 1. 354–5.

[121] Above, ch. ii. I am grateful to Dr R. S. Schofield for allowing me to read his unpublished paper on this subject.

this source of revenue to be eroded when it granted tonnage and poundage to each of the Tudor monarchs for life. But although this deprived Parliament of control from the beginning of each reign and created an expectation that the grant would automatically be made at the accession of every monarch, tonnage and poundage did still depend upon statutory control, as Charles I discovered in 1625. However, the rate at which it was levied did not depend on Parliament after 1558, when Mary issued on her own authority a fresh Book of Rates, a new impost on cloth, and an extra duty on sweet wines. There was some protest by merchants, but no opposition in Parliament, and the new duties were successfully levied. Between them they increased the yield from the customs by more than 150 per cent without any reference being made to Parliament. It was a precedent of which James I and Robert Cecil later took advantage.[122]

It has been argued by Dr Hurstfield that the Act of Proclamations of 1539 was originally intended by the Crown to enable it to act as sole legislator. The evidence for this belief lies in the wording of the preamble and in the opposition to the original bill in Parliament. Since this bill has not survived, its intentions can only be inferred. My own belief is that the wording of the preamble does not support Dr Hurstfield's view of Crown policy: a desire to use proclamations in a sudden emergency implies no sinister intent. Nor does the manner in which Cromwell and Henry actually used them. Dr Elton's arguments are to my mind convincing on this point, although he surely goes too far when he claims that the bill could never have been a threat because it rested on parliamentary consent. Evidently the bill would have given the Crown larger powers than the final act, but the arguments for despotic intentions are not convincing. In any case, it is agreed now by all parties that the final act did not allow the royal power to legislate by proclamation; if there was an attempt it failed.[123]

In only one significant respect—the imposing of new customs duties and rates—did the Tudor Crown free itself from legal limitations. But since the frontiers of the law were not always

---

[122] Dietz, *English Public Finance*, 1. 206–9. G. D. G. Hall, 'Impositions and the Courts, 1554–1606', *LQR* LXIX (1953).

[123] Hurstfield, loc. cit. Elton, 'Rule of Law', 271–4.

clearly drawn and reasons of state were often pressing, it did sometimes overstep the law. The first Tudor monarch was certainly harsh and probably unscrupulous in his use of legal weapons to control his subjects. The petition of Edmund Dudley, written from the Tower after the death of his master, is convincing in its account of Henry VII's methods. The King, he writes, 'was much set to have many persons in his danger and pleasure', and he gives plenty of detailed evidence to support this claim. The petition shows that Henry was less interested in money than in using fines, bonds, and recognizances as political weapons; and he used them in ways that at the very best skirted the fringes of illegality.[124]

Royal intervention in the proceedings of the law was probably more common under Henry VII than later, but neither Henry VIII nor Elizabeth was innocent of this. In November 1534 when the judges were divided over the critical case of the Dacre inheritance—in which the Crown was trying to overturn a trust—Henry summoned the judges to him and promised 'bon thanke' for their compliance; those who had at first been opposed to the Crown view conformed.[125] In 1579 John Stubbs was condemned to lose his right hand for writing a pamphlet, *The Gaping Gulf*, against Elizabeth's marriage with the Duke of Anjou. Various objections were made against his prosecution, on the ground that the statute employed was out of date and that Stubbs had libelled Anjou, not the Queen. Not merely were the objectors overruled, but one of them, James Dalton, was imprisoned, and Justice Monson of the Common Pleas was removed from the Bench.[126]

Although legal opinion from Sir John Fortescue to Edward Coke unequivocally stated that the use of torture was contrary to the common law, it was regularly used by the Privy Council in the sixteenth century. Holdsworth justified this on the ground that the resort to torture was part of the Crown's extraordinary authority in times of emergency. But in practice

---

[124] C. J. Harrison, 'The Petition of Edmund Dudley', *EHR* LXXXVII (1972). Also Lander, 'Bonds, Coercion and Fear', in *Florilegium Historiale*, ed. Rowe and Stockdale.

[125] E. W. Ives, 'The Genesis of the Statute of Uses', *EHR* LXXXII (1967), 691. See also the case of Lord Dacre of the South: *LP* XVI. 931, 932.

[126] W. Camden, *The True and Royal History of the Famous Empress Elizabeth* (1625), Bk III, 14 ff. For instances of royal intervention in civil cases see W. J. Jones, *Chancery*, 328–36.

torture was not confined to such occasions or purposes. Until 1570 it was generally used against murderers, thieves, and rioters. After that date it was certainly employed against men regarded as enemies of the state, but it continued to be inflicted on men suspected of ordinary crime, including the 'crime' of being a gipsy. It is hard to reconcile this practice with a scrupulous regard for the law.[127]

Elizabeth seems to have been less scrupulous than her predecessors in the use of proclamations. Two of her proclamations certainly anticipated Parliament in making new laws. One was issued in 1580 to prohibit the erection of any new buildings within three miles of the gates of the city of London; it specifically stated that the Queen was acting to prevent over-population 'until by some further good order to be had in Parliament or otherwise the same may be remedied'. It was not for another twelve years that a statute was carried to give this proclamation the force of law. In the meantime men were prosecuted under its provisions, which were of uncertain legality.[128] The other matter was more important, since it involved the law of treason. In 1582 a proclamation pronounced all Jesuits and seminary priests to be, *ipso facto*, traitors. This was a major extension of the treason laws, not merely easing the prosecutor's task, but introducing the new and alarming concept that a category of persons could be condemned as traitors without committing any overt act or speaking any treasonable words. For three years this definition of treason rested solely upon proclamation, until it was confirmed by statute in 1585. Such practice gave a wider power to proclamations than accepted common-law doctrines; but, although some criticism was made about prosecution under the building regulations, apparently none was voiced about the new treason 'law'.[129]

In one other respect Elizabeth's government seems to have flouted the law. It habitually raised troops for overseas campaigns from the county militia and in doing so contravened statutes of the reign of Edward III. When protest was publicly made against this by Sir John Smythe, an Essex gentleman,

[127] Jardine, *Torture*, 1–10. Holdsworth, v. 184–6.

[128] Hughes & Larkin, I, no. 649. 35 Elizabeth c. 6. Hawarde, 79.

[129] Hughes & Larkin, II, no. 660. See also nos. 650, 655. Youngs, 'Definitions of Treason', *HJ* XIV (1971).

he was imprisoned in the Tower, where he quickly retracted his apparently correct assertions, excusing himself on the ground that his mind had been unsettled by too much claret and white wine. Smyth was an expert on military affairs and evidently knew what he was talking about, in spite of the wine. But few people echoed or supported his protest. Perhaps the reason for this complacency lay in the composition of the levies, few of whom were men of any importance. The gentry, who would probably have complained had they been affected, were able to stay at home unless they wished to serve as volunteers.[130]

However, with these exceptions, the Tudor monarchs generally observed the law. On the whole, especially in its powers of coercion, it gave them the weapons they needed and only occasionally was there any reason for going outside it. But the law did not guarantee that justice was done. The conduct of treason trials might scrupulously follow the processes of the common law and still fall sadly short of just rule. The assessment of injustice is obviously more subjective than the assessment of legality; and men may reasonably differ about the justice of Tudor rule. But it is hard to believe that justice was served in treason trials by the denial of counsel to defendants, the obvious bias of the bench, or the inability of defendants to call witnesses in their own behalf. The summary jurisdiction exercised by the Privy Council probably had a foundation in the law; but arbitrary imprisonment, pillorying, and mutilation were not justice.

The limitations imposed upon the monarchy by law were supplemented by a genuine need to seek the consent of the political nation in Parliament. The independence of Parliament from the Crown was admittedly not yet complete. Accusations were made, especially under Henry VIII, that the government either packed it or cowed it into submission. Sir Thomas Tempest, one of the leaders of the Pilgrimage of Grace, complained that Henry's Parliaments would be more appropriately called 'councils of the King's appointment and not Parliaments'.[131]

[130] *CSPDom, 1595–7*, 259/16, 19, 21–2, 33–6, 51–2, 54–9; 263/59–61; 266/4. HMC, *Salisbury*, VI. 450. Cruickshank, *Elizabeth's Army*, 10.
[131] A. Fletcher, *Tudor Rebellions*, 126–7.

The Crown and its officials certainly interfered in some con-, stituencies during the elections of 1536 and 1539. Royal power over the House of Lords was probably greater still: peers known to be hostile to Crown policy could be persuaded to stay away; bishops, appointed and translated by the King, could be won over by threats or inducements. The monarch could curtail debates in both Houses, decide upon the dates for assembly and dissolution, sequester and imprison their members.[132]

Yet the Crown could never take the compliance of Parliament for granted. In 1523 an unknown correspondent told the Earl of Surrey that 'the greatest and sorest hold' had been made in the Commons over Wolsey's demand for revenue.[133] Parliament later opposed the Crown over the Statute of Uses, the Annates Act, the Royal Supremacy, the Treason Act, and the Proclamations Act.[134] Such opposition was not always successful, but Parliament hindered the royal will in various ways throughout the century. Bills were modified and amended in the course of their passage. Some of these revisions were slight, but at times major changes were made. The Poor Law proposed by Thomas Cromwell in 1536 was rejected and a much more conservative measure put in its place. The Parliament of 1563 added to a royal bill on wages additional provisions on apprenticeship and compulsory labour.[135] Occasionally bills proposed by the Crown were totally rejected: Henry VIII failed to secure an act against uses in 1532 and Mary's proposal to confiscate the property of exiles was defeated. Once or twice Parliament gained substantial concessions from the Crown: Mary in effect agreed in 1554 to allow the holders of monastic lands to keep them, so that the return to Roman jurisdiction might have a smooth passage; and Elizabeth promised in 1601 to revoke unpopular monopolies and to refer all complaints about them to the lawcourts. Several times in Elizabeth's reign Parliament acted as a pressure-group in conjunction with other political forces: unsuccessfully in the attempts to make her settle the succession; successfully, but only after several attempts, in securing

---

[132] S. E. Lehmberg, *Reformation Parliament*, 62–3, 253–6. J. S. Roskell, 'Perspectives in English Parliamentary History', in *Historical Studies of the English Parliament*, ed. E. Fryde and E. Miller, Vol. ii.   [133] Ellis, 1st ser. I. 219.

[134] Lehmberg, op. cit. 133–4, 137–8, 141, 180, 203–6.

[135] Elton, *Reform and Renewal*, 122–6. Bindoff, 'The Making of the Statute of Artificers', in *Elizabethan Government and Society*, ed. Bindoff *et al.*

the execution of Mary Stuart. At least once the fear of parliamentary opposition inhibited the Crown from putting forward a measure which it was anxious to secure. This certainly happened in 1555, when proposals for the coronation of Philip were abandoned; and such negative actions may be more frequent and important than they have seemed, for they leave little trace in the records.[136]

A large volume of legislation was carried up from below rather than imposed from above. The Poor Laws are an obvious example of grass-roots influence. The Cromwellian proposals for the relief of the poor, largely defeated in 1536, became law in the 1570s and acquired precise shape in 1597. It seems fair to suppose that experience of poor-relief schemes in London and Norwich—devised by city fathers, not by the Crown—was the critical force behind the legislation of 1572 and 1576.[137]

Viewed in the light of the seventeenth-century struggle, Parliament's record under the Tudors may not seem very impressive. But that is not the perspective in which it should be seen. Neither Crown nor Parliament regarded confrontation as their natural posture. They saw their relationship in terms of co-operation, in which disagreement might occur, but which was aimed—and aimed successfully—at securing an *agreed* body of statute law.[138] Parliament was an independent and important part of the machinery of government, capable under the Tudors, as it had been before 1485, of independent action. By means of discussion, criticism, and negotiation it participated in the production of a large volume of law.

Obviously the consent of Parliament was not equivalent to the agreement of the adult population. It was the consent of a minority: the political nation. The number of persons entitled to a voice in parliamentary elections may have been larger than is sometimes thought. While borough franchises were mostly restrictive, the freeholder franchise in the counties was wide, since the property qualification of 40s. p.a. was low and the status of freeholder was vague. Entitlement to a vote did not

[136] Jennifer Loach, 'Opposition to the Crown in Parliament, 1553–1558' (D. Phil. thesis, Oxford, 1974), ch. v. D. M. Loades, *Two Tudor Conspiracies*, 137–42.

[137] Elton, *Reform and Renewal*, 122–6. Above, 204–6.

[138] Elton, *Reform and Renewal*, ch. vii. Id., *Studies*, II, 58–61.

however necessarily provide the opportunity to cast one, for contested elections were rare. Furthermore, some influential men in the counties believed that elections should be decided as much by the status of voters as by their mere number. It therefore seems probable that in practice the House of Commons did represent only the small political nation: gentlemen, merchants, lawyers. But the width of the county franchise, the vagueness of its limits, and pressure for an extension of the suffrage in the towns helped to widen the political base of Parliament under the early Stuarts.[139]

As the doctrine of obedience and of unquestioning loyalty became firmly established in men's minds, the political nation offered a general acquiescence and consent to the regime. The intellectual chains which bound men to the monarchy had certainly been forged in the first place by royal servants. But by the time of Elizabeth they were devised as well as accepted by men of some independence; and high devotion to the monarchy had become an essential part of the consciousness of the articulate classes. It is hardly possible that an epic of the calibre of the *Faerie Queene* should have been written as a piece of contrived court flattery, or that the dazzling apparatus of pageants, tournaments, and poetry, eulogizing and elevating the monarch, should have been merely government propaganda or the contrivance of self-seeking courtiers.

Even those who detested or feared the policies of the Crown were reluctant to enter into open disobedience and regarded rebellion with distaste. Sir Thomas More, unshakeably opposed though he was to the divorce of Henry VIII, believed that it would be wrong for a layman openly to condemn policies or statutes, although it would be permissible for a cleric. The most that a layman could venture was private advice and dissent to the King: anything more would bring into contempt the law itself.[140] During the Pilgrimage of Grace, Archbishop Lee told the assembled pilgrims that it would be unlawful to do battle without the command of the King; and although many of the rank and file protested at this assertion, their leaders were evi-

---

[139] See Derek Hirst, *The Representative of the People?* (Cambridge, 1975), for a discussion of seventeenth-century developments and for useful remarks in the introduction on the sixteenth century. He rightly stresses the difficulty of estimating the extent of the franchise.

[140] Derrett, 'Trial of Sir Thomas More', *EHR* LXXIX (1964), 476–7.

dently, to judge from their actions, of the Archbishop's opinion.[141] In 1569, the Earl of Westmorland, just before he took up arms, voiced serious misgivings about rebelling for the sake of religion: 'Those that seem to take that quarrel in other countries are accounted as rebels; and therefore I will never blot my house which hath been this long preserved without staining.'[142]

Men condemned for rebellion generally accepted the justice of their own fate. Sir Thomas Wyatt expressed abhorrence at his own actions: 'Peruse the chronicles through, and you shall see that never rebellion against their natural prince and country prospered.'[143] Even those whose condemnation was obviously unjust acquiesced upon the scaffold. There were of course exceptions to this. Sir Thomas More insisted that his indictment was 'in law, amongst Christian men, insufficient to charge any Christian man'; Sir Walter Raleigh asserted his innocence in a speech from the scaffold that lasted forty-five minutes.[144] More typical of speeches from the Tudor scaffold was the oration of Anne Boleyn's brother, Lord Rochford, who instructed his audience that 'from my mishap ye may learn not to set your thoughts upon the vanities of this world'.[145]

This willing acceptance of a harsh regime is not difficult to understand. It has sometimes been explained as a reaction against painful memories of the Wars of the Roses; but it is unlikely that those limited and intermittent struggles had so profound or lasting an effect. The circumstances of the sixteenth century were probably more important in nurturing a belief in absolute obedience. The emphasis put by religious reformers upon the iniquity of man demanded in response an acceptance of strong government. Although Calvin, towards the end of his life, conceded the possibility of limited resistance to a heretical monarch, and although some of his continental followers, principally Béza, developed such notions further, the Reformed Church always insisted upon obedience to properly constituted

[141] *LP* xii. i. 1021.

[142] Reid, 'Rebellion of the Earls, 1569', *TRHS*, n.s. xx (1906), 192.

[143] Howell, *State Trials*, i. 861.

[144] R. W. Chambers, *Thomas More* (edn. of 1963), 325. S. J. Greenblatt, *Sir Walter Raleigh* (New Haven, 1973), 16–21.

[145] E. W. Ives, *History*, lvii (1972), 170. See L. B. Smith, 'English Treason Trials and Confession in the Sixteenth Century', *Journ. of the History of Ideas*, xv (1954).

and godly authority. Unless man's sinful nature were curbed by the painful bridle of government, chaos would ensue.

The teachings of religion were reinforced, from about 1540, by fears of invasion and civil war. In Mary's reign dislike of foreigners and abhorrence of Habsburg domination were widely spread; and in Elizabeth's, alarm at the apparent aggression of the Catholic powers was intensified. Sir Walter Raleigh, who had seen for himself the tragic strife in France, insisted that, had the Catholic priests and recusants in England gone unmolested, 'we should have had as furious a war both upon us and among us . . . if Pope Pius' bull could have gored as well as he could bellow'.[146] There was always the danger that, if the government's vigilance slackened, the whole social order would be overthrown by that 'many-headed monster', the common people of England. Here again there were terrifying events in Europe to provide a warning: the German peasants had risen in their thousands in 1525, and a few years later Jan of Leyden and his anabaptist followers had established a reign of terror in Munster. The riots and rebellions of mid-sixteenth-century England seemed to be symptoms of the same contagion. The hysterical tone of Cheke's attack upon the Norfolk rebels indicates the insecurity which gripped the propertied classes. In their view only total obedience could preserve the social order.[147]

That obedience was in a general way freely given. But acceptance of the regime, belief in obedience, abhorrence of rebellion, and devotion to monarchy did not guarantee that the political nation would actively comply with all the government's specific orders and demands. The adoring subjects of Gloriana could be remarkably obstinate about parting with their money or carrying out her more burdensome instructions. To secure such compliance the government had to bring pressures to bear. One example may, in conclusion, illustrate the point. When Henry VIII wished to raise a loan in 1542 he issued hundreds of letters under the privy seal to those of his faithful subjects who 'may and will gladly strain themselves'. The commissioners charged with collecting the money were given a list of taxpayers and

---

[146] A. L. Rowse, *The Times*, 8 Aug. 1970.

[147] C. Hill, 'The Many-headed Monster', in C. H. Carter (ed.), *From the Renaissance to the Counter-Reformation* (1966).

told to raise from them appropriate sums. Anyone who appeared 'stiff in condescending to the same' was to have his name taken and then to be ordered to keep his refusal secret so that others would not be encouraged by his example. The Crown's first appeal was to the loyalty of its subjects. But this was succeeded by coercive pressures from the commissioners, used in a subtle and tactically shrewd way. Compliance, if it were to be secured, would only come when the Crown manipulated both the devotion and the fears of its subjects; and the manipulation had to be skilfully done: above all, objectors must be isolated one from another.[148]

[148] *LP* xvii. 188, 190, 194.

XII

The Chains of Command

Who made up the links in the chains of command that ran between the central government and the regions? It is a truism that the Tudor monarchs had no local bureaucracy for enforcing their commands; and they certainly had nothing to compare with the hierarchy of competing officials who aided and obstructed the Kings of France. Early in the middle ages English monarchs had appointed their own unpaid representatives in the shires: the sheriffs, escheators, and coroners. Although the sheriff had by the fifteenth century lost his earlier pre-eminence in local affairs, he still collected the ancient revenues of the Crown, helped with the mustering of soldiers, held county and hundredal courts, and executed judicial writs from the central courts. Much of this work was mechanical, but he could influence the course of justice by empanelling partial juries, and his role as returning officer in parliamentary elections for the shire enabled him to manipulate arrangements to suit his favoured candidate, should he wish. The coroner, essential in the twelfth century as a check upon the sheriff and as the officer responsible for the pleas of the Crown, was limited at the end of the middle ages to examining witnesses in criminal cases and viewing the bodies of the dead. The escheator's role had become even more vestigial: responsible in early times for wardship dues and other feudal incidents, this unpaid, annually appointed officer had become thoroughly ineffective by Tudor times.[1]

The salaried local agents of government were few: the Exchequer and the Duchy of Lancaster employed local receivers of revenues; and the ports had staffs of customs officials, who sometimes acted directly on behalf of the Exchequer, sometimes

---

[1] On sheriffs see: C. H. Karraker, *The Seventeenth-Century Sheriff* (Chapel Hill, 1930), chs. i–v; T. G. Barnes, *Somerset*, ch. v.; W. B. Willcox, *Gloucestershire*, 38–49; Neale, *Elizabethan House of Commons*, ch. iii; *LP* II. i. 2579; v. 1051, 1130, 1516–18. On the coroner: A. Harding, *Social History of English Law*, 127. On the escheator: Hurstfield, *Queen's Wards*, 230–8.

on behalf of farmers leasing the right to collect duties from the Crown. In the sixteenth century the Crown developed the office of wardship feodary, a professional county officer responsible for looking after the Crown's feudal rights and supplementing the work of the unpaid and ineffective escheator.[2]

The most continuous and detailed control over the shires was exercised by the Justices of the Peace. Well-established by 1485, the J.P.s had extensive judicial authority over murders, felonies, misdemeanours, and offences against economic and social regulations. In practice they seem, in the course of the sixteenth century, to have yielded up to the assizes their jurisdiction over felonies and to have occupied themselves mainly with petty larceny, unlawful assembly, affray, riot, and forcible entry. In addition they were in principle burdened with the 'stacks of statutes' which Parliament expected them to enforce. But it is doubtful whether these burdens weighed upon them as heavily as they claimed, for many of the statutes were totally ignored in Quarter Sessions. Even so, J.P.s did have considerable duties 'out of sessions', which probably compensated for their virtual surrender of jurisdiction over felonies. Individual justices took sureties for good behaviour, ejected men who made forcible entries, examined suspects. A pair of justices could arrest rioters, send rogues to the house of correction, give or withhold bail, license alehouses, nominate overseers of the poor, and perform a score of other tasks. By the end of the sixteenth century a loose organization was being formed to assist them: divisions were created within counties for which particular justices were held responsible and they were beginning to hold regular divisional meetings, later to be known as 'petty sessions'.[3]

The most obvious chain of communication between the centre and these various local officials led from the Privy Council, via the royal messengers, to sheriffs and J.P.s. Along it passed proclamations, circular letters, and conciliar orders. But vital as this chain might be—and it generally carried the most solemn, formal, and legalistic matter—it was not sufficient, and the work of sheriffs and J.P.s had to be supple-

[2] Hurstfield, loc. cit.

[3] Harding, op. cit. 68–74. W. Lambarde, *Eirenarcha, passim*, for the most comprehensive contemporary account of the office of J.P. Barnes, *Somerset*, 67, 80–5, 149–50. Elton, *Tudor Constitution*, ch. x. Hurstfield, 'County Government', in *VCH, Wiltshire*, v. 80–110. Above, 218.

mented with other agencies which might convey orders and bind the localities to their performance. Some of these were personal; some were formal but temporary; others were permanent. Methods of control were devised, abandoned, resurrected, and transformed to meet immediate situations. Tudor rule was in many ways a triumph of the *ad hoc* response; and for that very reason it is exceptionally difficult to analyse.

Sometimes the Crown used noblemen to act on its behalf, in personal and informal ways, within the regions of their influence. Henry VIII sent the Duke of Norfolk into East Anglia to collect taxes, supervise arrangements for defence, and ensure the supply of food to the markets. The Dukes of Norfolk and Suffolk were jointly responsible for collecting—or failing to collect—the 'amicable grant' in the same area. Three years later, in 1528, Norfolk was busy suppressing riotous artisans in Bury St Edmunds, and, at the same time, urging clothiers to keep their men in work. In 1536 he was addressing the Mayor and aldermen of Norwich, exhorting them to assess themselves for taxes at a more realistic—that is to say, higher—level.[4] Under Elizabeth, the Earl of Pembroke habitually intervened in the affairs of Glamorgan even before he became President of the Council in the Marches. Relying on his position as the greatest landowner of the county he quelled a dispute between the influential families of Stradling and Carne; and he forced the county gentry into making a large contribution to the rebuilding of Cardiff Bridge.[5]

Bishops were also summoned to aid the secular government within their sees. Bishop Fox of Durham forced fifteen border thieves to submit by threatening them with excommunication in 1498; and Cardinal Wolsey attempted, unsuccessfully, to repeat this tactic at the request of the Warden of the Marches in 1524.[6] Archbishop Warham was called upon to levy the 'amicable grant' in Kent, the Bishop of Ely in Cambridgeshire, and the Bishop of Lincoln in Buckinghamshire, Bedfordshire, and Huntingdon.[7] In 1552 bishops were instructed by statute to admonish those laymen who were niggardly in contributing

[4] *LP* iv. ii. 4012, 4044; ix. 470.
[5] P. Williams, 'The Political and Administrative History of Glamorgan', in *Glamorgan County History*, iv, ed. Glanmor Williams, 175–91.
[6] M. E. James, *Family, Lineage and Civil Society*, 54.
[7] *LP* iv. i. 1243, 1263, 1267, 1272, 1305–6, 1330.

alms for the poor, while under Elizabeth they were ordered
by the Privy Council to arrange for ministers to preach on
the virtues of abstinence in times of dearth. This suggests an
attenuation of their secular role: under the early Tudors
bishops acted as the agents of royal power; Elizabeth confined them largely to exhortation, leaving execution to the
laity.[8]

Normally the Crown executed its will in the localities by issuing a commission.[9] The enforcement of royal orders was, more
than anything else, government by commission. Executive and
investigatory commissions were framed for particular purposes
and present the historian with a variety of forms particularly
difficult to describe. They ranged from permanent institutions
of government to inquiries into one man's lands. To convey
them to the reader in an intelligible way is to simplify and to
categorize something very complicated and undefined. However, many of them have already been mentioned in this book
and the following section is intended mainly to view from a
single and different perspective material which I have discussed
in separate contexts.

Some important commissions were inherited by the Tudors
from their predecessors and by 1485 made up part of the regular
system of government. They were usually valid only for limited
periods of time. Commissions of the peace were normally issued,
reissued, or renewed every two or three years. The circuit judges
operated under commissions of *oyer et terminer*, gaol delivery, and
assize which were directed to them at the beginning of each tour
of duty.[10] But although the authority granted was temporary,
the J.P.s and the assize-judges were a continuous part of
government. Commissions of array and of muster were issued
only when occasions of war, rebellion, or alarm demanded their
use; and commissions to levy fifteenths and tenths, or, in the
sixteenth century, subsidies, were used when Parliament had
authorized grants of money. These were not permanent institutions, but they were an accustomed instrument of government. I have said enough about most of these established local

---

[8] 5 & 6 Edward VI c. 2. *APC* XXVI. 383–6. R. B. Manning, 'The Crisis of Episcopal
Authority during the Reign of Elizabeth I', *Journal of British Studies*, XI (1971).

[9] Cf. P. S. Lewis, *Later Medieval France*, 158–60.

[10] Cockburn, *History of Assizes*, 59–60.

commissions in earlier chapters and with one exception will not discuss them further now.[11]

The role of the assize-judges, however, requires further comment. Their principal functions were to bring royal justice to the counties, to ensure that a uniform system of law was being administered, to try difficult or important cases of crime, and to deal with civil suits in the localities. But they also acquired during the sixteenth century a more general supervisory power over county government. It may be that they exercised such authority earlier but their history before the mid-sixteenth century remains obscure. In 1543 they were given statutory authority to fine J.P.s for neglect of duty.[12] At the beginning of Elizabeth's reign they were ordered by Lord Keeper Bacon to separate the bees from the drones among the J.P.s and report those that were negligent. That the circuit judges actually exercised this authority is suggested by a warning given by Francis Bacon in 1617 on their proper attitude to the local gentry: 'My meaning is not that you should be imperious and strange to the gentlemen of the county. You are above them in power, but your rank is not much unequal; and learn this, that power is ever of greatest strength when it is civilly carried.'[13]

The judges were also useful to the central government in recommending suitable men for the local benches in their circuit, although they were certainly not the only men to make proposals: Lord-Lieutenants, other nobles, major gentlemen, courtiers, and bishops all had their candidates. Justices of the Peace could be instructed in the law by watching the judges at work on the bench. The Privy Council might also use the judges as a channel of communication to pass on orders and exhortations. The judges might be addressed by the Lord Chancellor or Lord Keeper in Star Chamber and were expected to convey his commands in their own charges to the Grand Jury of each county. But this general charge to the judges seems only to have been used during periods of extreme social strain and unusual government activity: it was rarely given except during the 1590s and the time of Charles I's personal rule.[14]

---

[11] Above, chs. II, IV, VII.

[12] Cockburn, *History of Assizes*, 155–87 is my main source for this paragraph. 33 Henry VIII c. 10.

[13] Cockburn, *History of Assizes*, 166.　　　　　[14] Ibid. 183.

The work of assize-judges and J.P.s is well known; and although there is probably much more that could be discovered about the work of the commissions of the peace, their importance has always been fully recognized—indeed has usually been exaggerated. By contrast, the large number of *ad hoc* commissions issued by the Crown for executing specific policies has too often been ignored in discussions of Tudor government. Most of the major acts of Tudor policy were in practice carried through by such commissions. Henry VII's attempts to exact the full stint of his revenues is reflected in the issue of commissions throughout his reign for the management of the Crown's finances in the localities. Soon after his accession Henry authorized certain local gentlemen to collect the revenues of his manors in Cumberland and Westmorland. In 1488 the Lord Privy Seal, the Lord Treasurer, the Chief Baron of the Exchequer, Sir Reginald Bray, and two others were commissioned to lease out Crown lands and to appoint auditors and other officials. Four years later, Robert Willoughby and others were entrusted with the investigation of concealed lands and wardships in six counties: their commission became the pattern for a long series issued during the remaining years of the reign. Financial arrangements at the centre were flexible under Henry VII; in the localities they depended upon delegation to specific commissions, many of which were manned by members of the royal household or the Council.[15] After 1509 financial management became more systematic, permanent local feodaries, auditors, and receivers being appointed. Even so, occasional *ad hoc* financial commissions were still being issued a century later, in the early years of James I, for selling and leasing Crown lands and compounding for defective titles.[16]

Henry VIII opened his reign with an all-embracing commission of *oyer et terminer* for London, the Midlands, and the north, empowered to try by jury all cases of felony and all misdeeds and extortions by royal officers. In part at least the commission seems to have been an attempt by the new King to rescue the

---

[15] *CPR, Henry VII*, I. 56, 69, 133, 230, 415, 476; II. 33 and *passim*. W. C. Richardson, *Tudor Chamber Administration*, 64–7, 101–5, 119–21.

[16] G. E. Aylmer, 'Commissions for Crown Revenues', *BIHR* XLVI (1973). Also *CSPDom, 1581–90*, 227/31, 228/3, 229/11.

Crown from the unpopularity of Henry VII's harsh financial policy. In the event it uncovered relatively few cases of official misconduct and was revoked four months after its issue, having itself become unpopular with the common lawyers and perhaps with others.[17] In 1517 Wolsey issued the first of the great enclosure commissions of the century. Small sets of men, ranging in number from three to seven, were appointed for single shires or groups of counties and authorized to inquire through local juries what buildings had been destroyed, how much tillage had been converted to pasture, how many parklands had been enclosed. Essentially this was a nation-wide investigation whose results were to form the materials on which legal prosecution could be based; it was not, in itself, an instrument of enforcement.[18] The same could not be said of Wolsey's next major national commission, the 'general proscription' of 1522. Ostensibly intended to assess men for the arms which they should bear under the Statute of Winchester, the inquiry was in practice used for exacting a forced loan. Although the commissions issued for each shire necessarily included many of the notables, they were also manned by several of the King's own servants and officers.[19]

The most important commissions of Henry's reign were used to enforce his religious settlement. In 1534 a metropolitan visitation of every diocese was combined with a commission to take oaths binding men to the succession of Elizabeth and thus, by implication, to the royal supremacy. Legal problems impeded the operations of this commission, which was superseded by the unprecedented issue of a commission of Vicegerency to Thomas Cromwell, under which he was empowered to hear all ecclesiastical causes and to conduct visitations.[20] The Act of First Fruits of 1534 had authorized Henry to make valuations of every spiritual benefice. He appointed commissions in the following spring for each shire, except in Wales where diocesan

[17] J. P. Cooper, 'Henry VII's Last Years Reconsidered', *HJ* II (1959), 117–24. G. R. Elton, 'Henry VII: a Restatement', *HJ* IV (1961), 20–3.

[18] *LP* II. ii. 3297. M. W. Beresford, *The Lost Villages of England*, 106–29.

[19] J. J. Goring, 'The General Proscription of 1522', *EHR* LXXXVI (1971), 684–5. Above, 60–1.

[20] M. Bowker, 'The Supremacy and the Episcopate', *HJ* XVIII (1975). S. E. Lehmberg, 'Supremacy and Vicegerency', *EHR* LXXI (1966). Elton, *Policy and Police*, 220–30.

commissions were formed. Usually each commission consisted of the bishop, who directed its affairs, a group of local gentry, and one or two auditors. Their labours produced the massive *Valor Ecclesiasticus*, which recorded the financial state of every see and benefice in the kingdom.[21]

That same year the celebrated visitation of the monasteries was conducted by a much smaller group of men, of whom the most important were Richard Layton, clerk in chancery and Clerk to the Council; Thomas Legh, D.C.L.; John ap Rhys, a member of Cromwell's personal staff; and John Tregonwell, a judge in the Court of Admiralty. These men, with the help of one or two others, toured the entire country. Their reports on the monasteries were used to secure the passage of the statute dissolving the smaller monasteries, but the actual dissolution of these houses was conducted by yet another group of commissioners appointed on a county basis. Each county commission had six members: three were local gentlemen, two were officials of the Court of Augmentations, and one was the clerk attached to the commission for the *Valor Ecclesiasticus* of the previous year. The larger houses were extinguished later in a different way: a small number of men, including Legh and Layton, with the addition of William Petre and the notorious Warden of New College, Dr London, were authorized to take the 'voluntary surrenders' of the remaining houses.[22]

Edward VI's government used similar commissions for the enforcement of royal policy. The dissolution of the chantries was undertaken by small county commissions similar to those which had dealt with the lesser monasteries. Between five and thirteen men were appointed for each county: none of these commissions included a bishop, but most of them contained one or two officials of the Court of Augmentations, who did the real work, assisted by local gentlemen. Once their surveys had been completed, a central commission of two men, Walter Mildmay, Surveyor of Augmentations, and Robert Keilway, Surveyor of Liveries, decided which lands should be expropriated, what pensions should be paid, and so on. In the following year visitors were sent to the two universities for reform of their curricula,

---

[21] *LP* VIII. 149 (35–82).

[22] Joyce Youings, *The Dissolution of the Monasteries* (1971), 47–55, 67–75, 160–7, 176–86. D. Knowles, *Religious Orders in England*, III, chs. xxiv, xxvii.

destruction of religious monuments, and the expulsion of dissident fellows.[23]

In 1548 Protector Somerset and the Council issued a commission to John Hales and others to inquire into the decay of tillage in the midland counties. Like Wolsey's commission of 1517 it was intended to provide the material on which prosecutions could be based; but it had the additional objective of supplying the government with a general view of 'the whole state of the realm'. Separate commissions were evidently intended for other counties, but none was issued that year. The 1548 commission was ineffective and Somerset issued further commissions in 1549: their authority and scope remain obscure, but probably they covered a wider area than Hales's commission of the previous year. It is possible, but not at all certain, that this second group of commissions was empowered to try cases as well as collect information. But it does not seem to have been much more successful than its predecessor.[24]

A series of commissions was issued under Edward VI for surveying the financial system of the government and suggesting remedies for its defects. The most important of these was appointed in March 1552 under the chairmanship of Lord Darcy, with Walter Mildmay as its leading figure. It reported eight months later with a detailed account of royal revenues, a list of the principal weaknesses in each financial department, and a set of recommendations for reform. Although its proposals were not adopted, the work of this commission is impressive, by the standards of any age, for its speed, thoroughness, and perception.[25] The commissions for the chantries, enclosure, the universities, and the revenue system are only four examples of the ways in which *ad hoc* bodies were used under Edward VI to execute policy or collect information. Other instances are to be found in the survey of royal forts, the sale of Crown lands, the inquiry into heresies, and the naturalization of foreigners.[26]

Mary's government seems on the whole to have avoided large-scale national commissions, relying mainly upon the

[23] W. K. Jordan, *Edward VI: the Threshold of Power*, 187–8. Above, 297.

[24] *CPR, Edward VI*, I. 419. Hughes & Larkin, I. 309, 327, 334, 341. *TED* I. 39–47. M. L. Bush, *The Government Policy of Protector Somerset*, 43–8.

[25] W. C. Richardson (ed.), *The Report of the Royal Commission of 1552* (Morgantown, W. Virginia, 1974).

[26] *CPR, Edward VI*, I. 186; II. 57, 406; III. 165, 248–52, 347.

established ecclesiastical machinery and upon the J.P.s, although special commissioners were appointed for the visitation of the universities and for investigating the lands of exiles.[27] Elizabeth opened her reign with a major visitation of the entire kingdom to enforce the religious settlement of 1559. The realm was divided into six circuits, with commissions including Lord-Lieutenants, divines, lawyers, and gentlemen. Their task was the enforcement of subscriptions to the royal supremacy, the Prayer Book, and the ecclesiastical injunctions. The main burden of the work seems to have fallen upon two or three of the commissioners: in the northern circuit Edwin Sandys, soon to be Bishop of Worcester, and Henry Harvey, an ecclesiastical lawyer, conducted the visitations, while Edmund Scambler acted as their preacher.[28]

These *ad hoc* commissions were mostly intended to execute a specific piece of royal policy. In the first half of the sixteenth century the Crown was content to rely for more general and continuous authority in the shires upon the commissions of the peace, supplemented from time to time by commissions of array, musters, and subsidies. But as the tasks of government grew more complicated and security was more gravely threatened from within and without, these standing commissions came to seem alarmingly deficient. Although the monarch nominated their members, the heads of major county families in practice chose themselves, whatever their ability or disposition. The dangers of such a situation were perceptively described by Sir Thomas Smith, Secretary of State, in a letter to William Cecil in July 1549. Proclamations, he said, were issued so generally to the sheriff and all J.P.s in each shire that no one man felt responsible. He therefore suggested that, while proclamations be issued in the same way as before, one or two 'special men of trust' should be chosen in each county to execute Council commands, assemble the gentry, and suppress any disorders.[29]

Thinking of this kind gave rise to the development of the lieutenancy in the second half of the sixteenth century. Initially

[27] D. M. Loades, 'The Enforcement of Reaction, 1553–58', *Journ. Eccl. Hist.* XVI (1965) and 'The Essex Inquisition of 1556', *BIHR* XXXV (1962).

[28] C. J. Kitching (ed.), *The Royal Visitation of 1559: Act Book for the Northern Province* (Surtees Soc. CLXXXVII, 1975), *passim*.

[29] PRO, State Papers Domestic, Edward VI (SP 10), 8/33.

the appointment of Lord-Lieutenants was probably part of Northumberland's campaign to secure his own political position in the shires. From 1550 until 1553 Lieutenants were regularly sent into the counties to muster levies and act, if necessary, against rebels. Commissions of lieutenancy were issued only intermittently under Mary, but in the reign of Elizabeth they came to be a regular feature of county government. Early in her reign Lord-Lieutenants were assisted intermittently by three or four deputies, who came to be regularly appointed after 1585. The original and principal task of the lieutenancy was the mustering and training of the county militia. But it gradually became responsible as well for raising money, watching recusants, and enforcing miscellaneous regulations. The Lord-Lieutenant and his deputies were precisely what Thomas Smith had thought necessary: a group of men small enough to feel truly responsible for carrying out government orders. They provided a focal point in county administration which it had previously lacked; and, since the Lord-Lieutenant was usually a man of standing at court, they formed a close and invaluable link between the central government and the shires.[30]

While the lieutenancies were taking shape, the central government slowly developed other specialized local commissions for dealing with particular problems. Since I have discussed most of them in earlier chapters there is no need to do more than survey them briefly here. Ecclesiastical commissions were appointed from the beginning of Elizabeth's reign to enforce the religious settlement. High Commission, the best known of these, had a jurisdiction over the whole of England and Wales; but there was a separate northern commission for the province of York and diocesan commissions for at least eleven sees. From 1583 the Privy Council began to appoint trustworthy laymen for enforcing the statutes against recusancy, choosing committed Protestants from among the Justices of the Peace. After 1565 commissions were issued in the coastal shires for investigating pirates and their supporters on land. Commissioners for restraining the export of grain became an important part of the government's machinery for controlling

---

[30] Gladys Scott Thomson, *Lords Lieutenant in the Sixteenth Century*, *passim*. See J. Goring and J. Wake, *Northamptonshire Lieutenancy Papers, 1580–1614* (Northants Record Soc. XXVII, 1975) for examples of the work of the lieutenancy.

the food-supply. Apart from these commissions, which have all been discussed in earlier chapters, I would mention four others out of the multitude issued during the sixteenth century. Commissions for sewers had originally been appointed in the reign of Henry VI to maintain defences against flooding and to keep open inland waterways. Their authority was extended by a statute of 1532 and they became still more important towards the end of the century when projects were mooted for the drainage of the fens.[31] The Elizabethan Privy Council set up commissions in 1580 for improving the breed of horses and in 1586 for the relief of imprisoned debtors. A statute of 1601 authorized the appointment of charity-commissioners in each county to supervise the administration of charitable bequests.[32] Taken together these commissions show the steady growth of state intervention in national life.

The Crown also issued specific judicial commissions for the settlement of individual cases. Charges of treason, for instance, although they could legally be tried at assizes, were often heard by special commissions of *oyer et terminer*. Some of the 'rebels' of 1536 were condemned by martial law, but most went before special commissioners. So did the Earl of Surrey in 1546, Mary Stuart in 1587, and many others accused of treason throughout the century.[33] The Council, Star Chamber, Chancery, and the regular councils all used informal, *ad hoc* commissions for taking evidence and for settling cases by mediation or arbitration. Chancery especially favoured proceeding through arbitration procedures, under which local gentlemen would bring together the disputing parties and attempt to reach a solution by compromise and agreement. Although it is difficult to know how successful such referrals were in practice, they were a solution which the lawcourts often preferred to a full-scale hearing and judgement.[34]

[31] G. A. J. Hodgett, *Tudor Lincolnshire* (1975), 70–4, 80–2. A. E. B. Owen, 'Records of the Commissions of Sewers', *History*, LII (1967).

[32] *CSPDom, 1547–80*, 136/38–43; 137/17–19; *1581–90*, 190/21; 193/82; 195/6. T. G. Barnes, *Somerset, 1625–40*, 149–50.   [33] Elton, *Policy and Police*, 296–8.

[34] W. J. Jones, *The Elizabethan Court of Chancery*, 266–80. J. P. Dawson, *A History of Lay Judges*, 163 ff. Id., 'The Privy Council and Private Law', *Michigan Law Review*, XLVIII (1949/50), 410–28. J. A. Guy, 'The Early Tudor Star Chamber', in *Legal History Studies*, ed. D. Jenkins, 126. P. Williams, *Council in the Marches*, 77–8. M. J. Ingram in Cockburn, *Crime in England*, 125–7. J. A. Guy, *The Cardinal's Court*, 96–109. P. Clark, *English Provincial Society from the Reformation to the Revolution*, 135–8.

Commissions were not the only addition to the more formal machinery of enforcement. Partly because its institutions were inadequate to meet the massive demands of statute law, partly because local commissioners were sometimes reluctant to devote their time to the business of government, and partly because the Crown wished to reward its servants, the state often appealed to private profit. Two examples should make the point clear. One of the Crown's main financial problems' was the discovery of 'concealed lands'—that is to say, property which legally belonged to it, but from which it was receiving no benefit because its title had been forgotten or obscured. Henry VII issued several commissions for searching out concealed lands and his successors used the official machinery of the Court of Wards. But Elizabeth supplemented these methods by granting licences to search for concealed lands, the licensee being allowed to hold what property he discovered in fee-farm. Other men were sold the lands they uncovered on favourable terms. The practice was highly unpopular and occasionally the Crown called a halt, but seldom for long. After all inquiries had been forbidden in 1579, a patent was granted to Edward Stafford in 1581 which gave him a virtual monopoly in the field. Where Henry VII and Henry VIII had relied upon commissions of inquiry—local and national—Elizabeth saved money or encouraged her servants by putting the business out to farm.[35]

The second example is drawn from the wool trade. In 1590 Simon Bowyer was granted a commission to act as sole informer against all those who traded in wool contrary to the act of 1552. The penalties were to be shared between Bowyer and the Exchequer. In practice Bowyer did not object to other informers bringing prosecutions, provided that he received a proportion of their profits. The system does not however seem to have been especially successful, either in preventing illegal trade or in bringing revenue to the government.[36]

The Crown used many and varied agencies of enforcement to supplement those long-standing institutions, the assizes and the

---

[35] C. J. Kitching, 'The Quest for Concealed Lands', *TRHS* xxiv (1974). J. Hurstfield, *Queen's Wards*, ch. iii.

[36] P. J. Bowden, *The Wool Trade in Tudor and Stuart England*, 146–9. On the operation

commissions of the peace. Some of them were temporary creations for executing specific policies; others, like the lieutenancy, became permanent and continuous parts of local government; others, like the grain commissions, were intermittent; and others again were appointed to hear individual cases or to arbitrate in particular disputes. In general the great national commissions—the enclosure investigations, the visitation of the monasteries, the commissions for taking oaths—were characteristic of the period from 1509 to 1559. Thereafter, Elizabeth used in the main judges of assize, county justices, and the new semi-permanent local commissions, which provided each shire with a more complex structure of government under the general supervision of the Lord-Lieutenant.[37] The earlier commissions had given special authority to servants of the royal household or departmental officials sent down to the counties *en mission*. The later were very much in the hands of selected local land-owners. Most of the commissions, powerful and solemn though they might be, depended in the last resort upon the panels of local jurors who provided them with the information that they needed or gave the verdicts in criminal cases. Without the co-operation of those relatively humble men the agencies of the state were ineffective; and that co-operation, often grudging and partial, had to be won, for it could not be assumed.

---

of the profit-motive in local government, see especially A. Hassell Smith, *County and Court*. chs. xi, xii.

[37] Hassell Smith, op. cit., parts ii, iii. Clark, *English Provincial Society*, 118–38.

XIII

Who Ruled?

No government can rule in isolation from those sections of society which give it support in the expectation that their own goals will be promoted or their status maintained. In practice few regimes depend upon a single class or group: the dictatorship of the proletariat, for instance, is heavily adulterated by professional and managerial power. Early modern government demanded manipulation of several social interests: great magnates, county magnates, lawyers, clergy, merchants, professional administrators. The political levels ranged from the central élite in Council and at court, through the bureaucracy and the executive commissions, to the county administrations.

A full analysis of the political élite in Tudor England would have to include the Privy Council, the upper levels of the royal household, judges, bishops, diocesan officials, heads of Oxford and Cambridge colleges, Lord-Lieutenants and deputy lieutenants, officials of the central departments of state, J.P.s, members of other major commissions, and the ruling oligarchies of cities. Such an analysis would have to recognize that, since the weight of these groups varied from time to time, it could not work within a single frame of reference for the whole period. It would also demand a large book to itself. In this chapter I have set myself the much more modest aim of opening up the subject by examining the Privy Council at the centre and the regional élites in the provinces.[1]

The King's Council did not make up the whole of that central political élite which had a voice in the making of decisions and the distribution of patronage. Some men of influence and authority never belonged to it: Archbishop Parker and Sir Walter Raleigh are two obvious, but very different, examples. Nor was

[1] See W. L. Guttsman, *The British Political Elite* (1965), for an instructive analysis of the ruling élite in the nineteenth and twentieth centuries.

its membership clearly defined throughout the Tudor period. Until the middle of the reign of Henry VIII the royal council was a relatively large body and some of its members were fairly remote from the supreme élite represented by the Council's inner ring. After 1540 the Privy Council had a fixed and known membership which is easily subjected to analysis. Provided one remembers that it is only a sample of the upper élite—and a sample of uneven quality—the Privy Council can provide some useful insights into the ruling groups of Tudor England.

For most of the Lancastrian period the King had been assisted and advised by a small working council. Usually its members included several great magnates, although their attendance was irregular. Composition and attendance varied from time to time according to political circumstances; for instance, the magnates spent more time on the Council in the years immediately after 1406 and again after 1453. But the men who advised the monarch on decisions and helped to carry them out were the major officers of state—the Lord Chancellor, the Lord Treasurer, the Lord Privy Seal—the knights and esquires of the royal household, and some lay administrators.[2]

Henry VII appointed 227 councillors in the course of his reign, of whom 43 were peers, 45 were courtiers, 61 were clerics, 27 were lawyers, and 49 were lay administrators. Of this very large group about two dozen attended regularly. One or two peers counted for something, notably Lord Dinham, the Lord Treasurer, and the Earl of Surrey, who succeeded to that office in 1501. The clerical group was especially strong. John Alcock, Bishop of Worcester, became Chancellor in 1485; he was replaced by John Morton, Archbishop of Canterbury, in 1487, who was in turn succeeded by William Warham, also Archbishop of Canterbury. The Privy Seal was held by Peter Courtenay, Bishop of Exeter and of Winchester, and Richard Fox, successively Bishop of Exeter, Bath, Durham, and Winchester. Henry's four secretaries were all in holy orders and all became bishops: Richard Fox, Oliver King, Richard Sherborne, Thomas Ruthall. But to balance this strong group of clerics there were eight to ten laymen who exercised significant influ-

[2] A. L. Brown, 'The King's Councillors in Fifteenth-Century England', *TRHS*, 5th ser. XIX (1969). R. Virgoe, 'The Composition of the King's Council, 1437–61', *BIHR* XLIII (1970).

ence and power without holding any major office of state. Effective control of royal finances was in the hands of men like Reginald Bray, Thomas Lovell, Robert Southwell, John Hussey, and Edward Belknap, not because of any office they held but because they had specific and personal authority from the King. All these men were born into established and well-to-do families. Hussey's father was a judge, the others were knights or gentlemen. They had had a professional training in the law or in the management of land; and they were formally attached to Henry's service in his household. Important too were Poynings, Westby, Dudley, Empson, and Heron.[3]

The membership of the central élite is eclipsed, for the earlier part of the reign of Henry VIII, by the dominant personality of Cardinal Wolsey. But by 1540 the formal, defined Privy Council had emerged with a fixed list of members (Table I, p. 452).[4] Only three councillors were in holy orders: Cranmer, Tunstall, and Gardiner. Cranmer held no secular offices and attended infrequently; Gardiner was abroad on diplomatic missions for much of the time; and only Tunstall, Bishop of Durham, sat regularly at the Council board. Three men could be counted as magnates: Thomas Howard, Duke of Norfolk, was a member of a well-established ducal family; Charles Brandon, Duke of Suffolk, whose father had been standard-bearer to Henry Tudor at Bosworth, rose to favour in the royal household and on war-service, married the sister of Henry VIII, and was raised to his dukedom in 1514; Robert Radcliffe, Earl of Sussex, was a member of an old baronial family, and had been promoted in 1529. The other peers were of lesser standing and none of them had inherited their titles. Southampton, Hertford, Russell, and Sandys were all members of established landowning families who had been promoted to the peerage as a reward

---

[3] S. B. Chrimes, *Henry VII*, chs. iv, v. W. C. Richardson, *Tudor Chamber Administration*, 8, 112, 170, 201, 451–62.

[4] I have taken lists of attendance and membership from the Privy Council Registers: see Nicolas and *APC, passim*. Biographical details are mostly from *DNB* and *Complete Peerage*. Since I first drafted this chapter there appeared G. R. Elton, 'Tudor Government: the Points of Contact: i, The Council', *TRHS* xxv (1975). Professor Elton supplies important information on membership, especially for the period prior to 1540. His perspective on the Council's membership is rather different from mine; but I think that my account complements rather than contradicts his. For the membership of the Council under Edward VI see D. E. Hoak, *The King's Council in the Reign of Edward VI* (Cambridge, 1976), esp. ch. ii.

for diplomatic and military service. Each of them had been an esquire or knight of the body or a gentleman of the privy chamber in the royal household. The only peer to have risen by a different route was Lord Audley. Of obscure Essex origins, he had been trained in the law, had entered the service of Cardinal Wolsey, and became Lord Chancellor in 1533.

The commoners were of two distinct types. Sir Thomas Cheyney, Sir Anthony Wingfield, Sir William Kingston, Sir Anthony Browne, and Sir John Gage were all the sons of county landowners, had all held household office, and had all performed military or diplomatic service for the King. Cheyney was perhaps typical. His father had been sheriff of Kent and his uncle had fought with Henry Tudor at Bosworth. He himself had seen naval and diplomatic service under Henry VIII, who had made him first an esquire of the body and then Warden of the Cinque Ports. His kinship to Anne Boleyn may possibly have helped his promotion. The other four commoners had humbler origins and had risen in the world as professional administrators. Sir Thomas Wriothesley, son of a herald, had been Clerk of the Signet and assistant to Thomas Cromwell before becoming Secretary of State on his master's fall. Sir Ralph Sadler, his co-Secretary, was the son of an administrator and became a protégé of Cromwell, whom he served as a personal clerk. Sir Richard Rich and Sir John Baker were men of much more lowly and obscure origins, who had both been trained in the law. Rich became Solicitor-General in 1533 and Chancellor of Augmentations in 1536; Baker was successively Attorney-General, Chancellor of the Court of First Fruits, and Chancellor of the Exchequer.

The political élite had, by 1540, undergone changes. Membership of the Council was now almost, though not quite entirely, confined to the holders of the great offices of the state and the royal household.[5] The clerical and magnate groups in the Council were somewhat depleted. None of the major offices of state was held by a churchman; and Cranmer played little part in secular affairs. The only magnate of long standing was Norfolk; the other two had risen from lower ranks. But service

---

[5] Elton, loc. cit. 201–3. The principal authority on the Marian Council is the unpublished thesis by G. E. Lemasters, 'The Privy Council in the Reign of Queen Mary I' (Ph.D., Cambridge, 1970).

in the royal household, war, and diplomacy—usually combined in the course of a career—was still extremely important in the *cursus honorum* of a privy councillor. Eleven of the twenty men had held household offices at some point in their careers. Four councillors—Gardiner, Audley, Rich, and Baker—came from obscure and low-born families. It had always been common enough for churchmen to rise from the poor to high positions, but until this time it had been rare for a layman.

When we look at Elizabeth's first Privy Council, appointed in the early weeks of her reign, further changes in the élite are at once apparent.[6] The aristocratic element, much restored under Mary, was prominent. The Earls of Derby, Shrewsbury, and Arundel were members of established magnate families which wielded great power in their localities. Clinton and Howard, though hardly rising to the status of magnates, belonged to old noble families. William Parr, Marquis of Northampton, William Herbert, Earl of Pembroke, and Francis Russell, Earl of Bedford, were peers of recent creation. Northampton owed his success to his sister's marriage to Henry VIII, Pembroke to military and political service under Henry and Edward, Bedford, who had inherited the title, to to his father's service at court and on the battlefield. The clerical group had almost vanished: Nicholas Heath, Archbishop of York and Lord Chancellor under Mary, remained a privy councillor for only a few weeks under Elizabeth. Household men were well represented, though perhaps not quite so strongly as they had been in 1540. They also had less military experience. Sir Thomas Cheyney was still there, but not for long, since he died in December 1558. Sir Francis Knollys was the son of Henry VIII's Usher of the Chamber: he himself had been a gentleman pensioner to Henry VIII, had seen military service against the Scots, and was later appointed Vice-Chamberlain under Elizabeth. Sir Edward Rogers had been a squire of the body to Henry VIII, gentleman of the privy chamber under Edward VI, and on Elizabeth's accession became Captain of the Guard and Vice-Chamberlain. Sir Thomas Parry had been steward of Elizabeth's household before her accession and was appointed Controller of the royal

[6] Table II, p. 453. For more detailed comments on the members of Elizabeth's Privy Council see Wallace MacCaffrey, *The Shaping of the Elizabethan Regime* (1969), 30–5.

Household when she succeeded. Finally, there was a strong administrative element. William Paulet, Marquis of Winchester, had been Lord Treasurer since 1552 and survived the accessions of both Mary and Elizabeth. Three other administrators had also been in office under Mary: Sir John Mason, a specialist in diplomacy; Sir William Petre, who had begun as an official in Chancery and rose to become Secretary of State in 1544; and Sir Richard Sackville, who had studied at the Inns of Court and became Under-Treasurer of the Exchequer in 1538 and Chancellor of Augmentations in 1548. Of the newly appointed administrators William Cecil had already gained experience under Edward VI, Nicholas Bacon, his brother-in-law, had been Attorney to the Court of Wards and became Lord Keeper on Elizabeth's accession, and Sir Ambrose Cave was Chancellor of the Duchy of Lancaster.

Two other points are worth mentioning about Elizabeth's first Council. Three of its members came from very humble families: Mason was the son of a cowherd; Petre's family seems to have lain on the borderline between yeomen and lesser gentry; nothing is reliably known about the origins of Nicholas Bacon, except that they were lowly. Two others, Cheyney and Sackville, were related to Anne Boleyn; and Petre seems to have owed his start in life to the Boleyn family.

Some councillors attended very rarely. Sir Thomas Cheyney died a month after Elizabeth's accession and Archbishop Heath was soon deprived of office. The magnates from long-established families—Arundel, Derby, and Shrewsbury—attended seldom. Bedford was not often there, nor, surprisingly in a Lord Treasurer, was Winchester. The nucleus of regular councillors consisted of Cecil—easily the most constant member—Knollys, Clinton, Rogers, Howard, and Bacon. Cave and Sackville ran them fairly close. Thus the central direction of the realm was largely in the hands of great officers—the Lord Admiral, the Lord Keeper, and the Secretary of State—and of household men—the Lord Chamberlain, the Controller, and the Vice-Chamberlain.

For the next thirty years or so this pattern of membership and attendance was little changed.[7] From 1558 until the Armada only two churchmen, Dr Nicholas Wotton and Arch-

[7] Table III, p. 454.

bishop Whitgift, were appointed to the Privy Council. Several great noblemen were admitted: the Duke of Norfolk, the Earls of Leicester, Sussex, Shrewsbury, Warwick, and Derby, Lords Hunsdon, Howard of Effingham, Buckhurst, and Cobham. Most new entrants were either administrators, like Mildmay, Thomas Smith, Walsingham, Wilson, and Davison, or household men, like Croft, Hatton, and Heneage. The Council of 1586 shows a composition not much different from that of 1558.[8]

From the Armada until the death of Essex in 1601 the Council steadily contracted.[9] Although many of the noble councillors died in those years, they were not replaced. The Earl of Essex was the only great nobleman to enter the Council in the 1590s. Administrators and diplomats were represented by men like Robert Cecil, John Herbert, John Fortescue, and Edward Wotton. The household element was especially strong: Sir Thomas Heneage was Treasurer of the Chamber and Vice-Chamberlain, Lord North was Treasurer of the Household, Sir William Knollys was Controller and then Treasurer of the Household, Sir John Stanhope was Treasurer of the Chamber and then Lord Chamberlain. This group was, however, very different from the household men of the reign of Henry VIII. Few of them had been sent on diplomatic missions and fewer still had any military experience: they were, from first to last, courtiers. Indeed, of the Privy Council in 1597, only three men—Howard of Effingham, Essex, and Hunsdon—knew anything of war.

The Council of the 1590s was small and tightly knit. More than ever before it gives the impression of being a family group or an amalgam of three or four dominant families. Buckhurst, Fortescue, and Hunsdon were related to the Queen through her mother. William Knollys was the son of a former councillor, Sir Francis, and the father-in-law of Sir John Stanhope. The Cecil dynasty was notoriously powerful. This dominance of a few great families emphasizes by contrast another feature: the total absence of men of really humble origins.

After 1601 and the revolt of Essex the Queen brought into the Council two great noblemen, the Earls of Shrewsbury and Worcester, perhaps with the intention of placating the older

[8] Table IV, p. 455.   [9] Tables III, V, VI, pp. 454–6.

families. Shrewsbury's membership made little difference, since he rarely attended. But Worcester, who became Master of the Horse, was often at the Council-Board. Even so, the complexion of the Council in December 1601 was much the same as in 1597.

Reviewing the sixteenth century as a whole we can say that aristocratic birth and territorial power had ceased, by the later part of Elizabeth's reign, to be in themselves a qualification for entry to the central élite. The great noble families had been ousted from the Privy Council, which had largely become the preserve of major office-holders. Yet the nobles did not remain for long outside the Council chamber, and when they returned they stayed there for centuries. Palmerston's last Cabinet, which contained three dukes and two earls out of fifteen members, was socially far more elevated than the Privy Council of the 1590s.[10] Second, the churchmen, who controlled many of the great secular offices of state under Henry VII, had by 1558 been confined almost entirely to the ecclesiastical sphere. They were to make a brief, but disastrous, return to national politics in the reign of Charles I. Third, the demand for literate and lay administrators thrust into prominence, from about 1530 to about 1570, several low-born men: William Paget, son of a shearman and barber of London; Thomas Smith, son of a small sheep-farmer; John Mason, son of a cowherd; Nicholas Bacon, son of a man unknown; Walter Mildmay, son of a country mercer. But in the later part of Elizabeth's reign government service had virtually ceased to carry men, in one generation, from the bottom to the top of society. The landowning class had educated itself for public office and had closed ranks against the low-born. Indeed it was becoming difficult to enter the élite unless one was connected to certain families. Fourth, service in the royal household continued, throughout the sixteenth century, to be as sure a route as any to membership of the Privy Council.

In the early years of the Tudor dynasty, the Crown had to reckon with a dozen or so great families, well rooted in many parts of the realm.[11] The north was still dominated by the

[10] Guttsman, *British Political Elite*, 67.

[11] Among a large number of works relevant to this subject the following are especially

Nevilles, Earls of Westmorland, the Percies, Earls of Northumberland, the Cliffords, raised to the Earldom of Cumberland in 1525, and the Dacres of Naworth. In Lancashire the Stanleys were pre-eminent. The Talbots, Earls of Shrewsbury, and the Greys, Marquises of Dorset, controlled much of the Midlands. The Howards, Dukes of Norfolk, were supreme in East Anglia, the Fitzalan Earls of Arundel in Sussex, the Neville Lords of Burgavenny in Kent, and the Berkeleys in Gloucestershire. The Courtenays, Earls of Exeter, were still powerful in the south-west. Noble power was however less dominant in Wales and the Marches than it had been in the mid-fifteenth century. Dynastic warfare had brought the lordships of York and Neville to the Crown. Of the old Marcher magnates only the Staffords, Dukes of Buckingham, survived, ruling Brecknock and much of Gloucestershire. But two new families were rising in South Wales: the Devereux, Lords Ferrers, and the Somersets, later Earls of Worcester.[12]

The values and loyalties of fifteenth-century aristocratic society survived throughout the Tudor epoch and even beyond it. Sir Thomas Tresham explained in 1594 that all his tenants were obliged to furnish a man fit for service, to accompany himself or his son if they were sent to fight for the Queen overseas.[13] George Clarkson, writing in the 1560s, commented that 'it is most natural and no less honourable that his lordship [the Earl of Northumberland] should have the government and rule under the Prince here in this country of Northumber-

important: K. B. McFarlane, *The Nobility of Later Medieval England*. L. Stone, *The Crisis of the Aristocracy*, and *Family and Fortune*. R. B. Smith, *Land and Politics in the England of Henry VIII*. M. E. James, *Family, Lineage and Civil Society; Change and Continuity in the Tudor North; A Tudor Magnate and the Tudor State*; 'The First Earl of Cumberland and the Decline of Northern Feudalism', *Northern History*, 1 (1966); 'Obedience and Dissent', *P&P* 48 (1970); 'The Concept of Order and the Northern Rising of 1569', *P&P* 60 (1973). J. M. W. Bean, *The Estates of the Percy Family, 1416–1537*. A. Hassell Smith, *County and Court: Government and Politics in Norfolk, 1558–1603* (1974). Peter Clark, *English Provincial Society: Religion, Politics and Society in Kent, 1500–1640* (1977), is an important contribution which appeared too late for me to use extensively.

I also owe much to the D.Phil. thesis of Mrs J. R. Dias, 'Politics and Administration in Nottinghamshire and Derbyshire, 1590–1640' (Oxford, 1973).

Much of the biographical and genealogical information in this section is derived from *DNB* and *Complete Peerage*.

[12] W. Rees, *An Historical Atlas of Wales* (Cardiff, 1959), plates 53, 55. *LP* XIII. ii. 732: a list of English noblemen, *c.* 1538.

[13] *CSPDom, 1591–4*, 470–1.

land'.[14] Thirty years later—after the seventh earl had been executed for treason and the eighth had been found dead in the Tower—Robert Cecil echoed his words by recommending that Percy's power be restored to the borders in order to restrain the quarrels of the northern gentlemen: 'because their equality breeds emulation and contention, it was offered to th'Earl of Northumberland to be Warden of the Middle [Marches] and Lieutenant, for the time, to countenance justice, of the three shires ...'[15] Cecil's proposal was not taken up, but as late as 1619 Sir Henry Curwen testified to the deep-rooted loyalty felt by northern landowning families to the Percies: 'My ancestors always have been employed in service in that noble house of Northumberland, and although I acknowledge myself inferior to the meanest of them, yet none of them have ever borne a more faithful affection to that famous house.'[16] The Percies were not the only family to command such affection or to wield such power. In 1549, when enclosure riots broke out over much of southern England, the Earl of Arundel was sent by the Privy Council to Sussex, the centre of his influence. The Earl settled the disturbances, not by physical force, but by holding court at Arundel Castle, to which he summoned all who had cause for complaint. Landlords who were judged to have oppressed their tenants were ordered to reform matters, which they apparently did, while the ringleaders of revolt, 'as mutinying varlets', were put in the stocks. By this fair, but perhaps high-handed, use of his authority Arundel seems to have quietened the county. At the end of the sixteenth century Richard Topcliffe, the hunter of recusants, reminded the new Earl of Shrewsbury that 'you are a Prince (alone in effect) in two countries in the heart of England [Derbyshire and Nottinghamshire]'.[17]

But despite the survival of old families and the loyalties that attached men to them, the structure of power came in the Tudor period to differ markedly from that of the fifteenth century. To begin with, there were very few princes of the blood royal left by 1485. Edward IV had eliminated his brother Clarence; his own sons disappeared soon after his death; and

[14] James, *P&P* 60 (1973), 58–9.   [15] Lodge, III, 87–9.   [16] James, *Tudor Magnate*, 7.
[17] Stone, 'Patriarchy and Paternalism in Tudor England', *Journal of British Studies*, XIII (1974). Lodge, III. 22. I am grateful to Mrs J. R. Dias for this reference.

Richard of Gloucester fell at Bosworth. The only male members of the house of York to survive Henry's accession were the young Earl of Warwick, safely in the Tower, and the two de la Pole brothers, sons of Edward IV's sister. Warwick was executed in 1499; John de la Pole, Earl of Lincoln, fell at Stoke; and his brother was executed in 1513. The Tudors themselves produced few additions to the royal stock; Henry VII had no brothers and his only surviving uncle, Jasper, Duke of Bedford, died childless in 1495; only one of his sons, Henry VIII, survived to manhood; and Henry VIII in turn had only one son. Both Mary and Elizabeth were childless. The celebrated infertility of the Tudors led to serious problems for the succession to the throne. But it avoided that plague of royal uncles, brothers, and cousins which was so disruptive a feature of contemporary French politics under the Valois and the Bourbons. For the Tudor kith and kin were mostly women: the Grey sisters, Margaret Clifford, Margaret Douglas, and Mary Stuart. Elizabeth's male relations—the Sackvilles and Careys—belonged to her mother's family. The chief male claimants to the throne— the Earls of Derby and Huntingdon—showed no inclination whatever to play the over-mighty subject.[18]

Other magnate families had been seriously depleted during the Wars of the Roses. The lands of the Earl of Warwick, divided between Clarence and Gloucester, ultimately reverted to the Crown. The Herbert lordships in South Wales were seriously reduced in 1479 and finally passed to an heiress, Elizabeth, who was married off to Charles Somerset, companion-at-arms to Henry Tudor. The estates of the Holland Dukes of Exeter were dispersed among various royal relations and favourites. While mere baronial families suffered little, as a group, from the dynastic conflicts, the topmost branches of the aristocratic tree were heavily pruned.[19]

Henry VII was niggardly in granting new titles and the lands to sustain them, severe in his treatment of those magnates who stepped beyond the bounds of prudence and loyalty. Between 1485 and 1509 the numbers of the upper nobility fell from twenty to ten. Of the three dukes alive in 1485 Bedford

[18] See M. L. Bush, 'The Tudors and the Royal House', *History*, LV (1970).
[19] T. B. Pugh, 'Magnates, Knights, and Gentry', in *Fifteenth-Century England*, ed. S. B. Chrimes *et al.* (Manchester, 1972).

died without heirs and Suffolk was attainted; only Buckingham remained. The one marquisate, Dorset, temporarily disappeared in 1501 when Thomas Grey failed to succeed to his father's title. Four of the sixteen earldoms (Huntingdon, Nottingham, Rivers, Wiltshire) lapsed from lack of heirs; William Courtenay, heir to the Earldom of Exeter, was attainted in 1504; Lincoln was killed at Stoke and then attainted; Warwick was executed in 1499. Henry VII made no new creations of dukes, marquises, or earls; and he preferred to reward his followers by grants of offices, annuities, or wardships rather than with lands.[20]

In the past it had been usual for the Crown to reverse attainders after a few years so that the family of an attainted noble was not for ever deprived of its position. The Tudors sometimes followed this conventional path but were often much less generous. The Pole estates were never restored after the attainders of Lincoln and Suffolk. By contrast, the Courtenays, attainted in 1504 and in 1538, were twice restored in full: a fever in Italy in 1556, not the English executioner, finally ended that line. The lands of the third Duke of Norfolk, forfeit in 1547, were restored to his grandson in 1554; but that grandson's involvement in the Ridolfi plot eliminated the dukedom for about a century, the head of the family being reduced to the title of Earl of Arundel. The Percy inheritance, seized by the Crown in 1536–7, was restored under Mary; but the seventh Earl's treason in 1569 robbed the family of its northern influence, although the earldom and many of its lands survived in the family. After the Duke of Buckingham had been destroyed in 1521 his heirs recovered some of their lands, but lost the dukedom and the great lordship of Brecknock. The Nevilles, Earls of Westmorland, were destroyed by their treason in 1569. The Grey Dukedom of Suffolk was permanently extinguished after the Duke's rebellion in 1554.[21]

By the end of the sixteenth century political error, plain stupidity, and biological failure had destroyed many of those great families which had dominated English life at the beginning of the Tudor period. The Greys, Courtenays, Fitzalans, and Dacres had disappeared; of the Nevilles only the Burgavenny

[20] Ibid. 115, 128n. J. R. Lander, 'Attainder and Forfeiture', *HJ* IV (1961).
[21] Bush, op. cit. James, *Northern History*, I (1966), 67n.

branch survived, apparently less wealthy and certainly less influential than before. The political authority of the Staffords and the Veres had been almost eliminated. Percy influence was relegated to southern England. Howard hegemony in East Anglia had been destroyed, although several branches of the family continued to wield power in other parts of England, especially in Sussex and Cumberland. The Berkeleys had been seriously wounded by the decision of the sixth lord to leave his property to the Crown; and although they had recovered much of their wealth by the reign of Elizabeth, political folly and financial profligacy reduced them to relative insignificance. Only the Cliffords, the Stanleys, and the Talbots remained; and even the Talbots suffered eclipse in the seventeenth century.

Naturally enough, other families were promoted by the Tudor Crown to reward the claims of service, friendship, and blood.[22] Five were raised to high rank in the first half of the reign of Henry VIII: Brandon, Hussey, Somerset, Radcliffe, and Manners. Charles Brandon, companion and brother-in-law of the King, became Duke of Suffolk in 1514 and was endowed with the property of the de la Poles. To these he added the Willoughby lands by marrying his ward, Katherine Willoughby. But his impressive Lincolnshire estates, centred on Tattershall Castle, were dispersed when his two sons died of the sweating sickness in 1552. Sir John Hussey, Controller of the Household to Henry VII, who rewarded him well with offices and lands, was raised to the peerage in 1529. His alleged complicity in the Pilgrimage of Grace brought his line to an end.[23] The other three families were more fortunate. Charles Somerset, who fought for Henry Tudor at Bosworth, was married to the great Welsh heiress, Elizabeth Herbert, and created Earl of Worcester in 1514. He founded a dynasty which has survived, as Dukes of Beaufort, until the present day. Robert Radcliffe, heir to the old barony of Fitzwalter, was created Earl of Sussex in 1529. His successors maintained the line into the seventeenth century, but only the third Earl, Thomas, was a man of commanding political importance.

---

[22] The account of the Tudor peerage which follows is obviously highly selective. For fuller discussions see Stone, *Crisis of the Aristocracy* and W. K. Jordan, *Edward VI: the Young King*, 89–103.

[23] James, *P&P* 48 (1970), 41–7, 52–5.

Lastly, Thomas Manners of Belvoir, heir to another old baronial family—Ros—became Earl of Rutland in 1529. The favour of Henry VIII brought him grants of several offices and of large estates in the Midlands. His family and title—now a dukedom—survive.

The favoured courtiers promoted by Henry VIII to wealth and dignity after the Reformation played a greater part in national affairs than these earlier creations. By the last years of the reign Charles Brandon, John Hussey, Charles Somerset, Robert Radcliffe, and Thomas Manners were all dead. Hussey's family was destroyed in 1536–7; Brandon's heirs were children; the second Earls of Worcester, Sussex, and Rutland were of less account than their fathers. The men best placed to seize power, dignity, and wealth in the last days of the old King and the lavish minority of his son were Henry's two brothers-in-law, William Parr and Edward Seymour; Thomas Wriothesley, the Lord Chancellor; and the courtier soldiers, John Dudley and John Russell. Parr was created a baron in 1539 and was raised to be Marquis of Northampton on the accession of Edward VI. Deprived of his title in 1553, he was restored by Elizabeth but died childless, in spite of three marriages, in 1571; his property reverted to the Crown. Edward Seymour became Earl of Hertford in 1537, Duke of Somerset and Lord Protector in 1547. He was condemned for treason in 1552 and his son succeeded only to the earldom and to heavily depleted estates. John Dudley, created Viscount Lisle by Henry VIII, was made Earl of Warwick in 1547 and Duke of Northumberland in 1551. His immense power crumbled in 1553. Two of his sons were however promoted to the peerage under Elizabeth. Thomas Wriothesley, herald and bureaucrat, became Lord Chancellor and a baron in 1544, was promoted to the Earldom of Southampton in 1547. The rivalries of court politics quickly destroyed him and in 1548 he left office, to die in 1550. The family survived, materially weakened, into the seventeenth century. Of this quintet of Henrician creations only John Russell, first Baron Russell in 1539 and first Earl of Bedford in 1550, emerged unscathed from the infighting of mid-century politics.

Two men were outstanding among the nine peers created by Edward VI. William Herbert, brother-in-law to Catherine

Parr and gentleman of the privy chamber, was rewarded for his services to Henry and his loyalty to Dudley with substantial lands in Wiltshire and Glamorgan and with the title of Earl of Pembroke. He survived the accession of Mary and secured his dynasty by astute political trimming; the family still holds the earldom. The other new peer was William Paget, who became Lord Paget of Beaudesert in 1549. Paget rose from poor origins to become Secretary of State in 1543; his loyalty to Somerset brought him degradation in 1552, a piece of good fortune, since he was able easily to climb back into favour at the accession of Mary. He died in 1563 and the Catholicism of his successors excluded the family from effective national influence.[24]

Elizabeth was almost as niggardly in creating peers as her grandfather, Henry VII. Her first cousin, Henry Carey, became Lord Hunsdon in 1559; and a more remote kinsman, Thomas Sackville, was created Earl of Dorset in 1567. Edward Clinton became Earl of Lincoln in 1572. Walter Devereux, who succeeded as Viscount Hereford in 1558, was raised to the Earldom of Essex in 1572, and his son Robert became Elizabeth's favourite in the last years of the reign. Robert Dudley, son of the Duke of Northumberland, became Earl of Leicester in 1564, while his brother Ambrose was restored to the Earldom of Warwick in 1561. William Cecil, Secretary of State and Lord Treasurer, was made Lord Burghley in 1571. The remaining creations of her reign were relatively unimportant. Leicester and Essex were men of great influence, but their position rested very much upon the favour of the Queen. Leicester was certainly rich, but founded no dynasty. Essex, who did found a dynasty, was by aristocratic standards not well off. Cecil was the founder of two great dynasties, for his sons became Earls of Exeter and of Salisbury; but he himself derived his power from office and from the court, rather than from landed estates.[25]

Of all the Tudor creations only a few survived as dynasties to the end of the century. Earls of Worcester, Rutland, Sussex, Hertford, Bedford, Pembroke, Dorset, Nottingham, Southampton, and Essex lived on into the seventeenth century. But

[24] Jordan, loc. cit., for a more detailed account. I find Professor Jordan's remarks on p. 98 questionable. Stone, *Family and Fortune*, chs. vi, vii.
[25] For Elizabethan creations see Stone, *Crisis*, 756.

Hertford was in political eclipse until the death of the Queen, and Essex destroyed himself and endangered Southampton and Rutland by his attempted putsch of 1601. Only Arundel, Worcester, Bedford, Nottingham, and Pembroke entered the Stuart period as magnates of any importance, and they hardly stand comparison with the greatest of their predecessors. Had the bonanza of Edward VI's reign lasted longer, or had Elizabeth been more generous, brighter noble stars might have been burning in the sky by the end of the century. As things turned out, Tudor reluctance to reverse attainders, the biological accidents of death and infertility, the restraint of Henry VII and Elizabeth, helped to change the social firmament. In the late sixteenth century there were many clusters of stars, but there were fewer luminous planets than before and very few supernovae.

Even those magnate families which surmounted the hazards of the sixteenth century or rose, in spite of them, to prominence, found their political muscles slackening. By the reign of Elizabeth the development of lieutenancies, trained bands, and county militias had rendered the Crown less dependent upon noble retainers and the state had come nearer to effective control of physical force.[26] But the point should not be exaggerated. The Crown still depended upon privateers for its naval strength and upon landowners for cavalry. Nor was the diminished military role of the retainer necessarily decisive, for nobles had kept retainers as much for display and prestige as for the deployment of violence. In the sixteenth century noblemen continued to keep retainers for these purposes, even if they kept fewer of them. Equally important, those noblemen who had once led their bands of liveried servants now, in many cases, commanded the county militia as the Crown's Lord-Lieutenants and deputy lieutenants: like some fortunate captains of industry in our own day they found themselves, after nationalization, still running the business. The Crown was certainly restricted in its choice of lieutenants. Leading noblemen considered that they had a prescriptive right to lead their county's militia. Lord Chandos, for instance, complained vigorously in 1595 when he heard rumours that he would be displaced from the office of Lord-

---

[26] Stone, *Crisis*, 200, and ch. v, sect. i. Above, ch. iv. Professor Stone believes the 'royal monopoly of violence' to be more complete than I do.

Lieutenant or put in double harness with a partner. Either event would, he claimed, be a disgrace to a man like himself, whose ancestors had always held the post.[27] The Crown's limitations and opportunities are well illustrated by the history of the Sussex lieutenancy under Elizabeth. Initially, she had to accept as her Lieutenants the Earl of Arundel and Lord Lumley, both the heads of old Catholic families. They were discredited by the rising of 1569 and the Queen was able to replace them by Lord Buckhurst, a Protestant, and Lord Montague, a loyal Catholic. After 1585 she removed Montague in favour of the thoroughly Protestant Howard of Effingham. In some counties the hold of a great family was too strong to break. The Greys in Bedfordshire, the Stanleys in Cheshire and Lancashire, the Talbots in Derbyshire, the Brydges in Gloucestershire, the Cecils in Hertfordshire, the Hastings in Leicestershire and Rutland, the Herberts in Somerset and Wiltshire, and the Howards in Surrey had an almost hereditary lien upon the office. But elsewhere the monarch was generally able to exercise some freedom of choice.[28]

The Crown was also constrained by local interests and preferences in the appointment of deputy lieutenants and captains. Under Elizabeth the Privy Council preserved formal control over the nomination of deputy lieutenants. But only local gentlemen and landowners could lead the county militias. In 1587 the Earl of Pembroke described the trained bands of Wiltshire as 'by nature inclined and inured by custom most readily to follow their own countrymen'.[29] Under the Stuarts local interests seem to have encroached further upon the powers of the Crown; in the reign of James I Lord-Lieutenants gained the right to name their own deputies. In 1642 and again in 1688 the local militias were in many counties raised against the Crown. James II tried to subordinate the militia by replacing the traditional lieutenancy families with men of his own choosing and religion. His failure to accomplish this was apparent when the Yorkshire and Lancashire trained bands followed their aristocratic leaders against him in 1688; in doing so they

[27] HMC, *Salisbury*, v. 340; x. 15.
[28] Manning, *Religion and Society in Elizabethan Sussex*, ch. xi. J. C. Sainty, *Lieutenants of Counties, 1585–1642* (*BIHR* supplement, no. 8, 1970).
[29] Boynton, *Elizabethan Militia*, 104. Sainty, op. cit. 8.

showed that the militia was no mere arm of royal authority. The decline of retaining and the development of the militia did not replace unfettered magnate power by omnipotent state control. Before, during, and after the sixteenth century there was a complex balance of military and social forces; during the Tudor epoch it was shifting in favour of the Crown, but neither totally nor irrevocably so.

The monarchy achieved a similar success by confiscating many of the more important private castles.[30] The significance of this should not be exaggerated, since castles had played only a minor role in the Wars of the Roses. Even so, the magnates did lose many potential bastions of power. The attainder of Buckingham in 1521, for instance, brought Henry the castles of Tonbridge, Thornbury, Newport, Brecon, Hay, Huntingdon, Bronllys, Maxstoke, Kimbolton, and Stafford. Stafford was returned to the family; Maxstoke and Kimbolton were transferred to royal servants; but the others were kept by the Crown. More castles remained in private hands in the north, but even there the Crown took possession of Raby, Norham, Wolstry, Dalton, and the Piel of Fowdrey in the second half of the century. The Crown did not undertake the enormous expense of conserving all the castles which it took over after 1485. The Tower of London, Warwick, Carisbrooke, Berwick, Carlisle, and the castles of the Channel Islands were kept defensible. The new coastal forts established by Henry VIII were maintained as a principal defence against invasion. Some castles were kept up as seats of regional government, like Ludlow and Sheriff Hutton, or as royal residences, like Windsor or Tutbury. The rest slowly decayed and were usually described in royal surveys as 'utterly ruinated'. By 1603 very few nobles, if any, possessed a single castle in good defensible order. The Crown relied for defence upon Henry VIII's new coastal forts and upon the navy.

The shift in English military power from land to sea had other implications. Up to 1453 great reputations and sometimes great wealth had been gained by noblemen fighting in France.[31] Salaries, ransoms, plunder, lands, offices, and, of course, glory

---

[30] This paragraph is based on H. M. Colvin, 'Castles and Government in Tudor England', *EHR* LXXXIII (1968).

[31] McFarlane, *Nobility of Later Medieval England*, sect. I, ch. ii.

were won by nobles and captains at the expense of the French. Such opportunities recurred briefly under Henry VIII, many of whose closest advisers had been his companions in war. Charles Brandon, Duke of Suffolk, Thomas Howard, Duke of Norfolk, Edward Seymour, Earl of Hertford and Duke of Somerset, John Dudley, Earl of Warwick and Duke of Northumberland, John Russell, Earl of Bedford, and William Herbert, Earl of Pembroke, made their political way principally by skill at arms. But it is improbable that Henry's forays into France brought them the gains that had been won under Edward III and Henry V. Under Elizabeth the opportunities to display such qualities were very few, even if the skill had been there, which in the case of Robert Dudley and Robert Devereux it plainly was not. Two campaigns in France, long years of fighting as auxiliaries in the Netherlands, and debilitating, unglamorous struggles in the bogs of Ireland brought little in the way of glory, booty, or ransoms. Reward and reputation were to be won at sea—either in privateering raids or in combined-operations landings on the Spanish coast. The gains of these could be real enough but were highly speculative. They went usually to professional sailors, like Drake, and to their merchant backers, not to amateur noblemen like the third Earl of Cumberland, who vainly hoped to rebuild his family fortunes by privateering. Thus one great source of wealth and its replenishment was denied to the Tudor aristocracy. Instead they had to turn to the profit of court office—which again might be spectacular but involved large outlays of risk capital. The gains, even when they materialized, were made at the expense of Englishmen: taxpayers, merchants, recusants, consumers of monopoly goods. The political cost of a great fortune in the Tudor period was therefore far higher than it had been in Plantagenet times; and the aristocracy suffered accordingly in reputation. The great dynasties of Elizabethan and Jacobean England were created by men like Robert Cecil, Henry Howard, Earl of Northampton, and Thomas Howard, Earl of Suffolk. Their fortunes were extracted from the purses of other Englishmen and were in consequence unpopular.[32]

The dependence of noblemen upon their own tenants for

[32] K. R. Andrews, *Elizabethan Privateering* (Cambridge, 1964), chs. v, vii. L. Stone, 'Office under Queen Elizabeth', *HJ* x (1967).

political and military support may, by the end of the fifteenth century, have become fragile. Two great noblemen, at least, found in the reign of Henry VIII that their relations with their tenants had been embittered by their harsh policies of estate management. The last of the Stafford Dukes of Buckingham, compelled by Henry VIII to spend vast sums at the Field of the Cloth of Gold, had to squeeze his tenants so hard that he dared not go into Wales to collect his rents without a large escort of retainers. The first Earl of Cumberland set out in the 1520s and 1530s to realize the maximum returns from his estates; in doing so he alienated not merely the northern peasants but also those gentlemen who were his tenants. As the Duke of Norfolk acutely remarked, if the Earl were to serve the King on the Borders, 'he must ... not be so greedy to get money of his tenants'. At the latter end of the sixteenth century Robert Devereux came to be disliked by his Welsh tenants, thanks to the exactions of his steward Sir Gelly Meyrick; the Earl's fall in 1601 was said to be little regretted by them.[33]

Changes in the composition of the regional élites did not result simply from the destruction of old families and of the foundations, in stone or in men, of their power. The Crown also worked to establish a countervailing force at the centre and in the localities. With the increasing significance of communications, the importance of propaganda, the growth of paperwork, and the premium put upon information, the old-style aristocrat was at a disadvantage in Tudor politics. Important as the shires might be, the court was the real centre of politics and the skills required to manipulate it were highly professional. Men who wanted to make their way in the political world had to adopt the outlook of the court and to nurture roots in court life as well as in the shires. All this gave the Crown an opportunity for building its own bodies of supporters in the regions and establishing courtly values there. At the same time the demands being made by government upon the administration of the shires called for an élite different in its capacities from the old regional aristocracy. The Crown sought to train such an élite and to insert it into the crucial areas of power.[34]

[33] McFarlane, op. cit. 210–11, 223–6. C. Dyer, 'A Redistribution of Incomes in Fifteenth-Century England', *P&P* 39 (1968). James, *Northern History*, I (1966), esp. 55. HMC, *Salisbury*, XI. 81, 92, 102–8.   [34] James, *P&P* 60 (1973), esp. 56, 65–6.

The extent, the timing, and the processes of such changes varied from one region to another. No county can be described as typical. Nevertheless the transformation of the political élites can best be understood by examining some case-studies. This will indicate at least some of the possibilities, which ranged from stability and continuity in some shires to convulsive change in others.

In South Wales the Tudors inherited a political structure far more favourable to the Crown than the formidable array of independent Marcher lords which had confronted Henry VI twenty-five or so years before. On the eve of the Wars of the Roses, the house of York held the Earldom of March stretching from Ludlow into Central Wales, the lordships of Builth, Blaenllynfi, Ewyas, Lacy, and Usk. The earl of Warwick held the lordships of Glamorgan and of Elfael. Mowbray held Gower and Kilvey. On the Lancastrian side the Stafford Dukes of Buckingham held Brecknock and Newport, Jasper Tudor, Earl of Pembroke, held much of Pembrokeshire. The events of the next three decades brought into Crown hands the lordships possessed by the houses of York, Warwick, and Tudor. By 1485 only two important independent families survived in South Wales and the Marches: the Staffords, who had long been established in the area, and the Herberts, who owed the bulk of their lands to Yorkist favours after 1461.[35]

Early Tudor policy was highly pragmatic. Until the breach with Rome there was no attempt to change the political structure of the region. Indentures were signed with the independent Marcher lords, binding them to govern their lordships in accordance with the King's laws. The Council in the Marches of Wales, meeting somewhat intermittently, was established to supervise justice over the whole region. The Crown, far from showing hostility to the nobility or wishing to rule through some mythical middle class, built up two aristocratic families whose influence it could harness to the tasks of government. One of these was the Devereux, Lords Ferrers of Chartley, who had already acquired substantial estates in Herefordshire and the Midlands by skilfully arranged marriages.

---

[35] W. Rees, *Historical Atlas of Wales*, plates 53, 55. Pugh, 'Magnates, Knights and Gentry', in *Fifteenth-Century England*, ed. Chrimes *et al.* R. A. Griffiths, 'Wales and the Marches', in ibid.

During the Yorkist epoch Sir Walter Devereux was raised to
the rank of Baron Ferrers 'for his good service against Henry
VI and his accomplices'. Although Sir Walter was killed at Bosworth, his son, John, was quickly restored to the Devereux
estates. By John's death in 1501 the family had benefited from
two significant marriages, his own to Cicely Bourchier and that
of his son, another Walter, to the daughter of Thomas Grey,
Marquis of Dorset. Walter, the third Lord Ferrers, served
Henry VIII in military campaigns and on the Council in the
Marches; he was rewarded with honours and offices, rather
than with lands. The influence of the family in south-west Wales
and in the Marches was considerable, but it was neither based
upon nor reflected in great landed wealth: Lord Walter's gross
rental came to only £850 p.a. in 1548 and his grandson, the
first Earl of Essex, had only £400 p.a., with a reversionary interest in £530 p.a. It is not surprising that his son, Robert, the
second Earl, was chronically short of money.[36]

The other important family, that of Somerset, came to dominate Gower, Glamorgan, and Monmouth. In 1490 William
Herbert, Earl of Huntingdon, died, leaving his daughter Elizabeth as his sole heiress. Elizabeth, as a royal ward, was married
off by Henry Tudor to his cousin and companion-at-arms, Sir
Charles Somerset, an illegitimate son of the third Beaufort Duke
of Somerset. Through his wife Somerset acquired the lordships
of Gower, Kilvey, Crickhowell, Tretower, and Raglan. In 1509
he became permanent sheriff of Glamorgan and a few years
later was promoted to the peerage as first Earl of Worcester.
The combination of lands, offices, and title made him the most
powerful man in South Wales and the Crown's principal agent
for its government. By contrast with this careful grooming of
its own candidate in the southern region the Crown acted
dramatically in Brecknock. The third Duke of Buckingham was
allowed to rule there undisturbed until he quarrelled with Wolsey and was executed on false charges of treason in 1521.[37] This
swiftly changed the balance of power in South Wales. When
the breach with Rome made urgently necessary the establish-

[36] H. A. Lloyd, 'The Essex Inheritance', *WHR* vii. i (1974).

[37] Rhys Robinson, 'Early Tudor Policy towards Wales', *Bulletin Board of Celtic Studies*,
xx, xxi. Id., in *Glamorgan County History*, iii, ed. T. B. Pugh, ch. v (ii). M. Levine,
'The Fall of Edward, Duke of Buckingham', in A. J. Slavin (ed.), *Tudor Men and Institutions*.

ment of tighter government control, no one could resist the Crown's radical changes. The Marcher lordships were shired, English county government was established in the new counties, and a refurbished Council was set up to administer justice in the whole area. These administrative alterations were useful and important. But they could not themselves have achieved the Crown's political dominance in the region. Indeed they arose out of a political situation created by other means: the fortunate inheritance of 1485, the establishment of control through Worcester and Ferrers, the destruction of Buckingham.

The Acts of Union of 1536 and 1543 did not at once establish the complete supremacy of the ordinary legal processes in Glamorgan. The powers of the Earl of Worcester were diminished but not wholly eliminated by its provisions. Nor did the death of the second Earl in 1549 end the influence of a great lord in that part of the world, for his offices were transferred to a rising power at court, William Herbert, son of a Glamorgan landowner, gentleman of the privy chamber under Henry VIII, victor over the south-western rebels in 1549. Granted several Glamorgan lordships in the course of Edward's reign and created Earl of Pembroke in 1551, Herbert and his son became the dominant figures in Glamorgan politics for the rest of the century. Although the authority of Marcher lords had been substantially reduced by the Acts of Union, Pembroke's power was both the focal point of county controversy and the attractive force of local patronage. But gradually, under Elizabeth, the county gentry began to assert themselves, while the earls, now seated at Wilton, lost interest in most aspects of Glamorgan affairs apart from parliamentary elections. By the end of the sixteenth century Rice Merrick, clerk of the peace in Glamorgan, was able to draw a contrast with their situation under the old Marcher lords: 'for now life and death, lands and goods, resteth in this monarchy, and not in the pleasure of a subject'.[38]

The Tudors inherited a much less favourable situation in northern England. Percies, Nevilles (Earls of Westmorland), Cliffords, and Dacres were still entrenched. The Bishops of Durham ruled over the only palatinate jurisdiction not in the

---

[38] I have elaborated this story in 'The Political and Administrative History of Glamorgan, 1536–1642', *Glamorgan County History*, IV, ed. Glanmor Williams.

hands of the Crown. But the death in 1489 of the fourth Earl of Northumberland, when his son was still a minor, gave the Crown an opportunity to rule the northern marches independently of Percy support. Lord Dacre, head of a much less important family, was entrusted with the Wardenship of the Western March in 1486 and of the East and Middle Marches in 1515. The Crown at the same time did its best to create an affinity by attaching local gentlemen to its service by fees. Until his death in 1527 the fifth Earl of Northumberland was excluded from the great Wardenships which had been the natural preserve of his family for much of the fifteenth century. This exclusion, which might have freed the Crown from magnate support, was not a success: feuds and disorders multiplied and the Crown's agents were unable to check the pretensions of Percy retainers. Sir John and Sir William Heron insulted royal commissioners and protected the Tynedale raiders. Sir William Lisle, another Percy adherent, when challenged by the sheriff with the words 'Sir William Lisle, have we not a God and a King to live under?', replied: 'By God's blood, there is neither King nor his officers that shall take any distress on my ground, or have ado within the liberties of Felton, but I shall take another for it, if I be as strong as he, and able to make my party good.' Such an appeal to force was characteristic of Lisle and of his Percy patron.[39]

In 1527 the Crown was compelled temporarily to recognize realities and restore the new Earl of Northumberland to the Wardenship of the East and Middle Marches, leaving Dacre in the West. But Cromwell and Henry VIII soon resumed the attack upon the Percy influence. By intruding into the Percy household a Cromwellian agent, Sir Reynold Carnaby, they induced the childless, spendthrift, and timid sixth Earl to bequeath his lands to the Crown, disinheriting his two brothers. After the Pilgrimage of Grace—in part the response of the dispossessed Percies to this policy—the Percy estates were transferred to the Crown and the earldom lapsed. A concurrent attack was launched upon the Dacres, who ruled all three northern Marches from 1515 to 1525 and the Western March alone from 1528. In 1534 William, fourth Lord Dacre, was tried

---

[39] James, *Change and Continuity*, 11–12. Id., *Tudor Magnate*, 17–31.

for treasonable collusion with the Scots. The charges were brought by Sir William Musgrave, a long-standing enemy of the family, were encouraged by Thomas Cromwell, and were supported by the Earls of Northumberland and Cumberland. Even so, Dacre was acquitted by the Lords. But in escaping death he lost his offices and the Wardenship of the West March went to Cumberland.

The ruin of the Percies, the defeat of the Dacres, and the destruction of the Pilgrimage made necessary a reconstruction of northern government. There were three possibilities open to the Crown on the northern border: it could bring in an outside magnate, as Norfolk suggested, presumably with his own candidature in mind; it could rely upon the Earl of Cumberland, who had remained loyal to Henry VIII throughout the Pilgrimage; or it could entrust the government to border landowners of lesser power. The Crown chose the third option, promoting Sir Thomas Wharton to be deputy warden in the West March, Sir William Eure in the Middle March, and Sir John Widdrington in the East. Wharton's career was a remarkable illustration of the success that the Crown's favour could bring. Beginning as a modest landowner worth about £100 p.a., he first entered the service of the Percies and then switched his allegiance to the Crown. By the reign of Mary he was drawing £600–700 p.a. in fees and wages, held lands worth more than £750 p.a., and had become a baron.[40]

Government by men newly raised to power and affluence did not continue without a break. Somerset appointed Dacre to the Wardenship of the West March in 1549, and Mary restored the Earldom of Northumberland in 1557. Wharton had become deputy warden of all three Marches in 1552 and Warden of both the East and the Middle in 1555; but the revival of the Percy interest pushed him into the background.

However the resurrected power of the Dacres and the Percies did not survive for long. Between 1537 and 1557 the Percy lands had been held by the Crown. When Mary returned them to the seventh Earl the old bonds of loyalty seemed to have been restored. Lord Hunsdon's remark that Northumberland 'knew no Prince but a Percy' has often been quoted. But when the

[40] For this and preceding paragraph see James, *Change and Continuity*, and also Bean, *Estates of the Percy Family*.

test came in 1569 the peasants were reluctant to follow their lord and the traditional attachment had to be strengthened by the offer of wages.[41]

From her accession Elizabeth was reluctant to employ the Percies in the great border offices. In 1559 Lord Grey of Wilton was made Warden of the East and Middle Marches, Lord Dacre Warden of the West. The Dacres lost the Wardenship on the death of the fourth lord in 1563, and for the rest of her reign Elizabeth appointed to the Wardenships either southern nobles like Lord Grey, the Earl of Bedford, Lord Willoughby, Lord Hunsdon, and his two sons, Sir John and Sir Robert Carey, or lesser northern landowners like Lord Scrope, Lord Eure, and Sir John Forster.

During the first fifteen years of the reign the greatest magnate powers on the border were destroyed. The Dacre inheritance passed, on the death of the young sixth lord in 1569, to his three sisters, wards of the Duke of Norfolk, each married off to one of Norfolk's sons. Most of the Cumberland lands came in this way to Lord William Howard, 'belted Will', who came eventually to live at Naworth Castle. The seventh Earl of Northumberland was executed for treason in 1572; and although Sir Henry Percy, his brother, inherited the title and recovered most of the family lands, he never held office in the north and generally resided at Petworth. A suggestion by Robert Cecil that Northumberland be made Lieutenant in the North was never taken up. The Cliffords, Earls of Cumberland, survived as a northern power into the seventeenth century; but during most of Elizabeth's reign George, the third Earl, was mainly preoccupied with making his way at court and building a fortune by piracy. Only Lord William Howard emerged as a possible successor to the old-style magnates; and, powerful as he was, his Catholic sympathies inhibited the Crown from giving him office. In many ways the disappearance or absence of the great traditional families made government of the region harder. The southern lords resented their exile in the harsh and unrewarding borderland. The northern barons and gentlemen squabbled among themselves, levelled charges of corruption at one another, and sometimes had to be dismissed from office.

[41] James, *P&P* 60 (1973), 70–9.

But for good or evil, the old ruling hierarchy of the 'border country' had been decapitated and a new, broader élite governed in its place.[42]

In County Durham power was shared at the beginning of the sixteenth century between the bishop, who still held regalian powers throughout his palatinate, and the major landowners, headed by the Neville Earls of Westmorland and the Lumleys. In practice the bishop's palatinate power made the county much less independent than legal appearances suggested. The common law was administered by royal judges and episcopal power could easily be overridden by the King when it suited him to do so. The bishop was less a threat to the monarchy than a useful adjunct to royal power, and the political balance was not much altered by the abolition of palatinate jurisdiction in 1536.[43] Under Henry VIII an alliance of Crown, bishop, and gentry began to erode the traditional power of Nevilles and Lumleys, who recovered authority in Mary's reign when the Earl of Westmorland was created Lieutenant-General of the north. Elizabeth however reverted to the policy of her father and Westmorland's discontent aligned him with the Norfolk party in 1569. The rising of the northern earls was catastrophic for the Durham magnates. Westmorland died in exile, his lands confiscated, his title abolished. Lumley spent several years in the Tower and died without direct heirs. These events left the bishop very much in control once more, although southern noblemen were appointed to the lord-lieutenancy: Bedford after 1569 and Huntingdon in 1587. Through the bishop and the Lieutenants Crown interest was able to prevail. The pattern of change in Durham resembles very closely events in the border shires. In both regions the Crown was able to use countervailing social forces to edge the great magnates from the centre of the

---

[42] On the borderland under Elizabeth and the early Stuarts see the following: D. L. W. Tough, *The Last Years of a frontier* (Oxford, 1928). Thomas Hodgkin, *The Wardens of the Northern Marches* (1908). T. I. Rae, *The Administration of the Scottish Frontier, 1513–1603* (Edinburgh, 1966). M. E. James, *Estate Accounts of the Earls of Northumberland, 1562–1637* (Surtees Soc. CXLIII, 1948). H. S. Reinmuth, 'Border Society in Transition', in H. S. Reinmuth (ed.), *Early Stuart Studies* (Minneapolis, 1970). P. Williams, 'The Northern Borderland under the Early Stuarts', in *Historical Essays, 1600–1750*, ed. H. E. Bell and R. L. Ollard (1963). Robert Newton, 'The Decay of the Borders: Tudor Northumberland in Transition', in *Rural Change and Urban Growth, 1500–1800*, ed. C. W. Chalklin and M. A. Havinden (1974).

[43] 27 Henry VIII c. 24.

arena and then, when they rebelled, to destroy their independent power, substituting for it other alliances.[44]

Events were equally dramatic in Norfolk, where the Howard
Dukes of Norfolk had built an impressive regional power during
the first part of the sixteenth century. Their position rested upon
great wealth, large and concentrated estates, strong ties of local
loyalty, and influence at court. The family was seriously
imperilled at the very end of the reign of Henry VIII when
the third Duke and his son, the Earl of Surrey, were arrested.
Surrey was executed, but his father survived in the Tower, to
be released for a few months of freedom on the accession of
Mary. His grandson, Thomas, the fourth Duke, who succeeded
in 1554, should have attained pre-eminence in English politics.
He was certainly able to restore the Howard authority in East
Anglia and his position was not threatened by the accession of
Elizabeth. Yet he never achieved the influence at court wielded
by his grandfather, and he allowed himself to be drawn into
conspiracy with Mary Stuart. His relatively innocent proposal
to marry her drew him into the world of Catholic plots and
his life ended on Tower Hill in 1572. The dukedom remained
in abeyance for a century, and although his sons were well provided with lands, the great franchisal jurisdiction of the
Howards in East Anglia was destroyed for ever. Nor did Elizabeth replace the Duke with any new magnate. The lieutenancy
of Norfolk and Suffolk was granted to her cousin, Henry Carey,
Lord Hunsdon, who had few estates in East Anglia. No dominant local family emerged to seize the pre-eminence of the
Howards, and after 1572 Norfolk politics were riven by the
feuds of the leading gentry families.[45]

By contrast the authority of the Talbots in Nottinghamshire
and Derbyshire was slowly eroded by family feuds, personal inadequacies, and the final failure of the male line. The Earls
of Shrewsbury had long maintained a dominant position in
those two counties, which was inherited by George, the sixth
Earl, in 1560. His position was threatened by prolonged
absence from court, while he played the ungrateful role of custo-

---

[44] R. L. Storey, 'The North of England', in *Fifteenth-Century England*, ed. Chrimes
et al. 138–42. James, *Family, Lineage and Civil Society*, chs. ii, vi.

[45] A. Hassell Smith, *County and Court*, *passim*, esp. ch. ii. Neville Williams, *Thomas
Howard, fourth Duke of Norfolk*, *passim*.

dian to Mary Stuart, and by the monstrous behaviour towards him of his termagant wife, Bess of Hardwick. This enabled his enemies—the Manners, the Holles, and the Stanhopes—to sap his strength. Even so, his son Gilbert, who succeeded to the earl-dom in 1590, was seen as a prince in those two counties. But Gilbert's wife was a Catholic and his own connections with Ara-bella Stuart aroused suspicion. He succeeded to only one of his father's lieutenancies—Derbyshire—while the lieutenancy of Nottinghamshire was held in abeyance. Friendship with Robert Cecil enabled him to win some influence at court after 1598, but his local position was constantly under attack from rival families, who exploited his alleged unsoundness in reli-gion. However, the final destruction of Talbot power only came at Earl Gilbert's death in 1616, when the title passed to a cousin and the lands were divided among his three daughters.[46]

Changes in the power-structure of Kent were similarly pro-longed. At the beginning of the sixteenth century Kentish society was dominated by the Nevilles, Lords Abergavenny, by the Brookes, Lords Cobham, and by the Guldefordes of Halden. The decline of the Nevilles began in 1521 with the execution of Buckingham, to whom they were allied by marriage. The Guldeforde authority had gone by 1558. Only the Cobhams remained: but they never achieved the county influence under Elizabeth to which their ancient position might have entitled them. Increasingly power was shared among families of mid-dling prosperity, raised to authority by the Crown: families like the Sidneys, Twysdens, Wottons, Southwells, and Sackvilles, whose strength and riches were drawn from diverse sources. In the 1590s many of the most important Kentish families—the Brookes, Sackvilles, and Sidneys in particular—began to tire of county politics and turned their attention to the court.[47]

There were of course many counties which were already, in the fifteenth century, exempt from the dominating power of a great magnate and continued in this state throughout the six-teenth. Cheshire exemplifies a social and political continuity wholly different from the transformations which occurred in

[46] This paragraph is based on J. R. Dias, 'Politics and Administration in Nottingham-shire and Derbyshire, 1590–1640' (D.Phil. thesis, Oxford, 1973). I am grateful to Mrs Dias for allowing me to summarize some of her conclusions.

[47] Peter Clark, *English Provincial Society from the Reformation to the Revolution, passim,* esp. 6–7, 14–20, 50–3, 104, 125–32, 265–7.

South Wales, the northern Marches, Durham, and Norfolk. At the beginning of the fifteenth century it was ruled by a large group of landed families, united by close ties of kinship. This group survived with few changes to the end of the sixteenth century, indeed until the Civil War. Of the thirty-five families named by John Leland in the 1540s as belonging to the 'chiefest gentlemen' in Cheshire, twenty-five were still represented on the commission of the peace in 1640. Only two newcomers to the county could be found in the shire élite of Charles I's reign. With its separate institutions of local government Cheshire was more self-contained than most counties. But there were probably many in which the ruling oligarchy enjoyed a similar freedom from the control of magnates and a comparable stability.[48] However, there are large gaps in our knowledge of sixteenth-century county history; and we need to know more, especially about the Home Counties, before we can generalize with confidence.

There was only one city of real political significance in Tudor England: London. By the death of Elizabeth its population had reached 200,000, while its nearest competitor, Norwich, had only 15,000 inhabitants. Throughout the sixteenth century London was dominated by the small group of twenty-six aldermen who together controlled the general administration of the city and individually supervised the affairs of their own wards. They were supported by the larger Common Council, which apparently accepted and buttressed the authority of the Court of Aldermen. Closely linked together by their wealth, their family ties, and their membership of the great livery companies, the rulers of London were a cohesive and united group, devoted to the interests of their own community and invariably loyal to the Crown, which reinforced their power. This oligarchic control was the general rule in most towns of Tudor England; and, as in London, these lesser oligarchies tightened their authority during the century in a mutually beneficial alliance with the Crown.[49]

During the sixteenth century great and traditional accumulations of power were destroyed in certain regions and were not

---

[48] M. J. Bennett, 'A County Community', *Northern History*, VIII (1973). J. S. Morrill, *Cheshire, 1630–1660* (Oxford, 1974), ch. i.

[49] Frank Freeman Foster, *The Politics of Stability: a Portrait of the Rulers of Elizabethan*

replaced by new ones. The Tudor monarchs seem to have made grants to their favourites of dispersed pockets of land, preferring to avoid an undue concentration of private estates. Elizabeth was notably parsimonious in rewarding her servants: according to Lord Buckhurst, in a letter to the Earl of Shrewsbury, 'in the policy of this common wealth, we are not over ready to add increase of power and countenance to such great personages that you are'.[50] In many areas there was, without doubt, stability. In a few, rising families like the Herberts and the Russells built and maintained a regional authority. But in most of the counties where traditional magnates had exercised predominance their destruction was irreversible. Power which had once been concentrated was, by 1600, more widely diffused; and this seems to have been the consequence of political action, personal folly, and biological accident rather than of any general economic trend which undermined the power of the greatest lords. But while the peerage had usually to share its regional power with the major gentry by the end of the sixteenth century, it could not be discounted in national politics. Under the early Stuarts noblemen like Arundel, Pembroke, Bedford, and Southampton were to play a major role in the struggles at court and in Parliament.

It is difficult to say how far the upper élite of peers and county gentry was able to rule without taking into account the views of lesser gentlemen, merchants, and yeomen. The co-operation of such men, the 'middle sort of people', was essential to the working of local government: they were the constables, jurymen, churchwardens, and overseers of the poor. As such they were often dilatory, negligent, and obstructive; but on the whole they acquiesced, with occasional grumblings, in the rule of the propertied classes. Their participation did not however bring them much influence over national or county affairs. A substantial proportion of the adult male population may have been entitled to vote in parliamentary elections, but contested elections were rare and municipal oligarchies were tightening their hold over the boroughs. The élite was wider in 1600 than it had been in 1500, but it was still much more effectively

---

London (1977), *passim.* Peter Clark and Paul Slack, *English Towns in Transition, 1500–1700* (1976), ch. ix.

[50] Stone, *Crisis*, 237. Hassell Smith, op. cit. 42.

closed to influence from below than it was to be forty years later.[51]

TABLE I

The Privy Council, 1540

Thomas Cranmer, Archbishop of Canterbury
Lord Audley, Lord Chancellor
Duke of Norfolk, Lord Treasurer
Duke of Suffolk, Great Master of the Household
Earl of Southampton, Lord Privy Seal
Earl of Sussex, Great Chamberlain
Earl of Hertford
John, Lord Russell, Lord Admiral
Cuthbert Tunstall, Bishop of Durham
Stephen Gardiner, Bishop of Winchester
William, Lord Sandys, King's Chamberlain
Sir Thomas Cheyney, Warden of Cinque Ports and Treasurer of Household
Sir William Kingston, Comptroller of Household
Sir Anthony Browne, Master of the Horse
Sir Anthony Wingfield, Vice-Chamberlain
Sir Thomas Wriothesley, Secretary of State
Sir Ralph Sadler, Secretary of State
Sir Richard Rich, Chancellor of Augmentations
Sir John Baker, Chancellor of Tenths and First Fruits

---

[51] See the stimulating account of the opening-up of English politics, 1603–42, in Derek Hirst, *The Representative of the People?* (Cambridge, 1975).

TABLE II

Elizabeth's first Privy Council

The date in parentheses after each man's name represents that of his first recorded appearance at the Council in the reign of Elizabeth.

d=date of death.

*=men who were either members of Mary's Council or associated with her government.

*Marquis of Winchester (27.xi.58), Lord Treasurer	d. 1572
Marquis of Northampton (26.xi.58)	d. 1571
*Earl of Arundel (10.xii. 58), Lord Steward	d. 1580
*Earl of Derby (20.xi.58)	d. 1572
*Earl of Pembroke (20.xi.58)	d. 1570
*Earl of Shrewsbury (24.xi.58), President of Council in North	d. 1560
Earl of Bedford (21.xi.58)	d. 1585
*Lord Clinton (20.xi.58), Lord Admiral	d. 1585
*William, first Lord Howard of Effingham (20.xi.58), Lord Chamberlain	d. 1573
*Archbishop Heath (24.xi.58), Lord Chancellor. Deprived of office 1558; left Privy Council 1559; deprived of see of York 1559	d. 1579
Sir Nicholas Bacon (23.xii.58), Lord Keeper of Great Seal	d. 1579
*Sir Thomas Cheyney (24.xi.58), Treasurer of Household; Warden of Cinque Ports	d. Dec. 1558
*Sir John Mason (24.xi.58), Treasurer of Chamber	d. 1566
*Sir William Petre (24.xi.58)	d. 1572
*Sir Richard Sackville (20.xi.58), Under-Treasurer of Exchequer	d. 1566
Sir Ambrose Cave (20.xi.58), Chancellor of Duchy	d. 1568
Sir William Cecil (20.xi.58), Secretary of State	d. 1598
Sir Francis Knollys (16.i.59); succeeded Rogers as Vice-Chamberlain	d. 1596
Sir Thomas Parry (20.xi.58), Controller of Household; succeeded Cheyney as Treasurer of Household	d. 1560
Sir Edward Rogers (24.xi.58), Captain of the Guard and Vice-Chamberlain. Succeeded Parry as Controller of Household	d. 1567?

TABLE III

Additions to Elizabeth's Privy Council from 1560 to the end of the reign

The date in parentheses after a name indicates the date of the man's first recorded appearance at the Council in the case of those appointed before 1570, and the date of swearing-in as a councillor in the case of those appointed during and after 1570. In some instances, where the Council Registers are defective (especially between 1582 and 1586), these dates are not available and more approximate ones have been supplied.

Only the most important office or offices held by a man are given; and the date after the title of the office is the date of appointment to it.

d = date of death.

Dr Nicholas Wotton (28.v.62?), Dean of Canterbury and York	d. 1567
Lord Robert Dudley [Earl of Leicester]. Entered P.C. Jan. 1563? Master of Horse	d. 1588
Fourth Duke of Norfolk. Entered P.C. Jan. 1563?	d. 1572
Sir James Croft (8.x.66), Controller of Household *c.* 1566	d. 1590
Sir Ralph Sadler (8.x.66), Chancellor of Duchy 1568	d. 1587
Sir Walter Mildmay (17.xi.66), Chancellor of Exchequer 1559	d. 1589
Third Earl of Sussex (20.xii.70), President of North; Lord Chamberlain	d. 1583
Sir Thomas Smith. Entered P.C. Mar. 1571; Secretary of State 1572	d. 1577
Sixth Earl of Shrewsbury. Entered P.C. 1571; Lord Marshal	d. 1590
Earl of Warwick (5.ix.73), Master of Ordnance	d. 1590
Sir Francis Walsingham (21.xii.73), Secretary of State 1573	d. 1590
Sir Henry Sidney (31.xii.75), President of Wales 1560	d. 1586
Sir Christopher Hatton (12.xii.77), Vice-Chamberlain; Lord Chancellor 1587	d. 1591
Dr Thomas Wilson (12.xi.77), Secretary of State 1577	d. 1581
Lord Hunsdon (16.xi.77), Lord Chamberlain	d. 1596
Sir Thomas Bromley (11.iii.79), Lord Chancellor 1579	d. 1587
Sir Amyas Paulet. Entered P.C. *c.* Jan. 1585	d. 1588
Fourth Earl of Derby. Entered P.C. before 1586; Lord Steward	d. 1593
Charles, second Lord Howard of Effingham. Entered P.C. in or before Feb. 1586; Lord Admiral 1585	d. 1624
Lord Buckhurst. Entered P.C. in or before Feb. 1586; Lord Treasurer 1599	d. 1608
John Whitgift. Entered P.C. in or before Feb. 1586; Archbishop of Canterbury 1583	d. 1604
Tenth Lord Cobham. Entered P.C. in or before Feb. 1586; Warden of Cinque Ports 1558	d. 1596
William Davison (30.ix.86), Secretary of State 1586; suspended from office and dismissed from P.C. 1587	d. 1608

TABLE III *(cont.)*

John Wolley (30.ix.86), Latin Secretary 1568	d. 1596
Sir Thomas Heneage (6.ix.87), Vice-Chamberlain 1589	d. 1595
John Fortescue (10.ii.89), Chancellor of Exchequer 1589; Chancellor of Duchy 1601	d. 1607
Sir John Perrot (10.ii.89), Lord Deputy of Ireland 1584–8	d. 1592
Sir Robert Cecil (2.viii.91), Secretary of State 1596; Lord Treasurer 1608	d. 1612
Sir John Puckering (28.v.92), Lord Keeper 1592	d. 1596
Second Earl of Essex (25.ii.93), Master of Horse 1587; Earl Marshal 1597	d. 1601
Sir Thomas Egerton (6.v.96), Attorney-General 1592; Master of Rolls 1594–1603; Lord Keeper 1596	d. 1617
Roger, Lord North (30.viii.96), Treasurer of Household 1596	d. 1600
Sir William Knollys (30.viii.96), Controller of Household 1596; Treasurer of Household 1602	d. 1632
George, second Lord Hunsdon (17.iv.97), Lord Chamberlain 1597	d. 1603
Sir John Popham (13.v.99), Lord Chief Justice 1592	d. 1607
Dr John Herbert (10.v.1600), Second Secretary of State 1600	d. 1619
Seventh Earl of Shrewsbury (29.vi.1601)	d. 1616
Fourth Earl of Worcester (29.vi.1601), Master of Horse 1601	d. 1628
Sir John Stanhope (29.vi.1601), Treasurer of Chamber 1596; Vice-Chamberlain	d. 1621
Sir Edward Wotton (22.xii.1602), Controller of Household 1602	d. 1626

TABLE IV

The Privy Council in February 1586

J. Whitgift, Archbishop of Canterbury
Sir T. Bromley, Lord Chancellor
Lord Burghley, Lord Treasurer
Earl of Shrewsbury, Lord Marshal
Earl of Derby
Earl of Warwick, Master of Ordnance
Earl of Leicester, Master of Horse
Lord Howard of Effingham, Lord Admiral
Henry, first Lord Hunsdon, Lord Chamberlain
Lord Cobham, Warden of Cinque Ports
Lord Buckhurst
Sir F. Knollys, Treasurer of Household
Sir J. Croft, Controller of Household
Sir H. Sidney, President of Wales
Sir C. Hatton, Vice-Chamberlain
Sir F. Walsingham, Secretary of State
Sir R. Sadler, Chancellor of Duchy
Sir A. Paulet, Keeper of Mary Stuart
Sir W. Mildmay, Chancellor of Exchequer

TABLE V

The Privy Council in September 1597

J. Whitgift, Archbishop of Canterbury
Lord Burghley, Lord Treasurer
Earl of Essex, Master of Horse; Earl Marshal
Lord Howard of Effingham, Lord Admiral
George, second Lord Hunsdon, Lord Chamberlain
Lord Buckhurst
Roger, Lord North, Treasurer of Household
Sir J. Fortescue, Chancellor of Exchequer
Sir R. Cecil, Secretary of State
Sir T. Egerton, Lord Keeper of Great Seal
Sir William Knollys, Controller of Household

TABLE VI

The Privy Council in December 1601

J. Whitgift, Archbishop of Canterbury
Sir T. Egerton, Lord Keeper of Great Seal
Lord Buckhurst, Lord Treasurer
Earl of Nottingham (previously Howard of Effingham), Lord Admiral
Earl of Shrewsbury
Earl of Worcester, Master of Horse
George, second Lord Hunsdon, Lord Chamberlain
Sir William Knollys, Controller of Household
Sir J. Stanhope, Vice-Chamberlain and Treasurer of Chamber
Sir R. Cecil, Secretary of State and Master of Wards
Sir J. Fortescue, Chancellor of Exchequer
Sir J. Popham, Lord Chief Justice
Mr J. Herbert, Second Secretary of State

XIV

The Tudor Achievement

Some distinguished modern historians of sixteenth-century England have been sceptical about the power, durability, and effectiveness of Tudor rule.[1] Professor Lawrence Stone emphasized 'the instability of the Tudor polity', and commented that 'the Elizabethan state was remarkably deficient in some of the essential components of power'. Professor Joel Hurstfield, in the course of his study of wardship, concluded that 'the administrative resources of Elizabethan government, like its financial ones, were extremely limited'. In his opinion,

Early Tudor policy against enclosures and evictions was subverted by the slack and hostile responses of the men in the shire. Elizabethan thunderbolts against recusant Catholics landed harmlessly in some counties ... where local magnates sheltered their neighbours. The Elizabethan poor law fell short of its objectives ... because many justices of the peace stubbornly resisted the advancing claims of the welfare state.

Against these judgements, however, Professor Elton argued that a revolution in government during the 1530s had established both national sovereignty and the machinery of a bureaucratic state. The Tudor state, he asserted, was far from 'ramshackle' and the collapse of government under the early Stuarts was in no way inevitable. Commenting on Professor Stone's thesis he remarked that 'the description ... of governmental weakness under the later Tudors is heavily overdrawn. ... It should be said that Elizabethan government worked.'[2]

A review of the administrative machine and its resources does not suggest that the Tudors had created a new and powerful

[1] L. Stone, *The Causes of the English Revolution* (1972), 58–67. J. Hurstfield, *The Queen's Wards*, 230–1, 336.

[2] Dr Elton's review of Stone, op. cit., in *HJ* xvi (1973), 207. See also Elton, *TRG*, *passim*, and *Studies*, ii, chs. xxi, xxii, xxviii. It is only fair to point out that Dr Elton now seems to put less stress than before upon the purely bureaucratic elements in government. See his article in *TRHS* xxvi (1976).

state. The roles of Privy Council and Secretary of State were
certainly extended to meet the fresh demands upon government
and to assist the encroachments of the Crown into new areas
of activity. Printing and literacy provided the state with important means of control, multiplied the volume of paper, and
increased the amount of desk-work. But the men at the top
were supported by only the most rudimentary bureaucratic
apparatus. Councillors and Secretaries were inextricably involved in the minutiae of daily administration; and the Secretaries depended on their personal servants rather than a
permanent corps of royal bureaucrats. Intervention by government in the social and economic life of the nation was seldom
accompanied by the creation of new executive posts and
enforcement was generally left to the existing officials, to local
commissions, or to private enterprise. Nor was the bureaucracy
well suited for the conduct of effective administration. Offices
were held in plurality; meagre salaries tempted men to take
gratuities and bribes; and payment by fees sparked off fierce
demarcation disputes which often absorbed the energies of
officials.

Admittedly, substantial innovations were made under Henry
VIII and Edward VI in the extraction of royal revenue. The
parliamentary subsidy, developed in 1513–16, was based upon
assessments of personal wealth instead of regional quotas. The
acquisition of monastic and chantry property greatly extended
the landed estates of the Crown. Debasement of the coinage
added more than one million pounds to the Exchequer's
receipts between 1542 and 1551. Yet these gains were
ephemeral. Subsidy assessments became fixed at nominal
amounts. The sale of Crown lands and the reluctance of Elizabeth and Burghley to increase rents ensured that the real income from royal estates was no higher in 1603 than it had been
in 1509. After the recoinage of 1561 Elizabeth tacitly surrendered debasement as a possible source of income.[3] Nor did
she attempt to replenish her treasury by large-scale foreign borrowing. Wardship dues and customs duties, both increased by
Mary, were allowed to remain static in times of inflation. To
compensate for these deficiencies Elizabeth developed certain
local taxes, such as the poor-rate and the militia levies,

[3] I am indebted to Mr J. P. Cooper for this point.

exploited the royal right of purveyance, and granted monopolies as a means of rewarding courtiers. But in real terms the total impact of wartime taxation in the 1590s was much lighter than it had been fifty years earlier; and Englishmen were strikingly less burdened by taxes than were their contemporaries in France or Castile.[4]

The development of lord-lieutenancies and trained bands in the second half of the sixteenth century freed the Crown from its previous dependence upon baronial retainers. But the trained bands could not be fully relied upon to suppress internal revolts and they were never tested by foreign invasion. More important, they could only be commanded by local dignitaries and therefore failed to provide the Crown with sole control of armed force. The provision of cavalry continued to depend upon the personal service of noblemen and gentlemen. England's strength on land declined steadily during the second half of the century by comparison with her powerful neighbours. English sea-power on the other hand was by 1588 equal to any challenge; but it depended, not on the establishment of a regular royal navy, but on the profit-seeking enterprise of privateers.

Fifteenth-century monarchs had been expected only to do justice, keep order, defend their subjects from invasion or rebellion, and, when necessary, lead their armies in war.[5] Their successors were expected to do much more than this and they responded to those expectations by trying to impose on the kingdom a pattern of detailed and complex regulation. With only meagre resources in money, manpower, and institutions, they were often wholly unsuccessful: the enforcement of apprenticeship regulation is a case in point. Even in areas where the Crown might have been expected to apply its rules vigorously—for instance in preventing abuses in textile manufacture—its efforts were fitful and largely unavailing. It is not surprising that many historians, struck by the large gulf between royal command and practical achievement, should have concluded that Tudor government was feebly ineffective. This was the view which I held when I began to write this book,

---

[4] Professor Ralph Davis has suggested that whereas Elizabeth took only 3 per cent of England's national income for war in the 1590s, Philip II extracted 10 per cent of Castile's: see his *Rise of the Atlantic Economics* (1973), 211.

[5] Cf. J. R. Lander, *Crown and Nobility, 1450–1509* (1976), 48–9.

a view which I now believe to be mistaken. For it is essential to remember—and too often forgotten—that Tudor government, like any other administration, was seriously concerned only with a limited number of objectives, even though it might occasionally and half-heartedly pursue many others. To judge from the Privy Council register and the state papers, the Crown's primary concern in domestic affairs was with religious uniformity, the food-supply, vagrancy, law and order, and overseas trade. Its record must be tested in these fields.

Tudor government never imposed complete uniformity of belief or worship. But it did pull down the monasteries, disperse their monks, and abolish chantries. The work of destruction and the accompanying transfer of property were accomplished with relative ease. The imposition of Protestantism took longer and loopholes in the recusancy laws allowed Catholicism to survive. But by 1603 the English Catholic community was small in number, mostly loyal to the Crown, and largely deprived of social or political influence. England had become, once and for all, a Protestant country. Like most political victories this had been achieved at a price. Puritan clergy were more influential in sees, parishes, and universities than Elizabeth would have wished. But after the Presbyterian movement had been defeated in the 1590s, the Puritan leaders confined themselves to preaching and to prayer. It took the radical policies of Archbishop Laud to revive the disputes about Church government.

In the course of the sixteenth century the government developed detailed regulations to ensure the supply of corn, keep the poor alive, and control vagrants. The statutes, proclamations, and council orders promulgated under the Tudors were the foundations of a system which endured in England for two centuries and was probably unequalled for its complexity in any other large European state. The orders were certainly not enforced in every place at every time. Not until the seventeenth century did they take firm root in the minds of local administrators. But even in the sixteenth they probably helped to prevent the serious famines and disturbances which afflicted contemporary France.

The Crown was not completely successful in eliminating violence from the land or piracy from the sea. Without a professional and permanent police force this could not be done;

and the government probably hoped only to contain disorder within tolerable limits. This it achieved. Upper-class violence was substantially reduced. Provost-marshals curbed the excesses of highway robbers in the 1590s and quietened the alarms of Londoners. English pirates were attracted away from our shores by the greater rewards of the Mediterranean and the Caribbean. By comparison with the Kingdoms of Spain, where banditry was rife and uncontrolled, England had become a relatively well-ordered country by 1603.[6]

The pattern of overseas trade was substantially changed between 1485 and 1603. At the beginning of the Tudor period most foreign trade was conducted with the Low Countries and much of it was in the hands of foreign merchants, especially the Hansards. By 1603 the alien traders had been largely excluded from the export business and the direction of trade had been widely diversified, to take in Russia, the Baltic, the Mediterranean, and the Indian Ocean. Obviously this transformation was not entirely the work of government. But without the backing of the Crown it could not have been achieved by the great chartered companies.

Most important of all for the stability of the regime was the unification of Britain, finally achieved on Elizabeth's death, but foreshadowed in earlier years. Wales and the Marcher lordships were subjected to the direct rule of the Crown. The palatinates of Durham and Norfolk lost their independence. The security of the northern border was effectively established during the first fifteen years of the reign of Elizabeth. With the ejection of Mary Stuart from Scotland, the destruction of the Neville Earls of Westmorland, and the exclusion of Percy power from the borders, the north ceased to be a major threat. Diplomatic relations with Edinburgh continued to present difficulties; and the marches were still a source of minor disorders. But whereas the northern border had been one of the major preoccupations of the Privy Council until about 1570, it soon came to loom much less large. Its place was quickly taken by the troubles of Ireland. During the 1590s the Privy Council devoted as much energy and anxiety to Irish problems as it had in the 1560s to

---

[6] F. Braudel, *La Méditerranée et le monde Méditerranéen à l'époque de Philippe II* (2nd edn., Paris, 1966), II. 75–92. J. H. Elliott, *The Revolt of the Catalans* (Cambridge, 1963), chs. iii–v.

Scottish. Thanks to the ruthless and skilful generalship of Mountjoy, the Irish revolt was crushed at the end of Elizabeth's reign and she was thus able to hand to her successor a kingdom effectively united and secure—for the time being—from internal threats.

The Tudors certainly owed something of their success to the foundation of effective government laid by Edward IV, who expanded royal revenues and energetically administered justice. But Edward relied heavily upon great noble families, in particular upon the rival factions of the Woodvilles and of his brother, Richard of Gloucester, whose enmity tore the dynasty apart after his death. His most recent biographer, Dr Charles Ross, has criticized him for neglecting to enforce the statutes against livery and maintenance and for building up the power of new magnate families. He points out that Edward was the only English king since 1066 who died in safe possession of his throne but failed to secure it for his son; and he contrasts Edward's lenience and generosity towards the nobles with Henry VII's meanness and severity. Probably these criticisms are unfair. Edward could do little but use noble families for the establishment of royal control and he was bound to endow his own kinsmen. Henry was much more favourably placed: several of the great magnate properties had reverted to the Crown by 1485 and he had few relatives with a claim on the royal patrimony. Moreover he was able to draw upon Edward's financial practice to improve the royal revenues. The Tudor dynasty certainly inherited a monarchy more firmly established than that secured by Edward IV in 1461, thanks partly to the success of Yorkist methods, partly to the fortuitous destruction of several magnate houses, and partly to the waning interest of the surviving peerage in court politics. But this inheritance does not go far to explain the success of the Tudors.[7]

How then did they maintain a stable regime and impose their will, albeit incompletely, upon important areas of national life? They did not base their government, as Edward IV had done, upon an alliance with great magnate families. Nor, in my opinion, did their strength reside in the creation of a new

[7] C. Ross, *Edward IV* (1974), 332–41, 376–86, 412–13, 423–6. But see the review by B. P. Wolffe, *EHR* XCI (1976), 369–74, and the remarks by J. R. Lander, op. cit. 11–12, 20–32.

bureaucratic machine. In spite of the innovations of Cromwell and the attentiveness of Burghley the institutions of government remained slender and inadequate. Important as the Privy Council, the Secretaryship, and the lawcourts might be, they were stunted and fragile by comparison with the machinery of a modern state. But Tudor government should not be judged in such terms. The official bureaucracy conducted only one part of the political process. The driving thrust came from *ad hoc* commissions and the manipulation of landowning influence in the regions, both of them harnessed to energetic rule at the centre. The strength of Tudor government lay in a skilful combination of the formal and the informal, the official and the personal.

Dependent upon personal influence and relationships, Tudor government varied in style from one reign to another. Henry VII relied very much upon a corps of household servants and other officers operating under special commissions outside the normal institutions of government. Henry VIII put his trust in two great ministers, both of whom built up institutions which they could dominate: Wolsey developing Chancery and Star Chamber; Cromwell working through the Secretaryship and the new financial courts. Elizabeth enabled Burghley to continue and entrench the rule of Privy Council and Secretary at the centre, while permanent commissions were developed in the counties. In their relations with the nobility Henry VII and Elizabeth were niggardly with new creations and grants of land. Henry VIII and Edward VI by contrast raised many to the peerage and endowed them generously. The government of Henry VIII was bellicose in its foreign relations and extravagant in expenditure. The long period of peace under Elizabeth changed the attitudes of the nobility, deprived them of military experience, and enabled the Queen to lighten the fiscal burdens on her subjects until the 1590s.

Even when these variations are taken into the reckoning, the Tudor regime had enough common features to mark it off from its European contemporaries. At the furthest extreme from it lay the despotisms of Ottoman Turkey and Tsarist Russia. Giles Fletcher described the tyranny of Ivan IV in tones of firm disapproval: 'the manner of their government is much after the Turkish fashion'; 'it is plain tyrannical'. All powers were vested absolutely in the Tsar, to whom nobility and Church were sub-servient. Burghers had no seat in the *Zemsky Sobor*, which passed whatever laws the Tsar wished. Provinces were administered by minor nobles appointed by the monarch. The secret police, the *Oprichniki*, 6,000 in number, sustained a reign of terror.[8] The rulers of France and of the Spanish Kingdoms were subject to certain laws, but the state machines were vastly more power-ful than in England. The Valois and the Habsburgs maintained large standing armies and considerable bureaucracies. Taxa-tion in France and in Castile weighed much more heavily than in England. But social divisions, certainly in France, were a great deal sharper. Families like Guise, Bourbon, and Mont-morency in France, Mendoza and Ayala in Spain commanded larger areas, more tenants, and a wider jurisdiction than their English counterparts. Hereditary office-holders were viewed with hostility and envy by the middling nobility of France. Tax-farmers and taxpayers were fiercely divided. Landowners were sometimes prepared to encourage their tenants to revolt against the royal tax-collectors. The pressures of taxation, famine, and civil war often forced the peasantry of France into rebellion. The state machine in England could afford to be less developed. In a society where most of the peasantry enjoyed an adequate subsistence, where there were no sharp divisions between privi-leged and unprivileged, government by the informal mechan-isms of consent was possible.

Elizabeth has however been charged with bequeathing to her successor a state no longer capable of surviving the pressures laid upon it; and the 1590s have been viewed by some historians as a time of political and social crisis.[9] The financial resources of the state were slender for the conduct of war against a major power. Some of the devices employed by the Crown to reward its officials and to supply its needs were criticized and resisted. The local taxes required from the counties met with growing resistance during the final years of the war against Spain: many

[8] Giles Fletcher, *Of the Russe Commonwealth* (1591), chs. vii–xix, esp. p. 20. T. Szamuely, *The Russian Tradition* (1974), ch. iii.

[9] E.g. in Neale, *The Elizabethan Political Scene*, and Clark, *English Provincial Society*, chs. vii, viii.

men refused to contribute to the government loans; some tax commissioners had to be reprimanded for shifting the burden of taxation from the rich to the poor; demands for ship-money stirred discontent.[10] The initiatives taken by Robert Cecil to increase revenues after the death of his father were also unpopular. Although the main attacks upon them came principally during the reign of James, the financial policy of the Crown was already giving rise to suspicion among the subjects of Elizabeth and consequently to fears among her servants of a new spirit of opposition. At the end of the monopolies debate in 1601, Robert Cecil rebuked M.P.s for their conduct: 'The time was never more apt to disorder, or make ill interpretations of good meanings. I think those persons would be glad that all sovereignty were converted into popularity.'[11] Faction-fighting at court between the followers of Essex and Cecil had become intense; many courtiers, officers, and gentlemen felt thwarted of rewards and advancement by the meanness of the sovereign and the dominance of the Cecils. At the same time the high price of corn conjured up spectres of famine and the unrest of London apprentices alarmed the rulers of the City.

The combined and simultaneous pressures of war and bad harvests in the 1590s certainly tested the authority of government. But the fears of contemporaries and the diagnoses of later historians have been excessively alarmist. One must not assume that the Civil War of 1642 was foreshadowed in late Elizabethan England. More remarkable than the tensions and eruptions of those years was the success and stability of Tudor rule. Spanish attacks were repulsed, Irish revolts were defeated, the Presbyterian movement was broken, the Essex rebellion collapsed in a day. Parliament was, by medieval standards, restrained. During the fourteenth and fifteenth centuries the Commons had often attacked the 'evil councillors' of the monarch, calling for their replacement by men better fitted to advise their ruler. No sixteenth-century Parliament encroached in this way upon the royal prerogative of choosing ministers;

---

[10] *APC*, vols. XXI–XXXII are filled with reprimands from the Council to local officers for failing to meet contributions. e.g. *APC* XXI. 201; XXVI. 64; XXIX. 588. Also HMC, *Salisbury*, VI. 137, 534–6; XII. 700.

[11] *TED*, II. 289–92.

and such attempts were rarely made outside Parliament. Although the criticism of the Commons at the end of Elizabeth's reign grew out of issues that were strongly felt, there was no hint of a claim to parliamentary participation in government.

The social order held firm. Power was widely diffused throughout the political nation. There were no princes of the blood to claim special privileges or to challenge the throne. The ruling élite was supported by a substantial body of lesser gentry, yeomen farmers, merchants, and tradesmen; and the number of men with some stake in the country was large enough to provide an adequate defence of property.[12] Most important of all, the propertied classes were relatively cohesive. The threat of social disturbance was enough to keep them together, but not serious enough to be really dangerous. The low level of taxation removed one potential source of discontent, while the peasantry was too diverse a class to challenge the social hierarchy, and the destitute were too widely dispersed to create an effective force. Given sensitive and responsive leadership such a society could survive even the strains of war and dearth. The tight inner circle of English political leaders was able in 1603 to steer the country through the difficulties of the succession and to maintain their own power intact without meeting any serious opposition.

The government inherited by the Stuarts was of course limited in its capacity. It could not make large-scale or prolonged war, and it depended on the co-operation of the political nation to enforce its decrees. But these limitations were less constricting than they might appear. The landed classes accepted the notion that co-operation with the Crown was customary and normal. As Mr Conrad Russell has pointed out, the refusal of Parliament to grant taxes did not prevent the Crown from collecting them in the 1630s. Only the alienation and subsequent intervention of the Scots ultimately enabled Parliament to make legal limitations into a reality, and even then the political nation for the most part viewed the idea of armed resistance to the King with reluctance or even repugnance. The tensions at the end of the sixteenth century had certainly been disturbing; but the outbreak of civil war in 1642 should not

---

[12] Derek Hirst, *The Representative of the People?* ch. ii contains a valuable discussion of this point.

lead us to conclude that the monarchy had been in crisis fifty years before.[13]

[13] C. Russell, 'Parliamentary History in Perspective, 1604–29', *History*, LXI (1976). I have discussed some points of contrast between Tudor protests and the Civil War in 'Rebellion and Revolution in Early Modern England', in *War and Society: Essays in Memory of John Western*, ed. M. R. D. Foot (1973).

INDEX